PART V	**MONEY AND PRICES IN THE LONG RUN**	
Chapter 12	The monetary system	*The monetary system is crucial in determining the long-run behaviour of the price level, the inflation rate and other nominal variables.*
Chapter 13	Inflation: Its causes and costs	
PART VI	**THE MACROECONOMICS OF OPEN ECONOMIES**	
Chapter 14	Open-economy macroeconomics: Basic concepts	*A nation's economic interactions with other nations are described by its trade balance, net foreign investment and exchange rate.*
Chapter 15	A macroeconomic theory of the open economy	*A long-run model of the open economy explains the determinants of the trade balance, the real exchange rate and other real variables.*
PART VII	**SHORT-RUN ECONOMIC FLUCTUATIONS**	
Chapter 16	Aggregate demand and aggregate supply	*The model of aggregate demand and aggregate supply explains short-run economic fluctuations, the short-run effects of monetary and fiscal policy, and the short-run linkage between real and nominal variables.*
Chapter 17	The influence of monetary and fiscal policy on aggregate demand	
Chapter 18	The short-run trade-off between inflation and unemployment	
PART VIII	**FINAL THOUGHTS**	
Chapter 19	Five debates over macroeconomic policy	*A capstone chapter presents both sides of five major debates over economic policy.*

PRINCIPLES OF
Macroeconomics

PRINCIPLES OF Macroeconomics

Robin E. Stonecash
Australian Graduate School of Management

Joshua S. Gans
University of Melbourne

Stephen P. King
University of Melbourne

N. Gregory Mankiw
Harvard University

Sydney Fort Worth London Orlando Toronto

Harcourt Australia
30–52 Smidmore Street, Marrickville NSW 2204

Harcourt
24–28 Oval Road, London NW1 7DX

Harcourt
Orlando, Florida 32887

This edition copyright © 1999
by Harcourt Australia, ACN 000 910 583

About the cover   The cover illustrates, as Alfred Marshall pointed out a century ago, that economics is 'a study of mankind in the ordinary business of life'. Tom Roberts's classic artwork, *Bourke Street, Melbourne*, was chosen because of its beauty, elegance, simplicity and friendly appeal. It overlays a modern financial report containing graphs and numbers. The contrast between the artwork and the financial report represents the art and science of economics. Reproduced with permission of the National Library of Australia, Canberra.

About the interior illustrations   The interior illustrations are the work of Michael Steirnagle. Each illustration brings to life the economic markets and activities associated with the chapter topics presented in the book. Steirnagle, an award-winning illustrator and artist, teaches at Palomar College in San Marcos, California. He has been awarded two gold medals from the Society of Illustrators and has recently illustrated a children's book.

This publication is copyright. Except as expressly provided in the *Copyright Act 1968*, no part of this publication may be reproduced by any means (including electronic, mechanical, microcopying, photocopying, recording or otherwise) without prior written permission from the publisher.

National Library of Australia Cataloguing-in-Publication Data

Principles of macroeconomics.

Australian ed.
Includes index.
ISBN 0 7295 3264 X.

1. Macroeconomics. I. Stonecash, Robin Ellen.

339

Edited by Janette Whelan Publishing Consultancy
Index by Michael Wyatt
Picture and rights editor: Jan Stretton/Rhiain Hull
Publishing Services Manager: Helena Klijn
Cover design by Didona Design
Australian cover adaptation by Toni Darben
Typeset by Bookhouse Digital, Sydney
Printed in Singapore by SNP Printing Pte. Ltd

ABOUT THE AUTHORS

Robin Stonecash is a Senior Lecturer at the Australian Graduate School of Management at the University of New South Wales and the University of Sydney. She studied economics at Swarthmore College, the University of Wisconsin, and the University of New South Wales. She has taught a variety of courses in microeconomics, macroeconomics and international trade to undergraduates and graduates. She currently teaches industrial organisation and macroeconomics for managers to MBA students.

Dr Stonecash's research interests cover a wide range of topics, including R&D policy, competition policy, and privatisation and international trade and development. Her work has been published in the *Economic Record* and *Prometheus*. Dr Stonecash has also done several studies on the efficiency gains from outsourcing. She has consulted widely for private companies and government organisations such as AusAID and the Departments of Ageing and Disability and Community Services.

Dr Stonecash lives in Sydney with her partner, Bernd Luedecke.

Joshua Gans is an Associate Professor of Economics at the University of Melbourne. He studied economics at the University of Queensland and Stanford University. He currently teaches introductory economics and incentive theory to MBA students at the Melbourne Business School.

Professor Gans's research ranges over many fields of economics including economic growth, game theory, regulation and the economics of technological change and innovation. His work has been published in academic journals including the *American Economic Review, Journal of Economic Perspectives, Journal of Public Economics* and *Journal of Economic Behavior and Organization*. Currently, he is economics editor of the *Australian Journal of Management*. He has also undertaken consulting activities, advising governments and private firms on the impact of microeconomic reform and competition policy in Australia.

Professor Gans lives in Melbourne with his partner, Natalie Lippey, and their daughter, Belanna.

Stephen King is Professor of Economics at the University of Melbourne. After studying at the Australian National University and Monash University, he completed his PhD at Harvard University in 1991. Professor King has taught a variety of courses including introductory economics at Harvard and Melbourne.

Professor King specialises in industrial economics, although his research has covered a wide range of areas including game theory, corporate finance, privatisation and tax policy. His work has been published in academic journals such as the *Journal of Industry Economics, International Journal of Industrial Organization* and *Journal of Economic Behavior and Organization*. In addition, he has co-authored a book on industry reform in Australia, and has been consulted by various government organisations such as the Australian Competition and Consumer Commission.

Professor King lives in Melbourne with his wife, Mary, and their two children, Jacqui and Rebecca.

N. Gregory Mankiw is Professor of Economics at Harvard University. As a student, he studied economics at Princeton University and MIT. As a teacher, he has taught various courses, including macroeconomics, microeconomics, statistics and principles of economics.

Professor Mankiw is a prolific writer. His work has been published in academic journals, such as the *American Economic Review*, *Journal of Political Economy* and *Quarterly Journal of Economics*, and in more popular forums, such as the *New York Times*, *Boston Globe* and the *Wall Street Journal*. He is also the author of the best-selling textbook *Macroeconomics* (Worth Publishers). In addition to his teaching, research and writing, Professor Mankiw is Director of the Monetary Economics Program at the National Bureau of Economic Research, a non-profit think-tank in Cambridge, Massachusetts, and an adviser to the Federal Reserve Bank of Boston and the Congressional Budget Office.

Professor Mankiw lives in Wellesley, Massachusetts, with his wife, Deborah, their children, Catherine and Nicholas, and the family's border terrier, Keynes.

To

Mary Ellen Stonecash
Natalie and Belanna
Mary, Jacqui and Becky
Catherine and Nicholas

BRIEF CONTENTS

Preface to this edition xix
Preface to the original edition xxvii
To the student xxix

PART I INTRODUCTION 1
Chapter 1 Ten principles of economics 3
Chapter 2 Thinking like an economist 17
Chapter 3 Interdependence and the gains from trade 45

PART II SUPPLY AND DEMAND: HOW MARKETS WORK 59
Chapter 4 The market forces of supply and demand 61
Chapter 5 Elasticity and its application 87
Chapter 6 Supply, demand and government policies 109

PART III THE DATA OF MACROECONOMICS 129
Chapter 7 Measuring a nation's income 131
Chapter 8 Measuring the cost of living 149

PART IV THE REAL ECONOMY IN THE LONG RUN 167
Chapter 9 Production and growth 169
Chapter 10 Saving, investment and the financial system 195
Chapter 11 The natural rate of unemployment 221

PART V MONEY AND PRICES IN THE LONG RUN 247
Chapter 12 The monetary system 249
Chapter 13 Inflation: Its causes and costs 269

PART VI THE MACROECONOMICS OF OPEN ECONOMIES 295
Chapter 14 Open-economy macroeconomics: Basic concepts 297
Chapter 15 A macroeconomic theory of the open economy 319

PART VII SHORT-RUN ECONOMIC FLUCTUATIONS 341
Chapter 16 Aggregate demand and aggregate supply 343
Chapter 17 The influence of monetary and fiscal policy on aggregate demand 367
Chapter 18 The short-run trade-off between inflation and unemployment 393

PART VIII FINAL THOUGHTS 419
Chapter 19 Five debates over macroeconomic policy 421

Glossary 437
Credits 441
Index 443

CONTENTS

Preface to this edition xix
Preface to the original edition xxvii
To the student xxix

PART I
INTRODUCTION 1

CHAPTER 1
TEN PRINCIPLES OF ECONOMICS 3

How people make decisions 4
Principle 1: People face trade-offs 4
Principle 2: The cost of something is what you give up to get it 6
Principle 3: Rational people think at the margin 6
Principle 4: People respond to incentives 7

How people interact 8
Principle 5: Trade can make everyone better off 8
Principle 6: Markets are usually a good way to organise economic activity 9
Principle 7: Governments can sometimes improve market outcomes 10

How the economy as a whole works 11
Principle 8: A country's standard of living depends on its ability to produce goods and services 11
Principle 9: Prices rise when the government prints too much money 12
Principle 10: Society faces a short-run trade-off between inflation and unemployment 13

Conclusion 14
Summary 15
Key concepts 15
Questions for review 15
Problems and applications 15

CHAPTER 2
THINKING LIKE AN ECONOMIST 17

The economist as scientist 18
The scientific method: Observation, theory and more observation 18
The role of assumptions 19
Economic models 20
Our first model: The circular-flow diagram 20
Our second model: The production possibilities frontier 22
Microeconomics and macroeconomics 24

The economist as policymaker 25
Positive versus normative analysis 26
Economists in government 26

Why economists disagree 28
Differences in scientific judgements 28
Differences in values 29
Charlatans and cranks 29
Perception versus reality 30

Let's get going 31
Summary 32
Key concepts 32
Questions for review 32
Problems and applications 33
Appendix: Graphing—a brief review 34
Graphs of a single variable 34
Graphs of two variables: The coordinate system 34
Curves in the coordinate system 37
Slope and elasticity 39
Cause and effect 41

CHAPTER 3
INTERDEPENDENCE AND THE GAINS FROM TRADE 45

A parable for the modern economy 46
Production possibilities 46
Specialisation and trade 48

The principle of comparative advantage 50
Absolute advantage 51
Opportunity cost and comparative advantage 51
Comparative advantage and trade 52

Applications of comparative advantage 53
Should Michael Jordan mow his own lawn? 53
Should a country trade with other countries? 53
   FYI: The legacy of Adam Smith and David Ricardo 54

Conclusion 55

Summary 55

Key concepts 55

Questions for review 55

Problems and applications 56

PART II
SUPPLY AND DEMAND: HOW MARKETS WORK 59

CHAPTER 4
THE MARKET FORCES OF SUPPLY AND DEMAND 61

Markets and competition 62
Competitive markets 62
Competition: Perfect and otherwise 62

Demand 63
The determinants of individual demand 63
The demand schedule and the demand curve 64
Ceteris parabus 66
Market demand versus individual demand 66
Shifts in the demand curve 68
   Case study: Two ways to reduce the quantity of smoking demanded 69

Supply 70
The determinants of individual supply 71
The supply schedule and the supply curve 71
The market supply versus individual supply 72
Shifts in the supply curve 73

Supply and demand together 74
Equilibrium 76
Three steps to analysing changes in equilibrium 78

Conclusion: How prices allocate resources 82
   In the news: Supply, demand and the price of paper 83

Summary 84

Key concepts 84

Questions for review 85

Problems and applications 85

CHAPTER 5
ELASTICITY AND ITS APPLICATION 87

The elasticity of demand 88
The price elasticity of demand and its determinants 88
Calculating the price elasticity of demand 89
   FYI: Calculating elasticities using the midpoint method 90
The variety of demand curves 90
Total revenue and the price elasticity of demand 92
   Case study: Pricing admission to an art gallery 94
The income elasticity of demand 94
   FYI: Elasticity and total revenue along a linear demand curve 95
   In the news: On the road with elasticity 96

The elasticity of supply 96
The price elasticity of supply and its determinants 97
Calculating the price elasticity of supply 97
The variety of supply curves 98

Three applications of supply, demand and elasticity 98
Can good news for farming be bad news for farmers? 100
Why did OPEC fail to keep the price of oil high? 102
Do drug bans increase or decrease drug-related crime? 103

Conclusion 105

Summary 105

Key concepts 106

Questions for review 106

Problems and applications 106

CHAPTER 6
SUPPLY, DEMAND AND GOVERNMENT POLICIES   109

Controls on prices   110
How price ceilings affect market outcomes   110
    Case study: Lines at the petrol station   111
    Case study: Rent controls in the short run and long run   113
How price floors affect market outcomes   114
    In the news: Rent control in Mumbai, India   115
    Case study: Minimum wage rates   116
Evaluating price controls   118

Taxes   119
How taxes on buyers affect market outcomes   120
How taxes on sellers affect market outcomes   121
    Case study: Who pays the payroll tax?   123
Elasticity and tax incidence   124

Conclusion   125
Summary   125
Key concepts   126
Questions for review   126
Problems and applications   126

PART III
THE DATA OF MACROECONOMICS   129

CHAPTER 7
MEASURING A NATION'S INCOME   131

The economy's income and expenditure   132
The measurement of gross domestic product   134
'GDP is the market value…'   134
'…of all…'   134
'…final…'   135
'…goods and services…'   135
'…produced…'   135
'…within a country…'   135
'…in a given period of time.'   136

The components of GDP   137
    FYI: Three other measures of income   138

Real versus nominal GDP   140
A numerical example   140
The GDP deflator   142
    Case study: Real GDP over recent history   142

GDP and economic wellbeing   143
    Case study: International differences in GDP and the quality of life   144

Conclusion   145
Summary   146
Key concepts   146
Questions for review   146
Problems and applications   147

CHAPTER 8
MEASURING THE COST OF LIVING   149

    FYI: What's in the CPI basket?   150

The consumer price index   150
How the consumer price index is calculated   151
Problems in measuring the cost of living   153
    In the news: Changing our measure of inflation   154
    In the news: The CPI bias   156
The GDP deflator versus the consumer price index   157

Correcting economic variables for the effects of inflation   159
Dollar figures from different times   159
Indexation   160
Real and nominal interest rates   160
    In the news: Mr Index goes to Hollywood   161

Conclusion   163
Summary   163
Key concepts   163
Questions for review   164
Problems and applications   164

PART IV
THE REAL ECONOMY IN THE LONG RUN 167

CHAPTER 9
PRODUCTION AND GROWTH 169

Economic growth around the world 170
   FYI: The magic of compounding and the rule of 70 172
Productivity: Its role and determinants 173
Why productivity is so important 173
How productivity is determined 174
   Case study: Are natural resources a limit to growth? 175
The production function 177
   In the news: Computers and productivity 178
Economic growth and public policy 178
The importance of saving and investment 178
Diminishing returns and the catch-up effect 180
Investment from abroad 181
   In the news: The World Bank 182
Education 183
Property rights and political stability 184
   Case study: What causes famine? 185
Free trade 185
   In the news: The Sachs solution to the African problem 186
The control of population growth 188
Research and development 189
   Case study: The productivity slowdown 189
Conclusion: The importance of long-run growth 191
Summary 192
Key concepts 192
Questions for review 192
Problems and applications 193

CHAPTER 10
SAVING, INVESTMENT AND THE FINANCIAL SYSTEM 195

Financial institutions in the Australian economy 196
Financial markets 196
Financial intermediaries 198
   FYI: How to read the newspaper's share tables 199
Summing up 201
Saving and investment in the national income accounts 201
Some important identities 202
The meaning of saving and investment 203
The market for loanable funds 204
Supply of and demand for loanable funds 204
Policy 1: Taxes and saving 206
Policy 2: Taxes and investment 208
Policy 3: Government budget deficits 209
   FYI: Ricardian equivalence: An alternative view of government budget deficits 210
   Case study: A comparison of government debt and deficits in Australia and the United States 211
   In the news: Putting the budget deficit in perspective 214
Conclusion 214
   In the news: The balanced budget amendment 216
Summary 217
Key concepts 218
Questions for review 218
Problems and applications 218

CHAPTER 11
THE NATURAL RATE OF UNEMPLOYMENT 221

Identifying unemployment 222
How is unemployment measured? 222
   Case study: Labour-force participation of men and women in the Australian economy 225
Is unemployment measured correctly? 227
How long are the unemployed without work? 227
Why is there unemployment? 228
Minimum-wage laws 229
   In the news: Dealing with structural unemployment 230
Unions and collective bargaining 232
The economics of unions 232
Are unions good or bad for the economy? 233
   FYI: Why do strikes occur? 234
   Case study: Wage indexation 235
The theory of efficiency wages 236
Worker health 236
Worker turnover 237
Worker effort 237

Worker quality 237
  Case study: Henry Ford and the generous $5-a-day wage 238
Job search 239
The inevitability of search unemployment 239
  FYI: The economics of asymmetric information 240
Public policy and job search 241
Unemployment benefits 241
  Case study: The location of unemployment 242
Conclusion 243
Summary 244
Key concepts 244
Questions for review 244
Problems and applications 245

PART V
MONEY AND PRICES IN THE LONG RUN 247

CHAPTER 12
THE MONETARY SYSTEM 249

The meaning of money 250
The functions of money 250
Kinds of money 251
Money in the Australian economy 252
  In the news: Money on the island of Yap 253
  Case study: Where is all the currency? 254
The Reserve Bank of Australia (RBA) 255
  FYI: Credit cards, debit cards and money 255
Organisation of the RBA 256
Changes in the RBA's role 256
Banks and the money supply 258
The simple case of 100%-reserve banking 258
Money creation with fractional-reserve banking 259
The money multiplier 260
Monetary policy in Australia today 261

Problems in controlling the money supply 263
  Case study: Bank runs and the money supply 264
Conclusion 265
Summary 265
Key concepts 266
Questions for review 266
Problems and applications 266

CHAPTER 13
INFLATION: ITS CAUSES AND COSTS 269

The causes of inflation 270
The level of prices and the value of money 271
Money supply, money demand and monetary equilibrium 271
The effects of a monetary injection 272
A brief look at the adjustment process 273
The classical dichotomy and monetary neutrality 274
Velocity and the quantity equation 276
  Case study: Money and prices during four hyperinflations 278
The inflation tax 279
  In the news: Hyperinflation in Serbia 280
The Fisher effect 280
The costs of inflation 282
A fall in purchasing power? The inflation fallacy 282
Shoeleather costs 283
Menu costs 284
Relative-price variability and the misallocation of resources 284
Inflation-induced tax distortions 285
Confusion and inconvenience 286
A special cost of unexpected inflation: Arbitrary redistributions of wealth 287
  Case study: The Wizard of Oz and the free-silver debate 287
  In the news: How to protect your savings from inflation 288
Conclusion 290
Summary 291
Key concepts 291
Questions for review 292
Problems and applications 292

xvi CONTENTS

PART VI
THE MACROECONOMICS OF OPEN ECONOMIES 295

CHAPTER 14
OPEN-ECONOMY MACROECONOMICS: BASIC CONCEPTS 297

The international flows of goods and capital 298
The flow of goods: Exports, imports and net exports 298
   Case study: The importance of trade in the Australian economy 299
The flow of capital: Net foreign investment 301
   In the news: Do capital flows spread financial panic? 302
The equality of net exports and net foreign investment 302
Saving, investment and their relationship to the international flows 304
   In the news: Flows between the developing south and the industrial north 305
   Case study: Saving, investment and net foreign investment of Australia 306

The prices for international transactions: Real and nominal exchange rates 308
Nominal exchange rates 308
Real exchange rates 309

A first theory of exchange-rate determination: Purchasing-power parity 310
The basic logic of purchasing-power parity 310
   In the news: A baht depreciation and a tourist boom 311
Implications of purchasing-power parity 312
   Case study: The nominal exchange rate during hyperinflation 313
Limitations of purchasing-power parity 314

Conclusion 315
Summary 316
Key concepts 316
Questions for review 316
Problems and applications 316

CHAPTER 15
A MACROECONOMIC THEORY OF THE OPEN ECONOMY 319

Supply of and demand for loanable funds and foreign-currency exchange 320
The market for loanable funds 320
The market for foreign-currency exchange 322
   FYI: Purchasing-power parity as a special case 324

Equilibrium in the open economy 324
Net foreign investment: The link between the two markets 324
Simultaneous equilibrium in two markets 325
   FYI: The classical dichotomy once again 327

How policies and events affect an open economy 328
Government budget deficits 328
   Case study: The twin deficits in Australia 330
Trade policy 331
Political instability and capital flight 334
   In the news: Australia and the Asian crisis: She'll be right, mate 336

Conclusion 337
Summary 337
Key concepts 338
Questions for review 338
Problems and applications 338

PART VII
SHORT-RUN ECONOMIC FLUCTUATIONS 341

CHAPTER 16
AGGREGATE DEMAND AND AGGREGATE SUPPLY 343

Three key facts about economic fluctuations 344
Fact 1: Economic fluctuations are irregular and unpredictable 344

Fact 2: Most macroeconomic quantities fluctuate together   346
Fact 3: As output falls, unemployment rises   346
   FYI: Okun's law   347
Explaining short-run economic fluctuations   347
How the short run differs from the long run   348
The basic model of economic fluctuations   348
The aggregate-demand curve   350
Why the aggregate-demand curve is downward-sloping   350
Why the aggregate-demand curve might shift   352
The aggregate-supply curve   353
Why the aggregate-supply curve is vertical in the long run   353
Why the long-run aggregate-supply curve might shift   354
Why the aggregate-supply curve is upward-sloping in the short run   355
Why the short-run aggregate-supply curve might shift   357
Two causes of recession   358
The effects of a shift in aggregate demand   358
   In the news: Going for gold: How the Olympics building boom increases aggregate demand   360
The effects of a shift in aggregate supply   361
Conclusion: The origins of aggregate demand and aggregate supply   363
Summary   364
Key concepts   365
Questions for review   365
Problems and applications   365

CHAPTER 17
THE INFLUENCE OF MONETARY AND FISCAL POLICY ON AGGREGATE DEMAND   367

How monetary policy influences aggregate demand   368
The theory of liquidity preference   369
The downward slope of the aggregate-demand curve   372
Changes in the money supply   372
Interest-rate targets and RBA policy   375
How fiscal policy influences aggregate demand   375
Changes in government purchases   376
The multiplier effect   376
The crowding-out effect   377
   FYI: A formula for the government-purchases multiplier   378
Changes in taxes   379

   FYI: How fiscal policy might affect aggregate supply   380
Using policy to stabilise the economy   381
The case for active stabilisation policy   381
   Case study: Keynesian thinking today   382
The case against active stabilisation policy   383
Automatic stabilisers   384
   In the news: The independence of the Reserve Bank of Australia   385
The economy in the long run and the short run   386
   FYI: The long run and the short run: An algebraic explanation   387
Conclusion   388
Summary   388
Key concepts   389
Questions for review   389
Problems and applications   390

CHAPTER 18
THE SHORT-RUN TRADE-OFF BETWEEN INFLATION AND UNEMPLOYMENT   393

The Phillips curve   394
Origins of the Phillips curve   394
Aggregate demand, aggregate supply and the Phillips curve   395
   In the news: The effects of low unemployment   397
Shifts in the Phillips curve: The role of expectations   398
The long-run Phillips curve   398
Expectations and the short-run Phillips curve   401
   Case study: The US economy as the natural experiment for the natural-rate hypothesis   403
Shifts in the Phillips curve: The role of supply shocks   405
The cost of reducing inflation   408
The sacrifice ratio   409
Rational expectations and the possibility of costless disinflation   410
The Accord approach   411
A low inflation era   413
Conclusion   413
   In the news: Unemployment and its natural rate   414
Summary   415
Key concepts   415
Questions for review   415
Problems and applications   416

PART VIII
FINAL THOUGHTS 419

CHAPTER 19
FIVE DEBATES OVER MACROECONOMIC POLICY 421

That monetary and fiscal policymakers should try to stabilise the economy 422
Pro: Policymakers should try to stabilise the economy 422
Con: Policymakers should not try to stabilise the economy 422

That monetary policy should be made by rule rather than by discretion 424
Pro: Monetary policy should be made by rule 424
Con: Monetary policy should not be made by rule 425

That the central bank should aim for zero inflation 426
Pro: The central bank should aim for zero inflation 426
Con: The central bank should not aim for zero inflation 427

That the government should balance its budget 429
Pro: The government should balance its budget 429
Con: The government should not balance its budget 430

That the tax laws should be reformed to encourage saving 431
Pro: The tax laws should be reformed to encourage saving 432
Con: The tax laws should not be reformed to encourage saving 433

Conclusion 434
Summary 434
Questions for review 435
Problems and applications 435

Glossary 437
Credits 441
Index 443

PREFACE TO THIS EDITION

Studying economics should invigorate and enthral. It should challenge students' preconceptions and provide them with a powerful, coherent framework for analysing the world they live in. Yet, all too often, economics textbooks are dry and confusing. Rather than highlighting the important foundations of economic analysis, these books focus on the 'ifs' and 'buts'. The motto underlying this book is that it is 'the rule, not the exception' that is important. Our aim is to show the power of economic tools and the importance of economic ideas.

This book has been designed particularly for students in Australia and New Zealand. However, we are keenly aware of the diverse mix of students studying in these countries. When choosing examples and applications, we have kept an international focus. Whether the issue is rent control in Mumbai, tax policy in Australia or inflation targeting in New Zealand, examples have been chosen for their relevance and to highlight that the same economic questions are being asked in many countries. The specific context in which economics is applied may vary but the lessons and insights offered by the economic way of thinking are universal.

To boil economics down to its essentials, we had to consider what is truly important for students to learn in their first course in economics. As a result, this book differs from others not only in its length but also in its orientation.

It is tempting for professional economists writing a textbook to take the economist's point of view and to emphasise those topics that fascinate them and other economists. We have done our best to avoid that temptation. We have tried to put ourselves in the position of students seeing economics for the first time. Our goal is to emphasise the material that students should and do find interesting about the study of the economy.

One result is that more of this book is devoted to applications and policy, and less is devoted to formal economic theory, than is the case with many other books written for the principles course. For example, after students learn about the demand for and supply of loanable funds in chapter 10, they immediately apply these tools to answer important macroeconomic questions facing the Australian economy, such as: How do changes in government tax policy affect the nation's ability to invest in new capital equipment? These principles are extended to the open economy in chapter 15, where students learn about the demand for and supply of foreign exchange and immediately apply the new tools to explain capital flight from Indonesia during the Asian economic crisis.

Throughout this book we have tried to return to applications and policy questions as often as possible. Most chapters include 'Case Studies' illustrating how the principles of economics are applied. In addition, 'In the News' boxes offer excerpts from newspaper articles showing how economic ideas shed light on the current issues facing society. It is our hope that after students finish their first course in economics, they will think about news stories from a new perspective and with greater insight.

To write a brief and student-friendly book, we had to consider new ways to organise the material. This book includes all the topics that are central to a first course in economics, but the topics are not always arranged in the traditional order. What follows is a whirlwind tour of this text. This tour will, we hope, give instructors some sense of how the pieces fit together.

Chapter 1, 'Ten Principles of Economics', introduces students to the economist's view of the world. It previews some of the big ideas that recur throughout economics, such as opportunity cost, marginal decision making, the role of incentives, the gains from trade and the efficiency of market allocations. Throughout the book, we refer regularly to the *Ten Principles of Economics* in chapter 1 to remind students that these principles are the foundation for most economic analysis. A building-blocks icon in the margin calls attention to these references.

Chapter 2, 'Thinking Like an Economist', examines how economists approach their field of study. It discusses the role of assumptions in developing a theory and introduces the concept of an economic model. It also discusses the role of economists in making policy. The appendix to this chapter offers a brief refresher course on how graphs are used and how they can be abused.

Chapter 3, 'Interdependence and the Gains from Trade', presents the theory of comparative advantage. This theory explains why individuals trade with their neighbours, and why nations trade with other nations. Much of economics is about the coordination of economic activity through market forces. As a starting point for this analysis, students see in this chapter why economic interdependence can benefit everyone. This is done using a familiar example of trade in household chores among flatmates.

The next three chapters introduce the basic tools of supply and demand. Chapter 4, 'The Market Forces of Supply and Demand', develops the supply curve, the demand curve and the notion of market equilibrium. Chapter 5, 'Elasticity and Its Application', introduces the concept of elasticity and uses it in three applications to quite different markets. Chapter 6, 'Supply, Demand and Government Policies', uses these tools to examine price controls, such as rent control and the award wage system, and tax incidence.

Beginning in chapter 7, the book turns to the topics of macroeconomics. The coverage starts with the issues of measurement. Chapter 7, 'Measuring a Nation's Income', discusses the meaning of gross domestic product and related statistics from the national income accounts. Chapter 8, 'Measuring the Cost of Living', discusses the measurement and use of the consumer price index.

The next three chapters describe the behaviour of the real economy in the long run over which wages and prices are flexible. Chapter 9, 'Production and Growth', examines the determinants of the large variation in living standards over time and across countries. Chapter 10, 'Saving, Investment and the Financial System', discusses the types of financial institutions in our economy and examines the role of these institutions in allocating resources. Chapter 11, 'The Natural Rate of Unemployment', considers the long-run determinants of the unemployment rate, including minimum-wage laws, the market power of unions, the role of efficiency wages and the efficacy of job search.

Having described the long-run behaviour of the real economy, the book then turns to the long-run behaviour of money and prices. Chapter 12, 'The Monetary System', introduces the economist's concept of money and the role of the central bank in influencing the amount of money in the economy. Chapter 13, 'Inflation: Its Causes and Costs', develops the link between money growth and inflation and discusses the social costs of inflation.

The next two chapters present the macroeconomics of open economies. Chapter 14, 'Open-economy Macroeconomics: Basic Concepts', explains the relationship among saving, investment and the trade balance, the distinction between the nominal and real exchange rate, and the theory of purchasing-power parity. Chapter 15, 'A Macroeconomic Theory of the Open Economy', presents a classical model of the international flow of goods and capital. The model sheds light on various issues, including the link between budget deficits and trade deficits and the macroeconomic effects of trade policies. Because instructors differ in how much they emphasise this material, these chapters were written so they could be used in different ways. Some instructors may choose to cover chapter 14 but not chapter 15; others may skip both chapters; and others may choose to defer the analysis of open-economy macroeconomics until the end of their courses.

After fully developing the long-run theory of the economy in chapters 9 to 15, the book turns its attention to explaining short-run fluctuations around the long-run trend. This organisation simplifies the teaching of the theory of short-run fluctuations because, at this point in the course, students have a good grounding in many basic macroeconomic concepts. Chapter 16, 'Aggregate Demand and Aggregate Supply', begins with some facts about the business cycle and then introduces the model of aggregate demand and aggregate supply. Chapter 17, 'The Influence of Monetary and Fiscal Policy on Aggregate Demand', explains how policymakers can use the tools at their disposal to shift the aggregate-demand curve. Chapter 18, 'The Short-run Trade-off between Inflation and Unemployment', explains why policymakers who control aggregate demand face a trade-off between inflation and unemployment. It examines why this trade-off exists in the short run, why it shifts over time and why it does not exist in the long run.

The book concludes with chapter 19, 'Five Debates over Macroeconomic Policy'. This capstone chapter considers five controversial issues facing policymakers: the proper degree of policy activism in response to the business cycle, the choice between rules and discretion in the conduct of monetary policy, the desirability of reaching zero inflation, the importance of balancing the government's budget, and the need for tax reform to encourage saving. For each issue, the chapter presents both sides of the debate and encourages students to make their own judgements.

LEARNING TOOLS

The purpose of this book is to help students learn the fundamental lessons of economics and to show students how those lessons can be applied to the world in which they live. To that end, we have used various learning tools that recur throughout the book.

- **Chapter objectives** Every chapter begins with a list of the chapter's main objectives to give students a sense of where the chapter is heading. Each list has been kept brief in order to help students stay focused on the four or five key lessons presented in that chapter.
- **Case studies** Economic theory is useful and interesting only if it can be applied to understand actual events and policies. This book, therefore,

contains numerous case studies that apply the theory that has just been developed.

- **'In the news' boxes** One benefit from studying economics is that it gives students a new perspective and greater understanding about news from around the world. To highlight this benefit, we have included excerpts from many newspaper articles. These articles, together with the brief introductions, show how basic economic theory can be applied. Some of these articles are opinion columns written by prominent economists.

- **'FYI' boxes** These boxes provide additional material 'for your information'. Some of them give a glimpse into the history of economic thought. Others clarify difficult technical issues. Still others discuss supplementary topics that instructors might choose either to skip or discuss in their lectures.

- **Definitions of key concepts** When key concepts are introduced in the chapter, they are presented in **bold** typeface. In addition, their definitions are placed in the margins. This treatment should aid students in learning and reviewing the material.

- **Quick quizzes** After each major section, students are offered a 'quick quiz' to check their comprehension of what they have just learned. If students cannot readily answer these quizzes, they should stop and reread material before continuing.

- **Chapter summaries** Each chapter ends with a brief summary that reminds students of the most important lessons that they have just learned. It offers students an efficient way to review for exams.

- **List of key concepts** A list of key concepts at the end of each chapter allows students to test their understanding of the new terms that have been introduced. Page references are included so students can review the terms they do not understand.

- **Questions for review** At the end of each chapter are questions for review that test the chapter's main lessons. Students can use these questions to check their comprehension after finishing a chapter and to prepare for exams.

- **Problems and applications** Each chapter also contains a variety of problems and applications that ask students to apply the material they have learned. Some instructors may use these questions for homework assignments. Others may use them as a starting point for classroom discussions.

SUPPLEMENTS

Harcourt offers a variety of supplements for instructors and students who use this book. The goal of these ancillary resources is to provide an integrated package that makes teaching the principles of economics easy for the lecturer and learning them easy for the student.

Harcourt provides copies of these supplements free of charge to those instructors qualified under its adoption policy. Please contact your sales representative to learn how you may qualify, or call Harcourt on (02) 9517 8999.

FOR THE INSTRUCTOR

Teaching the principles of economics can be a demanding job. Often, classes are large and teaching assistants in short supply. The supplements designed for the instructor make that job less demanding and more fun.

The following supplements have been prepared specifically for use with this version of the textbook.

- ◆ **Test Bank** The test bank contains test questions consisting of multiple-choice questions and a large number of class-tested conceptual questions and problems. For the instructor's convenience, every question in the test bank is identified according to the chapter 'learning objective' the question covers, the chapter section in which the material is covered, the level of difficulty, and the type of question (multiple-choice, true–false, short answer, critical thinking, definition or graphical). Answers immediately follow each question.

- ◆ **Computerised Test Bank** Harcourt also offers a computerised version of the test bank (EXAMaster+) for IBM and Macintosh users. This software has many features that facilitate test preparation, scoring and grade recording. It also offers great flexibility. The order of test questions can be altered to create different versions of any given test, and it is easy to modify questions and reproduce any of the graphing questions to meet the instructor's needs.

- ◆ **Instructor's Resource Manual** The instructor's manual is aimed at helping both experienced and novice instructors prepare their lectures. It includes lecture notes for every chapter in this book. These notes briefly summarise the text material and provide additional examples and applications. The adjunct and teaching assistant guide offers extensive outlines of every chapter, even more examples, and classroom warm-up activities to help introduce chapter topics.

- ◆ **Electronic Instructor's Resource Manual** The entire *Instructor's Resource Manual* is also available in an electronic format (for Windows). Using these electronic files, instructors can create their own lecture notes or incorporate parts of the *Instructor's Resource Manual* into their PowerPoint presentations.

- ◆ **Solutions Manual** The solutions manual contains complete solutions for all the 'Questions for Review' and 'Problems and Applications' found in the text.

- ◆ **PowerPoint Presentation** The PowerPoint slide show can save instructors time as they prepare for class. This supplement covers all the essential topics presented in each chapter of this book. Graphs, tables, lists and concepts are developed sequentially, much as one might develop them on a blackboard. Additional examples and applications, pulled from the *Instructor's Resource Manual*, are used to reinforce major lessons. The slides are crisp, clear and colourful. Instructors may adapt or add slides to customise their lectures.

- ◆ **Web site** There is a state-of-the-art Web site to accompany this text. To appreciate this resource, we invite you to visit the site at http://www.dryden.com/econ. The ever-evolving Web site is both a teaching and economic research tool, with separate areas for students and instructors. Students visiting this page can learn from tutorials featuring interactive graphs, access a page of economic indicators, follow links relevant to each chapter, find out about career opportunities, and test their knowledge with our on-line quizzes. Instructors will be able to search a bank of news summaries and comprehension questions, download the instructor's resource material, and share ideas with others who are using this textbook.

The following supplements, published in the United States, are also available to instructors.

- **Classroom Activities, Demonstrations, and Games for Principles of Economics** This supplement helps instructors interested in incorporating 'cooperative learning' and 'learning by experiment' exercises into their courses. This supplement contains over 50 games, classroom experiments, in-class demonstrations and take-home and in-class assignments. Each activity is linked to a specific text chapter and lists the type of activity, topics covered, materials list, time required for completion and classroom limitations. Thorough directions are provided for the instructor. For the instructor's convenience, the supplement is three-hole punched and perforated; all pages are designed for easy overhead use and photocopying. The activities supplement is also available on the Web site.

- **The 'Ten Principles' video set** The Dryden Press has commissioned and produced ten video segments that illustrate the *Ten Principles of Economics* introduced in chapter 1. Instructors can show these videos as an interesting and visually appealing introduction to topics. Questions for use with the videos will be available.

- **Overhead Transparencies** For instructors who do not want to use PowerPoint presentations, overhead transparency acetates are available. These overhead transparencies consist of figures and tables from the text, allowing instructors to build text images into their lectures. Some of the more complex acetates are layered to show what happens graphically when curves shift.

FOR THE STUDENT

Harcourt makes supplements available for students who are studying the principles of economics. These supplements reinforce the basic lessons taught in this book and offer opportunities for additional practice and feedback.

- **Student Study Guide** Greg Parry (Edith Cowan University) has prepared a study guide that provides students with a useful summary and review of the important concepts presented in the text. Each study guide chapter includes a chapter overview, a chapter review, helpful hints and definitions. Students can test their understanding of the material with practice problems and a chapter self-test. Solutions to all study guide problems follow each chapter.

- **TAG: Tutorial-Analytical-Graphical Student Software** Andrew Foshee (McNeese State University) has customised for this book the award-winning educational software by Tod Porter and Teresa Riley (both of Youngstown University). This software contains an extensive chapter-by-chapter tutorial, a hands-on graphic section in which students are required to draw curves (with key strokes or a mouse), and a practice exam for each section. Students receive immediate feedback on their answers. It is available in both DOS and Windows formats.

ACKNOWLEDGEMENTS

In adapting this book, we have benefited from the input of a wide range of talented people. We would like to thank all those people who helped us with this task. First, we would like to thank Paul Barry and Janette Whelan for their marvellous work. Without their efforts this book would not have been possible. We would like to thank Ian Macfarlane and Glenn Stevens of the Reserve Bank of Australia for their helpful comments and Trevor Stegman of the University of New South Wales and Ian Harper of the University of Melbourne for useful discussions. We would also like to thank those economists who read and commented on portions of this manuscript, including:

Don Adams, Macquarie University
Jeff Borland, University of Melbourne
Vivek Chaudhri, University of Melbourne
Mark Crosby, University of Melbourne
Peter Dawkins, University of Melbourne
Laurel Dawson, Deakin University
Sarath Delpachitra, University of Southern Queensland
Robert Dixon, University of Melbourne
Paul Flatau, Murdoch University
John Freebairn, University of Melbourne
Mary Graham, Deakin University
Bob Gregory, Australian National University
Ian Harper, Melbourne Business School
John Hicks, Charles Sturt University
Sarah Jennings, University of Tasmania
Paul Jensen, Australian Graduate School of Management
Steven Kemp, Curtin University
Bruce Littleboy, University of Queensland
Bernd Luedecke, Macquarie University
Ian McDonald, University of Melbourne
Rod Maddock, La Trobe University
Alan Morris, Victoria University of Technology

Nilss Olekalns, University of Melbourne
David Owens, Swinburne University of Technology
Greg Parry, Edith Cowan University
Clive Reynoldson, Edith Cowan University
Shirley Richardson, Monash University
Sue Richardson, University of Adelaide
Amal Sanyal, Lincoln University
Martin Shanahan, University of South Australia
Leanne Smith, Massey University
Lindsay Smyrk, Victoria University of Technology
Rod St Hill, University of Southern Queensland
Judy Taylor, Monash University
Di Thomson, Deakin University
John Tressler, University of Waikato
Thea Vinnicombe, Bond University
Neil Warren, University of New South Wales
Philip Williams, University of Melbourne
Ed Wilson, University of Wollongong
John Wood, Edith Cowan University
Steffen Ziss, Sydney University

Finally, we give special acknowledgement to Sue Hornby, formerly of the Australian Graduate School of Management Frank Lowy Library, now head librarian for the Reserve Bank of Australia. She provided excellent research assistance. Thanks also to Pat Matthews.

Robin E. Stonecash
Joshua S. Gans
Stephen P. King
May 1999

PREFACE TO THE ORIGINAL EDITION

During my twenty-year career as a student, the course that excited me most was the two-semester sequence on the principles of economics I took during my freshman year in college. It is no exaggeration to say that it changed my life.

I had grown up in a family that often discussed politics over the dinner table. The pros and cons of various solutions to society's problems generated fervent debate. But, in school, I had been drawn to the sciences. Whereas politics seemed vague, rambling and subjective, science was analytic, systematic and objective. While political debate continued without end, science made progress.

My freshman course on the principles of economics opened my eyes to a new way of thinking. Economics combines the virtues of politics and science. It is, truly, a social science. Its subject matter is society—how people choose to lead their lives and how they interact with one another. But it approaches its subject with the dispassion of a science. By bringing the methods of science to the questions of politics, economics tries to make progress on the fundamental challenges that all societies face.

I was drawn to write this book in the hope that I could convey some of the excitement about economics that I felt as a student in my first economics course. Economics is a subject in which a little knowledge goes a long way. (The same cannot be said, for instance, of the study of physics or the Japanese language.) Economists have a unique way of viewing the world, much of which can be taught in one or two semesters. My goal in this book is to transmit this way of thinking to the widest possible audience and to convince readers that it illuminates much about the world around them.

I am a firm believer that everyone should study the fundamental ideas that economics has to offer. One of the purposes of general education is to make people more informed about the world in order to make them better citizens. The study of economics, as much as any discipline, serves this goal. Writing an economics textbook is, therefore, a great honor and a great responsibility. It is one way that economists can help promote better government and a more prosperous future. As the great economist Paul Samuelson put it, 'I don't care who writes a nation's laws, or crafts its advanced treaties, if I can write its economics textbooks.'

To reach a wide audience, I felt that one characteristic of this book would be especially important: its length. If you turn to the end of this book, you will find that it is hundreds of pages shorter than many of the standard texts used to teach the principles of economics. Moreover, the page count has not been reduced by cramming as much as possible on each page. As I requested, the designers of the book have given it an open, uncluttered and friendly look. Instead, brevity has been achieved by trying to present the principles of economics in the fewest words possible.

To explain this choice, I must make a confession: I am a slow reader. As a student, I rarely finished the readings I was assigned. I relied on Cliff's Notes an embarrassing number of times. I groaned whenever a professor gave the class a 1000-page tome to read (together, of course, with ancillary articles). I took some solace in the fact that my reaction was not unique. The Greek poet Callimachus put it succinctly: 'Big book, big bore.' Callimachus made that observation in 250 BC, so he was probably not referring to an economics textbook. But today his sentiment is echoed around the world every semester in the first lecture of many economics courses.

When I decided to write a text for the first course in economics, I wanted to write a book that as a student I would like to have read. My first and foremost goal, therefore, was brevity. I kept in mind a dictum from the great novelist Robertson Davies: 'One of the most important things about writing is to boil it down and not bore the hell out of everybody.'

All textbooks on economics teach that resources are scarce, but few textbook writers remember that student time is one of those scarce resources. I have tried to respect that scarcity by avoiding the bells, whistles and extraneous details that distract students from the key lessons. I hope this book lives up to the first word of its title, *Principles of Macroeconomics*.

N. Gregory Mankiw
August 1997

TO THE STUDENT

'Economics is a study of mankind in the ordinary business of life.' So wrote Alfred Marshall, the great nineteenth-century economist, in his textbook, *Principles of Economics*. Although we have learned much about the economy since Marshall's time, this definition of economics is as true today as it was in 1890, when the first edition of his text was published.

Why should you, as a student entering the twenty-first century, embark on the study of economics? There are three reasons.

The first reason to study economics is that it will help you understand the world in which you live. There are many questions about the economy that might spark your curiosity. Why are houses more expensive in Sydney than in Perth? Why do airlines charge less for a return ticket if the traveller stays over a Saturday night? Why is Pat Rafter paid so much to play tennis? Why are living standards so meagre in many African countries? Why do some countries have high rates of inflation while others have stable prices? Why are jobs easy to find in some years and hard to find in others? These are just a few of the questions that a course in economics will help you answer.

The second reason to study economics is that it will make you a more astute participant in the economy. As you go about your life, you make many economic decisions. While you are a student, you decide how many years you will continue with your studies. Once you take a job, you decide how much of your income to spend, how much to save and how to invest your savings. Someday you may find yourself running a small business or a large corporation, and you will decide what prices to charge for your products. The insights developed in the coming chapters will give you a new perspective on how best to make these decisions. Studying economics will not by itself make you rich, but it will give you some tools that may help in that endeavour.

The third reason to study economics is that it will give you a better understanding of the potential and limits of economic policy. As a voter, you help choose the policies that guide the allocation of society's resources. When deciding which policies to support, you may find yourself asking various questions about economics. What are the burdens associated with alternative forms of taxation? What are the effects of free trade with other countries? What is the best way to protect the environment? How does a government budget deficit affect the economy? These and similar questions are always on the minds of policymakers whether they work for a local council or the prime minister's office.

Thus, the principles of economics can be applied in many of life's situations. Whether the future finds you reading the newspaper, running a business or running a country, you will be glad that you studied economics.

Robin E. Stonecash
Joshua S. Gans
Stephen P. King
N. Gregory Mankiw
May 1999

I

INTRODUCTION

I

INTRODUCTION

1

TEN PRINCIPLES OF ECONOMICS

IN THIS CHAPTER YOU WILL

Learn that economics is about the allocation of scarce resources

Examine some of the trade-offs that people face

Learn the meaning of opportunity cost

See how to use marginal reasoning when making decisions

Discuss how incentives affect people's behaviour

Consider why trade among people or nations can be good for everyone

Discuss why markets are a good, but not perfect, way to allocate resources

Learn what determines some trends in the overall economy

The word *economy* comes from the Greek word for 'one who manages a household'. At first, this origin might seem peculiar. But, in fact, households and economies have much in common.

A household faces many decisions. It must decide which members of the household do which tasks and what each member gets in return. Who cooks dinner? Who does the laundry? Who gets the extra dessert at dinner? Who chooses what TV show to watch? In short, the household must allocate its scarce resources among its various members, taking into account each member's abilities, efforts and desires.

Like a household, a society faces many decisions. A society must decide what jobs will be done and who will do them. It needs some people to grow food, other people to make clothing, and still others to design computer software. Once society has allocated people (as well as land, buildings and machines) to various jobs, it must also allocate the output of the goods and services that they produce. It must decide who will eat caviar and who will eat potatoes. It must decide who will drive a Porsche and who will take the bus.

scarcity
the limited nature of society's resources

economics
the study of how society manages its scarce resources

The management of society's resources is important because resources are scarce. **Scarcity** means that society has less to offer than people wish to have. Just as a household cannot give every member everything he or she wants, a society cannot give every individual the highest standard of living to which he or she might aspire.

Economics is the study of how society manages its scarce resources. In most societies, resources are allocated not by a single central planner but through the combined actions of millions of households and firms. Economists, therefore, study how people make decisions—how much they work, what they buy, how much they save and how they invest their savings. Economists also study how people interact with one another. For instance, they examine how the many buyers and sellers of a good together determine the price at which the good is sold and the quantity that is sold. Finally, economists analyse forces and trends that affect the economy as a whole, including the growth in average income, the fraction of the population that cannot find work, and the rate at which prices are rising.

Although the study of economics has many facets, the field is unified by several central ideas. In the rest of this chapter, we look at the *Ten Principles of Economics*. These principles recur throughout this book and are introduced here to give you an overview of what economics is all about.

HOW PEOPLE MAKE DECISIONS

There is no mystery about what an 'economy' is. Whether we are talking about the economy of Sydney, of Australia, or of the whole world, an economy is just a group of people interacting with one another as they go about their lives. Because the behaviour of an economy reflects the behaviour of the individuals who make up the economy, we start our study of economics with four principles of individual decision making.

PRINCIPLE 1: People face trade-offs

The first lesson about making decisions is summarised in the adage: 'There is no such thing as a free lunch.' To get one thing that we like, we usually have to give up another thing that we like. Making decisions requires trading off one goal against another.

Consider a student who must decide how to allocate her most valuable resource—her time. She can spend all her time studying economics; she can spend all her time studying psychology; or she can divide her time between the two fields. For every hour she studies one subject, she gives up an hour she could have used studying the other. And for every hour she spends studying, she gives up an hour that she could have spent sleeping, bike riding, watching TV or working at her part-time job for some extra spending money.

Or consider parents deciding how to spend their family income. They can buy food or clothing, or have a holiday. Or they can save some of the family income for retirement or the children's education. When they choose to spend an extra dollar on one of these goods, they have one less dollar to spend on some other good.

When people are grouped into societies, they face different kinds of trade-offs. The classic trade-off is between 'guns and butter'. The more we spend on defence to protect our shores from foreign aggressors (guns), the less we can spend on personal goods to raise our standard of living at home (butter). Also important in modern society is the trade-off between a clean environment and a high level of income. Laws that require firms to reduce pollution raise the cost of producing goods and services. Because of the higher costs, these firms end up earning smaller profits, paying lower wages, charging higher prices, or some combination of these three. Thus, although pollution regulations give us the benefit of a cleaner environment and the improved health that comes with it, they have the cost of reducing the incomes of the firms' owners, workers and customers.

Another trade-off society faces is between efficiency and equity. **Efficiency** means that society is getting the most it can from its scarce resources. **Equity** means that the benefits of those resources are distributed fairly among society's members. In other words, efficiency refers to the size of the economic pie, and equity refers to how the pie is divided. Often, when government policies are being designed, these two goals conflict.

Consider, for instance, policies aimed at achieving a more equitable distribution of economic wellbeing. Some of these policies, such as the age pension or unemployment benefits, try to help those members of society who are most in need. Others, such as the individual income tax, ask the financially successful to contribute more than others to support the government. Although these policies have the benefit of achieving greater equity, they have a cost in terms of reduced efficiency. When the government redistributes income from the rich to the poor, it can reduce the reward for working hard; as a result, people may work less and produce fewer goods and services. In other words, as the government tries to cut the economic pie into more equitable slices, the pie may get smaller.

Recognising that people face trade-offs does not by itself tell us what decisions they will or should make. A student should not abandon the study of psychology just because doing so would increase the time available for the study of economics. Society should not stop protecting the environment just because environmental regulations reduce our material standard of living. The poor should not be ignored just because helping them distorts work incentives. Nonetheless, acknowledging life's trade-offs is important because people are likely to make good decisions only if they understand the options that they have available.

efficiency
the property of society getting the most it can from its scarce resources

equity
the property of distributing economic prosperity fairly among the members of society

CALVIN AND HOBBES by Bill Watterson

PRINCIPLE 2: The cost of something is what you give up to get it

Because people face trade-offs, making decisions requires comparing the costs and benefits of alternative courses of action. In many cases, however, the cost of some action is not as obvious as it might first appear.

Consider, for example, the decision whether to go to university. The benefit is intellectual enrichment and a lifetime of better job opportunities. But what is the cost? To answer this question, you might be tempted to add up the money you or your parents spend on fees, books, rent and food. Yet this total does not truly represent what you give up to spend a year at university.

The first problem with this answer is that it includes some things that are not really costs of university education. Even if you quit university, you would need a place to sleep and food to eat. Rent and food are costs of going to university only to the extent that they are more expensive because you are going to university. For instance, you might have to move cities to attend university and live away from home. Indeed, the cost of your room and food at your residential college or home might be less than the rent and food expenses that you would pay living on your own. In this case, the savings on the room and food are a benefit of going to university.

The second problem with this calculation of costs is that it ignores the largest cost of going to university—your time. When you spend a year listening to lectures, reading textbooks and writing assignments, you cannot spend that time working at a job. For most students, the wages given up to attend university are the largest single cost of their education.

The **opportunity cost** of an item is what you give up to get that item. When making any decision, such as whether to attend university, decision makers should be aware of the opportunity costs that accompany each possible action. In fact, they usually are. In the United States, athletes who can earn millions if they drop out of university and play professional sports are well aware that their opportunity cost of university is very high. It is not surprising that they often decide that the benefit is not worth the cost.

opportunity cost
whatever must be given up to obtain some item

PRINCIPLE 3: Rational people think at the margin

Many decisions in life involve making small incremental adjustments to an existing plan of action. Economists call these **marginal changes**. In many situations, people will make the best decisions by thinking at the margin.

Suppose, for instance, that a friend asks your advice about how many years to continue studying. If you were to compare the lifestyle of a person with a PhD with that of someone who did not complete secondary school, your friend might complain that this comparison is not helpful for his decision. Your friend is more likely to have some education already and to be deciding whether to spend an extra year or two studying. To make this decision, he needs to know the additional benefits that an extra year studying would offer and the additional costs that he would incur. By comparing these marginal benefits and marginal costs, he can evaluate whether the extra year is worthwhile.

As another example of how thinking at the margin helps decision making, consider an airline deciding how much to charge passengers who fly standby. Suppose that flying a 200-seat plane across the country costs the airline $100 000.

marginal changes
small incremental adjustments to a plan of action

In this case, the average cost of each seat is $100 000/200, which is $500. One might be tempted to conclude that the airline should never sell a ticket for less than $500.

Yet the airline can raise its profits by thinking at the margin. Suppose that a plane is about to take off with ten empty seats. A standby passenger is waiting at the gate, willing to pay $300 for a seat. Should the airline sell it to him? Of course it should. If the plane has empty seats, the cost of adding one more passenger is minuscule. Although the *average* cost of flying a passenger is $500, the *marginal* cost is merely the cost of the sandwich and coffee that the extra passenger will consume. As long as standby passengers pay more than the marginal cost, selling them a ticket is profitable.

As these examples show, individuals and firms can make better decisions by thinking at the margin. A rational decision maker takes an action if and only if the marginal benefit of the action exceeds the marginal cost.

PRINCIPLE 4: People respond to incentives

Because people make decisions by comparing costs and benefits, their behaviour may change when the costs or benefits change. That is, people respond to incentives. When the price of an apple rises, for instance, people decide to eat more pears and fewer apples, because the cost of buying an apple is higher. At the same time, apple orchards decide to hire more workers and harvest more apples, because the benefit of selling an apple is also higher.

The central role of incentives in determining behaviour is important for those designing public policy. Public policies often alter the costs or benefits of private actions. When policymakers fail to consider how behaviour might change as a result, their policies can have effects that they did not intend.

As an example of such unintended effects, consider public policy toward seat belts and car safety. In the 1950s, few cars had seat belts. Today all cars do, and the reason for the change is public policy. In the late 1960s, Ralph Nader, a famous US consumer advocate, wrote a book entitled *Unsafe at Any Speed* that generated much public concern over car safety. The US Congress responded with legislation requiring car companies to make various safety features, including seat belts, standard equipment on all new cars.

How does a seat belt law affect car safety? The direct effect is obvious. With seat belts in all cars, more people wear seat belts, and the probability of surviving a major car accident rises. In this sense, seat belts save lives. This direct impact of seat belts on safety is what motivated the US government to require seat belts.

Yet, to understand fully the effects of this law, one must recognise that people change their behaviour in response to the incentives they face. In this case, the relevant behaviour is the speed and care with which drivers operate their cars. Driving slowly and carefully is costly because it uses the driver's time and energy. When deciding how safely to drive, rational people compare the marginal benefit from safer driving with the marginal cost. They drive more slowly and carefully when the benefit of increased safety is high. This explains why people drive more slowly and carefully when roads are wet and slippery than when roads are clear.

Now consider how a seat belt law alters the cost–benefit calculation of a rational driver. Seat belts make accidents less costly for a driver because they reduce the probability of injury or death. Thus, a seat belt law reduces the benefits of slow and careful driving. People respond to seat belts as they would to an improvement in road conditions—by faster and less careful driving. The end result of a seat belt law, therefore, is a larger number of accidents.

How does the law affect the number of deaths from driving? Drivers who wear their seat belts are more likely to survive any given accident, but they are more likely to find themselves in an accident. The net effect is ambiguous. Moreover, the reduction in safe driving has a clear adverse effect on pedestrians (and on drivers who do not wear their seat belts). They are put in jeopardy by the law because they are more likely to find themselves in an accident but are not protected by a seat belt. Thus, a seat belt law tends to increase the number of pedestrian deaths.

At first, this discussion of incentives and seat belts might seem like idle speculation. Yet, in an article published in 1975, economist Sam Peltzman showed that the car safety laws have, in fact, had many of these effects. According to Peltzman's evidence, these laws produce both fewer deaths per accident and more accidents. The net result is little change in the number of driver deaths and an increase in the number of pedestrian deaths.

Peltzman's analysis of car safety is just one example of the general principle that people respond to incentives. Many of the incentives that economists study are more straightforward than those of the car safety laws. For example, no one is surprised that a tax on apples causes people to buy fewer apples. Yet, as the seat belt example shows, policies sometimes have effects that are not obvious in advance. In analysing any policy, one must consider not only the direct effects but also the indirect effects that work through incentives. If the policy changes incentives, it will cause people to alter their behaviour.

QUICK QUIZ List and briefly explain the four principles of individual decision making.

'For $5 a week you can watch cricket without being nagged to mow the lawn!'

HOW PEOPLE INTERACT

The first four principles discussed how individuals make decisions. As we go about our lives, many of our decisions affect not only ourselves but other people as well. The next three principles concern how people interact with one another.

PRINCIPLE 5: Trade can make everyone better off

You have probably heard on the news how Australian workers compete with overseas workers for jobs and Australian businesses compete with overseas firms for product sales. In some ways, this competition is real because Australian workers and firms produce many of the same goods that are produced overseas. Holden and Mazda compete for the same customers in the market for cars. Clothing firms in Victoria compete with those in Taiwan to sell shirts.

Yet it is easy to be misled when thinking about competition among countries. Trade between Australia and another country is not like a sports contest, where one side wins and the other side loses. In fact, the opposite is true—trade between two countries can make each country better off and, hence, workers (on average) better off.

To see why, consider how trade affects your family. When a member of your family looks for a job, he or she competes against members of other families who are looking for jobs. Families also compete against one another when they go shopping, because each family wants to buy the best goods at the lowest prices. So, in a sense, each family in the economy is competing with all other families.

Despite this competition, your family would not be better off isolating itself from all other families. If it did, your family would need to grow its own food, make its own clothes, and build its own home. Clearly, your family gains much from its ability to trade with others. Trade allows each person to specialise in the activities he or she does best, whether it is farming, sewing or home building. By trading with others, people can buy a greater variety of goods and services at lower cost.

Countries as well as families benefit from the ability to trade with one another. Trade allows countries to specialise in what they do best and to enjoy a greater variety of goods and services. The Japanese, the French, the Saudi Arabians and the Vietnamese are as much our partners in the world economy as they are our competitors.

PRINCIPLE 6: Markets are usually a good way to organise economic activity

The collapse of communism in the Soviet Union and Eastern Europe may be the most important change in the world during the past 50 years. Communist countries worked on the premise that central planners in the government were in the best position to guide economic activity. These planners decided what goods and services were produced, how much was produced, and who produced and consumed these goods and services. The theory behind central planning was that only the government could organise economic activity in a way that promoted economic wellbeing for the country as a whole.

Today, most countries that once had centrally planned economies have abandoned this system and are trying to develop market economies. In a **market economy**, the decisions of a central planner are replaced by the decisions of millions of firms and households. Firms decide whom to hire and what to make. Households decide which firms to work for and what to buy with their incomes. These firms and households interact in the marketplace, where prices and self-interest guide their decisions.

market economy
an economy that allocates resources through the decentralised decisions of many firms and households as they interact in markets for goods and services

At first glance, the success of market economies is puzzling. It might seem as if decentralised decision making by millions of self-interested households and firms would result in chaos. Yet this is not the case. Market economies have proven remarkably successful in organising economic activity in a way that promotes general economic wellbeing.

In his 1776 book *The Wealth of Nations*, economist Adam Smith made the most famous observation in all of economics—households and firms interacting in markets act as if they are guided by an 'invisible hand' that leads them to desirable market outcomes. One of our goals in this book is to understand how this invisible hand works its magic. As you study economics, you will learn that prices are the instrument with which the invisible hand directs economic activity. Prices reflect both the value of a good to society and the cost to society of making the good. Because households and firms look at prices when deciding what to buy and sell, they unknowingly take into account the social benefits and costs of their actions. As a result, prices guide these individual decision makers to reach outcomes that, in many cases, maximise the welfare of society as a whole.

There is an important corollary to the skill of the invisible hand in guiding economic activity—when the government prevents prices from adjusting naturally to supply and demand, it impedes the invisible hand's ability to coordinate the millions of households and firms that make up the economy. This corollary explains why taxes adversely affect the allocation of resources; taxes distort prices and thus the decisions of households and firms. It also explains the even greater harm caused by policies that directly control prices, such as rent control. And it explains the failure of communism. In communist countries, prices were not determined in the marketplace but were dictated by central planners. These planners lacked the information that gets reflected in prices when prices are free to respond to market forces. Central planners failed because they tried to run the economy with one hand tied behind their backs—the invisible hand of the marketplace.

PRINCIPLE 7: Governments can sometimes improve market outcomes

Although markets are usually a good way to organise economic activity, this rule has some important exceptions. There are two broad reasons for a government to intervene in the economy—to promote efficiency and to promote equity. That is, most policies aim either to enlarge the economic pie or to change how the pie is divided.

The invisible hand usually leads markets to allocate resources efficiently. Nonetheless, for various reasons, the invisible hand sometimes does not work. Economists use the term **market failure** to refer to a situation in which the market on its own fails to allocate resources efficiently.

One possible cause of market failure is an externality. An **externality** is the impact of one person's actions on the wellbeing of a bystander. Pollution is the classic example. If a chemical factory does not bear the entire cost of the smoke it emits, it is likely to emit too much. In this case, the government can raise economic wellbeing through environmental regulation.

Another possible cause of market failure is market power. **Market power** refers to the ability of a single person (or small group of people) to unduly influence market prices. For example, suppose that everyone in town needs water but there is only one well. The owner of the well has market power—in this case a *monopoly*—over the sale of water. The well owner is not subject to the rigorous competition with which the invisible hand normally keeps self-interest in check. You will learn that, in this case, regulating the price that the monopolist charges can potentially enhance economic efficiency.

The invisible hand is even less able to ensure that economic prosperity is distributed fairly. A market economy rewards people according to their ability to produce things that other people are willing to pay for. The world's best basketball player earns more than the world's best chess player simply because people are willing to pay more to see basketball than chess. The invisible hand

---

market failure
a situation in which a market left on its own fails to allocate resources efficiently

externality
the impact of one person's actions on the wellbeing of a bystander

market power
the ability of a single economic actor (or small group of actors) to have a substantial influence on market prices

does not ensure that everyone has sufficient food, decent clothing and adequate health care. A goal of many public policies, such as the tax and social welfare systems, is to achieve a more equitable distribution of economic wellbeing.

To say that the government *can* improve on market outcomes at times does not mean that it always *will*. Public policy is made not by angels but by a political process that is far from perfect. Sometimes policies are designed simply to reward the politically powerful. Sometimes they are made by well-intentioned leaders who are not fully informed. One goal of the study of economics is to help you judge when a government policy is justifiable to promote efficiency or equity and when it is not.

QUICK QUIZ List and briefly explain the three principles concerning economic interactions.

HOW THE ECONOMY AS A WHOLE WORKS

We started by discussing how individuals make decisions and then looked at how people interact with one another. All these decisions and interactions together make up 'the economy'. The last three principles concern the workings of the economy as a whole.

PRINCIPLE 8: A country's standard of living depends on its ability to produce goods and services

The differences in living standards around the world are staggering. In 1997, the average Australian had an income of about $24 000. In the same year, the average South Korean earned $15 000, and the average Nigerian earned $500. Not surprisingly, this large variation in average income is reflected in various measures of the quality of life. Citizens of high-income countries have more TV sets, more cars, better nutrition, better health care and longer life expectancy than citizens of low-income countries.

Changes in living standards over time are also large. In Australia, incomes have historically grown about 2% per year (after adjusting for changes in the cost of living). At this rate, average income doubles every 35 years. In some countries, economic growth has been even more rapid. In Japan, for instance, average income has doubled in the past 20 years, and in South Korea it has doubled in the past 10 years.

What explains these large differences in living standards among countries and over time? The answer is surprisingly simple. Almost all variation in living standards is attributable to differences in countries' **productivity**—that is, the amount of goods and services produced from each hour of a worker's time. In nations where workers can produce a large quantity of goods and services per unit of time, most people enjoy a high standard of living; in nations where workers are less productive, most people must endure a more meagre existence. Similarly, the growth rate of a nation's productivity determines the growth rate of its average income.

productivity
the quantity of goods and services produced from each hour of a worker's time

The fundamental relationship between productivity and living standards is simple, but its implications are far-reaching. If productivity is the primary determinant of living standards, other explanations must be of secondary importance. For example, it might be tempting to credit labour unions or award wages laws for the rise in living standards of Australian workers over the past century. Yet the real hero of Australian workers is their rising productivity. As another example, some commentators have claimed that increased competition from South-East Asia and other regions explains slow growth in domestic incomes in recent years. Yet the real villain is not competition from abroad but flagging productivity growth at home.

The relationship between productivity and living standards also has profound implications for public policy. When thinking about how any policy will affect living standards, the key question is how it will affect our ability to produce goods and services. To boost living standards, policymakers need to raise productivity by ensuring that workers are well educated, have the tools needed to produce goods and services, and have access to the best available technology.

Over the past decade, for example, much debate in Australia has centred on the government's budget deficit—the excess of government spending over government revenue. As we will see, concern over the budget deficit is based largely on its adverse impact on productivity. When the government needs to finance a budget deficit, it does so by borrowing in financial markets, much as a student might borrow to pay for postgraduate education or a firm might borrow to finance a new factory. As the government borrows to finance its deficit, therefore, it reduces the quantity of funds available for other borrowers. The budget deficit thereby reduces investment both in human capital (the student's education) and physical capital (the firm's factory). Because lower investment today means lower productivity in the future, budget deficits are generally thought to depress growth in living standards.

PRINCIPLE 9: Prices rise when the government prints too much money

In Germany in January 1921, a daily newspaper cost 0.30 of a mark. Less than 2 years later, in November 1922, the same newspaper cost 70 000 000 marks. All other prices in the economy rose by similar amounts. This episode is one of history's most spectacular examples of **inflation**, an increase in the overall level of prices in the economy.

inflation
an increase in the overall level of prices in the economy

Although Australia and New Zealand have never experienced inflation even close to that in Germany in the 1920s, inflation has at times been an economic problem. During the 1970s, for instance, the overall level of prices more than doubled, and political leaders lived under the catchcry 'Fight Inflation First!' In contrast, in the 1990s, inflation has been less than 3% per year; at this rate it would take over 20 years for prices to double. Because high inflation imposes various costs on society, keeping inflation at a low level is a goal of economic policymakers around the world.

What causes inflation? In most cases of large or persistent inflation, the culprit turns out to be the same—growth in the quantity of money. When a government creates large quantities of the nation's money, the value of the money falls. In Germany in the early 1920s, when prices were, on average, tripling every month, the quantity of money was also tripling every month. Although less

'Well, it may have been 68 cents when you got in line, but it's 74 cents now!'

dramatic, the economic history of Australia, New Zealand and the United States points to a similar conclusion—the high inflation of the 1970s was associated with rapid growth in the quantity of money, and the low inflation of the 1990s has been associated with slow growth in the quantity of money.

PRINCIPLE 10: Society faces a short-run trade-off between inflation and unemployment

If inflation is so easy to explain, why do policymakers sometimes have trouble ridding the economy of it? One reason is that reducing inflation is often thought to cause a temporary rise in unemployment. This trade-off between inflation and unemployment is called the **Phillips curve**, after the economist who first examined this relationship.

The Phillips curve remains a controversial topic among economists, but most economists today accept the idea that there is a short-run trade-off between inflation and unemployment. According to a common explanation, this trade-off arises because some prices are slow to adjust. Suppose, for example, that the government reduces the quantity of money in the economy. In the long run, the only result of this policy change will be a fall in the overall level of prices. Yet not all prices will adjust immediately. It may take several years before all firms issue new catalogues, all unions make wage concessions, and all restaurants print new menus. That is, prices are said to be *sticky* in the short run.

Because prices are sticky, various types of government policy have short-run effects that differ from their long-run effects. When the government reduces the quantity of money, for instance, it reduces the amount that people spend. Lower spending, together with prices that are stuck too high, reduces the quantity of goods and services that firms sell. Lower sales, in turn, cause firms to lay off workers. Thus, the reduction in the quantity of money raises unemployment temporarily until prices have fully adjusted to the change.

Phillips curve
the short-run trade-off between inflation and unemployment

The trade-off between inflation and unemployment is only temporary, but it can last for several years. The Phillips curve is, therefore, crucial for understanding many developments in the economy. In particular, policymakers can exploit this trade-off using various policy instruments. By changing the amount that the government spends, the amount it taxes and the amount of money it prints, policymakers can, in the short run, influence the combination of inflation and unemployment that the economy experiences. Because these instruments of monetary and fiscal policy are potentially so powerful, how policymakers should use these instruments to control the economy, if at all, is a subject of continuing debate.

QUICK QUIZ List and briefly explain the three principles that describe how the economy as a whole works.

CONCLUSION

You now have a taste of what economics is all about. In the coming chapters we will develop many specific insights about people, markets and economies. Mastering these insights will take some effort, but it is not an overwhelming task. The field of economics is based on a few basic ideas that can be applied in many different situations.

Throughout this book we will refer to the *Ten Principles of Economics* highlighted in this chapter and summarised in table 1.1. Whenever we do so, a 'building blocks' icon will show up in the margin, as it does now. But even when that icon is absent, you should keep these building blocks in mind. Even the most sophisticated economic analysis is built using the ten principles introduced here.

Table 1.1

TEN PRINCIPLES OF ECONOMICS

HOW PEOPLE MAKE DECISIONS	1:	People face trade-offs
	2:	The cost of something is what you give up to get it
	3:	Rational people think at the margin
	4:	People respond to incentives
HOW PEOPLE INTERACT	5:	Trade can make everyone better off
	6:	Markets are usually a good way to organise economic activity
	7:	Governments can sometimes improve market outcomes
HOW THE ECONOMY AS A WHOLE WORKS	8:	A country's standard of living depends on its ability to produce goods and services
	9:	Prices rise when the government prints too much money
	10:	Society faces a short-run trade-off between inflation and unemployment

Summary

- The fundamental lessons about individual decision making are that people face trade-offs among alternative goals, that the cost of any action is measured in terms of forgone opportunities, that rational people make decisions by comparing marginal costs and marginal benefits, and that people change their behaviour in response to the incentives they face.

- The fundamental lessons about interactions among people are that trade can be mutually beneficial, that markets are usually a good way of coordinating trade among people, and that the government can potentially improve market outcomes if there is some market failure or if the market outcome is inequitable.

- The fundamental lessons about the economy as a whole are that productivity is the ultimate source of living standards, that money growth is the ultimate source of inflation, and that society faces a short-run trade-off between inflation and unemployment.

Key concepts

scarcity, p. 4
economics, p. 4
efficiency, p. 5
equity, p. 5
opportunity cost, p. 6
marginal changes, p. 6
market economy, p. 9

market failure, p. 10
externality, p. 10
market power, p. 10
productivity, p. 11
inflation, p. 12
Phillips curve, p. 13

Questions for review

1. Give three examples of important trade-offs that you face in your life.
2. What is the opportunity cost of seeing a film?
3. Water is necessary for life. Is the marginal benefit of a glass of water large or small?
4. Why should policymakers think about incentives?
5. Why isn't trade among countries like a game with some winners and some losers?
6. What does the 'invisible hand' of the marketplace do?
7. What are 'efficiency' and 'equity', and what do they have to do with government policy?
8. Why is productivity important?
9. What is inflation, and what causes it?
10. How are inflation and unemployment related in the short run?

Problems and applications

1. Describe some of the trade-offs faced by:
   a. a family deciding whether to buy a new car
   b. a politician deciding whether to increase spending on national parks
   c. a company director deciding whether to open a new factory
   d. a professor deciding whether to prepare for a lecture.

2. You are trying to decide whether to take a holiday. Most of the costs of the holiday (airfare, hotel, forgone wages) are measured in dollars, but the benefits of the holiday are psychological. How can you compare the benefits with the costs?

3. You were planning to spend Saturday working at your part-time job, but a friend asks you to go skiing. What

is the true cost of going skiing? Now suppose that you had been planning to spend the day studying at the library. What is the cost of going skiing in this case? Explain.

4. You win $100 in a lottery. You have a choice between spending the money now or putting it away for a year in a bank account that pays 5% interest. What is the opportunity cost of spending the $100 now?

5. The company that you manage has invested $5 million in developing a new product, but the development is not quite finished. At a recent meeting, your salespeople report that the introduction of competing products has reduced the expected sales of *your* new product to $3 million. If it would cost $1 million to finish development, should you go ahead and do so? What is the most that you should pay to complete development?

6. The pension system provides income for people when they retire. Recipients with more income from other sources receive smaller benefits (after taxes) than recipients with less income from other sources.
   a. How does the provision of pensions affect people's incentive to save while working?
   b. How does the reduction in after-tax benefits associated with higher income affect people's incentive to work past retirement age?

7. There has been some discussion about changes to unemployment benefits that will result in payments being withdrawn after 2 years for those able to work.
   a. How do these changes in the laws affect the incentives for working?
   b. How might these changes represent a trade-off between equity and efficiency?

8. Your flatmate is a better cook than you are, but you can clean more quickly than your flatmate can. If your flatmate did all of the cooking and you did all of the cleaning, would your chores take you more or less time than if you divided each task evenly? Give a similar example of how specialisation and trade can make two countries both better off.

9. Suppose Australia adopted central planning for its economy, and you became the chief planner. Among the millions of decisions that you need to make for next year are how many compact discs to produce, what artists to record, and who should receive the discs.
   a. To make these decisions intelligently, what information would you need about the compact disc industry? What information would you need about each person in Australia?
   b. How would your decisions about CDs affect some of your other decisions, such as how many CD players to make or cassette tapes to produce? How might some of your other decisions about the economy change your views about CDs?

10. Explain whether each of the following government activities is motivated by a concern about equity or a concern about efficiency. In the case of efficiency, discuss the type of market failure involved.
    a. regulating local telephone prices
    b. providing some poor people with vouchers that can be used to buy food
    c. prohibiting smoking in public places
    d. breaking up the electricity industry into smaller generating companies
    e. imposing higher personal income tax rates on people with higher incomes
    f. instituting laws against driving while intoxicated

11. 'Everyone in society should be guaranteed the best health care possible.' Discuss this point of view from the standpoints of equity and efficiency.

12. In what ways is your standard of living different from that of your parents or grandparents when they were your age? Why have these changes occurred?

13. Suppose Australians decided to save more of their incomes. If banks lend this money to businesses, which use the money to build new factories, how might higher saving lead to faster productivity growth? Who do you suppose benefits from higher productivity? Is society getting a free lunch?

14. Suppose that when people wake up tomorrow, they discover that the government has given them an additional amount of money equal to the amount they already had. Explain what effect this doubling of the money supply is likely to have on:
    a. the total amount spent on goods and services
    b. the quantity of goods and services purchased if prices are sticky
    c. the prices of goods and services if prices can adjust.

15. Imagine that you are a policymaker trying to decide whether to reduce the rate of inflation. To make an intelligent decision, what would you need to know about inflation, unemployment and the trade-off between them?

2

THINKING LIKE AN ECONOMIST

IN THIS CHAPTER YOU WILL

See how economists apply the methods of science

Consider how assumptions and models can shed light on the world

Learn two simple models—the circular-flow diagram and the production possibilities frontier

Distinguish between microeconomics and macroeconomics

Learn the difference between positive and normative statements

Examine the role of economists in making policy

Consider why economists sometimes disagree with one another

Every field of study has its own language and its own way of thinking. Mathematicians talk about axioms, integrals and vector spaces. Psychologists talk about ego, id and cognitive dissonance. Lawyers talk about venue, torts and promissory estoppel.

Economics is no different. Supply, demand, elasticity, comparative advantage, consumer surplus, deadweight loss—these terms are part of the economist's language. In the coming chapters, you will encounter many new terms and some familiar words that economists use in specialised ways. At first, this new language may seem needlessly obscure. But, as you will see, its value lies in its ability to provide you with a new and useful way of thinking about the world in which you live.

The single most important purpose of this book is to help you learn the economist's way of thinking. Of course, just as you cannot become a mathematician, psychologist or lawyer overnight, learning to think like an economist will take some time. Yet with a combination of theory, case studies and examples of economics in the news, this book will give you ample opportunity to develop and practise this skill.

Before delving into the substance and details of economics, it is helpful to have an overview of how economists approach the world. This chapter, therefore, discusses the field's methodology. What is distinctive about how economists confront a question? What does it mean to think like an economist?

THE ECONOMIST AS SCIENTIST

Economists try to tackle their subject with a scientist's objectivity. They approach the study of the economy in much the same way as a physicist approaches the study of matter and a biologist approaches the study of life—they devise theories, collect data, and then analyse these data in an attempt to verify or refute their theories.

To beginners, it can seem odd to claim that economics is a science. After all, economists do not work with test tubes or telescopes. The essence of science, however, is the *scientific method*—the dispassionate development and testing of theories about how the world works. This method of inquiry is as applicable to studying a nation's economy as it is to studying the earth's gravity or a species' evolution. As Albert Einstein once put it, 'The whole of science is nothing more than the refinement of everyday thinking.'

Although Einstein's comment is as true for social sciences such as economics as it is for natural sciences such as physics, most people are not accustomed to looking at society through the eyes of a scientist. So let's discuss some of the ways in which economists apply the logic of science to examine how an economy works.

THE SCIENTIFIC METHOD: OBSERVATION, THEORY AND MORE OBSERVATION

Isaac Newton, the famous seventeenth-century scientist and mathematician, allegedly became intrigued one day when he saw an apple fall from an apple tree. This observation motivated Newton to develop a theory of gravity that applies not only to an apple falling to the earth but also to any two objects in the universe. Subsequent testing of Newton's theory has shown that it works well in many circumstances (although, as Einstein would later emphasise, not in all circumstances). Because Newton's theory has been so successful at explaining observation, the theory is still taught today in undergraduate physics courses around the world.

Peanuts

This interplay between theory and observation also occurs in the field of economics. An economist might live in a country experiencing rapid increases in prices and be moved by this observation to develop a theory of inflation. The theory might assert that high inflation arises when the government prints too much money. (As you may recall, this was one of the *Ten Principles of Economics* in chapter 1.) To test this theory, the economist could collect and analyse data on prices and money from many different countries. If growth in the quantity of money were not at all related to the rate at which prices are rising, the economist would start to doubt the validity of his theory of inflation. If money growth and inflation were strongly correlated in international data, as in fact they are, the economist would gain confidence in his theory.

Although economists use theory and observation like other scientists, they do face an obstacle that makes their task especially challenging—experiments are often difficult in economics. Physicists studying gravity can drop many objects in their laboratories to generate data to test their theories. In contrast, economists studying inflation are not allowed to control a nation's monetary policy simply to generate useful data. Economists, like astronomers and evolutionary biologists, usually have to make do with whatever data the world happens to give them.

To find a substitute for laboratory experiments, economists pay close attention to the natural experiments offered by history. When a war in the Middle East interrupts the flow of crude oil, for instance, oil prices skyrocket around the world. For consumers of oil and oil products, such an event depresses living standards. For economic policymakers, it poses a difficult choice about how best to respond. But for economic scientists, it provides an opportunity to study the effects of a key natural resource on the world's economies, and this opportunity persists long after the wartime increase in oil prices is over. Throughout this book, therefore, we consider many historical episodes. These episodes are valuable to study because they give us insight into the economy of the past and, more importantly, because they allow us to illustrate and evaluate economic theories of the present.

THE ROLE OF ASSUMPTIONS

If you ask physicists how long it would take for a marble to fall from the top of a ten-storey building, they will answer the question by assuming that the marble falls in a vacuum. Of course, this assumption is false. In fact, the building is surrounded by air, which exerts friction on the falling marble and slows it down. Yet physicists will correctly point out that friction on the marble is so small that its effect is negligible. Assuming the marble falls in a vacuum greatly simplifies the problem without substantially affecting the answer.

Economists make assumptions for the same reason—assumptions can make the world easier to understand. To study the effects of international trade, for example, we may assume that the world consists of only two countries and that each country produces only two goods. Of course, the real world consists of dozens of countries, each of which produces thousands of different types of goods. But by assuming two countries and two goods, we can focus our thinking. Once we understand international trade in an imaginary world with two countries and two goods, we are in a better position to understand international trade in the more complex world in which we live.

The art in scientific thinking—whether in physics, biology or economics—is deciding which assumptions to make. Suppose, for instance, that we were dropping a beach ball rather than a marble from the top of the building. Physicists would realise that the assumption of no friction is far less accurate in this case; friction exerts a greater force on a beach ball than on a marble. The assumption that gravity works in a vacuum is reasonable for studying a falling marble but not for studying a falling beach ball.

Similarly, economists use different assumptions to answer different questions. Suppose that we want to study what happens to the economy when the government changes the number of dollars in circulation. An important piece of this analysis, it turns out, is how prices respond. Many prices in the economy change infrequently; the newsagency prices of magazines, for instance, are changed only every few years. Knowing this fact may lead us to make different assumptions when studying the effects of the policy change over different time horizons. For studying the short-term effects of the policy, we may assume that prices do not change much. We may even make the extreme and artificial assumption that all prices are completely fixed. For studying the long-term effects of the policy, however, we may assume that all prices are completely flexible. Just as physicists use different assumptions when studying falling marbles and falling beach balls, economists use different assumptions when studying the short-term and long-term effects of a change in the quantity of money.

ECONOMIC MODELS

Secondary school biology teachers teach basic anatomy with plastic replicas of the human body. These models have all the major organs—the heart, the liver, the kidneys and so on. The models allow teachers to show their students in a simple way how the important parts of the body fit together. Of course, these plastic models are not actual human bodies, and no one would mistake the model for a real person. These models are stylised, and they omit many details. Yet despite this lack of realism—indeed, because of this lack of realism—studying these models is useful for learning how the human body works.

Economists also use models to learn about the world, but instead of being made of plastic, they are most often composed of diagrams and equations. Like a biology teacher's plastic model, economic models omit many details to allow us to see what is truly important. Just as the biology teacher's model does not include all of the body's muscles and capillaries, an economist's model does not include every feature of the economy.

As we use models to examine various economic issues throughout this book, you will see that all the models are built on assumptions. Just as a physicist begins the analysis of a falling marble by assuming away the existence of friction, economists assume away many of the details of the economy that are irrelevant for studying the question at hand. All models—in physics, biology or economics—simplify reality in order to improve our understanding of it.

OUR FIRST MODEL: THE CIRCULAR-FLOW DIAGRAM

The economy consists of millions of people engaged in many activities—buying, selling, working, hiring, manufacturing and so on. To understand how the economy works, we must find some way to simplify our thinking about all these activities. In other words, we need a model that explains, in general terms, how the economy is organised.

Figure 2.1 presents a visual model of the economy, called a **circular-flow diagram**. In this model, the economy has two types of decision makers—households and firms. Firms produce goods and services using various inputs, such as labour, land and capital (buildings and machines). These inputs are called the *factors of production*. Households own the factors of production and consume all the goods and services that the firms produce.

Households and firms interact in two types of markets. In the *markets for goods and services*, households are buyers, and firms are sellers. In particular, households buy the output of goods and services that firms produce. In the *markets for the factors of production*, households are sellers, and firms are buyers. In these markets, households provide firms with the inputs that the firms use to produce goods and services. The circular-flow diagram offers a simple way of organising all the economic transactions that occur between households and firms in the economy.

The inner loop of the circular-flow diagram represents the flows of goods and services between households and firms. The households sell the use of their

circular-flow diagram
a visual model of the economy that shows how dollars flow through markets among households and firms

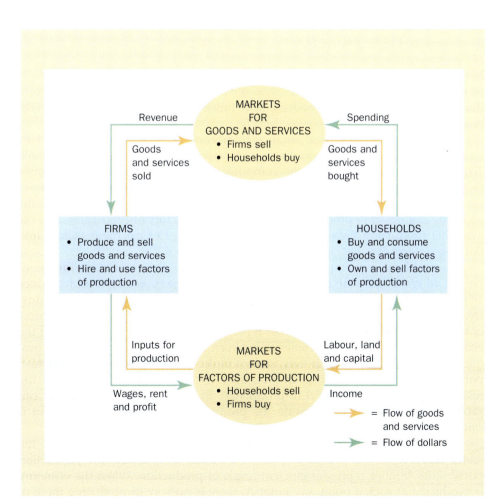

Figure 2.1

THE CIRCULAR FLOW. This diagram is a schematic representation of the organisation of the economy. Decisions are made by households and firms. Households and firms interact in the markets for goods and services (where households are buyers and firms are sellers) and in the markets for the factors of production (where firms are buyers and households are sellers). The outer set of arrows shows the flow of dollars, and the inner set of arrows shows the corresponding flow of goods and services.

labour, land and capital to the firms in the markets for the factors of production. The firms then use these factors to produce goods and services, which in turn are sold to households in the markets for goods and services. Hence, the factors of production flow from households to firms, and goods and services flow from firms to households.

The outer loop of the circular-flow diagram represents the corresponding flow of dollars. The households spend money to buy goods and services from the firms. The firms use some of the revenue from these sales to pay for the factors of production, such as the wages of their workers. What's left is the profit of the firm owners, who themselves are members of households. Hence, spending on goods and services flows from households to firms, and income in the form of wages, rent and profit flows from firms to households.

This circular-flow diagram is one simple model of the economy. It dispenses with various details that, for some purposes, are significant. A more complex and realistic circular-flow model would include, for instance, the roles of government and international trade. Yet these details are not crucial for a basic understanding of how the economy is organised. Because of its simplicity, this circular-flow diagram is useful to keep in mind when thinking about how the pieces of the economy fit together.

OUR SECOND MODEL: THE PRODUCTION POSSIBILITIES FRONTIER

Most economic models, unlike the circular-flow diagram, are built using the tools of mathematics. Here we consider one of the simplest models, called the production possibilities frontier, and see how this model illustrates some basic economic ideas.

Although real economies produce thousands of goods and services, let's imagine an economy that produces only two goods—cars and computers. Together the car industry and the computer industry use all of the economy's factors of production. The **production possibilities frontier** is a graph that shows the various combinations of output—in this case, cars and computers—that the economy can possibly produce given the available factors of production and the available production technology that firms can use to turn these factors into output.

Figure 2.2 is an example of a production possibilities frontier. In this economy, if all resources were used in the car industry, the economy would produce 1000 cars and no computers. If all resources were used in the computer industry, the economy would produce 3000 computers and no cars. The two end points of the production possibilities frontier represent these extreme possibilities. If the economy were to divide its resources between the two industries, it could produce 700 cars and 2000 computers, shown in the figure by point A. In contrast, point D is not a feasible outcome because the economy does not have the resources to support that level of production. In other words, the economy can produce at any point on or inside the production possibilities frontier, but it cannot produce at points outside the frontier.

An outcome is said to be *efficient* if the economy is getting all it can from the scarce resources it has available. Points on (rather than inside) the production possibilities frontier represent efficient levels of production. When the economy is producing at such a point, say point A, there is no way of producing more of

production possibilities frontier

a graph that shows the various combinations of output that the economy can possibly produce given the available factors of production and the available production technology

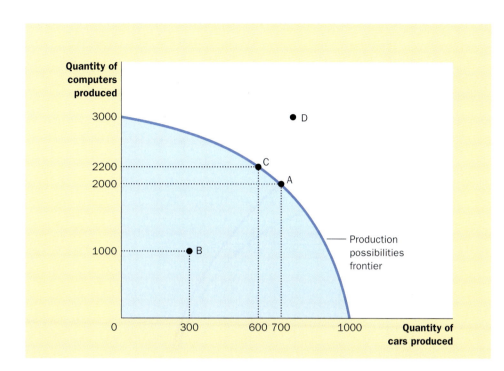

Figure 2.2

THE PRODUCTION POSSIBILITIES FRONTIER. The production possibilities frontier shows the combinations of output—in this case, cars and computers—that the economy can possibly produce. The economy can produce any combination on or inside the frontier. Points outside the frontier are not feasible given the economy's resources.

one good without producing less of the other. Point B represents an *inefficient* outcome. For some reason, perhaps widespread unemployment, the economy is producing less than it could from the resources it has available—it is producing only 300 cars and 1000 computers. If the source of the inefficiency were eliminated, the economy could move from point B to point A, increasing production of both cars (to 700) and computers (to 2000).

One of the *Ten Principles of Economics* discussed in chapter 1 is that people face trade-offs. The production possibilities frontier shows one trade-off that society faces. Once we have reached the efficient points on the frontier, the only way of getting more of one good is to get less of the other. When the economy moves from point A to point C, for instance, society produces more computers but at the expense of producing fewer cars.

Another of the *Ten Principles of Economics* is that the cost of something is what you give up to get it. This is called the *opportunity cost*. The production possibilities frontier shows the opportunity cost of one good as measured in terms of the other good. When society reallocates some of the factors of production from the car industry to the computer industry, moving the economy from point A to point C, it gives up 100 cars to get 200 additional computers. In other words, when the economy is at point A, the opportunity cost of 200 computers is 100 cars.

Notice that the production possibilities frontier in figure 2.2 is bowed outwards. This means that the opportunity cost of cars in terms of computers depends on how much of each good the economy is producing. When the economy is using most of its resources to make cars, the production possibilities frontier is quite steep. Because workers and machines best suited to making computers are being used to make cars, each car the economy gives up yields a substantial increase in the number of computers. In contrast, when the economy is using most of its resources to make computers, the production possibilities

Figure 2.3

A SHIFT IN THE PRODUCTION POSSIBILITIES FRONTIER. An economic advance in the computer industry shifts the production possibilities frontier outwards, increasing the number of cars and computers the economy can produce.

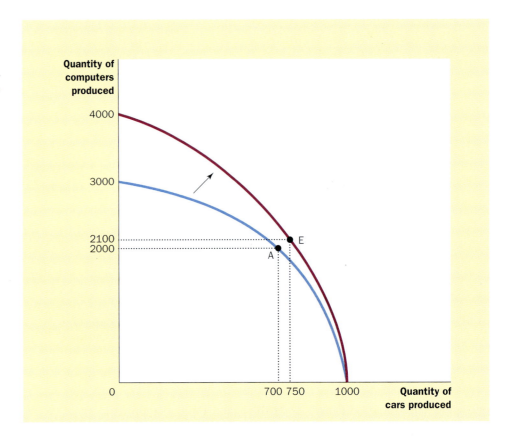

frontier is quite flat. In this case, the resources best suited to making computers are already in the computer industry, and each car the economy gives up yields only a small increase in the number of computers.

The production possibilities frontier shows the trade-off between the production of different goods at a given time, but the trade-off can change over time. For example, if a technological advance in the computer industry raises the number of computers that a worker can produce per week, the economy can make more computers for any given number of cars. As a result, the production possibilities frontier shifts outwards, as in figure 2.3. Because of this economic growth, society might move production from point A to point E, enjoying more computers and more cars.

The production possibilities frontier simplifies a complex economy in order to highlight and clarify some fundamental ideas. We have used it to illustrate some of the ideas mentioned briefly in chapter 1—efficiency, trade-offs, opportunity cost and economic growth. As you study economics, these ideas will recur in various forms. The production possibilities frontier offers one simple way of thinking about them.

MICROECONOMICS AND MACROECONOMICS

Many subjects are studied on various levels. Consider biology, for example. Molecular biologists study the chemical compounds that make up living things.

Cellular biologists study cells, which are made up of many chemical compounds and, at the same time, are themselves the building blocks of living organisms. Evolutionary biologists study the many varieties of animals and plants and how species change gradually over the centuries.

Economics is also studied on various levels. We can study the decisions of individual households and firms. Or we can study the interaction of households and firms in markets for specific goods and services. Or we can study the operation of the economy as a whole, which is just the sum of the activities of all these decision makers in all these markets.

The field of economics is traditionally divided into two broad subfields. **Microeconomics** is the study of how households and firms make decisions and how they interact in specific markets. **Macroeconomics** is the study of economy-wide phenomena. A microeconomist might study the effects of the discovery of a new gas reserve on energy production, the impact of foreign competition on the domestic car industry, or the effects of compulsory school attendance on workers' earnings. A macroeconomist might study the effects of borrowing by the federal government, the changes over time in the economy's rate of unemployment, or alternative policies to raise growth in national living standards.

microeconomics
the study of how households and firms make decisions and how they interact in markets

macroeconomics
the study of economy-wide phenomena, including inflation, unemployment and economic growth

Microeconomics and macroeconomics are closely intertwined. Because changes in the overall economy arise from the decisions of millions of individuals, it is impossible to understand macroeconomic developments without considering the associated microeconomic decisions. For example, a macroeconomist might study the effect of a cut in income tax on the overall production of goods and services. To analyse this issue, the macroeconomist must consider how the tax cut affects the decisions of households about how much to spend on goods and services.

Despite the inherent link between microeconomics and macroeconomics, the two fields are distinct. In economics, as in biology, it may seem natural to begin with the smallest unit and build up. Yet doing so is neither necessary nor always the best way to proceed. Evolutionary biology is, in a sense, built on molecular biology, since species are made up of molecules. Yet evolutionary biology and molecular biology are separate fields, each with its own questions and its own methods. Similarly, because microeconomics and macroeconomics tackle different questions, they sometimes take different approaches and are often taught in separate courses.

QUICK QUIZ In what sense is economics like a science? ◆ Define *microeconomics* and *macroeconomics*.

THE ECONOMIST AS POLICYMAKER

Often, economists are asked to explain the causes of economic events. Why, for example, is unemployment higher for teenagers than for older workers? Sometimes economists are asked to recommend policies to improve economic outcomes. What, for instance, should the government do to improve the economic wellbeing of teenagers? When economists are trying to explain the world, they are scientists. When they are trying to improve it, they are policymakers.

POSITIVE VERSUS NORMATIVE ANALYSIS

To help clarify the two roles that economists play, we begin by examining the use of language. Because scientists and policymakers have different goals, they use language in different ways.

For example, suppose that two people are discussing minimum-wage laws. Here are two statements you might hear:

POLLY: Minimum-wage laws cause unemployment.

NORMA: The government should raise the minimum wage.

Ignoring for now whether you agree with these statements, notice that Polly and Norma differ in what they are trying to do. Polly is speaking like a scientist—she is making a claim about how the world works. Norma is speaking like a policymaker—she is making a claim about how she would like to change the world.

In general, statements about the world are of two types. One type, such as Polly's, is positive. **Positive statements** are descriptive. They make a claim about how the world *is*. A second type of statement, such as Norma's, is normative. **Normative statements** are prescriptive. They make a claim about how the world *ought to be*.

A key difference between positive and normative statements is how we judge their validity. We can, in principle, confirm or refute positive statements by examining evidence. An economist might evaluate Polly's statement by analysing data on changes in minimum wages and changes in unemployment over time. In contrast, evaluating normative statements involves values as well as facts. Norma's statement cannot be judged using data alone. Deciding what is good or bad policy is not merely a matter of science. It also involves our views on ethics, religion and political philosophy.

Of course, positive and normative statements may be related. Our positive views about how the world works affect our normative views about what policies are desirable. Polly's claim that the minimum wage causes unemployment, if true, might lead us to reject Norma's conclusion that the government should raise the minimum wage. Yet our normative conclusions cannot come from positive analysis alone. Instead, they require both positive analysis and value judgements.

As you study economics, keep in mind the distinction between positive and normative statements. Much of economics just tries to explain how the economy works. Yet often the goal of economics is to improve how the economy works. When you hear economists making normative statements, you know they have crossed the line from scientist to policymaker.

positive statements
claims that attempt to describe the world as it is

normative statements
claims that attempt to prescribe how the world should be

ECONOMISTS IN GOVERNMENT

Former US President Harry Truman once said that he wanted to find a one-armed economist. When he asked his economists for advice, they always answered, 'On the one hand,…On the other hand,…'.

Truman was not alone in realising that economists' advice is often equivocal. This tendency is rooted in one of the *Ten Principles of Economics* in chapter 1—people face trade-offs. Economists are aware that trade-offs are involved in most policy decisions. A policy might increase efficiency at the cost of equity. It might help future generations but hurt current generations. An economist who says that all policy decisions are easy is an economist not to be trusted.

Nonetheless, economists play an important role in many areas of governmental decision making. In Australia, economists work in the Treasury and the Department of Finance to provide advice on taxation and fiscal policy. They give the government advice on microeconomic reform through research conducted at the Productivity Commission. Economists help construct statistical information at the Australian Bureau of Statistics and competition policy issues at the Australian Competition and Consumer Commission (ACCC). Economists skilled in macroeconomic, monetary and financial issues are employed at all levels of the Reserve Bank.

Similar roles are undertaken by economists in many countries. The president of the United States appoints a Council of Economic Advisers, which has three members and a staff of several dozen economists. The council has no duty other than to advise the president and to write the annual *Economic Report of the President*. Perhaps the most influential economist in the world is the person who chairs the Federal Reserve—the central bank of the United States. Financial markets around the world hang on any word, or indeed thought, of the current chairperson who has direct control over monetary policy in the United States.

'Let's switch. I'll make the policy, you implement it, and he'll explain it.'

The influence of economists on policy goes beyond their role as advisers and policymakers; their research and writings often affect policy indirectly. Economist John Maynard Keynes offered this observation:

> The ideas of economists and political philosophers, both when they are right and when they are wrong, are more powerful than is commonly understood. Indeed, the world is ruled by little else. Practical men, who believe themselves to be quite exempt from intellectual influences, are usually the slaves of some defunct economist. Madmen in authority, who hear voices in the air, are distilling their frenzy from some academic scribbler of a few years back.

Although these words were written in 1935, they remain true today. Indeed, the 'academic scribbler' now influencing public policy is often Keynes himself.

QUICK QUIZ Give an example of a positive statement and an example of a normative statement. ◆ Name three parts of government that regularly rely on advice from economists.

WHY ECONOMISTS DISAGREE

'If all economists were laid end to end, they would not reach a conclusion.' This quip from George Bernard Shaw is revealing. Economists as a group are often criticised for giving conflicting advice to policymakers. Former US President Ronald Reagan once joked that if the game Trivial Pursuit were designed for economists, it would have 100 questions and 3000 answers.

Why do economists so often appear to give conflicting advice to policymakers? There are three basic reasons:

◆ Economists may disagree about the validity of alternative positive theories about how the world works.
◆ Economists may have different values and, therefore, different normative views about what policies should try to accomplish.
◆ Economists may in fact agree, and yet the advice of charlatans or cranks obscures the consensus.

Let's discuss each of these reasons.

DIFFERENCES IN SCIENTIFIC JUDGEMENTS

Several centuries ago, astronomers debated whether the earth or the sun was at the centre of the heavens. More recently, meteorologists have debated whether the earth is experiencing 'global warming'. Science is a search for understanding about the world around us. It is not surprising that, as the search continues, scientists can disagree about the direction in which truth lies.

Economists often disagree for the same reason. Economics is a young science, and there is still much to be learned. Economists sometimes disagree because they have different hunches about the validity of alternative theories or about the size of important parameters.

For example, economists disagree about whether the government should levy taxes based on a household's income or its consumption (spending). Advocates of a switch from the current income tax system to a goods and services tax (GST) believe that the change would encourage households to save more, because income that is saved would not be taxed. Higher saving, in turn, would lead to more rapid growth in productivity and living standards. Advocates of the current income tax system believe that household saving would not respond much to a change in the tax laws. These two groups of economists hold different normative views about the tax system because they have different positive views about the responsiveness of saving to tax incentives.

DIFFERENCES IN VALUES

Suppose that Peter and Paul both take the same amount of water from the town well. To pay for maintaining the well, the town taxes its residents. Peter has income of $50 000 and is taxed $5000, or 10% of his income. Paul has income of $10 000 and is taxed $2000, or 20% of his income.

Is this policy fair? If not, who pays too much and who pays too little? Does it matter whether Paul's low income is due to a medical disability or to his decision to pursue a career in acting? Does it matter whether Peter's high income is due to a large inheritance or to his willingness to work long hours at a dreary job?

These are difficult questions on which people are likely to disagree. If the town hired two experts to study how the town should tax its residents to pay for the well, we would not be surprised if they offered conflicting advice.

This simple example shows why economists sometimes disagree about public policy. As we learned earlier in our discussion of normative and positive analysis, policies cannot be judged on scientific grounds alone. Economists give conflicting advice sometimes because they have different values. Perfecting the science of economics will not tell us whether it is Peter or Paul who pays too much.

CHARLATANS AND CRANKS

Fad weight-loss diets are popular because they promise amazing results with minimal effort. Many people want to lose weight but are not eager to pay the price of eating fewer kilojoules and exercising more regularly. These people are convinced all too easily by the reassuring words of some self-proclaimed expert selling a miraculous product. They *want* to believe that this new, easy-to-follow diet really will work.

Fad economics is also popular, for much the same reason. Anyone can adopt the title 'economist' and claim discovery of some easy fix to the economy's troubles. These fads often tempt politicians, who are eager to find easy and novel solutions to hard and persistent problems. Some fads come from charlatans who use crazy theories to gain the limelight and promote their own interests. Others come from cranks who believe that their theories really are true.

An example of fad economics occurred in 1980, when a small group of economists advised US presidential candidate Ronald Reagan that an across-the-board cut in income tax rates would raise tax revenue. They argued that if people could keep a higher fraction of their income, they would work harder to earn more income. Even though tax rates would be lower, income would rise by so much, they claimed, that tax revenue would rise. Almost all professional economists, including most of those who supported Reagan's proposal to cut taxes, viewed this outcome as far too optimistic. Lower tax rates might encourage people to work harder, and this extra effort would offset the direct effects of lower tax rates to some extent. But there was no credible evidence that work effort would rise by enough to cause tax revenues to rise in the face of lower tax rates. George Bush, also a presidential candidate in 1980 (who later became Reagan's vice-president), agreed with most of the professional economists; he called this idea 'voodoo economics'. Nonetheless, the argument was appealing to Reagan, and it shaped the 1980 presidential campaign and the economic policies of the 1980s.

People on fad diets put their health at risk but rarely achieve the permanent weight loss they desire. Similarly, when politicians rely on the advice of charlatans and cranks, they rarely get the desirable results they anticipate. After Reagan's election, the US Congress passed the cut in tax rates that Reagan advocated, but the tax cut did not cause tax revenue to rise. Instead, tax revenue fell, as most economists predicted it would, and the US federal government began a long period of deficit spending, leading to the largest peacetime increase in the government debt in that country's history.

Fads can make the experts seem less united than they actually are. It would be wrong to conclude that professional nutritionists are in disarray simply because fad diets are so popular. In fact, nutritionists have agreed on the basics of weight loss—exercise and a balanced low-fat diet—for many years. Similarly, when the economics profession appears in disarray, you should ask whether the disagreement is real or manufactured. It may be that some snake-oil seller is trying to sell a miracle cure for what ails the economy.

PERCEPTION VERSUS REALITY

Because of differences in scientific judgements and differences in values, some disagreement among economists is inevitable. Yet one should not overstate the amount of disagreement. In many cases, economists do offer a united view.

Table 2.1 contains ten propositions about economic policy. In a survey of economics professors in Australia, these propositions were endorsed by an overwhelming majority of respondents. The views of these economists reflect those generated by similar surveys around the world. Most of these propositions would fail to command a similar consensus among the general public.

The first proposition in the table is about rent control. For reasons we will discuss in chapter 6, almost all economists believe that rent control adversely affects the availability and quality of housing and is a very costly way of helping the most needy members of society. Nonetheless, governments in many countries choose to ignore the advice of economists and place ceilings on the rents that landlords may charge their tenants.

The second proposition in the table concerns tariffs and import quotas. For reasons we will discuss in chapter 3, almost all economists oppose such barriers to free trade. Nonetheless, over the years, governments in Australia and elsewhere have chosen to restrict the import of certain goods. Attempts to secure trade agreements, such as the North American Free Trade Agreement (between the United States, Canada and Mexico), the European Union, and APEC (Asia–Pacific Economic Cooperation), faced considerable domestic opposition in the respective countries, despite overwhelming support from economists. In

Table 2.1

Ten propositions about which most economists agree

Proposition and percentage of economists who agree

1. A ceiling on rents reduces the quantity and quality of housing available—96%
2. Tariffs and import quotas usually reduce general economic welfare—92%
3. Flexible and floating exchange rates offer an effective international monetary arrangement—77%
4. Fiscal policy (e.g. tax cut and/or government expenditure increase) has a significant stimulative impact on a less than fully employed economy—81%
5. In the short term, unemployment can be reduced by increasing the rate of inflation—60%
6. Cash payments increase the welfare of recipients to a greater degree than do transfers-in-kind of equal cash value—75%
7. Trade practices laws should be used vigorously to reduce monopoly power in Australia—81%
8. A minimum wage increases unemployment among young and unskilled workers—85%
9. The government should restructure the social security system along the lines of a 'negative income tax'—77%
10. Effluent taxes and marketable pollution permits represent a better approach to pollution control than imposition of pollution ceilings—87%

SOURCE: Adapted from Malcolm Anderson and Richard Blandy, 'What Australian economics professors think', *Australian Economic Review*, no. 100, 1992, pp. 17–40.

these cases, economists did offer united advice, but many politicians chose to ignore it.

Why do policies such as rent control and import quotas persist if the experts are united in their opposition? The reason may be that economists have not yet convinced the general public that these policies are undesirable. One of the purposes of this book is to make you understand the economist's view of these and other subjects and, perhaps, to persuade you that it is the right one.

QUICK QUIZ Give three reasons that two economic advisers to the federal government might disagree about a question of policy.

LET'S GET GOING

The first two chapters of this book have introduced you to the ideas and methods of economics. We are now ready to get to work. In the next chapter we start learning in more detail about the principles of economic behaviour and economic policy.

As you proceed through this book, you will be asked to draw on many of your intellectual skills. You might find it helpful to keep in mind some advice from the great economist John Maynard Keynes:

> The study of economics does not seem to require any specialised gifts of an unusually high order. Is it not...a very easy subject compared with the higher branches of philosophy or pure science? An easy subject, at which very few excel! The paradox finds its explanation, perhaps, in that the master-economist must possess a rare *combination* of gifts. He must be mathematician, historian, statesman, philosopher—in some degree. He must understand symbols and speak in words. He must contemplate the particular in terms of the general, and touch abstract and concrete in the same flight of thought. He must study the present in the light of the past for the purposes of the future. No part of man's nature or his institutions must lie entirely outside his regard. He must be purposeful and disinterested in a simultaneous mood; as aloof and incorruptible as an artist, yet sometimes as near the earth as a politician.

It is a tall order. But with practice, you will become more and more accustomed to thinking like an economist.

Summary

- Economists try to approach their subject with a scientist's objectivity. Like all scientists, they make appropriate assumptions and build simplified models in order to understand the world around them.

- The field of economics is divided into two subfields—microeconomics and macroeconomics. Microeconomists study decision making by households and firms and the interaction among households and firms in the marketplace. Macroeconomists study the forces and trends that affect the economy as a whole.

- A positive statement is an assertion about how the world *is*. A normative statement is an assertion about how the world *ought to be*. When economists make normative statements, they are acting more as policymakers than scientists.

- Economists who advise policymakers offer conflicting advice either because of differences in scientific judgements or because of differences in values. Sometimes policymakers get conflicting advice because some charlatan is offering an unrealistically easy solution to a hard problem. At other times, economists are united in the advice they offer, but policymakers may choose to ignore it.

Key concepts

circular-flow diagram, p. 21
production possibilities frontier, p. 22

microeconomics, p. 25
macroeconomics, p. 25

positive statements, p. 26
normative statements, p. 26

Questions for review

1. How is economics like a science?
2. Why do economists make assumptions?
3. Should an economic model describe reality exactly?
4. Draw and explain a production possibilities frontier for an economy that produces milk and biscuits. What happens to this frontier if a disease kills half of the economy's cow population?
5. What are the two subfields into which economics is divided? Explain what each subfield studies.
6. What is the difference between a positive and a normative statement? Give an example of each.
7. Why do economists sometimes offer conflicting advice to policymakers?

Problems and applications

1. Describe some unusual language used in one of the other fields that you are studying. Why are these special terms useful?

2. One common assumption in economics is that the products of different firms in the same industry are indistinguishable. For each of the following industries, discuss whether this is a reasonable assumption:
   a. steel
   b. novels
   c. wheat
   d. fast food.

3. Draw a circular-flow diagram. Identify the parts of the model that correspond to the flow of goods and services and the flow of dollars for each of the following activities:
   a. Sam pays a shopkeeper $1 for a litre of milk.
   b. Sally earns $4.50 per hour working at a fast-food restaurant.
   c. Serena spends $7 to see a film.
   d. Stuart earns $10 000 from his 10% ownership of Acme Industrial.

4. What important features of the economy does the circular-flow model ignore? Can you think of some questions for which it is reasonable to ignore these features, and some questions for which it is not?

5. The first principle of economics discussed in chapter 1 is that people face trade-offs. Use a production possibilities frontier to illustrate society's trade-off between a clean environment and high incomes. What do you suppose determines the shape and position of the frontier? Show what happens to the frontier if engineers develop a car engine with almost no emissions.

6. Classify the following topics as relating to microeconomics or macroeconomics:
   a. a family's decision about how much income to save
   b. the effect of government regulations on car emissions
   c. the impact of higher saving on economic growth
   d. a firm's decision about how many workers to hire
   e. the relationship between the inflation rate and changes in the quantity of money.

7. Classify each of the following statements as positive or normative. Explain.
   a. Society faces a short-term trade-off between inflation and unemployment.
   b. A reduction in the rate of growth of money will reduce the rate of inflation.
   c. The Reserve Bank should reduce the rate of growth of money.
   d. Society ought to require people on social security benefits to look for jobs.
   e. Lower tax rates encourage more work and more saving.

8. Classify each of the statements in table 2.1 as positive, normative or ambiguous. Explain.

9. If you were prime minister, would you be more interested in your economic advisers' positive views or their normative views? Why?

10. Who is the current head of the Reserve Bank of Australia and the Federal Reserve in the United States? Who is the current Australian Treasurer?

11. Would you expect economists to disagree less about public policy as time goes on? Why or why not? Can their differences be completely eliminated? Why or why not?

12. The chapter tells a story about Peter and Paul and the town well.
    a. Do you think that the tax policy in the example is a fair one? Why?
    b. What additional information would you like to have about Peter and Paul before reaching a judgement?
    c. In light of your answer to part (b), do you think that complicated tax systems are fairer than simple tax systems? What other considerations should affect the complexity of our tax system?

APPENDIX
GRAPHING—A BRIEF REVIEW

Many of the concepts that economists study can be expressed with numbers—the price of bananas, the quantity of bananas sold, the cost of growing bananas and so on. Often these economic variables are related to one another. When the price of bananas rises, people buy fewer bananas. One way of expressing the relationships among variables is with graphs.

Graphs serve two purposes. First, when economists develop economic theories, graphs offer a way to express visually ideas that might be less clear if described with equations or words. Second, when economists analyse economic data, graphs provide a way of finding how variables are, in fact, related in the world. Whether we are working with theory or with data, graphs provide a lens through which a recognisable forest emerges from a multitude of trees.

Numerical information can be expressed graphically in many ways, just as a thought can be expressed in words in many ways. A good writer chooses words that will make an argument clear, a description pleasing, or a scene dramatic. An effective economist chooses the type of graph that best suits the purpose at hand.

In this appendix we discuss how economists use graphs to study the mathematical relationships among variables. We also discuss some of the pitfalls that can arise in the use of graphical methods.

GRAPHS OF A SINGLE VARIABLE

Three common graphs are shown in figure 2A.1. The *pie chart* in panel (a) shows the sources of tax revenue in Australia. A slice of the pie represents each source's share of the total. The *bar graph* in panel (b) compares how much various large corporations are worth. The height of each bar represents the dollar value of each firm. The *time-series graph* in panel (c) traces the rising real income per capita of Australians over time. The height of the line shows real income per person in each year. You have probably seen similar graphs presented in newspapers and magazines.

GRAPHS OF TWO VARIABLES: THE COORDINATE SYSTEM

Although the three graphs in figure 2A.1 are useful in showing how a variable changes over time or across individuals, such graphs are limited in how much they can tell us. These graphs display information only on a single variable. Economists are often concerned with the relationships between variables. Thus, they need to be able to display two variables on a single graph. The *coordinate system* makes this possible.

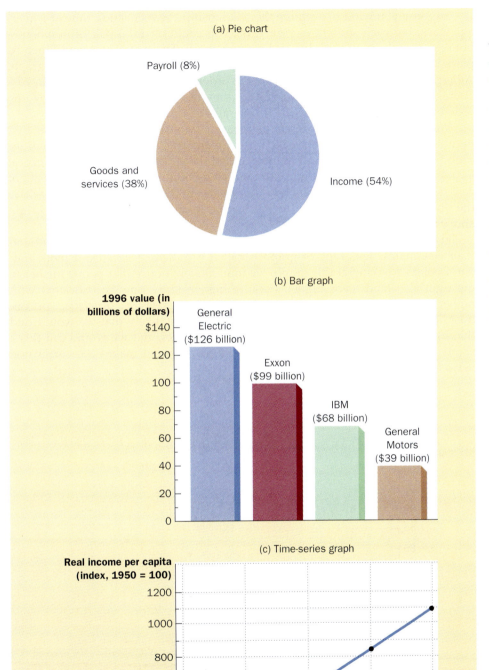

Figure 2A.1

TYPES OF GRAPHS. The pie chart in panel (a) shows the sources of tax revenue in Australia. The bar graph in panel (b) compares how much various large corporations are worth. The time-series graph in panel (c) traces the rising real income per capita of Australians over time.

SOURCES: (a) OECD, *Revenue Statistics of OECD Member Countries*, 1965–93, OECD Paris, 1994. (b) *Business Week*, 25 March 1996. (c) Robert Summers and Alan Heston, 'The Penn World (Mark 5): an expanded set of international comparisons, 1950–88', *Quarterly Journal of Economics*, vol. 106, no. 2, 1991, pp. 327–68; subsequently updated to Mark 5.5, available from National Bureau of Economic Research, Boston.

Suppose you want to examine the relationship between study time and average mark. For each student in your class, you could record a pair of numbers—hours per week spent studying and average mark. These numbers could then be placed in parentheses as an *ordered pair* and appear as a single point on the graph. Albert, for instance, is represented by the ordered pair (25 hours per week, 75% average), and his 'what-me-worry?' classmate Alfred is represented by the ordered pair (5 hours per week, 40% average).

We can graph these ordered pairs on a two-dimensional grid. The first number in each ordered pair, called the *x-coordinate*, tells us the horizontal location of the point. The second number, called the *y-coordinate*, tells us the vertical location of the point. The point with both an *x*-coordinate and a *y*-coordinate of zero is known as the *origin*. The two coordinates in the ordered pair tell us where the point is located in relation to the origin—*x* units to the right of the origin and *y* units above it.

Figure 2A.2 graphs average marks against study time for Albert, Alfred and their classmates. This type of graph is called a *scatterplot* because it plots scattered points. Looking at this graph, we immediately notice that points further to the right also tend to be higher. Because higher study time is associated with higher marks, we say that these two variables have a *positive correlation*. In contrast, if we were to graph party time and marks, it is likely that we would find that higher party time is associated with lower marks, and we would call this a *negative correlation*. In either case, the coordinate system makes the correlation between the two variables easy to see.

Figure 2A.2

USING THE COORDINATE SYSTEM. Average mark is measured on the vertical axis and study time on the horizontal axis. Albert, Alfred and their classmates are represented by various points. We can see from the graph that students who study more tend to get higher marks.

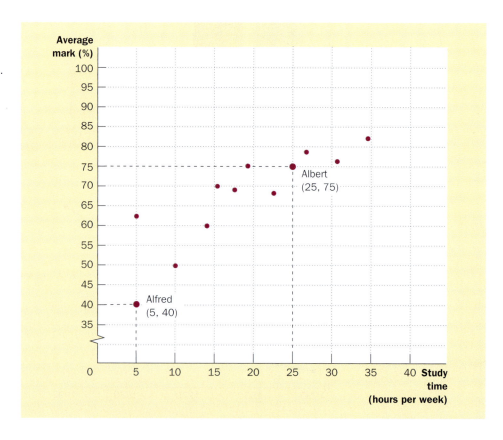

CURVES IN THE COORDINATE SYSTEM

Students who study more do tend to get higher marks, but other factors also influence a student's mark. Previous preparation is an important factor, for instance, as are talent, attention from teachers, even eating a good breakfast. A scatterplot like figure 2A.2 does not attempt to isolate the effect that study has on marks from the effects of other variables. Often, however, economists prefer looking at how one variable affects another, holding everything else constant.

One of the most important graphs in economics is the *demand curve*, which traces the effect of a good's price on the quantity of the good consumers want to buy. Table 2A.1 shows how the number of novels that Emma buys depends on her income and on the price of novels. When novels are cheap, Emma buys them in large quantities. As they become more expensive, she borrows books from the library instead of buying them or chooses to go to a film instead of reading. Similarly, at any given price, Emma buys more novels when she has a higher income. That is, when her income increases, she spends part of the additional income on novels and part on other goods.

We now have three variables—the price of novels, income and the number of novels purchased—which is more than we can represent in two dimensions. To put the information from table 2A.1 in graphical form, we need to hold one of the three variables constant and trace the relationship between the other two. Because the demand curve represents the relationship between price and quantity demanded, we hold Emma's income constant and show how the number of novels she buys varies with the price of novels.

Suppose that Emma's income is $30 000 per year. If we place the number of novels Emma purchases on the *x*-axis and the price of novels on the *y*-axis, we can graphically represent the third column of table 2A.1. When the points that represent these entries from the table—(5 novels, $10), (9 novels, $9) and so on—are connected, they form a line. This line, shown in figure 2A.3, is known as Emma's demand curve for novels; it tells us how many novels Emma purchases at any given price. The demand curve is downward-sloping, indicating that the quantity of novels demanded is negatively related to the price.

Now suppose that Emma's income rises to $40 000 per year. At any given price, Emma will purchase more novels than she did at her previous level of

Table 2A.1

NOVELS PURCHASED BY EMMA. This table shows the number of novels Emma buys at various incomes and prices. For any given level of income, the data on price and quantity demanded can be graphed to produce Emma's demand curve for novels.

	INCOME		
PRICE	$20 000	$30 000	$40 000
$10	2 novels	5 novels	8 novels
9	6	9	12
8	10	13	16
7	14	17	20
6	18	21	24
5	22	25	28
	Demand curve, D_3	Demand curve, D_1	Demand curve, D_2

Figure 2A.3

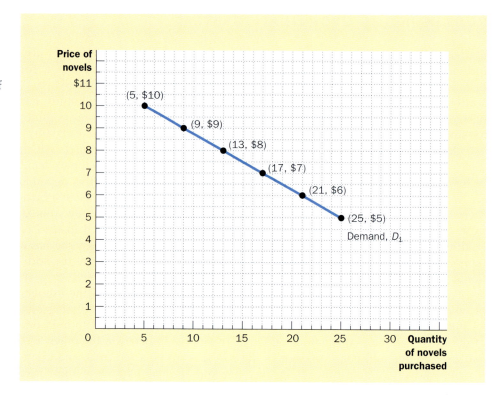

DEMAND CURVE. The line D_1 shows how Emma's purchases of novels depend on the price of novels when her income is held constant. Because the price and the quantity demanded are negatively related, the demand curve slopes downwards.

income. Just as earlier we drew Emma's demand curve for novels using the entries from the third column of table 2A.1, we now draw a new demand curve using the entries from the fourth column of the table. This new demand curve (curve D_2) is shown alongside the old one (curve D_1) in figure 2A.4; the new curve is a similar line drawn further to the right. We therefore say that Emma's demand curve for novels *shifts* to the right when her income increases. Likewise, if Emma's income were to fall to $20 000 per year, she would buy fewer novels at any given price and her demand curve would shift to the left (to curve D_3).

In economics, it is important to distinguish between *movements along a curve* and *shifts of a curve*. As we can see from figure 2A.3, if Emma earns $30 000 per year and novels cost $8 each, she will purchase 13 novels per year. If the price of novels falls to $7, Emma will increase her purchases of novels to 17 per year. The demand curve, however, stays fixed in the same place. Emma still buys the same number of novels *at each price*, but as the price falls she moves along her demand curve from left to right. In contrast, if the price of novels remains fixed at $8 but her income rises to $40 000, Emma increases her purchases of novels from 13 to 16 per year. Because Emma buys more novels *at each price*, her demand curve shifts out, as shown in figure 2A.4.

There is a simple way to tell when it is necessary to shift a curve. When a variable that is not named on either axis changes, the curve shifts. Income is on neither the *x*-axis nor the *y*-axis of the graph, so when Emma's income changes, her demand curve must shift. Any change that affects Emma's purchasing habits besides a change in the price of novels will result in a shift in her demand curve. If, for instance, the public library closes and Emma must buy all the books she wants to read, she will demand more novels at each price, and her demand curve

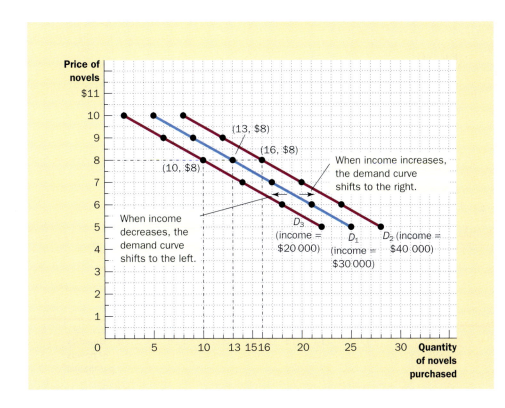

Figure 2A.4

SHIFTING DEMAND CURVES. The location of Emma's demand curve for novels depends on how much income she earns. The more she earns, the more novels she will purchase at any given price, and the further to the right her demand curve will lie. Curve D_1 represents Emma's original demand curve when her income is $30 000 per year. If her income rises to $40 000 per year, her demand curve shifts to D_2. If her income falls to $20 000 per year, her demand curve shifts to D_3.

will shift to the right. Or if the price of films falls and Emma spends more time at the pictures and less time reading, she will demand fewer novels at each price, and her demand curve will shift to the left. In contrast, when a variable on an axis of the graph changes, the curve does not shift. We read the change as a movement along the curve.

SLOPE AND ELASTICITY

One question we might want to ask about Emma is how much her purchasing habits respond to price. Look at the demand curve shown in figure 2A.5. If this curve is very steep, Emma purchases nearly the same number of novels regardless of whether they are cheap or expensive. If this curve is much flatter, Emma purchases many fewer novels when the price rises. To answer questions about how much one variable responds to changes in another variable, we can use the concept of *slope*.

The slope of a line is the ratio of the vertical distance covered to the horizontal distance covered as we move along the line. This definition is usually written out in mathematical symbols as follows:

$$\text{Slope} = \frac{\Delta y}{\Delta x}$$

where the Greek letter Δ (delta) stands for the change in a variable. In other words, the slope of a line is equal to the 'rise' (change in y) divided by the 'run' (change in x). The slope will be a small positive number for a fairly flat

Figure 2A.5

CALCULATING THE SLOPE OF A LINE. To calculate the slope of the demand curve, we can look at the changes in the x- and y-coordinates as we move from the point (21 novels, $6) to the point (13 novels, $8). The slope of the line is the ratio of the change in the y-coordinate (–2) to the change in the x-coordinate (+8), which equals –1/4.

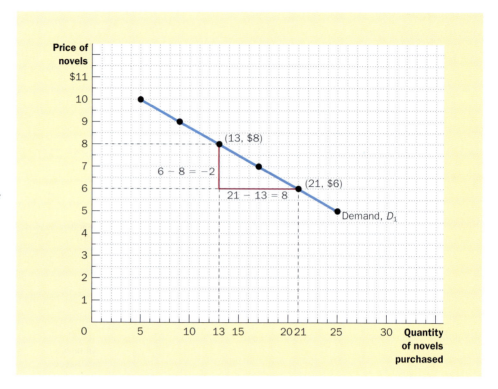

upward-sloping line, a large positive number for a steep upward-sloping line, and a negative number for a downward-sloping line. A horizontal line has a slope of zero because in this case the y-variable never changes; a vertical line is defined to have an infinite slope because the y-variable can take any value without the x-variable changing at all.

What is the slope of Emma's demand curve for novels? First of all, because the curve slopes down, we know the slope will be negative. To calculate a numerical value for the slope, we must choose two points on the line. With Emma's income at $30 000, she will purchase 21 novels at a price of $6 or 13 novels at a price of $8. When we apply the slope formula, we are concerned with the change between these two points; in other words, we are concerned with the difference between them, which lets us know that we will have to subtract one set of values from the other, as follows:

$$\text{Slope} = \frac{\text{first } y\text{-coordinate} - \text{second } y\text{-coordinate}}{\text{first } x\text{-coordinate} - \text{second } x\text{-coordinate}} = \frac{6-8}{21-13} = \frac{-2}{8} = \frac{-1}{4}$$

Figure 2A.5 shows graphically how this calculation works. Try calculating the slope of Emma's demand curve using two different points. You should get exactly the same result, –1/4. One of the properties of a straight line is that it has the same slope everywhere. This is not true of other types of curves, which are steeper in some places than in others.

The slope of Emma's demand curve tells us something about how responsive her purchases are to changes in the price. A small slope (a number close to zero) means that Emma's demand curve is relatively flat; in this case, she adjusts the number of novels she buys substantially in response to a price change. A larger slope (a number further from zero) means that Emma's demand curve is relatively steep; in this case, she adjusts the number of novels she buys only slightly in response to a price change.

The slope, however, is not a perfect measure of how much Emma responds to the price. The problem is that the slope depends on the units used to measure the variables on the x and y axes. If we measured the price of novels in cents instead of dollars, we would find that Emma's demand curve has a slope of $-100/4$ or -25, rather than $-1/4$ as we found originally. This is an equally valid calculation and tells us a useful fact—that Emma's demand for novels is less sensitive to a change in price of a certain number of cents than a change of the same number of dollars. Yet if we try to compare the slope of Emma's demand curve for novels with the price measured in dollars with the slope of Don's demand curve with the price measured in pesos or with the slope of David's demand curve with the price measured in pounds, great confusion will ensue. For this reason, economists often measure the sensitivity of one variable to changes in another variable not with slope but with *elasticity*, which uses the *percentage* change in a variable rather than the simple numerical magnitude of the change. A price decrease from $8 to $6 represents the same 25% drop as a price decrease from 800 cents to 600 cents. When we use elasticity, we no longer have to worry about whether variables are always expressed in the same units because percentage changes are the same no matter what units are used. We examine elasticities in more detail in chapter 5.

CAUSE AND EFFECT

Economists often use graphs to advance an argument about how the economy works. In other words, they use graphs to argue about how one set of events *causes* another set of events. With a graph like the demand curve, there is no doubt about cause and effect. Because we are varying price and holding all other variables constant, we know that changes in the price of novels cause changes in the quantity Emma demands. Remember, however, that our demand curve came from a hypothetical example. When graphing data from the real world, it is often more difficult to establish how one variable affects another.

The first problem is that it is difficult to hold everything else constant when measuring how one variable affects another. If we are not able to hold variables constant, we might decide that one variable on our graph is causing changes in the other variable when actually those changes are caused by a third *omitted variable* not pictured on the graph. Even if we have identified the correct two variables to look at, we might run into a second problem—*reverse causality*. In other words, we might decide that A causes B when in fact B causes A. The omitted-variable and reverse-causality traps require us to proceed with caution when using graphs to draw conclusions about causes and effects.

Omitted variables To see how omitting a variable can lead to a deceptive graph, let's consider an example. Imagine that the government, spurred by public concern about the large number of deaths from cancer, commissions an exhaustive study from Big Brother Statistical Services. Big Brother examines many of the items found in people's homes to see which of them are associated with the risk of cancer. Big Brother reports a strong relationship between two variables—the number of cigarette lighters that a household owns and the

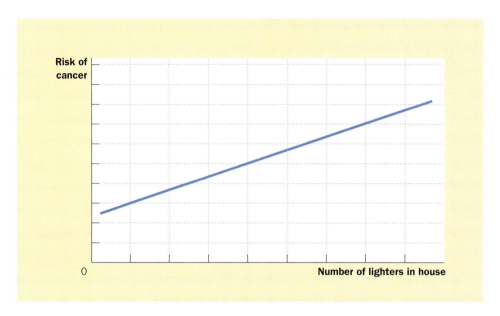

Figure 2A.6

GRAPH WITH AN OMITTED VARIABLE. The upward-sloping curve shows that households with more cigarette lighters are more likely to develop cancer. Yet we should not conclude that ownership of lighters causes cancer because the graph does not take into account the number of cigarettes smoked.

probability that someone in the household will develop cancer. Figure 2A.6 shows this relationship.

What should we make of this result? Big Brother advises a quick policy response. It recommends that the government discourage the ownership of cigarette lighters by taxing their sale. It also recommends that the government require warning labels—'Big Brother has determined that this lighter is dangerous to your health.'

In judging the validity of Big Brother's analysis, one question is paramount. Has Big Brother held constant every relevant variable except the one under consideration? If the answer is no, the results are suspect. An easy explanation for figure 2A.6 is that people who own more cigarette lighters are more likely to smoke cigarettes and that cigarettes, not lighters, cause cancer. If figure 2A.6 does not hold constant the amount of smoking, it does not tell us the true effect of owning a cigarette lighter.

This story illustrates an important principle—when you see a graph being used to support an argument about cause and effect, it is important to ask whether the movements of an omitted variable could explain the results you see.

Reverse causality Economists can also make mistakes about causality by misreading its direction. To see how this is possible, suppose the Association of Australian Anarchists commissions a study of crime in Australia and arrives at figure 2A.7, which plots the number of violent crimes per thousand people in major cities against the number of police officers per thousand people. The anarchists note the curve's upward slope and argue that since police increase rather than decrease the amount of urban violence, law enforcement should be abolished.

If we could run a controlled experiment, we would avoid the danger of reverse causality. To run an experiment, we would set the number of police officers in different cities randomly and then examine the correlation between police and crime. Figure 2A.7, however, is not based on such an experiment. We simply

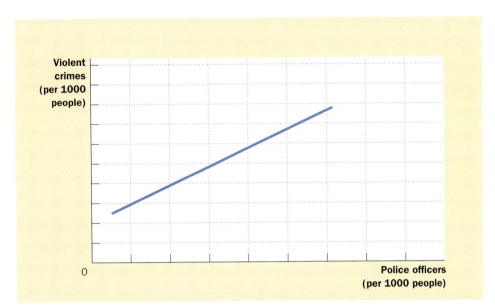

Figure 2A.7

GRAPH SUGGESTING REVERSE CAUSALITY. The upward-sloping curve shows that cities with a higher concentration of police are more dangerous. Yet the graph does not tell us whether police cause crime or crime-plagued cities hire more police.

observe that more dangerous cities have more police officers. The explanation for this may be that more dangerous cities hire more police. In other words, rather than police causing crime, crime may cause police. Nothing in the graph itself allows us to establish the direction of causality.

It might seem that an easy way to determine the direction of causality is to examine which variable moves first. If we see crime increase and then the police force expand, we reach one conclusion. If we see the police force expand and then crime increase, we reach the other. Yet there is also a flaw with this approach—often people change their behaviour not in response to a change in their present conditions but in response to a change in their *expectations* of future conditions. A city that expects a major crime wave in the future, for instance, might well hire more police now. This problem is even easier to see in the case of babies and station wagons. Couples often buy a station wagon in anticipation of the birth of a child. The station wagon comes before the baby, but we would not want to conclude that the sale of station wagons causes the population to grow!

There is no exhaustive set of rules that specifies when it is appropriate to draw causal conclusions from graphs. Yet just keeping in mind that cigarette lighters don't cause cancer (omitted variable) and station wagons don't cause babies (reverse causality) will keep you from falling for many faulty economic arguments.

3

INTERDEPENDENCE AND THE GAINS FROM TRADE

Consider your typical day. You wake up in the morning, and you pour yourself juice from oranges grown in the Riverina District of New South Wales and coffee from beans grown in Indonesia. Over breakfast, you watch a news program broadcast from Sydney on your television made in Japan. You get dressed in clothes made from cotton grown in the United States and sewn in factories in Thailand. You drive to university in a car made of parts manufactured in more than a dozen countries around the world. Then you open up your economics textbook written by one author living in Massachusetts and three others in Melbourne and Sydney, published by a company located in Sydney, and printed on paper made from trees grown in Tasmania.

Every day you rely on many people from around the world, most of whom you do not know, to provide you with the goods and services that you enjoy. Such interdependence is possible because people trade with one another. Those people who provide you with goods and services are not acting out of generosity or concern for your welfare. Nor is some government agency directing them to make what you want and to give it to you. Instead, people provide you and other consumers with the goods and services they produce because they get something in return.

In subsequent chapters we will examine how our economy coordinates the activities of millions of people with varying tastes and abilities. As a starting point for this analysis, here we consider the reasons for economic interdependence. One of the *Ten Principles of Economics* highlighted in chapter 1 is that trade can make everyone better off. This principle explains why people trade with their neighbours and why nations trade with other nations. In this chapter we

IN THIS CHAPTER YOU WILL

Consider how everyone can benefit when people trade with one another

Learn the meaning of absolute advantage and comparative advantage

See how comparative advantage explains the gains from trade

Apply the theory of comparative advantage to everyday life and national policy

examine this principle more closely. What exactly do people gain when they trade with one another? Why do people choose to become interdependent?

A PARABLE FOR THE MODERN ECONOMY

To understand why people choose to depend on others for goods and services and how this choice improves their lives, let's look at a simple economy—the economy inside a household. Imagine that there are two tasks that need to be completed in the household—cooking and laundry. And there are two people sharing the house—Monica (a cook by profession) and Rachel (a waitress)—each of whom likes to eat and wear clean and neatly ironed clothes.

The gains from trade are most obvious if Monica can only cook and Rachel can only do the laundry. In one scenario, Monica and Rachel could choose to have nothing to do with each other. Monica would cook for herself and Rachel would wash and iron her own clothes. Monica's clothes would never be cleaned. But after several months of eating cold meat and biscuits, Rachel might decide that self-sufficiency is not all it's cracked up to be. Monica, whose clothing could not have a worse odour, would be likely to agree. It is easy to see that trade would allow them to enjoy greater variety—each could eat well and wear clean clothes.

Although this scene illustrates very simply how everyone can benefit from trade, the gains would be similar if Monica and Rachel were each capable of doing the other task, but only at great cost. Suppose, for example, that Monica is able to wash and iron clothes, but that she is not very good at it. Similarly, suppose that Rachel is able to cook but has not had the experience and so can cook only a few basic dishes. In this case, it is easy to see that Monica and Rachel can each benefit by specialising in what she does best and then trading with the other.

The gains from trade are less obvious, however, when one person is better at producing *every* good. For example, suppose that Monica is better at cooking *and* better at washing and ironing than Rachel. In this case, should Monica or Rachel choose to remain self-sufficient? Or is there still reason for them to trade with each other? To answer this question, we need to look more closely at the factors that affect such a decision.

PRODUCTION POSSIBILITIES

Suppose that Monica and Rachel each have 12 spare hours a week to work on household tasks and can devote this time to cooking, laundry or a combination of the two. Table 3.1 shows the amount of time each person requires to produce 1 unit of each good—a decent meal and a basket of clean clothes. Rachel can wash and iron a basket of clothes in 4 hours and cook a meal in 2 hours. Monica, who is more productive in both activities, needs only half an hour to cook a meal and can wash and iron a basket of clothes in 3 hours.

Panel (a) of figure 3.1 illustrates the amounts of laundry and cooking that Rachel can produce. If Rachel devotes all 12 hours of her time to laundry, she cleans 3 baskets of clothes but does not cook. If she devotes all her time to

Table 3.1

THE PRODUCTION OPPORTUNITIES OF RACHEL AND MONICA

	HOURS NEEDED TO MAKE:		AMOUNT PRODUCED IN 12 HOURS:	
	1 MEAL	1 BASKET	MEALS	BASKETS
RACHEL	2	4	6	3
MONICA	1/2	3	24	4

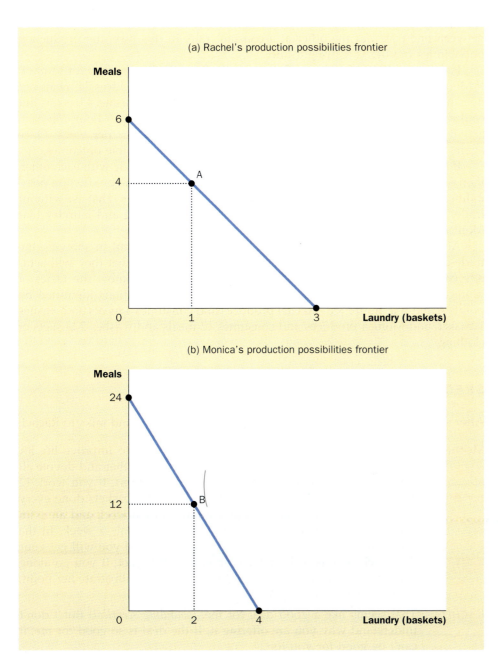

Figure 3.1

THE PRODUCTION POSSIBILITIES FRONTIER. Panel (a) shows the combinations of meals and laundry that Rachel can produce. Panel (b) shows the combinations of meals and laundry that Monica can produce. Both production possibilities frontiers are derived from table 3.1 and the assumption that Rachel and Monica each work 12 hours per week on domestic chores.

cooking, she produces 6 meals and washes no clothes. If Rachel spends 4 hours doing laundry and 8 hours cooking, she cooks 4 meals and washes and irons one basket of clothes. The figure shows these three possible outcomes and all others in between.

This graph is Rachel's production possibilities frontier. As we discussed in chapter 2, a production possibilities frontier shows the various mixes of output that an economy can produce. It illustrates one of the *Ten Principles of Economics* in chapter 1—people face trade-offs. Here Rachel faces a trade-off between time spent cooking and doing laundry. You may recall that the production possibilities frontier in chapter 2 was drawn bowed out; in this case, the trade-off between the two goods depends on the amounts being produced. Here, however, Rachel's 'technology' (as summarised in table 3.1) allows her to switch between one task and the other at a constant rate. In this case, the production possibilities frontier is a straight line.

Panel (b) of figure 3.1 shows the production possibilities frontier for Monica. If Monica devotes all 12 hours of her time to cooking, she produces 24 meals but does no laundry. If she devotes all her time to laundry, she washes 4 baskets but cooks no meals. If Monica divides her time equally, spending 6 hours on each activity, she cooks 12 meals and washes 2 baskets of clothes per week. Once again, the production possibilities frontier shows all the possible outcomes.

If Monica and Rachel choose to go it alone, rather than trade with each other, then each consumes exactly what she produces. In this case, the production possibilities frontier is also the consumption possibilities frontier. That is, without trade, figure 3.1 shows the possible combinations of cooking and laundry that Monica and Rachel can each consume.

Although these production possibilities frontiers are useful in showing the trade-offs that Monica and Rachel face, they do not tell us what they will actually choose to do. To determine their choices, we need to know the tastes of Monica and Rachel. Let's suppose they choose the combinations identified by points A and B in figure 3.1—Rachel produces and consumes 4 meals and washes 1 basket, and Monica produces and consumes 12 meals and washes 2 baskets of clothing.

SPECIALISATION AND TRADE

After several months of combination B, Monica gets an idea and talks to Rachel:

MONICA: Rachel, have I got a deal for you! I know how to improve life for both of us. I think you should stop cooking altogether and devote all your time to laundry. According to my calculations, if you work 12 hours a week washing and ironing, you'll get 3 baskets done every week. If you do 1 basket of laundry for me each week and an extra one every second week, then I'll cook you 5 meals a week. In the end, you'll be able to eat real food more often and you will get your clothes cleaner as well. Indeed, another half basket. If you go along with my plan, you'll eat well and look better! [To illustrate her point, Monica shows Rachel panel (a) of figure 3.2.]

RACHEL: That seems like a good deal for me. *(sounding sceptical)* But I don't understand why you are offering it. If the deal is so good for me, it can't be good for you too.

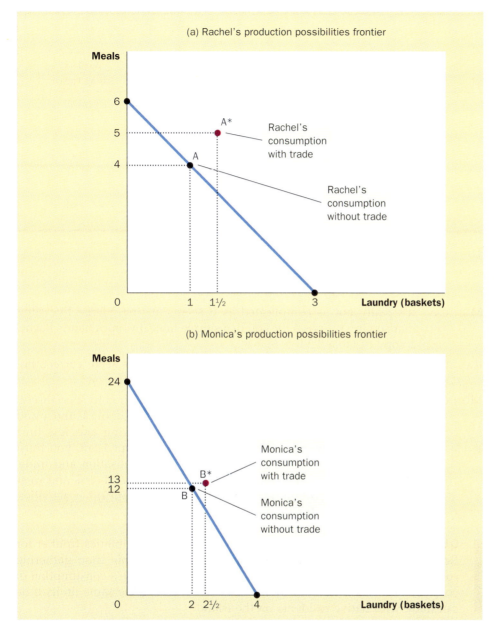

Figure 3.2

How trade expands the set of consumption opportunities. The proposed trade between Rachel and Monica offers each a combination of meals and baskets of clean clothes that would be impossible in the absence of trade. In panel (a), Rachel gets to consume at point A* rather than point A. In panel (b), Monica gets to consume at point B* rather than point B. Trade allows each to consume more meals and have more clean clothes.

MONICA: Oh, but it is! If I spend 9 hours a week cooking and 3 hours doing laundry, I'll make 18 meals and also have time spare to wash another basket. After I give you 5 meals in exchange for the extra basket-and-a-half you wash and iron, I'll be able to eat 13 meals at home but I'll have more clean shirts, pants and, most importantly, socks and underwear. In the end, I will be much happier than I am now. [She points out panel (b) of figure 3.2.]

RACHEL: I don't know…This sounds too good to be true. I don't want you coming back to me next week and complaining about having to do all the cooking.

	WITHOUT TRADE:	WITH TRADE:			
	PRODUCTION AND CONSUMPTION	PRODUCTION	TRADE	CONSUMPTION	GAINS FROM TRADE
RACHEL	4 meals	0 meals	Gets 5 meals	5 meals	1 meal
	1 basket	3 baskets	for 1½ baskets	1½ baskets	½ basket
MONICA	12 meals	18 meals	Gives 5 meals	13 meals	1 meal
	2 baskets	1 basket	for 1½ baskets	2½ baskets	½ basket

Table 3.2 THE GAINS FROM TRADE: A SUMMARY

MONICA: It's really not as complicated as it seems at first. Here—I've summarised my proposal for you in a simple table. [Monica hands Rachel a copy of table 3.2.]

RACHEL: *(after pausing to study the table)* These calculations seem correct, but I'm puzzled. How can this deal make us both better off?

MONICA: We can both benefit because trade allows each of us to specialise in doing what we do best. You will spend more time doing laundry and less time cooking. I will spend more time cooking and less time washing and ironing. I like to iron my clothes but I am, you must admit, a much better cook. As a result of specialisation and trade, each of us can consume more of the great meals that I cook and wear cleaner clothes without taking more time out of our other activities. Can it *be* more attractive?

QUICK QUIZ Draw an example of a production possibilities frontier for Robinson Crusoe, a shipwrecked sailor who spends his time gathering coconuts and catching fish. Does this frontier limit Crusoe's consumption of coconuts and fish if he lives by himself? Does he face the same limits if he can trade with native residents on the island?

THE PRINCIPLE OF COMPARATIVE ADVANTAGE

Monica's explanation of the gains from trade, though correct, poses a puzzle—if Monica is better at both cooking and laundry, how can Rachel ever specialise in doing what she does best? Rachel doesn't seem to do anything best. To solve this puzzle, we need to look at the principle of *comparative advantage*.

As a first step in developing this principle, consider the following question. In our example, who does the laundry at lower cost—Rachel or Monica? There are two possible answers, and in these two answers lie both the solution to our puzzle and the key to understanding the gains from trade.

ABSOLUTE ADVANTAGE

One way to answer the question about the cost of doing the laundry is to compare the inputs required by the two housemates. Monica needs only 3 hours to do a basket of laundry, whereas Rachel needs 4 hours. Based on this information, one might conclude that Monica has the lower cost of washing and ironing.

Economists use the term **absolute advantage** when comparing the productivity of one person, firm or nation with that of another. The producer that requires a smaller quantity of inputs to produce a good is said to have an absolute advantage in producing that good. In our example, Monica has an absolute advantage both in laundry and cooking, because she requires less time than Rachel to produce a unit of either good.

absolute advantage
the comparison among producers of a good according to their productivity

OPPORTUNITY COST AND COMPARATIVE ADVANTAGE

There is another way to look at the cost of laundry. Rather than comparing inputs required, we can compare the opportunity costs. Recall from chapter 1 that the **opportunity cost** of some item is what we give up to get that item. In our example, we assumed that Rachel and Monica each spend 12 hours a week on household tasks. Time spent doing laundry, therefore, takes away from time available for cooking. As Monica and Rachel change their allocations of time between producing the two goods, they move along their production possibility frontiers; in a sense, they are using one good to produce the other. The opportunity cost measures the trade-off that each faces.

opportunity cost
whatever must be given up to obtain some item

Let's first consider Monica's opportunity cost. Doing a basket of clothes takes her 3 hours of work. When Monica spends that 3 hours doing laundry, she spends 3 hours less cooking. Because Monica needs only half an hour to produce 1 meal, 3 hours of work would yield 6 meals. Hence, Monica's opportunity cost of 1 basket is 6 meals. Monica's production possibilities frontier reflects this opportunity cost—the downward-sloping line in panel (b) of figure 3.1 has a slope ('rise over run') equal to −6.

Now consider Rachel's opportunity cost. Washing and ironing one basket takes her 4 hours. Because she needs 2 hours to cook a meal, 4 hours would yield 2 meals. Hence, Rachel's opportunity cost of doing 1 basket is 2 meals. Rachel's production possibilities frontier in panel (a) of figure 3.1 reflects this opportunity cost by having a slope of −2.

Table 3.3 shows the opportunity cost of cooking and laundry for the housemates. Notice that the opportunity cost of cooking is the inverse of the opportunity cost of laundry. Because 1 clean basket costs Monica 6 meals, 1 meal costs

Table 3.3

THE OPPORTUNITY COST OF MEALS AND BASKETS OF CLEAN CLOTHES

	Opportunity cost of 1:	
	Meal (in terms of baskets given up)	Basket (in terms of meals given up)
Rachel	1/2	2
Monica	1/6	6

comparative advantage
the comparison among producers of a good according to their opportunity cost

Monica one-sixth of a basket. Similarly, because doing 1 basket costs Rachel 2 meals, 1 meal costs Rachel half a basket of clothing.

Economists use the term **comparative advantage** when describing the opportunity cost of two producers. The producer who has the smaller opportunity cost of producing a good is said to have a comparative advantage in producing that good. In our example, Rachel has a lower opportunity cost of laundry than Monica (2 versus 6 meals). Monica has a lower opportunity cost of cooking than Rachel ($1/6$ rather than $1/2$ of a basket). Thus, Rachel has a comparative advantage in laundry, and Monica has a comparative advantage in cooking.

Notice that it would be impossible for the same person to have a comparative advantage in both goods. Because the opportunity cost of one good is the inverse of the opportunity cost of the other, if a person's opportunity cost of one good is relatively high, his opportunity cost of the other good must be relatively low. Comparative advantage reflects the relative opportunity cost. Unless two people have exactly the same opportunity cost, one person will have a comparative advantage in one good, and the other person will have a comparative advantage in the other good.

COMPARATIVE ADVANTAGE AND TRADE

Differences in opportunity cost and comparative advantage create the gains from trade. When each person specialises in producing the good for which he or she has a comparative advantage, total production in the economy rises, and this increase in the size of the economic pie can be used to make everyone better off. In other words, as long as two people have different opportunity costs, each can benefit from trade by obtaining a good at a price lower than his or her opportunity cost of that good.

Consider the proposed deal from the viewpoint of Rachel. Rachel gets 5 meals in exchange for cleaning an extra one-and-a-half baskets. In other words, Rachel buys each meal for a price of $3/10$ of a basket of laundry. This price of a meal is lower than her opportunity cost of cooking, which is $1/2$ a basket. Thus, Rachel benefits from the deal because she gets to buy meals at a good price.

Now consider the deal from Monica's viewpoint. Monica buys a basket of laundry for a price of just over 3 meals. This price of laundry is lower than her opportunity cost of laundry, which is 6 meals. Thus, Monica benefits because she gets to buy a laundry service at a good price.

These benefits arise because each person concentrates on the activity for which she has the lower opportunity cost—Rachel spends more time doing laundry, and Monica spends more time cooking. As a result, the total production of clean clothing and the total production of meals both rise, and Rachel and Monica share the benefits of this increased production. The moral of the story of Monica and Rachel should now be clear—*trade can benefit everyone in society because it allows people to specialise in activities in which they have a comparative advantage.*

QUICK QUIZ Robinson Crusoe can gather 10 coconuts or catch 1 fish per hour. His friend Friday can gather 30 coconuts or catch 2 fish per hour. What is Crusoe's opportunity cost of catching 1 fish? What is Friday's? Who has an absolute advantage in catching fish? Who has a comparative advantage in catching fish?

APPLICATIONS OF COMPARATIVE ADVANTAGE

The principle of comparative advantage explains interdependence and the gains from trade. Because interdependence is so prevalent in the modern world, the principle of comparative advantage has many applications. Here are two examples, one fanciful and one of great practical importance.

SHOULD MICHAEL JORDAN MOW HIS OWN LAWN?

Michael Jordan is a great athlete. One of the best basketball players in the US competition, the NBA, he can jump higher and shoot better than most other people. Very likely, he is better at other activities, too. For example, Jordan can probably mow his lawn faster than anyone else. But just because he *can* mow his lawn fast, does this mean he *should*?

To answer this question, we can use the concepts of opportunity cost and comparative advantage. Let's say that Jordan can mow his lawn in 2 hours. In that same 2 hours, he could film a television commercial for sports shoes and earn $10 000. In contrast, Jennifer, the young woman next door, can mow Jordan's lawn in 4 hours. In that same 4 hours, she could work at McDonald's and earn $40.

In this example, Jordan's opportunity cost of mowing the lawn is $10 000, and Jennifer's opportunity cost is $40. Jordan has an absolute advantage in mowing lawns because he can do the work in less time. Yet Jennifer has a comparative advantage in mowing lawns because she has the lower opportunity cost.

The gains from trade in this example are tremendous. Rather than mowing his own lawn, Jordan should make the commercial and hire Jennifer to mow the lawn. As long as he pays her more than $40 and less than $10 000, both of them are better off.

SHOULD A COUNTRY TRADE WITH OTHER COUNTRIES?

Just as individuals can benefit from specialisation and trade with one another, as Monica and Rachel did, so can populations of people in different countries. Many of the goods that Australians enjoy are produced abroad, and many of the goods produced in Australia are sold abroad. Goods produced abroad and sold domestically are called **imports**. Goods produced domestically and sold abroad are called **exports**.

To see how countries can benefit from trade, suppose there are two countries, Australia and Japan, and two goods, food and cars. Imagine that the two countries produce cars equally well—an Australian worker and a Japanese worker can each produce 1 car per month. In contrast, because Australia has more and better land, it is better at producing food—an Australian worker can produce 2 tonnes of food per month, whereas a Japanese worker can produce only 1 tonne of food per month.

The principle of comparative advantage states that each good should be produced by the country that has the smaller opportunity cost of producing that good. Because the opportunity cost of a car is 2 tonnes of food in Australia but

imports
goods produced abroad and sold domestically

exports
goods produced domestically and sold abroad

only 1 tonne of food in Japan, Japan has a comparative advantage in producing cars. Japan should produce more cars than it wants for its own use and export some of them to Australia. Similarly, because the opportunity cost of a tonne of food is 1 car in Japan but only half a car in Australia, Australia has a comparative advantage in producing food. Australia should produce more food than it wants to consume and export some of it to Japan. Through specialisation and trade, both countries can have more food and more cars.

In reality, of course, the issues involved in trade among nations are more complex than this example suggests, as we will see in chapter 9. Most important among these issues is that each country has many citizens with different interests. International trade can make some individuals worse off, even as it makes the country as a whole better off. When Australia exports food and imports cars, the impact on an Australian farmer is not the same as the impact on an Australian car worker. Yet contrary to the opinions sometimes voiced by politicians and political commentators, international trade is not like war, in which some countries win and others lose. Trade allows all countries to achieve greater prosperity.

QUICK QUIZ Suppose that the world's fastest typist happens to be trained in brain surgery. Should that person type for herself or hire a secretary? Explain.

FYI

The legacy of Adam Smith and David Ricardo

DAVID RICARDO

ECONOMISTS HAVE LONG UNderstood the principle of comparative advantage. Here is how the great economist Adam Smith put the argument:

> It is a maxim of every prudent master of a family, never to attempt to make at home what it will cost him more to make than to buy. The tailor does not attempt to make his own shoes, but buys them of the shoemaker. The shoemaker does not attempt to make his own clothes but employs a tailor. The farmer attempts to make neither the one nor the other, but employs those different artificers. All of them find it for their interest to employ their whole industry in a way in which they have some advantage over their neighbours, and to purchase with a part of its produce, or what is the same thing, with the price of part of it, whatever else they have occasion for.

This quotation is from Smith's 1776 book *An Inquiry into the Nature and Causes of the Wealth of Nations*. This book was a landmark in the analysis of trade and economic interdependence. Many economists consider Smith to be the founder of modern economics.

Smith's book inspired David Ricardo, a millionaire stockbroker, to become an economist. In his 1817 book *Principles of Political Economy and Taxation*, Ricardo developed the principle of comparative advantage as we know it today. His defence of free trade was not a mere academic exercise. Ricardo put his economic beliefs to work as a member of the British Parliament, where he opposed the Corn Laws, which restricted the import of grain.

The conclusions of Adam Smith and David Ricardo on the gains from trade have held up well over time. Although economists often disagree on questions of policy, they are united in their support of free trade. Moreover, the central argument for free trade has not changed much in the past two centuries. Even though the field of economics has broadened its scope and refined its theories since the time of Smith and Ricardo, economists' opposition to trade restrictions is still based largely on the principle of comparative advantage.

CONCLUSION

The principle of comparative advantage shows that trade can make everyone better off. You should now understand more fully the benefits of living in an interdependent economy. But having seen why interdependence is desirable, you might naturally ask how it is possible. How do free societies coordinate the diverse activities of all the people involved in their economies? What ensures that goods and services will go from those who should be producing them to those who should be consuming them?

In a world with only two people, such as Monica and Rachel, the answer is simple—these two people can directly bargain and allocate resources between themselves. In the real world with millions of people, the answer is less obvious. We take up this issue in the next chapter, where we see that free societies allocate resources through the market forces of supply and demand.

Summary

- Each person consumes goods and services produced by many other people both in our country and around the world. Interdependence and trade are desirable because they allow everyone to enjoy a greater quantity and variety of goods and services.

- There are two ways to compare the ability of two people in producing a good. The person who can produce the good with the smaller quantity of inputs is said to have an *absolute advantage* in producing the good. The person who has the smaller opportunity cost of producing the good is said to have a *comparative*

  advantage. The gains from trade are based on comparative advantage, not absolute advantage.

- Trade makes everyone better off because it allows people to specialise in those activities in which they have a comparative advantage.

- The principle of comparative advantage applies to countries as well as to people. Economists use the principle of comparative advantage to advocate free trade among countries.

Key concepts

absolute advantage, p. 51
opportunity cost, p. 51
comparative advantage, p. 52

imports, p. 53
exports, p. 53

Questions for review

1. Explain how absolute advantage and comparative advantage differ.

2. Give an example in which one person has an absolute advantage in doing something but another person has a comparative advantage.

3. Is absolute advantage or comparative advantage more important for trade? Explain your answer using the example in your answer to question 2.

4. Why do economists oppose policies that restrict trade among nations?

Problems and applications

1. Consider Rachel and Monica from our example in this chapter. Explain why Rachel's opportunity cost of producing 1 basket of clean clothing is 2 meals. Explain why Monica's opportunity cost of producing 1 meal is $1/6$ of a washed and ironed basket of clothing.

2. Maria can read 20 pages of economics in an hour. She can also read 50 pages of sociology in an hour. She spends 5 hours per day studying.
   a. Draw Maria's production possibilities frontier for reading economics and sociology.
   b. What is Maria's opportunity cost of reading 100 pages of sociology?

3. Australian and Japanese workers can each produce 4 cars a year. An Australian worker can produce 10 tonnes of grain a year, whereas a Japanese worker can produce 5 tonnes of grain a year. To keep things simple, assume that each country has 100 million workers.
   a. For this situation, construct a table similar to table 3.1.
   b. Graph the production possibilities frontier of the Australian and Japanese economies.
   c. For Australia, what is the opportunity cost of a car? of grain? For Japan, what is the opportunity cost of a car? of grain? Put this information in a table similar to table 3.3.
   d. Which country has an absolute advantage in producing cars? in producing grain?
   e. Which country has a comparative advantage in producing cars? in producing grain?
   f. Without trade, half of each country's workers produce cars and half produce grain. What quantities of cars and grain does each country produce?
   g. Starting from a position without trade, give an example in which trade makes each country better off.

4. Joey and Chandler are flatmates. They spend most of their time working, but they leave some time for their favorite activities—making pizza and fine coffee. Chandler takes 5 minutes to make a pot of coffee and half an hour to make a pizza. Joey takes 15 minutes to make a pot of coffee and one hour to make a pizza.
   a. What is each flatmate's opportunity cost of making a pizza? Who has the absolute advantage in making pizza? Who has the comparative advantage in making pizza?
   b. If Joey and Chandler trade foods with each other, who will trade away pizza in exchange for coffee?
   c. The price of pizza can be expressed in terms of pots of coffee. What is the highest price at which pizza can be traded that would make both flatmates better off? What is the lowest price? Explain.

5. Suppose that there are 10 million workers in South Korea, and that each of these workers can produce either 2 cars or 30 bags of wheat in a year.
   a. What is the opportunity cost of producing a car in South Korea? What is the opportunity cost of producing a bag of wheat in South Korea? Explain the relationship between the opportunity costs of the two goods.
   b. Draw South Korea's production possibilities frontier. If South Korea chooses to consume 10 million cars, how much wheat can it consume without trade? Label this point on the production possibilities frontier.
   c. Now suppose that Thailand offers to buy 10 million cars from South Korea in exchange for 20 bags of wheat per car. If South Korea continues to consume 10 million cars, how much wheat does this deal allow South Korea to consume? Label this point on your diagram. Should South Korea accept the deal?

6. Consider a professor who is writing a book. The professor can both write the chapters and gather the needed data faster than anyone else at her university. Still, she pays a student to collect data at the library. Is this sensible? Explain.

7. England and Scotland both produce scones and jumpers. Suppose that an English worker can produce 50 scones per hour or 1 jumper per hour. Suppose that a Scottish worker can produce 40 scones per hour or 2 jumpers per hour.
   a. Which country has the absolute advantage in the production of each good? Which country has the comparative advantage?
   b. If England and Scotland decide to trade, which commodity will Scotland trade to England? Explain.
   c. If a Scottish worker could produce only 1 jumper per hour, would Scotland still gain from trade? Would England still gain from trade? Explain.

8. The following table describes the production possibilities of two cities in the country of Footballia:

	Maroon shirts per worker per hour	Blue shirts per worker per hour
Brisbane	3	3
Sydney	2	1

a. Without trade, what is the price of blue shirts (in terms of maroon shirts) in Brisbane? What is the price in Sydney?
b. Which city has an absolute advantage in the production of each colour shirt? Which city has a comparative advantage in the production of each colour shirt?
c. If the cities trade with each other, which colour shirt will each export?
d. What is the range of prices at which trade can occur?

9. Suppose that all goods can be produced with fewer worker hours in Germany than in France.
a. In what sense is the cost of all goods lower in Germany than in France?
b. In what sense is the cost of some goods lower in France?
c. If Germany and France traded with each other, would both countries be better off as a result? Explain in the context of your answers to parts (a) and (b).

10. Are the following statements true or false? Explain in each case.
a. 'Two countries can achieve gains from trade even if one of the countries has an absolute advantage in the production of all goods.'
b. 'Certain very talented people have a comparative advantage in everything they do.'
c. 'If a certain trade is good for one person, it can't be good for the other one.'

II

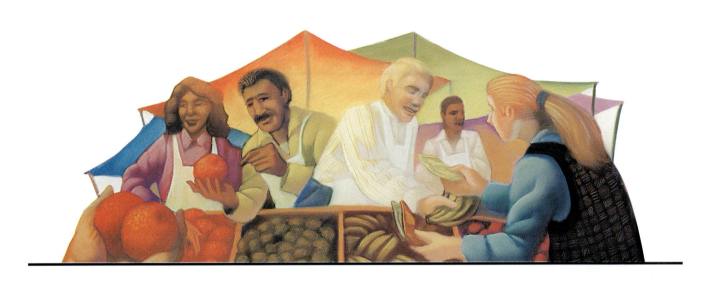

SUPPLY AND DEMAND: HOW MARKETS WORK

4

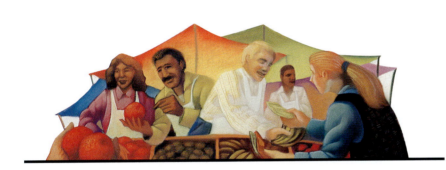

THE MARKET FORCES OF SUPPLY AND DEMAND

IN THIS CHAPTER YOU WILL

Learn what a competitive market is

Examine what determines the demand for a good in a competitive market

Examine what determines the supply of a good in a competitive market

See how supply and demand together set the price of a good and the quantity sold

Consider the key role of prices in allocating scarce resources in market economies

When a cyclone hits Queensland, the price of bananas rises in supermarkets throughout the country. When school holidays end, picture theatres discount tickets. When a war breaks out in the Middle East, the price of petrol in Australia and elsewhere rises, and the price of a used Ford Falcon falls. What do these events have in common? They all show the workings of supply and demand.

Supply and *demand* are the two words that economists use most often—and for good reason. Supply and demand are the forces that make market economies work. They determine the quantity of each good produced and the price at which it is sold. If you want to know how any event or policy will affect the economy, you must think first about how it will affect supply and demand.

This chapter introduces the theory of supply and demand. It considers how buyers and sellers behave and how they interact with one another. It shows how supply and demand determine prices in a market economy and how prices, in turn, allocate the economy's scarce resources.

MARKETS AND COMPETITION

The terms *supply* and *demand* refer to the behaviour of people as they interact with one another in markets. A **market** is a group of buyers and sellers of a particular good or service. The buyers as a group determine the demand for the product, and the sellers as a group determine the supply of the product. Before discussing how buyers and sellers behave, let's first consider more fully what we mean by a 'market' and the various types of markets we observe in the economy.

market
a group of buyers and sellers of a particular good or service

COMPETITIVE MARKETS

Markets take many forms. Sometimes markets are highly organised, such as the markets for many agricultural commodities. In these markets, buyers and sellers meet at a specific time and place, where an auctioneer helps set prices and arrange sales.

More often, markets are less organised. For example, consider the market for ice-cream in a particular town. Buyers of ice-cream do not meet together at any one time. The sellers of ice-cream are in different locations and offer somewhat different products. There is no auctioneer calling out the price of ice-cream. Each seller posts a price for an ice-cream, and each buyer decides how much ice-cream to buy at each store.

Even though it is not organised, the group of ice-cream buyers and ice-cream sellers forms a market. Each buyer knows that there are several sellers from which to choose, and each seller is aware that its product is similar to that offered by other sellers. The price of ice-cream and the quantity of ice-cream sold are not determined by any single buyer or seller. Rather, price and quantity are determined by all buyers and sellers as they interact in the marketplace.

The market for ice-cream, like most markets in the economy, is highly competitive. A **competitive market** is a market in which there are many buyers and many sellers so that each has a negligible impact on the market price. Each seller of ice-cream has limited control over the price because other sellers are offering similar products. A seller has little reason to charge less than the going price, and if he or she charges more, buyers will make their purchases elsewhere. Similarly, no single buyer of ice-cream can influence the price of ice-cream because each buyer purchases only a small amount.

competitive market
a market in which there are many buyers and many sellers so that each has a negligible impact on the market price

In this chapter we examine how buyers and sellers interact in competitive markets. We see how the forces of supply and demand determine both the quantity of the good sold and its price.

COMPETITION: PERFECT AND OTHERWISE

We assume in this chapter that markets are *perfectly competitive*. Perfectly competitive markets are defined by two main characteristics: (1) the goods being offered for sale are all the same, and (2) the buyers and sellers are so numerous that no single buyer or seller can influence the market price. Because buyers and sellers in perfectly competitive markets must accept the price the market determines, they are said to be *price takers*.

There are some markets in which the assumption of perfect competition applies perfectly. In the wheat market, for example, there are thousands of farmers who sell wheat and millions of consumers who use wheat and wheat products. Because no single buyer or seller can influence the price of wheat, each takes the price as given.

The markets for many goods and services, however, are not perfectly competitive. Some markets have only one seller, and this seller sets the price. Such a seller is called a *monopoly*. Your local water supplier, for instance, may be a monopoly. Residents of your suburb probably have only one water company from which to buy this service.

Some markets have only a few sellers, and these sellers do not always compete aggressively. This kind of market is called an *oligopoly*. For example, some international airline routes are oligopolies. If a route between two cities is serviced by only two or three carriers, it is likely that the carriers will try to avoid rigorous competition in order to keep prices high.

Some markets contain many sellers offering slightly different products. Because the products are not the same, each seller has some ability to set the price for its own product. Such a market is called *monopolistically competitive*. An example is the software industry. Many word-processing programs compete with one another for users, but every program is different from every other and has its own price.

Despite the diversity of market types we find in the world, we begin by studying perfect competition. Perfectly competitive markets are the easiest to analyse. Moreover, because some degree of competition is present in most markets, many of the lessons that we learn by studying supply and demand under perfect competition apply in more complicated markets as well.

QUICK QUIZ What is a market? ◆ What does it mean for a market to be competitive?

DEMAND

We begin our study of markets by examining the behaviour of buyers. Here we consider what determines the **quantity demanded** of any good, which is the amount of the good that buyers are willing and able to purchase. To focus our thinking, let's keep in mind a particular good—ice-cream.

quantity demanded
the amount of a good that buyers are willing and able to purchase

THE DETERMINANTS OF INDIVIDUAL DEMAND

Consider your own demand for ice-cream. How do you decide how much ice-cream to buy each month, and what factors affect your decision? Here are some of the answers you might give.

Price If the price of ice-cream rose to $20 per scoop, you would buy less ice-cream. You might buy frozen yoghurt instead. If the price of ice-cream fell to $0.20 per scoop, you would buy more. Because the quantity demanded falls as

law of demand
the claim that, other things being equal, the quantity demanded of a good falls when the price of the good rises

normal good
a good for which, other things being equal, an increase in income leads to an increase in quantity demanded

inferior good
a good for which, other things being equal, an increase in income leads to a decrease in quantity demanded

substitutes
two goods for which a decrease in the price of one good leads to a decrease in the demand for the other good

complements
two goods for which a decrease in the price of one good leads to an increase in the demand for the other good

the price rises and rises as the price falls, we say that the quantity demanded is *negatively related* to the price. This relationship between price and quantity demanded is true for most goods in the economy and, in fact, is so pervasive that economists call it the **law of demand**—other things being equal, when the price of a good rises, the quantity demanded of the good falls.

Income What would happen to your demand for ice-cream if you lost your job one summer? Most likely, it would fall. A lower income means that you have less to spend in total, so you would have to spend less on some—and probably most—goods. If the demand for a good falls when income falls, the good is called a **normal good**.

Not all goods are normal goods. If the demand for a good rises when income falls, the good is called an **inferior good**. An example of an inferior good might be bus rides. As your income falls, you are less likely to buy a car or take a taxi, and more likely to take the bus.

Prices of related goods Suppose that the price of frozen yoghurt falls. The law of demand says that you will buy more frozen yoghurt. At the same time, you will probably buy less ice-cream. Because ice-cream and frozen yoghurt are both cold, sweet, creamy desserts, they satisfy similar desires. When a fall in the price of one good reduces the demand for another good, the two goods are called **substitutes**. Other pairs of substitutes include hot dogs and hamburgers, CDs and cassettes, and film tickets and video rentals.

Now suppose that the price of chocolate topping falls. According to the law of demand, you will buy more chocolate topping. Yet, in this case, you will buy more ice-cream as well, since ice-cream and topping are often used together. When a fall in the price of one good raises the demand for another good, the two goods are called **complements**. Other pairs of complements include petrol and cars, computers and software, and skis and ski-lift tickets.

Tastes The most obvious determinant of your demand is your tastes. If you like ice-cream, you buy more of it. Economists normally do not try to explain people's tastes because tastes are based on historical and psychological forces that are beyond the realm of economics. Economists do, however, examine what happens when tastes change. For example, when people become more health conscious, they might tend to buy more frozen yoghurt and less ice-cream.

Expectations Your expectations about the future may affect your demand for a good or service today. For example, if you expect to earn a higher income next month, you may be more willing to spend some of your current savings buying ice-cream. As another example, if you expect the price of ice-cream to fall tomorrow, you may be less willing to buy an ice-cream at today's price.

THE DEMAND SCHEDULE AND THE DEMAND CURVE

We have seen that there are many variables that determine the quantity of ice-cream a person demands. Imagine for the moment that all these variables except price are held constant. Now let's consider how price affects quantity demanded.

Table 4.1 shows how many ice-creams Catherine buys each month at different prices of ice-cream. If ice-creams are free, Catherine eats 12. At $0.50 each, Catherine buys 10. As the price rises further, she demands fewer and fewer. When the price reaches $3.00, Catherine doesn't buy any ice-cream at all. Table 4.1 is a **demand schedule**, a table that shows the relationship between the price of a good and the quantity demanded.

Figure 4.1 graphs the numbers in table 4.1. By convention, the price of ice-cream is on the vertical axis, and the quantity of ice-cream demanded is on the horizontal axis. The downward-sloping line relating price and quantity demanded is called the **demand curve**.

demand schedule
a table that shows the relationship between the price of a good and the quantity demanded

demand curve
a graph of the relationship between the price of a good and the quantity demanded

PRICE OF AN ICE-CREAM	QUANTITY OF ICE-CREAMS DEMANDED
$0.00	12
0.50	10
1.00	8
1.50	6
2.00	4
2.50	2
3.00	0

Table 4.1

CATHERINE'S DEMAND SCHEDULE

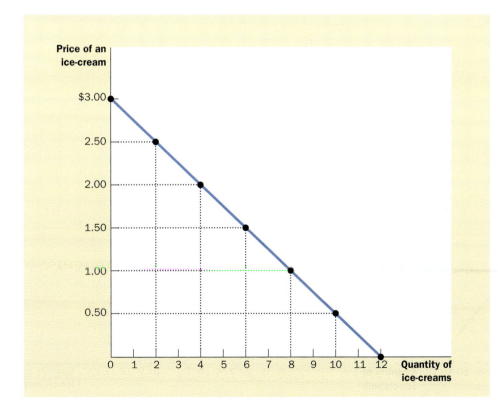

Figure 4.1

CATHERINE'S DEMAND CURVE. This demand curve, which graphs the demand schedule in table 4.1, shows how the quantity demanded of the good changes as its price varies. Because a lower price increases the quantity demanded, the demand curve slopes downwards.

CETERIS PARIBUS

Whenever you see a demand curve, remember that it is drawn holding many things fixed. Catherine's demand curve in figure 4.1 shows what happens to the quantity of ice-cream Catherine demands when only the price of ice-cream varies. The curve is drawn assuming that Catherine's income, tastes, expectations and the prices of related products are not changing.

Economists use the term *ceteris paribus* to signify that all the relevant variables, except those being studied at that moment, are held constant. The Latin phrase means 'other things being equal'. The demand curve slopes downwards because, *ceteris paribus*, lower prices mean a greater quantity demanded.

Although the term *ceteris paribus* refers to a hypothetical situation in which some variables are assumed to be constant, in the real world many things change at the same time. For this reason, when we use the tools of supply and demand to analyse events or policies, it is important to keep in mind what is being held fixed and what is not.

ceteris paribus
a Latin phrase, translated as 'other things being equal,' used as a reminder that all variables other than the ones being studied are assumed to be constant

MARKET DEMAND VERSUS INDIVIDUAL DEMAND

So far we have talked about an individual's demand for a product. To analyse how markets work, we need to determine the *market demand*, which is the sum of all the individual demands for a particular good or service.

Table 4.2 shows the demand schedules for ice-cream of two people—Catherine and Nicholas. At any price, Catherine's demand schedule tells us how much ice-cream she buys, and Nicholas's demand schedule tells us how much ice-cream he buys. The market demand is the sum of the two individual demands.

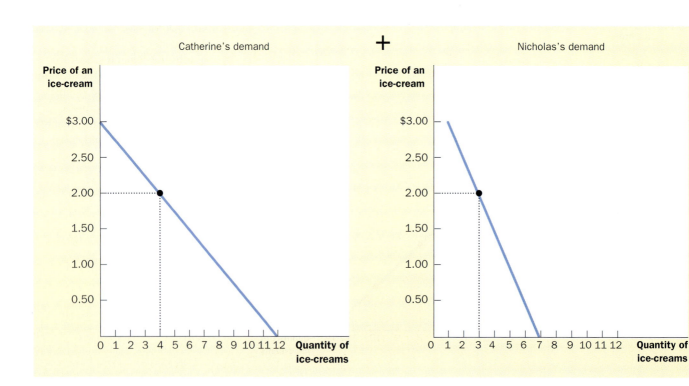

Because market demand is derived from individual demands, the quantity demanded in a market depends on those factors that determine the quantity demanded by individual buyers. Thus, the quantity demanded in a market depends not only on the price of the good but also on buyers' incomes, tastes, expectations and the prices of related goods. It also depends on the number of buyers. (If more consumers were to join Catherine and Nicholas, the quantity demanded in the market would be higher at every price.) The demand schedules in table 4.2 show what happens to quantity demanded as the price varies while all the other variables that determine quantity demanded are held constant.

Figure 4.2 shows the demand curves that correspond to these demand schedules. Notice that we add the individual demand curves *horizontally* to obtain the

Table 4.2

INDIVIDUAL AND MARKET DEMAND SCHEDULES

PRICE OF AN ICE-CREAM	CATHERINE		NICHOLAS		MARKET
$0.00	12	+	7	=	19
0.50	10		6		16
1.00	8		5		13
1.50	6		4		10
2.00	4		3		7
2.50	2		2		4
3.00	0		1		1

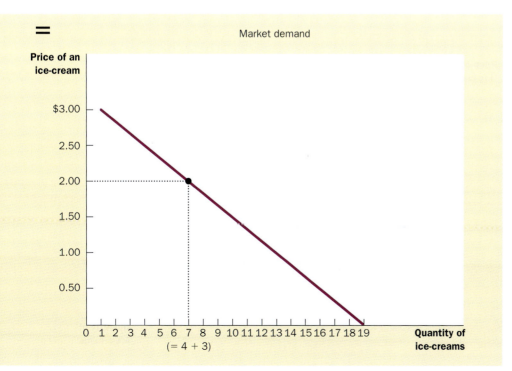

Figure 4.2

MARKET DEMAND AS THE SUM OF INDIVIDUAL DEMANDS. The market demand curve is found by adding horizontally the individual demand curves. At a price of $2, Catherine demands 4 ice-creams, and Nicholas demands 3 ice-creams. The quantity demanded in the market at this price is 7 ice-creams.

market demand curve. That is, to find the total quantity demanded at any price, we add the individual quantities found on the horizontal axis of the individual demand curves. Because we are interested in analysing how markets work, we will work most often with the market demand curve. The market demand curve shows how the total quantity demanded of a good varies as the price of the good varies.

SHIFTS IN THE DEMAND CURVE

Suppose that medical researchers suddenly announce a new discovery—people who regularly eat ice-cream live longer, healthier lives. How does this announcement affect the market for ice-cream? The discovery changes people's tastes and raises the demand for ice-cream. At any given price, buyers now want to purchase a larger quantity of ice-cream, and the demand curve for ice-cream shifts to the right.

Whenever any determinant of demand changes, other than the price, the demand curve shifts. As figure 4.3 shows, any change that increases the quantity demanded at every price shifts the demand curve to the right. Similarly, any change that reduces the quantity demanded at every price shifts the demand curve to the left.

Table 4.3 lists the variables that determine the quantity demanded in a market and how a change in the variable affects the demand curve. In summary, *the demand curve shows what happens to the quantity demanded of a good when its price varies, holding constant all other determinants of demand. When one of these other determinants changes, the demand curve shifts.*

Figure 4.3

SHIFTS IN THE DEMAND CURVE. Any change that raises the quantity that buyers wish to purchase at a given price shifts the demand curve to the right. Any change that lowers the quantity that buyers wish to purchase at a given price shifts the demand curve to the left.

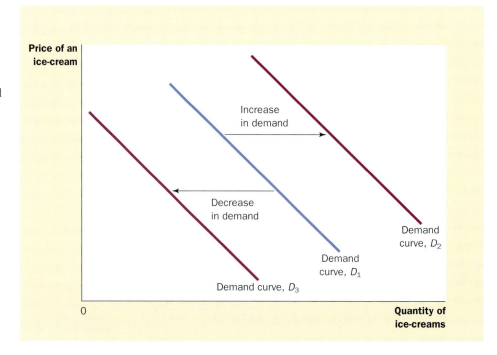

Table 4.3

THE DETERMINANTS OF DEMAND

VARIABLES THAT AFFECT QUANTITY DEMANDED	A CHANGE IN THIS VARIABLE...
Price	Represents a movement along the demand curve
Income	Shifts the demand curve
Prices of related goods	Shifts the demand curve
Tastes	Shifts the demand curve
Expectations	Shifts the demand curve
Number of buyers	Shifts the demand curve

CASE STUDY   **TWO WAYS TO REDUCE THE QUANTITY OF SMOKING DEMANDED**

Public policymakers often want to reduce the amount that people smoke. There are two ways that policy can attempt to achieve this goal.

One way to reduce smoking is to shift the demand curve for cigarettes and other tobacco products. Public service announcements, mandatory health warnings on cigarette packets, and the prohibition of cigarette advertising on television are all policies aimed at reducing the quantity of cigarettes demanded at any given price. If successful, these policies shift the demand curve for cigarettes to the left, as in panel (a) of figure 4.4.

Alternatively, policymakers can try to raise the price of cigarettes. If the government taxes the manufacture of cigarettes, for example, cigarette companies pass much of this tax on to consumers in the form of higher prices. A higher price encourages smokers to reduce the amount of cigarettes they smoke. In this case, the reduced amount of smoking does not represent a shift in the demand curve. Instead, it represents a movement along the same demand curve to a point with a higher price and lower quantity, as in panel (b) of figure 4.4.

How much does the amount of smoking respond to changes in the price of cigarettes? Economists have attempted to answer this question by studying what happens when the tax on cigarettes changes. They have found that a 10% increase in the price causes a 4% reduction in the quantity demanded. Teenagers are found to be especially sensitive to the price of cigarettes—a 10% increase in the price causes a 12% drop in teenage smoking.

What is the best way to stop this?

> **QUICK QUIZ** List the determinants of the demand for pizza. ◆ Give an example of a demand schedule for pizza, and graph the implied demand curve. ◆ Give an example of something that would shift this demand curve. ◆ Would a change in the price of pizza shift this demand curve?

Figure 4.4

SHIFTS IN THE DEMAND CURVE VERSUS MOVEMENTS ALONG THE DEMAND CURVE. If warnings on cigarette packets convince smokers to smoke less, the demand curve for cigarettes shifts to the left. In panel (a), the demand curve shifts from D_1 to D_2. At a price of $4 per packet, the quantity demanded falls from 20 to 10 cigarettes per day, as reflected by the shift from point A to point B. In contrast, if a tax raises the price of cigarettes, the demand curve does not shift. Instead, we observe a movement to a different point on the demand curve. In panel (b), when the price rises from $4 to $8, the quantity demanded falls from 20 to 12 cigarettes per day, as reflected by the movement from point A to point C.

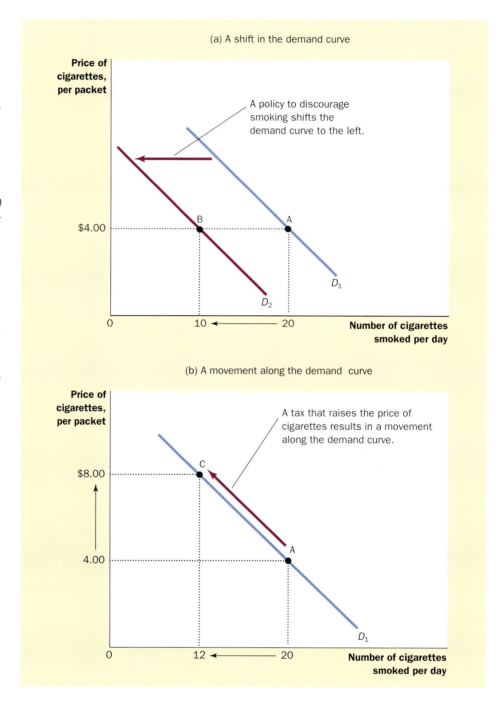

SUPPLY

quantity supplied
the amount of a good that sellers are willing and able to sell

We now turn to the other side of the market and examine the behaviour of sellers. The **quantity supplied** of any good or service is the amount that sellers are willing and able to sell. Once again, to focus our thinking, let's consider the market for ice-cream and look at the factors that determine the quantity supplied.

THE DETERMINANTS OF INDIVIDUAL SUPPLY

Imagine that you are running Student Sweets, a company that produces and sells ice-cream. What determines the quantity of ice-cream you are willing to produce and offer for sale? Here are some possible answers.

Price The price of ice-cream is one determinant of the quantity supplied. When the price of ice-cream is high, selling ice-cream is profitable, and so the quantity supplied is large. As a seller of ice-cream, you work long hours, buy many ice-cream machines, and hire many workers. In contrast, when the price of ice-cream is low, your business is less profitable, and so you will produce less ice-cream. At an even lower price, you may choose to go out of business altogether, and your quantity supplied falls to zero.

Because the quantity supplied rises as the price rises and falls as the price falls, we say that the quantity supplied is *positively related* to the price of the good. This relationship between price and quantity supplied is called the **law of supply**—other things being equal, when the price of a good rises, the quantity supplied of the good also rises.

law of supply
the claim that, other things being equal, the quantity supplied of a good rises when the price of the good rises

Input prices To produce its output of ice-cream, Student Sweets uses various inputs—cream, sugar, flavouring, ice-cream machines, the buildings in which the ice-cream is made, and the labour of workers to mix the ingredients and operate the machines. When the price of one or more of these inputs rises, producing ice-cream is less profitable, and your firm supplies less ice-cream. If input prices rise substantially, you might shut down your firm and supply no ice-cream at all. Thus, the quantity supplied of a good is negatively related to the price of the inputs used to make the good.

Technology The technology for turning the inputs into ice-cream is yet another determinant of the quantity supplied. The invention of the mechanised ice-cream machine, for example, reduced the amount of labour necessary to make ice-cream. By reducing firms' costs, the advance in technology raised the quantity of ice-cream supplied.

Expectations The quantity of ice-cream you supply today may depend on your expectations of the future. For example, if you expect the price of ice-cream to rise in the future, you will put some of your current production into storage and supply less to the market today.

THE SUPPLY SCHEDULE AND THE SUPPLY CURVE

Consider how the quantity supplied varies with the price, holding input prices, technology and expectations fixed. Table 4.4 shows the quantity supplied by Tony, an ice-cream seller, at various prices of ice-cream. At a price below $1.00, Tony does not supply any ice-cream at all. As the price rises, he supplies a greater and greater quantity. This table is called the **supply schedule**.

supply schedule
a table that shows the relationship between the price of a good and the quantity supplied

Table 4.4

TONY'S SUPPLY SCHEDULE

PRICE OF AN ICE-CREAM	QUANTITY OF ICE-CREAMS SUPPLIED
$0.00	0
0.50	0
1.00	1
1.50	2
2.00	3
2.50	4
3.00	5

Figure 4.5

TONY'S SUPPLY CURVE. This supply curve, which graphs the supply schedule in table 4.4, shows how the quantity supplied of the good changes as its price varies. Because a higher price increases the quantity supplied, the supply curve slopes upwards.

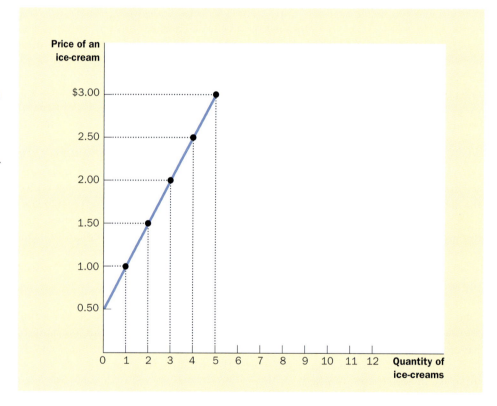

Figure 4.5 graphs the relationship between the quantity of ice-cream supplied and the price. The curve relating price and quantity supplied is called the **supply curve**. The supply curve slopes upwards because, *ceteris paribus*, a higher price means a greater quantity supplied.

MARKET SUPPLY VERSUS INDIVIDUAL SUPPLY

Just as market demand is the sum of the demands of all buyers, market supply is the sum of the supplies of all sellers. Table 4.5 shows the supply schedules for two ice-cream producers—Tony and Mick. At any price, Tony's supply schedule

supply curve
a graph of the relationship between the price of a good and the quantity supplied

Table 4.5

INDIVIDUAL AND MARKET SUPPLY SCHEDULES

Price of an ice-cream	Tony		Mick		Market
$0.00	0	+	0	=	0
0.50	0		0		0
1.00	1		0		1
1.50	2		2		4
2.00	3		4		7
2.50	4		6		10
3.00	5		8		13

tells us how much ice-cream Tony supplies, and Mick's supply schedule tells us how much ice-cream Mick supplies. The market supply is the sum of the two individual supplies.

The quantity supplied in a market depends on those factors that determine quantity supplied by individual sellers—the price of the good, the prices of inputs used to produce the good, the available technology and expectations. In addition, the quantity supplied in a market depends on the number of sellers. (If Tony or Mick were to retire from the ice-cream business, the quantity supplied in the market would fall.) The supply schedules in table 4.5 show what happens to quantity supplied as the price varies while all the other variables that determine quantity supplied are held constant.

Figure 4.6 shows the supply curves that correspond to the supply schedules in table 4.5. As with demand curves, we add the individual supply curves *horizontally* to obtain the market supply curve. That is, to find the total quantity supplied at any price, we add the individual quantities found on the horizontal axis of the individual supply curves. The market supply curve shows how the total quantity supplied varies as the price of the good varies.

SHIFTS IN THE SUPPLY CURVE

Suppose that the price of sugar falls. How does this change affect the supply of ice-cream? Because sugar is an input into producing ice-cream, the fall in the price of sugar makes selling ice-cream more profitable. This raises the supply of ice-cream; at any given price sellers are now willing to produce a larger quantity. Thus, the supply curve for ice-cream shifts to the right.

Whenever any determinant of supply, other than the price, changes, the supply curve shifts. As figure 4.7 shows, any change that raises quantity supplied at every price shifts the supply curve to the right. Similarly, any change that reduces the quantity supplied at every price shifts the supply curve to the left.

Table 4.6 lists the variables that determine the quantity supplied in a market and how a change in the variable affects the supply curve. In summary, *the supply curve shows what happens to the quantity supplied of a good when its price varies, holding constant all other determinants of supply. When one of these other determinants changes, the supply curve shifts.*

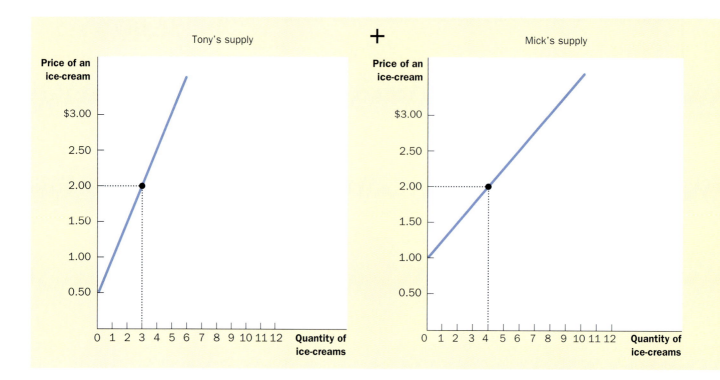

Table 4.6

THE DETERMINANTS OF SUPPLY

VARIABLES THAT AFFECT QUANTITY SUPPLIED	A CHANGE IN THIS VARIABLE...
Price	Represents a movement along the supply curve
Input prices	Shifts the supply curve
Technology	Shifts the supply curve
Expectations	Shifts the supply curve
Number of sellers	Shifts the supply curve

QUICK QUIZ List the determinants of the supply of pizza. ◆ Give an example of a supply schedule for pizza, and graph the implied supply curve. ◆ Give an example of something that would shift this supply curve. ◆ Would a change in the price of pizza shift this supply curve?

SUPPLY AND DEMAND TOGETHER

Having analysed supply and demand separately, we now combine them to see how they determine the quantity of a good sold in a market and its price.

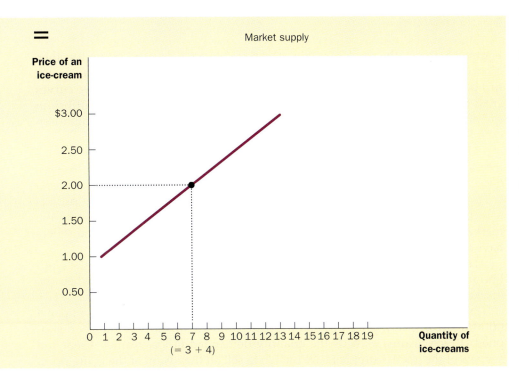

Figure 4.6

MARKET SUPPLY AS THE SUM OF INDIVIDUAL SUPPLIES. The market supply curve is found by adding horizontally the individual supply curves. At a price of $2, Tony supplies 3 ice-creams, and Mick supplies 4 ice-creams. The quantity supplied in the market at this price is 7 ice-creams.

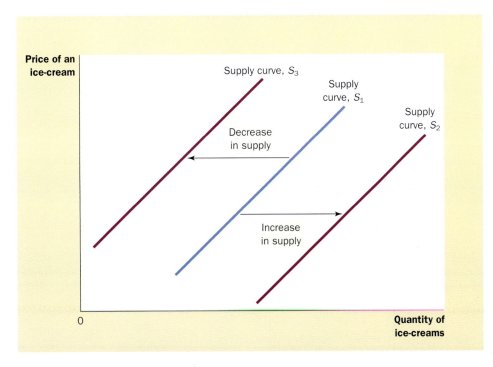

Figure 4.7

SHIFTS IN THE SUPPLY CURVE. Any change that raises the quantity that sellers wish to produce at a given price shifts the supply curve to the right. Any change that lowers the quantity that sellers wish to produce at a given price shifts the supply curve to the left.

EQUILIBRIUM

equilibrium
a situation in which supply and demand have been brought into balance

equilibrium price
the price that balances supply and demand

equilibrium quantity
the quantity supplied and the quantity demanded when the price has adjusted to balance supply and demand

Figure 4.8 shows the market supply curve and market demand curve together. Notice that there is one point at which the supply and demand curves intersect; this point is called the market's **equilibrium**. The price at which these two curves cross is called the **equilibrium price**, and the quantity is called the **equilibrium quantity**. Here the equilibrium price is $2.00 per ice-cream, and the equilibrium quantity is 7 ice-creams.

The dictionary defines the word *equilibrium* as a situation in which various forces are in balance—and this also describes a market's equilibrium. *At the equilibrium price, the quantity of the good that buyers are willing and able to buy exactly balances the quantity that sellers are willing and able to sell.* The equilibrium price is sometimes called the *market-clearing price* because, at this price, everyone in the market has been satisfied—buyers have bought all they want to buy, and sellers have sold all they want to sell.

The actions of buyers and sellers naturally move markets towards the equilibrium of supply and demand. To see why, consider what happens when the market price is not equal to the equilibrium price.

Suppose first that the market price is above the equilibrium price, as in panel (a) of figure 4.9. At a price of $2.50 per ice-cream, the quantity of the good supplied (10 ice-creams) exceeds the quantity demanded (4 ice-creams). There is a surplus of the good—suppliers are unable to sell all they want at the going price. This situation is called **excess supply**. When there is excess supply in the ice-cream market, for instance, sellers of ice-cream find their freezers increasingly full of ice-cream they would like to sell but cannot. They respond to the excess

excess supply
a situation in which quantity supplied is greater than quantity demanded

Figure 4.8

THE EQUILIBRIUM OF SUPPLY AND DEMAND. The equilibrium is found where the supply and demand curves intersect. At the equilibrium price, the quantity supplied equals the quantity demanded. Here the equilibrium price is $2. At this price, 7 ice-creams are supplied, and 7 ice-creams are demanded.

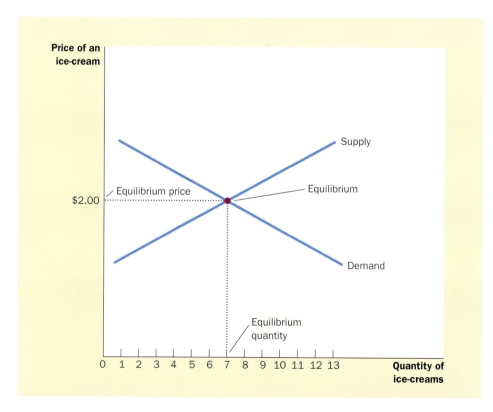

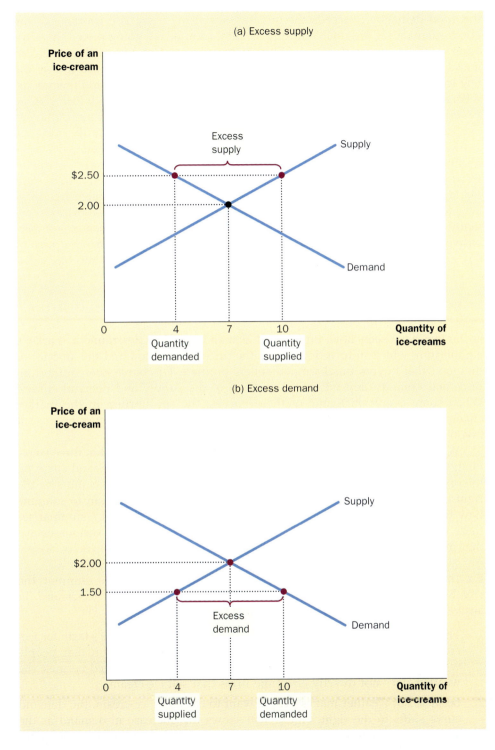

Figure 4.9

MARKETS NOT IN EQUILIBRIUM. In panel (a), there is excess supply. Because the market price of $2.50 is above the equilibrium price, the quantity supplied (10 ice-creams) exceeds the quantity demanded (4 ice-creams). Suppliers try to increase sales by cutting the price of an ice-cream, and this moves the price toward its equilibrium level. In panel (b), there is excess demand. Because the market price of $1.50 is below the equilibrium price, the quantity demanded (10 ice-creams) exceeds the quantity supplied (4 ice-creams). Because too many buyers are chasing too few goods, suppliers can take advantage of the shortage by raising the price. Hence, in both cases, the price adjustment moves the market towards the equilibrium of supply and demand.

supply by cutting their prices. Prices continue to fall until the market reaches the equilibrium.

Suppose now that the market price is below the equilibrium price, as in panel (b) of figure 4.9. In this case, the price is $1.50 per ice-cream, and the quantity of

excess demand
a situation in which quantity demanded is greater than quantity supplied

the good demanded exceeds the quantity supplied. There is a shortage of the good—demanders are unable to buy all they want at the going price. This situation is called **excess demand**. When excess demand occurs in the ice-cream market, for instance, buyers have to wait in long lines for a chance to buy the few ice-creams that are available. With too many buyers chasing too few goods, sellers can respond to excess demand by raising their prices without losing sales. As prices rise, the market once again moves towards the equilibrium.

Thus, the activities of the many buyers and sellers automatically push the market price towards the equilibrium price. Once the market reaches its equilibrium, all buyers and sellers are satisfied, and there is no upward or downward pressure on the price. How quickly equilibrium is reached varies from market to market, depending on how quickly prices adjust. In most free markets, however, surpluses and shortages are only temporary because prices eventually move towards their equilibrium levels. Indeed, this phenomenon is so pervasive that it is sometimes called the **law of supply and demand**—the price of any good adjusts to bring the supply and demand for that good into balance.

law of supply and demand
the claim that the price of any good adjusts to bring the supply and demand for that good into balance

THREE STEPS TO ANALYSING CHANGES IN EQUILIBRIUM

So far we have seen how supply and demand together determine a market's equilibrium, which in turn determines the price of the good and the amount of the good that buyers purchase and sellers produce. Of course, the equilibrium price and quantity depend on the position of the supply and demand curves. When some event shifts one of these curves, the equilibrium in the market changes. The analysis of such a change is called *comparative statics* because it involves comparing an old equilibrium and a new equilibrium.

When analysing how some event affects a market, we proceed in three steps. First, we decide whether the event shifts the supply curve, the demand curve or, in some cases, both curves. Second, we decide whether the curve shifts to the right or to the left. Third, we use the supply-and-demand diagram to examine how the shift affects the equilibrium price and quantity. Table 4.7 summarises these three steps. To see how this recipe is used, let's consider various events that might affect the market for ice-cream.

Example: A change in demand Suppose that one summer the weather is very hot. How does this event affect the market for ice-cream? To answer this question, let's follow our three steps.

1. The hot weather affects the demand curve by changing people's taste for ice-cream. That is, the weather changes the amount of ice-cream that people want to buy at any given price. The supply curve is unchanged because the weather does not directly affect the firms that sell ice-cream.

2. Because hot weather makes people want to eat more ice-cream, the demand curve shifts to the right. Figure 4.10 shows this increase in demand as the shift in the demand curve from D_1 to D_2. This shift indicates that the quantity of ice-cream demanded is higher at every price.

3. As figure 4.10 shows, the increase in demand raises the equilibrium price from $2.00 to $2.50 and the equilibrium quantity from 7 to 10 ice-creams. In other words, the hot weather increases the price of ice-cream and the quantity of ice-cream sold.

Table 4.7
A THREE-STEP PROGRAM FOR DOING COMPARATIVE STATICS

1. Decide whether the event shifts the supply or demand curve (or perhaps both).
2. Decide in which direction the curve shifts.
3. Use the supply-and-demand diagram to see how the shift changes the equilibrium.

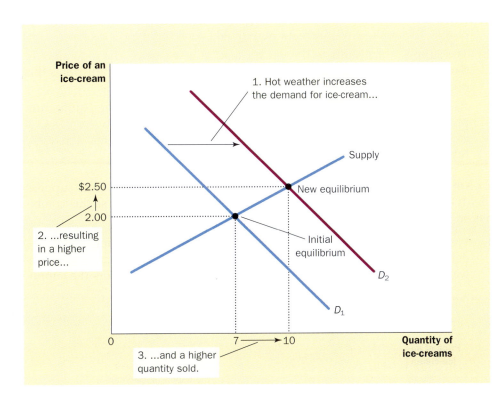

Figure 4.10

HOW AN INCREASE IN DEMAND AFFECTS THE EQUILIBRIUM. An event that raises quantity demanded at any given price shifts the demand curve to the right. The equilibrium price and the equilibrium quantity both rise. Here, an abnormally hot summer causes buyers to demand more ice-cream. The demand curve shifts from D_1 to D_2, which causes the equilibrium price to rise from $2.00 to $2.50 and the equilibrium quantity to rise from 7 to 10 ice-creams.

Shifts in curves versus movements along curves Notice that when hot weather drives up the price of ice-cream, the amount of ice-cream that firms supply rises, even though the supply curve remains the same. In this case, economists say there has been an increase in 'quantity supplied' but no change in 'supply'.

'Supply' refers to the position of the supply curve, whereas the 'quantity supplied' refers to the amount suppliers wish to sell. In this example, supply does not change because the weather does not alter firms' desire to sell at any given price. Instead, the hot weather alters consumers' desire to buy at any given price and thereby shifts the demand curve. The increase in demand causes the equilibrium price to rise. When the price rises, the quantity supplied rises. This increase in quantity supplied is represented by the movement along the supply curve.

To summarise, a shift *in* the supply curve is called a 'change in supply' and a shift *in* the demand curve is called a 'change in demand'. A movement *along* a fixed supply curve is called a 'change in the quantity supplied', and a movement *along* a fixed demand curve is called a 'change in the quantity demanded'.

Example: A change in supply Suppose that, during another summer, a bushfire destroys several ice-cream factories. How does this event affect the market for ice-cream? Once again, to answer this question, we follow our three steps.

1. The fire affects the supply curve. By reducing the number of sellers, the fire changes the amount of ice-cream that firms produce and sell at any given price. The demand curve is unchanged because the fire does not directly change the amount of ice-cream households wish to buy.

2. The supply curve shifts to the left because, at every price, the total amount that firms are willing and able to sell is reduced. Figure 4.11 illustrates this decrease in supply as a shift in the supply curve from S_1 to S_2.

3. As figure 4.11 shows, the shift in the supply curve raises the equilibrium price from $2.00 to $2.50 and lowers the equilibrium quantity from 7 to 4 ice-creams. As a result of the fire, the price of ice-cream rises, and the quantity of ice-cream sold falls.

Example: A change in both supply and demand Now suppose that the hot weather and the fire occur at the same time. To analyse this combination of events, we again follow our three steps.

1. We determine that both curves must shift. The hot weather affects the demand curve because it alters the amount of ice-cream that households want to buy at any given price. At the same time, the fire alters the supply

Figure 4.11

How a decrease in supply affects the equilibrium. An event that reduces quantity supplied at a given price shifts the supply curve to the left. The equilibrium price rises, and the equilibrium quantity falls. Here, a bushfire causes sellers to supply less ice-cream. The supply curve shifts from S_1 to S_2, which causes the equilibrium price to rise from $2.00 to $2.50 and the equilibrium quantity to fall from 7 to 4 ice-creams.

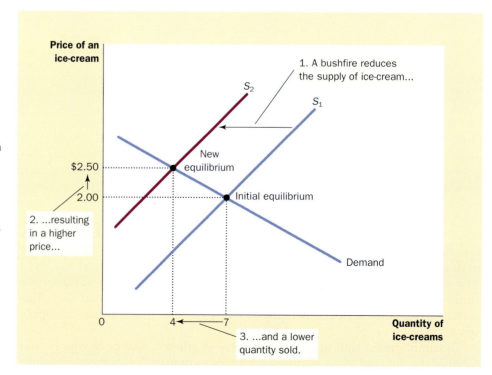

curve because it changes the amount of ice-cream that firms want to sell at any given price.

2. The curves shift in the same directions as they did in our previous analysis—the demand curve shifts to the right, and the supply curve shifts to the left. Figure 4.12 illustrates these shifts.

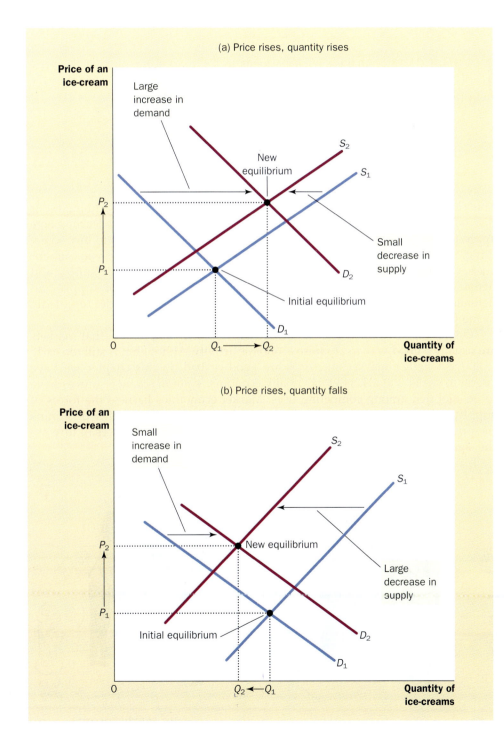

Figure 4.12

A SHIFT IN BOTH SUPPLY AND DEMAND. Here we observe a simultaneous increase in demand and decrease in supply. Two outcomes are possible. In panel (a), the equilibrium price rises from P_1 to P_2, and the equilibrium quantity rises from Q_1 to Q_2. In panel (b), the equilibrium price again rises from P_1 to P_2, but the equilibrium quantity falls from Q_1 to Q_2.

3. As figure 4.12 shows, there are two possible outcomes that might result, depending on the relative size of the demand and supply shifts. In both cases, the equilibrium price rises. In panel (a), where demand increases substantially and supply falls just a little, the equilibrium quantity also rises. In contrast, in panel (b), where supply falls substantially and demand rises just a little, the equilibrium quantity falls. Thus, these events certainly raise the price of ice-cream, but their impact on the amount of ice-cream sold is ambiguous.

QUICK QUIZ Analyse what happens to the market for pizza if the price of tomatoes rises. ◆ Analyse what happens to the market for pizza if the price of hamburgers falls.

CONCLUSION: HOW PRICES ALLOCATE RESOURCES

This chapter has analysed supply and demand in a single market. Although our discussion has centred around the market for ice-cream, the lessons learned here apply in most other markets as well. Whenever you go to a shop to buy something, you are contributing to the demand for that item. Whenever you look for a job, you are contributing to the supply of labour services. Because supply and demand are such pervasive economic phenomena, the model of supply and demand is a powerful tool for analysis. We will be using this model repeatedly in the following chapters.

One of the *Ten Principles of Economics* discussed in chapter 1 is that markets are usually a good way to organise economic activity. Although it is still too early to judge whether market outcomes are good or bad, in this chapter we have begun to see how markets work. In any economic system, scarce resources have to be allocated among competing uses. Market economies harness the forces of supply and demand to serve that end. Supply and demand together determine the prices of the economy's many different goods and services; prices in turn are the signals that guide the allocation of resources.

'Two dollars.'   '—and seventy-five cents.'

For example, consider the allocation of beachfront land. Because the amount of this land is limited, not everyone can enjoy the luxury of living by the beach. Who gets this resource? The answer is: whoever is willing to pay the price. The price of beachfront land adjusts until the quantity of land demanded exactly balances the quantity supplied. Thus, in market economies, prices are the mechanism for rationing scarce resources.

Similarly, prices determine who produces each good and how much is produced. For instance, consider farming. Because we need food to survive, it is crucial that some people work on farms. What determines who is a farmer and who is not? In a free society, there is no government planning agency making this decision and ensuring an adequate supply of food. Instead, the allocation of

IN THE NEWS

Supply, demand and the price of paper

THE FOLLOWING ARTICLE DESCRIBES developments in the paper market. As you read the article, try to identify shifts in the demand curve and shifts in the supply curve. Be careful to distinguish between shifts *in* the curves and movements *along* the curves.

Pulp Reality

BY JERRY ACKERMAN

Look no farther than the newsstand or your grocery bag for evidence of the worldwide economic turnaround: Soaring demand for paper has pushed prices to near-record levels.

Virtually no type of paper is immune. Facial tissue, office paper, newsprint, even stock for cardboard cartons—all today are ringing in at 25 to 40 percent more than in early 1994, and further increases are expected, perhaps as soon as summer.

'The mills tell me that things are going to be like this for the next six quarters,' says Edward Rosenbloom, president of Empire Paper Co., a Boston office-paper distributor.

Supermarket shoppers now must speak up if they want paper bags instead of plastic. Office managers are trying to limit the number of photocopies being made. Printers are taking extra steps to reduce waste to keep customer prices down. And newspapers are sometimes trimming features while raising prices to make up for higher newsprint costs.

Not surprisingly, papermakers are happy, saying that their industry has been absorbing losses through years of recession. Virgil Horton of the American Forest and Paper Association, a trade organization, says the papermaking industry has seen profits in only 3 of the past 14 years…

All this comes after a five-year recession-induced slump that industry leaders say was one of the worst ever in a business accustomed to cycles. Across the Americas, Europe, and Asia, reduced advertising brought thinner newspapers and magazines, and product sales declines meant less packaging.

But papermakers, primed by the boom of the 1980s, already were building new manufacturing capacity to meet expected growth. According to the American Forest and Paper Association, five huge newsprint machines came on line in the United States in 1990 and 1991, costing nearly $2 billion and increasing production capacity by 9.5 percent. The story was much the same in Canada; between them, the two nations produce three-quarters of the world's newsprint supply.

With bills to pay on the new machines, paper companies began running them even before deciding what to do with older units. The resulting paper glut pushed prices down. That is, until the economy turned around last year—not only in the United States but simultaneously in Europe, Asia, and much of Latin America.

Now, with the once-excess older machines out of service, rising demand is pushing prices to near record highs. According to *Pulp & Paper*, a trade journal, the average price of a metric ton of newsprint—a benchmark in the industry—rose from $445 at the end of 1993 to $515 in December. A separate survey by *The New York Times* pegged the price in January at $552, jumping to $600 at the beginning of March and due to hit $675 on May 1.

SOURCE: *Boston Globe*, 20 March 1995, p. 37.

workers to farms is based on the job decisions of millions of workers. This decentralised system works well because these decisions depend on prices. The prices of food and the wages of farm workers (the price of their labour) adjust to ensure that enough people choose to be farmers.

If a person had never seen a market economy in action, the whole idea might seem preposterous. Economies are large groups of people engaged in many interdependent activities. What prevents decentralised decision making from degenerating into chaos? What coordinates the actions of the millions of people with their varying abilities and desires? What ensures that what needs to get done does, in fact, get done? The answer, in a word, is *prices*.

Summary

- Economists use the model of supply and demand to analyse competitive markets. In a competitive market, there are many buyers and sellers, each of whom has little or no influence on the market price.

- The demand curve shows how the quantity of a good demanded depends on the price. According to the law of demand, as the price of a good falls, the quantity demanded rises. Therefore, the demand curve slopes downwards.

- In addition to price, other determinants of the quantity demanded include income, tastes, expectations, and the prices of substitutes and complements. If one of these other determinants changes, the demand curve shifts.

- The supply curve shows how the quantity of a good supplied depends on the price. According to the law of supply, as the price of a good rises, the quantity supplied rises. Therefore, the supply curve slopes upwards.

- In addition to price, other determinants of the quantity supplied include input prices, technology and expectations. If one of these other determinants changes, the supply curve shifts.

- The intersection of the supply and demand curves determines the market equilibrium. At the equilibrium price, the quantity demanded equals the quantity supplied.

- The behaviour of buyers and sellers naturally drives markets towards their equilibrium. When the market price is above the equilibrium price, there is excess supply, which causes the market price to fall. When the market price is below the equilibrium price, there is excess demand, which causes the market price to rise.

- To analyse how any event influences a market, we use the supply-and-demand diagram to examine how the event affects the equilibrium price and quantity. To do this we follow three steps. First, we decide whether the event shifts the supply curve or the demand curve. Second, we decide in which direction the curve shifts. Third, we compare the new equilibrium with the old equilibrium.

- In market economies, prices are the signals that guide economic decisions and thereby allocate scarce resources. For every good in the economy, the price ensures that supply and demand are in balance. The equilibrium price then determines how much of the good buyers choose to purchase and how much sellers choose to produce.

Key concepts

market, p. 62
competitive market, p. 62
quantity demanded, p. 63
law of demand, p. 64
normal good, p. 64
inferior good, p. 64
substitutes, p. 64

complements, p. 64
demand schedule, p. 65
demand curve, p. 65
ceteris paribus, p. 66
quantity supplied, p. 70
law of supply, p. 71
supply schedule, p. 71

supply curve, p. 72
equilibrium, p. 76
equilibrium price, p. 76
equilibrium quantity, p. 76
excess supply, p. 76
excess demand, p. 78
law of supply and demand, p. 78

Questions for review

1. What is a competitive market?
2. What determines the quantity of a good that buyers demand?
3. What are the demand schedule and the demand curve, and how are they related?
4. Why does the demand curve slope downwards?
5. Does a change in consumers' tastes lead to a movement along the demand curve or a shift in the demand curve? Does a change in price lead to a movement along the demand curve or a shift in the demand curve?
6. What determines the quantity of a good that sellers supply?
7. What are the supply schedule and the supply curve, and how are they related?
8. Why does the supply curve slope upwards?
9. Does a change in producers' technology lead to a movement along the supply curve or a shift in the supply curve? Does a change in price lead to a movement along the supply curve or a shift in the supply curve?
10. Define the equilibrium of a market. Describe the forces that move a market towards its equilibrium.
11. Beer and pies are complements because they are often enjoyed together. When the price of beer rises, what happens to the supply, demand, quantity supplied, quantity demanded and the price in the market for pies?
12. Describe the role of prices in market economies.

Problems and applications

1. Explain each of the following statements using supply-and-demand diagrams.
   a. When a cyclone hits Queensland, the price of bananas rises in supermarkets throughout the country.
   b. When school holidays end, the price of picture tickets plummets.
   c. When a war breaks out in the Middle East, the price of petrol rises, and the price of a used Ford Falcon falls.

2. 'An increase in the demand for notebooks raises the quantity of notebooks demanded, but not the quantity supplied.' Is this statement true or false? Explain.

3. Consider the market for mini-vans. For each of the events listed here, identify which of the determinants of demand or supply are affected. Also indicate whether demand or supply is increased or decreased.
   a. People decide to have more children.
   b. A strike by steelworkers raises steel prices.
   c. Engineers develop new automated machinery for the production of mini-vans.
   d. The price of station wagons rises.
   e. A stock market crash lowers people's wealth.

4. Using supply-and-demand diagrams, show the effect of the following events on the market for woollen jumpers:
   a. An outbreak of 'foot-and-mouth' disease hits sheep farms in New Zealand.
   b. The price of leather jackets falls.
   c. Alanis Morissette appears in a woollen jumper in her latest video.
   d. New knitting machines are invented.

5. Suppose that in the year 2000 the number of births is temporarily high. How does this baby boom affect the price of baby-sitting services in 2005 and 2015? (*Hint:* 5-year-olds need baby-sitters, whereas 15-year-olds can be baby-sitters.)

6. The case study presented in the chapter discussed cigarette taxes as a way to reduce smoking. Now think about the markets for other tobacco products such as cigars and pipe tobacco.
   a. Are these goods substitutes or complements for cigarettes?
   b. Using a supply-and-demand diagram, show what happens in the markets for cigars and pipe tobacco if the tax on cigarettes is increased.
   c. If policymakers wanted to reduce total tobacco consumption, what policies could they combine with the cigarette tax?

7. The market for pizza has the following demand and supply schedules:

Price	Quantity demanded	Quantity supplied
$4	135	26
5	104	53
6	81	81
7	68	98
8	53	110
9	39	121

   Graph the demand and supply curves. What is the equilibrium price and quantity in this market? If the actual price in this market were *above* the equilibrium price, what would drive the market towards the equilibrium? If the actual price in this market were *below* the equilibrium price, what would drive the market towards the equilibrium?

8. A technological breakthrough reduces the cost of producing computer chips. Using supply-and-demand diagrams, show the effect of this breakthrough on the equilibrium price and quantity in the following markets:
   a. the market for computers
   b. the market for computer software.

9. Because bagels and cream cheese are often eaten together, they are complements.
   a. We observe that both the equilibrium price of cream cheese and the equilibrium quantity of bagels have risen. What could be responsible for this pattern—a fall in the price of flour or a fall in the price of milk? Illustrate and explain your answer.
   b. Suppose instead that the equilibrium price of cream cheese has risen but the equilibrium quantity of bagels has fallen. What could be responsible for this pattern—a rise in the price of flour or a rise in the price of milk? Illustrate and explain your answer.

10. Suppose that the price of tickets at your local picture theatre is determined by market forces. Currently, the demand and supply schedules are as follows:

Price	Quantity demanded	Quantity supplied
$4	1000	800
8	800	800
12	600	800
16	400	800
20	200	800

    a. Draw the demand and supply curves. What is unusual about this supply curve? Why might this be true?
    b. What are the equilibrium price and quantity of tickets?
    c. Demographers tell you that next year there will be more film goers in the area. The additional people will have the following demand schedule:

Price	Quantity demanded
$ 4	400
8	300
12	200
16	100
20	0

    Now add the old demand schedule and the demand schedule for the new people to calculate the new demand schedule for the entire area. What will be the new equilibrium price and quantity?

11. An article in the *New York Times* (18 October 1990) described a successful marketing campaign by the French champagne industry. The article also noted: 'Many executives felt giddy about the stratospheric champagne prices. But they also feared that such sharp price increases would cause demand to decline, which would then cause prices to plunge.' What mistake are the executives making in their analysis of the situation? Illustrate your answer with a graph.

12. 'For a given increase in supply, the slopes of both the demand curve and the supply curve affect the change in equilibrium quantity.' Is this statement true or false? Explain with diagrams.

13. (This question requires the use of secondary school algebra.) Market research has revealed the following information about the market for bars of chocolate—the demand schedule can be represented by the equation $Q^D = 1600 - 300P$, where Q^D is the quantity demanded and P is the price. The supply schedule can be represented by the equation $Q^S = 1400 + 700P$, where Q^S is the quantity supplied. Calculate the equilibrium price and quantity in the market for bars of chocolate.

14. What do we mean by a perfectly competitive market? Do you think that the example of ice-cream used in this chapter fits this description? Is there another type of market that better characterises the market for ice-cream? Explain.

5

ELASTICITY AND ITS APPLICATION

IN THIS CHAPTER YOU WILL

Learn the meaning of the elasticity of demand

Examine what determines the elasticity of demand

Learn the meaning of the elasticity of supply

Examine what determines the elasticity of supply

Apply the concept of elasticity in three very different markets

Imagine yourself as a wheat farmer. Because you earn all your income from selling wheat, you devote much time and energy to making your land as productive as it can be. You monitor weather and soil conditions, check your fields for pests and disease, and study the latest advances in farm technology. You know that the more wheat you grow, the more you will have to sell after the harvest, and the higher your income and your standard of living will be.

One day the local university announces a major discovery. Researchers in its agronomy department have devised a new hybrid of wheat that raises the amount farmers can produce from each hectare of land by 20%. How should you react to this news? Should you use the new hybrid? Does this discovery make you better off or worse off than you were before? In this chapter we will see that these questions can have surprising answers. The surprise will come from applying the most basic tools of economics—supply and demand—to the market for wheat.

The previous chapter introduced supply and demand. In any competitive market, such as the market for wheat, the upward-sloping supply curve represents the behaviour of sellers, and the downward-sloping demand curve represents the behaviour of buyers. The price of the good adjusts to bring the quantity supplied and quantity demanded of the good into balance. To apply this basic analysis to understanding the impact of the agronomists' discovery, we must first develop one more tool—the concept of elasticity. Elasticity, a measure of how much buyers and sellers respond to changes in market conditions, allows us to analyse supply and demand with greater precision.

THE ELASTICITY OF DEMAND

When we discussed the determinants of demand in chapter 4, we noted that buyers usually demand more of a good when its price is lower, when their incomes are higher, when the prices of substitutes for the good are higher, or when the prices of complements of the good are lower. Our discussion of demand was qualitative, not quantitative. That is, we discussed the direction in which quantity demanded moves, but not the size of the change. To measure how much demand responds to changes in its determinants, economists use the concept of **elasticity**.

elasticity
a measure of the responsiveness of quantity demanded or quantity supplied to one of its determinants

THE PRICE ELASTICITY OF DEMAND AND ITS DETERMINANTS

The law of demand states that a fall in the price of a good raises the quantity demanded. The **price elasticity of demand** measures how much the quantity demanded responds to a change in price. Demand for a good is said to be *elastic* if the quantity demanded responds substantially to changes in the price. Demand is said to be *inelastic* if the quantity demanded responds only slightly to changes in the price.

price elasticity of demand
a measure of how much the quantity demanded of a good responds to a change in the price of that good, calculated as the percentage change in quantity demanded divided by the percentage change in price

What determines whether the demand for a good is elastic or inelastic? Since the demand for any good depends on consumer preferences, the price elasticity of demand depends on the many economic, social and psychological forces that shape individual desires. Based on experience, however, we can state some general rules about what determines the price elasticity of demand.

Necessities versus discretionary expenditure
Necessities tend to have inelastic demands, whereas goods that are discretionary have elastic demands. When the price of a visit to the doctor rises, people will not dramatically alter the number of times they go to the doctor, although they might go a little less often. In contrast, when the price of yachts rises, the quantity demanded falls substantially. The reason is that most people view visits to the doctor as a necessity and yachts as discretionary. Of course, whether a good is a necessity or discretionary depends not on the intrinsic properties of the good but on the preferences of the buyer. For an avid sailor with few health concerns, a yacht might be a necessity with inelastic demand and visits to the doctor a luxury with elastic demand.

Availability of close substitutes
Goods with close substitutes tend to have more elastic demand because it is easier for consumers to switch from that good to others. For example, butter and margarine are easily substitutable. A small increase in the price of butter, assuming the price of margarine is held fixed, causes the quantity of butter sold to fall by a large amount. In contrast, because eggs are a food without a close substitute, the demand for eggs is probably less elastic than the demand for butter.

Definition of the market
The elasticity of demand in any market depends on how we draw the boundaries of the market. Narrowly defined markets tend to have more elastic demand than broadly defined markets, since it is

easier to find close substitutes for narrowly defined goods. For example, food, a broad category, has a fairly inelastic demand because there are no good substitutes for food. Ice-cream, a more narrow category, has a more elastic demand because it is easy to substitute other desserts for ice-cream. Vanilla ice-cream, a very narrow category, has a very elastic demand because other flavours of ice-cream are almost perfect substitutes for vanilla.

Time horizon Goods tend to have more elastic demand over longer time horizons. When the price of petrol rises, the quantity of petrol demanded falls only slightly in the first few months. Over time, however, people buy more fuel-efficient cars, switch to public transport, or move closer to where they work. Within several years, the quantity of petrol demanded falls substantially.

CALCULATING THE PRICE ELASTICITY OF DEMAND

Now that we have discussed the price elasticity of demand in general terms, let's be more precise about how it is measured. Economists calculate the price elasticity of demand as the percentage change in the quantity demanded divided by the percentage change in the price. That is:

$$\text{Price elasticity of demand} = \frac{\text{Percentage change in quantity demanded}}{\text{Percentage change in price}}$$

For example, suppose that an increase in the price of an ice-cream from $2.00 to $2.20 causes the amount you buy to fall from 10 to 8 ice-creams per month. We calculate the percentage change in price as:

$$\text{Percentage change in price} = (2.20 - 2.00)/2.00 \times 100 = 10\%$$

Similarly, we calculate the percentage change in quantity demanded as:

$$\text{Percentage change in quantity demanded} = (10 - 8)/10 \times 100 = 20\%$$

In this case, your elasticity of demand is:

$$\text{Price elasticity of demand} = \frac{20\%}{10\%} = 2$$

In this example, the elasticity is 2, reflecting that the change in the quantity demanded is proportionately twice as large as the change in the price.

Because the quantity demanded of a good is negatively related to its price, the percentage change in quantity will always have the opposite sign to the percentage change in price. In this example, the percentage change in price is a *positive* 10% (reflecting an increase), and the percentage change in quantity demanded is a *negative* 20% (reflecting a decrease). For this reason, price elasticities of demand are sometimes reported as negative numbers. In this book we follow the common practice of dropping the minus sign and reporting all price elasticities as positive numbers. (Mathematicians call this the *absolute value*.) With this convention, a larger price elasticity implies a greater responsiveness of quantity demanded to price.

FYI

Calculating elasticities using the midpoint method

If you try calculating the price elasticity of demand between two points on a demand curve, you will quickly notice an annoying problem—the elasticity from point A to point B seems different from the elasticity from point B to point A. For example, consider these numbers:

Point A: Price = $4, Quantity = 120

Point B: Price = $6, Quantity = 80

Going from point A to point B, the price rises by 50%, and the quantity falls by 33%, indicating that the price elasticity of demand is 33/50, or 0.66. In contrast, going from point B to point A, the price falls by 33%, and the quantity rises by 50%, indicating that the price elasticity of demand is 50/33, or 1.5.

One way to avoid this problem is to use the *midpoint method* for calculating elasticities. Rather than calculating a percentage change using the standard way (by dividing the change by the initial level), the midpoint method calculates a percentage change by dividing the change by the midpoint of the initial and final levels. For instance, $5 is the midpoint of $4 and $6. Therefore, according to the midpoint method, a change from $4 to $6 is considered a 40% rise. (Why? Because $(6 - 4)/5 \times 100 = 40$.) Similarly, a change from $6 to $4 is considered a 40% fall.

Because the midpoint method gives the same answer regardless of the direction of change, it is often used when calculating the price elasticity of demand between two points. In our example, the midpoint between point A and point B is:

Midpoint: Price = $5, Quantity = 100

According to the midpoint method, when going from point A to point B, the price rises by 40%, and the quantity falls by 40%. Similarly, when going from point B to point A, the price falls by 40%, and the quantity rises by 40%. In both directions, the price elasticity of demand equals 1.

If you ever need to calculate elasticities, you should keep the midpoint method in mind. Throughout this book, however, we need to perform such calculations only rarely. For our purposes, what elasticity represents—the responsiveness of quantity demanded to price—is more important than how it is calculated.

THE VARIETY OF DEMAND CURVES

Economists classify demand curves according to their elasticity. Demand is *elastic* when the elasticity is greater than 1, so that quantity moves proportionately more than the price. Demand is *inelastic* when the elasticity is less than 1, so that quantity moves proportionately less than the price. If the elasticity is exactly 1, so that quantity moves the same amount proportionately as price, demand is said to have *unit elasticity*.

Because the price elasticity of demand measures how much quantity demanded responds to the price, it is closely related to the slope of the demand curve. (For a discussion of slope and elasticity, see the appendix to chapter 2.) The following rule of thumb is a useful guide: the flatter the demand curve that passes through a given point, the greater the price elasticity of demand; the steeper the demand curve that passes through a given point, the smaller the price elasticity of demand.

Figure 5.1 shows five cases. In the extreme case of a zero elasticity, demand is perfectly inelastic, and the demand curve is vertical. In this case, regardless of the price, the quantity demanded stays the same. As the elasticity rises, the demand curve gets flatter and flatter. At the opposite extreme is the case of perfectly elastic demand, which occurs as the price elasticity of demand

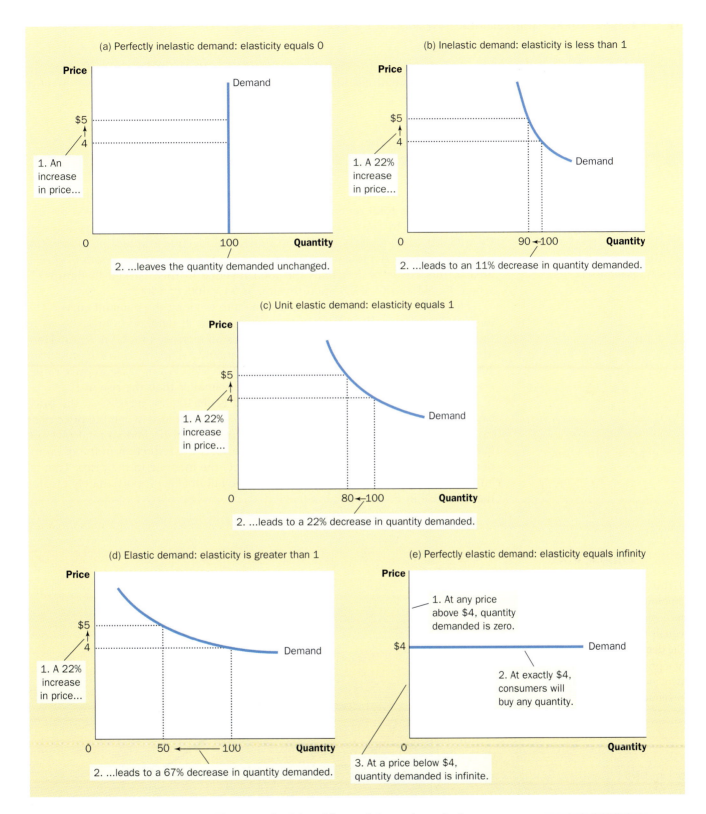

THE PRICE ELASTICITY OF DEMAND. The price elasticity of demand determines whether the demand curve is steep or flat. Note that all percentage changes are calculated using the midpoint method.

Figure 5.1

approaches infinity. In this case, the demand curve is horizontal, reflecting the fact that very small changes in the price lead to huge changes in the quantity demanded.

TOTAL REVENUE AND THE PRICE ELASTICITY OF DEMAND

When studying changes in supply or demand in a market, one variable we often want to study is **total revenue**, the amount paid by buyers and received by sellers of the good. In any market, total revenue is $P \times Q$, the price of the good times the quantity of the good sold. We can show total revenue graphically, as in figure 5.2. The height of the box under the demand curve is P, and the width is Q. The area of this box, $P \times Q$, equals the total revenue in this market. In figure 5.2, where $P = \$4$ and $Q = 100$, total revenue is $\$4 \times 100$, or $\$400$.

How does total revenue change as one moves along the demand curve? The answer depends on the price elasticity of demand. If demand is inelastic, as in figure 5.3, then an increase in the price causes an increase in total revenue. Here an increase in price from $1 to $3 causes the quantity demanded to fall only from 100 to 80, and so total revenue rises from $100 to $240. An increase in price raises $P \times Q$ because the fall in Q is proportionately smaller than the rise in P.

We obtain the opposite result if demand is elastic—an increase in the price causes a decrease in total revenue. In figure 5.4, for instance, when the price rises from $4 to $5, the quantity demanded falls from 50 to 20, and so total revenue falls from $200 to $100. Because demand is elastic, the reduction in the quantity demanded is so great that it more than offsets the increase in the price. That is, an increase in price reduces $P \times Q$ because the fall in Q is proportionately greater than the rise in P.

total revenue
the amount paid by buyers and received by sellers of a good, calculated as the price of the good times the quantity sold

Figure 5.2

TOTAL REVENUE. The total amount paid by buyers, and received as revenue by sellers, equals the area of the box under the demand curve, $P \times Q$. Here, at a price of $4, the quantity demanded is 100, and total revenue is $400.

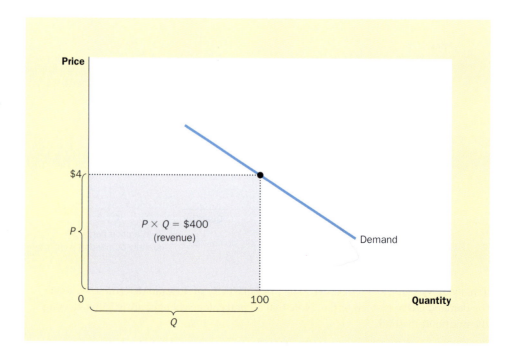

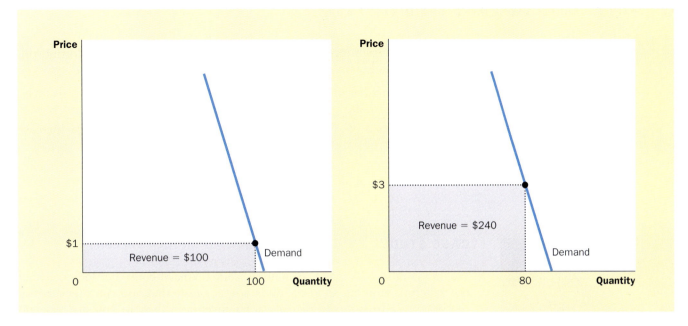

HOW TOTAL REVENUE CHANGES WHEN PRICE CHANGES: INELASTIC DEMAND.
With an inelastic demand curve, an increase in the price leads to a decrease in quantity demanded that is proportionately smaller. Therefore, total revenue (the product of price and quantity) increases. Here, an increase in the price from $1 to $3 causes the quantity demanded to fall from 100 to 80, and total revenue rises from $100 to $240.

Figure 5.3

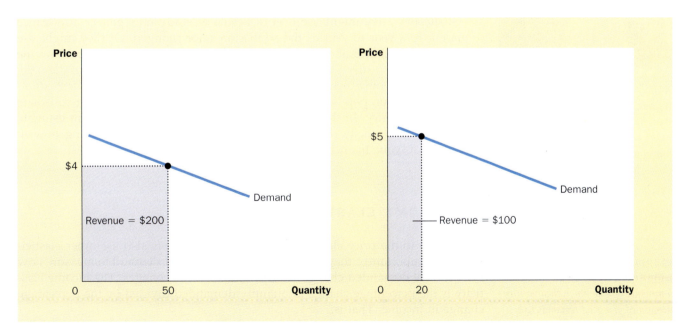

HOW TOTAL REVENUE CHANGES WHEN PRICE CHANGES: ELASTIC DEMAND.
With an elastic demand curve, an increase in the price leads to a decrease in quantity demanded that is proportionately larger. Therefore, total revenue (the product of price and quantity) decreases. Here, an increase in the price from $4 to $5 causes the quantity demanded to fall from 50 to 20, so total revenue falls from $200 to $100.

Figure 5.4

Although the examples in these two figures are extreme, they illustrate a general rule:

◆ When the price elasticity of demand is less than 1, a price increase raises total revenue, and a price decrease reduces total revenue.

◆ When the price elasticity of demand is greater than 1, a price increase reduces total revenue, and a price decrease raises total revenue.

◆ In the special case of demand with elasticity exactly equal to 1, a change in the price does not affect total revenue.

CASE STUDY   PRICING ADMISSION TO AN ART GALLERY

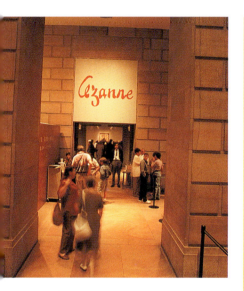

If the price of admission were higher, how much smaller would this crowd be?

You are curator of a major art gallery. Your financial controller tells you that the gallery is running short of funds and suggests that you consider altering the price of admission to increase total revenue. What do you do? Do you raise the price of admission, or do you lower it?

The answer depends on the elasticity of demand. If the demand for visits to the gallery is inelastic, then an increase in the price of admission would increase total revenue. But if the demand is elastic, then an increase in price would cause the number of visitors to fall by so much that total revenue would decrease. In this case, you should cut the price. The number of visitors would rise by so much that total revenue would increase.

To estimate the price elasticity of demand, you would need to turn to your statisticians. They might use historical data to study how gallery attendance varied from year to year as the admission price changed. Or they might use data on attendance at various galleries around the country to see how the admission price affects attendance. In studying either of these sets of data, the statisticians would need to take account of other factors that affect attendance—weather, population, size of collection and so on—in order to isolate the effect of price. In the end, such data analysis would provide an estimate of the price elasticity of demand, which you could use in deciding how to respond to your financial problem.

THE INCOME ELASTICITY OF DEMAND

income elasticity of demand
a measure of how much the quantity demanded of a good responds to a change in consumers' income, calculated as the percentage change in quantity demanded divided by the percentage change in income

In addition to the price elasticity of demand, economists also use other elasticities. Most importantly, they use the **income elasticity of demand** to measure how the quantity demanded changes as consumer income changes. The income elasticity is the percentage change in quantity demanded divided by the percentage change in income. That is:

$$\text{Income elasticity of demand} = \frac{\text{Percentage change in quantity demanded}}{\text{Percentage change in income}}$$

As we discussed in chapter 4, most goods are *normal goods*—higher income raises quantity demanded. Because quantity demanded and income move in the same direction, normal goods have positive income elasticities. A few goods,

FYI

Elasticity and total revenue along a linear demand curve

ALTHOUGH SOME DEMAND curves have an elasticity that is the same along the entire curve, that is not always the case. An example of a demand curve along which elasticity changes is a straight line, as shown in figure 5.5. A linear demand curve has a constant slope. Recall that slope is defined as 'rise over run', which here is the ratio of the change in price ('rise') to the change in quantity ('run'). In this case, the demand curve's slope is constant because each $1 increase in price causes the same 2-unit decrease in the quantity demanded.

Even though the slope of a linear demand curve is constant, the elasticity is not. The reason is that the slope is the ratio of *changes* in the two variables, whereas the elasticity is the ratio of *percentage changes* in the two variables. You can see this most easily by looking at table 5.1. This table shows the demand schedule for the linear demand curve in figure 5.5 and calculates the price elasticity of demand using the midpoint method discussed earlier. At points with low price and high quantity, the demand curve is inelastic. At points with a high price and low quantity, the demand curve is elastic.

Table 5.1 also presents total revenue at each point on the demand curve. These numbers illustrate the relationship between total revenue and elasticity. When the price is $1, for instance, demand is inelastic, and a price increase to $2 raises total revenue. When the price is $5, demand is elastic, and a price increase to $6 reduces total revenue. Between $3 and $4, demand is exactly unit elastic, and total revenue is the same at these two prices.

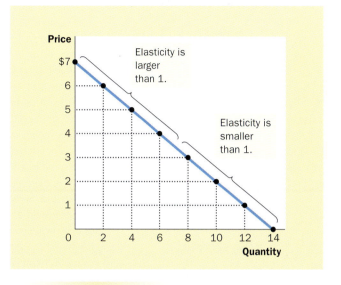

Figure 5.5

A LINEAR DEMAND CURVE. The slope of a linear demand curve is constant, but its elasticity is not.

Price	Quantity	Total revenue (price × quantity)	Per cent change in price	Per cent change in quantity	Elasticity	Description
$0	14	$ 0				
1	12	12	200%	15%	0.1	Inelastic
2	10	20	67	18	0.3	Inelastic
3	8	24	40	22	0.6	Inelastic
4	6	24	29	29	1.0	Unit elastic
5	4	20	22	40	1.8	Elastic
6	2	12	18	67	3.7	Elastic
7	0	0	15	200	13.0	Elastic

Table 5.1

CALCULATING THE ELASTICITY OF A LINEAR DEMAND CURVE
Note: Elasticity is calculated here using the midpoint method.

IN THE NEWS

On the road with elasticity

How should a firm that operates a private toll road set a price for its service? As the following article makes clear, answering this question requires an understanding of the demand curve and its elasticity.

Toll Traffic Jam Fear

BY KYLIE HANSEN

Melbourne's arterial roads would become clogged with drivers trying to avoid City Link tolls, transport groups warned yesterday.

They predicted chaos on Dandenong Rd, Kings Way, Nicholson St and Pascoe Vale Rd and called for off-peak toll discounts of 50 per cent to keep cars off residential roads.

The warning follows toll road operator Transurban's release of City Link charges up to March 2000. Private car drivers will pay a maximum of $3.77 for a one-way trip on City Link. Motorcyclists are set to pay a capped one-way fee of $1.89, with commercial vehicles paying a capped rate of $5.03 or $3.77 at night.

This means a person driving to and from work each day on City Link is facing costs of up to $37.70 per five-day week. RACV spokesman David Cumming said tolls at this level, with increases every quarter, would encourage people to look for alternative routes. 'People may pay in the morning but then find an alternative route at night when they have more time,' Mr Cumming said. 'They will take roads like Dandenong Rd, Mt Alexander Rd and Toorak Rd—anything on the edge of City Link. We need large reductions of 25–50 per cent offered during off peak to get people to use City Link.'

Moreland City Council spokesman Andrew Rowe said the toll would force people off the Tullamarine Freeway on to residential streets. Cr Rowe called on Transurban and the State Government to meet councils to develop ways of stopping drivers using local streets.

Opposition transport spokesman Peter Batchelor said secondary roads were not built to cope with freeway overflows. 'Many of these roads are already at capacity,' Mr Batchelor said.

But Transurban spokesman Rudi Michelson said: 'Our research tells us that only about 50 per cent of people volunteer support for the tolls even though 70 to 80 per cent support City Link. The research also indicates consumers will not accept tolls unless they deliver value. Our task is to demonstrate that the substantial benefits…will make them significantly better off,' he said.

SOURCE: *Herald Sun,* 30 March 1998, p. 8.

---

such as second-hand clothes, are *inferior goods*—higher income lowers the quantity demanded. Because quantity demanded and income move in opposite directions, inferior goods have negative income elasticities.

Even among normal goods, income elasticities vary substantially in size. Necessities, such as food and clothing, tend to have small income elasticities because consumers, regardless of how low their incomes, choose to buy some of these goods. Luxuries, such as caviar and furs, tend to have large income elasticities because consumers feel that they can do without these goods altogether if their income is too low.

QUICK QUIZ Define *price elasticity of demand*. ◆ Explain the relationship between total revenue and the price elasticity of demand.

THE ELASTICITY OF SUPPLY

When we discussed the determinants of supply in chapter 4, we noted that sellers of a good increase the quantity supplied when the price of the good rises, when their input prices fall, or when their technology improves. To turn from qualitative to quantitative statements about supply, we once again use the concept of elasticity.

THE PRICE ELASTICITY OF SUPPLY AND ITS DETERMINANTS

The law of supply states that higher prices raise the quantity supplied. The **price elasticity of supply** measures how much the quantity supplied responds to changes in the price. Supply of a good is said to be *elastic* if the quantity supplied responds substantially to changes in the price. Supply is said to be *inelastic* if the quantity supplied responds only slightly to changes in the price.

The price elasticity of supply depends on the flexibility of sellers to change the amount of the good they produce. For example, beachfront land has an inelastic supply because it is almost impossible to produce more of it. In contrast, manufactured goods, such as books, cars and televisions, have elastic supplies because the firms that produce them can run their factories longer in response to a higher price.

In most markets, a key determinant of the price elasticity of supply is the time period being considered. Supply is usually more elastic in the long run than in the short run. Over short periods of time, firms cannot easily change the size of their factories to make more or less of a good. Thus, in the short run, the quantity supplied is not very responsive to the price. In contrast, over longer periods, firms can build new factories or close old ones. In addition, new firms can enter a market, and old firms can shut down. Thus, in the long run, the quantity supplied can respond substantially to the price.

> **price elasticity of supply**
> *a measure of how much the quantity supplied of a good responds to a change in the price of that good, calculated as the percentage change in quantity supplied divided by the percentage change in price*

CALCULATING THE PRICE ELASTICITY OF SUPPLY

Now that we have some idea about what the price elasticity of supply is, let's be more precise. Economists calculate the price elasticity of supply as the percentage change in the quantity supplied divided by the percentage change in the price. That is:

$$\text{Price elasticity of supply} = \frac{\text{Percentage change in quantity supplied}}{\text{Percentage change in price}}$$

For example, suppose that an increase in the price of milk from $1.00 to $1.10 a litre raises the amount that dairy farmers produce from 10 000 to 11 500 litres per month. We calculate the percentage change in price as:

$$\text{Percentage change in price} = (1.10 - 1.00)/1.00 \times 100 = 10\%$$

Similarly, we calculate the percentage change in quantity supplied as:

$$\text{Percentage change in quantity supplied} = (11\,500 - 10\,000)/10\,000 \times 100 = 15\%$$

In this case, the price elasticity of supply is:

$$\text{Price elasticity of supply} = \frac{15\%}{10\%} = 1.5$$

In this example, the elasticity of 1.5 is greater than 1, which reflects the fact that the quantity supplied moves proportionately more than the price.

THE VARIETY OF SUPPLY CURVES

Because the price elasticity of supply measures the responsiveness of quantity supplied to the price, it is reflected in the appearance of the supply curve. Figure 5.6 shows five cases. In the extreme case of a zero elasticity, supply is perfectly inelastic, and the supply curve is vertical. In this case, the quantity supplied is the same regardless of the price. As the elasticity rises, the supply curve gets flatter, which shows that the quantity supplied responds more to changes in the price. At the opposite extreme is the case of perfectly elastic supply, which occurs as the price elasticity of supply approaches infinity. In this case, the supply curve is horizontal, reflecting the fact that very small changes in the price lead to very large changes in the quantity supplied.

In some markets, the elasticity of supply is not constant but varies over the supply curve. Figure 5.7 shows a typical case for an industry in which firms have factories with a limited capacity for production. For low levels of quantity supplied, the elasticity of supply is high, indicating that firms respond substantially to changes in the price. In this region, firms have capacity for production that is not being used, such as plant and equipment sitting idle for all or part of the day. Small increases in price make it profitable for firms to begin using this idle capacity. As the quantity supplied rises, firms begin to reach capacity. Once capacity is fully used, increasing production further requires the construction of new factories. To induce firms to incur this extra expense, the price must rise substantially, so supply becomes less elastic.

Figure 5.7 on page 100 presents a numerical example of this phenomenon. When the price rises from $3 to $4 (a 33% increase), the quantity supplied rises from 100 to 200 (a 100% increase). Because quantity supplied moves proportionately more than the price, the supply curve has elasticity greater than 1. In contrast, when the price rises from $12 to $15 (a 25% increase), the quantity supplied rises from 500 to 525 (a 5% increase). In this case, quantity supplied moves proportionately less than the price, so the elasticity is less than 1.

QUICK QUIZ Define *price elasticity of supply*. ◆ Explain why the price elasticity of supply might be different in the long run than in the short run.

THREE APPLICATIONS OF SUPPLY, DEMAND AND ELASTICITY

Can good news for farming be bad news for farmers? Why did OPEC, the Organization of Petroleum Exporting Countries, fail to keep the price of oil high? Does greater enforcement of drug laws increase or decrease drug-related crime? At first, these questions might seem to have little in common. Yet all three questions are about markets, and all markets are subject to the forces of supply and demand. Here we apply the versatile tools of supply, demand and elasticity to answer these seemingly complex questions.

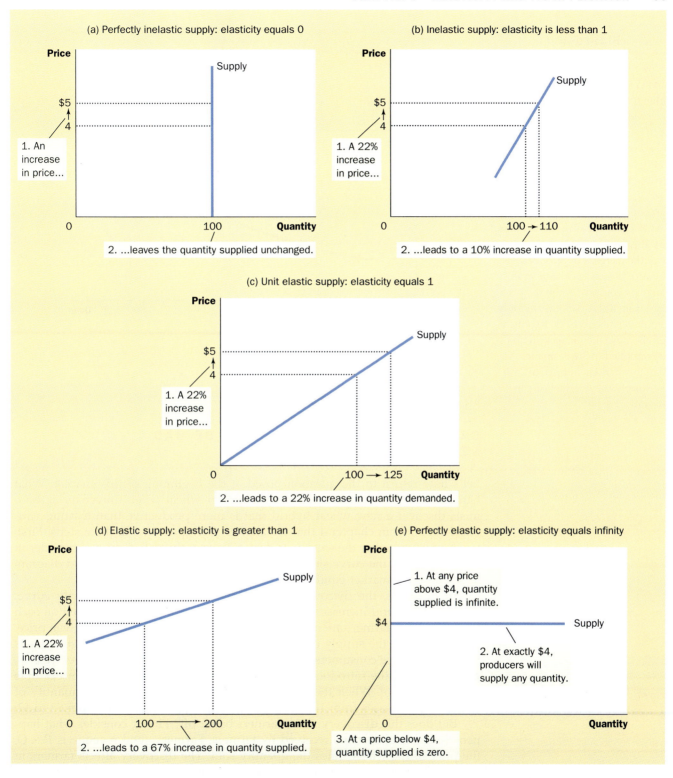

THE PRICE ELASTICITY OF SUPPLY. The price elasticity of supply determines whether the supply curve is steep or flat. Note that all percentage changes are calculated using the midpoint method.

Figure 5.6

Figure 5.7

HOW THE PRICE ELASTICITY OF SUPPLY CAN VARY. Because firms often have a maximum capacity for production, the elasticity of supply may be very high at low levels of quantity supplied and very low at high levels of quantity supplied. Here, an increase in price from $3 to $4 increases the quantity supplied from 100 to 200. Because the increase in quantity supplied of 100% is larger than the increase in price of 33%, the supply curve is elastic in this range. In contrast, when the price rises from $12 to $15, the quantity supplied rises from 500 to only 525. Because the increase in quantity supplied of 5% is smaller than the increase in price of 25%, the supply curve is inelastic in this range.

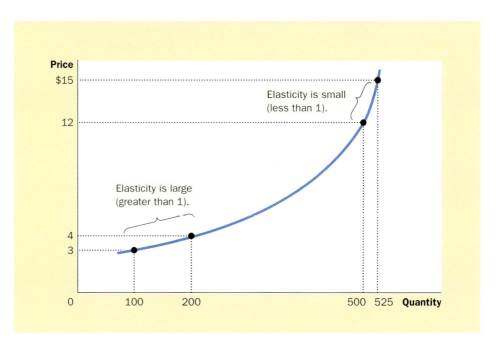

CAN GOOD NEWS FOR FARMING BE BAD NEWS FOR FARMERS?

Let's now return to the question posed at the beginning of this chapter. What happens to wheat farmers and the market for wheat when university agronomists discover a new wheat hybrid that is more productive than existing varieties? Recall from chapter 4 that we answer such questions in three steps. First, we examine whether the supply or demand curve shifts. Second, we consider in which direction the curve shifts. Third, we use the supply-and-demand diagram to see how the market equilibrium changes.

In this case, the discovery of the new hybrid affects the supply curve. Because the hybrid increases the amount of wheat that can be produced on each hectare of land, farmers are now willing to supply more wheat at any given price. In other words, the supply curve shifts to the right. The demand curve remains the same because consumers' desire to buy wheat products at any given price is not affected by the introduction of a new hybrid. Figure 5.8 shows an example of such a change. When the supply curve shifts from S_1 to S_2, the quantity of wheat sold increases from 100 to 110, and the price of wheat falls from $3 to $2.

But does this discovery make farmers better off? Firstly, consider what happens to the total revenue received by farmers. Farmers' total revenue is $P \times Q$, the price of the wheat times the quantity sold. The discovery affects farmers in two conflicting ways. The hybrid allows farmers to produce more wheat (Q rises), but now each bag of wheat sells for less (P falls).

Whether total revenue rises or falls depends on the elasticity of demand. In practice, the demand for basic foodstuffs such as wheat is usually inelastic, for these items are relatively inexpensive and have few good substitutes. When the demand curve is inelastic, as it is in figure 5.8, a decrease in price causes total revenue to fall. You can see this in the figure—the price of wheat falls substantially, whereas the quantity of wheat sold rises only slightly. Total revenue falls from $300 to $220. Thus, the discovery of the new hybrid lowers the total revenue that farmers receive for the sale of their crops.

If farmers are made worse off by the discovery of this new hybrid, why do they adopt it? The answer to this question goes to the heart of how competitive markets work. Because each farmer is a small part of the market for wheat, he or she takes the price of wheat as given. For any given price of wheat, it is better to use the new hybrid in order to produce and sell more wheat. Yet when all farmers do this, the supply of wheat rises, the price falls and farmers are worse off.

This analysis of the market for farm products also helps to explain a seeming paradox of public policy—certain farm policies try to help farmers by getting farmers to plough under some of their crops. Why do these programs do this? Their purpose is to reduce the supply of farm products and thereby raise prices. Because demand is inelastic, farmers as a group receive greater total revenue if they supply a smaller crop to the market. No single farmer would choose to destroy crops alone, since each takes the market price as given. But if all farmers do so together, each can be better off.

When analysing the effects of farm technology or farm policy, it is important to keep in mind that what is good for farmers is not necessarily good for society as a whole. Improvement in farm technology can be bad for farmers who become increasingly unnecessary, but it is surely good for consumers who pay less for food. Similarly, a policy aimed at reducing the supply of farm products may raise the incomes of farmers, but it does so at the expense of consumers.

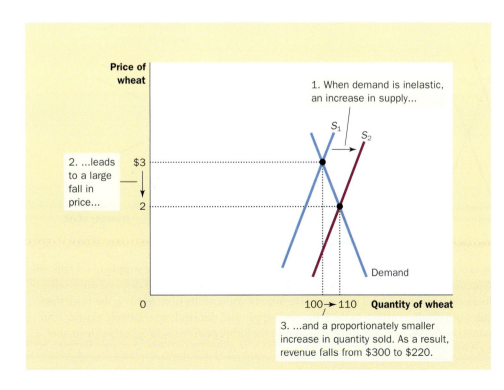

Figure 5.8

AN INCREASE IN SUPPLY IN THE MARKET FOR WHEAT. When an advance in farm technology increases the supply of wheat from S_1 to S_2, the price of wheat falls. Because the demand for wheat is inelastic, the increase in the quantity sold from 100 to 110 is proportionately smaller than the decrease in the price from $3 to $2. As a result, farmers' total revenue falls from $300 ($3 × 100) to $220 ($2 × 110).

WHY DID OPEC FAIL TO KEEP THE PRICE OF OIL HIGH?

Many of the most disruptive events for the world's economies over the past several decades have originated in the world market for oil. In the 1970s, members of the Organization of Petroleum Exporting Countries (OPEC) decided to raise the world price of oil in order to increase their incomes. These countries accomplished this goal by jointly reducing the amount of oil they supplied. From 1973 to 1974, the price of oil (adjusted for overall inflation) rose more than 50%. Then, a few years later, OPEC did the same thing again. The price of oil rose 14% in 1979, followed by 34% in 1980, and 34% in 1981.

Yet OPEC found it difficult to maintain a high price. From 1982 to 1985, the price of oil steadily declined at about 10% per year. Dissatisfaction and disarray soon prevailed among the OPEC countries. In 1986 cooperation among OPEC members completely broke down, and the price of oil plunged 45%. In 1990 the price of oil (adjusted for overall inflation) was back to where it was in 1970, and has stayed at that low level throughout most of the 1990s.

This episode shows how supply and demand can behave differently in the short run and in the long run. In the short run, both the supply and demand for oil are relatively inelastic. Supply is inelastic because the quantity of known oil reserves and the capacity for oil extraction cannot be changed quickly. Demand is inelastic because buying habits do not respond immediately to changes in

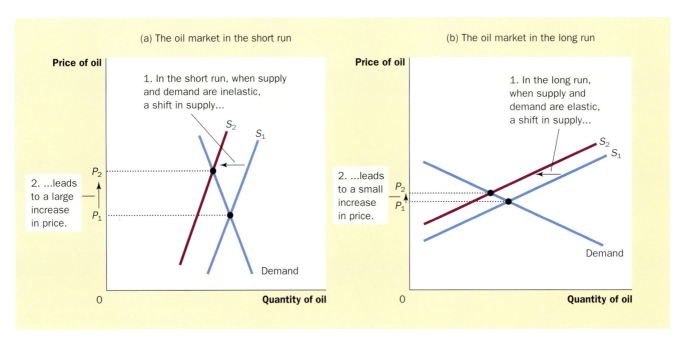

Figure 5.9

A REDUCTION IN SUPPLY IN THE WORLD MARKET FOR OIL. When the supply of oil falls, the response depends on the time horizon. In the short run, supply and demand are relatively inelastic, as in panel (a). Thus, when the supply curve shifts from S_1 to S_2, the price rises substantially. In contrast, in the long run, supply and demand are relatively elastic, as in panel (b). In this case, the same size shift in the supply curve (S_1 to S_2) causes a smaller increase in the price.

price. Many drivers with old cars that 'guzzle' petrol and oil, for instance, will just pay the higher price. Thus, as panel (a) of figure 5.9 shows, the short-run supply and demand curves are steep. When the supply of oil shifts from S_1 to S_2, the price increase from P_1 to P_2 is large.

The situation is very different in the long run. Over long periods of time, producers of oil outside of OPEC respond to high prices by increasing oil exploration and by erecting new drilling rigs. Consumers respond with greater conservation, for instance by replacing old inefficient cars with newer efficient ones. Thus, as panel (b) of figure 5.9 shows, the long-run supply and demand curves are more elastic. In the long run, the shift in the supply curve from S_1 to S_2 causes a much smaller increase in the price.

This analysis shows why OPEC succeeded in maintaining a high price of oil only in the short run. When OPEC countries agreed to reduce their production of oil, they shifted the supply curve to the left. Even though each OPEC member sold less oil, the price rose by so much in the short run that OPEC incomes rose. In contrast, in the long run when supply and demand are more elastic, the same reduction in supply, measured by the horizontal shift in the supply curve, caused a smaller increase in the price. Thus, OPEC's coordinated reduction in supply proved less profitable in the long run.

OPEC still exists today. You will occasionally hear in the news about meetings of officials from the OPEC countries. Cooperation among OPEC countries is now rare, however, in part because of the organisation's past failure at maintaining a high price.

DO DRUG BANS INCREASE OR DECREASE DRUG-RELATED CRIME?

A persistent problem facing our society is the use of illegal drugs, such as heroin, cocaine and crack. Drug use has several adverse effects. One is that drug dependency can ruin the lives of drug users and their families. Another is that drug addicts often turn to robbery and other violent crimes to obtain the money needed to support their habit. To discourage the use of illegal drugs, many governments devote billions of dollars each year to reduce the flow of drugs into their countries. Let's use the tools of supply and demand to examine this policy of drug prohibition.

Suppose the Australian government increases the number of customs inspectors and police officers devoted to preventing imports of drugs. What happens in the market for illegal drugs? As is usual, we answer this question in three steps. First, we consider whether the supply or demand curve shifts. Second, we consider the direction of the shift. Third, we see how the shift affects the equilibrium price and quantity.

Although the purpose of drug prohibition is to reduce drug use, its direct impact is on the sellers of drugs rather than the buyers. When the government stops some drugs from entering the country and arrests more smugglers, it raises the cost of selling drugs and, therefore, reduces the quantity of drugs supplied at any given price. The demand for drugs—the amount buyers want at any given price—is not changed. As panel (a) of figure 5.10 shows, prohibition shifts the supply curve to the left from S_1 to S_2 and leaves the demand curve the same. The equilibrium price of drugs rises from P_1 to P_2, and the equilibrium quantity

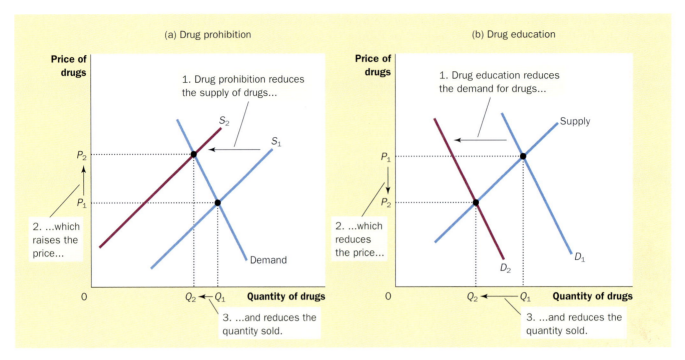

Figure 5.10

POLICIES TO REDUCE THE USE OF ILLEGAL DRUGS. Drug prohibition reduces the supply of drugs from S_1 to S_2, as in panel (a). If the demand for drugs is inelastic, then the total amount paid by drug users rises, even as the amount of drug use falls. In contrast, drug education reduces the demand for drugs from D_1 to D_2, as in panel (b). Because both price and quantity fall, the amount paid by drug users falls.

falls from Q_1 to Q_2. The fall in the equilibrium quantity shows that drug prohibition does reduce drug use.

But what about the amount of drug-related crime? To answer this question, consider the total amount that drug users pay for the drugs they buy. Because few drug addicts are likely to break their destructive habits in response to a higher price, it is likely that the demand for drugs is inelastic, as it is drawn in the figure. If demand is inelastic, then an increase in price raises total revenue in the drug market. That is, because drug prohibition raises the price of drugs proportionately more than it reduces drug use, it raises the total amount of money that drug users pay for drugs. Addicts who already had to steal to support their habits would have an even greater need for quick cash. Thus, drug bans could increase drug-related crime.

Because of this adverse effect of drug prohibition, some analysts argue for alternative approaches to the drug problem. Rather than trying to reduce the supply of drugs, policymakers might try to reduce the demand by pursuing a policy of drug education. Successful drug education has the effects shown in panel (b) of figure 5.10. The demand curve shifts to the left from D_1 to D_2. As a result, the equilibrium quantity falls from Q_1 to Q_2, and the equilibrium price falls from P_1 to P_2. Total revenue, which is price times quantity, also falls. Thus, in contrast to drug prohibition, drug education can reduce both drug use and drug-related crime.

Advocates of drug prohibition might argue that the effects of this policy are different in the long run than in the short run, because the elasticity of demand may depend on the time horizon. The demand for drugs is probably inelastic over short periods of time because higher prices do not substantially affect drug use by established addicts. But demand may be more elastic over longer periods of time because higher prices would discourage experimentation with drugs among the young and, over time, lead to fewer drug addicts. In this case, drug prohibition would increase drug-related crime in the short run but decrease it in the long run.

QUICK QUIZ How might a drought that destroys half of all farm crops be good for farmers? If such a drought is good for farmers, why don't farmers destroy their own crops in the absence of a drought?

CONCLUSION

According to an old quip, even a parrot can become an economist simply by learning to say 'supply and demand'. The last two chapters should have convinced you that there is much truth in this statement. The tools of supply and demand allow you to analyse many of the most important events and policies that shape the economy. You are now well on your way to becoming an economist (or, at least, a well-educated parrot).

Summary

- The price elasticity of demand measures how much the quantity demanded responds to changes in the price. Demand tends to be more elastic if the good is a luxury rather than a necessity, if close substitutes are available, if the market is narrowly defined, or if buyers have substantial time to react to a price change.

- The price elasticity of demand is calculated as the percentage change in quantity demanded divided by the percentage change in price. If the elasticity is less than 1, so that quantity demanded moves proportionately less than the price, demand is said to be inelastic. If the elasticity is greater than 1, so that quantity demanded moves proportionately more than the price, demand is said to be elastic.

- Total revenue, the total amount paid for a good, equals the price of the good times the quantity sold. For inelastic demand curves, total revenue rises as price rises. For elastic demand curves, total revenue falls as price rises.

- The income elasticity of demand measures how much the quantity demanded responds to changes in income. It is defined to be the percentage change in quantity demanded divided by the percentage change in income.

- The price elasticity of supply measures how much the quantity supplied responds to changes in the price. This elasticity often depends on the time horizon under consideration. In most markets, supply is more elastic in the long run than in the short run.

- The price elasticity of supply is calculated as the percentage change in quantity supplied divided by the percentage change in price. If the elasticity is less than 1, so that quantity supplied moves proportionately less than the price, supply is said to be inelastic. If the elasticity is greater than 1, so that quantity supplied moves proportionately more than the price, supply is said to be elastic.

- The tools of supply and demand can be applied in many different kinds of markets. This chapter uses them to analyse the market for wheat, the market for oil and the market for illegal drugs.

Key concepts

elasticity, p. 88
price elasticity of demand, p. 88
total revenue, p. 92
income elasticity of demand, p. 94
price elasticity of supply, p. 97

Questions for review

1. Define the price elasticity of demand and the income elasticity of demand.
2. List and explain some of the determinants of the price elasticity of demand.
3. If the elasticity is greater than 1, is demand elastic or inelastic? If the elasticity equals 0, is demand perfectly elastic or perfectly inelastic?
4. On a supply-and-demand diagram, show total spending by consumers. How does this compare with total revenue received by producers?
5. If demand is elastic, how will an increase in price change total revenue? Explain.
6. What do we call a good whose income elasticity is less than 0?
7. What is the formula for the price elasticity of supply? Explain what this measures.
8. What is the price elasticity of supply of Picasso paintings?
9. Is the price elasticity of supply usually larger in the short run or in the long run? Why?
10. In the 1970s, OPEC caused a dramatic increase in the price of oil. What prevented the organisation from maintaining this high price through the 1980s?

Problems and applications

1. For each of the following pairs of goods, which good would you expect to have more elastic demand and why?
    a. required textbooks or mystery novels
    b. Beethoven recordings or classical music recordings in general
    c. heating oil during the next 6 months or heating oil during the next 5 years
    d. lemonade or water
2. Suppose that business travellers and holiday-makers have the following demand for airline tickets from Sydney to Melbourne:

Price	Quantity demanded (business travellers)	Quantity demanded (holiday-makers)
$150	2100	1000
200	2000	800
250	1900	600
300	1800	400

    a. As the price of tickets rises from $200 to $250, what is the price elasticity of demand for (i) business travellers and (ii) holiday-makers?
    b. Why might holiday-makers have a different elasticity than business travellers?

3. Suppose that your demand schedule for compact discs is as follows:

Price	Quantity demanded (income = $10 000)	Quantity demanded (income = $12 000)
$ 8	40	50
10	32	45
12	24	30
14	16	20
16	8	12

    a. Calculate your price elasticity of demand as the price of compact discs increases from $8 to $10 if (i) your income is $10 000, and (ii) your income is $12 000.
    b. Calculate your income elasticity of demand as your income increases from $10 000 to $12 000 if (i) the price is $12, and (ii) the price is $16.
4. Emily has decided always to spend one-third of her income on clothing.

a. What is her income elasticity of clothing demand?
b. What is her price elasticity of clothing demand?
c. If Emily's tastes change and she decides to spend only a quarter of her income on clothing, how does her demand curve change? What is her income elasticity and price elasticity now?

5. The *New York Times* (17 February 1996) reported that subway use declined after a fare increase: 'There were nearly four million fewer riders in December 1995, the first full month after the price of a token increased 25 cents to $1.50, than in the previous December, a 4.3% decline.'
   a. Use these data to estimate the price elasticity of demand for subway rides.
   b. According to your estimate, what happens to the revenue when the fare rises?
   c. Why might your estimate of the elasticity be unreliable?

6. Two drivers—Tom and Jerry—each drive up to a petrol station. Before looking at the price, each places an order. Tom says, 'I'd like 10 litres of petrol.' Jerry says, 'I'd like $10 of petrol.' What is each driver's price elasticity of demand?

7. Economists have observed that spending on restaurant meals declines more during economic downturns than does spending on food to be eaten at home. How might the concept of elasticity help to explain this phenomenon?

8. Consider public policy aimed at smoking.
   a. Studies indicate that the price elasticity of demand for cigarettes is about 0.4. If a packet of cigarettes currently costs $8 and the government wants to reduce smoking by 20%, by how much should it increase the price?
   b. If the government permanently increases the price of cigarettes, will the policy have a larger effect on smoking 1 year from now or 5 years from now?
   c. Studies also find that teenagers have a higher price elasticity than do adults. Why might this be true?

9. Would you expect the price elasticity of *supply* to be larger in the market for all ice-cream or the market for vanilla ice-cream? Explain.

10. Flooding in the Queensland Granite Belt destroyed thousands of hectares of grapevines.
    a. Vineyard owners whose vines were destroyed by the floods were much worse off, but those whose vines were not destroyed benefited from the floods. Why?
    b. What information would you need about the market for wine in order to assess whether vineyard owners as a group were hurt or helped by the floods?

11. Explain why the following might be true. A drought around the world raises the total revenue that farmers receive from the sale of grain, but a drought only in Queensland reduces the total revenue that Queensland farmers receive.

12. Because better weather makes farmland more productive, farmland in regions with good weather conditions is more expensive than farmland in regions with bad weather conditions. Over time, however, as advances in technology have made all farmland more productive, the price of farmland (adjusted for overall inflation) has fallen. Use the concept of elasticity to explain why productivity and farmland prices are positively related across space but negatively related over time.

13. In the 1980s, the government imposed a sales tax on the purchase of luxury cars. The revenue collected from the tax equals the tax rate multiplied by total spending on such cars. There have been suggestions that the government could earn more tax revenue by increasing the tax rate on luxury cars. Would such an increase necessarily raise tax revenue? Explain.

6

SUPPLY, DEMAND AND GOVERNMENT POLICIES

IN THIS CHAPTER YOU WILL

Examine the effects of government policies that place a ceiling on prices

Examine the effects of government policies that put a floor under prices

Consider how a tax on a good affects the price of the good and the quantity sold

Learn that taxes levied on buyers and taxes levied on sellers are equivalent

See how the burden of a tax is split between buyers and sellers

Economists have two roles. As scientists, they develop and test theories to explain the world around them. As policymakers, they use their theories to try to change the world for the better. The focus of the past two chapters has been scientific. We have seen how supply and demand determine the price of a good and the quantity of the good sold. We have also seen how various events shift supply and demand and thereby change the equilibrium price and quantity.

This chapter offers our first look at policy. Here we analyse various types of government policies using only the tools of supply and demand. As you will see, the analysis yields some surprising results. Policies often have effects that their architects did not intend or anticipate.

We begin by considering policies that directly control prices. For example, rent-control laws dictate a maximum rent that landlords may charge tenants. Minimum-wage laws dictate the lowest wage that firms may pay workers. Price controls are usually imposed when policymakers believe that the market price of a good or service is unfair to buyers or sellers. Yet, as we will see, these policies can generate inequities of their own.

After our discussion of price controls, we next consider the impact of taxes. Policymakers use taxes both to influence market outcomes and to raise revenue for public purposes. Although the prevalence of taxes in our economy is obvious, their effects are not. For example, when the government levies a tax on the amount that firms pay their workers, do the firms or the workers bear the burden of the tax? The answer is not at all clear—until we apply the powerful tools of supply and demand.

CONTROLS ON PRICES

To see how price controls affect market outcomes, let's look once again at the market for ice-cream. As we saw in chapter 4, if ice-cream is sold in a competitive market free of government regulation, the price of ice-cream adjusts to balance supply and demand—at the equilibrium price, the quantity of ice-cream that buyers want to buy exactly equals the quantity that sellers want to sell. To be concrete, suppose the equilibrium price is $3 per ice-cream.

Not everyone may be happy with the outcome of this free-market process. Let's say the Australian Association of Ice-cream Eaters complains that the $3 price is too high for everyone to enjoy an ice-cream a day (their recommended diet). Meanwhile, the National Organisation of Ice-cream Makers complains that the $3 price—the result of 'cutthroat competition'—is depressing the incomes of its members. Each of these groups lobbies the government to pass laws that alter the market outcome by directly controlling prices.

Of course, because buyers of any good always want a lower price and sellers want a higher price, the interests of the two groups conflict. If the Ice-cream Eaters are successful in their lobbying, the government imposes a legal maximum on the price at which ice-cream can be sold, called a **price ceiling**. If the Ice-cream Makers are successful, the government imposes a legal minimum on the price, called a **price floor**. Let us consider the effects of these policies in turn.

price ceiling
a legal maximum on the price at which a good can be sold

price floor
a legal minimum on the price at which a good can be sold

HOW PRICE CEILINGS AFFECT MARKET OUTCOMES

When the government, moved by the complaints of the Ice-cream Eaters, imposes a price ceiling on the market for ice-cream, two outcomes are possible. In panel (a) of figure 6.1, the government imposes a price ceiling of $4 per ice-cream. In this case, because the price that balances supply and demand ($3) is below the ceiling, the price ceiling is *not binding*. Market forces naturally move the economy to the equilibrium, and the price ceiling has no effect.

Panel (b) of figure 6.1 shows the other, more interesting, possibility. In this case, the government imposes a price ceiling of $2 per ice-cream. Because the equilibrium price of $3 is above the price ceiling, the ceiling is a *binding constraint* on the market. The forces of supply and demand tend to move the price towards the equilibrium price, but when the market price hits the ceiling, it can rise no further. Thus, the market price equals the price ceiling. At this price, the quantity of ice-cream demanded (125 ice-creams in the figure) exceeds the quantity supplied (75 ice-creams). There is a shortage of ice-cream, so some people who want to buy ice-cream at the going price are unable to.

When a shortage of ice-cream develops because of this price ceiling, some mechanism for rationing ice-cream will naturally develop. The mechanism could be long lines—buyers who are willing to arrive early and wait in line get an ice-cream, whereas those unwilling to wait do not. Alternatively, sellers could ration ice-cream according to their own personal biases, selling it only to friends, relatives or members of their own racial or ethnic group. Notice that even though the price ceiling was motivated by a desire to help buyers of ice-cream, not all buyers benefit from the policy. Some buyers do get to pay a lower price, although they may have to wait in line to do so, but other buyers cannot get any ice-cream at all.

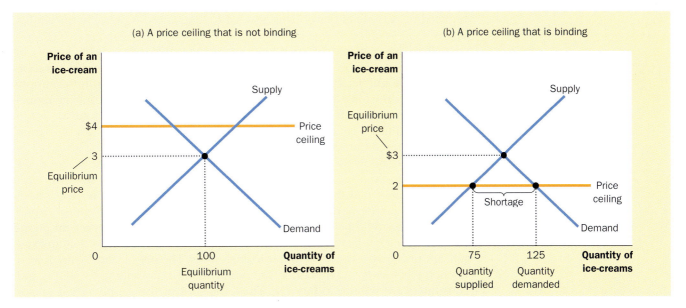

A MARKET WITH A PRICE CEILING. In panel (a), the government imposes a price ceiling of $4. Because the price ceiling is above the equilibrium price of $3, the price ceiling has no effect, and the market can reach the equilibrium of supply and demand. In this equilibrium, quantity supplied and quantity demanded both equal 100 ice-creams. In panel (b), the government imposes a price ceiling of $2. Because the price ceiling is below the equilibrium price of $3, the market price equals $2. At this price, 125 ice-creams are demanded and only 75 are supplied, so there is a shortage of 50 ice-creams.

Figure 6.1

This example in the market for ice-cream shows a general result—*when the government imposes a binding price ceiling on a competitive market, a shortage of the good arises, and sellers must ration the scarce goods among the large number of potential buyers.* The rationing mechanisms that develop under price ceilings are rarely desirable. Long lines are inefficient, because they waste buyers' time. Discrimination according to seller bias is both inefficient (because the good does not go to the buyer who values it most highly) and potentially unfair. In contrast, the rationing mechanism in a free, competitive market is both efficient and impersonal. When the market for ice-cream reaches its equilibrium, anyone who wants to pay the market price can get an ice-cream. Free markets ration goods with prices.

CASE STUDY   LINES AT THE PETROL STATION

Most major Australian cities receive their petrol from a single refinery. When the refinery reduces output, owing to a labour dispute, for example, then the supply of petrol to the city is cut. Long lines at petrol stations become commonplace, and motorists often have to wait for hours to buy only a few litres of petrol. A similar phenomenon occurred in the United States in 1973. Then, as we discussed in the last chapter, the Organization of Petroleum Exporting Countries (OPEC) raised the price of crude oil in world oil markets. Because crude oil is the major component used in making petrol, the higher oil prices reduced the supply of petrol. This also led to long lines for petrol in the United States.

Who is responsible for such long lines at petrol stations? If the supply of petrol has been cut because of a strike, most people blame either the oil companies or the unions. But the industrial dispute explains the cut in the supply of petrol, not the long lines. Similarly, the OPEC action also explains the reduction in the supply of petrol, but not the queues. These, most economists would argue, are due to government regulations that prevent petrol stations from raising the price they can charge for petrol.

Figure 6.2 shows what happens. As panel (a) shows, before the labour dispute, the supply of petrol is given by S_1 and the equilibrium price is P_1. But panel (b) shows that the dispute at the refinery cuts the supply of petrol back to S_2. If the petrol market were unregulated, the price of petrol would rise to P_2 and there would be no shortage. Instead, state governments prevent petrol stations from significantly raising the price of petrol. It is claimed that any significant price rises would be unfair to customers. The petrol stations are forced to charge below P_2. At this price, the petrol stations are willing to sell Q_S and consumers are willing to buy Q_D. Thus, the shift in the supply curve causes a severe shortage.

The ban on price rises not only creates long lines at petrol stations, it also reduces the incentive for producers to ship petrol in from other states. If the

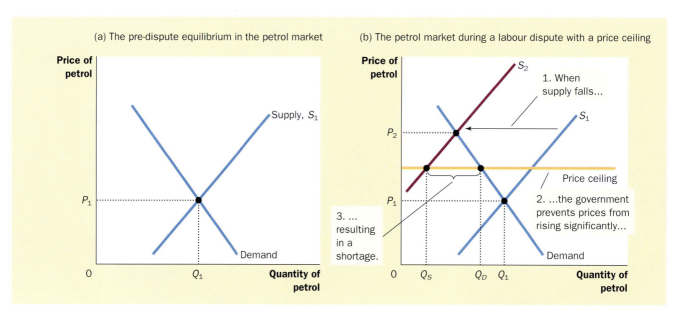

Figure 6.2

THE MARKET FOR PETROL WITH A PRICE CEILING. Panel (a) shows the petrol market when there is no price ceiling. The equilibrium price is P_1, and petrol sales are Q_1. Panel (b) shows the petrol market during an industrial dispute. The supply curve shifts to the left from S_1 to S_2. In the absence of government intervention, the price would have risen from P_1 to P_2. If the government imposes a price ceiling, this cannot happen. At the binding price ceiling, consumers are willing to buy Q_D, but producers of petrol are willing to sell only Q_S. The difference between quantity demanded and quantity supplied, $Q_D - Q_S$, measures the petrol shortage.

price of petrol increased to P_2, it would pay enterprising petrol station owners to buy petrol in an area unaffected by the dispute and have it delivered to their stations. By not allowing the price to rise, the government eliminates this incentive to bring in petrol supplies.

When the government prevents the price of petrol from rising during an industrial dispute, it says that it is protecting customers from 'price gouging' (increases in prices after strikes or disasters). Governments also prevent price gouging after natural disasters, when the supply of food and water is cut and the equilibrium price of these goods rises sharply. While governments prevent prices from rising for equity reasons—so that poorer people trapped by the disaster are not forced to pay higher prices—the laws against price gouging create shortages and reduce the incentives to ship more food and water into the affected regions.

CASE STUDY **RENT CONTROL IN THE SHORT RUN AND LONG RUN**

One common example of a price ceiling is rent control. In many cities around the world, local governments place a ceiling on rents that landlords may charge their tenants. The goal of this policy is to help the poor by making housing more affordable. Economists often criticise rent control, arguing that it is a highly inefficient way to help the poor raise their standard of living. One economist called rent control 'the best way to destroy a city, other than bombing'.

The adverse effects of rent control are less apparent to the general population because these effects occur over many years. In the short run, landlords have a fixed number of flats to rent, and they cannot adjust this number quickly as market conditions change. Moreover, the number of people searching for housing in a city may not be highly responsive to rents in the short run because people take time to adjust their housing arrangements. Therefore, the short-run supply of and demand for housing are relatively inelastic.

Panel (a) of figure 6.3 shows the effects in the short run of rent control on the housing market. As with any price ceiling, rent control causes a shortage. Yet because supply and demand are inelastic in the short run, the initial shortage caused by rent control is small. The main effect in the short run is to reduce rents.

In the long run, the story is very different because the buyers and sellers of rental housing respond more to market conditions as time passes. On the supply side, landlords respond to low rents by not building new flats and by failing to maintain existing ones. On the demand side, low rents encourage people to find their own accommodation (rather than living with their parents or sharing flats with friends) and induce more people to move into a city. Therefore, both supply and demand are more elastic in the long run.

Panel (b) of figure 6.3 illustrates the housing market in the long run. When rent control depresses rents below the equilibrium level, the quantity of flats supplied falls substantially, and the quantity of flats demanded rises substantially. The result is a large shortage of housing.

In cities with rent control, landlords use various mechanisms to ration housing. Some landlords keep long waiting lists. Others give a preference to tenants without children. Still others discriminate on the basis of race. Sometimes, flats are allocated to those willing to offer under-the-table payments to

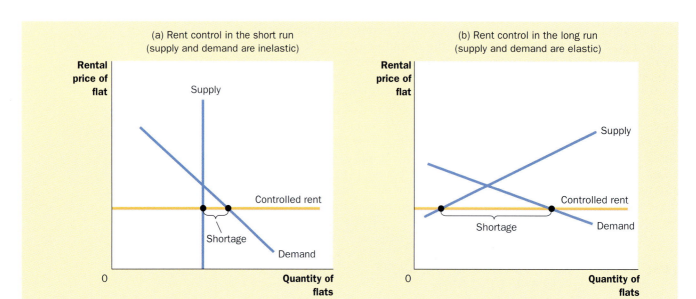

Figure 6.3

RENT CONTROL IN THE SHORT RUN AND IN THE LONG RUN. Panel (a) shows the effects in the short run of rent control—because the supply of and demand for flats are relatively inelastic, the price ceiling imposed by a rent-control law causes only a small shortage of housing. Panel (b) shows the effects in the long run of rent control—because the supply of and demand for flats are more elastic, rent control causes a large shortage.

real estate agents. In essence, these bribes bring the total price of a flat (including the bribe) closer to the equilibrium price.

To understand fully the effects of rent control, we have to remember one of the *Ten Principles of Economics* from chapter 1—people respond to incentives. In free markets, landlords try to keep their buildings clean and safe because desirable flats or home units command higher prices. In contrast, when rent control creates shortages and waiting lists, landlords lose their incentive to be responsive to tenants' concerns. Why should a landlord spend money to maintain and improve the property when people are waiting to get in as it is? In the end, tenants get lower rents, but they also get lower quality housing.

Policymakers often react to the effects of rent control by imposing additional regulations. For example, there are laws that make racial discrimination in housing illegal and require landlords to provide minimally adequate living conditions. These laws, however, are difficult and costly to enforce. In contrast, when rent control is eliminated and the market for housing is regulated by the forces of competition, such laws are less necessary. In a free market, the price of housing adjusts to eliminate the shortages that give rise to undesirable landlord behaviour.

HOW PRICE FLOORS AFFECT MARKET OUTCOMES

To examine the effects of another kind of government price control, let's return to the market for ice-cream. Imagine now that the government is persuaded by

IN THE NEWS

Rent control in Mumbai, India

RENT CONTROL PLAYS A LARGE ROLE IN some of the world's largest cities. Rent control issues in New York City, the largest city in the United States, are a regular issue in sitcoms such as 'Seinfeld' and 'Friends'. But in other cities the consequences are more extreme. Here is a description of how rent control has affected the Indian city of Mumbai, one of the world's largest cities.

New Homes for Old

MUMBAI—Driving along the Queen's Necklace, a sweep of waterfront in Mumbai, as Bombay prefers to be called these days, the taxi driver notes that its residences used to shine, but now look tattered. 'Rent control,' he explains.

Rent control has left much of Mumbai shabby, and not just the once splendid buildings on the waterfront. Because rent control has been so stringently enforced for so long, there has been little incentive to build housing, even though the city's population has tripled, to almost 13m people, since 1960. This accounts for the odd sight of briefcase-carrying middle managers emerging from crumbling housing which looks no less squalid for being adorned with satellite-television dishes. Though many people have the means to move out of the mean streets, there has been nowhere to move to.

That may be changing. Maharashtra state has found a way to encourage property improvement without removing rent control. In the past, building regulations stipulated that only so many square feet of housing could be built on so many square feet of land. Squatters made their own rules by, well, squatting, but even they were prevented from building more than one storey above the ground.

Moreover, because rents were depressed by law, landlords were discouraged from developing or improving their property. The only way they could increase revenues was to allow the land to be overrun by squatters and then send heavies to collect rents. Now they can do it legally: under the new rules, landowners, or 70% of squatters themselves, can apply to increase the land-use density.

The change this has brought about is already obvious. In Mumbai's Kanhyacha Pada district, for example, a one-storey, tin-roofed slum with no legal water supply, electricity or sanitation has been converted into a decent-looking seven-storey block with gardens and basic amenities.

For the slum tenants, the carrot is that their position is made legal, and the city authorities will provide them with services for about $10 a month. The landlord gets more rent, and a sellable property. Given the Mumbai boom, this is valuable, even though squatters and sitting tenants have to be rehoused by the landlord.

Mumbai's new approach has brought much-needed life to a moribund property market. About 100 000 people living in squalor have been rehoused under the plan in the past couple of years. That leaves just 6m to go.

SOURCE: *Economist*, 29 June 1996, p. 33.

---

the pleas of the National Organisation of Ice-cream Makers. In this case, the government might institute a price floor. Price floors, like price ceilings, are an attempt by the government to maintain prices at other than equilibrium levels. Whereas a price ceiling places a legal maximum on prices, a price floor places a legal minimum.

When the government imposes a price floor on the ice-cream market, two outcomes are possible. If the government imposes a price floor of $2 per ice-cream when the equilibrium price is $3, we obtain the outcome in panel (a) of figure 6.4. In this case, because the equilibrium price is above the floor, the price floor is not binding. Market forces naturally move the economy to the equilibrium, and the price floor has no effect.

Panel (b) of figure 6.4 shows what happens when the government imposes a price floor of $4 per ice-cream. In this case, because the equilibrium price of

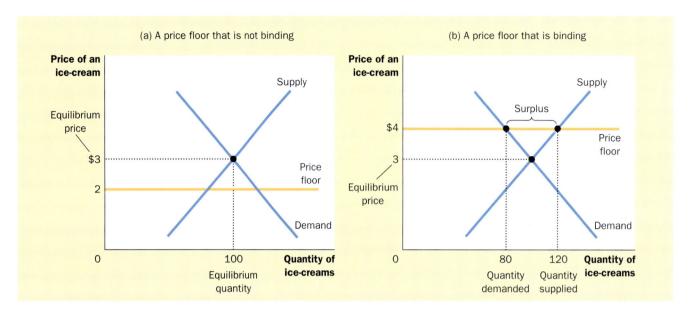

Figure 6.4

A MARKET WITH A PRICE FLOOR. In panel (a), the government imposes a price floor of $2. Because this is below the equilibrium price of $3, the price floor has no effect. The market price adjusts to balance supply and demand. At the equilibrium, quantity supplied and quantity demanded both equal 100 ice-creams. In panel (b), the government imposes a price floor of $4, which is above the equilibrium price of $3. Therefore, the market price equals $4. Because 120 ice-creams are supplied at this price and only 80 are demanded, there is a surplus of 40 ice-creams.

$3 is below the floor, the price floor is a binding constraint on the market. The forces of supply and demand tend to move the price towards the equilibrium price, but when the market price hits the floor, it can fall no further. The market price equals the price floor. At this floor, the quantity of ice-cream supplied (120 ice-creams) exceeds the quantity demanded (80). Some people who want to sell ice-cream at the going price are unable to. Thus, *a binding price floor causes a surplus*.

Just as price ceilings and shortages can lead to undesirable rationing mechanisms, so can price floors and surpluses. In the case of a price floor, some sellers are unable to sell all they want at the market price. The sellers who appeal to the personal biases of the buyers, perhaps because of racial or familial ties, are better able to sell their goods than those who do not. In contrast, in a free market, the price serves as the rationing mechanism, and sellers can sell all they want at the equilibrium price.

CASE STUDY   MINIMUM WAGE RATES

An important example of a price floor is a minimum wage. Minimum-wage laws dictate the lowest price for labour that any employer may pay. In Australia, the Australian Industrial Relations Commission (AIRC) sets **awards**

awards
the minimum wage rates that can be paid to particular workers in particular industries

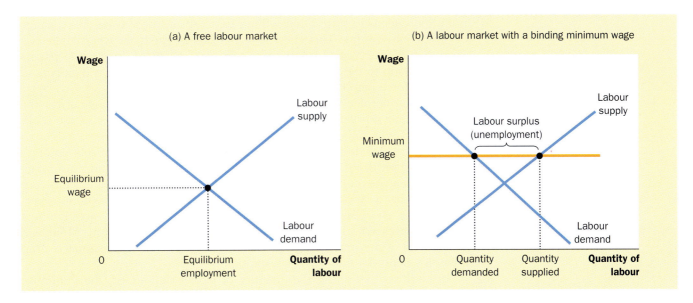

HOW THE MINIMUM WAGE AFFECTS THE LABOUR MARKET. Panel (a) shows a labour market in which the wage adjusts to balance labour supply and labour demand. Panel (b) shows the impact of a binding minimum or award wage. Because the minimum wage is a price floor, it causes a surplus—the quantity of labour supplied exceeds the quantity demanded. The result is unemployment.

Figure 6.5

which are the minimum wage rates that can be paid to particular workers in particular industries. Unlike other countries, such as the United States, Australia does not have a single minimum wage but a system of awards.

To examine the effects of a minimum wage or award rate, we must consider the market for labour in a particular industry. Panel (a) of figure 6.5 shows the labour market which, like all markets, is subject to the forces of supply and demand. Workers determine the supply of labour, and firms determine the demand. In the absence of government intervention, the wage adjusts to balance labour supply and labour demand.

Panel (b) of figure 6.5 shows the labour market with a minimum or award wage. If the minimum wage is above the equilibrium level, as it is here, the quantity of labour supplied exceeds the quantity demanded. The result is unemployment. Thus, the minimum wage raises the incomes of those workers who have jobs, but it lowers the incomes of those workers who cannot find jobs.

To fully understand the minimum or award wage, it is important to keep in mind that the economy contains not a single labour market, but many labour markets for different types of workers. The impact of the minimum wage depends on the skill and experience of the worker. Workers with high skills and much experience are not affected, because their equilibrium wages are well above the minimum. For these workers, award wage rates are not binding.

Minimum wages have their greatest impact on the market for teenage labour. The equilibrium wages of teenagers tend to be low because teenagers are among the least skilled and least experienced members of the labour force.

In addition, teenagers are often willing to accept a lower wage in exchange for on-the-job training. This effect is recognised in Australia where there is a separate minimum wage for teenagers—the 'junior' award. Even so, teenagers are more likely to be paid at this minimum rate, whereas other members of the labour force may be paid above-award wages.

Many economists have examined how minimum-wage laws affect the teenage labour market. These researchers compare the changes in the minimum wage over time with the changes in teenage employment. Although there is some debate about how much the minimum wage affects employment, the typical study finds that a 10% increase in the minimum wage depresses teenage employment between 1% and 3%. In interpreting this estimate, note that a 10% increase in the minimum wage does not raise the average wage of teenagers by 10%. A change in the law does not directly affect those teenagers who are already paid well above the minimum. Moreover, enforcement of minimum-wage laws is not perfect. Thus, the estimated drop in employment of 1% to 3% is substantial.

In addition to altering the quantity of labour demanded, the minimum wage also alters the quantity supplied. Because the minimum wage raises the wage that teenagers can earn, it increases the number of teenagers who choose to look for jobs. Studies have found that a higher minimum wage influences which teenagers are employed. When the minimum wage rises, some teenagers who are still attending school choose to drop out and take jobs. These new drop-outs displace other teenagers who had already dropped out of school and who now become unemployed.

The minimum wage is a frequent topic of political debate. Advocates of the minimum wage view the policy as one way to raise the income of the working poor. They correctly point out that workers who earn the minimum wage can afford only a meagre standard of living. In 1996, for instance, the Australian Council of Trade Unions—representing employees—argued to the Australian Industrial Relations Commission that the minimum wage applying to all workers should be $12 per hour. Their argument was based on the idea that all workers should be entitled to a 'living wage'. Many advocates of the minimum wage admit that it potentially has some adverse effects, including unemployment, but they believe that these effects are small and that, all things considered, a higher minimum wage makes the poor better off.

Opponents of the minimum wage contend that it is not the best way to combat poverty. They note that high minimum wages and junior wages cause unemployment, encourage teenagers to drop out of school, and prevent some unskilled workers from getting the on-the-job training they need. Moreover, opponents of the minimum wage point out that the minimum wage is a poorly targeted policy. Not all award-wage workers are heads of households trying to help their families escape poverty. Many award-wage earners are teenagers from middle-class homes working at part-time jobs for extra spending money.

EVALUATING PRICE CONTROLS

One of the *Ten Principles of Economics* discussed in chapter 1 is that markets are usually a good way to organise economic activity. This principle explains why economists almost always oppose price ceilings and price floors. To economists, prices are not the outcome of some haphazard process. Prices, they contend, are the result of the millions of business and consumer decisions that lie behind the supply and demand curves. Prices have the crucial job of balancing supply and demand and, thereby, coordinating economic activity. When policymakers set prices by legal decree, they obscure the signals that normally guide the allocation of society's resources.

Another one of the *Ten Principles of Economics* is that governments can sometimes improve market outcomes. Indeed, policymakers are led to control prices because they view the market's outcome as unfair. Price controls are often aimed at helping the poor. For instance, rent-control laws try to make housing affordable for everyone, and minimum-wage laws try to help people escape poverty.

Yet price controls often hurt those they are trying to help. Rent control may keep rents low, but it also discourages landlords from maintaining their buildings and makes housing hard to find. Minimum-wage laws may raise the incomes of some workers, but they also cause other workers to be unemployed.

Helping those in need can be accomplished in ways other than controlling prices. For instance, the government can make housing more affordable by paying a fraction of the rent for poor families. Unlike rent control, such rent subsidies do not reduce the quantity of housing supplied and, therefore, do not lead to housing shortages. Similarly, wage subsidies raise the living standards of the working poor without discouraging firms from hiring them.

Although these alternative policies are often better than price controls, they are not perfect. Rent and wage subsidies cost the government money and, therefore, require higher taxes. As we see in the next section, taxation has costs of its own.

QUICK QUIZ Define price ceiling and price floor, and give an example of each. Which leads to a shortage? Which leads to a surplus? Why?

TAXES

All governments—from the federal government in Canberra to local governments in small towns—use taxes to raise revenue for public purposes. Taxes are an important policy instrument, and they affect our lives in many ways. In this section we study how taxes affect the economy.

To set the stage for our analysis, imagine that a local government decides to hold an annual ice-cream celebration—with a parade, fireworks and speeches by town officials. To raise revenue to pay for the event, it decides to place a $0.50 tax on the sale of ice-creams. When the plan is announced, our two lobbying groups swing into action. The National Organisation of Ice-cream Makers claims that its members are struggling to survive in a competitive market, and it argues that *buyers* of ice-cream should have to pay the tax. The Australian Association of Ice-cream Eaters claims that consumers of ice-cream are having trouble making ends meet, and it argues that *sellers* of ice-cream should pay the tax. The mayor, hoping to reach a compromise, suggests that half the tax be paid by the buyers and half be paid by the sellers.

tax incidence

the study of who bears the burden of taxation

To analyse these proposals, we need to consider a simple but subtle question. When the government levies a tax on a good, who bears the burden of the tax—the people buying the good or the people selling the good? Or, if buyers and sellers share the tax burden, what determines how the burden is divided? Can the government simply legislate the division of the burden, as the mayor is suggesting, or is the division determined by more fundamental forces in the economy? Economists use the term **tax incidence** to refer to these questions about the distribution of a tax burden. As we will see, we can learn some surprising lessons about tax incidence just by applying the tools of supply and demand.

HOW TAXES ON BUYERS AFFECT MARKET OUTCOMES

We first consider a tax levied on buyers of a good. Suppose, for instance, that our local government passes a law requiring buyers of ice-creams to send $0.50 to the government for each ice-cream they buy. How does this law affect the buyers and sellers of ice-cream? To answer this question, we can follow the three steps in chapter 4 for analysing supply and demand: (1) we decide whether the law affects the supply or demand curve; (2) we decide which way the curve shifts; and (3) we examine how the shift affects the equilibrium.

The initial impact of the tax is on the demand for ice-cream. The supply curve is not affected because, for any given price of ice-cream, sellers have the same incentive to provide ice-cream to the market. In contrast, buyers now have to pay a tax to the government (as well as the price to the sellers) whenever they buy ice-cream. Thus, the tax shifts the demand curve for ice-cream.

The direction of the shift is easy to see. Because the tax on buyers makes buying ice-cream less attractive, buyers demand a smaller quantity of ice-cream at every price. As a result, the demand curve shifts to the left (or, equivalently, downwards).

We can, in this case, be more precise about how much the curve shifts. Because of the $0.50 tax levied on buyers, the effective price to buyers is now $0.50 higher than the market price. For example, if the market price of an ice-cream happened to be $2.00, the effective price to buyers would be $2.50. Because buyers look at their total cost including the tax, they demand a quantity of ice-cream as if the market price were $0.50 higher than it actually is. In other words, to induce buyers to demand any given quantity, the market price must now be $0.50 lower to make up for the effect of the tax.

Figure 6.6 shows how a tax of $0.50 shifts the demand curve downwards from D_1 to D_2 by exactly the size of the tax. To see the effect of the tax, we compare the old equilibrium and the new equilibrium. You can see in the figure that the equilibrium price of ice-cream falls from $3.00 to $2.80 and the equilibrium quantity falls from 100 to 90 ice-creams. Because sellers sell less and buyers buy less in the new equilibrium, the tax on ice-cream reduces the size of the ice-cream market.

Now let's return to the question of tax incidence. Who pays the tax? Although buyers send the entire tax to the government, buyers and sellers share the burden. Because the market price falls from $3.00 to $2.80 when the tax is introduced, sellers receive $0.20 less for each ice-cream than they did without the tax. Thus, the tax makes sellers worse off. Buyers pay sellers a lower price

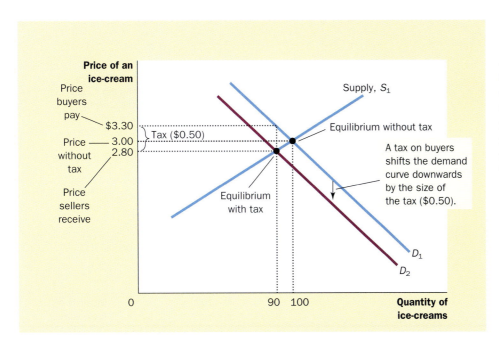

Figure 6.6

A TAX ON BUYERS. When a tax of $0.50 is levied on buyers, the demand curve shifts down by $0.50 from D_1 to D_2. The equilibrium quantity falls from 100 to 90 ice-creams. The price that sellers receive falls from $3.00 to $2.80. The price that buyers pay (including the tax) rises from $3.00 to $3.30. Even though the tax is levied on buyers, buyers and sellers share the burden of the tax.

($2.80), but the effective price including the tax rises from $3.00 before the tax to $3.30 with the tax ($2.80 + $0.50 = $3.30). Thus, the tax also makes buyers worse off.

To sum up, the analysis yields two general lessons:

◆ Taxes discourage market activity. When a good is taxed, the quantity of the good sold is smaller in the new equilibrium.

◆ Buyers and sellers share the burden of taxes. In the new equilibrium, buyers pay more for the good, and sellers receive less.

HOW TAXES ON SELLERS AFFECT MARKET OUTCOMES

Now consider a tax levied on sellers of a good. Suppose the local government passes a law requiring sellers of ice-creams to send $0.50 to the government for each one they sell. What are the effects of this law?

In this case, the initial impact of the tax is on the supply of ice-cream. Because the tax is not levied on buyers, the quantity of ice-cream demanded at any given price is the same, so the demand curve does not change. In contrast, the tax on sellers raises the cost of selling ice-cream, and this leads sellers to supply a smaller quantity at every price. The supply curve shifts to the left (or, equivalently, upwards).

Once again, we can be precise about the magnitude of the shift. For any market price of ice-cream, the effective price to sellers—the amount they get to keep after paying the tax—is $0.50 lower. For example, if the market price of an ice-cream happened to be $2.00, the effective price received by sellers would be $1.50. Whatever the market price, sellers will supply a quantity of ice-cream as if the price were $0.50 lower than it is. Put differently, to induce sellers to supply

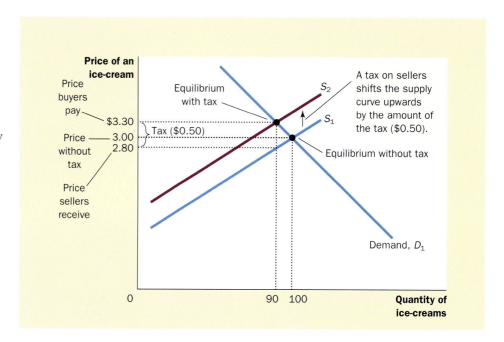

Figure 6.7

A TAX ON SELLERS. When a tax of $0.50 is levied on sellers, the supply curve shifts up by $0.50 from S_1 to S_2. The equilibrium quantity falls from 100 to 90 ice-creams. The price that buyers pay rises from $3.00 to $3.30. The price that sellers receive (after paying the tax) falls from $3.00 to $2.80. Even though the tax is levied on sellers, buyers and sellers share the burden of the tax.

any given quantity, the market price must now be $0.50 higher to compensate for the effect of the tax.

Figure 6.7 shows how the supply curve shifts upwards from S_1 to S_2 by exactly the size of a $0.50 tax. When the market moves from the old to the new equilibrium, the equilibrium price of ice-cream rises from $3.00 to $3.30, and the equilibrium quantity falls from 100 to 90 ice-creams. Once again, the tax reduces the size of the ice-cream market. And once again, buyers and sellers share the burden of the tax. Because the market price rises, buyers pay $0.30 more for each ice-cream than they did before the tax was imposed. Sellers receive a higher price than they did without the tax, but the effective price (after paying the tax) falls from $3.00 to $2.80.

Comparing figures 6.6 and 6.7 leads to a surprising conclusion—*taxes on buyers and taxes on sellers are equivalent*. In both cases, the tax places a wedge between the price that buyers pay and the price that sellers receive. The wedge between the buyers' price and the sellers' price is the same, regardless of whether the tax is levied on buyers or sellers. In either case, the wedge shifts the relative position of the supply and demand curves. In the new equilibrium, buyers and sellers share the burden of the tax. The only difference between taxes on buyers and taxes on sellers is who sends the money to the government.

The equivalence of these two taxes is perhaps easier to understand if we imagine that the government collects the $0.50 ice-cream tax in a bowl on the counter of each ice-cream shop. When the government levies the tax on buyers, the buyer is required to place $0.50 in the bowl every time an ice-cream is bought. When the government levies the tax on sellers, the seller is required to place $0.50 in the bowl after the sale of each ice-cream. Whether the $0.50 goes directly from the buyer's pocket into the bowl, or indirectly from the buyer's pocket into the seller's hand and then into the bowl, does not matter. Once the market reaches its new equilibrium, buyers and sellers share the burden, regardless of how the tax is levied.

CASE STUDY   WHO PAYS THE PAYROLL TAX?

If you have ever received a pay packet, you probably noticed that taxes were deducted from the amount you earned. In Australia, this tax is income tax imposed by the federal government. However, there are other taxes that affect workers. In particular, state governments in Australia levy payroll taxes on medium and large employers. In 1998, the standard payroll tax was 5% of the total payments a firm makes to its employees. However, in some states this rate was higher (up to 7%).

Who do you think bears the burden of this payroll tax—firms or workers? Payroll tax is imposed on employers so governments often argue that it is different from a tax on income. But is it true that payroll tax is really paid by employers?

Our analysis of tax incidence shows that the distribution of the burden of a tax is determined by more than who physically pays it. To illustrate, we can analyse payroll tax as merely a tax on a good, where the good is labour and the price is the wage. The key feature of the payroll tax is that it places a wedge between the wages that firms pay and the wages that workers receive. Figure 6.8 shows the outcome. When a payroll tax is imposed, the wages received by workers fall, and the wages paid by firms rise. In the end, workers and firms share the burden of the tax. So the division of the tax burden between workers and firms has nothing to do with who actually hands over the money. Workers effectively bear some of the tax burden.

This example shows that the most basic lesson of tax incidence is often overlooked in public debate. Law-makers can decide whether a tax comes from the buyer's pocket or from the seller's, but they cannot legislate the true burden of a tax. Rather, tax incidence depends on the forces of supply and demand.

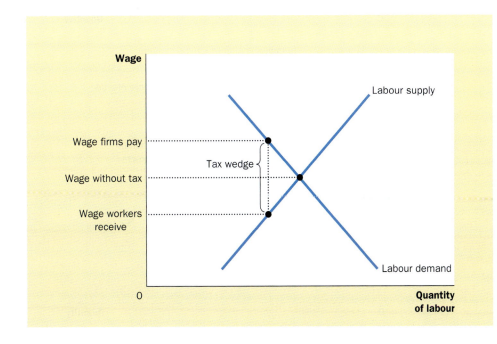

Figure 6.8

A PAYROLL TAX. A payroll tax places a wedge between the wages that workers receive and the wages that firms pay. Comparing wages with and without the tax, you can see that workers and firms share the tax burden. This division of the tax burden between workers and firms does not depend on whether the government levies the tax on workers, levies the tax on firms, or divides the tax equally between the two groups.

ELASTICITY AND TAX INCIDENCE

When a good is taxed, buyers and sellers of the good share the burden of the tax. But how exactly is the tax burden divided? Only rarely will it be shared equally. To see how the burden is divided, consider the impact of taxation in the two markets in figure 6.9. In both cases, the figure shows the initial demand curve, the initial supply curve, and a tax that drives a wedge between the amount paid by buyers and the amount received by sellers. (Not drawn in either panel of the figure is the new supply or demand curve. Which curve shifts depends on whether the tax is levied on buyers or sellers. As we have seen, this is irrelevant for the incidence of the tax.) The difference in the two panels is the relative elasticity of supply and demand.

Figure 6.9

How the burden of a tax is divided. In panel (a), the supply curve is elastic, and the demand curve is inelastic. In this case, the price received by sellers falls only slightly, and the price paid by buyers rises substantially. Thus, buyers bear most of the burden of the tax. In panel (b), the supply curve is inelastic, and the demand curve is elastic. In this case, the price received by sellers falls substantially, and the price paid by buyers rises only slightly. Thus, sellers bear most of the burden of the tax.

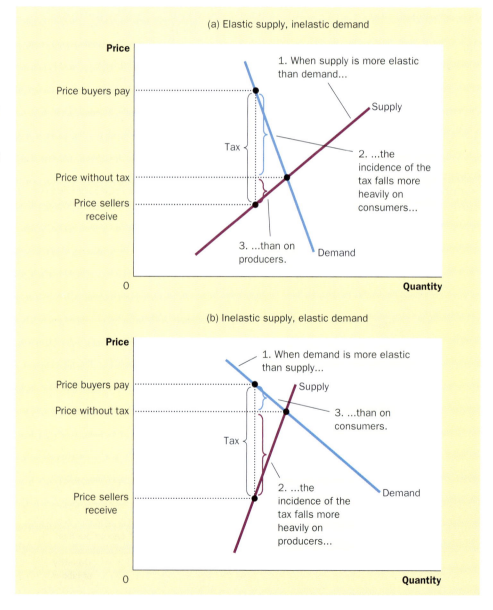

Panel (a) of figure 6.9 shows a tax in a market with very elastic supply and relatively inelastic demand—that is, sellers are very responsive to the price of the good, whereas buyers are not very responsive. When a tax is imposed on a market with these elasticities, the price received by sellers does not fall much, so sellers bear only a small burden. In contrast, the price paid by buyers rises substantially, indicating that buyers bear most of the burden of the tax.

Panel (b) of figure 6.9 shows a tax in a market with relatively inelastic supply and very elastic demand. In this case, sellers are not very responsive to the price, whereas buyers are very responsive. The figure shows that when a tax is imposed, the price paid by buyers does not rise much, and the price received by sellers falls substantially. Thus, sellers bear most of the burden of the tax.

The two panels of figure 6.9 show a general lesson about how the burden of a tax is divided—*a tax burden falls more heavily on the side of the market that is less elastic*. Why is this true? In essence, the elasticity measures the willingness of buyers or sellers to leave the market when conditions become unfavourable. A small elasticity of demand means that buyers do not have good alternatives to consuming this particular good. A small elasticity of supply means that sellers do not have good alternatives to producing this particular good. When the good is taxed, the side of the market with fewer good alternatives cannot easily leave the market and must, therefore, bear more of the burden of the tax.

> **QUICK QUIZ** In a supply-and-demand diagram, show how a tax on car buyers of $1000 per car affects the quantity of cars sold and the price of cars. In another diagram, show how a tax on car sellers of $1000 per car affects the quantity of cars sold and the price of cars. In both diagrams, show the change in the price paid by car buyers and the change in the price received by car sellers.

CONCLUSION

The economy is governed by two kinds of laws—the laws of supply and demand and the laws enacted by governments. In this chapter we have begun to see how these laws interact. Price controls and taxes are common in various markets in the economy, and their effects are frequently debated in the press and among policymakers. Even a little bit of economic knowledge can go a long way towards understanding and evaluating these policies.

In subsequent chapters we will analyse many government policies in greater detail and consider a broader range of policies than we considered here. Yet the basic lessons of this chapter will not change—when analysing government policies, supply and demand are the first and most useful tools of analysis.

Summary

- A price ceiling is a legal maximum on the price of a good or service. An example is rent control. If the price ceiling is below the equilibrium price, the quantity demanded exceeds the quantity supplied. Because of the resulting shortage, sellers must in some way ration the good or service among buyers.

- A price floor is a legal minimum on the price of a good or service. An example is a minimum or award wage. If the price floor is above the equilibrium price, the quantity supplied exceeds the quantity demanded. Because of the resulting surplus, buyers' demands for the good or service must in some way be rationed among sellers.

- When the government levies a tax on a good, the equilibrium quantity of the good falls. That is, a tax on a market shrinks the size of the market.

- A tax on a good places a wedge between the price paid by buyers and the price received by sellers. When the market moves to the new equilibrium, buyers pay more for the good and sellers receive less for it. In this sense, buyers and sellers share the tax burden. The incidence of a tax does not depend on whether the tax is levied on buyers or sellers.

- The incidence of a tax depends on the price elasticities of supply and demand. The burden tends to fall on the side of the market that is less elastic because that side of the market can respond less easily to the tax by changing the quantity bought or sold.

Key concepts

price ceiling, p. 110   price floor, p. 110   awards, p. 116   tax incidence, p. 120

Questions for review

1. Give an example of a price ceiling and of a price floor.
2. Which causes a shortage of a good—a price ceiling or a price floor? Which causes a surplus?
3. Explain why economists usually oppose controls on prices.
4. What is the difference between a tax paid by buyers and a tax paid by sellers?
5. How does a tax on a good affect the price paid by buyers, the price received by sellers and the quantity sold?
6. What determines how the burden of a tax is divided between buyers and sellers? Why?

Problems and applications

1. Suppose the federal government requires beer drinkers to pay a $2 tax on each carton of beer purchased. (In fact, both the federal and state governments impose beer taxes of some sort.)
   a. Draw a supply-and-demand diagram of the market for beer without the tax. Show the price paid by consumers, the price received by producers and the quantity of beer sold. What is the difference between the price paid by consumers and the price received by producers?
   b. Now draw a supply-and-demand diagram for the beer market with the tax. Show the price paid by consumers, the price received by producers, and the quantity of beer sold. What is the difference between the price paid by consumers and the price received by producers? Has the quantity of beer sold increased or decreased?

2. The government has decided that the free-market price of cheese is too low.
   a. Suppose the government imposes a binding price floor in the cheese market. Use a supply-and-demand diagram to show the effect of this policy on the price of cheese and the quantity of cheese sold. Is there a shortage or surplus of cheese?
   b. Farmers complain that the price floor has reduced their total revenue. Is this possible? Explain.
   c. In response to farmers' complaints, the government agrees to purchase all of the surplus cheese at the price floor. Compared with the basic price floor, who benefits from this new policy? Who loses?

3. If the government places a $500 tax on luxury cars, will the price paid by consumers rise by more than $500, less than $500 or exactly $500? Explain.

4. A recent study found that the demand and supply schedules for frisbees are as follows:

Price per frisbee	Quantity demanded	Quantity supplied
$11	1 million	15 million
10	2	12
9	4	9
8	6	6
7	8	3
6	10	1

   a. What are the equilibrium price and quantity of frisbees?
   b. Frisbee manufacturers persuade the government that frisbee production improves scientists' understanding of aerodynamics and thus is important for national security. A concerned government votes to impose a price floor $2 above the equilibrium price. What is the new market price? How many frisbees are sold?
   c. Irate university students march on Canberra and demand a reduction in the price of frisbees. An even more concerned Parliament votes to repeal the price floor and impose a price ceiling $1 below the former price floor. What is the new market price? How many frisbees are sold?

5. The federal government decides that Australia should reduce air pollution by reducing its use of petrol. The government imposes a $0.50 tax for each litre of petrol sold.
   a. Should this tax be imposed on producers or consumers? Explain carefully using a supply-and-demand diagram.
   b. If the demand for petrol were more elastic, would this tax be more effective or less effective in reducing the quantity of petrol consumed? Explain using both words and a diagram.
   c. Are consumers of petrol helped or hurt by this tax? Why?
   d. Are workers in the oil industry helped or hurt by this tax? Why?

6. A case study in this chapter discusses minimum or award wages.
   a. Suppose the award wage in a particular industry is above the equilibrium wage in the market for unskilled labour. Using a supply-and-demand diagram of the market for unskilled labour, show the market wage, the number of workers who are employed, and the number of workers who are unemployed. Also show the total wage payments to unskilled workers.
   b. Now suppose the Industrial Relations Commission proposes an increase in the award wage. What effect would this increase have on employment? Does the change in employment depend on the elasticity of demand, the elasticity of supply, both elasticities, or neither?
   c. What effect would this increase in the award wage have on unemployment? Does the change in unemployment depend on the elasticity of demand, the elasticity of supply, both elasticities, or neither?
   d. If the demand for unskilled labour were inelastic, would the proposed increase in the award wage raise or lower total wage payments to unskilled workers? Would your answer change if the demand for unskilled labour were elastic?

7. Consider the following policies, each of which is aimed at reducing violent crime by reducing the use of guns. Illustrate each of these proposed policies in a supply-and-demand diagram of the gun market.
   a. a tax on gun buyers
   b. a tax on gun sellers
   c. a price floor on guns
   d. a tax on ammunition

8. The Australian government administers two programs that affect the market for cigarettes. Media campaigns and labelling requirements are aimed at making the public aware of the dangers of cigarette smoking. At the same time, there is a tax on cigarettes.
   a. How do these two programs affect cigarette consumption? Use a graph of the cigarette market in your answer.
   b. What is the combined effect of these two programs on the price of cigarettes?

9. (This question requires the use of secondary school algebra.) The market for tickets to the symphony can be described by the following demand and supply curves:

$$Q^D = 20\,000 - 90P$$
$$Q^S = 10\,000 + 110P$$

   a. What are the equilibrium price and quantity in the ticket market?
   b. Lovers of classical music persuade the government

to impose a price ceiling of $40 per ticket. How many tickets are now sold in the market? Does this policy get more or fewer people to attend classical music concerts?

10. (This question requires the use of secondary school algebra.) Suppose the demand curve for pizza can be represented by the equation $Q^D = 20 - 2P$, where Q^D is the quantity demanded and P is the price. The supply curve for pizza can be represented by the equation $Q^S = P - 1$, where Q^S is the quantity supplied. Suppose the government imposes a $3 tax per pizza. How much more will consumers now pay for a pizza? (*Hint:* The prices in the demand and supply equations are no longer equal. The price that determines quantity demanded now equals the price that determines quantity supplied plus $3.)

11. A subsidy is the opposite of a tax. With a $0.50 tax on the buyers of ice-creams, the government collects $0.50 for each ice-cream purchased; with a $0.50 subsidy for the buyers of ice-creams, the government pays buyers $0.50 for each ice-cream purchased.
   a. Show the effect of a $0.50 subsidy per ice-cream on the demand curve for ice-creams, the effective price paid by consumers, the effective price received by sellers and the quantity of ice-creams sold.
   b. Do consumers gain or lose from this policy? Do producers gain or lose? Does the government gain or lose?

THE DATA OF MACROECONOMICS

7

MEASURING A NATION'S INCOME

When you finish university and start looking for a full-time job, your experience will, to a large extent, be shaped by prevailing economic conditions. In some years, firms throughout the economy are expanding their production of goods and services, employment is rising, and jobs are easy to find. In other years, firms are cutting back on production, employment is declining, and finding a good job takes a long time. Not surprisingly, any university graduate would rather enter the labour force in a year of economic expansion than in a year of economic contraction.

Because the condition of the overall economy profoundly affects all of us, changes in economic conditions are widely reported by the media. Indeed, it is hard to pick up a newspaper without seeing some newly reported statistic about the economy. The statistic might measure the total income of everyone in the economy (GDP), the rate at which average prices are rising (inflation), the percentage of the labour force that is out of work (unemployment), total spending at stores (retail sales), or the imbalance of trade between Australia and the rest of the world (the trade deficit). All these statistics are macroeconomic. Rather than telling us about a particular household or firm, they tell us something about the entire economy.

IN THIS CHAPTER YOU WILL

Consider why an economy's total income equals its total expenditure

Learn how gross domestic product (GDP) is defined and calculated

See the breakdown of GDP into its four major components

Learn the distinction between real GDP and nominal GDP

Consider whether GDP is a good measure of economic wellbeing

microeconomics
the study of how households and firms make decisions and how they interact in markets

macroeconomics
the study of economy-wide phenomena, including inflation, unemployment and economic growth

As you may recall from chapter 2, economics is divided into two branches—microeconomics and macroeconomics. **Microeconomics** is the study of how individual households and firms make decisions and how they interact with one another in markets. **Macroeconomics** is the study of the economy as a whole. The goal of macroeconomics is to explain the economic changes that affect many households, firms and markets at once. Macroeconomists consider diverse questions: Why is average income high in some countries and low in others? Why do prices rise rapidly in some periods of time but are more stable in other periods? Why do production and employment expand in some years and contract in others? These diverse questions are all macroeconomic because they concern the workings of the entire economy.

Because the economy as a whole is just a collection of many households and many firms interacting in many markets, microeconomics and macroeconomics are closely linked. The basic tools of supply and demand, for instance, are as central to macroeconomic analysis as they are to microeconomic analysis. Yet studying the economy in its entirety raises some new and intriguing challenges.

In this chapter and the next one, we discuss some of the data that economists and policymakers use to monitor the overall economy. These data reflect the economic changes that macroeconomists try to explain. This chapter considers *gross domestic product*, or simply GDP, which measures the total income of a nation. GDP is the most closely watched economic statistic because it is thought to be the best single measure of a society's economic wellbeing.

THE ECONOMY'S INCOME AND EXPENDITURE

If you were to judge how a person is doing economically, you might first look at his or her income. A person with a high income can more easily afford life's necessities and luxuries. It is no surprise that people with higher incomes enjoy higher standards of living—better housing, better health care, fancier cars, more opulent holidays, and so on.

The same logic applies to a nation's overall economy. When judging whether the economy is doing well or poorly, it is natural to look at the total income that everyone in the economy is earning. That is the task of gross domestic product (GDP).

GDP measures two things at once—the total income of everyone in the economy and the total expenditure on the economy's output of goods and services. The reason that GDP can perform the trick of measuring both total income and total expenditure is that these two things are really the same. *For an economy as a whole, income must equal expenditure.*

Why is this true? The reason that an economy's income is the same as its expenditure is simply that every transaction has two parties: a buyer and a seller. Every dollar of spending by some buyer is a dollar of income for some seller. Suppose, for instance, that Karen pays Doug $100 to mow her lawn. In this case, Doug is a seller of a service, and Karen is a buyer. Doug earns $100, and Karen spends $100. Thus, the transaction contributes equally to the economy's income and to its expenditure. GDP, whether measured as total income or total expenditure, rises by $100.

Another way to see the equality of income and expenditure is with the circular-flow diagram in figure 7.1. (You may recall this circular-flow diagram from chapter 2.) This diagram describes all the transactions between households and firms in a simple economy. In this economy, households buy goods and services from firms; these expenditures flow through the markets for goods and services. The firms in turn use the money they receive from sales to pay workers' wages, landowners' rent and firm owners' profit; this income flows through the markets for the factors of production. In this economy, money continuously flows from households to firms and then back to households.

We can calculate GDP for this economy in one of two ways—by adding up the total expenditure by households or by adding up the total income (wages, rent and profit) paid by firms. Because all expenditure in the economy ends up as someone's income, GDP is the same regardless of how we calculate it.

The real economy is, of course, more complicated than the one illustrated in figure 7.1. In particular, households do not spend all of their income. Households pay some of their income to the government in taxes, and they save and invest some of their income for use in the future. In addition, households do not buy all goods and services produced in the economy. Some goods and services are bought by governments, and some are bought by firms that plan to use them in

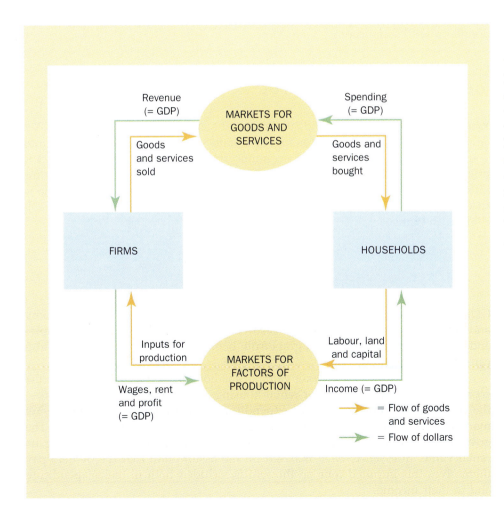

Figure 7.1

THE CIRCULAR-FLOW DIAGRAM. Households buy goods and services from firms, and firms use their revenue from sales to pay wages to workers, rent to landowners and profit to firm owners. GDP equals the total amount spent by households in the market for goods and services. It also equals the total wages, rent and profit paid by firms in the markets for the factors of production.

the future to produce their own output. Yet, regardless of whether a household, government or firm buys a good or service, the transaction has a buyer and seller. Thus, for the economy as a whole, expenditure and income are always the same.

QUICK QUIZ What two things does gross domestic product measure? How can it measure two things at once?

THE MEASUREMENT OF GROSS DOMESTIC PRODUCT

Now that we have discussed the meaning of gross domestic product in general terms, let's be more precise about how this statistic is measured. Here is a definition of GDP:

◆ **Gross domestic product (GDP)** is the market value of all final goods and services produced within a country in a given period of time.

This definition might seem simple enough. But, in fact, many subtle issues arise when calculating an economy's GDP. Let's therefore consider each phrase in this definition with some care.

gross domestic product (GDP)
the market value of all final goods and services produced within a country in a given period of time

'GDP IS THE MARKET VALUE...'

You have probably heard the adage 'You can't compare apples and oranges'. Yet GDP does exactly that. GDP adds together many different kinds of products into a single measure of the value of economic activity. To do this, it uses market prices. Because market prices measure the amount people are willing to pay for different goods, they reflect the value of those goods. If the price of an apple is twice the price of an orange, then an apple contributes twice as much to GDP as does an orange.

'...OF ALL...'

GDP tries to be comprehensive. It includes all items produced in the economy and sold legally in markets. GDP measures the market value of not just apples and oranges, but also pears and grapefruit, books and films, haircuts and health care, and so on.

GDP also includes the market value of the housing services provided by the economy's stock of housing. For rental housing, this value is easy to calculate—the rent equals both the tenant's expenditure and the landlord's income. Yet many people own the place where they live and, therefore, do not pay rent. The government includes this owner-occupied housing in GDP by estimating its rental value. In essence, GDP is based on the assumption that the owners pay themselves this imputed rent, so the rent is included both in their expenditure and in their income.

There are some products, however, that GDP excludes because measurement of them is so difficult. GDP excludes items produced and sold illicitly, such as illegal drugs. It also excludes most items that are produced and consumed at home and, therefore, never enter the marketplace. Vegetables you buy at the supermarket are part of GDP; vegetables you grow in your garden are not.

These exclusions from GDP can at times lead to paradoxical results. For example, when Karen pays Doug to mow her lawn, that transaction is part of GDP. If Karen were to marry Doug, the situation would change. Even though Doug may continue to mow Karen's lawn, the value of the mowing is now left out of GDP because Doug's service is no longer sold in a market. Thus, when Karen and Doug marry, GDP falls.

'...FINAL...'

When Australian Allied Paper makes paper which Hallmark uses to make a greeting card, the paper is called an *intermediate good*, and the card is called a *final good*. GDP includes only the value of final goods. The reason is that the value of intermediate goods is already included in the prices of the final goods. Adding the market value of the paper to the market value of the card would be double counting. That is, it would (incorrectly) count the paper twice.

An important exception to this principle arises when an intermediate good is produced and, rather than being used, is added to a firm's inventory to be used or sold at a later date. In this case, the intermediate good is taken to be 'final' for the moment, and its value as inventory investment is added to GDP. When the inventory of the intermediate good is later used or sold, the firm's inventory investment is negative, and GDP for the later period is reduced accordingly.

'...GOODS AND SERVICES...'

GDP includes both tangible goods (food, clothing, cars) and intangible services (haircuts, house cleaning, doctor visits). When you buy a CD by your favourite band, you are buying a good, and the purchase price is part of GDP. When you pay to hear a concert by the same group, you are buying a service, and the ticket price is also part of GDP.

'...PRODUCED...'

GDP includes goods and services currently produced. It does not include transactions involving items produced in the past. When Ford produces and sells a new car, the value of the car is included in GDP. When one person sells a used car to another person, the value of the used car is not included in GDP.

'...WITHIN A COUNTRY...'

GDP measures the value of production within the geographic confines of a country. When Japanese citizens work temporarily in Australia, their production is

gross national product (GNP)

the market value of all final goods and services produced by permanent residents of a nation within a given period of time

part of Australian GDP. When an Australian citizen owns a factory in Malaysia, the profit from production at that factory is not part of Australian GDP (it is part of Malaysia's GDP). Thus, items are included in a nation's GDP if they are produced domestically, regardless of the nationality of the producer.

Another statistic, called **gross national product (GNP)**, takes a different approach to dealing with the goods and services produced by foreigners. GNP is the value of the production of a nation's permanent residents. When Japanese citizens work temporarily in Australia, their production is not part of Australian GNP (it is part of Japan's GNP). When an Australian citizen owns a factory in Malaysia, the profit from production at the factory is part of Australian GNP. Thus, income is included in a nation's GNP if it is earned by the nation's permanent residents (called *nationals*), regardless of where they earn it.

Throughout this book, we follow the standard practice of using GDP to measure the value of economic activity. For most purposes, however, the distinction between GDP and GNP is not very important. In Australia and most other countries, domestic residents are responsible for most domestic production, so GDP and GNP are quite close.

'...IN A GIVEN PERIOD OF TIME.'

GDP measures the value of production that takes place within a specific interval of time. Usually that interval is a year or a quarter (3 months). GDP measures the economy's flow of income and expenditure during that interval.

When the government reports the GDP for a quarter, it usually presents GDP 'at an annual rate'. This means that the figure reported for quarterly GDP is the amount of income and expenditure during the quarter multiplied by 4. The government uses this convention so that quarterly and annual figures on GDP can be compared more easily.

In addition, when the government reports quarterly GDP, it presents the data after they have been modified by a statistical procedure called *seasonal adjustment*. The unadjusted data show clearly that the economy produces more goods and services during some times of the year than during others. (As you might guess, December's Christmas shopping season is a high point.) When monitoring the condition of the economy, economists and policymakers often want to look beyond these regular seasonal changes. Therefore, government statisticians adjust the quarterly data to take out the seasonal cycle. The GDP data reported in the news are always seasonally adjusted.

Now let's repeat the definition of GDP:

◆ Gross domestic product (GDP) is the market value of all final goods and services produced within a country in a given period of time.

It should now be apparent that GDP is a sophisticated measure of the value of economic activity. In advanced courses in macroeconomics, you will learn more of the subtleties that arise in its calculation. But even now you can see that each phrase in this definition is packed with meaning.

QUICK QUIZ Which contributes more to GDP—the production of a kilogram of mince or the production of a kilogram of caviar? Why?

THE COMPONENTS OF GDP

Spending in the economy takes many forms. At any moment, the Brown family may be having lunch at Pizza Hut; General Motors–Holden may be building a car factory; the Navy may be procuring a submarine; and Qantas may be buying an aeroplane from Boeing. GDP accounts for all of these various forms of spending on goods and services.

To understand how the economy is using its scarce resources, economists are often interested in studying the composition of GDP among various types of spending. To do this, GDP (which we denote as Y) is divided into four components: consumption (C), investment (I), government purchases (G) and net exports (NX):

$$Y = C + I + G + NX$$

This equation is an *identity*—an equation that must be true by the way the variables in the equation are defined. In this case, because each dollar of expenditure included in GDP is placed into one of the four components of GDP, the total of the four components must be equal to GDP.

We have just seen an example of each component. **Consumption** is spending by households on goods and services, such as the Browns' lunch at Pizza Hut. **Investment** is the purchase of new capital equipment, inventories and structures, such as the General Motors–Holden factory. Investment also includes expenditure on new housing. (By convention, expenditure on new housing is the one form of household spending categorised as investment rather than consumption.) **Government purchases** include spending on goods and services by local, state and federal governments, such as the Navy's purchase of a submarine. **Net exports** equal the purchases of domestically produced goods by foreigners (exports) minus the domestic purchases of foreign goods (imports). A domestic firm's purchase from a producer in another country, such as the Qantas purchase of a plane from Boeing, decreases net exports.

The 'net' in 'net exports' refers to the fact that imports are subtracted from exports. This subtraction is made because imports of goods and services are included in other components of GDP. For example, suppose that a household buys a $50 000 car from Volvo, the Swedish car-maker. That transaction increases consumption by $50 000 because car purchases are part of consumer spending. It also reduces net exports by $50 000 because the car is an import. In other words, net exports include goods and services produced abroad (with a minus sign) because these goods and services are included in consumption, investment and government purchases (with a plus sign). Thus, when a domestic household, firm or government buys a good or service from abroad, the purchase reduces net exports—but because it also raises consumption, investment or government purchases, it does not affect GDP.

The meaning of 'government purchases' also requires clarification. When the government pays the salary of an Army general, that salary is part of government purchases. But what happens when the government pays a pension benefit to one of the elderly? Such government spending is called a *transfer payment* because it is not made in exchange for a currently produced good or service. From a macroeconomic standpoint, transfer payments are like a tax rebate. Like taxes, transfer payments alter household income, but they do not reflect the economy's production. No new goods or services are produced in the process of the

consumption
spending by households on goods and services, with the exception of purchases of new housing

investment
spending on new capital equipment, inventories and structures, including household purchases of new housing

government purchases
spending on goods and services by local, state and federal governments

net exports
spending on domestically produced goods by foreigners (exports) minus spending on foreign goods by domestic residents (imports)

FYI

Three other measures of income

When the Australian Bureau of Statistics (ABS) calculates the nation's GDP every 3 months, it uses three approaches to calculate the value of national output. The first measure, GDP(E), uses the expenditure approach to calculate national income. This is the approach described in the text. The other measures are GDP(I), the income approach, and GDP(P), the production approach. Conceptually, the three measures are the same but, in practice, they can differ because of the different data sources for each measure. They also differ more in the short run. Over time, more accurate estimates of the data become available, which allow the ABS to update its calculation of GDP. The ABS also calculates various other measures of income for the economy. These other measures differ from GDP by excluding or including certain categories of income. What follows is a brief description of the other two measures of GDP. Figure 7.2 shows the relationship between other income measures.

◆ *Gross domestic product income approach (GDP(I))* is the sum of factor incomes, consumption of fixed capital (depreciation) and net indirect taxes. Factor incomes include wages, salaries and supplements paid to labour and profit received by both private and public businesses. Depreciation is the wear and tear on the economy's stock of equipment and structures, such as trucks rusting and lightbulbs burning out. In the national income accounts prepared by the ABS, depreciation is called the 'consumption of fixed capital'.

◆ *Gross domestic product production approach (GDP(P))* involves taking the market value of goods and services produced by an industry and deducting the cost of goods and services used up by the industry in the productive process, or what is referred to by the ABS as 'intermediate consumption'. This approach uses a concept called **value added** to calculate GDP. When a firm produces a good, it must buy inputs. In the process of production, the firm transforms the inputs into something else. The additional value which is added to the value of the inputs is referred to as the 'value added'. When the ABS uses this approach to calculate GDP, the value of the inputs must be subtracted from the value of the final product to avoid double counting because GDP is the value of final goods and services.

Although the various measures of income differ in detail, they almost always tell the same story about economic conditions. When GDP is growing rapidly, these other measures of income are usually growing rapidly. And when GDP is falling, these other measures are usually falling as well. For monitoring fluctuations in the overall economy, it does not matter much which measure of income we use.

value added
the value of a firm's output minus the value of its inputs

government giving a transfer payment to an individual. Because GDP is intended to measure the income from (and expenditure on) the production of goods and services, transfer payments are not counted as part of government purchases.

Table 7.1 shows the composition of Australian GDP in 1997. In this year, the GDP of Australia was about $512 billion. If we divide this number by the 1997 Australian population of 18.5 million, we find that GDP per person—the amount of expenditure for the average Australian—was $27 567. Consumption made up just under two-thirds of GDP, or $17 140 per person. Investment was $4718 per person. Government purchases were $5548 per person. Net exports were $161 per person. This number is positive because Australians earned more from selling to foreigners than we spent on foreign goods. In three of the four years from 1993 to 1997, this number was negative—indicating that the value of our imports was greater than the value of our exports in those years.

QUICK QUIZ List the four components of expenditure. Which is the largest?

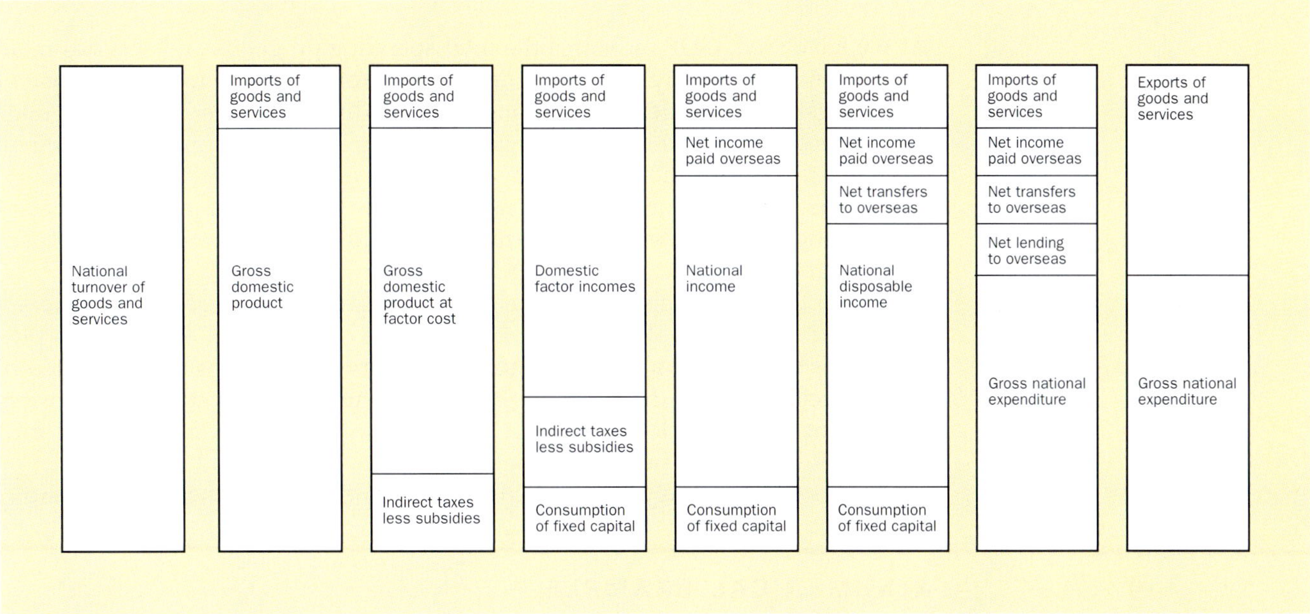

RELATIONSHIPS AMONG OTHER INCOME MEASURES. The figure shows the relationships among various measures of expenditure, income and output. National turnover is the total of expenditure on all goods and services, including expenditure on imports. Gross domestic product subtracts imports from national turnover to get a value of goods and services produced within the domestic economy. The value of domestic production can also be obtained by adding up the incomes of domestic factors of production. The figure shows how taxes and subsidies, payments to and receipts from overseas, and borrowing and lending are accounted for in the national income accounts.

Figure 7.2

SOURCE: Australian Bureau of Statistics

	TOTAL (IN BILLIONS OF DOLLARS)	PER PERSON (IN DOLLARS)	PER CENT OF TOTAL
Gross domestic product	$512	$27 567	100%
Consumption	319	17 140	62
Investment	88	4 718	17
Government purchases	103	5 548	20
Net exports	3	161	1

SOURCE: Australian Bureau of Statistics.

Table 7.1

GDP AND ITS COMPONENTS. This table shows total GDP for the Australian economy in 1997 and the breakdown of GDP into its four components.

REAL VERSUS NOMINAL GDP

As we have seen, GDP measures the total spending on goods and services in all markets in the economy. If total spending rises from one year to the next, one of two things must be true: (1) the economy is producing a larger output of goods and services, or (2) goods and services are being sold at higher prices. When studying changes in the economy over time, economists want to separate these two effects. In particular, they want a measure of the total quantity of goods and services the economy is producing that is not affected by changes in the prices of those goods and services.

To do this, economists use a measure called *real* GDP. Real GDP answers a hypothetical question: What would be the value of the goods and services produced this year if we valued these goods and services at prices that prevailed in some specific year in the past? By evaluating current production using prices that are fixed at past levels, real GDP shows how the economy's overall production of goods and services changes over time.

To see more precisely how real GDP is constructed, let's consider an example.

A NUMERICAL EXAMPLE

Table 7.2 shows some data for an economy that produces only two goods—meat pies and kebabs. The table shows the quantities of the two goods produced and their prices in the years 2001, 2002 and 2003.

To calculate total spending in this economy, we multiply the quantities of meat pies and kebabs by their prices. In the year 2001, 100 meat pies are sold at a price of $1 per meat pie, so expenditure on meat pies equals $100. In the same year, 50 kebabs are sold for $2 per kebab, so expenditure on kebabs also equals $100. Total expenditure in the economy—the sum of expenditure on meat pies and expenditure on kebabs—is $200. This amount, the production of goods and services valued at current prices, is called **nominal GDP**.

nominal GDP
the production of goods and services valued at current prices

The table shows the calculation of nominal GDP for these 3 years. Total spending rises from $200 in 2001 to $600 in 2002 and then to $1200 in 2003. Part of this rise is attributable to the increase in the quantities of meat pies and kebabs, and part is attributable to the increase in the prices of meat pies and kebabs.

real GDP
the production of goods and services valued at constant prices

To obtain a measure of the amount produced that is not affected by changes in prices, we use **real GDP**, which is the production of goods and services valued at constant prices. We calculate real GDP by first choosing one year as a *base year*. We then use the prices of meat pies and kebabs in the base year to calculate the value of goods and services in all of the years. In other words, the prices in the base year provide the basis for comparing quantities in different years.

Suppose that we choose 2001 to be the base year in our example. We can then use the prices of meat pies and kebabs in 2001 to calculate the value of goods and services produced in 2001, 2002 and 2003. Table 7.2 shows these calculations. To calculate real GDP for 2001, we use the prices of meat pies and kebabs in 2001 (the base year) and the quantities of meat pies and kebabs produced in 2001. (Thus, for the base year, real GDP always equals nominal GDP.) To calculate real GDP for 2002, we use the prices of meat pies and kebabs in 2001 (the base year) and the quantities of meat pies and kebabs produced in 2002.

	Price and quantities			
Year	Price of meat pies	Quantity of meat pies	Price of kebabs	Quantity of kebabs
2001	$1	100	$2	50
2002	2	150	3	100
2003	3	200	4	150

Year	Calculating nominal GDP
2001	($1 per meat pie × 100 meat pies) + ($2 per kebab × 50 kebabs) = $200
2002	($2 per meat pie × 150 meat pies) + ($3 per kebab × 100 kebabs) = $600
2003	($3 per meat pie × 200 meat pies) + ($4 per kebab × 150 kebabs) = $1200

Year	Calculating real GDP (base year 2001)
2001	($1 per meat pie × 100 meat pies) + ($2 per kebab × 50 kebabs) = $200
2002	($1 per meat pie × 150 meat pies) + ($2 per kebab × 100 kebabs) = $350
2003	($1 per meat pie × 200 meat pies) + ($2 per kebab × 150 kebabs) = $500

Year	Calculating the GDP deflator
2001	($200/$200) × 100 = 100
2002	($600/$350) × 100 = 171
2003	($1200/$500) × 100 = 240

Table 7.2

REAL AND NOMINAL GDP. This table shows how to calculate real GDP, nominal GDP and the GDP deflator for a hypothetical economy that produces only meat pies and kebabs.

Similarly, to calculate real GDP for 2003, we use the prices in 2001 and the quantities in 2003. When we find that real GDP has risen from $200 in 2001 to $350 in 2002 and then to $500 in 2003, we know that the increase is attributable to an increase in the quantities produced, because the prices are held fixed at base-year levels.

To sum up—*nominal GDP uses current prices to place a value on the economy's production of goods and services; real GDP uses constant base-year prices to place a value on the economy's production of goods and services.* Because real GDP is not affected by changes in prices, changes in real GDP reflect only changes in the amounts being produced. Thus, real GDP is a measure of the economy's production of goods and services.

Our goal in calculating GDP is to gauge how well the overall economy is performing. Because real GDP measures the economy's production of goods and services, it reflects the economy's ability to satisfy people's material needs and desires. Thus, real GDP is a better gauge of economic wellbeing than is nominal GDP. When economists talk about the economy's GDP, they usually mean real rather than nominal GDP. And when they talk about growth in the economy, they measure that growth using the percentage change in real GDP from an earlier period.

THE GDP DEFLATOR

From nominal GDP and real GDP, we can calculate a third useful statistic—the GDP deflator. The GDP deflator measures the current level of prices relative to the level of prices in the base year. In other words, the GDP deflator tells us the rise in nominal GDP that is attributable to a rise in prices rather than a rise in the quantities produced.

The **GDP deflator** is calculated as follows:

$$\text{GDP deflator} = \frac{\text{Nominal GDP}}{\text{Real GDP}} \times 100$$

GDP deflator
a measure of the price level calculated as the ratio of nominal GDP to real GDP times 100

This formula shows why the GDP deflator measures the level of prices in the economy. A change in the price of some good or service, without any change in the quantity produced, affects nominal GDP but not real GDP. This price change, therefore, is reflected in the GDP deflator.

The GDP deflator in our example is calculated at the bottom of table 7.2. For the year 2001, nominal GDP is $200 and real GDP is $200, so the GDP deflator is 100. (The GDP deflator is always 100 in the base year.) For the year 2002, nominal GDP is $600 and real GDP is $350, so the GDP deflator is 171. Because the GDP deflator rose in year 2002 from 100 to 171, we can say that the price level increased by 71%.

The GDP deflator is one measure that economists use to monitor the average level of prices in the economy. We examine another—the consumer price index—in the next chapter.

CASE STUDY   REAL GDP OVER RECENT HISTORY

Now that we know how real GDP is defined and measured, let's look at what this macroeconomic variable tells us about the recent history of Australia. Figure 7.3 shows quarterly data on real GDP for the Australian economy since 1970.

The most obvious feature of these data is that real GDP grows over time. The real GDP of the Australian economy in 1998 was over twice its level in 1970. Put differently, the output of goods and services produced in Australia has grown on average about 3.3% per year. This continued growth in real GDP enables the typical Australian to enjoy greater economic prosperity than his or her parents and grandparents did.

A second feature of the GDP data is that growth is not steady. The upward climb of real GDP is occasionally interrupted by periods of decline, called *recessions*. Figure 7.3 marks recessions with shaded vertical bars. Recessions are associated not only with lower incomes but also with other forms of economic distress—rising unemployment, falling profits, increased bankruptcies and so on.

Much of macroeconomics is aimed at explaining the long-run growth and short-run fluctuations in real GDP. As we will see in the coming chapters, we need different explanatory frameworks or 'models' for these two purposes. Because short-run fluctuations represent deviations from the long-run trend, we first examine the behaviour of the economy in the long run. In particular, chapters 9 to 15 examine how key macroeconomic variables, including real GDP, are determined in the long run. We then build on this analysis to explain short-run fluctuations in chapters 16 to 18.

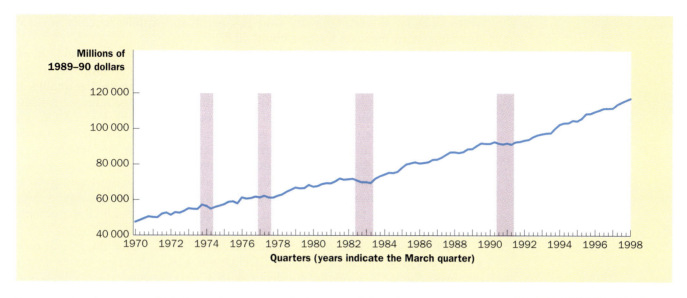

REAL GDP IN AUSTRALIA. This figure shows quarterly data on real GDP for the Australian economy since 1970. Recessions—periods of falling real GDP—are marked with the shaded vertical bars.

SOURCE: Australian Bureau of Statistics.

Figure 7.3

QUICK QUIZ Define real and nominal GDP. Which is a better measure of economic wellbeing? Why?

GDP AND ECONOMIC WELLBEING

Earlier in this chapter, GDP was called the best single measure of the economic wellbeing of a society. Now that we know what GDP is, we can evaluate this claim.

As we have seen, GDP measures both the economy's total income and the economy's total expenditure on goods and services. Thus, GDP per person tells us the income and expenditure of the average person in the economy. Because most people prefer to receive higher income and enjoy higher expenditure, GDP per person seems a natural measure of the economic wellbeing of the average individual.

Yet some people dispute the validity of GDP as a measure of welfare. When he was running for president in 1968, US Senator Robert Kennedy gave a moving critique of such economic measures:

> [Gross domestic product] does not allow for the health of our children, the quality of their education, or the joy of their play. It does not include the beauty of our poetry or the strength of our marriages, the intelligence of our public debate or the integrity of our public officials. It measures neither our courage, nor our wisdom, nor our devotion to our country. It measures everything, in short, except that which makes life worthwhile, and it can tell us everything about America except why we are proud that we are Americans.

Much of what Robert Kennedy said is correct and applies equally well to Australia. Why, then, do we care about GDP?

The answer is that a large GDP does in fact help us to lead enjoyable lives. GDP does not measure the health of children, but nations with larger GDP can afford better health care for their children. GDP does not measure the quality of education, but nations with larger GDP can afford better educational systems. GDP does not measure the beauty of poetry, but nations with larger GDP can afford to teach more of their citizens to read and to enjoy poetry. GDP does not take account of our intelligence, integrity, courage, wisdom or devotion to country, but all of these laudable attributes are easier to foster when people are less concerned about being able to afford the material necessities of life. In short, GDP does not directly measure those things that make life worthwhile, but it does measure our ability to satisfy material needs, and these are essential ingredients of comfortable, enjoyable and worthwhile lives.

GDP is not, however, a perfect measure of wellbeing. Some things that contribute to a good life are left out of GDP. One is leisure. Suppose, for instance, that everyone in the economy suddenly started working every day of the week, rather than enjoying leisure on weekends. More goods and services would be produced, and GDP would rise. Yet, despite the increase in GDP, we should not conclude that everyone would be better off. The welfare loss from reduced leisure would offset the welfare gain from producing and consuming a greater quantity of goods and services.

Another thing that GDP excludes is the quality of the environment. Imagine that the government eliminated all environmental regulations. Firms could then produce goods and services without considering the pollution they create, and GDP might rise. Yet it is most likely that wellbeing would fall. The deterioration in the quality of air and water would more than offset the welfare gain from greater production.

Because GDP uses market prices to value goods and services, it also excludes the value of almost all activity that takes place outside of markets. Child-rearing and volunteer work, for instance, contribute to the wellbeing of those in society, but GDP does not reflect these contributions. If parents decided to spend fewer hours at their jobs in order to spend more time with their children, the economy would produce fewer goods and services, and GDP would fall, but that change would not necessarily reflect a lower quality of life.

In the end, we conclude that GDP is a good measure of welfare for most—but not all—purposes. It is important to keep in mind what GDP includes as well as what it leaves out.

CASE STUDY   INTERNATIONAL DIFFERENCES IN GDP AND THE QUALITY OF LIFE

One way to gauge the usefulness of GDP as a measure of economic wellbeing is to examine international data. Rich and poor countries have vastly different levels of GDP per person. If a large GDP leads to a higher standard of living, then we should observe GDP to be strongly correlated with measures of the quality of life. And, in fact, we do.

Table 7.3 shows ten of the world's most populous countries, as well as Australia and New Zealand, ranked in order of GDP per person. The table also shows life expectancy (the expected life span at birth) and literacy (the

Country	Real GDP per Person (1994)	Life Expectancy	Adult Literacy
United States	$26 397	76 years	99%
Japan	21 581	80	99
Germany	19 675	76	99
Australia	19 285	78	99
New Zealand	16 851	76	99
Russia	4 760	67	99
Indonesia	3 270	63	83
China	2 330	69	80
Pakistan	2 160	62	36
Nigeria	1 540	51	54
Bangladesh	1 290	56	37
India	1 240	61	51

SOURCE: *Human Development Report 1997*, United Nations.

Table 7.3

GDP, LIFE EXPECTANCY AND LITERACY. The table shows GDP per person and two measures of the quality of life for 12 major countries.

percentage of the adult population who can read). These data show a clear pattern. In rich countries, such as the United States, Japan and Australia, people can expect to live well into their seventies, and almost all of the population can read. In poor countries, such as Nigeria, Bangladesh and India, people typically live only into their fifties, and only about half of the population is literate.

Although data on other aspects of the quality of life are less complete, they tell a similar story. Countries with low GDP per person tend to have more infants with low birthweight, higher rates of infant mortality, higher rates of maternal mortality, higher rates of child malnutrition, and less common access to safe drinking water. In countries with low GDP per person, fewer school-age children are in fact in school, and those who are in school must learn with fewer teachers per student. These countries also tend to have fewer radios, fewer televisions, fewer telephones, fewer paved roads and fewer households with electricity. International data leave no doubt that a nation's GDP is closely associated with its citizens' standard of living.

■ **QUICK QUIZ** Why should policymakers care about GDP?

CONCLUSION

This chapter has discussed how economists measure the total income of a nation. Measurement is, of course, only a starting point. Much of macroeconomics is aimed at revealing the long-run and short-run determinants of a nation's gross domestic product. Why, for example, is GDP higher in Australia and Japan than in India and Nigeria? What can the governments of the poorest countries do to promote more rapid growth in GDP? Why does GDP in Australia rise rapidly in some years and fall in others? What can Australian policymakers do to reduce the severity of these fluctuations in GDP? These are the questions we will take up shortly.

At this point, it is important to acknowledge the importance of just measuring GDP. We all get some sense of how the economy is doing as we go about our lives. But economists who study changes in the economy and policymakers who formulate economic policies need more than this vague sense—they need concrete data on which to base their judgements. Quantifying the behaviour of the economy with statistics such as GDP is, therefore, the first step in developing a science of macroeconomics.

Summary

- Because every transaction has a buyer and a seller, the total expenditure in the economy must equal the total income in the economy.

- Gross domestic product (GDP) measures an economy's total expenditure on newly produced goods and services and the total income earned from the production of these goods and services. More precisely, GDP is the market value of all final goods and services produced within a country in a given period of time.

- GDP is divided among four components of expenditure—consumption, investment, government purchases and net exports. Consumption includes spending on goods and services by households, with the exception of purchases of new housing. Investment includes spending on new equipment and structures, including households' purchases of new housing. Government purchases include spending on goods and services by local, state and federal governments. Net exports equal the value of goods and services produced domestically and sold abroad (exports) minus the value of goods and services produced abroad and sold domestically (imports).

- Nominal GDP uses current prices to value the economy's production of goods and services. Real GDP uses constant base-year prices to value the economy's production of goods and services. The GDP deflator—calculated from the ratio of nominal to real GDP—measures the level of prices in the economy.

- GDP is a good measure of economic wellbeing because people prefer higher to lower incomes. But it is not a perfect measure of wellbeing. For example, GDP excludes the value of leisure and the value of a clean environment.

Key concepts

microeconomics, p. 132
macroeconomics, p. 132
gross domestic product (GDP), p. 134
gross national product (GNP), p. 136
consumption, p. 137
investment, p. 137

government purchases, p. 137
net exports, p. 137
value added, p. 138
nominal GDP, p. 140
real GDP, p. 140
GDP deflator, p. 142

Questions for review

1. Explain why an economy's income must equal its expenditure.

2. Which contributes more to GDP—the production of a family car or the production of a luxury car? Why?

3. A farmer sells wheat to a baker for $2. The baker uses the wheat to make bread, which is sold for $3. What is the contribution to GDP?

4. Many years ago, Sharon paid $500 to put together a record collection. Today she sold her albums at a garage sale for $100. How does this sale affect current GDP?

5. List the four components of GDP. Give an example of each.

6. In the year 2001, the economy produces 100 loaves of bread that sell for $2 each. In the year 2002, the economy produces 200 loaves of bread that sell for $3 each. Calculate nominal GDP, real GDP and the GDP deflator for each year. (Use 2001 as the base year.) By what percentage does each of these three statistics rise from one year to the next?

7. Why is it desirable for a country to have a large GDP? Give an example of something that would raise GDP and yet be undesirable.

Problems and applications

1. What components of GDP (if any) would each of the following transactions affect? Explain.
   a. A family buys a new refrigerator.
   b. Aunt Jane buys a new house.
   c. Ford sells a Laser from its inventory.
   d. You buy a pizza.
   e. The government of New South Wales resurfaces the Pacific Highway.
   f. Your parents buy a bottle of French wine.
   g. Toyota expands its factory in Altona, Victoria.

2. The 'government purchases' component of GDP does not include spending on transfer payments such as pension benefits. Thinking about the definition of GDP, explain why transfer payments are excluded.

3. Why do you think households' purchases of new housing are included in the investment component of GDP rather than the consumption component? Can you think of a reason that households' purchases of new cars should also be included in investment rather than in consumption? To what other consumption goods might this logic apply?

4. As the chapter states, GDP does not include the value of used goods that are resold. Why would including such transactions make GDP a less informative measure of economic wellbeing?

5. What is the advantage of measuring GDP using the prices, rather than the sizes or weights, of different goods?

6. Consider the following data on Australian GDP:

YEAR	NOMINAL GDP (IN BILLIONS)	GDP DEFLATOR (BASE YEAR 1989–90)
1995–96	$492	113
1996–97	512	116

   a. What was the growth rate of nominal income between 1995–96 and 1996–97? (*Note:* The growth rate is the percentage change from one period to the next. The ABS calculates annual GDP on a financial year basis, from July one year to June the next.)
   b. What was the growth rate of the GDP deflator between 1995–96 and 1996–97?
   c. What was real income in 1995–96 measured in 1989–90 prices?
   d. What was real income in 1996–97 measured in 1989–90 prices?
   e. What was the growth rate of real income between 1995–96 and 1996–97?
   f. Was the growth rate of nominal income higher or lower than the growth rate of real income? Explain.

7. If prices rise, people's income from selling goods increases. The growth of real GDP ignores this gain, however. Why, then, do economists prefer real GDP as a measure of economic wellbeing?

8. Revised estimates of Australian GDP are usually released by the government near the end of each month. Go to a library and find a newspaper article that reports on the most recent release. Or look it up on the ABS Web site, http://www.statistics.gov.au/. Discuss the recent changes in real and nominal GDP and in the components of GDP.

9. If a farmer sells the same amount of corn as last year, but at a higher price per ear, her income has increased. Can you tell whether she is better off? Explain.

10. A friend tells you that the GDP of China is three times the GDP of Sweden. Does this imply that China is better off economically than Sweden? Why or why not?

11. Goods and services that are not sold in markets, such as food produced and consumed at home, are

generally not included in GDP. Can you think of how this might cause the numbers in the second column of table 7.3 to be misleading in a comparison of the economic wellbeing of Australia and India? Explain.

12. Until the early 1990s, the US government emphasised GNP rather than GDP as a measure of economic wellbeing, whereas most other countries emphasised GDP. Which measure should the US government prefer if it cares about the total income of Americans? Which measure should it prefer if it cares about the total amount of economic activity occurring in the United States? Why would Australia and the United States look at different measures of economic activity?

13. The participation of women in the Australian labour force has risen dramatically since 1965.
    a. How do you think this rise affected GDP?
    b. Now imagine a measure of wellbeing that includes time spent working in the home and taking leisure. How would the change in this measure of wellbeing compare with the change in GDP?
    c. Can you think of other aspects of wellbeing that are associated with the rise in women's labour-force participation? Would it be practical to construct a measure of wellbeing that includes these aspects?

8

MEASURING THE COST OF LIVING

IN THIS CHAPTER YOU WILL

Learn how the consumer price index (CPI) is constructed

Consider why the CPI is an imperfect measure of the cost of living

Compare the CPI and the GDP deflator as measures of the overall price level

See how to use a price index to compare dollar amounts from different times

Learn the distinction between real and nominal interest rates

In 1930, as the Australian economy was suffering through the Great Depression, famed racehorse Phar Lap earned £9429 at the Melbourne Cup. At the time, these earnings were extraordinary, even for great racehorses. The prime minister, James Scullin, received a parliamentary allowance of about £1000. When Australia switched from pounds to decimal currency in 1966, a pound was designated to be worth $2, so in dollar terms, these earnings would have been $19 000 and $2000 respectively. (See the FYI box, 'The change to decimal currency'.) Phar Lap may be more famous than Prime Minister Scullin, but neither amount seems much when compared with the winnings for the 1998 Melbourne Cup.

Today the Melbourne Cup pays $1.5 million to the winning horse, about 80 times what Phar Lap won. And Phar Lap is still considered one of the greatest racehorses ever to have lived. At first, this fact might lead you to think that horseracing has become much more lucrative over the past seven decades. But, as everyone knows, the prices of goods and services have also risen. In 1930, an ice-cream would have cost about 2 cents and a ticket to the local picture theatre about 5 cents. Because these prices were so much lower in Phar Lap's day than they are in ours, it is not clear whether Phar Lap's owners enjoyed a higher or lower standard of living than today's horse owners.

In the preceding chapter we looked at how economists use gross domestic product (GDP) to measure the quantity of goods and services that the economy is producing. This chapter examines how economists measure the overall cost of living. To compare Phar Lap's earnings of $19 000 with prize money of today, we need to find some way of turning dollar figures into meaningful measures of purchasing power. That is exactly the job of a statistic called the *consumer price index*. After seeing how the consumer price index is constructed, we discuss how we can use such a price index to compare dollar figures from different points in time.

The consumer price index is used to monitor changes in the cost of living over time. When the consumer price index rises, the typical family has to spend more dollars to maintain the same standard of living. Economists use the term *inflation* to describe a situation in which the economy's overall price level is rising. The *inflation rate* is the percentage change in the price level from the previous period. As we will see in the coming chapters, inflation is a closely watched aspect of macroeconomic performance and is a key variable guiding macroeconomic policy. This chapter provides the background for that analysis by showing how economists measure the inflation rate using the consumer price index.

FYI

The change to decimal currency

IMAGINE THAT, INSTEAD OF the name 'dollar', the currency in Australia was called the 'inflato'. That was one of the names suggested to Prime Minister Holt for the new decimal currency introduced in 1966. The 'royal' was the most favoured name, but others suggested were 'austral', 'A.B.C.D.', 'aborroo', 'anzac', 'centimate', 'decicur', 'dollauster', 'kanoala', 'howzat', 'macquarie', 'oz' and 'sheepsback'. It's hard to imagine a shopkeeper saying 'That'll be five sheepsbacks, please'!

The day Australia changed to decimal currency was 14 February 1966. The currency used before the change was the pound (£). One pound was worth 20 shillings, and 1 shilling was worth 12 pence. The conversion rate was $2 for every pound. A shilling became 10 cents, and 1 penny was equivalent to 5/6 of a cent. This is not an exchange rate, though. It is simply the rate chosen for converting old currency to new. If you found a pound in your attic, it would still be equivalent to $2. How much that pound would buy today compared with how much it would have bought 50 years ago is another matter. What we are discussing in this chapter is what happens to the purchasing power of a unit of currency over time as a result of inflation, that is, a rise in the prices of goods and services.

At the time of the conversion, people predicted that inflation would result from the change. For example, a box of matches sold for 2 pence in the old currency. At the standard conversion rate of 1 penny to 5/6 of a cent, the price in the new currency would be 1.67 cents. But there were no units of currency smaller than a cent, so this would be rounded up to 2 cents, a price increase of roughly 20%. However, these increases would have occurred only for goods that were very low in price and an insignificant part of anyone's budget, so the predicted inflationary effects did not occur.

Other costs of the conversion included changing acccounting machines, cash registers and electronic data processing machines to handle decimal currency. There was a government compensation scheme to help business people with the costs of the changeover. Despite concerns that conversion would be costly and inflationary, the transition to decimal currency was made with relatively little fuss.

THE CONSUMER PRICE INDEX

consumer price index (CPI)

a measure of the overall cost of the goods and services bought by a typical consumer

The **consumer price index (CPI)** is a measure of the overall cost of the goods and services bought by a typical consumer. Each month the Australian Bureau of Statistics calculates and reports the consumer price index. In this section, we discuss how the consumer price index is calculated and what problems arise in its measurement. We also consider how this index compares with the GDP deflator, another measure of the overall level of prices, which we examined in the last chapter.

HOW THE CONSUMER PRICE INDEX IS CALCULATED

When the Australian Bureau of Statistics (ABS) calculates the consumer price index and the inflation rate, it uses data on the prices of thousands of goods and services. To see exactly how these statistics are constructed, let's consider a simple economy in which consumers buy only two goods—meat pies and apples. Table 8.1 shows the five steps that the ABS follows.

1. *Fix the basket.* The first step in calculating the consumer price index is to determine which prices are most important to the typical consumer. If the typical consumer buys more apples than meat pies, then the price of apples is more important than the price of meat pies and, therefore, should be given greater weight in measuring the cost of living. The ABS sets these weights by surveying consumers and finding the basket of goods and services that

Table 8.1

CALCULATING THE CONSUMER PRICE INDEX AND THE INFLATION RATE: AN EXAMPLE. This table shows how to calculate the consumer price index and the inflation rate for a hypothetical economy in which consumers buy only meat pies and apples.

STEP 1: SURVEY CONSUMERS TO DETERMINE A FIXED BASKET OF GOODS

4 apples, 2 meat pies

STEP 2: FIND THE PRICE OF EACH GOOD IN EACH YEAR

YEAR	PRICE OF APPLES	PRICE OF MEAT PIES
2001	$1	$2
2002	2	3
2003	3	4

STEP 3: CALCULATE THE COST OF THE BASKET OF GOODS IN EACH YEAR

YEAR	COST OF BASKET
2001	($1 per apple × 4 apples) + ($2 per meat pie × 2 meat pies) = $8
2002	($2 per apple × 4 apples) + ($3 per meat pie × 2 meat pies) = $14
2003	($3 per apple × 4 apples) + ($4 per meat pie × 2 meat pies) = $20

STEP 4: CHOOSE ONE YEAR AS A BASE YEAR (2001) AND CALCULATE THE CONSUMER PRICE INDEX IN EACH YEAR

YEAR	CONSUMER PRICE INDEX
2001	($8/$8) × 100 = 100
2002	($14/$8) × 100 = 175
2003	($20/$8) × 100 = 250

STEP 5: USE THE CONSUMER PRICE INDEX TO CALCULATE THE INFLATION RATE FROM PREVIOUS YEAR

YEAR	INFLATION RATE
2002	(175 − 100)/100 × 100 = 75%
2003	(250 − 175)/175 × 100 = 43%

the typical consumer buys. In the example in the table, the typical consumer buys a basket of 4 apples and 2 meat pies.

2. *Find the prices.* The second step in calculating the consumer price index is to find the prices of each of the goods and services in the basket for each point in time. The table shows the prices of meat pies and apples for 3 different years.

3. *Calculate the basket's cost.* The third step is to use the data on prices to calculate the cost of the basket of goods and services at different times. The table shows this calculation for each of the 3 years. Notice that only the prices in this calculation change. By keeping the basket of goods the same (4 apples and 2 meat pies), we are isolating the effects of price changes from the effect of any quantity changes that might be occurring at the same time.

4. *Choose a base year and calculate the index.* The fourth step is to designate one year as the base year, which is the benchmark with which other years are compared. To calculate the index, the price of the basket of goods and services in each year is divided by the price of the basket in the base year, and this ratio is then multiplied by 100. The resulting number is the consumer price index.

   In the example in the table, the year 2001 is the base year. In this year, the basket of meat pies and apples costs $8. Therefore, the price of the basket in all years is divided by $8 and multiplied by 100. The consumer price index is 100 in 2001. (The index is always 100 in the base year.) The consumer price index is 175 in 2002. This means that the price of the basket in 2002 is 175% of its price in the base year. Put differently, a basket of goods that costs $100 in the base year costs $175 in 2002. Similarly, the consumer price index is 250 in 2003, indicating that the price level in 2003 is 250% of the price level in the base year.

5. *Calculate the inflation rate.* The fifth and final step is to use the consumer price index to calculate the **inflation rate**, which is the percentage change in the price index from the preceding period. In our example, the consumer price index rose by 75% from 2001 to 2002 and by 43% from 2002 to 2003. The inflation rate is said to be 75% in 2002 and 43% in 2003.

inflation rate
the percentage change in the price index from the preceding period

Although this example simplifies the real world by including only two goods, it shows how the ABS calculates the consumer price index and the inflation rate. The ABS collects and processes data on the prices of thousands of goods and services at least once each quarter and, by following the five steps described above, determines how quickly the cost of living for the typical consumer is rising. When the ABS makes its quarterly announcement of the inflation rate calculated from the consumer price index, you can usually hear the number on the evening television news or see it in the next day's newspaper.

In addition to the consumer price index for the overall economy, the ABS calculates several other price indexes. It reports the index for the capital cities (Sydney, Melbourne, Perth, Adelaide, Brisbane, Hobart, Darwin) and Canberra as well as for some narrow categories of goods and services (such as food, clothing and housing). It also calculates the **producer price index**, which measures the cost of a basket of goods and services bought by firms rather than by consumers. Because firms eventually pass on their costs to consumers in the form of higher consumer prices, changes in the producer price index are often thought to be useful in predicting changes in the consumer price index.

producer price index
a measure of the cost of a basket of goods and services bought by firms

FYI

What is in the CPI's basket?

When constructing the consumer price index, the Australian Bureau of Statistics tries to include all the goods and services that the typical consumer buys. Moreover, it tries to weight these goods and services according to how much consumers buy of each item.

Figure 8.1 shows the breakdown of consumer spending into the major categories of goods and services. The basics of living are the most significant categories. Housing and household equipment and operation make up the largest component of the typical consumer's budget, at 34%. Housing (16%) includes rent, mortgage interest charges, and local government rates and charges as well as insurance. Household equipment and operation (18%) includes fuel and other utilities (2%) and household furnishings and operation (13.5%). This category also includes consumer credit charges (2.5%). The next largest category at 18% is food and beverages; this includes food at home (13%) and food away from home (5%). Alcoholic beverages and tobacco products are in a separate category (7.5%). The next category, at 16%, is transport, which includes spending on cars, petrol, buses, trains and so on. Next are recreation and education at 11%, health and personal care at 7%, and clothing at 6%.

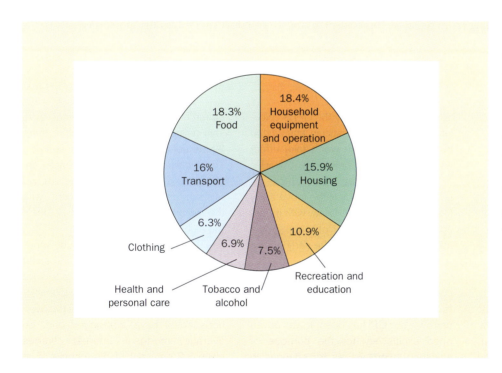

Figure 8.1

The basket of goods and services. This figure shows how the typical consumer divides his or her spending among various categories of goods and services. The Australian Bureau of Statistics calls each percentage the 'relative importance' of the category.

Source: Based on statistical data from the Australian Bureau of Statistics.

PROBLEMS IN MEASURING THE COST OF LIVING

The consumer price index is a measure of the aggregate price level in the economy. The goal of the index is to measure changes in the cost of living. In other words, the consumer price index can be used to gauge how much incomes must rise in order to maintain a constant standard of living. The consumer price index, however, is not a perfect measure of the cost of living. Three problems with the index are widely acknowledged but difficult to solve.

The first problem is called *substitution bias*. When prices change from one year to the next, they do not all change proportionately—some prices rise by more than others. Consumers respond to these differing price changes by buying less of the goods whose prices have risen by large amounts and by buying more of the goods whose prices have risen less or have even fallen. That is, consumers substitute goods that have become relatively less expensive. Yet the consumer price index is calculated assuming a fixed basket of goods. By not taking into account the possibility of consumer substitution, the index overstates the increase in the cost of living from one year to the next.

Let's consider a simple example. Imagine that, in the base year, apples are cheaper than pears, and so consumers buy more apples than pears. When the ABS constructs the basket of goods, it will include more apples than pears. Suppose that next year pears are cheaper than apples. Consumers will naturally respond to the price changes by buying more pears and fewer apples. Yet, when calculating the consumer price index, the ABS uses a fixed basket, which in essence assumes that consumers continue buying the now-expensive apples in the same quantities as before. For this reason, the index will measure a much larger increase in the cost of living than consumers actually perceive.

IN THE NEWS

Changing our measure of inflation

AUSTRALIA HAS BEEN UNDERGOING THE process of microeconomic reform for the last decade. These changes are now affecting how we measure inflation. The following article examines how the CPI is being changed.

Micro Reform Reaches the CPI

BY ROSS GITTINS

Is nothing sacred? Micro-economic reform has changed many aspects of our lives over the last decade. Now it's reached even the Consumer Price Index.

This is what binds together the various changes to the way the CPI is calculated, which the Statistician announced last week (but which won't take effect until the September quarter next year).

The reform that's done most to prompt those changes is the move away from centralised wage fixing, with its on-again, off-again history of wage indexation stretching back to the early part of this century.

Every country has a CPI as its most commonly used measure of inflation but few people realise how peculiar—and narrow—our CPI has been. It was developed exclusively for the purpose of adjusting award wages for changes in the cost of living of wage-earners. (Which is why the ACTU still regards the CPI as its private property.)

You see this from the CPI's 'reference group'. The CPI is based on the expenditure patterns of only those capital-city households that derive at least three-quarters of their income from wages and salaries but excluding the top 10 per cent of them (which means it doesn't even include salary-earners). This group is surprisingly small: a mere 29 per cent of all Australian households. The decision to widen the reference population to all capital-city households will raise its coverage to 64 per cent (with the remaining 36 per cent living outside the eight capitals).

The move in 1987 to include mortgage interest charges in the CPI basket was consistent with its role as a tool for use by the Industrial Relations Commission. About 43 per cent of employee households have mortgages and, on average, mortgage interest charges claim 5.2 per cent of the income of *all* employee households.

Including mortgage interest charges raised the CPI's credibility as a measure of living costs in the eyes of wage-earners. At the same time, however, it lowered the CPI's credibility in the eyes of the 75 per cent of households (no, it's not a misprint) that *don't* have a mortgage.

Included in this category is a group

The second problem with the consumer price index is the *introduction of new goods*. When a new good is introduced, consumers have more variety from which to choose. Greater variety, in turn, makes each dollar more valuable, so consumers need fewer dollars to maintain any given standard of living. Yet because the consumer price index is based on a fixed basket of goods, it does not reflect this change in the purchasing power of the dollar.

Again, let's consider an example. When VCRs were introduced, consumers could watch their favourite films at home. This new good increased consumers' wellbeing by expanding their consumption choices. A perfect cost-of-living index would reflect this change as a decrease in the cost of living. The consumer price index, however, did not decrease in response to the introduction of the VCR. Eventually, the ABS did revise the basket of goods to include VCRs, and subsequently the index reflected changes in VCR prices. But the reduction in the cost of living associated with the initial introduction of the VCR never showed up in the index.

The third problem with the consumer price index is *unmeasured quality change*. If the quality of a good deteriorates from one year to the next, the value of a dollar falls, even if the price of the good stays the same. (A dollar buys a

---

perceiving itself to have a vital interest in CPI movements: age pensioners. On average, mortgage interest charges claim less than 0.3 per cent of the income of age pensioner households.

(In truth, however, the CPI is no longer as important to pensioners as they imagine. Pensions are now indexed effectively to male average weekly earnings —which will almost always be rising a lot faster than the CPI. This is why the claim that removing mortgage interest charges from the CPI basket at a time when mortgage rates are at a cyclical low will cheat the pensioners is mistaken.)

Now we've moved away from centralised and cost of living-based wage fixing, it's appropriate to end the CPI's exclusive focus on the living costs of wage-earners. The CPI becomes a better measure of inflation for all households, as well as more consistent with other countries' CPIs.

And, with this new focus, there's less to be lost by removing mortgage interest charges from the basket. They're a less important item in the budgets of *all* households.

But the influence of micro reform on the CPI doesn't end with the reform of wage fixing. The decision to include a new category for the cost of 'financial services' can be attributed to the deregulation of banking. As deregulation and competition from non-banks have prompted the banks to 'unbundle' their various services (that is, unwind their cross-subsidies), bank fees and charges have become a significant item in household budgets. They're sure to become more so.

Also included in the new category will be the cost of the 'intermediation service' provided by banks. This is the price they charge for bringing together lenders (depositors) and borrowers. In other words, their gross interest margin.

It's a price the Statistician will find very hard to calculate accurately. But it has to be included because as competition squeezes the banks' interest margins they resort to higher fees and charges on transactions. To leave margins out of the basket would be to bias (upward) the measure of the cost of financial services.

Another influence on the CPI changes has been the reform of institutional arrangements for conducting monetary policy.

The Statistician makes it clear that his decision to drop interest rates from the basket was influenced by the Reserve Bank's move to targeting inflation and the fact that 'the shaping of inflationary expectations of the Australian population is attracting much more focus as an economic policy imperative'.

Excluding interest rates will make CPI movements less volatile and closer to the underlying rate of inflation, thus permitting the public to form more realistic inflation expectations.

SOURCE: *Sydney Morning Herald*, 17 November 1997, p. 37.

good of lower quality.) Similarly, if the quality rises from one year to the next, the value of a dollar rises. The ABS does its best to account for quality change. When the quality of a good in the basket changes—for example, when a car model has more horsepower or gets better petrol consumption per kilometre from one year to the next—the ABS adjusts the price of the good to account for the quality change. It is, in essence, trying to calculate the price of a basket of goods of constant quality. Nonetheless, changes in quality remain a problem, because quality is so hard to measure.

There is still much debate among economists about how severe these measurement problems are and what should be done about them. The issue is important because many government programs use the consumer price index to adjust for changes in the overall level of prices. Some economists have suggested modifying these programs to correct for the measurement problems. For example, most studies conclude that the consumer price index overstates inflation by 0.5 to 2.0 percentage points per year. In response to these findings, the federal government could change benefits programs so that benefits increased every year by the measured inflation rate minus 1 percentage point. Such a change would

IN THE NEWS

The CPI bias

OUR CPI IS PROBABLY LESS BIASED THAN America's, but CPI bias may still be a serious economic problem. In this article from the *Australian Financial Review*, Alan Mitchell reviews the biases in Australia's index.

CPI Bias Can Have Significant Impact

BY ALAN MITCHELL

How well does Australia's consumer price index work? A good deal better, by all accounts, than the US consumer price index. According to the US Congress' Boskin Commission, the US CPI over- states inflation by around 1.1 percent a year. One result of this bias is that indexed welfare and other US Government spending has been artificially inflated. The Boskin Commission claims that the bias in the CPI could add $148 billion to the Federal Budget deficit by the year 2006. Needless to say, the prospect of any serious reform of the CPI has horrified US welfare recipients—a warning, if one was needed, of the potential political pitfalls of CPI reform here.

No-one thinks the Australian CPI is overstating inflation by 1.1 percent. But no-one thinks that it is free of bias either. It's a design limitation of consumer prices indexes that they tend to overstate inflation.

All these estimates of CPI bias are controversial, but the bias of the Canadian CPI has been put at up to 0.5 percent, while that of the British CPI has been estimated at between 0.35 and 0.8 percent.

While public attention has focused on the problems of measuring changes in quality and of taking account of the effects of new products, there are in fact several other sources of bias in most CPIs. One relates to the failure of the indexes to take adequate account of people's ability to substitute between goods and services. Most CPIs measure the change in the cost of a more or less fixed basket of goods and services. However, in practice, people don't consume a fixed basket of goods and services. When the price of beef goes up, people switch to cheaper chicken. When the dollar is weak and the price of imported cars heads for the sky, we turn to cheaper Holdens or Fords. This failure to take adequate account of people's ability to substitute cheaper goods and services for more expensive ones is called 'item substitution bias'. In the US, the CPI substitution bias is estimated to have added about 0.4 percent to the measured inflation rate.

Another form of bias relates to the substitution between retail outlets. People economise, not just by switching to cheaper goods and services, but by purchasing their goods and services from cheaper outlets, such as supermarkets and discount stores. To the extent

THE GDP DEFLATOR VERSUS THE CONSUMER PRICE INDEX

In the preceding chapter, we saw another measure of the overall level of prices in the economy—the GDP deflator. The GDP deflator is the ratio of nominal GDP to real GDP. Because nominal GDP is current output valued at current prices and real GDP is current output valued at base-year prices, the GDP deflator reflects the current level of prices relative to the level of prices in the base year.

Economists and policymakers monitor both the GDP deflator and the consumer price index to gauge how quickly prices are rising. Usually, these two statistics tell a similar story. Yet there are two important differences that can cause them to diverge.

The first difference is that the GDP deflator reflects the prices of all goods and services *produced domestically*, whereas the consumer price index reflects the

---

that a cost of living index is tied to a fixed basket of goods and services purchased from a fixed set of retailers, it will miss this economising behaviour.

There is also the potential for bias inherent in the arithmetical processes of combining individual goods and services into indexes. There are a variety of techniques for doing this, but each is based on a set of assumptions, and to the extent that these assumptions don't fit reality, the result may be biased.

Finally, there are the well known biases that arise from the failure to adequately take account of improvements in quality and the introduction of new goods and services. A 1997 Holden is a very different car to a Holden of 20 years ago. Any attempt to measure the change in the cost of a Holden over that period would have to take into account the change that has also occurred in the quality of the product. But in many cases, measuring the change in quality is more easily said than done. New goods are potentially important because of the way their prices tend to fall after they are introduced. In the US, the Boskin Commission cites the examples of domestic air conditioners, microwave ovens and VCRs, all of which were widely sold for several years before being included in the CPI.

The failure to take adequate account of quality change and new goods is estimated by the Boskin Commission to add about 0.6 percent a year to the US CPI.

What of Australia? As in the US, the Australian CPI is based on a 'fixed' basket of goods and services. However, the Australian basket is updated every five years, whereas the US basket is updated only every 10 years. In addition, the Australian basket is not rigidly fixed between five-yearly reviews. New goods are introduced and, at the lower levels of aggregation, weights are regularly changed. The ABS has put considerable effort into adjusting the CPI for changes in quality. It believes its quality adjustments are adequate for most manufactured goods.

It's the services, such as health care and telecommunications, that give the bureau the major problems in quality adjustment. However, the ABS statisticians claim that only about one-tenth of the CPI is in danger of being seriously under-adjusted for quality. If the continuous annual rate of quality improvement were 1 percent, the quality bias of our CPI would be 0.1 percent.

What does that all add up to? Well, the truth is that no-one's quite sure yet. The ABS is currently trying to assess the extent of bias in the Australian index. However, even if the Australian index is overstating inflation by only 0.3 percent —which is the bottom end of the range of bias in the UK—it would be a serious enough problem in the current economic environment. One third of a per cent reduction in the measured rate of inflation would have kept inflation within the Reserve Bank's target in 1996–97. And that, it is fair to say, would have made a significant difference to inflationary expectations. One of the reasons that wage bargains have been running at excessive levels is that many employers have not believed inflation would be kept within the RBA target range.

SOURCE: *Australian Financial Review*, 2 April 1997, p. 17.

prices of all goods and services *bought by consumers*. For example, suppose that the price of a ship produced by Australian shipbuilders and sold to the Navy rises. Even though the ship is part of GDP, it is not part of the basket of goods and services bought by a typical consumer. Thus, the price increase shows up in the GDP deflator but not in the consumer price index.

As another example, suppose that Volvo raises the price of its cars. Because Volvos are made in Sweden, the car is not part of Australian GDP. But some Australian consumers do buy Volvos, and so the car is part of the typical consumer's basket of goods. Hence, a price increase in an imported consumption good, such as a Volvo, shows up in the consumer price index but not in the GDP deflator.

This first difference between the consumer price index and the GDP deflator is particularly important if a country imports a significant proportion of its oil. As a result, oil and oil products such as petrol and heating oil are a much larger share of consumer spending than they are of GDP. When the price of oil rises, the consumer price index rises by much more than does the GDP deflator. This is more significant in some countries than others. Australia is a net exporter of oil products, so a change in the price of oil is reflected both in the GDP deflator *and* the consumer price index.

The second and more subtle difference between the GDP deflator and the consumer price index concerns how various prices are weighted to yield a single number for the overall level of prices. The consumer price index compares the price of a *fixed* basket of goods and services with the price of the basket in the base year. The ABS changes the basket of goods once every 4 or 5 years. In contrast, the GDP deflator compares the price of *currently produced* goods and services with the price of the same goods and services in the base year. Thus, the group of goods and services used to calculate the GDP deflator changes

Figure 8.2

TWO MEASURES OF INFLATION. This figure shows the inflation rate—the percentage change in the level of prices—as measured by the GDP deflator and the consumer price index using annual data since 1970. Notice that the two measures of inflation generally move together.

SOURCE: Reserve Bank of Australia, 1996.

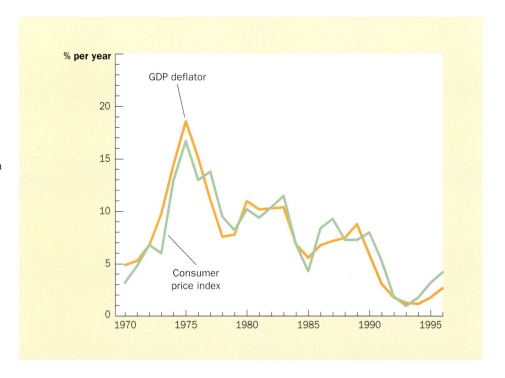

automatically over time. This difference is not important when all prices are changing proportionately. But if the prices of different goods and services are changing by varying amounts, the way we weight the various prices matters for the overall inflation rate.

Figure 8.2 shows the inflation rate as measured by both the GDP deflator and the consumer price index for each year since 1970. You can see that sometimes the two measures diverge. When they do diverge, it is possible to go behind these numbers and explain the divergence with the two differences we have discussed. The figure shows, however, that divergence between these two measures is the exception rather than the rule. In the mid-1970s, both the GDP deflator and the consumer price index show high rates of inflation. In the mid-1980s and mid-1990s, both measures showed low rates of inflation.

> **QUICK QUIZ** Explain briefly what the consumer price index is trying to measure and how it is constructed.

CORRECTING ECONOMIC VARIABLES FOR THE EFFECTS OF INFLATION

The purpose of measuring the overall level of prices in the economy is to permit comparison between dollar figures from different points in time. Now that we know how price indexes are calculated, let's see how we might use such an index to compare a dollar figure from the past with a dollar figure in the present.

DOLLAR FIGURES FROM DIFFERENT TIMES

We first return to the issue of Phar Lap's winnings. Were his earnings of $19 000 in 1930 high or low compared with the earnings in today's race?

To answer this question, we need to know the level of prices in 1930 and the level of prices today. Part of the increase in prize money just compensates the owners of racehorses for the higher level of prices today. To compare Phar Lap's winnings with those of today's horses, we need to inflate Phar Lap's winnings to turn 1930 dollars into today's dollars. A price index determines the size of this inflation correction. (Remember that Phar Lap's earnings were in pounds, but we are using the equivalent dollar amounts.)

Government statistics give a price index of 4.7 for 1930 and 121 for 1998. (The base year is 1989–90.) Thus, the overall level of prices has risen by a factor of 25.7 (which equals 121/4.7). We can use these numbers to measure Phar Lap's winnings in 1998 dollars. The calculation is:

$$\text{Winnings in 1998 dollars} = \frac{\text{Winnings in 1930 dollars} \times \text{Price level in 1998}}{\text{Price level in 1930}}$$

$$= \frac{\$19\,000 \times 121}{4.7}$$

$$= \$488\,300$$

'The price may seem a little high, but you have to remember that's in today's dollars.'

We find that Phar Lap's 1930 winnings are equivalent to winnings today of just over $488 000. That is a lot of money for a horse, but nothing like what the Melbourne Cup winner earns today. It is closer to the amount that the second-placed horse receives. The example does show that it is important to make these comparisons using the same dollars. Half a million dollars looks much better than $19 000.

Let's also examine Prime Minister Scullin's 1930 salary of £1000, or roughly $2000. To translate that figure into 1998 dollars, we again multiply the ratio of the price levels in the 2 years. We find that Scullin's salary is equivalent to $2000 × (121/4.7), or $51 489 in 1998 dollars. This is well below John Howard's salary of $232 000. It seems that Prime Minister Scullin did not earn very much compared with the famous racehorse or today's prime minister.

INDEXATION

As we have just seen, price indexes are used to correct for the effects of inflation when comparing dollar figures from different times. This type of correction shows up in many places in the economy. When some dollar amount is automatically corrected for inflation by law or contract, the amount is said to be **indexed** for inflation.

indexation
the automatic correction of a dollar amount for the effects of inflation by law or contract

For example, for many years, the basic wage in Australia was indexed to the consumer price index. Such a provision automatically raises the wage whenever the consumer price index rises.

Indexation is also a feature of many laws. Pension benefits, for example, are frequently adjusted to compensate the elderly for increases in prices. There are, however, many ways in which the tax system is not indexed for inflation, even when perhaps it should be. For example, the brackets of income tax—the income levels at which the tax rates change—are not indexed for inflation. We discuss these issues more fully when we discuss the costs of inflation later in this book.

REAL AND NOMINAL INTEREST RATES

Correcting economic variables for the effects of inflation is particularly important, and somewhat tricky, when we look at data on interest rates. When you deposit your savings in a bank account, you will earn interest on your deposit. Conversely, when you borrow from a bank to pay for a car, you will pay interest on your loan. Interest represents a payment in the future for a transfer of money in the past. As a result, interest rates always involve comparing amounts of money at different points in time. To fully understand interest rates, we need to know how to correct for the effects of inflation.

Let's consider an example. Suppose that Sally Saver deposits $1000 in a bank account that pays an annual interest rate of 10%. After a year passes, Sally has accumulated $100 in interest. Sally then withdraws her $1100. Is Sally $100 richer than she was when she made the deposit a year earlier?

The answer depends on what we mean by the word 'richer'. Sally does have $100 more than she had before. In other words, the number of dollars has risen by 10%. But if prices have risen at the same time, each dollar now buys less than it did a year ago. Thus, her purchasing power has not risen by 10%. If the

IN THE NEWS

Mr Index goes to Hollywood

WHAT WAS THE MOST POPULAR FILM OF all time? As the following article notes, answering this question requires an understanding of price indexes.

Winner and Still Champ

Rumour has it that when the storyline for the film *Titanic* was suggested, the pitch went something like this. 'I've got this great idea for a movie. Romeo and Juliet

'FRANKLY, MY DEAR, I DON'T GIVE A DAMN ABOUT THE EFFECTS OF INFLATION.'

on a boat. Oh, and the boat sinks.' The film not only took out seven Academy Awards, it also topped the box office, earning $600 million the year it was released.

But those records are for dollars not adjusted for inflation. Exhibitor Relations, a Los Angeles firm that tracks box office receipts, used today's dollars to calculate the gross takings of movies old and new. Its list indicates that *Titanic*, even with a take of $600 million, will still fall far short of what Scarlett and Rhett accomplished more than a half century ago.

SOURCE: Web site: http://www.washingtonpost.com

TOP 20 FILMS, ADJUSTED FOR INFLATION

TITLE	YEAR OF RELEASE	ESTIMATED US GROSS IN 1997 DOLLARS
Gone with the Wind	1939	$865 million
Star Wars	1977	775
Titanic	1997	601
E.T.	1982	594
The Ten Commandments	1956	572
The Sound of Music	1965	571
Jaws	1975	560
Doctor Zhivago	1965	542
Jungle Book	1967	485
Snow White	1937	476
Ben-Hur	1959	471
101 Dalmatians	1961	460
The Empire Strikes Back	1980	432
Return of the Jedi	1983	414
The Exorcist	1973	412
The Sting	1973	399
Raiders of the Lost Ark	1981	381
Jurassic Park	1993	377
The Graduate	1967	374
Fantasia	1940	363

inflation rate was 4%, then the amount of goods she can buy has increased by only 6%. And if the inflation rate was 15%, then the price of goods has increased proportionately more than the number of dollars in her account. In that case, Sally's purchasing power has actually fallen by 5%.

nominal interest rate
the interest rate as usually reported without a correction for the effects of inflation

real interest rate
the interest rate corrected for the effects of inflation

The interest rate that the bank pays is called the **nominal interest rate**, and the interest rate corrected for inflation is called the **real interest rate**. We can write the relationship of the nominal interest rate, the real interest rate and inflation as follows:

Real interest rate = Nominal interest rate − Inflation rate.

The real interest rate is the difference between the nominal interest rate and the rate of inflation. The nominal interest rate tells you how fast the number of dollars in your bank account rises over time. The real interest rate tells you how fast the purchasing power of your bank account rises over time.

Figure 8.3 shows real and nominal interest rates in Australia since 1970. The nominal interest rate is the interest rate on 90-day bank bills. The real interest rate is calculated by subtracting inflation—the percentage change in the consumer price index—from this nominal interest rate.

You can see that real and nominal interest rates do not always move together. For example, in the mid-1970s, nominal interest rates were high. But since inflation was very high, real interest rates were low. Indeed, in some years, real interest rates were negative, for inflation eroded people's savings more quickly than nominal interest payments increased them. In contrast, in both 1985 and 1990, even though nominal interest rates were high, low inflation meant that real interest rates were relatively high. In the coming chapters, when we study the causes and effects of changes in interest rates, it will be important for us to keep in mind the distinction between real and nominal interest rates.

> **QUICK QUIZ** Henry Ford paid his workers $5 a day in 1914. If a price index was 11 in 1914 and 131 in 1996, how much was the Ford paycheque worth in 1996 dollars?

Figure 8.3

REAL AND NOMINAL INTEREST RATES. This figure shows nominal and real interest rates using annual data since 1970. The nominal interest rate is the rate on a 90-day bank bill. The real interest rate is the nominal interest rate minus the inflation rate as measured by changes in the consumer price index. Notice that nominal and real interest rates often do not move together.

SOURCE: Reserve Bank of Australia.

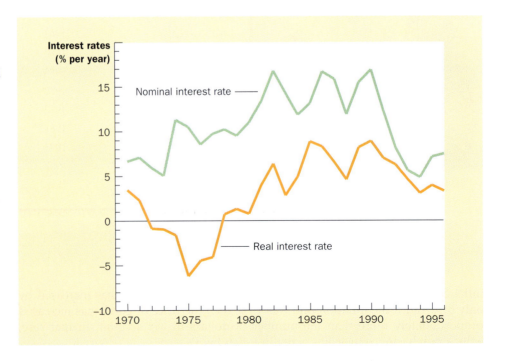

CONCLUSION

When McDonalds was introduced into Australia, a Big Mac, fries and a Coke cost about a dollar. Now the same meal costs $4.50. A dollar's not worth what it used to be. Indeed, throughout recent history, the purchasing power of the dollar has not been stable. Persistent increases in the overall level of prices have been the norm. Such inflation reduces the purchasing power of each unit of money over time. When comparing dollar figures from different times, it is important to keep in mind that a dollar today is not the same as a dollar 20 years ago or, most likely, 20 years from now.

This chapter has discussed how economists measure the overall level of prices in the economy and how they use price indexes to correct economic variables for the effects of inflation. This analysis is only a starting point. We have not yet examined the causes and effects of inflation or how inflation interacts with other economic variables. To do that, we need to go beyond issues of measurement. Indeed, that is our next task. Having explained how economists measure macroeconomic quantities and prices in the past two chapters, we are now ready to develop the models that explain long-run and short-run movements in these variables.

Summary

- The consumer price index shows the cost of a basket of goods and services relative to the cost of the same basket in the base year. The index is used to measure the overall level of prices in the economy. The percentage change in the consumer price index measures the inflation rate.

- The consumer price index is an imperfect measure of the cost of living for three reasons. First, it does not take into account consumers' ability to substitute goods that become relatively cheaper over time. Second, it does not take into account increases in the purchasing power of the dollar due to the introduction of new goods. Third, it is distorted by unmeasured changes in the quality of goods and services. Because of these measurement problems, the CPI overstates annual inflation by about 1 percentage point.

- Although the GDP deflator also measures the overall level of prices in the economy, it differs from the consumer price index because it includes goods and services produced rather than goods and services consumed. As a result, imported goods affect the consumer price index but not the GDP deflator. In addition, whereas the consumer price index uses a fixed basket of goods, the GDP deflator automatically changes the group of goods and services over time as the composition of GDP changes.

- Dollar figures from different points in time cannot be used to make valid comparisons of purchasing power. To compare a dollar figure from the past with a dollar figure today, the older figure should be inflated using a price index.

- Various laws and private contracts use price indexes to correct for the effects of inflation. The tax laws, however, are only partially indexed for inflation.

- A correction for inflation is especially important when looking at data on interest rates. The nominal interest rate is the interest rate usually reported; it is the rate at which the number of dollars in a savings account increases over time. In contrast, the real interest rate takes into account changes in the value of the dollar over time. The real interest rate equals the nominal interest rate minus the rate of inflation.

Key concepts

consumer price index (CPI), p. 150
inflation rate, p. 152

producer price index, p. 152
indexation, p. 160

nominal interest rate, p. 162
real interest rate, p. 162

Questions for review

1. Which do you think has a greater effect on the consumer price index: a 10% increase in the price of chicken or a 10% increase in the price of caviar? Why?

2. Describe the three problems that make the consumer price index an imperfect measure of the cost of living.

3. If the price of a Navy submarine rises, is the consumer price index or the GDP deflator affected more? Why?

4. Over a long period of time, the price of a Mars bar rose from $0.10 to $0.60. Over the same period, the consumer price index rose from 150 to 300. Adjusted for overall inflation, how much did the price of the Mars bar change?

5. Explain the meaning of *nominal interest rate* and *real interest rate*. How are they related?

Problems and applications

1. Suppose that people consume only three goods, as shown in this table:

	TENNIS BALLS	TENNIS RACQUETS	GATORADE
2001 price	$2	$40	$1
2001 quantity	100	10	200
2002 price	$2	$60	$2
2002 quantity	100	10	200

   a. What is the percentage change in the price of each of the three goods? What is the percentage change in the overall price level?

   b. Do tennis racquets become more or less expensive relative to Gatorade? Does the wellbeing of some people change relative to the wellbeing of others? Explain.

2. Suppose that the residents of Veggieland spend all of their income on cauliflower, broccoli and carrots. In 2001, they buy 100 heads of cauliflower for $200, 50 bunches of broccoli for $75 and 500 carrots for $50. In 2002 they buy 75 heads of cauliflower for $225, 80 bunches of broccoli for $120 and 500 carrots for $100. If the base year is 2001, what is the CPI in both years? What is the inflation rate in 2002?

3. From 1950 to 1998 the consumer price index in Australia rose around 1500%. Use this fact to adjust each of the following 1950 prices for the effects of inflation. Which items cost less in 1998 than in 1950 after adjusting for inflation? Which items cost more?

ITEM	1950 PRICE	1998 PRICE
A day at the cricket	$0.25	$20
Woman's Day magazine	$0.05	$2.80
Orange marmalade	$0.12	$2.30
A Holden sedan	$700	$29 000
Sending a package by air from Sydney to the UK	$1.28	$4.50

4. Beginning in 1994, environmental regulations have required that petrol contain a new additive to reduce air pollution. This requirement raised the cost of petrol. The Australian Bureau of Statistics (ABS) decided that this increase in cost represented an improvement in quality.

   a. Given this decision, did the increased cost of petrol raise the CPI?

   b. What is the argument in favour of the ABS's decision? What is the argument for a different decision?

5. Which of the problems in the construction of the CPI might be illustrated by each of the following situations? Explain.

   a. the invention of the Sony Walkman

   b. the introduction of air bags in cars

   c. increased personal computer purchases in response to a decline in their price

   d. more scoops of sultanas in each package of Sultana Bran

   e. greater use of fuel-efficient cars after petrol prices increase

6. The *Sydney Morning Herald* cost $0.05 in 1970 and $0.50 in 1990. The average wage in manufacturing was $3.35 per hour in 1970 and $10.82 in 1990.

   a. By what percentage did the price of a newspaper rise?

   b. By what percentage did the wage rise?

   c. In each year, how many minutes does a worker have to work to earn enough to buy a newspaper?

   d. Did workers' purchasing power in terms of newspapers rise or fall?

7. The chapter explains that pension benefits could be increased each year roughly in proportion to the increase in the CPI, even though most economists believe that the CPI overstates actual inflation.

a. If the elderly consume the same market basket as other people, do pension benefits provide the elderly with an improvement in their standard of living each year? Explain.

b. In fact, the elderly consume more health care than younger people, and health care costs have risen faster than overall inflation. What would you do to determine whether the elderly are actually better off from year to year?

8. Suppose that a borrower and a lender agree on the nominal interest rate to be paid on a loan. Then inflation turns out to be higher than they both expected.
   a. Is the real interest rate on this loan higher or lower than expected?
   b. Does the lender gain or lose from this unexpectedly high inflation? Does the borrower gain or lose?
   c. Inflation during the 1970s was much higher than most people expected when the decade began. How did this affect homeowners who obtained fixed-rate mortgages during the 1960s? How did it affect the banks that lent the money?

9. The chapter defines the real interest rate as the nominal interest rate less inflation. Because, under Australian tax laws, nominal interest income is taxed, we can define the after-tax real interest rate as the nominal interest rate after taxes, less inflation.
   a. Suppose that the inflation rate is 0%, the nominal interest rate is 3%, and the tax rate is 33%. What is the real interest rate? What is the after-tax real interest rate? What is the effective tax rate on real interest income (the percentage reduction in real interest income due to taxes)?
   b. Now suppose that the inflation rate rises to 3%, and the nominal interest rate rises to 6%. What is the real interest rate now? What is the after-tax real interest rate? What is the effective tax rate on real interest income?
   c. Some economists argue that because of our tax system, inflation discourages saving. Use your answers to parts (a) and (b) to explain this view.

10. In Australia, income tax brackets are not indexed. When inflation pushed up nominal incomes, what do you think happened to real tax revenue? (*Hint:* This phenomenon was known as 'bracket creep'.)

IV

THE REAL ECONOMY IN THE LONG RUN

VI

THE REAL ECONOMY
IN THE LONG RUN

9

PRODUCTION AND GROWTH

IN THIS CHAPTER YOU WILL

See how much economic growth differs around the world

Consider why productivity is the key determinant of a country's standard of living

Analyse the factors that determine a country's productivity

Examine how a country's policies influence its productivity growth

When you travel around the world, you see tremendous variation in the standard of living. The average person in a rich country, such as Australia, the United States or Japan, has an income more than ten times as high as the average person in a poor country, such as India, Indonesia or Nigeria. These large differences in income are reflected in large differences in the quality of life. Richer countries have more cars, more telephones, more televisions, better nutrition, safer housing, better health care and longer life expectancy.

Even within a country, there are large changes in the standard of living over time. In Australia over the past 100 years, average income as measured by real GDP per person has grown by just over 1% per year. Although 1% might seem small, this rate of growth implies that average income doubles every 70 years. Because of this growth, average income today is about 3.5 times as high as average income 100 years ago. As a result, the typical Australian today enjoys much greater economic prosperity than did an Australian in 1900.

Growth rates vary substantially from country to country. In some East Asian countries, such as Hong Kong, Singapore, South Korea and Taiwan, average income has risen about 7% per year in recent decades. At this rate, average income doubles every 10 years. These countries have, in the length of one generation, gone from being among the poorest countries in the world to being among the richest. In contrast, in some African countries, such as Chad, Ethiopia and Nigeria, average income has been stagnant for many years.

The effects of these difference in growth rates can be seen in Australia. Even though the typical Australian enjoys a greater level of economic prosperity now relative to his or her ancestors in Australia, the Australian standard of living has not increased as rapidly as it has in some other countries. For example, in 1870, GDP per capita in Australia was 1.4 times GDP per capita in the United States. In 1990, Australian GDP per capita was only three-quarters of US GDP per capita. The fact that Australia has slipped in the rankings of GDP per capita is not necessarily cause for concern, but it does indicate that we are not growing as rapidly as we perhaps could.

What explains these diverse experiences? How can the rich countries be sure to maintain their high standard of living? What policies should the poor countries pursue to promote more rapid growth in order to join the developed world? These are among the most important questions in macroeconomics. As economist Robert Lucas put it, 'The consequences for human welfare in questions like these are simply staggering: Once one starts to think about them, it is hard to think about anything else.'

In the previous two chapters we discussed how economists measure macroeconomic quantities and prices. In this chapter we start studying the forces that determine these variables. As we have seen, an economy's gross domestic product (GDP) measures both the total income earned in the economy and the total expenditure on the economy's output of goods and services. The level of real GDP is a good gauge of economic prosperity, and the growth of real GDP is a good gauge of economic progress. Here we focus on the long-run determinants of the level and growth of real GDP. Later in this book we will study the short-run fluctuations of real GDP around its long-run trend.

We proceed here in three steps. First, we examine international data on real GDP per person. These data will give you some sense of how much the level and growth of living standards vary around the world. Second, we examine the role of *productivity*—the amount of goods and services produced for each hour of a worker's time. In particular, we see that a nation's standard of living is determined by the productivity of its workers, and we consider the factors that determine a nation's productivity. Third, we consider the link between productivity and the economic policies that a nation pursues.

ECONOMIC GROWTH AROUND THE WORLD

As a starting point for our study of long-run growth, let's look at the experiences of some of the world's economies. Table 9.1 shows data on real GDP per person for 15 countries. For each country, the data cover about a century of history. The first and second columns of the table present the countries and time periods. (The time periods differ somewhat from country to country because of differences in data availability.) The third and fourth columns show real GDP per person about a century ago and for a recent year.

The data on real GDP per person show that living standards vary widely from country to country. Income per person in Australia, for instance, is about 8 times that in China and 20 times that in India. The poorest countries have average levels of income that have not been seen in Australia for many decades. The typical Argentinian in 1987 had about as much real income as the typical

Country	Period	Real GDP per person at beginning of period*	Real GDP per person at end of period*	Growth rate (per year)
Japan	1890–1990	$ 842	$16 144	3.00%
Brazil	1900–1987	436	3 417	2.39
Canada	1870–1990	1 330	17 070	2.15
West Germany	1870–1990	1 223	14 288	2.07
United States	1870–1990	2 244	18 258	1.76
China	1900–1987	401	1 748	1.71
Mexico	1900–1987	649	2 667	1.64
United Kingdom	1870–1990	2 693	13 589	1.36
Australia	1870–1990	3 143	13 514	1.22
Argentina	1900–1987	1 284	3 302	1.09
Thailand	1900–1987	626	2 294	1.09
Indonesia	1900–1987	499	1 200	1.01
Pakistan	1900–1987	413	885	0.88
India	1900–1987	378	662	0.65
Bangladesh	1900–1987	349	375	0.08

The variety of growth experiences

Table 9.1

* Real GDP is measured in 1985 dollars.
Source: Robert J. Barro and Xavier Sala-i-Martin, *Economic Growth* (New York: McGraw-Hill, 1995), tables 10.2 and 10.3; and authors' calculations.

Australian in 1870. The typical person in India in 1987 had about one-fifth the real income of a typical Australian a century ago.

The last column of the table shows each country's growth rate. The growth rate measures how rapidly real GDP per person grew in the typical year. In Australia, for example, real GDP per person was $3143 in 1870 and $13 514 in 1990. The growth rate was 1.22% per year. This means that if real GDP per person, beginning at $3143, were to increase by 1.22% for each of 120 years, it would end up at $13 514. Of course, real GDP per person did not actually rise exactly 1.22% every year—there are short-run fluctuations around the long-run trend. The growth rate of 1.22% represents an average rate of growth for real GDP per person over many years.

The countries in table 9.1 are ordered by their growth rate from the most to the least rapid. Japan tops the list with a growth rate of 3.00% per year. A hundred years ago, Japan was not a rich country. Japan's average income was only somewhat higher than Mexico's, and it was well behind Argentina's. To put the issue another way, Japan's 1890 income was close to Pakistan's 1987 income. But because of its spectacular growth, Japan is today an economic superpower, with average income about the same as the United States. At the bottom of the list of countries is Bangladesh, which has experienced hardly any growth at all over the past century. The typical resident of Bangladesh lives in abject poverty similar to that experienced by his or her great-grandparents.

Because of differences in growth rates, the ranking of countries by income changes substantially over time. As we have seen, Japan is a country that has risen relative to others. Two countries that have fallen behind are the United Kingdom and Argentina. In 1870, the United Kingdom was one of the richest countries in the world, with average income about 20% higher than that of the United States and about twice that of Canada. Today, average income in the United Kingdom is well below average income in its two former colonies. In 1900, Argentina had about three times the income of its South American neighbour, Brazil. Today, Argentina is on a par with Brazil. Australia's story is somewhere in between these two. In 1900, Australia had the highest per capita income in the world, but by 1970 it had fallen to around seventh in the rankings. By 1991, Australia was no longer in the top 10, and had fallen behind most Western European countries in relative terms.

These data show that the world's richest countries have no guarantee that they will stay the richest and that the world's poorest countries are not doomed forever to remain in poverty. But what explains these changes over time? Why do some countries zoom ahead while others lag behind? These are precisely the questions that we take up next.

FYI

The magic of compounding and the rule of 70

IT MAY BE TEMPTING TO DISMISS differences in growth rates as insignificant. If one country grows at 1% while another grows at 3%, so what? What difference can 2% make?

The answer is a big difference. Even growth rates that seem small when written in percentage terms seem large after they are compounded for many years. *Compounding* refers to the accumulation of a growth rate over a period of time.

Consider an example. Suppose that two university graduates—Elle and Kylie—both take their first jobs at the age of 22 earning $30 000 a year. Elle lives in an economy where all incomes grow at 1% per year, whereas Kylie lives in one where incomes grow at 3% per year. Straightforward calculations show what happens. Forty years later, when both are 62 years old, Elle earns $45 000 a year, and Kylie earns $98 000. Because of that difference of 2 percentage points in the growth rate, Kylie's salary in old age is more than twice Elle's.

An old rule of thumb, called the *rule of 70*, is helpful in understanding growth rates and the effects of compounding. According to the rule of 70, if some variable grows at a rate of $x\%$ per year, then that variable doubles in approximately $70/x$ years. In Elle's economy, incomes grow at 1% per year, so it takes about 70 years for incomes to double. In Kylie's economy, incomes grow at 3% per year, so it takes about 70/3, or 23, years for incomes to double.

The rule of 70 applies not only to a growing economy but also to a growing savings account. Here is an example. Suppose that, when Governor Phillip left office in 1792, he gave $5000 to be invested for a period of 200 years to benefit scientific research into early Australian history. If this money had earned 7% per year (which would, in fact, have been very possible to do), the investment would have doubled in value every 10 years. Over 200 years, it would have doubled 20 times. At the end of 200 years of compounding, the investment would have been worth $2^{20} \times \$5000$, which is about $5 billion.

As these examples show, growth rates compounded over many years can lead to some spectacular results. That is probably why Albert Einstein once called compounding 'the greatest mathematical discovery of all time'.

> **QUICK QUIZ** What is the approximate growth rate of real GDP per person in Australia? Name a country that has had faster growth and a country that has had slower growth.

PRODUCTIVITY: ITS ROLE AND DETERMINANTS

Explaining the large variation in living standards around the world is, in one sense, very easy. As we will see, the explanation can be summarised in a single word—*productivity*. But, in another sense, the international variation is deeply puzzling. To explain why incomes are so much higher in some countries than in others, we must look at the many factors that determine a nation's productivity.

WHY PRODUCTIVITY IS SO IMPORTANT

Let's begin our study of productivity and economic growth by developing a simple model based loosely on Daniel Defoe's famous novel, *Robinson Crusoe*. Robinson Crusoe, as you may recall, is a sailor stranded on a desert island. Because Crusoe lives alone, he catches his own fish, grows his own vegetables and makes his own clothes. We can think of Crusoe's activities—his production and consumption of fish, vegetables and clothing—as being a simple economy. By examining Crusoe's economy, we can learn some lessons that also apply to more complex and realistic economies.

What determines Crusoe's standard of living? The answer is obvious. If Crusoe is good at catching fish, growing vegetables and making clothes, he lives well. If he is bad at doing these things, he lives poorly. Because Crusoe gets to consume only what he produces, his living standard is tied to his productive ability.

The term **productivity** refers to the quantity of goods and services that a worker can produce for each hour of work. In the case of Crusoe's economy, it is easy to see that productivity is the key determinant of living standards and that growth in productivity is the key determinant of growth in living standards. The more fish Crusoe can catch per hour, the more he eats at dinner. If Crusoe finds a better place to catch fish, his productivity rises. This increase in productivity makes Crusoe better off—he could eat the extra fish, or he could spend less time fishing and devote more time to making other goods he enjoys.

productivity
the amount of goods and services produced from each hour of a worker's time

The key role of productivity in determining living standards is as true for nations as it is for stranded sailors. Recall that an economy's gross domestic product (GDP) measures two things at once—the total income earned by everyone in the economy and the total expenditure on the economy's output of goods and services. The reason GDP can measure these two things simultaneously is that, for the economy as a whole, they must be equal. Put simply, an economy's income is the economy's output.

Like Crusoe, a nation can enjoy a high standard of living only if it can produce a large quantity of goods and services. Australians live better than Nigerians because Australian workers are more productive than Nigerian workers. The Japanese have enjoyed more rapid growth in living standards than Argentinians because Japanese workers have experienced more rapidly growing productivity.

Indeed, one of the *Ten Principles of Economics* in chapter 1 is that a country's standard of living depends on its ability to produce goods and services.

Hence, to understand the large differences in living standards we observe across countries or over time, we must focus on the production of goods and services. But seeing the link between living standards and productivity is only the first step. It leads naturally to the next question: Why are some economies so much better at producing goods and services than others?

HOW PRODUCTIVITY IS DETERMINED

Although productivity is uniquely important in determining Robinson Crusoe's standard of living, many factors determine Crusoe's productivity. Crusoe will be better at catching fish, for instance, if he has more fishing rods, if he has been trained in the best fishing techniques, if his island has a plentiful fish supply, and if he has figured out the best places on his island to fish. Each of these determinants of Crusoe's productivity—which we can call *physical capital*, *human capital*, *natural resources* and *technological knowledge*—has a counterpart in more complex and realistic economies. Let's consider each of these factors in turn.

physical capital
the stock of equipment and structures that are used to produce goods and services

Physical capital Workers are more productive if they have tools with which to work. The stock of equipment and structures that are used to produce goods and services is called **physical capital**, or just *capital*. For example, when woodworkers make furniture, they use saws, lathes and drill presses. More tools allow work to be done more quickly and more accurately. That is, a worker with only basic hand tools can make less furniture each week than a worker with sophisticated and specialised woodworking equipment.

As you may recall from chapter 2, the inputs used to produce goods and services—labour, capital and so on—are called the *factors of production*. An important feature of capital is that it is a *produced* factor of production. That is, capital is an input into the production process that in the past was an output from the production process. The woodworker uses a lathe to make the leg of a table. Earlier, the lathe itself was the output of a firm that manufactures lathes. The lathe manufacturer in turn used other equipment to make its product. Thus, capital is a factor of production used to produce all kinds of goods and services, including more capital.

human capital
the knowledge and skills that workers acquire through education, training and experience

Human capital A second determinant of productivity is human capital. **Human capital** is the economist's term for the knowledge and skills that workers acquire through education, training and experience. Human capital includes the skills accumulated in early childhood programs, primary school, secondary school, university, and on-the-job training for adults in the labour force.

Although education, training and experience are less tangible than lathes, bulldozers and buildings, human capital is like physical capital in many ways. Like physical capital, human capital raises a nation's ability to produce goods and services. Also like physical capital, human capital is a produced factor of production. Producing human capital requires inputs in the form of teachers, libraries and student time. Indeed, students can be viewed as 'workers' who have the important job of producing the human capital that will be used in future production.

Natural resources A third determinant of productivity is **natural resources**. Natural resources are inputs into production that are provided by nature, such as land, rivers and mineral deposits. Natural resources take two forms—renewable and non-renewable. A forest is an example of a renewable resource. When one tree is cut down, a seedling can be planted in its place to be harvested in the future. Oil is an example of a non-renewable resource. Because oil is produced by nature over many thousands of years, there is only a limited supply. Once the supply of oil is depleted, it is impossible to create more.

Differences in natural resources are responsible for some of the differences in standards of living around the world. The historical success of Australia was driven in part by the large supply of land well suited to agriculture. Today, some countries in the Middle East, such as Kuwait and Saudi Arabia, are rich because they are on top of some of the largest pools of oil in the world.

Although natural resources can be important, they are not necessary for an economy to be highly productive in producing goods and services. Japan, for instance, is one of the richest countries in the world, despite having few natural resources. International trade makes Japan's success possible. Japan imports many of the natural resources it needs, such as oil, and exports its manufactured goods to economies rich in natural resources.

natural resources
the inputs into the production of goods and services that are provided by nature, such as land, rivers and mineral deposits

CASE STUDY ARE NATURAL RESOURCES A LIMIT TO GROWTH?

The world's population is far larger today than it was a century ago, and many people are enjoying a much higher standard of living. A perennial debate concerns whether this growth in population and living standards can continue in the future.

Many commentators have argued that natural resources provide a limit to how much the world's economies can grow. At first, this argument might seem hard to ignore. If the world has only a fixed supply of non-renewable natural resources, how can population, production and living standards continue to grow over time? Eventually, won't supplies of oil and minerals start to run out? When these shortages start to occur, won't they stop economic growth and, perhaps, even force living standards to fall?

Despite the apparent appeal of such arguments, most economists are less concerned about such limits to growth than one might guess. They argue that technological progress often yields ways to avoid these limits. If we compare the economy today with the economy of the past, we see various ways in which the use of natural resources has improved. Modern cars require fewer litres per kilometre. New houses have better insulation and require less energy to heat and cool them. More efficient oil rigs waste less oil in the process of extraction. Recycling allows some non-renewable resources to be reused. The development of alternative fuels, such as ethanol instead of petrol, allows us to substitute renewable for non-renewable resources.

Fifty years ago, some conservationists were concerned about the excessive use of tin and copper. At the time, these were crucial commodities—tin was used to make many food containers, and copper was used to make telephone wire. Some people advocated mandatory recycling and rationing of tin and copper so that supplies would be available for future generations. Today, however, plastic has replaced tin as a material for making many food containers,

What happens when these wells run dry?

and phone calls often travel over fibre-optic cables, which are made from sand. Technological progress has made once-crucial natural resources less necessary.

But are all these efforts enough to permit continued economic growth? One way to answer this question is to look at the prices of natural resources. In a market economy, scarcity is reflected in market prices. If the world were running out of natural resources, then the prices of those resources would be rising over time. But, in fact, the opposite is more nearly true. The prices of most natural resources (adjusted for overall inflation) are stable or falling. It appears that our ability to conserve these resources is growing more rapidly than their supplies are dwindling. Market prices give no reason to believe that natural resources are a limit to economic growth.

technological knowledge
society's understanding of the best ways to produce goods and services

Technological knowledge A fourth determinant of productivity is **technological knowledge**—the understanding of the best ways to produce goods and services. A hundred years ago, most Australians worked on farms, because farm technology required a high input of labour in order to feed the entire population. Today, thanks to advances in the technology of farming, a small fraction of the population can produce enough food to feed the entire country. This technological change made labour available to produce other goods and services.

Technological knowledge takes many forms. Some technology is common knowledge—after it becomes used by one person, everyone becomes aware of it. For example, once Henry Ford successfully introduced production in assembly lines, other car-makers quickly followed suit. Other technology is proprietary —it is known only by the company that discovers it. Only the Coca-Cola Company, for instance, knows the secret recipe for making its famous soft drink. Still other technology is proprietary for a short time. When a drug company discovers a new drug, the patent system gives that company a temporary right to be the exclusive manufacturer of this particular drug. When the patent expires, however, other companies are allowed to make the drug. All these forms of technological knowledge are important for the economy's production of goods and services.

It is worthwhile to distinguish between technological knowledge and human capital. Although they are closely related, there is an important difference. Technological knowledge refers to society's understanding about how the world works. Human capital refers to the resources expended transmitting this understanding to the labour force. To use a relevant metaphor, knowledge is the quality of society's textbooks, whereas human capital is the amount of time that the population has devoted to reading them. Workers' productivity depends on both the quality of textbooks they have available and the amount of time they have spent studying them.

THE PRODUCTION FUNCTION

Economists often use a *production function* to describe the relationship between the quantity of inputs used in production and the quantity of output from production. For example, suppose Y denotes the quantity of output, L the quantity of labour, K the quantity of physical capital, H the quantity of human capital and N the quantity of natural resources. Then we might write:

$$Y = A\,F(L, K, H, N)$$

where $F(\ )$ is a function that shows how the inputs are combined to produce output. A is a variable that reflects the available production technology. As technology improves, A rises, so the economy produces more output from any given combination of inputs.

Many production functions have a property called *constant returns to scale*. If a production function has constant returns to scale, then a doubling of all the inputs causes the amount of output to double as well. Mathematically, we write that a production function has constant returns to scale if, for any positive number x:

$$xY = A\,F(xL, xK, xH, xN)$$

A doubling of all inputs is represented in this equation by $x = 2$. The right-hand side shows the inputs doubling, and the left-hand side shows output doubling.

Production functions with constant returns to scale have an interesting implication. To see what it is, set $x = 1/L$. Then the equation above becomes:

$$Y/L = A\,F(1, K/L, H/L, N/L)$$

Notice that Y/L is output per worker, which is a measure of productivity. This equation says that productivity depends on physical capital per worker (K/L), human capital per worker (H/L), and natural resources per worker (N/L). Productivity also depends on the state of technology, as reflected by the variable A. Thus, this equation provides a mathematical summary of the four determinants of productivity we have just discussed.

QUICK QUIZ List and describe four determinants of a country's productivity.

IN THE NEWS

Computers and productivity

One determinant of productivity is technological knowledge, and one recent advance in technological knowledge has been the computer revolution. As the following article describes, however, this revolution has not yet had the great impact on productivity that many people expected.

What Has the Computer Done for Us Lately?

BY LOUIS UCHITELLE

At the end of the nineteenth century, railroads and electric motors were expected to transform America, making a young industrial economy far more productive than any seen before. And they did. At the end of the twentieth century, computers were supposed to perform the same miracle.

They haven't.

Computers do wonderful things. But in purely economic terms, their contribution has been less than a transforming force; they have failed to bring back the strong growth that characterized so many decades of the American century. By that standard, they have been a disappointment.

'It is a pipe dream to think that computers will lead us back to a promised land,' said Alan Krueger, a Princeton University economist.

The issue is productivity. Those who look to computers for economic miracles, and there are many, insist that measuring their contribution only in dollars misses the less tangible improvement in quality that computers have made possible. But quality is often in the eyes of the beholders rather than in their wallets.

Through decades of invention and change, productivity has been measured as the amount of 'output', in dollars, that comes from an hour of labor. A worker who makes 100 pencils in an hour, each valued at $0.50, produces $50 of output. And the more output from each of the nation's workers, the greater the national wealth.

Or, put more broadly, productivity is the amount of output in dollars that comes from various 'inputs', not only a worker's labor, but the tools he or she uses to carry out that labor: a machine or a computer or a wrench or an air conditioner that makes work more comfortable in summer. People work faster or concentrate better, and that shows up quickly in tangible output.

By this definition, the output resulting from the computer revolution of the last 25 years has been disappointing. Computers have, of course, contributed to productivity and economic growth. But that contribution has failed to register in government statistics as the kind

ECONOMIC GROWTH AND PUBLIC POLICY

So far, we have determined that a society's standard of living depends on its ability to produce goods and services and that its productivity depends on physical capital, human capital, natural resources and technological knowledge. Let's now turn to the question faced by policymakers around the world: What can government policy do to raise productivity and living standards?

THE IMPORTANCE OF SAVING AND INVESTMENT

Because capital is a produced factor of production, a society can change the amount of capital it has. If today the economy produces a large quantity of new capital goods, then tomorrow it will have a larger stock of capital and be able to produce more of all types of goods and services. Thus, one way to raise future productivity is to invest more current resources in the production of capital.

PRODUCTIVITY—OR SOLITAIRE?

of robust catalyst that made the 1950s and 1960s such prosperous years.

If computers have fallen short of expectations, that would help explain an apparent paradox that has puzzled economists and policymakers for two decades: how rapid technological progress and a booming stock market took place during a period of sluggish economic performance—sluggish, that is, relative to earlier decades.

One possibility is that the statistics are wrong. A panel of economists came to this conclusion in a report to Congress last week, suggesting that growth has actually been quite robust but that this fact has been obscured by overstating the amount of output lost to inflation. This happened, the panel hinted, partly because the beneficial economic role of computers was not correctly taken into account. Some price increases that registered as inflation should really have registered as increases in output from computers.

But there is another explanation. Perhaps the computer is one of those inventions, like the lightbulb early in the century, that makes life much better without adding as much to tangible national wealth as appearances might suggest. That is because, while the lightbulb allowed factories to operate night shifts and students to study more easily, the measurable result was less impressive than the great improvement in the quality of life that the electric lightbulb made possible.

Given the computer's ubiquity and convenience, should the calculation of productivity and wealth be changed to give more dollar value to the conveniences the computer has wrought?

That kind of recalculation has not been done over generations of technological change, largely because convenience is too hard to quantify and translate into dollars. Too often, convenience increases consumption more than production. With computers, 'most of the recent use has been on the consumption side,' said Zvi Griliches, a Harvard economist. 'The time you waste surfing the Internet is not an output.'

Others take a broader view. Children using home computers for schoolwork—gathering data from the Internet, for example—become better students, they say. In time, that will translate into rising workplace skills and greater measurable output. But it hasn't yet, and standard practice dictates that the nation wait until it shows up in the numbers before proclaiming the computer's great contribution to productivity.

SOURCE: *New York Times*, 8 December 1996, Week in Review, Section 4, pp. 1, 4.

One of the *Ten Principles of Economics* presented in chapter 1 is that people face trade-offs. This principle is especially important when considering the accumulation of capital. Because resources are scarce, devoting more resources to producing capital requires devoting fewer resources to producing goods and services for current consumption. That is, for society to invest more in capital, it must consume less and save more of its current income. The growth that arises from capital accumulation is not a free lunch—it requires that society sacrifice consumption of goods and services in the present in order to enjoy higher consumption in the future.

The next chapter examines in more detail how the economy's financial markets coordinate saving and investment. It also examines how government policies influence the amount of saving and investment that takes place. At this point it is important to note that encouraging saving and investment is one way that a government can encourage growth and, in the long run, raise the economy's standard of living.

To see the importance of investment for economic growth, consider figure 9.1, which displays data on 14 countries. Panel (a) shows each country's growth rate over a 31-year period. The countries are ordered by their growth rates, from

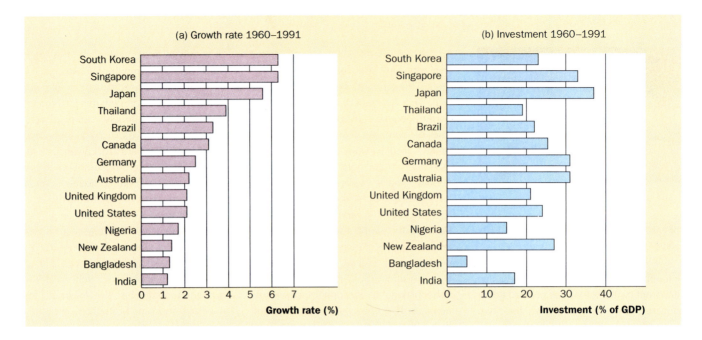

Figure 9.1

GROWTH AND INVESTMENT. Panel (a) shows the average annual growth rate of GDP per person for 14 countries over the period 1960–1991. Panel (b) shows the percentage of GDP that each country devoted to investment over this period. The figure shows that investment and growth are positively correlated.

most to least rapid. Panel (b) shows the percentage of GDP that each country devotes to investment. The correlation between growth and investment, although not perfect, is strong. Countries that devote a large share of GDP to investment, such as Singapore and Japan, tend to have high growth rates. Countries that devote a small share of GDP to investment, such as Bangladesh, tend to have low growth rates. Studies that examine a more comprehensive list of countries confirm this strong correlation between investment and growth.

There is, however, a problem in interpreting these data. As the appendix to chapter 2 discussed, a correlation between two variables does not establish which variable is the cause and which is the effect. It is possible that high investment causes high growth, but it is also possible that high growth causes high investment. (Or, perhaps, high growth and high investment are both caused by a third variable that has been omitted from the analysis.) The data by themselves cannot tell us the direction of causation. Nonetheless, because capital accumulation affects productivity so clearly and directly, many economists interpret these data as showing that high investment leads to more rapid economic growth.

DIMINISHING RETURNS AND THE CATCH-UP EFFECT

Suppose that a government, convinced by the evidence in figure 9.1, pursues policies that raise the nation's saving rate—the percentage of GDP devoted to saving rather than consumption. What happens? With the nation saving more, fewer resources are needed to make consumption goods, and more resources are available to make capital goods. As a result, the capital stock increases, leading to rising productivity and more rapid growth in GDP. But how long does this higher rate of growth last? Assuming that the saving rate remains at its new higher level, does the growth rate of GDP stay high indefinitely or only for a period of time?

The traditional view of the production process is that capital is subject to **diminishing returns**—as the stock of capital rises, the extra output produced from an additional unit of capital falls. In other words, when workers already have a large quantity of capital to use in producing goods and services, giving them an additional unit of capital increases their productivity only slightly. Because of diminishing returns, an increase in the saving rate leads to higher growth only for a while. As the higher saving rate allows more capital to be accumulated, the benefits from additional capital become smaller over time, and so growth slows down. *In the long run, the higher saving rate leads to a higher level of productivity and income, but not to higher growth in these variables.* Reaching this long run, however, can take quite a while. According to studies of international data on economic growth, increasing the saving rate can lead to substantially higher growth for a period of several decades.

diminishing returns
the property whereby the benefit from an extra unit of an input declines as the quantity of the input increases

The diminishing returns on capital has another important implication—other things being equal, it is easier for a country to grow fast if it starts out relatively poor. This effect of initial conditions on subsequent growth is sometimes called the **catch-up effect**. In poor countries, workers lack even the most rudimentary tools and, as a result, have low productivity. Small amounts of capital investment would substantially raise these workers' productivity. In contrast, workers in rich countries have large amounts of capital with which to work, and this partly explains their high productivity. Yet with the amount of capital per worker already so high, additional capital investment has a relatively small effect on productivity. Studies of international data on economic growth confirm this catch-up effect—controlling for other variables, such as the percentage of GDP devoted to investment, poor countries do tend to grow faster than rich countries.

catch-up effect
the property whereby countries that start off poor tend to grow more rapidly than countries that start off rich

This catch-up effect can help explain some of the puzzling results in figure 9.1. Over this 31-year period, Australia and Singapore devoted a similar share of GDP to investment. Yet Australia experienced only mediocre growth of about 2%, whereas Singapore experienced spectacular growth of more than 6%. The explanation is the catch-up effect. In 1960, Singapore had GDP per person around one-fifth the Australian level, in part because previous investment had been so low. With a small initial capital stock, the benefits to capital accumulation were much greater in Singapore, and this gave Singapore a higher subsequent growth rate.

This catch-up effect shows up in other aspects of life. When a school gives an end-of-year award to the 'most improved' student, that student is usually one who began the year with relatively poor performance. Students who began the year not studying find improvement easier than students who always worked hard. Note that it is good to be 'most improved', given the starting point, but it is even better to be 'best student'. Similarly, economic growth over the last several decades has been much more rapid in Singapore than in Australia, but GDP per person is still higher in Australia.

INVESTMENT FROM ABROAD

So far we have discussed how policies aimed at increasing a country's saving rate can increase investment and, thereby, long-term economic growth. Yet

IN THE NEWS

The World Bank

AS THE FOLLOWING ARTICLE DESCRIBES, the World Bank encourages firms to invest in some of the world's poorest, and politically least stable, countries.

World Bank Focusing on Areas Shunned by Western Business

BY PAUL LEWIS

WASHINGTON—The World Bank announced a plan today to attract private investment to developing countries that Western businesses have largely shunned.

The agency's International Finance Corporation said it had selected 16 countries and regions either very poor or troubled by their social past as the focus of its efforts. It said it would send investment officers to the areas to generate business opportunities for local and foreign entrepreneurs. The areas include Albania, Bosnia and Herzegovina, Cambodia, Kazakstan, Uzbekistan, Mongolia, El Salvador, and the West Bank and Gaza.

At the same time, Jannik Lindbaek, the International Finance Corporation's executive vice-president, said the agency had approved a record $3.2 billion in financing for 264 private investment projects in the developing world last year, a rise of 12 percent from 1994 and the fifth consecutive double-digit increase. Private industry invested $16.4 billion in the same projects, he added. 'There is a continuing trend in favor of the private sector in the developing world,' Mr Lindbaek said.

The decision to set up shop in distressed countries as well as the overall increase in activities in the Third World are part of the development strategy that the World Bank's president, James D. Wolfensohn, has been pushing since he took over the United Nations agency in June 1995. Under his leadership, the World Bank has tried to compensate for declines in foreign aid from richer countries by stimulating private-sector investment in the developing world and spreading it around more evenly.

As part of that drive, the agency plans to offer foreign companies more generous guarantees against the political risks of investing in the developing world, such as unexpected government price controls or outright expropriations of property. It is also working with the International Monetary Fund on a plan for reducing the debts of the most highly indebted poor countries.

While official aid has stagnated at $55 billion to $65 billion annually in recent years, such private investment has nearly quadrupled to $167 billion last year from $44 billion in 1990.

SOURCE: *New York Times*, 19 September 1996, p. D2.

---

saving by domestic residents is not the only way for a country to invest in new capital. The other way is investment by foreigners.

Investment from abroad takes several forms. An Australian university might build a university in Thailand. A capital investment that is owned and operated by a foreign entity is called *foreign direct investment*. Alternatively, an Australian might buy shares in a Thai corporation (that is, buy a share of the ownership of the corporation); the Thai corporation can use the proceeds from the sale of shares to build a new factory. An investment that is financed with foreign money but operated by domestic residents is called *foreign portfolio investment*. In both cases, Australians provide the resources necessary to increase the stock of capital in Thailand. That is, Australian saving is being used to finance Thai investment.

When foreigners invest in a country, they do so because they expect to earn a return on their investment. If the University of Melbourne were to open a Thai campus, that would increase the Thai capital stock and, therefore, increase Thai productivity and Thai GDP. Yet, in this case, the university takes some of this additional income back to Australia in the form of profit. Similarly, when an Australian investor buys shares in a Thai corporation, the investor has a right to a portion of the profit that the Thai corporation earns.

Investment from abroad, therefore, affects GDP and GNP differently. Recall that gross domestic product is the income earned within a country by both residents and non-residents, whereas gross national product is the income earned by residents of a country both at home and abroad. If the University of Melbourne opens a campus in Thailand, some of the income the university generates accrues to people who do not live in Thailand. As a result, this investment raises Thailand's GDP more than it raises Thailand's GNP.

Investment from abroad is one way for a country to grow. Even though some of the benefits from this investment flow back to the foreign owners, this investment does increase the economy's stock of capital, leading to higher productivity and higher wages. Moreover, investment from abroad is one way for poor countries to learn the state-of-the-art technologies developed and used in richer countries. For these reasons, many economists who advise governments in less developed economies advocate policies that encourage investment from abroad. Often this means removing restrictions that governments have imposed on foreign ownership of domestic capital.

An organisation that tries to encourage the flow of investment to poor countries is the World Bank. This international organisation obtains funds from the world's advanced countries, such as Australia, and uses these resources to make loans to less developed countries so that they can invest in roads, sewer systems, schools and other types of capital. It also offers the countries advice about how the funds might best be used. The World Bank, together with its sister organisation, the International Monetary Fund, was set up after World War II. One lesson from the war was that economic distress often leads to political turmoil, international tensions and military conflict. Thus, every country has an interest in promoting economic prosperity around the world. The World Bank and the International Monetary Fund aim at achieving that common goal.

EDUCATION

Education—investment in human capital—is at least as important as investment in physical capital for a country's long-run economic success. In Australia, each year of schooling raises a person's wage on average by about 8%. In less developed countries, where human capital is especially scarce, the gap between the wages of educated and uneducated workers is even larger. Thus, one way in which government policy can enhance the standard of living is to provide good schools and to encourage the population to take advantage of them.

Investment in human capital, like investment in physical capital, has an opportunity cost. When students are in school or university, they forgo the wages they could have earned. In less developed countries, children often drop out of school at an early age, even though the benefit of additional schooling is very high, simply because their labour is needed to help support the family.

Some economists have argued that human capital is particularly important for economic growth because human capital conveys positive externalities. An *externality* is the effect of one person's actions on the wellbeing of a bystander. An educated person, for instance, might generate new ideas about how best to produce goods and services. If these ideas enter society's pool of knowledge so everyone can use them, then the ideas are an external benefit of education. In this case, the return on schooling is even greater for society than for the individual. This argument would justify the large subsidies for human-capital investment that we observe in the form of public education.

One problem facing some countries is the *brain drain*—the emigration of many of the most highly educated workers to rich countries, where these workers can enjoy a higher standard of living. This is particularly a problem for poor countries, but Australia also suffers from brain drain. If human capital does have positive externalities, then this brain drain makes those people left behind poorer than they otherwise would be. This problem offers policymakers a dilemma. On the one hand, Australia and the United States and other rich countries have better systems of higher education, and it would seem natural for poor countries to send their best students abroad to earn higher degrees. On the other hand, those students who have spent time abroad may choose not to return home, and this brain drain will reduce the poor nation's stock of human capital even further.

PROPERTY RIGHTS AND POLITICAL STABILITY

Another way in which policymakers can foster economic growth is by protecting property rights and promoting political stability. As we first noted when we discussed economic interdependence in chapter 2, production in market economies arises from the interactions of millions of individuals and firms. When you buy a car, for instance, you are buying the output of a car dealer, a car manufacturer, a steel company, an iron ore mining company and so on. This division of production among many firms allows the economy's factors of production to be used as effectively as possible. To achieve this outcome, the economy has to coordinate transactions among these firms, as well as between firms and consumers. Market economies achieve this coordination through market prices. That is, market prices are the instrument with which the 'invisible hand of the marketplace' brings supply and demand into balance. (In his 1776 landmark book, *The Wealth of Nations*, economist Adam Smith referred to the seemingly undirected operation of the marketplace as being guided by an 'invisible hand'.)

An important prerequisite for the price system to work is an economy-wide respect for *property rights*. Property rights refer to the ability of people to exercise authority over the resources they own. A mining company will not make the effort to mine iron ore if it expects the ore to be stolen. The company mines the ore only if it is confident that it will benefit from the ore's subsequent sale. For this reason, courts serve an important role in a market economy—they enforce property rights. Through the criminal justice system, the courts discourage direct theft. In addition, through the civil justice system, the courts ensure that buyers and sellers live up to their contracts.

Although people in developed countries tend to take property rights for granted, those living in less developed countries understand that lack of property rights can be a major problem. In many countries, the system of justice does not work well. Contracts are hard to enforce, and fraud often goes unpunished. In more extreme cases, the government not only fails to enforce property rights but actually infringes upon them. To do business in some countries, firms are expected to bribe powerful government officials. Such corruption impedes the coordinating power of markets. It also discourages domestic saving and investment from abroad.

One threat to property rights is political instability. When revolutions and coups are common, there is doubt about whether property rights will be respected in the future. If a revolutionary government might confiscate the capital of some businesses, as was often true after communist revolutions, domestic residents have less incentive to save, invest and start new businesses. At the same time, foreigners have less incentive to invest in the country. Even the threat of revolution can act to depress a nation's standard of living.

Thus, economic prosperity depends in part on political prosperity. A country with an efficient court system, honest government officials and a stable political system will enjoy a higher economic standard of living than a country with a poor court system, corrupt officials, and frequent revolutions and coups.

CASE STUDY   WHAT CAUSES FAMINE?

A recurring problem facing the world's poorest countries is famine. Every few years, haunting pictures of starving people in an underdeveloped country show up on the nightly news. Such tragedies are surely among the most serious economic problems the world's nations face.

It is tempting to think that the problem of famine is simply due to excessive population. After all, if there were fewer people, then each person could get a larger share of the available food supply. Reducing population growth would seem to be the natural remedy for recurrent famine. It turns out, however, that this straightforward logic is not correct.

In many cases, famine is caused not by an inadequate *supply* of food but by an inadequate *distribution* of food. That is, food is available, but it is not getting to the people who need it. The failure of distribution, in turn, is caused by political instability and poor enforcement of property rights. An example is the famine in Papua New Guinea in 1998. A lack of funding for transport and poor government control over resources prevented food supplies from being distributed to outer provinces. Eventually, Australian troops coordinated the relief effort to allow the available food to be distributed properly.

Papua New Guinea—too many people was not the problem.

FREE TRADE

Some of the world's poorest countries have tried to achieve more rapid economic growth by pursuing *inward-oriented policies*. These policies are aimed at raising productivity and living standards within the country by avoiding interaction with the rest of the world. Domestic firms sometimes claim they need protection from foreign competition in order to compete and grow. This 'infant industry' argument, together with a general distrust of foreigners, has at times led policy-makers in less developed countries to impose tariffs and other trade restrictions.

Most economists today believe that poor countries are better off pursuing *outward-oriented policies* that integrate these countries into the world economy. Chapter 3 showed how international trade can improve the economic wellbeing of a country's citizens. Trade is, in some ways, a type of technology. When a country exports wheat and imports steel, the country benefits in the same way

IN THE NEWS

The Sachs solution to the African problem

ECONOMIST JEFFREY SACHS HAS BEEN A prominent adviser to governments seeking to reform their economies in order to promote more rapid economic growth. Over the past decade, Bolivia, Poland and Russia have been among his many clients. Sachs has also been a critic of the World Bank and the International Monetary Fund (IMF), which are international policy organisations that dispense both advice and money to struggling countries. In the following article, Sachs discusses how the countries of Africa can escape their continuing poverty.

Growth in Africa: It Can Be Done

BY JEFFREY SACHS

In the old story, the peasant goes to the priest for advice on saving his dying chickens. The priest recommends prayer, but the chickens continue to die. The priest then recommends music for the chicken coop, but the deaths continue unabated. Pondering again, the priest recommends repainting the chicken coop in bright colors. Finally, all the chickens die. 'What a shame,' the priest tells the peasant. 'I had so many more good ideas.'

Since independence, African countries have looked to donor nations—often their former colonial rulers—and to the international finance institutions for guidance on growth. Indeed, since the onset of the African debt crises of the 1980s, the guidance has become a kind of economic receivership, with the policies of many African nations decided in a seemingly endless cycle of meetings with the IMF, the World Bank, donors and creditors.

What a shame. So many good ideas, so few results. Output per head fell 0.7 percent between 1978 and 1987, and 0.6 percent during 1987–1994. Some growth is estimated for 1995 but only at 0.6 percent—far below the faster-growing developing countries…

The IMF and World Bank would be absolved of shared responsibility for slow growth if Africa were structurally incapable of growth rates seen in other parts of the world or if the continent's low growth were an impenetrable mystery. But Africa's growth rates are not huge mysteries. The evidence on cross-country growth suggests that Africa's chronically low growth can be explained by standard economic variables linked to identifiable (and remediable) policies…

Studies of cross-country growth show that per capita growth is related to:

- the initial income level of the country, with poorer countries tending to grow faster than richer countries
- the extent of overall market orientation, including openness to trade, domestic market liberalization, private rather than state ownership, protection of private property rights, and low marginal tax rates
- the national saving rate, which in turn is strongly affected by the government's own saving rate
- the geographic and resource structure of the economy…

These four factors can account broadly for Africa's long-term growth predicament. While it should have grown faster than other developing areas because of relatively low income per head (and hence larger opportunity for 'catch-up' growth), Africa grew more slowly. This was mainly because of much higher trade barriers; excessive tax rates; lower saving rates; and adverse structural conditions, including an unusually high incidence of inaccessibility to the sea (15 of 53 countries are landlocked)…

If the policies are largely to blame, why, then, were they adopted? The historical origins of Africa's antimarket orientation are not hard to discern. After almost a century of colonial depredations, African nations understandably if erroneously viewed open trade and

as if it had invented a technology for turning wheat into steel. A country that eliminates trade restrictions will, therefore, experience the same kind of economic growth that would occur after a major technological advance.

The adverse impact of inward orientation becomes clear when one considers the small size of many less developed economies. The total GDP of Fiji, for instance, is about that of Sydney. Imagine what would happen if Sydney residents were prohibited from trading with people living outside the city. Without

A CONTINENT WITH PROBLEMS

foreign capital as a threat to national sovereignty. As in Sukarno's Indonesia, Nehru's India, and Peron's Argentina, 'self-sufficiency' and 'state leadership', including state ownership of much of industry, became the guideposts of the economy. As a result, most of Africa went into a largely self-imposed economic exile…

Adam Smith in 1755 famously remarked that 'little else is requisite to carry a state to the highest degrees of opulence from the lowest barbarism, but peace, easy taxes, and tolerable administration of justice'. A growth agenda need not be long and complex. Take his points in turn.

Peace, of course, is not so easily guaranteed, but the conditions for peace on the continent are better than today's ghastly headlines would suggest. Several of the large-scale conflicts that have ravaged the continent are over or nearly so…The ongoing disasters, such as in Liberia, Rwanda and Somalia, would be better contained if the West were willing to provide modest support to African-based peacekeeping efforts.

'Easy taxes' are well within the ambit of the IMF and World Bank. But here, the IMF stands guilty of neglect, if not malfeasance. African nations need simple, low taxes, with modest revenue targets as a share of GDP. Easy taxes are most essential in international trade, since successful growth will depend, more than anything else, on economic integration with the rest of the world. Africa's largely self-imposed exile from world markets can end quickly by cutting import tariffs and ending export taxes on agricultural exports. Corporate tax rates should be cut from rates of 40 percent and higher now prevalent in Africa, to rates between 20 percent and 30 percent, as in the outward-oriented East Asian economies…

Adam Smith spoke of a 'tolerable' administration of justice, not perfect justice. Market liberalization is the primary key to strengthening the rule of law. Free trade, currency convertibility and automatic incorporation of business vastly reduce the scope for official corruption and allow the government to focus on the real public goods—internal public order, the judicial system, basic public health and education, and monetary stability…

All of this is possible only if the government itself has held its own spending to the necessary minimum. The Asian economies show how to function with government spending of 20 percent of GDP or less (China gets by with just 13 percent). Education can usefully absorb around 5 percent of GDP; health, another 3 percent; public administration, 2 percent; the army and police, 3 percent. Government investment spending can be held to 5 percent of GDP but only if the private sector is invited to provide infrastructure in telecommunications, port facilities, and power…

This fiscal agenda excludes many popular areas for government spending. There is little room for transfers or social spending beyond education and health (though on my proposals, these would get a hefty 8 percent of GDP). Subsidies to publicly owned companies or marketing boards should be scrapped. Food and housing subsidies for urban workers cannot be financed. And, notably, interest payments on foreign debt are not budgeted for. This is because most bankrupt African states need a fresh start based on deep debt-reduction, which should be implemented in conjunction with far-reaching domestic reforms.

SOURCE: *Economist*, 29 June 1996, pp. 19–21.

being able to take advantage of the gains from trade, Sydney would need to produce all the goods it consumes. It would also have to produce all its own capital goods, rather than importing state-of-the-art equipment from other cities. Living standards in Sydney would fall immediately, and the problem would be likely to get worse over time. This is precisely what happens when countries pursue inward-oriented policies, such as Argentina did throughout much of the twentieth century. In contrast, countries pursuing outward-oriented policies, such as South Korea, Singapore and Taiwan, have enjoyed high rates of economic growth.

The amount that a nation trades with others is determined not only by government policy but also by geography. Countries with good natural seaports find trade easier than countries without this resource. It is not a coincidence that many of the world's major cities, such as New York, Singapore and Hong Kong, are located next to oceans. Similarly, because landlocked countries find international trade more difficult, they tend to have lower levels of income than countries with easy access to the world's waterways.

THE CONTROL OF POPULATION GROWTH

A country's productivity and living standard are determined in part by its population growth. Obviously, population is a key determinant of a country's labour force. It is no surprise, therefore, that countries with large populations (such as the United States and Japan) tend to produce greater GDP than countries with small populations (such as Australia and New Zealand). But *total* GDP is not a good measure of economic wellbeing. For policymakers concerned about living standards, GDP *per person* is more important, for it tells us the quantity of goods and services available for the typical individual in the economy.

How does growth in the number of people affect the amount of GDP per person? The answer is that high population growth reduces GDP per person. The reason is that rapid growth in the number of workers forces the other factors of production to be spread more thinly. In particular, when population growth is rapid, equipping each worker with a large quantity of capital is more difficult. A smaller quantity of capital per worker leads to lower productivity and lower GDP per worker.

This problem is most apparent in the case of human capital. Countries with high population growth have large numbers of school-age children. This places a larger burden on the educational system. It is not surprising, therefore, that educational attainment tends to be low in countries with high population growth.

The differences in population growth around the world are large. In developed countries, such as Australia, the United States and countries in western Europe, the population has risen about 1% per year in recent decades, and it is expected to rise even more slowly in the future. In contrast, in many poor African countries, population growth is about 3% per year. At this rate, the population doubles every 23 years.

Reducing the rate of population growth is widely thought to be one way less developed countries can try to raise their standards of living. In some countries, this goal is accomplished directly with laws regulating the number of children families may have. China, for instance, allows only one child per family; couples who violate this rule are subject to substantial fines. In countries with greater freedom, the goal of reduced population growth is accomplished less directly by increasing awareness of birth control techniques.

The final way in which a country can influence population growth is to apply one of the *Ten Principles of Economics*—people respond to incentives. Bearing a child, like any decision, has an opportunity cost. When the opportunity cost rises, people will choose to have smaller families. In particular, women with the opportunity to receive good education and desirable employment tend to want fewer children than those with fewer opportunities outside the home. Hence, policies that foster equal treatment of women are one way for less developed economies to reduce the rate of population growth.

RESEARCH AND DEVELOPMENT

The main reason that living standards are higher today than they were a century ago is that technological knowledge has advanced. The telephone, the transistor, the computer and the internal combustion engine are among the thousands of innovations that have improved the ability to produce goods and services.

Although most technological advances come from private research by firms and individual inventors, there is also a public interest in promoting these efforts. To a large extent, knowledge is a *public good*—once one person discovers an idea, the idea enters society's pool of knowledge, and other people can freely use it. Just as government has a role in providing a public good such as national defence, it also has a role in encouraging the research and development of new technologies.

The Australian government has long played a major role in the creation and dissemination of technological knowledge. Government spending on research and development in Australia outstrips private sector spending by a ratio of 2:1. The government funds research in organisations such as the CSIRO (the Commonwealth Scientific and Industrial Research Organisation). It also provides funding for research in universities across the country through research grants from the Australian Research Council and the National Health and Medical Research Council, and with tax breaks for firms engaging in research and development.

Yet another way in which government policy encourages research is through the patent system. When a person or firm invents a new product, such as a new drug, the inventor can apply for a patent. If the product is deemed truly original, the government awards the patent, which gives the inventor the exclusive right to make the product for a specified number of years. In essence, the patent gives the inventor a property right over the invention, turning the new idea from a public good into a private good. By allowing inventors to profit from their inventions—even if only temporarily—the patent system enhances the incentive for individuals and firms to engage in research.

CASE STUDY   THE PRODUCTIVITY SLOWDOWN

From 1964 to 1984, productivity, as measured by output per hour worked in Australian businesses, grew at a rate of 2.6% per year. From 1984 to 1994, productivity grew by only 1.2% per year. Not surprisingly, this slowdown in productivity growth has been reflected in reduced growth in real wages and family incomes. It is also reflected in a general sense of economic anxiety. Because it has accumulated over so many years, this fall in productivity growth of 1.4 percentage points has had a large effect on incomes. If this slowdown had not occurred, the income of the average Australian would today be much higher.

The slowdown in economic growth has been one of the most important problems facing economic policymakers. Economists are often asked what caused the slowdown and what can be done to reverse it. Unfortunately, despite much research on these questions, the answers remain elusive.

Two facts are well established. First, the slowdown in productivity growth is a worldwide phenomenon. Sometime in the mid-1970s, economic growth slowed in industrial countries, including the United States, Canada, France, Germany, Italy, Japan and the United Kingdom. (Australia's productivity slowdown began in the 1980s.) Although some of these countries have had more rapid growth than Australia, all of them have had slow growth compared with their own past experience. To explain the slowdown in Australian growth, therefore, it seems necessary to look beyond our borders.

Second, the slowdown cannot be traced to those factors of production that are most easily measured. Economists can measure directly the quantity of physical capital that workers have available. They can also measure human capital in the form of years of schooling. It appears that the slowdown in productivity is not primarily attributable to reduced growth in these inputs.

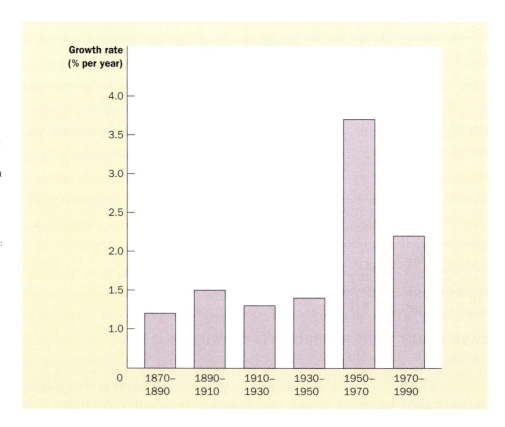

Figure 9.2

THE GROWTH IN REAL GDP PER PERSON. This figure shows the average growth rate of real GDP per person for 16 advanced economies, including the major countries of Europe, Canada, the United States, Japan and Australia. Notice that the growth rate rose substantially after 1950 and then fell after 1970.

SOURCE: Robert J. Barro and Xavier Sala-i-Martin, *Economic Growth* (New York: McGraw-Hill, 1995), p. 6.

Technology appears to be one of the few remaining culprits. That is, having ruled out most other explanations, many economists attribute the slowdown in economic growth to a slowdown in the creation of new ideas about how to produce goods and services. Because the quantity of 'ideas' is hard to measure, this explanation is difficult to confirm or refute.

In some ways, it is odd to say that the last 20 years have been a period of slow technological progress. This period has witnessed the spread of computers across the economy—an historic technological revolution that has affected almost every industry and almost every firm. Yet, for some reason, this change has not yet been reflected in more rapid economic growth. As economist Robert Solow put it, 'You can see the computer age everywhere but in the productivity statistics.'

What does the future of economic growth hold? An optimistic scenario is that the computer revolution will rejuvenate economic growth once these new machines are integrated into the economy and their potential is fully understood. Economic historians note that the discovery of electricity took many decades to have a large impact on productivity and living standards because people had to figure out the best ways to use the new resource. Perhaps the computer revolution will have a similar delayed effect.

A more pessimistic scenario is that, after a period of rapid scientific and technological advance, we have entered a new phase of slower growth in knowledge, productivity and incomes. Data from a longer span of history seem to support this conclusion. Figure 9.2 shows the average growth of real GDP per person in the developed world going back to 1870. The productivity slowdown is apparent in the last two entries—around 1970, the growth rate slowed from 3.7% to 2.2%. But compared with earlier periods of history, the anomaly is not the slow growth of recent years but rather the rapid growth during the 1950s and 1960s. Perhaps the decades after World War II were a period of unusually rapid technological advance, and growth has slowed down simply because technological progress has returned to a more normal rate.

QUICK QUIZ Describe three ways in which a government policymaker can try to raise the growth in living standards in a society. Are there any drawbacks to these policies?

CONCLUSION: THE IMPORTANCE OF LONG-RUN GROWTH

In this chapter we have discussed what determines the standard of living in a nation and how policymakers can endeavour to raise the standard of living through policies that promote economic growth. Most of this chapter is summarised in one of the *Ten Principles of Economics*—a country's standard of living depends on its ability to produce goods and services. Policymakers who want to encourage growth in standards of living must aim to increase their nation's productive ability by encouraging rapid accumulation of the factors of production and ensuring that these factors are employed as effectively as possible.

Economists differ in their views of the role of government in promoting economic growth. At the very least, government can lend support to the invisible

Summary

- Economic prosperity, as measured by GDP per person, varies substantially around the world. The average income in the world's richest countries is more than ten times that in the world's poorest countries. Because growth rates of real GDP also vary substantially, the relative positions of countries can change dramatically over time.

- The standard of living in an economy depends on the economy's ability to produce goods and services. Productivity, in turn, depends on the amounts of physical capital, human capital, natural resources and technological knowledge available to workers.

- Government policies can influence the economy's growth rate in many ways—encouraging saving and investment, encouraging investment from abroad, fostering education, maintaining property rights and political stability, allowing free trade, controlling population growth, and promoting the research and development of new technologies.

- The accumulation of capital is subject to diminishing returns—the more capital an economy has, the less additional output the economy gets from an extra unit of capital. Because of diminishing returns, higher saving leads to higher growth for a period of time, but growth eventually slows down as the economy approaches a higher level of capital, productivity and income. Also because of diminishing returns, the return on capital is especially high in poor countries. Other things being equal, these countries can grow faster because of the catch-up effect.

Key concepts

productivity, p. 173
physical capital, p. 174
human capital, p. 174
natural resources, p. 175
technological knowledge, p. 176
diminishing returns, p. 181
catch-up effect, p. 181

Questions for review

1. What two things does GDP measure? What does this dual meaning tell us about the determinants of the standard of living in a society?

2. List and describe four determinants of productivity.

3. In what way is a university degree a form of capital?

4. Explain how higher saving leads to a higher standard of living. What might deter a policymaker from trying to raise the rate of saving?

5. Does a higher rate of saving lead to higher growth temporarily or indefinitely?

6. Why would removing a trade restriction, such as a tariff, lead to more rapid economic growth?

7. How does the rate of population growth influence the level of GDP per person?

8. Describe two ways in which the Australian government tries to encourage advances in technological knowledge.

Problems and applications

1. Most countries, including Australia, import substantial amounts of goods and services from other countries. Yet the chapter says that a nation can enjoy a high standard of living only if it can produce a large quantity of goods and services itself. Can you reconcile these two facts?

2. List the capital inputs necessary to produce each of the following:
   a. cars
   b. secondary school education
   c. plane travel
   d. fruits and vegetables.

3. Australian income per person today is roughly four times what it was a century ago. Many other countries have also experienced significant growth over that period. What are some specific ways in which your standard of living differs from that of your great-grandparents?

4. The chapter discusses how employment has declined relative to output in the farm sector. Can you think of another sector of the economy where the same phenomenon has occurred more recently? Would you consider the change in employment in this sector to represent a success or a failure from the standpoint of society as a whole?

5. Suppose that society decided to reduce consumption and increase investment.
   a. How would this change affect economic growth?
   b. What groups in society would benefit from this change? What groups might be hurt?

6. Societies choose what share of their resources to devote to consumption and what share to devote to investment. Some of these decisions involve private spending; others involve government spending.
   a. Describe some forms of private spending that represent consumption, and some forms that represent investment.
   b. Describe some forms of government spending that represent consumption, and some forms that represent investment.

7. What is the opportunity cost of investing in capital? Do you think a country can 'over-invest' in capital? What is the opportunity cost of investing in human capital? Do you think a country can 'over-invest' in human capital? Explain.

8. Suppose that a car manufacturing company owned entirely by German citizens opens a new factory in Victoria.
   a. What sort of foreign investment would this represent?
   b. What would be the effect of this investment on Australian GDP? Would the effect on Australian GNP be larger or smaller?

9. In the 1980s, Japanese investors made significant direct and portfolio investments in Australia. At the time, many Australians were unhappy that this investment was occurring.
   a. In what way was it better for Australia to receive this Japanese investment than not to receive it?
   b. In what way would it have been better still for Australians to have engaged in this investment?

10. In the countries of South Asia in 1992, only 56 young women were enrolled in secondary school for every 100 young men. Describe several ways in which greater educational opportunities for young women could lead to faster economic growth in these countries.

11. Suppose the government increased the number of years for which a patent lasts. What would be the effect of this change on the incentive to do research? Could this change produce a decline in the growth rate of GDP? Explain.

12. International data show a positive correlation between political stability and economic growth.
    a. Through what mechanism could political stability lead to strong economic growth?
    b. Through what mechanism could strong economic growth lead to political stability?

10

SAVING, INVESTMENT AND THE FINANCIAL SYSTEM

IN THIS CHAPTER YOU WILL

Learn about some of the important financial institutions in the Australian economy

Consider how the financial system is related to key macroeconomic variables

Develop a model of the supply of and demand for loanable funds in financial markets

Use the loanable funds model to analyse various government policies

Consider how government budget deficits affect the Australian economy

Imagine that you have just graduated from university (with a degree in economics, of course) and you decide to start your own business—an economic forecasting firm. Before you make any money selling your forecasts, you have to incur substantial costs to set up your business. You have to buy computers with which to make your forecasts, as well as desks, chairs and filing cabinets to furnish your new office. Each of these is a type of capital that your firm will use to produce and sell its services.

How do you obtain the funds to invest in these capital goods? Perhaps you are able to pay for them out of your past savings. More likely, however, like most entrepreneurs, you do not have enough money of your own to finance the start of your business. As a result, you have to get the money you need from other sources.

There are various ways for you to finance these capital investments. You could borrow the money, perhaps from a bank or from a friend or relative. In this case, you would promise not only to return the money at a later date but also to pay interest for the use of the money. Alternatively, you could convince someone to provide the money you need for your business in exchange for a share of your future profits, whatever they might happen to be. In either case, your investment in computers and office equipment is being financed by someone else's saving.

financial system
the group of institutions in the economy that help to match one person's saving with another person's investment

The **financial system** consists of those institutions in the economy that help to match one person's saving with another person's investment. As we discussed in the previous chapter, saving and investment are key ingredients to economic growth. When a country saves a large portion of its GDP, more resources are available for investment in capital, and higher capital raises a country's productivity and living standard. But that chapter did not explain how the economy coordinates saving and investment. At any time, some people want to save some of their income for the future, and others want to borrow in order to finance investments in new and growing businesses. What brings these two groups of people together? What ensures that the supply of funds from those who want to save balances the demand for funds from those who want to invest?

This chapter examines how the financial system works. First, we discuss the large variety of institutions that make up the financial system in our economy. Second, we discuss the relationship between the financial system and some key macroeconomic variables—notably saving and investment. Third, we develop a model of the supply of and demand for funds in financial markets. In the model, the interest rate is the price that adjusts to balance supply and demand. The model shows how various government policies affect the interest rate and, thereby, society's allocation of scarce resources.

FINANCIAL INSTITUTIONS IN THE AUSTRALIAN ECONOMY

At the broadest level, the financial system moves the economy's scarce resources from savers (people who spend less than they earn) to borrowers (people who spend more than they earn). Savers save for various reasons—to put a child through university in several years or to retire comfortably in several decades. Similarly, borrowers borrow for various reasons—to buy a house in which to live or to start a business with which to make a living. Savers supply their money to the financial system with the expectation that they will get it back with interest at a later date. Borrowers demand money from the financial system with the knowledge that they will be required to pay it back with interest at a later date.

The financial system is made up of various financial institutions that help coordinate savers and borrowers. As a prelude to analysing the economic forces that drive the financial system, let's discuss the most important of these institutions. Financial institutions can be grouped into two categories—financial markets and financial intermediaries. We consider each category in turn.

FINANCIAL MARKETS

financial markets
financial institutions through which savers can directly provide funds to borrowers

Financial markets are the institutions through which a person who wants to save can directly supply funds to a person who wants to borrow. The two most important financial markets in our economy are the bond market and the stock market.

The bond market When BHP, the big Australian steel company, wants to borrow to finance construction of a new steel processing plant, it can borrow directly from the public. It does this by selling bonds. A **bond** (a **security**) is a certificate of indebtedness that specifies the obligations of the borrower to the holder of the bond. Put simply, a bond is just an IOU. It identifies the time at which the loan will be repaid, called the *date of maturity*, and the rate of interest that will be paid periodically until the loan matures. Buyers of bonds give their money to BHP in exchange for the promise of interest and eventual repayment of the amount borrowed (called the principal). Buyers can hold the bonds until maturity or sell them at an earlier date to someone else.

bond (security)
a certificate of indebtedness

There are literally hundreds of different kinds of bonds in the Australian economy. When large corporations or the federal or state governments need to borrow to finance the purchase of a new factory or a new jet fighter, they usually do so by issuing bonds. If you look at the *Australian Financial Review* or the business section of your local newspaper, you will find a listing of the prices and interest rates on some of the most important bond issues. Although these bonds differ in many ways, three characteristics of bonds are most important.

The first characteristic is a bond's *term*—the length of time until the bond matures. Some bonds have short terms, such as a few months, and others have terms as long as 100 years. (The British government has even issued a bond that never matures, called a *perpetuity*. This bond pays interest forever, but the principal is never repaid.) The interest rate on a bond depends, in part, on its term. Long-term bonds are riskier than short-term bonds because holders of long-term bonds have to wait longer for repayment of principal. If a holder of a long-term bond needs the money earlier than the distant date of maturity, the buyer has no choice but to sell the bond to someone else, perhaps at a reduced price. To compensate for this risk, long-term bonds usually pay higher interest rates than short-term bonds do.

The second important characteristic of a bond is its *credit risk*—the probability that the borrower will fail to pay some of the interest or principal. Such a failure to pay is called a *default*. Borrowers can (and sometimes do) default on their loans by declaring bankruptcy. When bond buyers perceive that the probability of default is high, they demand a higher interest rate to compensate them for this risk. Because the Australian government is considered a safe credit risk, government bonds tend to pay low interest rates. In contrast, financially shaky corporations raise money by issuing *junk bonds*, which pay very high interest rates. Buyers of bonds can judge credit risk by checking with various private credit-rating agencies, such as Standard & Poor's or Moody's, which rate the credit risk of different bonds.

The third important characteristic of a bond is its *tax treatment*—the way in which the tax laws treat the interest earned on the bond. The interest on most bonds is taxable income, so the bond owner has to pay a portion of the interest in income taxes. In some countries, state and local governments issue bonds. When state and local governments issue bonds in the United States, called *municipal bonds*, the bond owners are not required to pay federal income tax on the interest income. Because of this tax advantage, bonds issued by state and local governments in the United States pay a lower interest rate than bonds issued by corporations or the federal government. However, in Australia, interest earned on bonds is treated as any other type of income and taxed at the normal rate.

The stock market Another way for BHP to raise funds to build a new steel processing factory is to sell shares in the company. **Shares** represent ownership in a firm and are, therefore, a claim to the profits that the firm makes. For

share
a claim to partial ownership in a firm

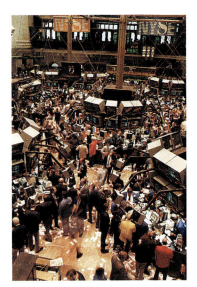

One of the world's largest trading floors

example, if BHP sells a total of 1 000 000 shares, then each share represents ownership of 1/1 000 000 of the business.

The sale of shares to raise money is called *equity finance*, whereas the sale of bonds is called *debt finance*. Although corporations use both equity and debt finance to raise money for new investments, shares and bonds are very different. The owner of shares in BHP is a part-owner of BHP; the owner of a BHP bond is a creditor of the corporation. If BHP is very profitable, the shareholders enjoy the benefits of these profits, whereas the bondholders get only the interest on their bonds. And if BHP runs into financial difficulty, the bondholders are paid what they are due before shareholders receive anything at all. Compared with bonds, shares offer the holder both higher risk and potentially higher return.

After a corporation sells shares to the public, these shares trade among shareholders on organised stock exchanges. In these transactions, the corporation itself receives no money when its shares change hands. The most important stock exchange in the Australian economy is the Australian Stock Exchange (ASX), but our stock market is also influenced by stock markets overseas. Some of the important overseas markets are the New York Stock Exchange, the American Stock Exchange, and NASDAQ (National Association of Securities Dealers Automated Quotation system) in the United States, the Tokyo Stock Exchange, the Stock Exchange of Hong Kong and the London Stock Exchange. Most of the world's countries have their own stock exchanges on which the shares of local companies trade.

The prices at which shares trade on stock exchanges are determined by the supply of and demand for the shares in these companies. Because shares represent ownership in a corporation, the demand for a share (and thus its price) reflects people's perception of the corporation's future profitability. When people become optimistic about a company's future, they raise their demand for its shares and thereby bid up the price of a share. Conversely, when people come to expect a company to have little profit or even losses, the price of a share falls.

Various share indexes are available to monitor the overall level of share prices. A share index is calculated as an average of a group of share prices. The Australian share index is the All Ordinaries, which is an index of common shares listed on the Australian Stock Exchange. One of the world's most famous share indexes is the Dow Jones Industrial Average in the United States, which has been calculated regularly since 1896. It is now based on the prices of the shares of 30 major US companies, such as General Motors, General Electric, Coca-Cola, AT&T and IBM. Other well-known share indexes include the Nikkei in Tokyo, the Hang Seng in Hong Kong, the FTSE in London and Standard & Poor's 500 Index in the United States. Because share prices reflect expected profitability, these share indexes are watched closely as possible indicators of future economic conditions.

FINANCIAL INTERMEDIARIES

Financial intermediaries are financial institutions through which savers can indirectly provide funds to borrowers. The term *intermediary* reflects the role of these institutions in standing between savers and borrowers. Here we consider two of the most important financial intermediaries—banks and managed funds.

Banks Chris owns a small grocery store and wants to finance a business expansion. The strategy taken is probably quite different from that of BHP. Unlike BHP, Chris would find it difficult to raise funds in the bond and stock

financial intermediaries
financial institutions through which savers can indirectly provide funds to borrowers

FYI

How to read the newspaper's share tables

Most daily newspapers include share tables, which contain information about recent trading in the shares of several thousand companies. Here is the kind of information these tables usually provide:

- *Price.* The single most important piece of information about a share is its price. The newspaper usually presents several prices. The 'last' or 'closing' price is the price of the last transaction that occurred before the stock exchange closed the previous day. Many newspapers also give the 'high' and 'low' prices over the past day of trading and, sometimes, over the past year as well.
- *Volume.* Most newspapers present the number of shares sold during the past week of trading. This figure is called the *weekly volume*.
- *Dividend.* Corporations pay out some of their profits to their shareholders; this amount is called the *dividend*. (Profits not paid out are called *retained profits* and are used by the corporation for additional investment.) Newspapers often report the dividend paid over the previous year for each share. They sometimes report the *dividend yield*, which is the dividend expressed as a percentage of the share's price.
- *Price–earnings ratio.* A corporation's profit is the amount of revenue it receives for the sale of its products minus its costs of production as measured by its accountants. Some of the profits are used to pay dividends; the rest is kept in the firm to make new investments. The price–earnings ratio, often called the P/E ratio, is the price of a corporation's share divided by the amount the corporation earned per share over the past year. Historically, the typical price–earnings ratio is about 15. A higher P/E indicates that a corporation's shares are expensive relative to its recent earnings; this might indicate either that people expect earnings to rise in the future or that the shares are overvalued. Conversely, a lower P/E indicates that a corporation's shares are cheap relative to its recent earnings; this might indicate either that people expect earnings to fall or that the shares are undervalued.

Why does the newspaper report all these data every day? Many people who invest their savings in shares follow these numbers closely when deciding which shares to buy and sell. In contrast, other shareholders follow a buy-and-hold strategy —they buy the shares of well-run companies, hold them for long periods of time, and do not respond to the daily fluctuations reported in the newspaper.

ASX Code	Stock	Market Capital $m	Last Sale Price	12 Months High	12 Months Low	Change on Week	Price	Price/ Earnings Ratio	Div Yield %	Weekly Volume (000s)
NCP	News Corp.	41222	11.30	13.65	8.48	−.14	0.18	25.22	0.26	25613
NAB	Nat. Bank	39447	26.85	27.42	18.99	+.23	2.81	19.17	3.79	73578
TLS	Telstra	35410	8.21	9.20	6.03	−.38	7.80	26.99	—	47260
BHP	BHP	25111	12.09	16.10	10.62	+.35	176.27	n/c	4.21	37455
CBA	Cwlth Bank	22623	24.20	25.60	16.86	−.25	3.14	18.62	4.42	47294
WBC	Westpac	20223	10.64	11.73	8.36	−.30	2.34	15.18	1.97	38417
AMP	AMP	19794	18.23	45.00	18.10	−1.02	2.58	18.85	—	23948
ANZ	ANZ Bank	16164	10.40	12.04	8.28	−.16	2.08	14.32	5.00	18939
CWO	C&W Optus	13292	3.54	4.16	2.51	+.04	2.43	n/c	—	49042

Symbol for company's shares · Name of company · Total value of all shares traded · Highest and lowest price of the shares over the past year · Increase or decrease in price in the last week · Dividend yield

markets. Most buyers of shares and bonds prefer to buy those issued by larger, more familiar companies. Chris, a small grocer, therefore, is most likely to finance his business expansion with a loan from a local bank.

Banks are the financial intermediaries with which people are most familiar. One of the main jobs of banks is to take in deposits from people who want to save and use these deposits to make loans to people who want to borrow. Banks pay depositors interest on their deposits and charge borrowers slightly higher interest on their loans. The difference between these rates of interest covers the banks' costs and returns some profit to the owners of the banks.

Besides being financial intermediaries, banks play a second important role in the economy—they facilitate purchases of goods and services by allowing people to write cheques against their deposits. In other words, banks help create a special asset that people can use as a *medium of exchange*. A medium of exchange is an item that people can easily use to make payments. A bank's role in providing a medium of exchange distinguishes it from many other financial institutions. Shares and bonds, like bank deposits, are a possible *store of value* for the wealth that people have accumulated in past saving, but access to this wealth is not as easy, cheap and immediate as just writing a cheque. For now, we ignore this second role of banks, but we will return to it when we discuss the monetary system in a later chapter.

Managed funds A financial intermediary of increasing importance in the Australian economy is the managed fund. A **managed fund** is a type of financial investment that allows investors to own a selection, or *portfolio*, of various types of shares, bonds, or both shares and bonds without buying them individually. When an individual investor puts money into a managed fund, a manager or trustee makes the decisions about which shares or bonds to purchase. However, the individual investor in the managed fund accepts all the risk and return associated with the portfolio. If the value of the portfolio rises, the investor benefits; if the value of the portfolio falls, the investor suffers the loss.

The main advantage of managed funds is that they allow people with small amounts of money to diversify. Buyers of shares and bonds are well advised to heed the adage 'don't put all your eggs in one basket'. Because the value of any single share or bond is tied to the fortunes of one company, holding a single kind of share or bond is very risky. In contrast, people who hold a diverse portfolio of shares and bonds face less risk because they have only a small stake in each company. Managed funds make this diversification easy. With only a few hundred dollars, a person can buy shares in a managed fund and, indirectly, become the part owner or creditor of hundreds of major companies. For this service, the company operating the managed fund charges shareholders a fee, usually between 0.5% and 2.0% of assets each year.

A second advantage claimed by managed fund companies is that managed funds give ordinary people access to the skills of professional money managers. The managers of most managed funds pay close attention to the developments and prospects of the companies in which they buy shares. These managers buy the shares of those companies that they view as having a profitable future and sell the shares of companies with less promising prospects. This professional management, it is argued, should increase the return that managed fund depositors earn on their savings.

Financial economists, however, are often sceptical of this second argument. With thousands of money managers paying close attention to each company's

managed fund
a type of financial investment that allows investors to own a portfolio of various types of shares and/or bonds

prospects, the price of a company's share is usually a good reflection of the company's true value. As a result, it is hard to 'beat the market' by buying good shares and selling bad ones. In fact, managed funds called *index funds*, which buy all the shares in a given share index, perform somewhat better on average than managed funds that engage the services of professional money managers. The explanation for the superior performance of index funds is that they keep costs low by buying and selling very rarely and by not having to pay the salaries of the professional money managers.

SUMMING UP

The Australian economy contains a large variety of financial institutions. In addition to the bond market, the stock market, banks and managed funds, there are also credit unions, insurance companies, and even the local loan shark. These institutions differ in many ways. When analysing the macroeconomic role of the financial system, however, it is more important to keep in mind the similarities of these institutions rather than the differences. These financial institutions all serve the same goal—directing the resources of savers into the hands of borrowers.

> **QUICK QUIZ**   What are shares? What are bonds? How are they different? How are they similar?

SAVING AND INVESTMENT IN THE NATIONAL INCOME ACCOUNTS

Events that occur within the financial system are central to understanding developments in the overall economy. As we have just seen, the institutions that make up this system—the bond market, the stock market, banks and managed funds—have the role of coordinating the economy's saving and investment. And as we saw in the previous chapter, saving and investment are important determinants of long-run growth in GDP and living standards. As a result, macroeconomists need to understand how financial markets work and how various events and policies affect them.

As a starting point for an analysis of financial markets, we discuss in this section the key macroeconomic variables that measure activity in these markets. Our emphasis here is not on behaviour but on accounting. *Accounting* refers to how various numbers are defined and added up. A personal accountant might help individuals add up their income and expenses. A national income accountant does the same thing for the economy as a whole. The national income accounts include, in particular, GDP and the many related statistics.

The rules of national income accounting include several important identities. Recall that an *identity* is an equation that must be true because of the way the variables in the equation are defined. Identities are useful to keep in mind, for they clarify how different variables are related to one another. Here we consider some accounting identities that shed light on the macroeconomic role of financial markets.

SOME IMPORTANT IDENTITIES

Recall that gross domestic product (GDP) is both total income in an economy and the total expenditure on the economy's output of goods and services in a given period of time. GDP (denoted as Y) is divided into four components of expenditure: consumption (C), investment (I), government purchases (G) and net exports (NX). We write:

$$Y = C + I + G + NX$$

This equation is an identity because every dollar of expenditure that shows up on the left-hand side also shows up in one of the four components on the right-hand side. Because of the way each of the variables is defined and measured, this equation must always hold.

In this chapter, we simplify our analysis by assuming that the economy we are examining is closed. A *closed economy* is one that does not interact with other economies. In particular, a closed economy does not engage in international trade in goods and services, nor does it engage in international borrowing and lending. Of course, actual economies are *open economies*, that is, they interact with other economies around the world. (We will examine the macroeconomics of open economies later in this book.) Nonetheless, assuming a closed economy is a useful simplification with which we can learn some lessons that apply to all economies. Moreover, this assumption applies perfectly to the world economy (since interplanetary trade is not yet common).

Because a closed economy does not engage in international trade, imports and exports are exactly zero. Therefore, net exports (NX) are also zero. In this case, we can write:

$$Y = C + I + G$$

This equation states that GDP is the sum of consumption, investment and government purchases. Each unit of output sold in a closed economy is consumed, invested or bought by the government.

To see what this identity can tell us about financial markets, subtract C and G from both sides of this equation. We obtain:

$$Y - C - G = I$$

The left-hand side of this equation (Y − C − G) is the total income in the economy that remains after paying for consumption and government purchases. This amount is called **national saving**, or just **saving**, and is denoted S. Substituting S for Y − C − G, we can write the last equation as:

$$S = I$$

This equation states that saving equals investment.

To understand the meaning of national saving, it is helpful to manipulate the definition a bit more. Let T denote the amount that the government collects from households in taxes minus the amount it pays back to households in the form of transfer payments (such as pension benefits or social security payments). We can then write national saving in either of two ways:

$$S = Y - C - G$$

or

$$S = (Y - T - C) + (T - G)$$

national saving (saving)
the total income in the economy that remains after paying for consumption and government purchases

These equations are the same, since the two Ts in the second equation cancel each other, but each reveals a different way of thinking about national saving. In particular, the second equation separates national saving into two pieces: private saving ($Y - T - C$) and public saving ($T - G$).

Consider each of these two pieces. **Private saving** is the amount of income that households have left after paying their taxes and paying for their consumption. In particular, because households receive income of Y, pay taxes of T and spend C on consumption, private saving is $Y - T - C$. **Public saving** is the amount of tax revenue that the government has left after paying for its spending. The government receives T in tax revenue and spends G on goods and services. If T exceeds G, the government runs a **budget surplus** because it receives more money than it spends. This surplus of $T - G$ represents public saving. If the government spends more than it receives in tax revenue (as has been the case for the most part in recent Australian history), then G is larger than T. In this case, the government runs a **budget deficit**, and public saving $T - G$ is a negative number.

Now consider how these accounting identities are related to financial markets. The equation $S = I$ reveals an important fact—*for the economy as a whole, saving must be equal to investment*. Yet this fact raises some important questions. What mechanisms lie behind this identity? What coordinates those people who are deciding how much to save and those people who are deciding how much to invest? The answer is the financial system. The bond market, the stock market, banks, managed funds and other financial markets and intermediaries stand between the two sides of the $S = I$ equation. They take in the nation's saving and channel it to the nation's investors.

private saving
the income that households have left after paying for taxes and consumption

public saving
the tax revenue that the government has left after paying for its spending

budget surplus
an excess of tax revenue over government spending

budget deficit
when government spending exceeds tax revenue

THE MEANING OF SAVING AND INVESTMENT

The terms *saving* and *investment* can sometimes be confusing. Most people use these terms casually and sometimes interchangeably. In contrast, the macroeconomists who put together the national income accounts use these terms carefully and distinctly.

Consider an example. Suppose that Larry earns more than he spends and deposits his unspent income in a bank or uses it to buy a bond or some shares from a corporation. Because Larry's income exceeds his consumption, he adds to the nation's saving. Larry might think of himself as 'investing' his money, but a macroeconomist would call Larry's act 'saving' rather than 'investment'.

In the language of macroeconomics, investment refers to the purchase of new capital, such as equipment or buildings. When Moe borrows from the bank to build himself a new house, he adds to the nation's investment. Similarly, when the Curly Corporation sells some shares and uses the proceeds to build a new factory, it also adds to the nation's investment.

Although the accounting identity $S = I$ shows that saving and investment are equal for the economy as a whole, this does not have to be true for every individual household or firm. Larry's saving can be greater than his investment, and he can deposit the excess in a bank. Moe's saving can be less than his investment, and he can borrow the shortfall from a bank. Banks and other financial institutions make these individual differences between saving and investment possible by allowing one person's saving to finance another person's investment.

> **QUICK QUIZ** Define private saving, public saving, national saving and investment. How are they related?

THE MARKET FOR LOANABLE FUNDS

Having discussed some of the important financial institutions in our economy and the macroeconomic role of these institutions, we are ready to build a model of financial markets. Our purpose in building this model is to explain how financial markets coordinate the economy's saving and investment. The model also gives us a tool with which we can analyse various government policies that influence saving and investment.

To keep things simple, we assume that the economy has only one financial market, called the **market for loanable funds**. All savers go to this market to deposit their saving, and all borrowers go to this market to get their loans. In this market, there is one interest rate, which is both the return on saving and the cost of borrowing.

The assumption of a single financial market, of course, is not literally true. As we have seen, the economy has many types of financial institutions. But, as we discussed in chapter 2, the art in building an economic model is simplifying the world in order to explain it. For our purposes here, we can ignore the diversity of financial institutions and assume that the economy has a single financial market.

market for loanable funds
the market in which those who want to save supply funds and those who want to borrow to invest demand funds

SUPPLY OF AND DEMAND FOR LOANABLE FUNDS

The economy's market for loanable funds, like other markets in the economy, is governed by supply and demand. To understand how the market for loanable funds operates, therefore, we first look at the sources of supply and demand in that market.

The supply of loanable funds comes from those people who have some extra income they want to save and lend out, and from the government when government revenue is in excess of government expenditure. This lending can occur directly, such as when a household buys a bond from a firm, or it can occur indirectly, such as when a household makes a deposit in a bank which in turn uses the funds to make loans. In both cases, saving is the source of the supply of loanable funds.

The demand for loanable funds comes from households and firms who wish to borrow to make investments. This demand includes families taking out mortgages to buy homes. It also includes firms borrowing to buy new equipment or build factories. In both cases, investment is the source of the demand for loanable funds.

The interest rate is the price of a loan. It represents the amount that borrowers pay for loans and the amount that lenders receive on their saving. Because a high interest rate makes borrowing more expensive, the quantity of loanable funds demanded falls as the interest rate rises. Similarly, because a high interest rate makes saving more attractive, the quantity of loanable funds supplied rises as the interest rate rises. In other words, the demand curve for loanable funds slopes downwards, and the supply curve for loanable funds slopes upwards.

Figure 10.1 shows the interest rate that balances the supply of and demand for loanable funds. In the equilibrium shown, the interest rate is 5%, and the quantity of loanable funds demanded and the quantity of loanable funds supplied both equal $1200 million. The adjustment of the interest rate to the equilibrium level occurs for the usual reasons. If the interest rate were lower than the equilibrium level, the quantity of loanable funds supplied would be less than the quantity of loanable funds demanded. The resulting shortage of loanable funds would encourage lenders to raise the interest rate they charge. Conversely, if the interest rate were higher than the equilibrium level, the quantity of loanable funds supplied would exceed the quantity of loanable funds demanded. As lenders competed for the scarce borrowers, interest rates would be driven down. In this way, the interest rate approaches the equilibrium level at which the supply of and demand for loanable funds exactly balance.

Recall that economists distinguish between the real interest rate and the nominal interest rate. The nominal interest rate is the interest rate as usually reported—the monetary return on saving and the cost of borrowing. The real interest rate is the nominal interest rate corrected for inflation; it equals the nominal interest rate minus the inflation rate. Because inflation erodes the value of money over time, the real interest rate more accurately reflects the real return on saving and the cost of borrowing. Therefore, the supply of and demand for loanable funds depend on the real (rather than nominal) interest rate, and the equilibrium in figure 10.1 should be interpreted as determining the real interest rate in the economy. For the rest of this chapter, when you see the term *interest rate*, you should remember that we are talking about the real interest rate.

This model of the supply of and demand for loanable funds shows that financial markets work much like other markets in the economy. In the market

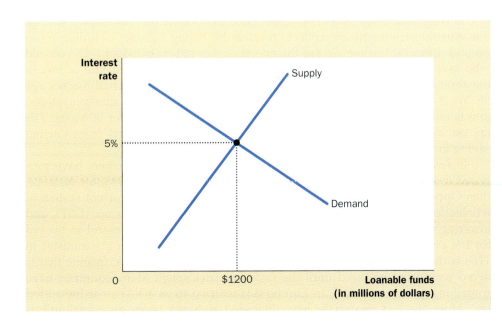

Figure 10.1

THE MARKET FOR LOANABLE FUNDS. The interest rate in the economy adjusts to balance the supply of and demand for loanable funds. The supply of loanable funds comes from national saving, including both private saving and public saving. The demand for loanable funds comes from firms and households that want to borrow for purposes of investment. Here the equilibrium interest rate is 5%, and $1200 million of loanable funds are supplied and demanded.

for milk, for instance, the price of milk adjusts so that the quantity of milk supplied balances the quantity of milk demanded. In this way, the invisible hand coordinates the behaviour of dairy farmers and the behaviour of milk drinkers. Once we realise that saving represents the supply of loanable funds and investment represents the demand, we can see how the invisible hand coordinates saving and investment. When the interest rate adjusts to balance supply and demand in the market for loanable funds, it coordinates the behaviour of people who want to save (the suppliers of loanable funds) and the behaviour of people who want to invest (the demanders of loanable funds).

We can now use this analysis of the market for loanable funds to examine various government policies that affect the economy's saving and investment. Because this model is just supply and demand in a particular market, we analyse any policy using the three steps discussed in chapter 4. First, we decide whether the policy shifts the supply curve or the demand curve. Second, we determine the direction of the shift. Third, we use the supply-and-demand diagram to see how the equilibrium changes.

POLICY 1: TAXES AND SAVING

Australian families save a smaller fraction of their incomes than their counterparts in many other countries, such as Japan and Germany. Although the reasons for these international differences are unclear, many Australian policy-makers view the low level of Australian saving as a major problem. One of the *Ten Principles of Economics* in chapter 1 is that a country's standard of living depends on its ability to produce goods and services. And, as we discussed in the last chapter, saving is an important long-run determinant of a nation's productivity. If Australia could somehow raise its saving rate to the level that prevails in other countries, the growth rate of GDP would increase and, over time, Australian citizens would enjoy a higher standard of living.

Another of the *Ten Principles of Economics* is that people respond to incentives. Many economists have used this principle to suggest that the low saving rate in Australia is at least partly attributable to tax laws that discourage saving. The Australian government collects revenue by taxing income, including interest and dividend income. To see the effects of this policy, consider a 25-year-old who saves $1000 and buys a 30-year bond that pays an interest rate of 9%. In the absence of taxes, the $1000 grows to $13 268 when the individual reaches age 55. Yet if that interest is taxed at a rate of, say, 33%, then the after-tax interest rate is only 6%. In this case, the $1000 grows to only $5743 after 30 years. The tax on interest income substantially reduces the future payoff from current saving and, as a result, reduces the incentive for people to save.

In response to this problem, many economists and law-makers have proposed changing the tax laws to encourage greater saving. In 1993, for instance, then Opposition Leader John Hewson proposed replacing the current system of wholesale taxes with a consumption tax or goods and services tax (GST), and lowering income tax rates. Although John Hewson wasn't successful in his bid for the prime minister's job, John Howard was re-elected as prime minister in 1998 with another proposal for a GST. Under a consumption tax, income that is saved would not be taxed until the saving is later spent. Many countries have something similar to a GST; in Europe it is referred to as a VAT or value-added tax. More modest proposals have included reduced taxes on contributions to superannuation funds that allow people to shelter some of their saving from taxation. Let's consider the effect of such a saving incentive on the market for loanable funds, as illustrated in figure 10.2.

First, which curve would this policy affect? Because the tax change would alter the incentive for households to save *at any given interest rate*, it would affect the quantity of loanable funds supplied at each interest rate. Thus, the supply of loanable funds would shift. Because the tax change would not directly affect the amount that borrowers want to borrow at any given interest rate, the demand for loanable funds would be unchanged.

Second, which way would the supply curve shift? Because saving would be taxed less heavily than under current law, households would increase their saving by consuming a smaller fraction of their income. Households would use this additional saving to increase their deposits in banks or to buy more bonds. The supply of loanable funds would increase, and the supply curve would shift to the right from S_1 to S_2, as shown in figure 10.2.

Finally, we compare the old and new equilibria. In the figure, the increased supply of loanable funds reduces the interest rate from 5% to 4%. The lower interest rate raises the quantity of loanable funds demanded from $1200 million to $1600 million. That is, the shift in the supply curve moves the market equilibrium along the demand curve. With a lower cost of borrowing, households and firms are motivated to borrow more to finance greater investment. Thus, *if a change in the tax laws encouraged greater saving, the result would be lower interest rates and greater investment.*

Although this analysis of the effects of increased saving is widely accepted among economists, there is less consensus about what kinds of tax changes should be enacted. Many economists endorse tax reform aimed at increasing saving in order to stimulate investment and growth. Yet others are sceptical that

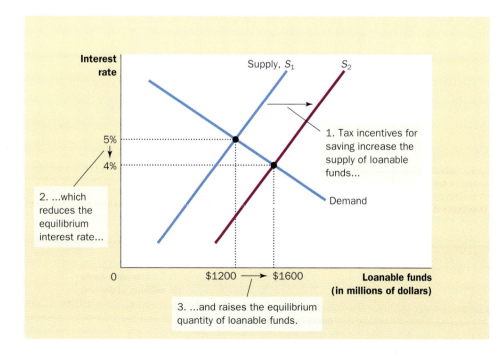

Figure 10.2

AN INCREASE IN THE SUPPLY OF LOANABLE FUNDS. A change in the tax laws to encourage Australians to save more would shift the supply of loanable funds to the right from S_1 to S_2. As a result, the equilibrium interest rate would fall, and the lower interest rate would stimulate investment. Here the equilibrium interest rate falls from 5% to 4%, and the equilibrium quantity of loanable funds saved and invested rises from $1200 million to $1600 million.

these tax changes would have much effect on national saving. These sceptics also doubt the equity of the proposed reforms. They argue that, in many cases, the benefits of the tax changes would accrue primarily to the wealthy, who are least in need of tax relief. We examine this debate more fully in the final chapter of this book.

POLICY 2: TAXES AND INVESTMENT

Suppose that Parliament passed a law giving a tax reduction to any firm building a new factory. In essence, this is what the government does when it institutes an *investment tax credit*, which it does from time to time. Let's consider the effect of such a law on the market for loanable funds, as illustrated in figure 10.3.

First, would the law affect supply or demand? Because the tax credit would alter the incentive of firms to borrow and invest in new capital, it would alter the demand for loanable funds. In contrast, because the tax credit would not affect the amount that households save at any given interest rate, it would not affect the supply of loanable funds.

Second, which way would the demand curve shift? Because firms would have an incentive to increase investment at any interest rate, the quantity of loanable funds demanded would be higher at any given interest rate. Thus, the demand curve for loanable funds would shift to the right from D_1 to D_2, as shown in the figure.

Third, consider how the equilibrium would change. In figure 10.3, the increased demand for loanable funds raises the interest rate from 5% to 6%, and the higher interest rate in turn increases the quantity of loanable funds supplied from $1200 million to $1400 million, as households respond by increasing the amount they save. This change in household behaviour is represented here as a

Figure 10.3

AN INCREASE IN THE DEMAND FOR LOANABLE FUNDS. If the passage of an investment tax credit encouraged Australian firms to invest more, the demand for loanable funds would increase. As a result, the equilibrium interest rate would rise, and the higher interest rate would stimulate saving. Here, when the demand curve shifts from D_1 to D_2, the equilibrium interest rate rises from 5% to 6%, and the equilibrium quantity of loanable funds saved and invested rises from $1200 million to $1400 million.

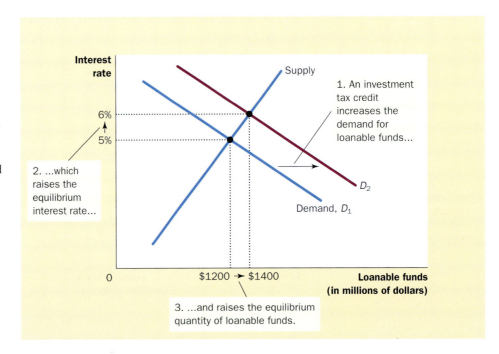

movement along the supply curve. Thus, *if a change in the tax laws encouraged greater investment, the result would be higher interest rates and greater saving.*

POLICY 3: GOVERNMENT BUDGET DEFICITS

One of the most pressing policy issues of the past decade has been the government budget deficit. When the government spends more than it receives in tax revenue, the shortfall is called the *budget deficit*. The accumulation of past budget deficits is called the *government debt*. In recent years, the Australian government has usually run large budget deficits, resulting in a growing government debt. As a result, much public debate has centred on the effects of these deficits both on the allocation of the economy's scarce resources and on long-run economic growth.

We can analyse the effects of a budget deficit by following our three steps in the market for loanable funds, which is illustrated in figure 10.4. First, which curve shifts when the budget deficit rises? Recall that national saving—the source of the supply of loanable funds—is composed of private saving and public saving. A change in the government budget deficit represents a change in public saving and, thereby, in the supply of loanable funds. Because the budget deficit does not influence the amount that households and firms want to borrow to finance investment at any given interest rate, it does not alter the demand for loanable funds.

Second, which way does the supply curve shift? When the government runs a budget deficit, public saving is negative, and this reduces national saving. In other words, when the government borrows to finance its budget deficit, it reduces the supply of loanable funds available to finance investment by households and firms. Thus, a budget deficit shifts the supply curve for loanable funds to the left from S_1 to S_2, as shown in figure 10.4.

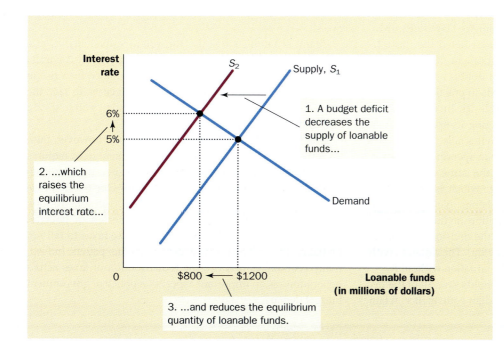

Figure 10.4

THE EFFECT OF A GOVERNMENT BUDGET DEFICIT. When the government spends more than it receives in tax revenue, the resulting budget deficit lowers national saving. The supply of loanable funds decreases, and the equilibrium interest rate rises. Thus, when the government borrows to finance its budget deficit, it crowds out households and firms who otherwise would borrow to finance investment. Here, when the supply shifts from S_1 to S_2, the equilibrium interest rate rises from 5% to 6%, and the equilibrium quantity of loanable funds saved and invested falls from $1200 million to $800 million.

crowding out
a decrease in investment that results from government borrowing

Third, we compare the old and new equilibria. In the figure, when the budget deficit reduces the supply of loanable funds, the interest rate rises from 5% to 6%. This higher interest rate then alters the behaviour of the households and firms that participate in the loan market. In particular, many demanders of loanable funds are discouraged by the higher interest rate. Fewer families buy new homes, and fewer firms choose to build new factories. The fall in investment because of government borrowing is called **crowding out** and is represented in the figure by the movement along the demand curve from a quantity of $1200 million in loanable funds to a quantity of $800 million. That is, when the government borrows to finance its budget deficit, it crowds out private borrowers who are trying to finance investment.

Thus, the most basic lesson about budget deficits follows directly from their effects on the supply of and demand for loanable funds—*when the government reduces national saving by running a budget deficit, the interest rate rises and investment falls.* Because investment is important for long-run economic growth, government budget deficits reduce the economy's growth rate.

FYI

Ricardian equivalence: An alternative view of government budget deficits

ALTHOUGH MOST ECONOMISTS accept the view that government budget deficits reduce national saving and crowd out investment, a small group questions this conclusion. They advance a theory called *Ricardian equivalence*. This view is named after the famous nineteenth-century economist David Ricardo, who first noted the theoretical argument (and who also raised doubts about whether it holds in practice).

The Ricardian argument runs as follows. Imagine that the government cuts taxes without changing its spending. As a result of the budget deficit, public saving falls. But if households save all of the tax cut, rather than spending some of it, private saving will rise by exactly the same amount that public saving falls. National saving, which is the sum of public and private saving, will not change. Neither will the supply of loanable funds nor the equilibrium interest rate. In fact, nothing will change (except for the division of national saving between public and private saving). The situation with the budget deficit is equivalent to the situation without it.

Why, you might ask, would households save all of the tax cut? According to the theory of Ricardian equivalence, when people see the government running a budget deficit, they understand that the government will need to raise their taxes in the future in order to pay off the debt that it is now accumulating. A tax cut and budget deficit do not reduce households' overall tax bill; they merely postpone it. In a sense, a tax cut financed by a budget deficit is more of a loan from the government than a gift. Because the policy does not make people any richer than they were, they should not use it to increase their spending. Instead, they should save the tax cut for the day when the loan comes due in the form of higher taxes.

Many economists dismiss Ricardian equivalence as idle speculation. Certainly, the large budget deficits in Australia since the early 1980s have not been accompanied by a rise in private saving, as the Ricardian theory suggests. In fact, the opposite is more nearly the case. As Australian public saving fell, so did Australian private saving.

The theory of Ricardian equivalence does, however, raise an intriguing question. If a rise in government debt requires higher taxes in the future, as surely it does, why aren't households saving in anticipation of these taxes? One possibility is that people are too short-sighted in their decisions to look ahead to the ramifications of current government policies. Another possibility is that they expect these taxes to fall not on themselves but on future generations of taxpayers. Indeed, many economists point to the redistribution of taxes across generations as an important aspect of a policy of government budget deficits.

CASE STUDY A COMPARISON OF GOVERNMENT DEBT AND DEFICITS IN AUSTRALIA AND THE UNITED STATES

Discussions regarding the Australian federal budget are often filled more with rhetoric than with reason. For example, when the Howard government brought down its 1997–98 budget, it was claimed that the government's reversal of the '$10.3 billion deficit black hole' inherited by the government into a $1.6 billion surplus was the 'first ever serious and sustainable attack on public debt by a federal government, which [had] inherited a legacy of endemic overspending, endless deficits and rising debt'. However, a look at the history of Australia's budget position tells a different story.

Figure 10.5 shows the debt of the federal government expressed as a percentage of Australian GDP. From the 1950s to the early 1980s, the debt–GDP ratio declined. Although the government did run budget deficits during some of these years, the deficits were sufficiently small that the size of the government's debt grew less rapidly than the overall economy. Because GDP is a rough measure of the government's ability to raise tax revenue, a declining debt–GDP ratio indicates the economy is, in some sense, living within its means. In contrast, when the budget deficits increased in the early 1980s, the government debt started rising more rapidly than the overall economy. As a result, the debt–GDP ratio started to rise. The increase in the debt–GDP ratio was short-lived, though. It rose from 1982 to 1986, but then fell sharply from 1986 to 1991 and then rose again until 1995. The highest level it reached in this period was around 26%.

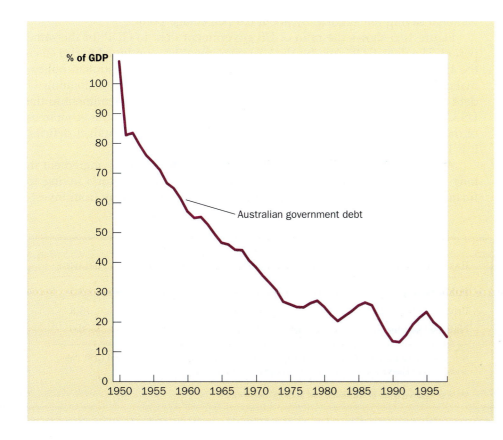

Figure 10.5

THE AUSTRALIAN GOVERNMENT DEBT. The debt of the federal government, expressed here as a percentage of GDP, was high after the large expenditures of World War II but has declined significantly until the 1980s. Since then it has fluctuated around 20% of GDP.

SOURCE: Reserve Bank of Australia.

'Our deficit-reduction plan is simple, but it will require a great deal of money.'

Table 10.1 shows the impact of this policy on various measures of saving. During the 1970s and early 1980s, the Australian government was running budget deficits. When the government started running budget surpluses, public saving as a percentage of GDP rose by 3.2 percentage points. At the same time, private saving rates also fell significantly, by 3.8 percentage points. National saving fell slightly, by about 0.6 percentage points.

Figure 10.6 shows the ratio of US government debt to GDP for the same period. The debt–GDP ratio for the US government has continued to rise since the 1970s, when, at its lowest levels, it reached levels that Australian policy-makers have considered dangerously high, around 25%. The ballooning of debt in the United States led to calls for a balanced budget amendment to the US Constitution. Although there are significant differences in the economies of the two countries and therefore in their abilities to finance budget deficits, it is important to keep Australia's debt position in perspective.

As we saw in the previous chapter, national saving is a key ingredient in long-run economic growth. By using some of the private sector's saving to finance the budget deficit, the government pulls resources away from invest-

Table 10.1

SAVING IN THE AUSTRALIAN ECONOMY

RATE OF:	SYMBOL	1971–82	1988–96	CHANGE
Public saving	$T - G$	–1.9	1.3	3.2
Private saving	$Y - T - C$	7.6	3.8	–3.8
National saving	$Y - C - G$	5.7	5.1	–0.6

Note: The saving rates are gross nominal amounts expressed as a percentage of nominal GDP. Public saving is calculated from federal government outlays and receipts.

SOURCE: Reserve Bank of Australia; and authors' calculations.

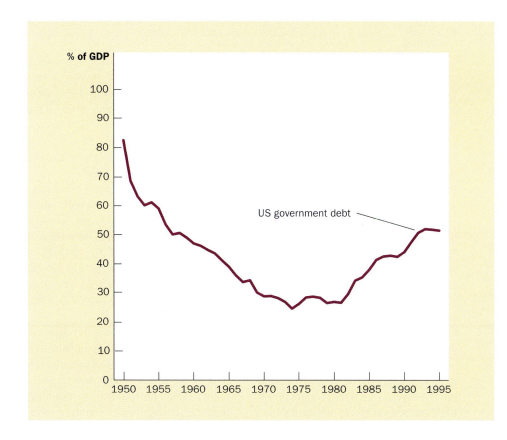

Figure 10.6

THE US GOVERNMENT DEBT. The debt of the US federal government, expressed here as a percentage of GDP, was high after the large expenditures of World War II but then declined throughout the 1950s and 1960s. It began rising again in the early 1980s when President Reagan's tax cuts were not accompanied by similar cuts in government spending.

SOURCE: US Department of the Treasury; US Department of Commerce.

ment in new capital and, thereby, depresses the living standards of future generations. Policymakers from both political parties accept this basic argument and view persistent budget deficits as an important policy problem. When John Howard became prime minister in 1996, deficit reduction was one of his major goals. By the end of the Coalition's first term in office, it had substantially reduced the size of the government budget deficit, producing a budget surplus in 1996–97.

Why, if there is such unanimity, have previous Australian governments run budget deficits? Part of the answer is that there is disagreement about how to eliminate the deficit. The Coalition has achieved the budget surplus by cutting back on expenditure on social services. Others would like to cut some taxes in order to stimulate private saving. They would balance the budget through deeper cuts in government spending than social welfare groups think is wise. In this way, disagreement over the details of deficit reduction, together with a general reluctance to make hard decisions, has allowed government budget deficits to persist.

Like most policy debates, the debate over the government budget deficit has many facets. We discuss more of these in the final chapter of this book. But the basic elements of this debate should already be clear. Whenever policymakers consider the government's budget deficit and its impact on the economy, foremost in their minds are saving, investment and interest rates.

QUICK QUIZ If more Australians adopted a 'live for today' approach to life, how would this affect saving, investment and the interest rate?

IN THE NEWS

Putting the budget deficit in perspective

POLITICIANS OFTEN REFER TO THE LATEST economic 'crisis' that they face, but in the following article, John Pitchford considers whether or not we really do have an economic crisis in the budget. John Pitchford is an emeritus professor of economics at the Australian National University.

Blackhole is Convenient 'Crisis'

BY JOHN PITCHFORD

Economic policy in the latter part of the 1980s involved the setting of very high interest rates and a program of cuts in government spending. We were told that the reason for this tight monetary and fiscal policy was to reduce the current account deficit.

This deficit had been declared our major macroeconomic problem. Attempts at its 'solution' dominated policy actions and, in the long run, were largely unsuccessful.

In the 1990s the approach was changed with the Reserve Bank now directing monetary policy at controlling inflation and promoting growth rather than at a current account target. Those who believe the current account is a problem now see its solution coming from greater public and private saving rather than higher interest rates. To that extent, we are now free of policy making by crisis.

However, the primacy presently being given to the Commonwealth budget deficit means we again have a declared crisis where any and every policy is to be justified by the supposed need to achieve this latest target. Government by crisis is appropriate when there is a crisis, but is not in the national interest unless it can be convincingly established that a crisis exists.

If one looks at the data and considers the significance of the budget deficit, the Commonwealth Government's fiscal situation does not suggest a state of crisis. First, both government spending and receipts are particularly sensitive to the level of activity in the economy. This is because spending on welfare and unemployment benefits rises in recessions and falls in periods of recovery and taxation receipts fall in recessions and rise with high growth.

Hence the budget deficit rises in recessions and falls during recoveries. Because the fall in unemployment has been slow following the 1990–92 downturn, the recession pattern has been particularly evident until the past two years.

Now, after several years of reasonable growth, data on Commonwealth outlays and receipts to the end of 1995 show the budget deficit is closing rapidly. If the economy were to achieve high growth rates through 1996 and 1997, there is every likelihood that these automatic responses would close the deficit.

The second piece of relevant data is Commonwealth government debt, which stood at 107 percent of gross domestic product in 1949–50, largely as a result of financing World War II. By 1979–80 it was down to 25 percent and in 1994–95 it was 23 percent. Policy making by crisis was not needed to achieve these long-run reductions.

In addition to checking the data, we need to ask what the appropriate size for government deficits and debts is. Situations in which responsible governments might borrow include financing defence during wars, financing economic development and ensuring equity among generations.

For instance, much of public investment yields returns which will substantially benefit future generations. It would be inequitable and impracticable to expect present generations to bear their full capital cost, particularly as future generations are likely to be richer.

On the other hand, there is the problem that government spending is electorally popular and taxes are unpopular, so biasing fiscal outcomes towards deficits that future generations would have to finance without enjoying the benefits of

CONCLUSION

'Neither a borrower nor a lender be,' Polonius advises his son in Shakespeare's *Hamlet*. If everyone followed this advice, this chapter would have been unnecessary.

PARLIAMENT HOUSE IN CANBERRA

the spending. For this and other reasons, it is most difficult to decide what is an appropriate level for deficits and debt.

One formal way of appraising fiscal situations, developed in the United States, is 'generational accounting', which asks whether future generations will bear a larger taxation burden than present generations, given current government programs. For the US, the answer seems to be that future generations will pay higher taxes, but calculations for Australia by John Ablett of the University of New South Wales suggest that it is present generations that are 'over-taxed' here.

Unfortunately, in its present state of development, generational accounting does not take account of critical issues such as how to choose an appropriate level of government investment or how to ensure that each generation pays the costs of the government services it consumes.

Of course, any deficit creates a crisis for those who advocate balanced budgets whatever the cost. The private-sector equivalent to this view would be to appraise a firm from a single item in its balance sheet, namely its level of borrowing—a procedure which would get most managers the sack.

Those who had the balanced budget view should note that there are worse things than government debt that we can bequeath to future generations. There are circumstances in which inadequate public infrastructure, a workforce with degraded skills or the social ills resulting from high rates of long-term unemployment could all be more costly to our heirs than inheriting public debt.

Another critical aspect of the Government Budget is the effect it is liable to have on current economic activity. It is probable that the confidence effects of expenditure cuts will be negative and that their net outcome will be contractionary.

This will mean that taxes will fall and so any given expenditure reduction will lead to a smaller reduction in the deficit. If the economy is likely to be growing strongly in any case, the expenditure cuts could help to curb excessive growth.

However, at present the signals for Australia's growth in the next year or so are mixed.

Moreover, the Reserve Bank's recent interest rate reduction suggests that it does not believe that excessive growth is likely. Indeed, lower interest rates may well be needed to offset the contractionary effect of expenditure cuts.

In short, there is little to support the view that the present budgetary situation is in crisis. Given this, there is no economic reason preventing the Government from arguing for expenditure cuts on their own merits. Also, it follows that if the economy turns out to be weak, it would be prudent to phase in the cuts so as not to exacerbate this weakness.

It is also to be hoped that Australian governments of either persuasion are now sufficiently responsible to appreciate the need to look at all aspects of their legacies to the future, not just the level of and change in public debt.

SOURCE: *Australian*, 20 August 1996, p. 13.

Few economists would agree with Polonius. In our economy, people borrow and lend often, and usually for good reason. You may borrow one day to start your own business or to buy a home. And people may lend to you in the hope that the interest you pay will allow them to enjoy a more prosperous retirement. The financial system has the job of coordinating all this borrowing and lending activity.

In many ways, financial markets are like other markets in the economy. The price of loanable funds—the interest rate—is governed by the forces of supply and demand, just as other prices in the economy are. And we can analyse shifts in supply or demand in financial markets as we do in other markets. One of the *Ten Principles of Economics* introduced in chapter 1 is that markets are usually a good way to organise economic activity. This principle applies to financial markets as well. When financial markets bring the supply of and demand for loanable funds into balance, they help allocate the economy's scarce resources to their most efficient uses.

In one way, however, financial markets are special. Financial markets, unlike most other markets, serve the important role of linking the present and the future. Those who supply loanable funds—savers—do so because they want to convert some of their current income into future purchasing power. Those who demand loanable funds—borrowers—do so because they want to invest today in order to have additional capital in the future to produce goods and services. Thus, well-functioning financial markets are important not only for current generations but also for future generations who will inherit many of the resulting benefits.

IN THE NEWS

The balanced budget amendment

IN RECENT YEARS, SOME MEMBERS OF the US Congress have advocated a constitutional amendment that would require the US federal government to balance its budget. President Clinton, however, has opposed the amendment. In the following opinion column, economist Robert Eisner presents the case against it. Although the arguments are written with the US constitutional amendment in mind, the general comments about the wisdom of a balanced budget for the entire country apply to the Australian economy as well.

Balanced Budget: Bad Economics

BY ROBERT EISNER

Along with two Nobel laureates, Robert Solow of MIT and James Tobin of Yale, I have been soliciting economists' endorsements of a statement opposing a balanced budget amendment to the Constitution. We have initial support from 35 distinguished members of the profession, including seven other Nobel laureates…

The problem is that the amendment would violate the principles of sound economics that many of us have been teaching for decades. Any good accountant—or informed investor—knows how difficult and arbitrary measures of 'balance', the difference between profit and loss, can be for a company. What is a current expense, how fast do you depreciate, what do you amortize, how do you price inventories, when do you put in special charges, how do you handle pension funds, what do you do about 'deferred' taxes? The issues are more complex—much more complex—for the federal government…

Consider the handling of portfolio transactions. When an individual buys a stock or bond he hardly classifies that as a current expenditure that may put him into 'deficit' or reduce his saving. By federal accounting it would. Thus, a few years ago, when the Treasury was financing the purchase of savings and loans' assets, as part of the S&L bailout, the deficit soared, fueling further, misinformed warnings that the deficit was destroying national saving and hence jeopardizing our future. Then, when the government sold off the old S&L portfolios, our 'deficit' miraculously came down.

Another problem: The federal government has no separate capital budget. If federal accounting were to be consistent with that of private business, it would include not current capital outlays but only depreciation charges on existing capital in its measure of surplus or deficit, the counterpart of a firm's profit-and-loss statement. But then how would we measure depreciation? How fast is our vast defense arsenal becoming obsolete? With the end of the Cold War, should we take a special charge and write off much

Summary

- The Australian financial system is made up of many types of financial institutions, such as the bond market, the stock market, banks and managed funds. All these institutions act to direct the resources of households who want to save some of their income into the hands of households and firms who want to borrow.

- National income accounting identities reveal some important relationships among macroeconomic variables. In particular, for a closed economy, national saving must equal investment. Financial institutions are the mechanism through which the economy matches one person's saving with another person's investment.

- The interest rate is determined by the supply of and demand for loanable funds. The supply of loanable funds comes from households who want to save some of their income and lend it out. The demand for loanable funds comes from households and firms who want to borrow for investment. To analyse how any policy or event affects the interest rate, one must consider how it affects the supply of and demand for loanable funds.

- National saving equals private saving plus public saving. A government budget deficit represents negative public saving and, therefore, reduces national saving and the supply of loanable funds available to finance investment. When a government budget deficit crowds out investment, it reduces the growth of productivity and GDP.

---

of it? What also should be done about the increasing amounts of investment in intangible capital, in computer software, in research and development, in education and training, and in health?

These are just a few of the oddities of current federal accounting. One may wonder if the congressional supporters of a constitutional amendment intend to order that all accounting rules that would determine 'balance' be kept in place. Would we set up commissions to revise them from time to time? Or would we leave it to the courts to determine which rules fit the 'intent' of the amendment?...

As proposed in the last Congress, the amendment would allow federal borrowing only if approved by three-fifths majorities of all of the members, a very difficult hurdle. Many say, 'I balance my checkbook, and state and local governments have balanced budget provisions in their constitutions, why can't the federal government be the same? Why must it borrow?' In fact, almost all of us borrow—to finance our homes, to send our children to college, and to buy cars and other durable goods. Businesses borrow—look at the corporate bond market. State and local governments generally have separate capital budgets; the constraints of balance apply only to current or operating budgets. They borrow for all kinds of capital investment. The balanced budget amendment would put only our federal government under that strict limitation to borrowing.

Finally, the amendment is ludicrous —perhaps fortunately—in its pretense of enforceability. In one section it declares, 'Prior to each fiscal year, the President shall transmit to the Congress a proposed budget for the United States Government for that fiscal year, in which total outlays do not exceed total receipts.' What would stop the president from simply estimating prospective receipts high enough to equal outlays? Given the general uncertainty and inaccuracy of such projections, this could be done with reasonable honesty.

Section 1 indeed declares, 'Total outlays for any fiscal year shall not exceed total receipts for that year…'. But who can say what will actually happen to outlays or receipts? Suppose more people get sick and use more Medicare or Medicaid. Suppose there is a fall in income and tax revenues decline. This section might as well assert that the waves of the Atlantic Ocean shall not cross a certain line. What if they do? Do we put the president or Congress in jail?

On the matter of evasion, I should probably welcome passage of the amendment and set up a consulting firm to make millions by advising how to get around it. One simple technique would be the sale of government assets, which under federal accounting would count as offsets to outlays. We could begin with our national parks, federal land in general, our oil reserves and all parts of the federally owned transportation infrastructure…We could then go on to public buildings, including the Capitol and the White House, perhaps renting them back for current use…Of course, eventually we would run out of public assets to sell. But by then perhaps, as with Prohibition, there would be sufficient awareness of the folly of it all for the amendment to be repealed.

SOURCE: *Wall Street Journal*, 22 January 1997, p. A14.

Key concepts

financial system, p. 196
financial markets, p. 196
bond (security), p. 197
share, p. 197
financial intermediaries, p. 198
managed fund, p. 200
national saving (saving), p. 202
private saving, p. 203
public saving, p. 203
budget surplus, p. 203
budget deficit, p. 203
market for loanable funds, p. 204
crowding out, p. 210

Questions for review

1. What is the role of the financial system? Name and describe two markets that are part of the financial system in our economy. Name and describe two financial intermediaries.

2. What is national saving? What is private saving? What is public saving? How are these three variables related?

3. What is investment? How is it related to national saving?

4. Describe a change in the tax laws that might increase private saving. If this policy were implemented, how would it affect the market for loanable funds?

5. What is a government budget deficit? How does it affect interest rates, investment and economic growth?

Problems and applications

1. For each of the following pairs, which bond would you expect to pay a higher interest rate? Explain.
    a. a bond of the Australian government or a bond of an Eastern European government
    b. a bond that repays the principal in the year 2005 or a bond that repays the principal in the year 2025
    c. a bond from Coca-Cola or a bond from a software company you run in your garage
    d. a bond issued by the federal government or a bond issued to finance part of the 2000 Olympics in Sydney.

2. The 'yield curve' is a graph of the interest rates on bonds of different terms, with the term shown on the horizontal axis and the interest rate shown on the vertical axis.
    a. Based on the discussion in the chapter, would you expect the yield curve to be upward-sloping or downward-sloping?
    b. Using the business section of a recent newspaper, graph the yield curve for Australian government bonds. Does the curve have the slope you expected?

3. A US president once said, 'There is no moral difference between gambling at cards or in lotteries or on the race track and gambling in the stock market.' What social purpose do you think is served by the existence of the stock market?

4. Declines in share prices are sometimes viewed as harbingers of future declines in real GDP. Why do you suppose that might be true?

5. The chapter explains that managed funds allow people with small amounts of money to buy a diverse portfolio of shares and bonds. What is the advantage of owning a diverse portfolio rather than holding shares or bonds from a single company?

6. Many workers hold large amounts of shares issued by the firms at which they work. Why do you suppose companies encourage this behaviour? Why might people *not* want to hold shares in the company where they work?

7. Your room-mate says that he buys shares only in companies that everyone believes will experience big increases in profits in the future. How do you suppose the price–earnings ratio of these companies compares with the price–earnings ratio of other companies? What

might be the disadvantage of buying shares in these companies?

8. Explain the difference between saving and investment as defined by a macroeconomist. Which of the following situations represent investment? saving? Explain.
   a. Your family takes out a mortgage and buys a new house.
   b. You use your $200 paycheque to buy shares in Boral.
   c. Your roommate earns $100 and deposits it in her account at a bank.
   d. You borrow $1000 from a bank to buy a car to use in your pizza delivery business.

9. Suppose that BHP is considering building a new steel processing plant.
   a. Assuming that BHP needs to borrow money in the bond market, why would an increase in interest rates affect BHP's decision about whether to build the factory?
   b. If BHP has enough of its own funds to finance the new factory without borrowing, would an increase in interest rates still affect BHP's decision about whether to build the factory? Explain.

10. Suppose the government borrows $20 million more next year than this year.
    a. Use a supply-and-demand diagram to analyse this policy. Does the interest rate rise or fall?
    b. What happens to investment? to private saving? to public saving? to national saving? Compare the size of the changes with the $20 million of extra government borrowing.
    c. How does the elasticity of supply of loanable funds affect the size of these changes? (*Hint:* See chapter 5 to review the definition of elasticity.)
    d. How does the elasticity of demand for loanable funds affect the size of these changes?
    e. Suppose households believe that greater government borrowing today implies higher taxes to pay off the government debt in the future. What does this belief do to private saving and the supply of loanable funds today? Does it increase or decrease the effects you discussed in parts (a) and (b)?

11. Over the past 10 years, new computer technology has enabled firms to reduce substantially the amount of inventories they hold for each dollar of sales. Illustrate the effect of this change on the market for loanable funds. (*Hint:* Expenditure on inventories is a type of investment.) What do you think has been the effect on investment in factories and equipment?

12. 'Some economists worry that the aging populations of industrial countries are going to start running down their savings just when the investment appetite of emerging economies is growing' (*Economist*, 6 May 1995). Illustrate the effect of these phenomena on the world market for loanable funds.

13. This chapter explains that investment can be increased both by reducing taxes on private saving and by reducing the government budget deficit.
    a. Why is it difficult to implement both of these policies at the same time?
    b. What would you need to know about private saving in order to judge which of these two policies would be a more effective way to raise investment?

11

THE NATURAL RATE OF UNEMPLOYMENT

IN THIS CHAPTER YOU WILL

Learn about the data used to measure the level of unemployment

Consider how unemployment can result from minimum-wage laws

See how unemployment can arise from union wage bargaining and efficiency wages

Consider how unemployment arises from the process of job search

Losing a job can be the most distressing economic event in a person's life. Most people rely on their labour earnings to maintain their standard of living, and many people get from their work not only income but also a sense of personal accomplishment. A job loss means a lower living standard in the present, anxiety about the future and reduced self-esteem. It is not surprising, therefore, that politicians, campaigning for office, often speak about how their proposed policies will help create jobs.

In the last two chapters, we have seen some of the forces that determine the level and growth of a country's standard of living. A country that saves and invests a high fraction of its income, for instance, enjoys more rapid growth in its capital stock and its GDP than a similar country that saves and invests less. An even more obvious determinant of a country's standard of living is the amount of unemployment it typically experiences. People who would like to work but cannot find a job are not contributing to the economy's production of goods and services. Although some degree of unemployment is inevitable in a complex economy with thousands of firms and millions of workers, the amount of unemployment varies substantially over time and across countries. When a country keeps its workers as fully employed as possible, it achieves a higher level of GDP than it would if it left many of its workers standing idle.

This chapter begins our study of unemployment. The problem of unemployment is usefully divided into two categories—the long-run problem and the short-run problem. The economy's *natural rate of unemployment* refers to the amount of unemployment that the economy normally experiences. *Cyclical unemployment* refers to the year-to-year fluctuations in unemployment around its natural rate, and it is closely associated with the short-run ups and downs of economic activity. Cyclical unemployment has its own explanation, which we defer until we study short-run economic fluctuations later in this book. In this chapter we discuss the determinants of an economy's natural rate of unemployment. As we will see, the designation *natural* does not in any way imply that this rate of unemployment is desirable or inevitable. It merely means that this unemployment does not go away on its own, even in the long run.

We begin the chapter by looking at some of the relevant facts that describe unemployment. In particular, we examine three questions: How does the government measure the economy's rate of unemployment? What problems arise in interpreting the unemployment data? How long are the unemployed typically without work?

We then turn to the reasons that economies always experience some unemployment and the ways in which policymakers can help the unemployed. We discuss four potential explanations for the economy's natural rate of unemployment —minimum-wage laws, unions, efficiency wages and job search. As we will see, long-run unemployment does not arise from a single problem that has a single solution. Instead, it reflects a variety of related problems. As a result, there is no easy way for policymakers to reduce the economy's natural rate of unemployment and, at the same time, to alleviate the hardships experienced by the unemployed.

IDENTIFYING UNEMPLOYMENT

We begin this chapter by examining more precisely what the term *unemployment* means. We consider how the government measures unemployment, what problems arise in interpreting the unemployment data, and how long the typical spell of unemployment lasts.

HOW IS UNEMPLOYMENT MEASURED?

Measuring unemployment is the job of the Australian Bureau of Statistics (ABS). Every month the ABS produces data on unemployment and on other aspects of the labour market, such as types of employment, length of the average working week and the duration of unemployment. These data come from a regular survey of 0.6% of Australian households, called the Labour Force Survey. Other data come from the Department of Social Security which keeps information on the number of people receiving unemployment benefits.

Based on the answers to survey questions, the ABS places each adult (aged 15 years and older) in each surveyed household into one of three categories:

- employed
- unemployed
- not in the labour force.

A person is considered employed if he or she spent at least 1 hour of the previous week working at a paid job (including self-employment) or family business. A person is unemployed if he or she is on temporary layoff, is looking for a job, or is waiting to start a new job. A person who fits neither of the first two categories, such as a full-time student, homemaker, or retiree, is not in the labour force. Figure 11.1 shows this breakdown for 1998.

Once the ABS has placed all the individuals covered by the survey in a category, it calculates various statistics to summarise the state of the labour market. The ABS defines the **labour force** as the sum of the employed and the unemployed:

$$\text{Labour force} = \text{Number of employed} + \text{Number of unemployed}$$

labour force
the total number of workers, including both the employed and the unemployed

The ABS defines the **unemployment rate** as the percentage of the labour force that is unemployed:

$$\text{Unemployment rate} = \frac{\text{Number of unemployed}}{\text{Labour force}} \times 100$$

unemployment rate
the percentage of the labour force that is unemployed

The ABS calculates unemployment rates for the entire adult population and for more narrow groups—men, women, youth and so on.

The ABS uses the same survey to produce data on labour-force participation. The **labour-force participation rate** measures the percentage of the total adult population of Australia that is in the labour force:

$$\text{Labour-force participation rate} = \frac{\text{Labour force}}{\text{Adult population}} \times 100$$

labour-force participation rate
the percentage of the adult population that is in the labour force

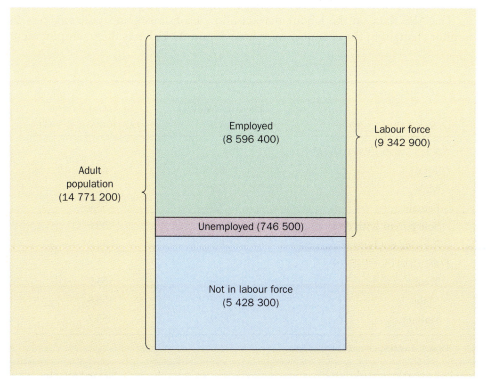

Figure 11.1

THE BREAKDOWN OF THE POPULATION IN 1998. The Australian Bureau of Statistics divides the adult population into three categories: employed, unemployed, and not in the labour force.

SOURCE: Based on statistical data from the Australian Bureau of Statistics.

This statistic tells us the fraction of the population that has chosen to participate in the labour market. The labour-force participation rate, like the unemployment rate, is calculated both for the entire adult population and for more narrow groups.

To see how these data are calculated, consider the figures for 1998. In that year, about 8.6 million people were employed, and about 746 000 people were unemployed. The labour force was:

$$\text{Labour force} = 8.6 + 0.74 = 9.34 \text{ million}$$

The unemployment rate was:

$$\text{Unemployment rate} = (0.74/9.34) \times 100 = 8.0\%$$

Because the adult population was 14.7 million, the labour-force participation rate was:

$$\text{Labour-force participation rate} = (9.3/14.7) \times 100 = 63\%$$

Hence, in 1998, a little less than two-thirds of the Australian adult population were participating in the labour market, and 8.0% of those labour-market participants were unemployed.

Table 11.1 shows the statistics on unemployment and labour-force participation for various groups within the Australian population. Three comparisons are most apparent. First, women have lower rates of labour-force participation than men, but once in the labour force, women have similar rates of unemployment. Second, migrants to Australia have both higher unemployment rates and lower participation rates than the overall population. Third, teenagers have lower rates of labour-force participation and much higher rates of unemployment than the overall population. More generally, these data show that labour-market experiences vary widely among groups within the economy.

The ABS data on the labour market allow economists and policymakers to monitor changes in the economy over time. Figure 11.2 shows the unemployment

Table 11.1

THE LABOUR-MARKET EXPERIENCES OF VARIOUS DEMOGRAPHIC GROUPS. This table shows the unemployment rate and the labour-force participation rate of various groups in the population for 1998.

DEMOGRAPHIC GROUP	UNEMPLOYMENT RATE	LABOUR-FORCE PARTICIPATION RATE
ADULTS (AGED 15 AND OVER)		
Total	8.0%	63.3%
Male	8.2	72.9
Female	7.7	53.9
Sole parent with dependants	15.7	55.6
Persons not born in Australia	9.5	59.2
TEENAGERS (AGED 15–19)		
Total	18.9	55.7
Male	19.9	55.8
Female	17.9	55.7

SOURCE: Australian Bureau of Statistics.

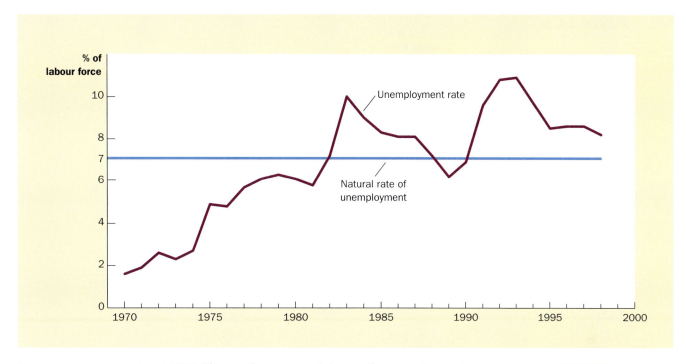

UNEMPLOYMENT RATE SINCE 1970. This graph uses annual data on the unemployment rate to show the fraction of the labour force without a job.

Figure 11.2

SOURCE: Based on statistical data from the Australian Bureau of Statistics.

rate in Australia since 1970. The figure shows that the economy always has some unemployment and that the amount changes from year to year. The normal rate of unemployment around which the unemployment rate fluctuates is called the **natural rate of unemployment**, and the deviation of unemployment from its natural rate is called **cyclical unemployment**. In the figure, the natural rate is shown as a horizontal line at 7%, which is a rough estimate of the natural rate for the Australian economy during this period. Later in this book, we discuss short-run economic fluctuations, including the year-to-year fluctuations in unemployment around its natural rate. In the rest of this chapter, however, we ignore the short-run fluctuations and examine why unemployment is a chronic problem for market economies.

natural rate of unemployment
unemployment accounted for by structural factors around which the actual unemployment rate fluctuates

cyclical unemployment
the deviation of unemployment from its natural rate

CASE STUDY   LABOUR-FORCE PARTICIPATION OF MEN AND WOMEN IN THE AUSTRALIAN ECONOMY

Women's role in Australian society has changed dramatically over the past century. Social commentators have pointed to many causes for this change. In part, it is attributable to new technologies, such as the washing machine, clothes dryer, refrigerator, freezer and dishwasher, which have reduced the amount of time required to complete routine household tasks. In part, it is attributable to improved birth control, which has reduced the number of

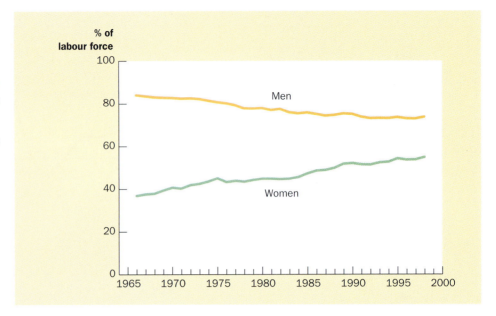

Figure 11.3

LABOUR-FORCE PARTICIPATION RATES FOR MEN AND WOMEN SINCE 1966. Over the past several decades, women have entered the labour force and men have left it.

SOURCE: Based on statistical data from the Australian Bureau of Statistics.

children born to the typical family. And, of course, the change in women's role is also partly attributable to changing political and social attitudes. Together, these developments have had a profound impact on society in general and on the economy in particular.

Nowhere is that impact more obvious than in data on labour-force participation. Just after World War II, men and women had very different roles in society. Only around 30% of women were working or looking for work, in contrast to over 85% of men. Figure 11.3 shows the labour-force participation rates of men and women in Australia since 1966. Over the past several decades, the difference between the participation rates of men and women has gradually diminished, as growing numbers of women have entered the labour force and some men have left it. Data for 1998 show that 54% of women were in the labour force, in contrast to 73% of men. As measured by labour-force participation, men and women are now playing a more equal role in the economy.

More women are working now than ever before.

The increase in women's labour-force participation is easy to understand, but the fall in men's may seem puzzling. There are several reasons for this decline. First, young men now stay in school longer than their fathers and grandfathers did. Second, older men now retire earlier and live longer. Third, with more women employed, more fathers now stay at home to raise their children. Full-time students, retirees, and stay-at-home fathers are all counted as out of the labour force. Finally, there is much concern that technological progress and a lack of opportunities and incentives for learning new skills has contributed to the unemployment of older men.

IS UNEMPLOYMENT MEASURED CORRECTLY?

Measuring the amount of unemployment in the economy might seem straightforward. In fact, it is not. Although it is easy to distinguish between a person with a full-time job and a person who is not working at all, it is much harder to distinguish between a person who is unemployed and a person who is not in the labour force.

Movements into and out of the labour force are, in fact, very common. More than one-third of the unemployed are recent entrants into the labour force. These entrants include young workers looking for their first jobs, such as recent university graduates. They also include, in greater numbers, older workers who had previously left the labour force but have now returned to look for work. Moreover, not all unemployment ends with the job seeker finding a job. Almost half of all spells of unemployment end when the unemployed person leaves the labour force.

Because people move into and out of the labour force so often, statistics on unemployment are difficult to interpret. On the one hand, some of those who report being unemployed may not, in fact, be trying hard to find a job. They may be calling themselves unemployed in order to qualify for one of the government programs that provide financial assistance for the unemployed. It would be more realistic to view some of these individuals as out of the labour force. On the other hand, some of those who report being out of the labour force may, in fact, want to work. These individuals may have tried to find a job but have given up after an unsuccessful search. Such individuals, called **discouraged workers**, do not show up in unemployment statistics, even though they are truly workers without jobs.

discouraged workers
individuals who would like to work but have given up looking for a job

There is no easy way to fix the unemployment rate as reported by the ABS to make it a more reliable indicator of conditions in the labour market. In the end, it is best to view the reported unemployment rate as a useful but imperfect measure of joblessness.

HOW LONG ARE THE UNEMPLOYED WITHOUT WORK?

In judging how serious the problem of unemployment is, one question to consider is whether unemployment is typically a short-term or long-term condition. If unemployment is short term, one might conclude that it is not a big problem. Workers may require a few weeks between jobs to find the openings that best suit their skills and tastes. Yet if unemployment is long term, one might conclude that it is a serious problem. Workers unemployed for many months are more likely to suffer economic and psychological hardship.

Because the duration of unemployment can affect our view about how big a problem unemployment is, economists have devoted much energy to studying data on the duration of unemployment spells. In this work, they have uncovered a result that is important, subtle and seemingly contradictory—*most spells of unemployment are short, and most unemployment observed at any given time is long term.*

To see how this statement can be true, consider an example. Suppose that you visited an unemployment office every week for a year to survey the unemployed. Each week you find that there are four unemployed workers. Three of these workers are the same individuals for the whole year, whereas the fourth person changes every week. Based on this experience, would you say that unemployment is typically short term or long term?

Some simple calculations help answer this question. In this example, you meet a total of 55 unemployed people—52 of them are unemployed for 1 week, and 3 are unemployed for the full year. Thus, 52/55, or 95%, of unemployment spells end in 1 week. That is, most spells of unemployment are short. Yet consider the total amount of unemployment. The 3 people unemployed for 1 year (52 weeks) make up a total of 156 weeks of unemployment. Together with the 52 people unemployed for 1 week, this makes 208 weeks of unemployment. In this example, 156/208, or 75%, of unemployment is attributable to those individuals who are unemployed for a full year. Thus, most unemployment observed at any given time is long term.

This subtle conclusion implies that economists and policymakers must be careful when interpreting data on unemployment and when designing policies to help the unemployed. Most people who become unemployed will soon find jobs. Yet most of the economy's unemployment problem is attributable to the relatively few workers who are jobless for long periods of time.

WHY IS THERE UNEMPLOYMENT?

We have discussed how the government measures the amount of unemployment, the problems that arise in interpreting unemployment statistics, and the findings of labour economists on the duration of unemployment. You should now have a good idea about what unemployment is.

This discussion, however, has not explained why economies experience unemployment. In most markets in the economy, prices adjust to bring quantity supplied and quantity demanded into balance. In an ideal labour market, wages would adjust to balance the quantity of labour supplied and the quantity of labour demanded. This adjustment of wages would ensure that all workers are always fully employed.

Of course, reality does not resemble this ideal. There are always some workers without jobs, even when the overall economy is doing well. In other words, the unemployment rate never falls to zero; instead, it fluctuates around the natural rate of unemployment. To understand this natural rate, we now examine four reasons that actual labour markets depart from the ideal of full employment—minimum-wage laws, unions, efficiency wages and job search.

QUICK QUIZ How is the unemployment rate measured? How might the unemployment rate overstate the amount of joblessness? How might it understate it?

MINIMUM-WAGE LAWS

We begin by reviewing how unemployment arises from minimum-wage laws—a topic we first analysed in chapter 6. Although minimum wages are not the predominant reason for unemployment in our economy, they may have an important effect on certain groups with particularly high unemployment rates. Moreover, the analysis of minimum wages is a natural place to start because, as we will see, it can be used to understand some of the more common reasons for unemployment.

Figure 11.4 reviews the basic economics of a minimum wage. When a minimum-wage law forces the wage to remain above the level that balances supply and demand, it raises the quantity of labour supplied and reduces the quantity of labour demanded compared with the equilibrium level. There is a surplus of labour. Because there are more workers willing to work than there are jobs, some workers are unemployed.

Because we discussed minimum-wage laws extensively in chapter 6, we will not discuss them further here. It is, however, important to note why minimum-wage laws are *not* a predominant reason for unemployment—most workers in the economy earn above-award wages. Minimum-wage laws are binding most often for the least skilled and least experienced members of the labour force. It is only among these workers that minimum-wage laws explain the existence of unemployment.

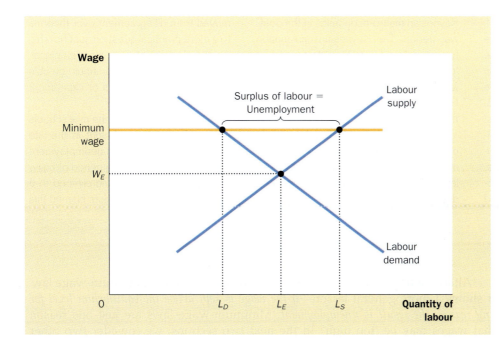

Figure 11.4

UNEMPLOYMENT FROM A WAGE ABOVE THE EQUILIBRIUM LEVEL. In this labour market, the wage at which supply and demand balance is W_E. At this equilibrium wage, the quantity of labour supplied and the quantity of labour demanded both equal L_E. In contrast, if the wage is forced to remain above the equilibrium level, perhaps because of a minimum-wage law, the quantity of labour supplied rises to L_S, and the quantity of labour demanded falls to L_D. The resulting excess supply of labour, $L_S - L_D$, represents unemployment.

IN THE NEWS

Dealing with structural unemployment

ECONOMISTS RECOGNISE THAT STRUCTURAL unemployment is a serious problem in Australia. The key question is how much choice do policymakers have in influencing the level of unemployment? The following article summarises the debate.

Five Find Workable Way to Bridge Divide

BY ROSS GITTINS

In the five economists' plan for lower unemployment we see the resolution of a debate which has for many years divided economists into rival camps: what exactly is the cause of unemployment?

What various interest groups have missed in their knee-jerk reaction to the economists' plan is that it's a golden compromise, an attempt to break the deadlock by finding the middle ground. It's a compromise on many levels: between the rival explanations of unemployment, between neo-classical economists and Keynesian economists, between micro-economics and macro-economics, between efficiency and equity, and between Liberal and Labor policy references.

The oldest school of thought among economists is that unemployment is caused by wage rates that are too high. If not all the labour people are seeking to supply is being bought by firms, the solution is obvious: lower the price being charged for the labour until supply and demand balance.

In this respect, employers are just like any consumer: how much we decide to buy of some item is influenced by the price we're being asked to pay compared with the value we expect to derive. Businesses use labour and capital equipment to produce the goods or services they sell. They need a fair bit of both but, at the margin, they choose between a bit more capital and a bit less labour or vice versa.

When the cost of labour is low relative to the cost of capital, they'll substitute labour for capital; when the cost of labour is high relative to capital, they'll do the reverse. This theory is simple neo-classical micro-economics, which is why it's known as the 'classical' explanation for unemployment.

The rival theory came with the rise of Keynesian macro-economics in the post-war period. The Keynesian explanation for unemployment is that it's caused by 'deficient demand'. Businesses' demand for labour is 'derived demand'—derived from the demand for the products they're selling.

When the demand for a business's products is strong, it needs to produce more and to do so it has to hire more labour. But when the demand is weak, it doesn't hire more workers and may actually put some off. So if we have workers who are unemployed, the reason must be that the community's demand for goods and services is deficient. And the solution is for the government to stimulate demand by increasing its spending or cutting taxes (fiscal policy), or by cutting interest rates (monetary policy).

Professor John Quiggin of James Cook University in Townsville further elucidated the differences between the classical and Keynesian explanations in a recent article. Neo-classical economists thought mostly in terms of prices, he said, whereas Keynesian economists thought mostly in terms of quantities.

'A more precise way of putting things is that economists who think mostly about prices tend to believe that the elasticities (sensitivity) of demand and supply are large, so that small reductions in the price of a good will lead to large increases in the quantity demanded,' he said.

'Economists who focus on quantities tend to believe that elasticities are low and that adjustment processes are slow and prone to breakdown.' Ah. Do you see what's happened here? We've moved from disagreement over theories to a more practical question: just how big are the elasticities? This is an 'empirical' question—a question we should be able to answer by observation or experiment with a real live economy.

The debate between the rival schools of thought was at its height in the late 70s, when it was clear unemployment had broken out of its long period of being 2 per cent or less and had climbed to 6 per cent. The neo-classicists blamed this

Although figure 11.4 was drawn to show the effects of a minimum-wage law, it shows a more general lesson—*if the wage is kept above the equilibrium level for any reason, the result is unemployment*. Minimum-wage laws are just one reason that wages may be 'too high'. In the next two sections, we consider two other

on the huge leap in the level of real wages that occurred in the early Whitlam years, whereas the Keynesians blamed it on the recession of 1974–75 and the weak growth that followed.

It was the same story in the early 1980s, when the unemployment rate jumped from 6 per cent to 10. The Keynesians blamed this on the severe recession of 1982–83; the neo-classicists pointed out that the recession had been preceded by another blowout in real wages. But then, in the rest of the 80s, we had an episode that went in the opposite direction. With the co-operation of the unions, the Hawke Government used the Accord to achieve a fall in real wages, but accompanied this by fairly easy fiscal and monetary policies.

The economy grew strongly and the unemployment rate fell quite rapidly, ultimately getting back down to 6 per cent by the end of the decade. These three unintended experiments gave economists enough data to do a thorough study of all the factors that had been at work in the economy over that long period and draw some reasonably firm conclusions about the size of elasticities at the macro level.

In 1988, two economists at the Reserve Bank, Bill Russell and Warren Tease, published what became a seminal study, effectively resolving the long-running debate over the causes of unemployment. They found that neither theory captured all the truth, but both captured part of it. The truth—surprise, surprise—was in the middle. Specifically, they estimated that a 1 per cent rise in output (aggregate demand) during a quarter led to a 0.65 per cent rise in employment over the following 18 months or so, while a 1 per cent fall in real labour costs per unit of production led to a 0.6 per cent rise in employment over the same period.

As Professor Quiggin commented recently, 'in any economic system, prices and quantities are determined jointly, so it is wrong to focus exclusively on one or the other'. This spirit of compromise—or, as economists would put it, 'eclecticism'—informs the five economists' plans for striking a new blow against unemployment, which, at 8 per cent, seems unlikely to go much lower unless we try something different.

More specifically, it's an attempt to apply the findings of another, much more recent study by the Reserve Bank economists, Guy Debelle and James Vickery. They found that slower growth in wages of 2 per cent for a year could lead to a lasting reduction in the unemployment rate of about 1 percentage point.

In a sense, what the five economists want to do is repeat the successful Accord experiment of the 80s. Their problem, of course, is that the Accord no longer exists and the centralised wage-fixing system of that time has been replaced by one of uncontrolled bargaining at the enterprise level. The one part of the present wage-fixing system that remains within the Government's ability to influence directly is the safety net of award wage rates, which underpins enterprise bargaining.

As you know, the level of award wages is raised each year by the Industrial Relations Commission—usually by $12 or $14 a week. But the only workers affected by this are the minority who haven't benefited from a higher increase achieved through enterprise bargaining or informal arrangements. This minority tends to be those workers who are less skilled and weakly unionised.

The economists' plan involves holding award wages steady for four years which, they calculate, would cause real average wages to rise over the period by 3 to 4 percentage points less than otherwise. And this, according to Debelle and Vickery's elasticities, would cause the unemployment rate to be 1.5 to 2 percentage points lower than otherwise.

Three points to note. First, low-income workers who suffered from the absence of award-wage rises would be protected by being given special, annually increasing tax credits. (This is a novel feature of the proposal. It acknowledges the equity implications of the plan. And it echoes the wage/tax trade-offs of the Accord era while fitting well with the Government's tax package.) Second, the plan operates not at the neo-classical, micro level but at the Keynesian, macro level.

Third, the plan works on both prices and quantities. Because the average price of labour would rise by less, inflation would rise by less. And this means the managers of the economy could allow aggregate demand to grow faster. The stimulus would come partly from the cost of the tax credits to the Budget and partly from the Reserve Bank's ability to lower interest rates.

From the five economists' perspective, their plan offers a golden compromise.

SOURCE: *Sydney Morning Herald*, 7 November 1998, p. 62.

reasons that wages may be kept above the equilibrium level—unions and efficiency wages. The basic economics of unemployment in these cases is the same as that shown in figure 11.4, but these explanations of unemployment can apply to many more of the economy's workers.

> **QUICK QUIZ** Draw the supply curve and the demand curve for a labour market in which the wage is fixed above the equilibrium level. Show the quantity of labour supplied, the quantity demanded and the amount of unemployment.

UNIONS AND COLLECTIVE BARGAINING

In some industries, labour markets do not operate according to the simple principles of supply and demand. In industries such as transport, teaching and mining, wages are determined by negotiations between unions and employers. A **union** is a type of cartel. Like any cartel, a union is a group of sellers acting together in the hope of exerting their joint market power. Many workers in the economy discuss their wages, benefits and working conditions with their employers as individuals. In contrast, workers in a union do so as a group. The process by which unions and firms agree on the terms of employment is called **collective bargaining**.

The role of unions has been the source of considerable debate in Australia. Every year it seems that workers and employers in another industry, whether it be air transport, meat processing or the waterfront, are in a dispute. Unionisation was partly a response to very poor working conditions in those industries. There was a time that being a member of a union was seen as very important to achieving better work conditions. Recently, however, economic changes have altered this pattern. As depicted in table 11.2, trade union membership rates are on the decline in Australia.

union
a worker association that bargains with employers over wages and working conditions

collective bargaining
the process by which unions and firms agree on the terms of employment

THE ECONOMICS OF UNIONS

When a union bargains with a firm, it asks for higher wages, better benefits and better working conditions than the firm would offer in the absence of a union. If the union and the firm do not reach agreement, the union can organise a withdrawal of labour from the firm, called a **strike**. Because a strike reduces

strike
the organised withdrawal of labour from a firm by a union

Table 11.2

UNIONISATION RATE—UNION MEMBERS AS A PERCENTAGE OF EMPLOYEES

YEAR	UNIONISATION RATE
1976	53%
1982	54
1986	50
1990	46
1994	38
1996	35

SOURCE: Anne Hawke and Mark Wooden, 'The changing face of Australian industrial relations', *Economic Record*, vol. 74, no. 224, 1998, pp. 74–88.

production, sales and profit, a firm facing a strike threat is likely to agree to pay higher wages than it otherwise would.

When a union raises the wage above the equilibrium level, it raises the quantity of labour supplied and may reduce the quantity of labour demanded, resulting in unemployment. Those workers who remain employed are better off, but those who were previously employed and are now unemployed at the higher wage are worse off. Indeed, unions are often thought to cause conflict between different groups of workers—between the *insiders* who benefit from high union wages and the *outsiders* who do not get the union jobs.

The outsiders can respond to their status in one of two ways. Some of them remain unemployed and wait for the chance to become insiders and earn the high union wage. Others take jobs in firms that are not unionised. Thus, when unions raise wages in one part of the economy, the supply of labour increases in other parts of the economy. This increase in labour supply, in turn, reduces wages in industries that are not unionised. In other words, workers in unions reap the benefit of collective bargaining, whereas workers not in unions bear some of the cost.

The end result is that the existence of unions can cause wages to be higher and, hence, some workers to be unemployed. However, the ability of unions to exert this control depends on their specific goals. Many unions are explicitly concerned about unemployment levels and are willing to negotiate arrangements that promote existing employment levels. During the 1980s, these negotiations were assisted by the Hawke Labor government which offered workers tax cuts in order to preserve after-tax real incomes.

ARE UNIONS GOOD OR BAD FOR THE ECONOMY?

Economists disagree about whether unions are good or bad for the economy as a whole. Let's consider both sides of the debate.

Critics argue that unions are merely a type of cartel. When unions raise wages above the level that would prevail in competitive markets, they reduce the quantity of labour demanded, cause some workers to be unemployed, and reduce the wages in the rest of the economy. The resulting allocation of labour is, critics argue, both inefficient and inequitable. It is inefficient because high union wages reduce employment in unionised firms below the efficient, competitive level. It is inequitable because some workers benefit at the expense of other workers.

Advocates of unions contend that unions are a necessary antidote to the market power of the firms that hire workers. The extreme case of this market power is the 'company town', where a single firm does most of the hiring in a geographic region. In a company town, if workers do not accept the wages and working conditions that the firm offers, they have little choice but to move or stop working. In the absence of a union, therefore, the firm could use its market power to pay lower wages and offer worse working conditions than would prevail if it had to compete with other firms for the same workers. In this case, a union may balance the firm's market power and protect the workers from being at the mercy of the firm owners.

Advocates of unions also claim that unions are important for helping firms respond efficiently to workers' concerns. Whenever a worker takes a job, the worker and the firm must agree on many attributes of the job in addition to the

FYI

Why do strikes occur?

STRIKES ARE COSTLY TO BOTH firms and workers. To firms they represent lost output; to workers, lost income. The longer the strike, the more costly to both parties. So why do they occur?

In reality, strikes occur because negotiations do not always run so smoothly. Negotiations break down. During times of disagreement, unions wish to demonstrate their resolve by striking and being willing to forgo income. Management also wants to demonstrate to the union that it can weather a strike and hold out as well. In this case, disagreements are the result of 'brinkmanship'—an attempt by both parties to temporarily use threats to demonstrate the value of their work to the firm.

If both unions and management had a better understanding of the costs of strike action, brinkmanship might not occur. In this way, strikes can be seen as the result of a lack of information. Unions might believe that a company does not appreciate their full value. Management might believe that unions do not appreciate the willingness of their company's shareholders to hold out and earn high profits.

Nonetheless, in the past—whether because of simple misunderstandings or differences in information—many workdays were lost to industrial action in Australia. Australia has always had government involvement in the resolution of industrial disputes. At its core is a dispute resolution body—the Industrial Relations Commission. Whenever a union contemplated strike action, the Commission's task was to step in and arbitrate the dispute. Its rulings were binding.

The arbitration system was strengthened considerably during the 1980s. Also during that time the Labor government struck an Accord with the trade unions to agree to wage restraint. The result of this was a dramatic reduction in strike action. As depicted in figure 11.5, this resulted in a reduction in workdays lost due to industrial disputes. In recent years, under the Coalition government, there has been an increase in the number of disputes.

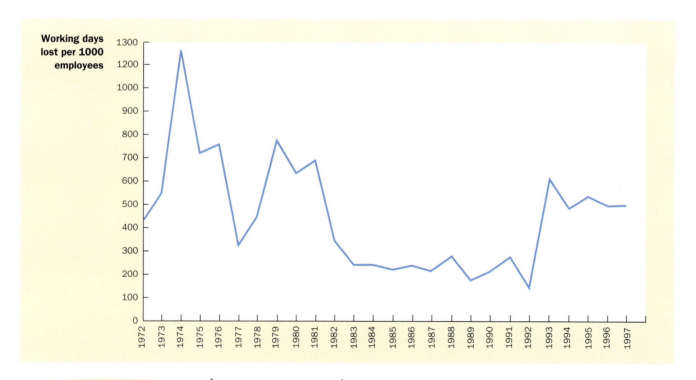

Figure 11.5 INDUSTRIAL DISPUTES IN AUSTRALIA
SOURCE: Based on statistical data from the Australian Bureau of Statistics, various years, Cat. No. 6101.0.

wage—hours of work, overtime, annual leave, sick leave, health benefits, promotion schedules, job security and so on. By representing workers' views on these issues, unions allow firms to provide the right mix of job attributes. Even if unions have the adverse effect of pushing wages above the equilibrium level and causing unemployment, they have the benefit of helping firms keep a happy and productive workforce.

In the end, there is no consensus among economists about whether unions are good or bad for the economy. Like many institutions, their influence is probably beneficial in some circumstances and adverse in others.

> **QUICK QUIZ** How does a union in the car industry affect wages and employment at holden and ford? How does it affect wages and employment in other industries?

CASE STUDY   WAGE INDEXATION

As discussed in chapter 6, Australia has a system of minimum wages that take the form of awards. These are minimum wage levels that are set for certain jobs in broad industry categories. In contrast to a simple minimum wage, therefore, the award system affords some flexibility in the system to take into account differences in industry conditions and job skills.

These awards are still, however, minimum wages. It is often the case that individual employees can obtain better wage and salary conditions from their employers. When a union negotiates new wage conditions, awards serve as their best option. The superior negotiating power afforded by collective bargaining allows unions to realise better outcomes for their members.

For this reason, Australia's award wages have historically been set by including the arguments of both employer groups and unions. The Australian Industrial Relations Commission periodically conducts hearings into the structure of awards in which employers, unions and the government present their views. However, given the potential ability of unions to circumvent awards with individual employers, their agreement is critical. For if such agreement is not forthcoming, wages will rise and this could increase both inflation and unemployment.

Although wage increases that pass on the gains from productivity improvements will not have this effect, a particularly difficult issue was how to treat the consequences of inflation. Recall that inflation raises prices across the economy. This reduces the purchasing power of the current income of workers and puts pressure on those incomes to rise. In Australia, this pressure has been recognised and has periodically been a part of the determination of awards (from 1921 to 1952, and since 1975 to 1980). Under wage indexation, wages would rise in line with inflation. If the inflation rate was 8%, award wages would automatically rise by at least 8%.

The problem with this policy is that wages are part of the costs of production. So when wages rise for reasons other than an increase in productivity, production costs rise. This, in turn, leads to higher prices for goods and services and, hence, inflation. If this inflation is again passed through to higher wages, the cycle continues. The result, as occurred during the late 1970s, is an ever-rising inflation rate. In 1980, partial indexation was seen as a way of stopping the 'wage–price spiral'. However, union pressure meant that real wages continued to rise.

In 1983, the Labor Party, under Bob Hawke, decided to use its close relationship with the Australian Council of Trade Unions (ACTU) to break this cycle. As part of their election policy, they entered into a Prices and Income Accord (known simply as the Accord). This Accord would limit wage increases, guarantee productivity increases and, at the same time, maintain worker incomes. In return, unions received assurances of the use of macroeconomic policies that would expand employment rather than fight inflation.

The Accord was renegotiated over the next decade to include guarantees of tax cuts in return for wage restraint. As we will see in a later chapter, wages policy became an integral part of macroeconomic stabilisation policy.

THE THEORY OF EFFICIENCY WAGES

One explanation for different earnings might come from different practices designed to improve workplace performance. Firms may set wages high so as to motivate workers to perform well in their jobs. This wage is called an **efficiency wage**. Efficiency wages are necessarily above-equilibrium wages that would result when supply equals demand. Thus, efficiency wages can potentially explain unemployment as well as earnings.

efficiency wages
above-equilibrium wages paid by firms in order to increase worker productivity

Why should firms want to keep wages high? In some ways, this decision seems odd, for wages are a large part of firms' costs. Normally, we expect profit-maximising firms to want to keep costs—and therefore wages—as low as possible. The novel insight of efficiency-wage theory is that paying high wages might be profitable because it might raise the efficiency of a firm's workers by more than it costs.

There are several types of efficiency-wage theory. Each type suggests a different explanation for why firms may want to pay high wages. Let's now consider four of these theories.

WORKER HEALTH

The first and simplest type of efficiency-wage theory emphasises the link between wages and worker health. Better paid workers eat a more nutritious diet, and workers who eat a better diet are healthier and more productive. A firm may find it more profitable to pay high wages and have healthy, productive workers than to pay lower wages and have less healthy, less productive workers.

This type of efficiency-wage theory is not relevant for firms in rich countries such as Australia. In these countries, the equilibrium wages for most workers are well above the level needed for an adequate diet. Firms are not concerned that paying equilibrium wages would place their workers' health in jeopardy.

Paying higher wages to raise worker health is more relevant for firms in less developed countries where inadequate nutrition is a more common problem. Unemployment is high in the cities of many poor African countries, for example.

In these countries, firms may fear that cutting wages would adversely influence their workers' health and productivity. Concern over nutrition may explain why firms do not cut wages despite a surplus of labour.

WORKER TURNOVER

A second type of efficiency-wage theory emphasises the link between wages and worker turnover. Workers quit jobs for many reasons—to take jobs in other firms, to move to other parts of the country, to leave the labour force and so on. The frequency with which they quit depends on the entire set of incentives they face, including the benefits of leaving and the benefits of staying with their current employer. The more a firm pays its workers, the less often its workers will choose to leave. Thus, a firm can reduce turnover among its workers by paying them a high wage.

Why do firms care about turnover? The reason is that it is costly for firms to hire and train new workers. Moreover, even after they are trained, newly hired workers are not as productive as experienced workers. Firms with higher turnover, therefore, will tend to have higher production costs. Firms may find it profitable to pay wages above the equilibrium level in order to reduce worker turnover.

WORKER EFFORT

A third type of efficiency-wage theory emphasises the link between wages and worker effort. In many jobs, workers have some discretion over how hard to work. As a result, firms monitor the efforts of their workers, and workers caught shirking their responsibilities are fired. But not all shirkers are caught immediately because monitoring workers is costly and imperfect. A firm can respond to this problem by paying wages above the equilibrium level. High wages make workers more eager to keep their jobs and, thereby, give workers an incentive to put forward their best effort.

This particular type of efficiency-wage theory is similar to the old Marxist idea of the 'reserve army of the unemployed'. Marx thought that employers benefited from unemployment because the threat of unemployment helped to discipline those workers who had jobs. In the worker-effort variant of efficiency-wage theory, unemployment fills a similar role. If the wage were at the level that balanced supply and demand, workers would have less reason to work hard because, if they were fired, they could quickly find new jobs at the same wage. Therefore, firms find it profitable to raise wages above the equilibrium level. This causes unemployment while providing an incentive for workers not to shirk their responsibilities.

WORKER QUALITY

A fourth and final type of efficiency-wage theory emphasises the link between wages and worker quality. When a firm hires new workers, it cannot perfectly gauge the quality of the applicants. By paying a high wage, the firm attracts a better pool of workers to apply for its jobs.

To see how this might work, consider a simple example. Waterwell Company owns one well and needs one worker to pump water from the well. Two workers, Bill and Ben, are interested in the job. Bill, a proficient worker, is willing to work for $10 per hour. Below that wage, he would rather start his own lawn-mowing business. Ben, a complete incompetent, is willing to work for anything above $2 per hour. Below that wage, he would rather sit on the beach. Economists say that Bill's *reservation wage*—the lowest wage he would accept—is $10, and Ben's reservation wage is $2.

What wage should the firm set? If the firm were interested in minimising labour costs, it would set the wage at $2 per hour. At this wage, the quantity of workers supplied (one) would balance the quantity demanded. Ben would take the job, and Bill would not apply for it. Yet suppose Waterwell knows that only one of these two applicants is competent, but it does not know whether it is Bill or Ben. If the firm hires the incompetent worker, he will damage the well, causing the firm huge losses. In this case, the firm has a better strategy than paying the equilibrium wage of $2 and hiring Ben. It can offer $10 per hour, inducing both Bill and Ben to apply for the job. By choosing randomly between these two applicants and turning the other away, the firm has a fifty-fifty chance of hiring the competent worker. In contrast, if the firm offers any lower wage, it is sure to hire the incompetent worker.

This story illustrates a general phenomenon. When a firm has an excess supply of workers, it might seem profitable to reduce the wage it is offering. But by reducing the wage, the firm induces an adverse change in the mix of workers. In this case, at a wage of $10, Waterwell has two workers applying for one job. But if Waterwell responds to this excess supply by reducing the wage, the competent worker (who has better alternative opportunities) will not apply. Thus, it is profitable for the firm to pay a wage above the level that balances supply and demand.

CASE STUDY   HENRY FORD AND THE GENEROUS $5-A-DAY WAGE

Henry Ford was an industrial visionary. As founder of the Ford Motor Company, he was responsible for introducing modern techniques of production. Rather than building cars with small teams of skilled craftsmen, Ford built cars on assembly lines in which unskilled workers were taught to perform the same simple tasks over and over again. The output of this assembly process was the Model T Ford, one of the most famous early cars.

In 1914, Ford introduced another innovation—the $5 workday. This might not seem like much today, but back then $5 was about twice the going wage. It was also far above the wage that balanced supply and demand. When the new $5-a-day wage was announced, long lines of job seekers formed outside the Ford factories. The number of workers willing to work at this wage far exceeded the number of workers Ford needed.

Ford's high-wage policy had many of the effects predicted by efficiency-wage theory. Turnover fell, absenteeism fell and productivity rose. Workers were so much more efficient that Ford's production costs were lower even though wages were higher. Thus, paying a wage above the equilibrium level was profitable for the firm. Henry Ford himself called the $5-a-day wage 'one of the finest cost-cutting moves we ever made'.

Historical accounts of this episode are also consistent with efficiency-wage theory. An historian of the early Ford Motor Company wrote, 'Ford and his associates freely declared on many occasions that the high-wage policy turned out to be good business. By this they meant that it had improved the discipline of the workers, given them a more loyal interest in the institution, and raised their personal efficiency.'

Why did it take Henry Ford to introduce this efficiency wage? Why were other firms not already taking advantage of this seemingly profitable business strategy? According to some analysts, Ford's decision was closely linked to his use of the assembly line. Workers organised in an assembly line are highly interdependent. If one worker is absent or works slowly, other workers are less able to complete their own tasks. Thus, while assembly lines made production more efficient, they also raised the importance of low worker turnover, high worker quality, and high worker effort. As a result, paying efficiency wages may have been a better strategy for the Ford Motor Company than for other businesses at the time.

QUICK QUIZ Give four explanations for why firms might find it profitable to pay wages above the level that balances quantity of labour supplied and quantity of labour demanded.

JOB SEARCH

A fourth reason economies always experience some unemployment, besides minimum-wage laws, unions and efficiency wages, is job search. **Job search** is the process of matching workers with appropriate jobs. If all workers and all jobs were the same, so that all workers were equally well suited for all jobs, job search would not be a problem. Laid-off workers would quickly find new jobs that were well suited to them. But, in fact, workers differ in their tastes and skills, jobs differ in their attributes, and information about job candidates and job vacancies is disseminated slowly among the many firms and households in the economy.

The unemployment that arises because of job search is, in an important sense, different from the unemployment that arises because of minimum-wage laws, unions and efficiency wages. In the previous three cases, the wage is above the equilibrium level, so the quantity of labour supplied exceeds the quantity of labour demanded; workers are unemployed because they are *waiting* for jobs to open up. In contrast, job search is not due to the failure of wages to balance labour supply and labour demand. When job search is the explanation for unemployment, workers are *searching* for the jobs that best suit them.

THE INEVITABILITY OF SEARCH UNEMPLOYMENT

Search unemployment is often the result of changes in the demand for labour among different firms. When consumers decide that they prefer Compaq over Dell computers, Compaq increases employment, and Dell lays off workers. The former Dell workers must now search for new jobs, and Compaq must decide

job search
the process by which workers find appropriate jobs given their tastes and skills

FYI

The economics of asymmetric information

In many situations in life, information is asymmetric—one person in a transaction knows more about what is going on than the other person. This possibility raises a variety of interesting problems for economic theory. We have just seen some of these problems raised in the context of developing the theory of efficiency wages. These problems, however, go beyond the study of unemployment.

The worker-quality variant of efficiency-wage theory illustrates a general principle called *adverse selection*. Adverse selection arises when one person knows more about the attributes of a good than another and, as a result, the uninformed person runs the risk of being sold a good of low quality. In the worker-quality story, for instance, workers have better information about their own abilities than firms do. When a firm cuts the wage it pays, the selection of workers changes in a way that is adverse to the firm.

Adverse selection arises in many other circumstances. Here are two examples:

- Sellers of used cars know their cars' defects whereas buyers often do not. Because owners of the worst cars are more likely to sell them than are the owners of the best cars, car buyers are correctly apprehensive about getting a 'lemon'. As a result, many people avoid buying cars in the used-car market.

- Buyers of private health insurance know more about their own health problems than do health funds. Because people with greater hidden health problems are more likely to buy private health insurance than are other people, the price of health insurance reflects the costs of a sicker-than-average person. As a result, people with average health problems are discouraged from buying private health insurance.

In each case, the market for the product—used cars or private health insurance—does not work as well as it might because of the problem of adverse selection.

Similarly, the worker-effort variant of efficiency-wage theory illustrates a general phenomenon called *moral hazard*. Moral hazard arises when one person, called the *agent*, is performing some task on behalf of another person, called the *principal*. Because the principal cannot perfectly monitor the agent's behaviour, the agent tends to undertake less effort than the principal considers desirable. The term 'moral hazard' refers to the risk of dishonest or otherwise inappropriate behaviour by the agent. In such a situation, the principal tries various ways to encourage the agent to act more responsibly.

In an employment relationship, the firm is the principal and the worker is the agent. The moral-hazard problem is the temptation of imperfectly monitored workers to shirk their responsibilities. According to the worker-effort variant of efficiency-wage theory, the principal can encourage the agent not to shirk by paying a wage above the equilibrium level because then the agent has more to lose if caught shirking. In this way, high wages reduce the problem of moral hazard.

Moral hazard arises in many other situations. Here are some examples:

- A homeowner with fire insurance buys too few fire extinguishers. The reason is that the homeowner bears the cost of the extinguisher whereas the insurance company receives much of the benefit.

- A babysitter allows children to watch more television than the parents of the children prefer. The reason is that more educational activities require more energy from the babysitter, even though they are beneficial for the children.

- A family lives near a river with a high risk of flooding. The reason it continues to live there is that the family enjoys the scenic views, and the government will bear part of the cost when it provides disaster relief after a flood.

Can you identify the principal and the agent in each of these situations? How do you think the principal in each case might solve the problem of moral hazard?

---

which new workers to hire for the various jobs that have opened up. The result of this transition is temporary unemployment.

Similarly, because different regions of the country produce different goods, employment can rise in one region and fall in another. Consider, for instance, what happens when the world price of coal falls. Coal mines in Western Australia respond to the lower price by cutting back on production and employment. At the same time, cheaper coal reduces electricity costs, so aluminium refineries in Queensland that are electricity-intensive raise production and employment. Changes in the composition of demand among industries or regions are called *sectoral shifts*. Because it takes time for workers to search for jobs in the new sectors, sectoral shifts temporarily cause unemployment.

Search unemployment is inevitable simply because the economy is always changing. A century ago, the sectors with the largest employment in Australia were primary industries such as agriculture and mining. Today, the largest employers are in services including information technology and financial services. As this transition took place, jobs were created in some firms and were destroyed in others. The end result of this process has been higher productivity and higher living standards. But, along the way, workers in declining industries found themselves out of work and searching for new jobs.

PUBLIC POLICY AND JOB SEARCH

Even if some search unemployment is inevitable, public policy can nonetheless affect its prevalence. To the extent that policy can reduce the time it takes unemployed workers to find new jobs, it can reduce search unemployment.

Government programs try to facilitate job finding in various ways. One way is through government-sponsored employment agencies, which give out information about job vacancies in order to match workers and jobs more quickly. Another way is through public training programs, which aim to ease the transition of workers from declining to growing industries and to help disadvantaged groups escape poverty. The Australian government now spends more than half a billion dollars each year on job training and related programs.

Critics of these programs question whether the government should get involved with the process of job search. They argue that it is better to let the private market match workers and jobs. In fact, most job search in our economy takes place without intervention by the government. Newspaper advertisements, job newsletters, university placement offices, headhunters and word of mouth all help spread information about job openings and job candidates. Similarly, much worker education is done privately, either through schools or through on-the-job training. These critics contend that the government is no better—and most likely worse—at disseminating the right information to the right workers and deciding what kinds of worker training would be most valuable. They claim that these decisions are best made privately by workers and employers.

UNEMPLOYMENT BENEFITS

One government program that increases the amount of search unemployment, without intending to do so, is **unemployment benefits**. This program is designed to offer workers partial protection against income loss. Any person who becomes unemployed is eligible for such benefits. However, in recent times, the length of eligibility has been lowered to about 6 months if a person does not undertake

unemployment benefits
a government program that partially protects workers' incomes when they become unemployed

reasonable efforts to regain employment. Regardless, unemployment benefits are usually only a fraction of a worker's previous wage.

Although unemployment benefits reduce the hardship of unemployment, they also increase the amount of unemployment. The explanation is based on one of the *Ten Principles of Economics* in chapter 1—people respond to incentives. Because unemployment benefits stop when a worker takes a new job, the unemployed devote less effort to job search and are more likely to turn down unattractive job offers. In addition, because unemployment benefits makes unemployment less onerous, workers are less likely to seek guarantees of job security when they negotiate with employers over the terms of employment.

Many studies by labour economists have examined the incentive effects of unemployment benefits. One study examined an experiment run by the US state of Illinois in 1985. When unemployed workers applied to collect unemployment benefits, the state randomly selected some of them and offered each a $500 bonus if they found new jobs within 11 weeks. This group was then compared with a control group not offered the incentive. The average spell of unemployment for the group offered the bonus was 7% shorter than the average spell for the control group. This experiment shows that the design of the unemployment benefits system influences the effort that the unemployed devote to job search.

Several other studies examined search effort by following a group of workers over time. In the United States, unemployment benefits, rather than lasting for many years (subject to job search requirements), usually run out after 6 months or a year. These studies found that when the unemployed become ineligible for benefits, the probability of their finding a new job rises markedly. Thus, receiving unemployment benefits does reduce the search effort of the unemployed.

Even though unemployment benefits reduce search effort and raise unemployment, we should not necessarily conclude that the policy is a bad one. The program does achieve its primary goal of reducing the income uncertainty that workers face. In addition, when workers turn down unattractive job offers, they have the opportunity to look for jobs that better suit their tastes and skills. Some economists have argued that unemployment benefits improve the ability of the economy to match each worker with the most appropriate job.

The study of unemployment benefits shows that the unemployment rate is an imperfect measure of a nation's overall level of economic wellbeing. Most economists agree that eliminating unemployment benefits would reduce the amount of unemployment in the economy. Yet economists disagree on whether economic wellbeing would be enhanced or diminished by this change in policy.

QUICK QUIZ How would an increase in the world price of oil affect the amount of search unemployment? Is this unemployment undesirable? What public policies might affect the amount of unemployment caused by this price change?

CASE STUDY   THE LOCATION OF UNEMPLOYMENT

Popular discussions of unemployment rarely consider the composition of the unemployed. Even though unemployment in certain groups is sometimes targeted (for instance, youth or ethnic minority), there is still a tendency to view unemployment in the aggregate around the country. Recent research by Bob

Gregory and Boyd Hunter suggests that location of the unemployed is a critical feature of the problem.

Some neighbourhoods and cities have much lower rates of unemployment than others. More importantly, however, the differences are growing. Gregory and Hunter found that between 1976 and 1991, the poorest areas of Australia's cities lost one-third of their employment. Although it is perhaps not surprising that affluent neighbourhoods report lower rates of unemployment than less affluent ones, it is disturbing to find that when a neighbourhood starts from a position of high unemployment, its position worsens over time. The reverse is true for more affluent neighbourhoods. Indeed, in 1976, although incomes differed, a person living in a poor neighbourhood was just as likely to have a job as a person living in an affluent one. Today, that is no longer true. This suggests a growing regional inequality that is part of the unemployment problem.

To be sure, it is a basic fact of economic life that poor people, who happen to be poor because they do not have a job, congregate in poor neighbourhoods. Gregory and Hunter are concerned, however, that the causation might run the other way—it may be harder to find a job precisely because you are living in a poor neighbourhood. They point to signs that job search relies on word of mouth among friends and contacts who live close to you. If your neighbours are not employed, that in turn reduces your chance of landing a job. The result is potentially diminishing prospects for job seekers in poor neighbourhoods relative to those at the fashionable end of town.

Job search is not the only potential cause of growing inequality. Public housing policy and the decline of manufacturing may also play a role. In the United States, where ghettos are a pervasive problem, the influence of crime, segregation and discrimination and their impact on public services can also make it difficult for those living in poor areas to find employment. Nonetheless, the differences between locations suggest that broad-based national solutions to unemployment problems should be complemented by programs that target specific geographic areas.

CONCLUSION

In this chapter, we discussed the measurement of unemployment and the reasons economies always experience some degree of unemployment. We have seen how minimum-wage laws, unions, efficiency wages and job search can all help explain why some workers do not have jobs. Which of these four explanations for the natural rate of unemployment are the most important for the Australian economy and other economies around the world? Unfortunately, there is no easy way to tell. Economists therefore differ in which of these explanations of unemployment they consider most important.

Unemployment is not a simple problem with a simple solution. Instead, it has various explanations and is affected by various public policies. When politicians debate the minimum wage, the laws regulating collective bargaining, or unemployment benefits, one issue is always the impact of these policies on the economy's natural rate of unemployment.

Summary

- The unemployment rate is the percentage of those who would like to work but do not have jobs. The Australian Bureau of Statistics calculates this statistic monthly based on a survey of thousands of households.

- The unemployment rate is an imperfect measure of joblessness. Some people who call themselves unemployed may actually not want to work, and some people who would like to work have left the labour force after an unsuccessful search.

- In the Australian economy, most people who become unemployed find work within a short period of time. Nonetheless, most unemployment observed at any given time is attributable to the few people who are unemployed for long periods of time.

- One reason our economy always has some unemployment is minimum-wage laws. By raising the wage of unskilled and inexperienced workers above the equilibrium level, minimum-wage laws raise the quantity of labour supplied and reduce the quantity demanded. The resulting excess supply of labour represents unemployment.

- A second reason for unemployment is the market power of unions. When unions push the wages in unionised industries above the equilibrium level, they create an excess supply of labour.

- A third reason for unemployment is suggested by the theory of efficiency wages. According to this theory, firms find it profitable to pay wages above the equilibrium level. High wages can improve worker health, lower worker turnover, increase worker effort and raise worker quality.

- A fourth reason for unemployment is the time it takes for workers to search for jobs that best suit their skills and tastes. The unemployment benefit is a government policy that, while protecting workers' incomes, increases the amount of search unemployment.

Key concepts

labour force, p. 223
unemployment rate, p. 223
labour-force participation rate, p. 223
natural rate of unemployment, p. 225
cyclical unemployment, p. 225
discouraged workers, p. 227

union, p. 232
collective bargaining, p. 232
strike, p. 232
efficiency wages, p. 236
job search, p. 239
unemployment benefits, p. 241

Questions for review

1. What are the three categories into which the Australian Bureau of Statistics divides everyone? How does it calculate the labour force, the unemployment rate and the labour-force participation rate?

2. Is unemployment typically short term or long term? Explain.

3. Are minimum-wage laws a better explanation for unemployment among teenagers or among university graduates? Why?

4. How do unions affect the natural rate of unemployment?

5. What claims do advocates of unions make to argue that unions are good for the economy?

6. Explain four ways in which a firm might increase its profits by raising the wages it pays.

7. Why is search unemployment inevitable? How might the government reduce the amount of search unemployment?

Problems and applications

1. The Australian Bureau of Statistics announced that, in June 1998, of all adult Australians, 8 610 500 were employed, 733 700 were unemployed, and 5 417 400 were not in the labour force. How big was the labour force? What was the labour-force participation rate? What was the unemployment rate?

2. As shown in figure 11.3, the overall labour-force participation rate of men declined between 1978 and 1998. This overall decline reflects different patterns for different age groups, however, as shown in the following table:

	ALL MEN	MEN 15–24	MEN 25–54	MEN 55 AND OVER
1978	78%	80%	92%	54%
1998	73	71	91	44

   Which group experienced the largest decline? Given this information, what factor may have played an important role in the decline in overall male labour-force participation over this period?

3. Are the following workers more likely to experience short-term or long-term unemployment? Explain.
   a. a construction worker laid off because of bad weather
   b. a manufacturing worker who loses her job at a plant in an isolated area
   c. a blacksmith laid off because of competition from cars
   d. a cook in a fast-food outlet who loses his job when a new restaurant opens across the street
   e. an expert welder with little formal education who loses her job when the company installs automatic welding machinery

4. Using a diagram of the labour market, show the effect of an increase in the minimum wage on the wage paid to workers, the number of workers supplied, the number of workers demanded and the amount of unemployment.

5. Do you think that firms in small towns or cities have more market power in hiring? Do you think that firms generally have more market power in hiring today than 50 years ago or less? How do you think this change over time has affected the role of unions in the economy? Explain.

6. Consider an economy with two labour markets, neither of which is unionised. Now suppose a union is established in one market.
   a. Show the effect of the union on the market in which it is formed. In what sense is the quantity of labour employed in this market an inefficient quantity?
   b. Show the effect of the union on the non-unionised market. What happens to the equilibrium wage in this market?

7. Each of the following situations involves moral hazard. In each case, identify the principal and the agent, and explain why there is asymmetric information. How does the action described reduce the problem of moral hazard?
   a. Landlords require tenants to pay security deposits.
   b. Firms compensate top executives with options to buy company shares at a given price in the future.
   c. Car insurance companies offer discounts to customers who install anti-theft devices in their cars.

8. Suppose that the Live-Long-and-Prosper Health Fund charges $5000 annually for family health cover. The fund's managing director suggests that the firm raise the annual price to $6000 in order to increase its profits. If the firm followed this suggestion, what economic problem might arise? Would the firm's pool of customers tend to become more or less healthy on average? Would the firm's profits necessarily increase?

9. (This problem is challenging.) Suppose that the federal government passes a law requiring employers to provide employees some benefit (such as private health care) that raises the cost of an employee by $4 per hour.
   a. What effect does this legal requirement have on the demand for labour? (In answering this and the following questions, be quantitative when you can.)
   b. If employees place a value on this benefit exactly equal to its cost, what effect does this legal requirement have on the supply of labour?
   c. If the wage is free to balance supply and demand, how does this legal requirement affect the wage and the level of employment? Are employers better or worse off? Are employees better or worse off?
   d. If a minimum-wage law prevents the wage from balancing supply and demand, how does the legal requirement to provide the benefit affect the wage, the level of employment and the level of unemployment? Are employers better or worse off? Are employees better or worse off?
   e. Now suppose that workers do not value the benefit at all. How does this alternative assumption change your answers to parts (b), (c) and (d) above?

V

MONEY AND PRICES
IN THE LONG RUN

12

THE MONETARY SYSTEM

IN THIS CHAPTER YOU WILL

Consider what money is and what functions money has in the economy

Learn about the Reserve Bank of Australia

Examine how the banking system helps determine the supply of money

See what tools the Reserve Bank of Australia uses to influence the supply of money

When you walk into a restaurant to buy a meal, you get something of value—your hunger satisfied. To pay for this service, you might hand the restaurateur several worn-out pieces of coloured plastic decorated with strange symbols, government buildings and the portraits of famous dead Australians. Or you might hand over a plastic card that is used to electronically access your cheque or savings account. Whether you pay by cash or debit card, the restaurateur is happy to work hard to satisfy your gastronomical desires in exchange for these pieces of plastic, which, in and of themselves, are worthless.

To anyone who has lived in a modern economy, this social custom is not at all odd. Even though plastic money has no intrinsic value, the restaurateur is confident that, in the future, some third person will accept it in exchange for something that the restaurateur does value. And that third person is confident that some fourth person will accept the money, with the knowledge that yet a fifth person will accept the money…and so on. To the restaurateur and to other people in our society, your cash represents a claim to goods and services in the future.

The social custom of using money for transactions is extraordinarily useful in a large, complex society. Imagine, for a moment, that there was no item in the economy widely accepted in exchange for goods and services. People would have to rely on *barter*—the exchange of one good or service for another—to obtain the things they need. To get your restaurant meal, for instance, you would have to offer the restaurateur something of immediate value. You could offer to wash some dishes, clean the floor, or give away your family's secret recipe for lamb roast. An economy that relies on barter will have trouble allocating its scarce resources efficiently. In such an economy, trade is said to require the *double coincidence of wants*—the unlikely occurrence that two people each have a good or service that the other wants at the same time.

The existence of money makes trade easier. Our restaurateur, George, does not care whether you can produce a valuable good or service for him. He is happy to accept your money, knowing that other people will do the same for him. Such a convention allows trade to be roundabout—a coincidence of desires to trade is not required. George accepts your money and uses it to pay Ellen, his chef; Ellen uses her paycheque to send her child to day care; the day care centre uses these fees to pay Tom, a teacher; and Tom hires you to mow his lawn. As money flows from person to person in the economy, it facilitates production and trade, thereby allowing people to specialise in what they do best and raising everyone's standard of living.

In this chapter, we begin to examine the role of money in the economy. We discuss what money is, the various forms that money takes, how the banking system helps create money, and how the government influences the quantity of money in circulation. Because money is so important in the economy, we devote much effort in the rest of this book to learning how changes in the quantity of money affect various economic variables, including inflation, interest rates, production and employment. Consistent with our long-run focus in the last three chapters, we will examine the long-run effects of changes in the quantity of money in the next chapter. The short-run effects of monetary changes are a more complex topic, which we take up later in the book. This chapter provides the background for all of this further analysis.

THE MEANING OF MONEY

What is money? This might seem like an odd question. When you read that billionaire Kerry Packer has a lot of money, you know what that means—he is so rich that he can buy almost anything he wants. In this sense, the term *money* is used to mean *wealth*.

money
the set of assets in an economy that people regularly use to buy goods and services from other people

Economists, however, use the word in a more specific sense. **Money** is the set of assets in the economy that people regularly use to buy goods and services from other people. The cash in your wallet is money because you can use it to buy a meal at a restaurant or a shirt at a clothing shop. In contrast, if you happened to be a major shareholder in Publishing and Broadcasting Limited, as Kerry Packer is, you would be wealthy, but this asset is not considered a form of money. You could not buy a meal or a shirt with this wealth without first obtaining some money. According to the economist's definition, money includes only those few types of wealth that are regularly accepted by sellers in exchange for goods and services.

THE FUNCTIONS OF MONEY

Money has three functions in the economy—it is a *medium of exchange*, a *unit of account*, and a *store of value*. These three functions together distinguish money from other assets.

A **medium of exchange** is an item that buyers give to sellers when they purchase goods and services. When you buy a shirt at a clothing shop, the shop gives you the shirt, and you give the shop your money. This transfer of money from buyer to seller allows the transaction to take place. When you walk into a shop, you are confident that the shop will accept your money for the items it is selling because money is the commonly accepted medium of exchange.

A **unit of account** is the yardstick people use to post prices and record debts. When you go shopping, you might observe that a shirt costs $20 and a meat pie costs $2. Even though it would be accurate to say that the price of a shirt is 10 meat pies and the price of a meat pie is 1/10 of a shirt, prices are never quoted in this way. Similarly, if you take out a loan from a bank, the size of your future loan repayments will be measured in dollars, not in a quantity of goods and services. When we want to measure and record economic value, we use money as the unit of account.

A **store of value** is an item that people can use to transfer purchasing power from the present to the future. When a seller accepts money today in exchange for a good or service, that seller can hold the money and become a buyer of another good or service at another time. Of course, money is not the only store of value in the economy. A person can also transfer purchasing power from the present to the future by holding shares, bonds, real estate, art, or even old stamps. The term *wealth* is used to refer to the total of all stores of value, including both money and non-monetary assets.

Economists use the term **liquidity** to describe the ease with which an asset can be converted into the economy's medium of exchange. Because money is the economy's medium of exchange, it is the most liquid asset available. Other assets vary widely in their liquidity. Most shares and bonds can be sold easily at little or no cost, so they are relatively liquid assets. In contrast, selling a house, a Rembrandt painting, or a 1948 Don Bradman cricket bat requires more time and effort, so these assets are less liquid.

When people decide in what form to hold their wealth, they have to balance the liquidity of each possible asset against the asset's usefulness as a store of value. Money is the most liquid asset, but it is far from perfect as a store of value. When prices rise, the value of money falls. In other words, when goods and services become more expensive, each dollar in your wallet can buy less. This link between the price level and the value of money will turn out to be important for understanding how money affects the economy.

KINDS OF MONEY

When money takes the form of a commodity with intrinsic value, it is called **commodity money**. The term *intrinsic value* means that the item would have value even if it were not used as money. One example of commodity money is gold. Gold has intrinsic value because it is used in industry and in the making of jewellery. Although today we no longer use gold as money, historically gold has been a common form of money because it is relatively easy to carry, measure and verify for impurities. When an economy uses gold as money (or uses plastic or paper money that is convertible into gold on demand), it is said to be operating under a *gold standard*.

Another example of commodity money is cigarettes. In prisoner-of-war camps during World War II, prisoners traded goods and services with one

medium of exchange
an item that buyers give to sellers when they want to purchase goods and services

unit of account
the yardstick people use to post prices and record debts

store of value
an item that people can use to transfer purchasing power from the present to the future

liquidity
the ease with which an asset can be converted into the economy's medium of exchange

commodity money
money that takes the form of a commodity with intrinsic value

another using cigarettes as the store of value, unit of account and medium of exchange. Similarly, as the Soviet Union was breaking up in the late 1980s, cigarettes started replacing the rouble as the preferred currency in Moscow. In both cases, even non-smokers were happy to accept cigarettes in an exchange, knowing that they could use the cigarettes to buy other goods and services. In the early days of the Australian colonies, rum was used as commodity money. Workers were paid in gallons of rum and they then used this as a medium of exchange. It didn't serve as much of a store of value, though—you could say it was a very liquid asset.

Money without intrinsic value is called **fiat money**. A *fiat* is simply an order or decree, and fiat money is established as money by government decree. For example, compare the plastic dollars in your wallet (printed by the Reserve Bank of Australia) and the paper dollars from a game of Monopoly (printed by the Parker Brothers game company). Why can you use the first to pay your bill at a restaurant but not the second? The answer is that the Australian government has decreed its dollars to be valid money. Each note in your wallet reads 'This Australian note is legal tender throughout Australia and its territories'.

Although the government is central to establishing and regulating a system of fiat money (such as by prosecuting counterfeiters), other factors are also required for the success of such a monetary system. To a large extent, the acceptance of fiat money depends as much on expectations and social convention as on government decree. The Soviet government in the 1980s never abandoned the rouble as the official currency. Yet the people of Moscow preferred to accept cigarettes (or even American dollars) in exchange for goods and services, because they were more confident that these alternative monies would be accepted by others in the future. The same thing happened more recently in Indonesia, where the value of the rupiah dropped dramatically in a short period of time. Some places in Indonesia would accept only American dollars in payment for goods or services.

fiat money
money without intrinsic value that is used as money because of government decree

MONEY IN THE AUSTRALIAN ECONOMY

As we will see, the quantity of money circulating in the economy, called the **money supply**, has a powerful influence on many economic variables. But before we consider why that is true, we need to ask a preliminary question. What is the quantity of money? In particular, suppose you were given the task of measuring how much money there is in the Australian economy. What would you include in your measure?

The most obvious asset to include is **currency**—the plastic notes and coins in the hands of the public. Currency is clearly the most widely accepted medium of exchange in our economy. There is no doubt that it is part of the money supply.

Yet currency is not the only asset that you can use to buy goods and services. Most shops today also accept debit cards, or offer EFTPOS facilities. (EFTPOS stands for 'electronic funds transfer at point of sale'. There is a distinction between the plastic card itself and the funds in savings or cheque accounts that the card allows consumers to access. See the FYI box 'Credit cards, debit cards and money'.) Some shops also accept personal cheques. Wealth held in your savings or cheque account is almost as convenient for buying things as wealth held in your wallet. To measure the money supply, therefore, you might

money supply
the quantity of money circulating in the economy

currency
the plastic notes and coins in the hands of the public

IN THE NEWS

Money on the island of Yap

The role of social custom in the monetary system is most apparent in foreign cultures with customs very different from our own. The following article describes the money on the island of Yap. As you read the article, ask yourself whether Yap is using a type of commodity money, a type of fiat money, or something in between.

Fixed Assets, or Why a Loan in Yap Is Hard to Roll Over

BY ART PINE

YAP, MICRONESIA—On this tiny South Pacific island, life is easy and the currency is hard.

Elsewhere, the world's troubled monetary system creaks along; floating exchange rates wreak havoc on currency markets, and devaluations are commonplace. But on Yap the currency is as solid as a rock. In fact, it is rock. Limestone to be precise.

For nearly 2000 years the Yapese have used large stone wheels to pay for major purchases, such as land, canoes and permissions to marry. Yap is a US trust territory, and the dollar is used in grocery stores and gas stations. But reliance on stone money, like the island's ancient caste system and the traditional dress of loincloths and grass skirts, continues.

Buying property with stones is 'much easier than buying it with US dollars', says John Chodad, who recently purchased a building lot with a 30-inch stone wheel. 'We don't know the value of the US dollar...'

Stone wheels don't make good pocket money, so for small transactions, Yapese use other forms of currency, such as beer. Beer is proffered as payment for all sorts of odd jobs, including construction. The 10 000 people on Yap consume 40 000 to 50 000 cases a year, mostly of Budweiser...

The people of Yap have been using stone money ever since a Yapese warrior named Anagumang first brought the huge stones from limestone caverns on neighboring Palau, some 1500 to 2000 years ago. Inspired by the moon, he fashioned the stone into large circles. The rest is history.

Yapese lean the stone wheels against their houses or prop up rows of them in village 'banks'. Most of the stones are 2½ to 5 feet in diameter, but some are as much as 12 feet across. Each has a hole in the center so it can be slipped onto the trunk of a fallen betel nut tree and carried. It takes 20 men to lift some stones.

By custom, the stones are worthless when broken. You never hear people on Yap musing about wanting a piece of the rock. Rather than risk a broken stone—or back—Yapese tend to leave the larger stones where they are and make a mental accounting that the ownership

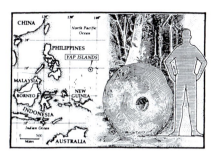

MONEY ON THE ISLAND OF YAP: NOT EXACTLY SMALL CHANGE

has been transferred—much as gold bars used in international transactions change hands without leaving the vaults of the New York Federal Reserve Bank...

There are some decided advantages to using massive stones for money. They are immune to black-market trading, for one thing, and they pose formidable obstacles to pickpockets. In addition, there aren't any sterile debates about how to stabilize the Yapese monetary system. With only 6600 stone wheels remaining on the island, the money supply stays put...

Meanwhile, Yap's stone money may be about to take on international significance. Just yesterday, Washington received notice that Tosiho Nakayama, the president of Micronesia, plans to bring a stone disk when he visits the United States next month. It will be flown by Air Force jet.

Officials say Mr Nakayama intends the stone as Micronesia's symbolic contribution toward reducing the US budget deficit.

SOURCE: *Wall Street Journal*, 29 March 1984, p. A1.

---

want to include **current deposits**—balances in bank accounts that depositors can access on demand simply by using a debit card or writing a cheque.

Once you start to consider balances in savings or cheque accounts as part of the money supply, you are led to consider the large variety of other accounts

current deposits
balances in bank accounts that depositors can access on demand by using a debit card or writing a cheque

Table 12.1

Three measures of the money supply for the Australian economy

Measure	Amount in 1998	What's included
Currency	$21 096 million	Notes and coins
M3	$335 192 million	Current deposits with banks Traveller's cheques Savings deposits Certificates of deposit
Broad money	$401 257 million	Everything in M3 Deposits in non-bank financial institutions less currency and bank deposits by non-bank financial institutions

SOURCE: Reserve Bank Bulletin.

that people hold at banks and other financial institutions. Bank depositors usually cannot write cheques against the balances in their savings accounts, but they can easily transfer funds from other accounts into cheque accounts or use debit cards to access their funds. Thus, these accounts should plausibly be part of the Australian money supply.

In a complex economy such as ours, it is not easy to draw a line between assets that can be called 'money' and assets that cannot. The coins in your pocket are clearly part of the money supply, and the Sydney Opera House clearly is not, but there are many assets in between these extremes for which the choice is less clear. Therefore, various measures of the money supply are available for the Australian economy. Table 12.1 shows the three most important monetary aggregates—currency, M3 and broad money. Each of these measures uses a slightly different criterion for distinguishing monetary from non-monetary assets.

For our purposes in this book, we need not dwell on the differences between the various measures of money. The important point is that the money supply for the Australian economy includes not just currency but also deposits in banks and other financial institutions that can be readily accessed and used to buy goods and services.

CASE STUDY   WHERE IS ALL THE CURRENCY?

One puzzle about the money supply of the US economy concerns the amount of currency. In 1996 there was about $380 billion of currency outstanding. To put this number in perspective, we can divide it by 200 million, the number of adults (age 16 and over) in the United States. This calculation implies that the average adult holds about $1900 of currency. Most people are surprised to learn that the economy has so much currency because they carry far less than this in their wallets.

Who is holding all this currency? No one knows for sure, but there are two plausible explanations.

The first explanation is that much of the currency is being held outside the United States. In countries without a stable monetary system, people often prefer US dollars to domestic assets. It is, in fact, not unusual to see US dollars being used overseas as the medium of exchange, unit of account and store of value.

The second explanation is that much of the currency is being held by drug dealers, tax evaders and other criminals. For most people in the US economy, currency is not a particularly good way to hold wealth. Currency can be lost or stolen. Moreover, currency does not earn interest, whereas money in a bank account does. Thus, most people hold only small amounts of currency. In contrast, criminals may prefer not to hold their wealth in banks. A bank deposit would give police a paper trail with which to trace their illegal activities. For criminals, currency may be the best store of value available.

■ **QUICK QUIZ** List and describe the three functions of money.

THE RESERVE BANK OF AUSTRALIA (RBA)

Whenever an economy relies on a system of fiat money, as the Australian economy does, some agency must be responsible for regulating the system. In Australia, that agency is the **Reserve Bank of Australia (RBA)**. If you look at an

Reserve Bank of Australia (RBA)
the central bank of Australia

FYI

Credit cards, debit cards and money

IT MIGHT SEEM NATURAL TO include credit cards as part of the economy's supply of money. After all, people use credit cards to make many of their purchases. Aren't credit cards, therefore, a medium of exchange?

Although at first this argument may seem persuasive, credit cards are excluded from all measures of the quantity of money. The reason is that credit cards are not really a method of payment but a method of *deferring* payment. When you buy a meal with a credit card, the bank that issued the card pays the restaurant what is due. At a later date, you will have to repay the bank (perhaps with interest). When the time comes to pay your credit card bill, you will probably do so by writing a cheque on your cheque account. The balance in this cheque account is part of the economy's supply of money.

Notice that credit cards are very different from debit cards, which automatically withdraw funds from a bank account to pay for items bought. Rather than allowing the user to postpone payment for a purchase, a debit card allows the user immediate access to deposits in a bank account. In this sense, a debit card is more similar to a cheque than to a credit card. The account balances that lie behind debit cards are included in measures of the quantity of money.

Even though credit cards are not considered a form of money, they are nonetheless important in analysing the monetary system. People who have credit cards can pay many of their bills all at once at the end of the month, rather than sporadically as they make purchases. As a result, people who have credit cards probably carry less money on average than people who do not have credit cards. Thus, the introduction and increased popularity of credit cards may reduce the amount of money that people choose to carry.

IS THIS MONEY?

central bank

an institution designed to oversee the banking system and regulate the quantity of money in the economy

Australian note, you will see that it is signed by the Secretary to the Treasury and the Governor of the Reserve Bank of Australia. The RBA is an example of a **central bank**—an institution designed to oversee the banking system and financial conditions of the economy. Other major central banks around the world include the Federal Reserve System of the United States, the Bank of England, the Bank of Japan and Germany's Bundesbank.

ORGANISATION OF THE RBA

The origins of the RBA are in the Commonwealth Bank of Australia, which was established in 1911 in response to the banking crisis of the 1890s. It combined the roles of a commercial bank and a central bank. Central bank functions developed gradually until World War II when the powers of the central banking arm were increased to include control over exchange rates and administration of monetary and banking policy. In 1945, these powers were formalised in the Commonwealth Bank Act and the Banking Act. The RBA was created in its current form by the Reserve Bank Act of 1959, when it was separated from the Commonwealth Bank and given its own Board.

The Reserve Bank Board is responsible for determining the bank's monetary and banking policy. The Board consists of nine members, including the Governor and Deputy Governor and the Secretary to the Treasury. The Governor and Deputy Governor are appointed by the Governor-General on the recommendation of the government. The remaining members of the Board are drawn from industry, universities and, in the past, the trade union movement. Individuals who are employed by banks are not eligible to be members of the Board as this would represent a conflict of interest.

The Reserve Bank Board determines monetary policy after advice from the various departments within the RBA. The Economic Group is responsible for economic analysis of international and domestic markets, forecasting and research relevant to the framing of monetary policy. The Financial Markets Group is responsible for implementation of policy decisions. The RBA operates independently of the government of the day, but in cases of irreconcilable differences over policy, legislation provides for the government to be able to overrule the RBA. However, this is clearly a measure of last resort. The procedures required to do this are politically demanding and thus reinforce the RBA's independence. For the most part, the RBA and the government interact on a consultative basis.

CHANGES IN THE RBA'S ROLE

The RBA has, historically, had three related jobs. The first is to monitor individual banks and ensure their stability. The RBA monitors each bank's financial condition and makes recommendations to the bank if it is experiencing financial difficulties and is unable to meet depositors' demands. This is known as *prudential supervision*. A related role is acting as a guarantor of stability in the banking system. As part of this role, the RBA also facilitates bank transactions by clearing cheques. This helps ensure that the banking system has sufficient liquidity at any one time.

Unlike the Federal Reserve in the United States, the RBA does not act as a lender of last resort. In the United States, when financially troubled banks find themselves short of cash, the Federal Reserve acts as a lender to those who cannot borrow anywhere else—in order to maintain stability in the overall banking system. In Australia, the RBA has not specifically acted in this capacity. Instead, it has ensured financial stability by monitoring liquidity in the system and assisting troubled banks to find a solution to their problems. For instance, the RBA has played a role in facilitating mergers and acquisitions of troubled banks by other banks.

The RBA's third job is to determine monetary policy. **Monetary policy** is the management by the central bank of liquidity conditions in the economy. **Liquidity conditions** refers to the price and availability of funding for the economy's expenditure. According to the RBA's charter, the objectives of monetary policy are to '…contribute to stability of the currency…, the maintenance of full employment; and the economic prosperity and welfare of the people of Australia'. The RBA's main contribution to these objectives is to control inflation. It has an announced target for monetary policy of keeping inflation to around 2–3% over time.

monetary policy
the management by the central bank of liquidity conditions in the economy

liquidity conditions
the price and availability of funding for the economy's expenditure

The long-run objective of monetary policy is to influence the rate of growth in the economy and the level of prices. When overall economic growth is too fast, and the economy is overheating, this puts upward pressure on prices. The RBA will implement a tightening of monetary policy to slow the economy. On the other hand, when the economy is experiencing slow growth, the RBA will implement expansionary monetary policy. This process is described in detail below.

The functions of the RBA have changed recently. An inquiry into the financial sector, known as the Wallis Inquiry, recommended the separation of these three roles. A new regulatory body, the Australian Prudential Regulation Authority (APRA), was created in 1998. APRA will perform many of the functions of prudential supervision of banks, as well as other financial institutions, that the RBA had previously performed, and the RBA will be left in charge of monetary policy and operation of the payments system, or the settlement of cheques between banks. In the past, the RBA used its instruments of monetary policy to exercise prudential control over the banking system, but with changes in the implementation of monetary policy and innovations in the financial sector in the last two decades, these controls were no longer considered useful. Under the new regulatory structure, the RBA no longer has an obligation to protect the interests of bank depositors, nor will it supervise any individual financial institution. Instead, it will concentrate more broadly on the overall stability of the financial system.

We discuss later in this chapter how the RBA actually influences the amount of cash in the economy, but it is worth noting here that the RBA's main tool is *open-market operations*—the purchase and sale of Australian government securities. (Recall that an Australian government security is a certificate of indebtedness of the federal government.) If the RBA decides it wants to change the amount of cash in the economy, it can either purchase government securities from financial institutions or sell them to financial institutions in the nation's bond markets.

The RBA is an important institution because changes in monetary policy can profoundly affect the economy. One of the *Ten Principles of Economics* in chapter 1 is that prices rise when the government prints too much money. Another of the *Ten Principles of Economics* is that society faces a short-run trade-off between inflation and unemployment. The power of the RBA rests on these principles.

For reasons we discuss more fully in the coming chapters, the RBA's policy decisions have an important influence on the economy's rate of inflation in the long run and the economy's employment and production in the short run.

■ **QUICK QUIZ** What role does the RBA play in the Australian economy?

BANKS AND THE MONEY SUPPLY

So far we have introduced the concept of 'money' and discussed how the RBA influences the liquidity or cash in the system by buying and selling government securities in open-market operations. We now extend our analysis to explain how changes in the amount of cash in the system affect the amount of money in the economy. We do this by examining the central role that banks play in the monetary system.

Recall that the amount of money you hold includes both currency (the notes in your wallet and coins in your pocket) and deposits at banks (the balances in your savings and cheque accounts). Because deposits are held in banks, the behaviour of banks can influence the quantity of deposits in the economy and, therefore, the money supply. This section examines how banks affect the money supply and how they complicate the job of controlling the interest rate and thus the money supply.

THE SIMPLE CASE OF 100%-RESERVE BANKING

To see how banks influence the money supply, it is useful to imagine first a world without any banks at all. In this simple world, currency is the only form of money. To be concrete, let's suppose that the total quantity of currency is $100. The supply of money is, therefore, $100.

Now suppose that someone opens a bank, called First State Bank. First State Bank is only a depository institution. That is, the bank accepts deposits but does not make loans. The purpose of the bank is to give depositors a safe place to keep their money. Whenever people deposit some money, the bank keeps the money in its vault until the depositors come to withdraw it or write cheques against their balances. Deposits that banks have received but have not loaned out are called **reserves**. In this imaginary economy, all deposits are held as reserves, so this system is called *100%-reserve banking*.

reserves
deposits that banks have received but have not lent out

We can express the financial position of First State Bank with a *T-account*, which is a simplified accounting statement that shows changes in a bank's assets and liabilities. Here is the T-account for First State Bank if the economy's entire $100 of money is deposited in the bank:

FIRST STATE BANK

Assets		Liabilities	
Reserves	$100.00	Deposits	$100.00

On the left-hand side of the T-account are the bank's assets of $100 (the reserves it holds in its vaults). On the right-hand side of the T-account are the bank's liabilities of $100 (the amount it owes to its depositors). Notice that the assets and liabilities of First State Bank exactly balance.

Now consider the money supply in this imaginary economy. Before First State Bank opens, the money supply is the $100 of currency that people are holding. After the bank opens and people deposit their currency, the money supply is the $100 of current deposits. (There is no longer any currency outstanding, for it is all in the bank vault.) Each deposit in the bank reduces currency and raises current deposits by exactly the same amount, leaving the money supply unchanged. Thus, *if banks hold all deposits in reserve, banks do not influence the supply of money.*

MONEY CREATION WITH FRACTIONAL-RESERVE BANKING

Eventually, the bankers at First State Bank may start to reconsider their policy of 100%-reserve banking. Leaving all that money sitting idle in their vaults seems unnecessary. Why not use some of it to make loans? Families buying houses, firms building new factories, and students paying for university would all be happy to pay interest to borrow some of that money for a while. Of course, First State Bank has to keep some reserves so that currency is available if depositors want to make withdrawals. But if the flow of new deposits is roughly the same as the flow of withdrawals, First State needs to keep only a fraction of its deposits in reserve. Thus, First State adopts a system called **fractional-reserve banking**.

Let's suppose that First State decides to keep 10% of its deposits in reserve and to lend the rest. Banks may hold reserves because people may want to withdraw some cash from their accounts. We say that the **reserve ratio**—the fraction of total deposits that the bank holds as reserves—is 10%. Now let's look again at the bank's T-account:

fractional-reserve banking
a banking system in which banks hold only a fraction of deposits as reserves

reserve ratio
the fraction of deposits that banks hold as reserves

FIRST STATE BANK

Assets		Liabilities	
Reserves	$10.00	Deposits	$100.00
Loans	90.00		

First State still has $100 in liabilities because making the loans did not alter the bank's obligation to its depositors. But now the bank has two kinds of assets—it has $10 of reserves in its vault, and it has loans of $90. (These loans are liabilities of the people taking out the loans but they are assets of the bank making the loans, because the borrowers will later repay the bank.) In total, First State's assets still equal its liabilities.

Once again consider the supply of money in the economy. Before First State makes any loans, the money supply is the $100 of deposits in the bank. Yet when First State makes these loans, the money supply increases. The depositors still have current deposits totalling $100, but now the borrowers hold $90 in currency. The money supply (which equals currency plus current deposits) equals $190. Thus, *when banks hold only a fraction of deposits in reserve, banks create money.*

At first, this creation of money by fractional-reserve banking may seem too good to be true because it appears that the bank has created money out of thin air. To make this creation of money seem less miraculous, note that when First State Bank lends some of its reserves and creates money, it does not create any

'I've heard a lot about money, and now I'd like to try some.'

wealth. Loans from First State give the borrowers some currency and thus the ability to buy goods and services. Yet the borrowers are also taking on debts, so the loans do not make them any richer. In other words, as a bank creates the asset of money, it also creates a corresponding liability for its borrowers. At the end of this process of money creation, the economy is more liquid in the sense that there is more of the medium of exchange, but the economy is no wealthier than before.

THE MONEY MULTIPLIER

The creation of money does not stop with First State Bank. Suppose the borrower from First State uses the $90 to buy something from someone who then deposits the currency in Second State Bank. Here is the T-account for Second State Bank:

SECOND STATE BANK

Assets		Liabilities	
Reserves	$ 9.00	Deposits	$90.00
Loans	81.00		

After the deposit, this bank has liabilities of $90. If Second State also has a reserve ratio of 10%, it keeps assets of $9 in reserve and makes $81 in loans. In this way, Second State Bank creates an additional $81 of money. If this $81 is eventually deposited in Third State Bank, which also has a reserve ratio of 10%, this bank keeps $8.10 in reserve and makes $72.90 in loans. Here is the T-account for Third State Bank:

THIRD STATE BANK

Assets		Liabilities	
Reserves	$ 8.10	Deposits	$81.00
Loans	72.90		

The process goes on and on. Each time that money is deposited and a bank loan is made, more money is created.

How much money is eventually created in this economy? Let's add it up:

Original deposit	=	$ 100.00
First State lending	=	90.00 [= 0.9 × $100.00]
Second State lending	=	81.00 [= 0.9 × $90.00]
Third State lending	=	72.90 [= 0.9 × $81.00]
•		•
•		•
•		•
Total money supply	=	$1000.00

It turns out that even though this process of money creation can continue forever, it does not create an infinite amount of money. If you laboriously add the infinite sequence of numbers in the foregoing example, you find the $100 of reserves generates $1000 of money. The amount of money the banking system generates with each dollar of reserves is called the **money multiplier**. In this imaginary economy, where the $100 of reserves generates $1000 of money, the money multiplier is 10.

What determines the size of the money multiplier? It turns out that the answer is simple—*the money multiplier is the reciprocal of the reserve ratio*. If R is the reserve ratio for all banks in the economy, then each dollar of reserves generates $1/R$ dollars of money. In our example, $R = 1/10$, so the money multiplier is 10.

This reciprocal formula for the money multiplier makes sense. If a bank holds $1000 in deposits, then a reserve ratio of 1/10 (10%) means that the bank must hold $100 in reserves. The money multiplier just turns this idea around—if the banking system holds a total of $100 in reserves, it can have only $1000 in deposits. Similarly, if the reserve ratio were 1/5 (20%), the banking system must have five times as much in deposits as in reserves, implying a money multiplier of 5. The higher the reserve ratio, the less of each deposit banks lend, and the smaller the money multiplier. In the special case of 100%-reserve banking, the reserve ratio is 1, the money multiplier is 1, and banks do not create money.

money multiplier
the amount of money the banking system generates with each dollar of reserves

MONETARY POLICY IN AUSTRALIA TODAY

As we have already discussed, the RBA is responsible for influencing the amount of liquidity in the system. Now that we understand how fractional-reserve banking works, we are in a better position to understand how the RBA uses its control over liquidity to influence the money supply in the economy. Because the banking system creates money in a system of fractional-reserve banking, the RBA cannot directly control the money supply. It can only affect the amount of cash in the system in the short-run. **Cash** refers to the amount of currency and bank reserves in the economy. When the RBA changes the amount of cash, it indirectly influences the amount of money created through fractional-reserve banking.

The instrument that the RBA uses for monetary policy in Australia today is control of the overnight interest rate in the short-term money market—what is referred to as the *cash rate*. The **cash rate** is the interest rate that financial institutions can earn on overnight loans of their currency or reserves. The RBA influences the amount of cash in the system by setting a target for the interest rate

cash
the amount of currency and bank reserves in the economy

cash rate
the interest rate that financial institutions can earn on overnight loans of their currency or reserves

at which banks can lend or borrow money in the overnight market. When the RBA decides that it wants to implement a change in monetary policy, it announces a new target for the cash rate. It then stands ready to buy or sell government securities through *open-market operations* to guarantee that its target rate is the equilibrium interest rate in the short-term money market. In essence, the RBA is setting the 'price' of money, and allowing the quantity to adjust to achieve that price.

The cash rate is significant because it is the interest rate that is the foundation for all other interest rates in the economy. The cash rate is like a wholesale rate that financial institutions charge one another for borrowing and lending. When financial institutions then decide to lend to businesses or private individuals, they use the cash rate as a basis for determining the interest rates they will charge.

How does the change in the cash rate affect the level of economic activity throughout the economy? If the economy is growing too fast, the RBA will raise short-term interest rates. This tends to push up deposit and borrowing rates at financial institutions in general. For some borrowers, it will now not make sense to borrow money for previously intended purposes, whether it be an investment project, a consumer item or the acquisition of financial assets. Hence there are fewer opportunities for banks and other financial institutions to profitably expand their balance sheets by making more loans. The pace of money and credit creation slows as a result. In addition, the demand for real goods and services falls or grows more slowly, and pressure on resource usage in the economy lessens, resulting in a fall in prices or in their rate of increase. This process will be described in more detail in chapter 17, but this brief explanation helps us understand how the RBA's actions in the short-term money market affect the long-run position of the economy.

Open-market operations The RBA uses open-market operations to influence the cash rate. An **open-market operation** is the purchase or sale of Australian government securities. The cash rate is the interest rate that equates the demand for funds that financial institutions borrow overnight with the supply of funds financial institutions want to lend overnight. If the RBA sees that there is an excess supply of funds in the overnight market at the target interest rate, it will withdraw funds from the market by selling government securities. When it sells government securities, it takes in cash from the financial institutions purchasing the government securities, thus reducing the cash in the system. If there is an excess demand for funds at the target interest rate, the RBA will buy government securities, thus increasing the cash in the system. When the RBA increases or decreases the amount of cash in the system, this changes the price of cash—the cash rate.

Open-market operations are easy to conduct. In fact, the RBA's purchases and sales of government securities in the nation's bond markets are similar to the transactions that individuals might undertake for their own portfolios. (Of course, when an individual buys or sells a security, money changes hands, but the amount of money in circulation remains the same.) In addition, the RBA can use open-market operations to effect small or large changes in the cash rate on any day without major changes in laws or banking regulations.

Reserve requirements The RBA has used **reserve requirements** in the past to influence the money supply. Reserve requirements are regulations on the minimum amount of reserves that banks must hold against deposits. They

open-market operations
the purchase and sale of Australian government securities by the RBA

reserve requirements
regulations on the minimum amount of reserves that banks must hold against deposits

influence how much money the banking system can create with each dollar of reserves. An increase in reserve requirements means that banks must hold more reserves and, therefore, can lend less of each dollar that is deposited; as a result, it raises the reserve ratio, lowers the money multiplier and decreases the money supply. Conversely, a decrease in reserve requirements lowers the reserve ratio, raises the money multiplier and increases the money supply. Changing reserve requirements can be disruptive to the business of banking. If the central bank changes reserve requirements, some banks would find themselves short of reserves, even though there had been no change in deposits. As a result, they would have to curtail lending until they built their level of reserves to the new required level. The RBA no longer uses changes in reserve requirements because the decisions about the amount of reserves to hold is more a matter of prudential control. The RBA concentrates on control of the cash rate, as described above.

PROBLEMS IN CONTROLLING THE MONEY SUPPLY

The RBA's control over the cash rate has a powerful effect on the money supply. Yet the RBA's control of the money supply is not precise. The RBA must wrestle with two problems, each of which arises because much of the money supply is created by our system of fractional-reserve banking.

The first problem is that the RBA does not control the amount of money that households choose to hold as deposits in banks. The more money that households deposit, the more reserves banks have, and the more money the banking system can create. The less money that households deposit, the less reserves banks have, and the less money the banking system can create. To see why this is a problem, suppose that one day people begin to lose confidence in the banking system and, therefore, decide to withdraw deposits and hold more currency. When this happens, the banking system loses reserves and creates less money. The money supply falls, even without any RBA action.

The second problem of monetary control is that the RBA does not control the amount that bankers choose to lend. Once money is deposited in a bank, it creates more money only when the bank lends it out. Yet banks can choose the amount of reserves they wish to hold. To see why variations in the amount of reserves complicate control of the money supply, suppose that one day bankers become more cautious about economic conditions and decide to make fewer loans and hold greater reserves. In this case, the banking system creates less money than it otherwise would. Because of the bankers' decision, the money supply falls.

Hence, in a system of fractional-reserve banking, the amount of money in the economy depends in part on the behaviour of depositors and bankers. Because the RBA cannot control or perfectly predict this behaviour, it cannot perfectly control the money supply. Partly for this reason, the RBA chose to shift its emphasis from controlling the money supply to targeting interest rates. The RBA still collects data on deposits and reserves from banks and non-bank financial institutions (NBFIs) every week, so it is quickly aware of any changes in depositor or banker behaviour. However, it has much more control over the cash rate and can implement changes in the cash rate fairly quickly. This can be seen in figure 12.1 (p. 264), where the target cash rate is graphed against the actual cash rate. This graph shows that when the RBA sets a target cash rate, it is able to achieve this rate fairly precisely.

Figure 12.1

THE TARGET CASH RATE AND THE ACTUAL CASH RATE. This graph shows the cash rate the RBA targets and the overnight interest rate actually obtained.

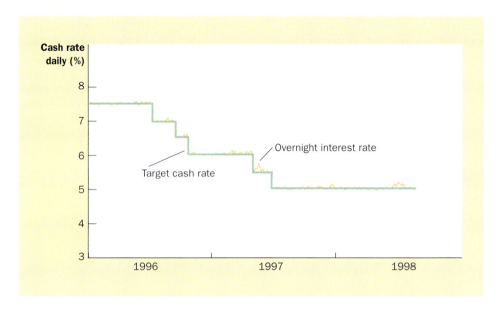

CASE STUDY   BANK RUNS AND THE MONEY SUPPLY

Although bank runs are infrequent occurrences, they do happen occasionally. There were bank runs in Victoria in 1990–91. A bank run occurs when depositors suspect that a bank may go bankrupt and, therefore, 'run' to the bank to withdraw their deposits.

Bank runs are a problem for banks under fractional-reserve banking. Because a bank holds only a fraction of its deposits in reserve, it cannot satisfy withdrawal requests from all depositors. Even if the bank is in fact *solvent* (meaning that its assets exceed its liabilities), it will not have enough cash on hand to allow all depositors immediate access to all of their money. When a run occurs, the bank is forced to close its doors until some bank loans are repaid or until some arrangement is made by the RBA to provide it with the currency it needs to satisfy depositors.

Bank runs complicate the control of the money supply. An important example of this problem occurred during the Great Depression in the early 1930s. After a wave of bank runs and bank closures, households and bankers became more cautious. Households withdrew their deposits from banks, preferring to hold their money in the form of currency. This decision reversed the process of money creation, as bankers responded to falling reserves by reducing bank loans. At the same time, bankers increased their reserve ratios so that they would have enough cash on hand to meet their depositors' demands in any future bank runs. The higher reserve ratio reduced the money multiplier, which also reduced the money supply. This contraction in money supply occurred even though there was no deliberate action by the Commonwealth Bank of Australia.

However, the effects of the contraction in deposits were less severe in Australia than in other countries. Many economists nonetheless point to this fall in the money supply to explain the high unemployment and falling prices that prevailed during this period. (In future chapters we examine the mechanisms by which changes in the money supply affect unemployment and prices.)

Today, bank runs are not a major problem for the banking system or the RBA. Even though the RBA and APRA do not specifically guarantee the safety of deposits at banks, they discourage bank runs through ensuring stability of the financial system. As a result, most people see bank runs only in films. In some other countries, though, other means are used to prevent people from making runs on banks. During the recent Asian financial crisis, authorities in different countries imposed controls on various types of financial transactions to prevent people from withdrawing their deposits from the banking system.

■ **QUICK QUIZ** Describe how banks create money.

CONCLUSION

Several years ago, a book made the best-seller list in the United States with the title *Secrets of the Temple: How the Federal Reserve Runs the Country*. Although no doubt an exaggeration, this title highlights the important role of the monetary system in our daily lives. Whenever we buy or sell anything, we are relying on the extraordinarily useful social convention called 'money'. Now that we know what money is and what determines its supply, we can discuss how changes in the quantity of money affect the economy. We begin to discuss that topic in the next chapter.

Summary

- The term *money* refers to assets that people regularly use to buy goods and services.

- Money serves three functions. As a medium of exchange, it provides the item used to make transactions. As a unit of account, it provides the way in which prices and other economic values are recorded. As a store of value, it provides a way of transferring purchasing power from the present to the future.

- Commodity money, such as gold, is money that has intrinsic value—it would be valued even if it were not used as money. Fiat money, such as plastic dollars, is money without intrinsic value—it would be worthless if it were not used as money.

- In the Australian economy, money takes the form of currency and various types of bank deposits, such as cheque accounts.

- The Reserve Bank of Australia, Australia's central bank, is responsible for regulating the Australian monetary system. The RBA sets interest rates to reach a target range of inflation. It does this through open-market operations—the purchase of government securities increases the amount of cash in the economy, thus lowering the interest rate, and the sale of government securities decreases the amount of cash in the economy, thus increasing the interest rate.

- When banks lend some of their deposits, they increase the quantity of money in the economy. Because of this role of banks in determining the money supply, the RBA's control of the money supply is imperfect.

Key concepts

money, p. 250
medium of exchange, p. 251
unit of account, p. 251
store of value, p. 251
liquidity, p. 251
commondity money, p. 251
fiat money, p. 252
money supply, p. 252

currency, p. 252
current deposits, p. 253
Reserve Bank of Australia (RBA), p. 255
central bank, p. 256
monetary policy, p. 257
liquidity conditions, p. 257
reserves, p. 258
fractional-reserve banking, p. 259

reserve ratio, p. 259
money multiplier, p. 261
cash, p. 261
cash rate, p. 261
open-market operations, p. 262
reserve requirements, p. 262

Questions for review

1. What distinguishes money from other assets in the economy?

2. What is commodity money? What is fiat money? Which kind do we use?

3. What are current deposits, and why should they be included in the supply of money?

4. If the RBA wants to increase the money supply with open-market operations, what does it do?

5. What is the cash rate? What happens to the money supply when the RBA raises the cash rate?

6. What are reserve requirements? Why doesn't the RBA use reserve requirements to control the money supply?

7. Why can't the RBA control the money supply perfectly?

8. What is meant by 'prudential supervision'? Which agency is now responsible for this function in the Australian financial system?

Problems and applications

1. Which of the following are money in the Australian economy? Which are not? Explain your answers by discussing each of the three functions of money.
   a. an Australian dollar coin
   b. an Indian rupee
   c. a painting by Brett Whitely
   d. a plastic credit card

2. In some places, people try to barter goods and services rather than pay for them. Here is an example from a newspaper column: 'Will swap custom-designed wedding gown and up to 6 bridesmaids' gowns for 2 return tickets and 3 nights' lodging in Tasmania.'
   a. Why would it be difficult to run our economy using barter instead of money?
   b. In light of your answer to part (a), why might newspaper notices like the one above exist?

3. What characteristics of an asset make it useful as a medium of exchange? as a store of value?

4. Consider how the following situations would affect the economy's monetary system.
   a. Suppose that the people on Yap discovered an easy way to make limestone wheels. How would this development affect the usefulness of stone wheels as money? Explain.
   b. Suppose that someone in Australia discovered an easy way to counterfeit $100 notes. How would this development affect the Australian monetary system? Explain.

5. Your uncle repays a $100 loan from Tenth State Bank (TSB) by writing a $100 cheque on his TSB cheque account. Use T-accounts to show the effect of this transaction on your uncle and on TSB. Has your uncle's wealth changed? Explain.

6. Beleaguered State Bank (BSB) holds $250 million in deposits and maintains a reserve ratio of 10%.
   a. Show a T-account for BSB.
   b. Now suppose that BSB's largest depositor

withdraws $10 million from her account in cash. If BSB decides to restore its reserve ratio by reducing the amount of loans outstanding, show its new T-account.
  c. Explain what effect BSB's action will have on other banks.
  d. Why might it be difficult for BSB to take the action described in part (b)? Discuss another way for BSB to return to its original reserve ratio.

7. You take $100 you had kept under your pillow and deposit it in your bank account. If this $100 stays in the banking system as reserves and if banks hold reserves equal to 10% of deposits, by how much does the total amount of deposits in the banking system increase? By how much does the money supply increase?

8. The RBA conducts a $10 million open-market purchase of government bonds. If the required reserve ratio is 10%, what is the largest possible increase in the money supply that could result? Explain. What is the smallest possible increase? Explain.

9. Suppose that the T-account for First State Bank is as follows:

FIRST STATE BANK

Assets		Liabilities	
Reserves	$100 000	Deposits	$500 000
Loans	400 000		

  a. Suppose APRA, in response to the Asian financial crisis, suggests that banks hold 5% of deposits as reserves. How much in excess reserves does First State now hold?
  b. Assume that all other banks hold only the required amount of reserves. If First State decides to reduce its reserves to only the required amount, by how much would the economy's money supply increase?

10. Suppose that banks hold reserves of 10% against cheque account deposits.
  a. If the RBA sells $1 million of government securities, what is the effect on the economy's reserves and money supply?
  b. Suppose banks decide to lower their reserves to 5%. Why might banks choose to do so? What is the overall change in the money multiplier and the money supply as a result of these actions?

11. Assume that the banking system has total reserves of $100 billion. Assume also that reserves are 10% of cheque account deposits.
  a. What is the money multiplier? What is the money supply?
  b. Under what circumstances might banks raise their reserves to 20% of deposits? What is the change in reserves and the change in the money supply?

12. (This problem is challenging.) The economy of Elmendyn contains 2000 $1 notes.
  a. If people hold all money as currency, what is the quantity of money?
  b. If people hold all money as current deposits and banks maintain 100% reserves, what is the quantity of money?
  c. If people hold equal amounts of currency and current deposits and banks maintain 100% reserves, what is the quantity of money?
  d. If people hold all money as current deposits and banks maintain a reserve ratio of 10%, what is the quantity of money?
  e. If people hold equal amounts of currency and current deposits and banks maintain a reserve ratio of 10%, what is the quantity of money?

13

INFLATION: ITS CAUSES AND COSTS

Although today you need a dollar or two to buy yourself an ice-cream, life was very different 50 years ago. If you were walking along Bondi Beach on a hot summer's day and wanted to buy an ice-cream, it would cost you about 5 cents.

You are probably not surprised at the increase in the price of ice-cream. In our economy, most prices tend to rise over time. This increase in the overall level of prices is called *inflation*. Earlier in the book we examined how economists measure the inflation rate as the percentage change in the consumer price index, the GDP deflator, or some other index of the overall price level. These price indexes show that, over the past 50 years, prices have risen on average about 5% per year. Accumulated over so many years, a 5% annual inflation rate leads to almost a 15-fold increase in the price level.

Inflation may seem natural and inevitable to a person who grew up in Australia during the second half of the twentieth century, but in fact it is not inevitable at all. There were long periods in the nineteenth century during which most prices fell—a phenomenon called *deflation*. The average level of prices in the Australian economy was 20% lower in 1898 than in 1889. Farmers who had accumulated large debts suffered when the fall in crop prices reduced their incomes and thus their ability to pay off their debts. It was a time of great turmoil in the colonies.

Although inflation has been the norm in more recent history, there has been substantial variation in the rate at which prices rise. From 1990 to 1998, prices

IN THIS CHAPTER YOU WILL

See why inflation results from rapid growth in the money supply

Learn the meaning of the classical dichotomy and monetary neutrality

See why some countries print so much money that they experience hyperinflation

Examine how the nominal interest rate responds to the inflation rate

Consider the various costs that inflation imposes on society

rose at an average rate of about 2% per year. In contrast, in the 1970s, prices rose by almost 11% per year, which meant the price level increased by more than 2½ times over the decade. The public often views such high rates of inflation as a major economic problem. In fact, when Malcolm Fraser led the Coalition to victory in the 1975 election, high inflation was one of the major issues of the campaign. Fraser promised to 'fight inflation first'.

International data show an even broader range of inflation experiences. Germany after World War I experienced a spectacular example of inflation. The price of a newspaper rose from 0.3 of a mark in January 1921 to 70 000 000 marks less than 2 years later. Other prices rose by similar amounts. An extraordinarily high rate of inflation such as this is called *hyperinflation*. The German hyperinflation had such an adverse effect on the German economy that it is often viewed as one contributor to the rise of Nazism and, as a result, World War II. Over the past 50 years, with this episode still in mind, German policymakers have been especially averse to inflation, and Germany has had much lower inflation than Australia. New Zealand had such high inflation in the 1970s and 1980s that the central bank made low inflation its number one priority in the 1990s. In 1996, the Reserve Bank of New Zealand announced an inflation target of between 0% and 3% per year.

What determines whether an economy experiences inflation and, if so, how much? This chapter answers the question by developing the *quantity theory of money*. Chapter 1 summarised this theory as one of the *Ten Principles of Economics* —prices rise when the government prints too much money. This insight has a long and venerable tradition among economists. The quantity theory was discussed by the famous eighteenth-century philosopher David Hume, and has been advocated more recently by the prominent economist Milton Friedman. This theory of inflation can explain both moderate inflations, such as those we have experienced in Australia, and hyperinflations, such as those experienced in interwar Germany and, more recently, in some Latin American countries.

After developing a theory of inflation, we turn to a related question: Why is inflation a problem? At first glance, the answer to this question may seem obvious—inflation is a problem because people don't like it. In the 1970s, when Australia experienced relatively high rates of inflation, opinion polls placed inflation as one of the most important issues facing the nation. This sentiment was echoed in other countries as well. In the United States, President Ford called inflation 'public enemy number one'. Ford briefly wore a 'WIN' button on his lapel—for Whip Inflation Now.

But what, exactly, are the costs that inflation imposes on a society? The answer may surprise you. Identifying the various costs of inflation is not as straightforward as it first appears. As a result, although all economists decry hyperinflation, some economists argue that the costs of moderate inflation are not nearly as large as the general public believes.

THE CAUSES OF INFLATION

We begin our study of inflation by developing the quantity theory of money. Most economists rely on this theory for explaining the long-run determinants of the price level and the inflation rate.

THE LEVEL OF PRICES AND THE VALUE OF MONEY

Suppose we observe over some period of time the price of an ice-cream rising from 5 cents to a dollar. What conclusion should we draw from the fact that people are willing to give up so much more money in exchange for an ice-cream? It is possible that people have come to enjoy ice-cream more (perhaps because some chemist has developed a miraculous new flavour). Yet that is probably not the case. It is more likely that people's enjoyment of ice-cream has stayed roughly the same and that, over time, the money used to buy ice-cream has become less valuable. Indeed, the first insight about inflation is that it is more about the value of money than about the value of goods.

This insight helps point the way towards a theory of inflation. When the consumer price index and other measures of the price level rise, commentators are often tempted to look at the many individual prices that make up these price indexes: 'The CPI rose by 3% last month, led by a 20% rise in the price of coffee and a 30% rise in the price of heating oil.' Although this approach does contain some interesting information about what's happening in the economy, it also misses a key point—inflation is an economy-wide phenomenon that concerns, first and foremost, the value of the economy's medium of exchange.

The economy's overall price level can be viewed in two ways. So far, we have viewed the price level as the price of a basket of goods and services. When the price level rises, people have to pay more for the goods and services they buy. Alternatively, we can view the price level as a measure of the value of money. A rise in the price level means a lower value of money because each dollar in your wallet now buys a smaller quantity of goods and services.

It may help to express these ideas mathematically. Suppose P is the price level as measured, for instance, by the consumer price index or the GDP deflator. Then P measures the number of dollars needed to buy a basket of goods and services. Now turn this idea around—the quantity of goods and services that can be bought with \$1 equals $1/P$. In other words, if P is the price of goods and services measured in terms of money, $1/P$ is the value of money measured in terms of goods and services. Thus, when the overall price level rises, the value of money falls.

MONEY SUPPLY, MONEY DEMAND AND MONETARY EQUILIBRIUM

What determines the value of money? The answer to this question, like many in economics, is supply and demand. Just as the supply of and demand for bananas determines the price of bananas, the supply of and demand for money determines the value of money. Thus, our next step in developing the quantity theory of money is to consider the determinants of money supply and money demand.

First consider money supply. In the last chapter, we discussed how the Reserve Bank of Australia (RBA), together with the banking system, determines the supply of money. Through open-market operations, the RBA can change the quantity of reserves available to banks, which in turn influences the quantity of money that the banking system can create. For our purposes in this chapter, we ignore most of the complications introduced by the banking system and simply take the quantity of money supplied as a policy variable that the RBA controls directly. We do this even though the RBA influences the money supply indirectly, through its control over the cash rate, as we explained in the last chapter.

Now consider money demand. There are many determinants of the quantity of money demanded, just as there are many determinants of the quantity demanded of other goods and services. How much money people choose to hold in their wallets, for instance, depends on how much they rely on credit cards and on whether an automatic teller machine is easy to find. And, as we will emphasise in a later chapter, the quantity of money demanded depends on the interest rate that a person could earn by using the money to buy an interest-bearing bond rather than leaving it in a wallet or low-interest cheque account.

Although many variables affect the demand for money, one variable stands out in importance—the average level of prices in the economy. People hold money because it is the medium of exchange. Unlike other assets, such as bonds or shares, people can use money to buy the goods and services on their shopping lists. How much money they choose to hold for this purpose depends on the prices of those goods and services. The higher prices are, the more money the typical transaction requires, and the more money people will choose to hold in their wallets and cheque accounts. That is, a higher price level (a lower value of money) increases the quantity of money demanded.

What ensures that the quantity of money the RBA supplies balances the quantity of money people demand? The answer, it turns out, depends on the time horizon being considered. Later in this book we will examine the short-run answer, and we will see that interest rates play a key role. In the long run, however, the answer is different and much simpler. *In the long run, the overall level of prices adjusts to the level at which the demand for money equals the supply.* If the price level is above the equilibrium level, people will want to hold more money than the RBA has created, so the price level must fall to balance supply and demand. If the price level is below the equilibrium level, people will want to hold less money than the RBA has created, and the price level must rise to balance supply and demand. At the equilibrium price level, the quantity of money that people want to hold exactly balances the quantity of money supplied by the RBA.

Figure 13.1 illustrates these ideas. The horizontal axis of this graph shows the quantity of money. The left-hand vertical axis shows the value of money, and the right-hand vertical axis shows the price level. Notice that the price-level axis is inverted—when the value of money is high (as measured on the left axis), the price level is low (as measured on the right axis). The supply curve for money in this figure is vertical, indicating that the RBA has fixed the quantity of money available. The demand curve for money is downward-sloping, indicating that when the value of money is low, people demand a larger quantity of it to buy goods and services. At the equilibrium, shown in the figure as point A, the quantity of money demanded balances the quantity of money supplied. This equilibrium of money supply and money demand determines the value of money and the price level.

THE EFFECTS OF A MONETARY INJECTION

Let's now consider the effects of a change in monetary policy. To do so, imagine that the economy is in equilibrium and then, suddenly, the RBA does as economist Milton Friedman suggested and doubles the supply of money by printing some more and dropping it around the country from helicopters. (Or, less dramatically and more realistically, the RBA could inject money into the economy by buying some government bonds from the public in open-market operations.)

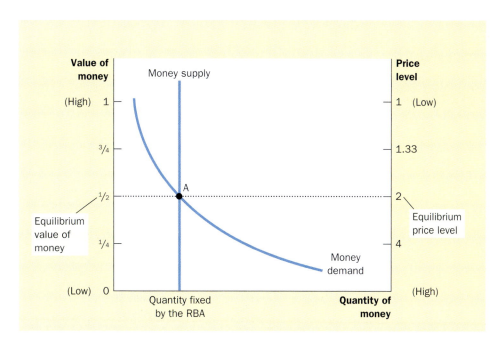

Figure 13.1

HOW THE SUPPLY OF AND DEMAND FOR MONEY DETERMINE THE EQUILIBRIUM PRICE LEVEL. The horizontal axis shows the quantity of money. The left vertical axis shows the value of money, and the right vertical axis shows the price level. The supply curve for money is vertical because the quantity of money supplied is fixed by the RBA. The demand curve for money is downward-sloping because people want to hold a larger quantity of money when each dollar buys less. At the equilibrium, point A, the value of money (on the left axis) and the price level (on the right axis) have adjusted to bring the quantity of money supplied and the quantity of money demanded into balance.

What happens after such a monetary injection? How does the new equilibrium compare with the old one?

Figure 13.2 on page 274 shows what happens. The monetary injection shifts the supply curve to the right from MS_1 to MS_2, and the equilibrium moves from point A to point B. As a result, the value of money (shown on the left axis) decreases from ½ to ¼, and the equilibrium price level (shown on the right axis) increases from 2 to 4. In other words, when an increase in the money supply makes dollars more plentiful, the result is an increase in the price level that makes each dollar less valuable.

This explanation of how the price level is determined and why it might change over time is called the **quantity theory of money**. According to the quantity theory, the quantity of money available in the economy determines the value of money, and growth in the quantity of money is the primary cause of inflation. As Milton Friedman once put it, 'Inflation is always and everywhere a monetary phenomenon.'

quantity theory of money
a theory asserting that the quantity of money available determines the price level and that the growth rate in the quantity of money available determines the inflation rate

A BRIEF LOOK AT THE ADJUSTMENT PROCESS

So far we have compared the old equilibrium and the new equilibrium after an injection of money. How does the economy get from the old to the new equilibrium? A complete answer to this question requires an understanding of short-run fluctuations in the economy, which we examine later in this book. Yet, even now, it is instructive to consider briefly the adjustment process that occurs after a change in money supply.

The immediate effect of a monetary injection is to create an excess supply of money. Before the injection, the economy was in equilibrium (point A in figure 13.2). At the prevailing price level, people had exactly as much money as they

Figure 13.2

AN INCREASE IN THE MONEY SUPPLY. When the RBA increases the supply of money, the money supply curve shifts from MS_1 to MS_2. The value of money (on the left axis) and the price level (on the right axis) adjust to bring supply and demand back into balance. The equilibrium moves from point A to point B. Thus, when an increase in the money supply makes dollars more plentiful, the price level increases, making each dollar less valuable.

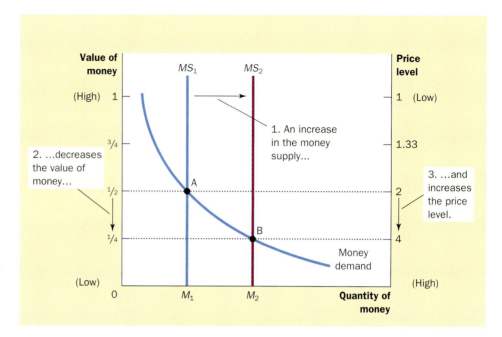

wanted. But after the helicopters drop the new money and people pick it up in the streets, people have more dollars in their wallets than they want. At the prevailing price level, the quantity of money supplied now exceeds the quantity demanded.

People try to get rid of this excess supply of money in various ways. They might buy goods and services with their excess holdings of money. Or they might use this excess money to make loans to others by buying bonds or by depositing the money in a bank savings account. These loans allow other people to buy goods and services. In either case, the injection of money increases the demand for goods and services.

Because the economy's ability to produce goods and services has not changed, this greater demand for goods and services causes the prices of goods and services to increase. The increase in the price level, in turn, increases the quantity of money demanded. Eventually, the economy reaches a new equilibrium (point B in figure 13.2) at which the quantity of money demanded again equals the quantity of money supplied. In this way, the overall price level for goods and services adjusts to bring money supply and money demand into balance.

THE CLASSICAL DICHOTOMY AND MONETARY NEUTRALITY

We have seen how changes in the money supply lead to changes in the average level of prices of goods and services. How do these monetary changes affect other important macroeconomic variables, such as production, employment, real wages and real interest rates? This question has long intrigued economists. Indeed, the great philosopher David Hume wrote about it in the eighteenth century. The answer we give today owes much to Hume's analysis.

Hume and his contemporaries suggested that all economic variables should be divided into two groups. The first group consists of **nominal variables**—variables measured in monetary units. The second group consists of **real variables**—variables measured in constant units. For example, the price of corn is a nominal variable because it is measured in dollars, and the value of a dollar is not constant. The amount of corn produced is a real variable because it is measured in kilograms, and a kilogram is a constant unit of measurement. Similarly, nominal GDP is a nominal variable because it measures the dollar value of the economy's output of goods and services, whereas real GDP is a real variable because it measures the value of the total quantity of goods and services produced in constant units.

Although prices quoted in terms of money are nominal variables, *relative* prices are real variables. For instance, the price of corn and the price of wheat are both nominal variables, but the price of corn relative to the price of wheat is a real variable because it is measured in kilograms of wheat per kilogram of corn. Similarly, the real wage (the dollar wage adjusted for inflation) is a real variable because it measures the rate at which the economy exchanges goods and services for each unit of labour. The real interest rate (the nominal interest rate adjusted for inflation) is a real variable because it measures the rate at which the economy exchanges goods and services produced today for goods and services produced in the future.

The division of variables into these two groups is called the **classical dichotomy**. Hume suggested that the classical dichotomy is useful in analysing the economy because different forces influence real and nominal variables. In particular, he argued, nominal variables are heavily influenced by developments in the economy's monetary system, whereas the monetary system is largely irrelevant for understanding the determinants of important real variables.

Notice that Hume's idea was implicit in our earlier discussions of the real economy in the long run. In previous chapters, we examined how real GDP, saving, investment, real interest rates and unemployment are determined without any mention of the existence of money. As explained in that analysis, the economy's production of goods and services depends on productivity and factor supplies, the real interest rate adjusts to balance the supply of and demand for loanable funds, the real wage adjusts to balance the supply of and demand for labour, and unemployment results when the real wage is, for some reason, kept above its equilibrium level. These important conclusions have nothing to do with the quantity of money supplied.

Changes in the supply of money, according to Hume, affect nominal variables but not real variables. When the central bank doubles the money supply, the price level doubles, the dollar wage doubles, and all other dollar values double. Real variables, such as production, employment, real wages and real interest rates, are unchanged. This irrelevance of monetary changes for real variables is called **monetary neutrality**.

An analogy sheds light on the meaning of monetary neutrality. Recall that, as the unit of account, money is the yardstick we use to measure economic transactions. When a central bank doubles the money supply, all prices double, and the value of the unit of account falls by half. A similar change would occur if the government were to reduce the length of a metre from 100 centimetres to 50 centimetres—as a result of the new unit of measurement, all *measured* distances (nominal variables) would double, but the *actual* distances (real variables) would

nominal variables
variables measured in monetary units

real variables
variables measured in constant units

classical dichotomy
the theoretical separation of nominal and real variables

monetary neutrality
the proposition that changes in the money supply do not affect real variables

remain the same. The dollar, like the metre, is merely a unit of measurement, so a change in its value should not have important real effects.

Is this conclusion of monetary neutrality a realistic description of the world in which we live? The answer is 'not completely'. A change in the length of a metre from 100 to 50 centimetres would not matter much in the long run, but in the short run it would certainly lead to confusion and various mistakes. Similarly, most economists today believe that over short periods of time-within the span of a year or two—there is reason to think that monetary changes do have important effects on real variables. Hume himself also doubted that monetary neutrality would apply in the short run. (We will turn to the study of short-run non-neutrality in a later chapter, and this topic will shed light on the reasons the RBA changes the supply of money over time.)

Yet most economists today accept Hume's conclusion as a description of the economy in the long run. Over the course of a decade, for instance, monetary changes have important effects on nominal variables but only negligible effects on real variables. When studying long-run changes in the economy, the neutrality of money offers a good description of how the world works.

VELOCITY AND THE QUANTITY EQUATION

We can obtain another perspective on the quantity theory of money by considering the following question: How many times per year is the typical dollar coin used to pay for a newly produced good or service? The answer to this question is given by a variable called the **velocity of money**. In physics, the term *velocity* refers to the speed (and direction) at which an object travels. In economics, the velocity of money refers to the speed at which the typical note or coin travels around the economy from wallet to wallet.

To calculate the velocity of money, we divide the nominal value of output (nominal GDP) by the quantity of money. If P is the price level (the GDP deflator), Y the quantity of output (real GDP) and M the quantity of money, then velocity is:

$$V = (P \times Y)/M$$

velocity of money
the rate at which money changes hands

To see why this makes sense, imagine a simple economy that produces only pizza. Suppose that the economy produces 100 pizzas in a year, that a pizza sells for $10, and that the quantity of money in the economy is $50 consisting of 50 dollar coins. Then the velocity of money is:

$$V = (\$10 \times 100)/\$50$$
$$= 20$$

In this economy, people spend a total of $1000 per year on pizza. For this $1000 of spending to take place with only $50 of money, each dollar coin must change hands 20 times per year.

With slight algebraic rearrangement, this equation can be rewritten as:

$$M \times V = P \times Y$$

This equation states that the quantity of money (M) times the velocity of money (V) equals the price of output (P) times the amount of output (Y). It is called the

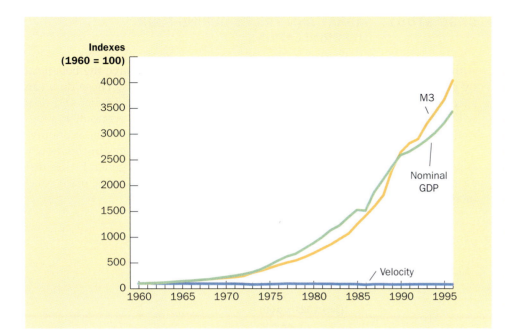

Figure 13.3

NOMINAL GDP, THE QUANTITY OF MONEY AND THE VELOCITY OF MONEY. This figure shows the nominal value of output as measured by nominal GDP, the quantity of money as measured by M3 (see table 12.1), and the velocity of money as measured by their ratio. For comparability, all three series have been scaled to equal 100 in 1960. Notice that nominal GDP and the quantity of money have grown dramatically over this period, while velocity has been relatively stable.

SOURCE: Reserve Bank of Australia.

quantity equation because it relates the quantity of money (M) to the nominal value of output ($P \times Y$). The quantity equation shows that an increase in the quantity of money in an economy must be reflected in one of the other three variables—the price level must rise, the quantity of output must rise, or the velocity of money must fall.

In many cases, it turns out that the velocity of money is relatively stable. For example, figure 13.3 shows nominal GDP, the quantity of money (as measured by M3, see table 12.1, page 254), and the velocity of money for the Australian economy since 1960. Although the velocity of money is not exactly constant, it has not changed dramatically. In contrast, the money supply and nominal GDP during this period have increased more than tenfold. Thus, for some purposes, the assumption of constant velocity may be a good approximation.

We now have all the elements necessary to explain the equilibrium price level and inflation rate. Here they are:

1. The velocity of money is relatively stable over time.
2. Because velocity is stable, when the RBA changes the quantity of money (M), it causes proportionate changes in the nominal value of output ($P \times Y$).
3. The economy's output of goods and services (Y) is primarily determined by factor supplies and the available technology. In particular, because money is neutral, money does not affect output.
4. With output (Y) determined by factor supplies and technology, when the RBA alters the money supply (M) and induces parallel changes in the nominal value of output ($P \times Y$), these changes are reflected in changes in the price level (P).
5. Therefore, when the RBA increases the money supply rapidly, the result is a high rate of inflation.

These five steps are the essence of the quantity theory of money.

quantity equation
the equation $M \times V = P \times Y$, which relates the quantity of money, the velocity of money and the dollar value of the economy's output of goods and services

CASE STUDY MONEY AND PRICES DURING FOUR HYPERINFLATIONS

Although earthquakes can wreak havoc on a society, they have the beneficial by-product of providing much useful data for seismologists. These data can shed light on alternative theories and, thereby, help society predict and deal with future threats. Similarly, hyperinflations offer monetary economists a natural experiment they can use to study the effects of money on the economy.

Hyperinflations are interesting in part because the changes in the money supply and price level are so large. Indeed, hyperinflation is generally defined as inflation that exceeds 50% *per month*. This means that the price level increases more than 100-fold over the course of a year.

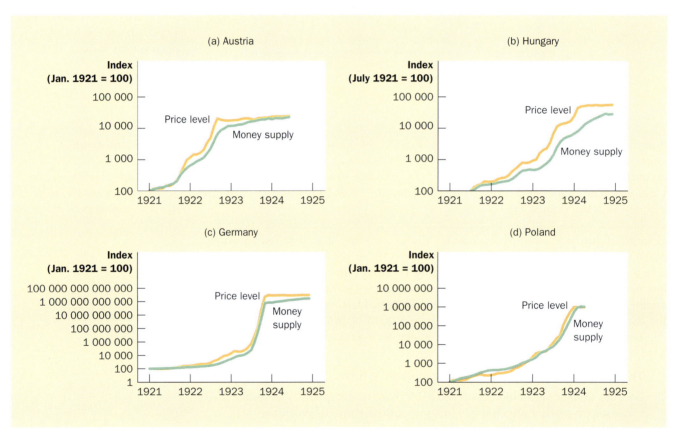

Figure 13.4

MONEY AND PRICES DURING FOUR HYPERINFLATIONS. This figure shows the quantity of money and the price level during four hyperinflations. (Note that these variables are graphed on *logarithmic* scales. This means that equal vertical distances on the graph represent equal *percentage* changes in the variable.) In each case, the quantity of money and the price level move closely together. The strong association between these two variables is consistent with the quantity theory of money, which states that growth in the money supply is the primary cause of inflation.

SOURCE: Adapted from Thomas J. Sargent, 'The end of four big inflations,' in Robert Hall, ed., *Inflation* (Chicago: University of Chicago Press, 1983), pp. 41–93.

The data on hyperinflation show a clear link between the quantity of money and the price level. Figure 13.4 graphs data from four classic hyperinflations that occurred during the 1920s in Austria, Hungary, Germany and Poland. Each graph shows the quantity of money in the economy and an index of the price level. The slope of the money line represents the rate at which the quantity of money was growing, and the slope of the price line represents the inflation rate. The steeper the lines, the higher the rates of money growth or inflation.

Notice that in each graph the quantity of money and the price level are almost parallel. In each instance, growth in the quantity of money is moderate at first, and so is inflation. But over time, the quantity of money in the economy starts growing faster and faster. At about the same time, inflation also takes off. Then when the quantity of money stabilises, the price level stabilises as well. These episodes illustrate well one of the *Ten Principles of Economics*—prices rise when the government prints too much money.

THE INFLATION TAX

If inflation is so easy to explain, why do countries experience hyperinflation? That is, why do the central banks of these countries choose to print so much money that its value is certain to fall rapidly over time?

The answer is that the governments of these countries are using money creation as a way to pay for their spending. When the government wants to build roads, pay salaries to police officers, or give transfer payments to the poor or elderly, it first has to raise the necessary funds. Normally, the government does this by levying taxes, such as income and sales taxes, and by borrowing from the public by selling government bonds. Yet the government can also pay for spending by simply printing the money it needs.

When the government raises revenue by printing money, it is said to levy an **inflation tax**. The inflation tax is not exactly like other taxes, however, because no one receives a bill from the government for this tax. Instead, the inflation tax is more subtle. When the government prints money, the price level rises, and the dollars in your wallet are less valuable. Thus, *the inflation tax is like a tax on everyone who holds money*.

inflation tax
the revenue the government raises by creating money

The importance of the inflation tax varies from country to country and over time. In Australia in the 1970s, the inflation tax was a significant source of revenue. However, one of the most striking examples was the German hyperinflation after World War I. The German government was required to pay war reparations to the Allies, but it was unable to collect sufficient tax revenue to meet the debt. It financed the debt by borrowing freshly minted money from the Reichsbank, the German central bank. By 1922, prices were 1475 times their pre-war level.

Almost all hyperinflations follow the same pattern as the hyperinflation following World War I in Germany. The government has high spending, inadequate tax revenue and limited ability to borrow. As a result, it turns to the printing press to pay for its spending. The massive increases in the quantity of money lead to massive inflation. The inflation ends when the government institutes fiscal reforms—such as cuts in government spending—that eliminate the need for the inflation tax.

IN THE NEWS

Hyperinflation in Serbia

Whenever governments turn to the printing press to finance substantial amounts of spending, the result is hyperinflation. Residents of Serbia learned that lesson in the early 1990s.

Special, Today Only: 6 Million Dinars for a Snickers Bar

BY ROGER THUROW

BELGRADE, YUGOSLAVIA—At the Luna boutique, a Snickers bar costs 6 million dinars. Or at least it does until manager Tihomir Nikolic reads the overnight fax from his boss.

'Raise prices 99 percent,' the document tersely orders. It would be an even 100 percent except that the computers at the boutique, which would be considered a dime store in other parts of the world, can't handle three-digit changes.

So for the second time in three days, Mr Nikolic sets about raising prices. He jams a mop across the door frame to keep customers from getting away with a bargain. The computer spits out the new prices on perforated paper. The manager and two assistants rip the paper into tags and tape them to the shelves. They used to put the prices directly on the goods, but there were so many stickers it was getting difficult to read the labels.

After four hours, the mop is removed from the door. The customers wander in, rub their eyes and squint at the tags, counting the zeros. Mr Nikolic himself squints as the computer prints another price, this one for a video recorder.

'Is that billions?' he asks himself. It is: 20 391 560 223 dinars, to be precise. He points to his T-shirt, which is emblazoned with the words 'Far Out', the name of a fruit juice he once sold. He suggests it is an ideal motto for Serbia's bizarre economic situation. 'It fits the craziness,' he says.

How else would you describe it? Since the international community imposed economic sanctions, the inflation rate has been at least 10 percent daily. This translates to an annual rate in the quadrillions—so high as to be meaningless. In Serbia, one US dollar will get you 10 million dinars at the Hyatt hotel, 12 million from the shady money changers on Republic Square, and 17 million from a bank run by Belgrade's underworld. Serbs complain that the dinar is as worthless as toilet paper. But for the moment, at least, there is plenty of toilet paper to go around.

The government mint, hidden in the park behind the Belgrade racetrack, is said to be churning out dinars 24 hours a day, furiously trying to keep up with the inflation that is fueled, in turn, by its own nonstop printing. The government, which believes in throwing around money to damp dissent, needs dinars to pay workers for not working at closed factories and offices. It needs them to buy the harvest from the farmers. It needs them to finance its smuggling forays and other ways to evade the sanctions, bringing in everything from oil to Mr Nikolic's Snickers bars. It also needs them to supply brother Serbs fighting in Bosnia-Herzegovina and Croatia.

The money changers, whose fingertips detect the slightest change in paper quality, insist that the mint is even contracting out to private printers to meet demand.

'We're experts. They can't fool us,' says one of the changers as he hands over 800 million worth of 5-million-dinar bills. 'These,' he notes confidently, 'are fresh from the mint.' He says he got them from a private bank, which got them from the central bank, which got them from the mint—an unholy circuit linking the black market with the Finance Ministry. 'It's collective lunacy,' the money changer says, laughing wickedly.

SOURCE: *Wall Street Journal*, 4 August 1993, p. A1.

THE FISHER EFFECT

According to the principle of monetary neutrality, an increase in the rate of money growth raises the rate of inflation but does not affect any real variable. An important application of this principle concerns the effect of money on interest rates. Interest rates are important variables for macroeconomists to understand because they link the economy of the present and the economy of the future through their effects on saving and investment.

To understand the relationship between money, inflation and interest rates, recall the distinction between the nominal interest rate and the real interest rate. The *nominal interest rate* is the interest rate you hear about at your bank. If you have a savings account, for instance, the nominal interest rate tells you how fast the number of dollars in your account will rise over time. The *real interest rate* corrects the nominal interest rate for the effect of inflation in order to tell you how fast the purchasing power of your savings account will rise over time. The real interest rate is the nominal interest rate minus the inflation rate:

Real interest rate = Nominal interest rate − Inflation rate

For example, if the bank posts a nominal interest rate of 7% per year and the inflation rate is 3% per year, then the real value of the deposits grows by 4% per year.

We can rewrite this equation to show that the nominal interest rate is the sum of the real interest rate and the inflation rate:

Nominal interest rate = Real interest rate + Inflation rate

This way of looking at the nominal interest rate is useful because different economic forces determine each of the two terms on the right-hand side of this equation. As we discussed in an earlier chapter, the supply of and demand for loanable funds determines the real interest rate. And, according to the quantity theory of money, growth in the money supply determines the inflation rate.

Let's now consider how the growth in the money supply affects interest rates. In the long run over which money is neutral, a change in money growth should not affect the real interest rate. The real interest rate is, after all, a real variable. For the real interest rate not to be affected, the nominal interest rate must adjust one-for-one to changes in the inflation rate. Thus, *when the RBA increases the rate of money growth, the result is both a higher inflation rate and a higher nominal interest rate*. This adjustment of the nominal interest rate to the inflation

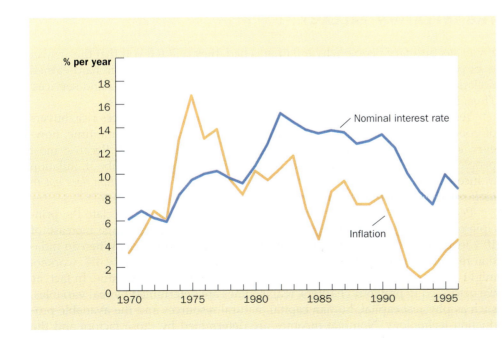

Figure 13.5

THE NOMINAL INTEREST RATE AND THE INFLATION RATE. This figure uses annual data since 1970 to show the nominal interest rate on 10-year Treasury bonds and the inflation rate as measured by the consumer price index. The close association between these two variables is evidence for the Fisher effect—when the inflation rate rises, so does the nominal interest rate.

SOURCE: Reserve Bank of Australia.

Fisher effect
the one-for-one adjustment of the nominal interest rate to the inflation rate

rate is called the **Fisher effect**, after economist Irving Fisher (1867–1947), who first studied it.

The Fisher effect is, in fact, crucial for understanding changes over time in the nominal interest rate. Figure 13.5 shows the nominal interest rate and the inflation rate in the Australian economy since 1970. The close association between these two variables is clear. The nominal interest rate rose from 1973 to 1975 because inflation was also rising during this time. Similarly, the nominal interest rate fell from the early 1980s to the mid-1990s because the RBA finally got inflation under control.

> **QUICK QUIZ** The government of a country increases the growth rate of the money supply from 5% per year to 50% per year. What happens to prices? What happens to nominal interest rates? Why might the government be doing this?

THE COSTS OF INFLATION

In the early 1980s, when the Australian inflation rate was above 10% per year, inflation dominated debates over economic policy. Even though inflation dropped significantly during the first half of the 1990s, inflation remained a closely watched macroeconomic variable. One 1996 study found that *inflation* was the economic term mentioned most often in Australian newspapers and magazines.

Inflation is closely watched and widely discussed because it is thought to be a serious economic problem. But is that true? And if so, why?

A FALL IN PURCHASING POWER? THE INFLATION FALLACY

If you ask ordinary people why inflation is bad, they will tell you that the answer is obvious—inflation robs them of the purchasing power of their hard-earned dollars. When prices rise, each dollar of income buys fewer goods and services. Thus, it might seem that inflation directly lowers living standards.

Yet further thought reveals a fallacy in this answer. When prices rise, buyers of goods and services do pay more for what they buy. At the same time, however, sellers of goods and services get more for what they sell. Because most people earn their incomes by selling their services, such as their labour, inflation in incomes goes hand in hand with inflation in prices. Thus, *inflation does not in itself reduce people's real purchasing power*.

People believe the inflation fallacy because they do not appreciate the principle of monetary neutrality. Workers who receive an annual wage increase of 10% tend to view it as a reward for their own talents and efforts. When an inflation rate of 6% reduces the real value of that wage increase to only 4%, workers might feel that they have been cheated of what is rightfully their due. In fact, as we discussed in previous chapters, real incomes are determined by real variables, such as physical capital, human capital, natural resources and the available production technology. Nominal incomes are determined by those factors and the overall price level. If the RBA were to lower the inflation rate from 6% to zero, workers' annual wage increase would fall from 10% to 4%. They might feel less robbed by inflation, but their real income would not rise more quickly.

But if nominal incomes tend to keep pace with rising prices, why then is inflation a problem? It turns out that there is no single answer to this question. Instead, economists have identified several costs of inflation. Each of these costs shows some way in which persistent growth in the money supply does, in fact, have some effect on real variables.

SHOELEATHER COSTS

As we have discussed, inflation is like a tax on the holders of money. The tax itself is not a cost to society—it is only a transfer of resources from households to the government. Yet most taxes give people an incentive to alter their behaviour to avoid paying the tax, and this distortion of incentives causes efficiency losses for society as a whole. Like other taxes, the inflation tax also causes efficiency losses, as people waste scarce resources trying to avoid it.

How can a person avoid paying the inflation tax? Because inflation erodes the real value of the money in your wallet, you can avoid the inflation tax by holding less money. One way to do this is to go to the bank more often. For example, rather than withdrawing $200 every 4 weeks, you might withdraw $50 once a week. By making more frequent trips to the bank, you can keep more of your wealth in your interest-bearing savings account and less in your wallet, where inflation erodes its value.

The cost of reducing your money holdings is called the **shoeleather cost** of inflation because making more frequent trips to the bank causes your shoes to wear out more quickly. Of course, this term is not to be taken literally—the actual cost of reducing your money holdings is not the wear and tear on your shoes but the time and convenience you must sacrifice to keep less money on hand than you would if there were no inflation.

The shoeleather costs of inflation may seem trivial. And, in fact, they are in the Australian economy, which has had only moderate inflation in recent years. But this cost is magnified in countries experiencing hyperinflation. Here is a description of one person's experience in Bolivia during its hyperinflation (as reported in the 13 August 1985 issue of the *Wall Street Journal*, p. 1):

> When Edgar Miranda gets his monthly teacher's pay of 25 million pesos, he hasn't a moment to lose. Every hour, pesos drop in value. So, while his wife rushes to market to lay in a month's supply of rice and noodles, he is off with the rest of the pesos to change them into black-market dollars.
>
> Mr Miranda is practising the First Rule of Survival amid the most out-of-control inflation in the world today. Bolivia is a case study of how runaway inflation undermines a society. Price increases are so huge that the figures build up almost beyond comprehension. In one six-month period, for example, prices soared at an annual rate of 38 000 percent. By official count, however, last year's inflation reached 2000 percent, and this year's is expected to hit 8000 percent—though other estimates range many times higher. In any event, Bolivia's rate dwarfs Israel's 370 percent and Argentina's 1100 percent—two other cases of severe inflation.
>
> It is easier to comprehend what happens to the thirty-eight-year-old Mr Miranda's pay if he doesn't quickly change it into dollars. The day he was paid

shoeleather costs
the resources wasted when inflation encourages people to reduce their money holdings

25 million pesos, a dollar cost 500 000 pesos. So he received $50. Just days later, with the rate at 900 000 pesos, he would have received $27.

As this story shows, the shoeleather costs of inflation can be substantial. With the high inflation rate, Mr Miranda does not have the luxury of holding the local money as a store of value. Instead, he is forced to convert his pesos quickly into goods or into US dollars, which offer a more stable store of value. The time and effort that Mr Miranda expends to reduce his money holdings are a waste of resources. If the monetary authority pursued a low-inflation policy, Mr Miranda would be happy to hold pesos, and he could put his time and effort to more productive use. In fact, shortly after this article was written, the Bolivian inflation rate was reduced substantially with more restrictive monetary policy.

MENU COSTS

Most firms do not change the prices of their products every day. Instead, firms often announce prices and leave them unchanged for weeks, months or even years. One survey found that the typical Australian firm changes its prices about once a year.

Firms change prices infrequently because there are costs of changing prices. Costs of price adjustment are called **menu costs**, a term derived from a restaurant's cost of printing a new menu. Menu costs include the cost of printing new price lists and catalogues, the cost of sending these new price lists and catalogues to dealers and customers, the cost of advertising the new prices, the cost of deciding on new prices, and even the cost of dealing with customer annoyance over price changes.

Inflation increases the menu costs that firms must bear. In the current Australian economy, with its low inflation rate, annual price adjustment is an appropriate business strategy for many firms. But when high inflation makes firms' costs rise rapidly, annual price adjustment is impractical. During hyperinflations, for example, firms must change their prices daily or even more often just to keep up with all the other prices in the economy.

menu costs
the costs of changing prices

RELATIVE-PRICE VARIABILITY AND THE MISALLOCATION OF RESOURCES

Suppose that the Eatabit Eatery prints a new menu with new prices every January and then leaves its prices unchanged for the rest of the year. If there is no inflation, Eatabit's relative prices—the prices of its meals compared with other prices in the economy—would be constant over the course of the year. In contrast, if the inflation rate is 12% per year, Eatabit's relative prices will automatically fall by 1% each month. The restaurant's prices will be relatively high in the early months of the year, just after it has printed a new menu, and relatively low in the later months. And the higher the inflation rate, the greater this automatic variability. Thus, because prices change only once in a while, inflation causes relative prices to vary more than they otherwise would.

Why does this matter? The reason is that market economies rely on relative prices to allocate scarce resources. Consumers decide what to buy by comparing the quality and prices of various goods and services. Through these decisions, they determine how the scarce factors of production are allocated among industries and firms. When inflation distorts relative prices, consumer decisions are distorted, and markets are less able to allocate resources to their best uses.

INFLATION-INDUCED TAX DISTORTIONS

Almost all taxes distort incentives, cause people to alter their behaviour, and lead to a less efficient allocation of the economy's resources. Many taxes, however, become even more problematic in the presence of inflation. The reason is that law-makers often fail to take inflation into account when writing the tax laws. Economists who have studied the tax laws conclude that inflation tends to raise the tax burden on income earned from savings.

One example is the tax treatment of interest income. Income tax treats the *nominal* interest earned on savings as income, even though part of the nominal interest rate merely compensates for inflation. To see the effects of this policy, consider the numerical example in table 13.1. The table compares two economies, both of which tax interest income at a rate of 25%. In Economy 1, inflation is zero, and the nominal and real interest rates are both 4%. In this case, the 25% tax on interest income reduces the real interest rate from 4% to 3%. In Economy 2, the real interest rate is again 4%, but the inflation rate is 8%. As a result of the Fisher effect, the nominal interest rate is 12%. Because the income tax treats this entire 12% interest as income, the government takes 25% of it, leaving an after-tax nominal interest rate of only 9% and an after-tax real interest rate of only 1%. In this case, the 25% tax on interest income reduces the real interest rate from 4% to 1%. Because the after-tax real interest rate provides the incentive to save, saving is much less attractive in the economy with inflation (Economy 2) than in the economy with stable prices (Economy 1).

The taxes on nominal interest income are one example of how tax laws interact with inflation. There are many others. Because of these inflation-induced tax changes, higher inflation tends to discourage people from saving. Recall that the

Table 13.1

HOW INFLATION RAISES THE TAX BURDEN ON SAVING. In the presence of zero inflation, a 25% tax on interest income reduces the real interest rate from 4% to 3%. In the presence of 8% inflation, the same tax reduces the real interest rate from 4% to 1%.

	ECONOMY 1 (PRICE STABILITY)	ECONOMY 2 (INFLATION)
Real interest rate	4%	4%
Inflation rate	0	8
Nominal interest rate (real interest rate + inflation rate)	4	12
Reduced interest due to 25% tax (0.25 × nominal interest rate)	1	3
After-tax nominal interest rate (0.75 × nominal interest rate)	3	9
After-tax real interest rate (after-tax nominal interest rate − inflation rate)	3	1

economy's saving provides the resources for investment, which in turn is a key ingredient to long-run economic growth. Thus, when inflation raises the tax burden on saving, it tends to depress the economy's long-run growth rate. There is, however, no consensus among economists about the size of this effect.

One solution to this problem, other than eliminating inflation, is to index the tax system. That is, the tax laws could be rewritten to take account of the effects of inflation. This is already done in the case of capital gains. A *capital gain* is the profit made by selling an asset for more than its purchase price. For example, if you purchased shares in BHP in 1980 for $10 and then sold the same shares in 1998 for $50, you would have made a capital gain of $40. But if the overall price level had doubled between 1980 and 1998, then the increase in the value of your asset was really only $20. If the tax laws did not take into account the effects of inflation, you would pay tax on the profit of $40 instead of $20. The tax laws in Australia adjust the purchase price using a price index and assess the tax only on the real gain.

In the case of interest income, the government could tax only real interest income by excluding that portion of the interest income that merely compensates for inflation. To some extent, the tax laws have moved in the direction of indexation, as demonstrated above with capital gains. However, the income levels at which marginal income tax rates change are not adjusted automatically for inflation.

In an ideal world, the tax laws would be written so that inflation would not alter anyone's real tax liability. In the world in which we live, however, tax laws are far from perfect. More complete indexation would probably be desirable, but it would further complicate tax laws that many people already consider too complex.

CONFUSION AND INCONVENIENCE

Imagine that we took a poll and asked people the following question: 'This year the metre is 100 centimetres. How long do you think it should be next year?' Assuming we could get people to take us seriously, they would tell us that the metre should stay the same length—100 centimetres. Anything else would just complicate life needlessly.

What does this finding have to do with inflation? Recall that money, as the economy's unit of account, is what we use to quote prices and record debts. In other words, money is the yardstick with which we measure economic transactions. The job of the RBA is a bit like the job of Standards Australia—to ensure the reliability of a commonly used unit of measurement. When the RBA increases the money supply and creates inflation, it erodes the real value of the unit of account.

It is difficult to judge the costs of the confusion and inconvenience that arise from inflation. Earlier we discussed how the tax laws incorrectly measure real incomes in the presence of inflation. Similarly, accountants incorrectly measure firms' profits when prices are rising over time. Because inflation causes dollars at different times to have different real values, calculating a firm's profit—the difference between its revenue and costs—is more complicated in an economy with inflation. Therefore, to some extent, unexpected inflation makes investors less able to sort out successful from unsuccessful firms, which in turn impedes financial markets in their role of allocating the economy's saving to alternative types of investment.

A SPECIAL COST OF UNEXPECTED INFLATION: ARBITRARY REDISTRIBUTIONS OF WEALTH

So far, most of the costs of inflation we have discussed occur even if inflation is steady and predictable. Inflation has an additional cost, however, when it comes as a surprise. Unexpected inflation redistributes wealth among the population in a way that has nothing to do with either merit or need. These redistributions occur because many loans in the economy are specified in terms of the unit of account—money.

Consider an example. Suppose that Sam Student takes out a $20 000 loan at a 7% interest rate from Bigbank to attend university. In 10 years, the loan will come due. After his debt has compounded for 10 years at 7%, Sam will owe Bigbank $40 000. The real value of this debt will depend on inflation over the decade. If Sam is lucky, the economy will have hyperinflation. In this case, wages and prices will rise so high that Sam will be able to pay the $40 000 debt out of small change. In contrast, if the economy goes through a major deflation, then wages and prices will fall, and Sam will find the $40 000 debt a greater burden than he anticipated.

This example shows that unexpected changes in prices redistribute wealth among debtors and creditors. Hyperinflation enriches Sam at the expense of Bigbank because it diminishes the real value of the debt; Sam can repay the loan in dollars that are less valuable than he anticipated. Deflation enriches Bigbank at Sam's expense because it increases the real value of the debt; in this case, Sam has to repay the loan in dollars that are more valuable than he anticipated. If inflation were predictable, then Bigbank and Sam could take inflation into account when setting the nominal interest rate. (Recall the Fisher effect.) But if inflation is hard to predict, it imposes risk on Sam and Bigbank that both would prefer to avoid.

This cost of unexpected inflation is important to consider together with another fact—inflation is especially volatile and uncertain when the average rate of inflation is high. This is seen most simply by examining the experience of different countries. Countries with low average inflation, such as Germany in the late twentieth century, tend to have stable inflation. Countries with high average inflation, such as many countries in Latin America, tend also to have unstable inflation. There are no known examples of economies with high, stable inflation. This relationship between the level and volatility of inflation points to another cost of inflation. If a country pursues a high-inflation monetary policy, it will have to bear not only the costs of high expected inflation but also the arbitrary redistributions of wealth associated with unexpected inflation.

CASE STUDY   THE WIZARD OF OZ AND THE FREE-SILVER DEBATE

As a child, you may have seen the film *The Wizard of Oz*, based on a children's book written in 1900. The film and book tell the story of a young girl, Dorothy, who finds herself lost in a strange land far from home. You probably did not know, however, that the story is actually an allegory about US monetary policy in the late nineteenth century.

From 1880 to 1896, the price level in the US economy fell by 23%. Because this event was unanticipated, it led to a major redistribution of wealth. Most farmers in the western part of the country were debtors. Their creditors were

IN THE NEWS

How to protect your savings from inflation

As we have seen, unexpected changes in the price level redistribute wealth among debtors and creditors. This would no longer be true, however, if debt contracts were written in real, rather than nominal, terms. Indexed bonds have been available in Australia since the mid-1980s. The first of the following two articles discuss the merits of indexed bonds, and the second looks at the range of indexed bonds (securities) available in Australia.

Inflation Fighters for the Long Term

BY JOHN Y. CAMPBELL AND ROBERT J. SHILLER

[US] Treasury Secretary Robert Rubin announced on Thursday that the government plans to issue inflation-indexed bonds—that is, bonds whose interest and principal payments are adjusted upward for inflation, guaranteeing their real purchasing power in the future.

This is a historic moment. Economists have been advocating such bonds for many long and frustrating years. Indexed bonds were first called for in 1822 by the economist Joseph Lowe. In the 1870s, they were championed by the British economist William Stanley Jevons. In the early part of this century, the legendary Irving Fisher made a career of advocating them.

In recent decades, economists of every political stripe—from Milton Friedman to James Tobin, Alan Blinder to Alan Greenspan—have supported them. Yet, because there was little public clamor for such an investment, the government never issued indexed bonds.

Let's hope this lack of interest does not continue now that they will become available. The success of the indexed bonds depends on whether the public understands them—and buys them. Until now, inflation has made government bonds a risky investment. In 1966, when the inflation rate was only 3 percent, if someone had bought a 30-year government bond yielding 5 percent, he would have expected that by now his investment would be worth 180 percent of its original value. However, after years of higher-than-expected inflation, the investment is worth only 85 percent of its original value.

Because inflation has been modest in recent years, many people today are not worried about how it will affect their savings. This complacency is dangerous: Even a low rate of inflation can seriously erode savings over long periods of time.

Imagine that you retire today with a pension invested in Treasury bonds that pay a fixed $10 000 each year, regardless

the bankers in the east. When the price level fell, it caused the real value of these debts to rise, which enriched the banks at the expense of the farmers.

According to populist politicians of the time, the solution to the farmers' problem was the free coinage of silver. During this period, the United States was operating with a gold standard. The quantity of gold determined the money supply and, thereby, the price level. The free-silver advocates wanted silver, as well as gold, to be used as money. If adopted, this proposal would have increased the money supply, pushed up the price level, and reduced the real burden of the farmers' debts.

The debate over silver was heated, and it was central to the politics of the 1890s. A common election slogan of the populists was 'We are mortgaged; all but our votes'. One prominent advocate of free silver was William Jennings Bryan, the Democrat nominee for president in 1896. He is remembered in part for a speech at the Democratic Party's nominating convention in which he said, 'You shall not press down upon the brow of labor this crown of thorns. You shall not crucify mankind upon a cross of gold.' Rarely since then have politicians waxed so poetic about alternative approaches to monetary policy.

of inflation. If there is no inflation, in 20 years the pension will have the same purchasing power that it does today. But if there is an inflation rate of only 3 percent per year, in 20 years your pension will be worth only $5540 in today's dollars. Five percent inflation over 20 years will cut your purchasing power to $3770, and 10 percent will reduce it to a pitiful $1390. Which of these scenarios is likely? No one knows. Inflation ultimately depends on the people who are elected and appointed as guardians of our money supply.

At a time when Americans are living longer and planning for several decades of retirement, the insidious effects of inflation should be of serious concern. For this reason alone, the creation of inflation-indexed bonds, with their guarantee of a safe return over long periods of time, is a welcome development.

SOURCE: *New York Times*, 18 May 1996, Section 1, p. 19.

A Taste of the Big League

BY EDNA CAREW

They're complex, conservative and have been available in Australia for more than a decade, but inflation-linked securities are only now gaining a higher public profile as a number of intermediaries identify growing retail demand. Typically these securities have been bought by the major super funds and insurance companies as a hedge against the inflation-linked products they sell, but there is a growing belief that they have considerable retail potential, particularly among the do-it-yourself superannuation funds and other low-tax-paying entities.

Worldwide, the profile of securities offering protection against inflation has received a boost with the US announcing in May that it plans to introduce this type of bond for the first time, and New Zealand has re-issued the securities after a pause of more than a decade. The Australian market in inflation-linked securities was mostly the preserve of the Commonwealth Government until 1987, when state government authorities began issuing in greater volume.

These securities are government-guaranteed investments offering a return above inflation of about 4.75 per cent, which compares well with the typical performance objective of 3 per cent above inflation, before tax, of most large superannuation funds.

Whether inflation-linked securities appeal to you or not depends largely on your inflation expectations. They are attractive to investors who believe inflation will hold about 4 per cent or higher over the next 10 years. Some say there is great potential retail demand, but others contend that inflation-linked securities are too complicated for the average retail investor.

Promoters of these securities emphasis three key features: a government guarantee; protection of capital against inflation while producing income; and an attractive investment return compared with other asset classes.

SOURCE: Excerpts from *Personal Investment*, August 1996, p. 79.

Nonetheless, Bryan lost the election to Republican William McKinley, and the United States remained on the gold standard.

L. Frank Baum, the author of *The Wizard of Oz*, was a midwestern journalist. When he sat down to write a story for children, he made the characters represent protagonists in the major political battle of his time. Although modern commentators on the story differ somewhat in the interpretation they assign to each character, there is no doubt that the story highlights the debate over monetary policy. Here is how economic historian Hugh Rockoff, writing in the August 1990 issue of the *Journal of Political Economy*, interprets the story:

DOROTHY: Traditional American values
TOTO: Prohibitionist party, also called the Teetotallers
SCARECROW: Farmers
TIN WOODSMAN: Industrial workers
COWARDLY LION: William Jennings Bryan [Democrat nominee for president in 1896]

MUNCHKINS:	Citizens of the east
WICKED WITCH OF THE EAST:	Grover Cleveland [Democrat president 1893–97]
WICKED WITCH OF THE WEST:	William McKinley [Republican president 1897–1901]
WIZARD:	Marcus Alonzo Hanna [chairman of the Republican party at the time]
OZ:	Abbreviation for ounce of gold
YELLOW BRICK ROAD:	Gold standard

In the end of Baum's story, Dorothy does find her way home, but it is not by just following the yellow brick road. After a long and perilous journey, she learns that the wizard is incapable of helping her or her friends. Instead, Dorothy finally discovers the magical power of her *silver* slippers. (When *The Wizard of Oz* was made into a film in 1939, Dorothy's slippers were changed from silver to ruby. Apparently, the Hollywood filmmakers were not aware that they were telling a story about nineteenth-century monetary policy.)

Although the populists lost the debate over the free coinage of silver, they did eventually get the monetary expansion and inflation that they wanted. In 1898 prospectors discovered gold near the Klondike River in Alaska. Increased supplies of gold also arrived from the Canadian Yukon and the gold mines of South Africa. As a result, the money supply and the price level started to rise in the United States and other countries operating on the gold standard. Within 15 years, prices in the United States were back to the levels that had prevailed in the 1880s, and farmers were better able to handle their debts.

An early debate over monetary policy

■ **QUICK QUIZ** List and describe six costs of inflation.

CONCLUSION

This chapter discussed the causes and costs of inflation. The main cause of inflation is simply growth in the quantity of money. When the central bank creates money in large quantities, the value of money falls quickly over time. To maintain stable prices, the central bank must maintain strict control over the money supply or interest rates.

The costs of inflation are more subtle. They include shoeleather costs, menu costs, increased variability of relative prices, unintended changes in tax liabilities, confusion and inconvenience, and arbitrary redistributions of wealth. Are these costs, in total, large or small? All economists agree that they become huge during hyperinflation. But their size for moderate inflation—when prices rise by less than 10% per year—is more open to debate.

Although this chapter presented many of the most important lessons about inflation, the discussion is incomplete. When the RBA reduces the rate of money growth, prices rise less rapidly, as the quantity theory suggests. Yet as the economy makes the transition to this lower inflation rate, the change in monetary policy will have disruptive effects on production and employment. That is, even though monetary policy is neutral in the long run, it has profound effects on real variables in the short run. Later in this book we will examine the reasons for short-run monetary non-neutrality in order to enhance our understanding of the causes and costs of inflation.

Summary

- The overall level of prices in an economy adjusts to bring money supply and money demand into balance. When the central bank increases the supply of money, it causes the price level to rise. Persistent growth in the quantity of money supplied leads to continuing inflation.

- The principle of monetary neutrality asserts that changes in the quantity of money influence nominal variables but not real variables. Most economists believe that monetary neutrality approximately describes the behaviour of the economy in the long run.

- A government can pay for some of its spending simply by printing money. When countries rely heavily on this 'inflation tax', the result is hyperinflation.

- One application of the principle of monetary neutrality is the Fisher effect. According to the Fisher effect, when the inflation rate rises, the nominal interest rate rises by the same amount, so that the real interest rate remains the same.

- Many people think that inflation makes them poorer because it raises the cost of what they buy. This view is a fallacy, however, because inflation also raises nominal incomes.

- Economists have identified six costs of inflation: shoeleather costs associated with reduced money holdings, menu costs associated with more frequent adjustment of prices, increased variability of relative prices, unintended changes in tax liabilities due to non-indexation of the tax laws, confusion and inconvenience resulting from a changing unit of account, and arbitrary redistributions of wealth between debtors and creditors. Many of these costs are large during hyperinflation, but the size of these costs for moderate inflation is less clear.

Key concepts

quantity theory of money, p. 273
nominal variables, p. 275
real variables, p. 275
classical dichotomy, p. 275
monetary neutrality, p. 275
velocity of money, p. 276

quantity equation, p. 277
inflation tax, p. 279
Fisher effect, p. 282
shoeleather costs, p. 283
menu costs, p. 284

Questions for review

1. Explain how an increase in the price level affects the real value of money.

2. According to the quantity theory of money, what is the effect of an increase in the quantity of money?

3. Explain the difference between nominal and real variables, and give two examples of each. According to the principle of monetary neutrality, which variables are affected by changes in the quantity of money?

4. In what sense is inflation like a tax? How does thinking about inflation as a tax help explain hyperinflation?

5. According to the Fisher effect, how does an increase in the inflation rate affect the real interest rate and the nominal interest rate?

6. What are the costs of inflation? Which of these costs do you think are most important for the Australian economy?

7. If inflation is less than expected, who benefits—debtors or creditors? Explain.

Problems and applications

1. As mentioned in the chapter, the Reserve Bank of New Zealand has a goal of keeping inflation low, in the 0–3% range. Suppose they tried to reduce the New Zealand inflation rate to zero. If we assume that velocity is constant, does this zero-inflation goal require that the rate of money growth equal zero? If so, explain why. If not, explain what the rate of money growth should equal.

2. The chapter preceding this one showed that there are several different measures of the money stock, with the larger measures including more types of assets than the smaller ones. How can the quantity equation hold for all of these measures? How can the quantity theory of money hold for all of these measures?

3. The economist John Maynard Keynes wrote: 'Lenin is said to have declared that the best way to destroy the capitalist system was to debauch the currency. By a continuing process of inflation, governments can confiscate, secretly and unobserved, an important part of the wealth of their citizens.' Justify Lenin's assertion.

4. Suppose that a country's inflation rate increases sharply. What happens to the inflation tax on the holders of money? Why is wealth that is held in savings accounts *not* subject to a change in the inflation tax? Can you think of any way in which holders of savings accounts are hurt by the increase in the inflation rate?

5. Hyperinflations are extremely rare in countries whose central banks are independent of the rest of the government. Why might this be so?

6. Suppose that Bob is a bean farmer and Rita is a rice farmer. Bob and Rita are the only people in the economy, and both always consume equal amounts of rice and beans. In 1998 the price of beans was $1 and the price of rice was $3.
   a. Suppose that in 1999 the price of beans was $2 and the price of rice was $6. What was inflation? Was Bob better off, worse off, or unaffected by the changes in prices? What about Rita?
   b. Now suppose that in 1999 the price of beans was $2 and the price of rice was $4. What was inflation? Was Bob better off, worse off, or unaffected by the changes in prices? What about Rita?
   c. Finally, suppose that in 1999 the price of beans was $2 and the price of rice was $1.50. What was inflation? Was Bob better off, worse off, or unaffected by the changes in prices? What about Rita?

7. What are your shoeleather costs of going to the bank? How might you measure these costs in dollars? How do you think the shoeleather costs of your university Vice-Chancellor differ from your own?

8. Recall that money serves three functions in the economy. What are those functions? How does inflation affect the ability of money to serve each of these functions?

9. Suppose that Australians expect inflation to equal 3% in 2000, but in fact prices rise by 5%. How would this unexpectedly high inflation rate help or hurt the following?

a. the federal government
b. a homeowner with a fixed-rate mortgage
c. a union worker in the second year of a labour contract
d. a private school that has invested some of its endowment in Treasury bonds

10. Explain one harm associated with unexpected inflation that is *not* associated with expected inflation. Then explain one harm associated with both expected and unexpected inflation.

11. Explain whether the following statements are true, false, or uncertain.
    a. 'Inflation hurts borrowers and helps lenders, because borrowers must pay a higher rate of interest.'
    b. 'If prices change in a way that leaves the overall price level unchanged, then no one is made better or worse off.'
    c. 'Inflation does not reduce the purchasing power of most workers.'

VI

THE MACROECONOMICS OF OPEN ECONOMIES

IV

14

OPEN-ECONOMY MACROECONOMICS: BASIC CONCEPTS

IN THIS CHAPTER YOU WILL

Learn how net exports measure the international flow of goods and services

Learn how net foreign investment measures the international flow of capital

Consider why net exports must always equal net foreign investment

See how saving, domestic investment and net foreign investment are related

Learn the meaning of the nominal exchange rate and the real exchange rate

Examine purchasing-power parity as a theory of how exchange rates are determined

When you graduate from university and decide to buy a car, you may compare the latest models offered by Ford and Mazda. When you take your next holiday, you may consider spending it on a beach in Queensland or in Bali. When you get a job and begin to save for your retirement, you may choose between a managed fund that buys shares in Australian companies and one that buys shares in foreign companies. In all of these cases, you will be participating not just in the Australian economy but in economies around the world.

There are clear benefits to an economy that is open to international trade—trade allows people to produce what they produce best and to consume the great variety of goods and services produced around the world. Indeed, one of the *Ten Principles of Economics* highlighted in chapter 1 is that trade can make everyone better off. Chapter 3 examined the gains from trade more fully. We learned that international trade can raise living standards in all countries by allowing each country to specialise in producing those goods and services in which it has a comparative advantage.

So far, our development of macroeconomics has largely ignored the economy's interaction with other economies around the world. For some economies, such as that of the United States, many questions in macroeconomics can be discussed without considering international issues. However, for some economies, such as the Australian economy, the effects of international trade are very important. We ignored the effects of international trade when we discussed topics such as the natural rate of unemployment and the causes of inflation to keep our

closed economy
an economy that does not interact with other economies in the world

open economy
an economy that interacts freely with other economies around the world

exposition simple and focused. Indeed, to keep their analysis simple, macroeconomists often assume a **closed economy**—an economy that does not interact with other economies.

To build a complete picture of the economy, though, we need to examine an **open economy**—an economy that interacts freely with other economies around the world. This chapter and the next one, therefore, provide an introduction to open-economy macroeconomics. We begin in this chapter by discussing the key macroeconomic variables that describe an open economy's interactions in world markets. You may have noticed mention of these variables—exports, imports, the trade balance and exchange rates—when reading the newspaper or watching the nightly news. Our first job is to understand what these data mean. In the next chapter we develop a model to explain how these variables are determined and how they are affected by various government policies.

THE INTERNATIONAL FLOWS OF GOODS AND CAPITAL

An open economy interacts with other economies in two ways—it buys and sells goods and services in world product markets, and it buys and sells financial assets in world financial markets. Here we discuss these two activities and the close relationship between them.

THE FLOW OF GOODS: EXPORTS, IMPORTS AND NET EXPORTS

exports
goods and services that are produced domestically and sold abroad

imports
goods and services that are produced abroad and sold domestically

As we first noted in chapter 3, **exports** are domestically produced goods and services that are sold abroad, and **imports** are foreign-produced goods and services that are sold domestically. When Boeing, the US aircraft manufacturer, builds a plane and sells it to Qantas, the sale is an export for the United States and an

'But we're not just talking about buying a car—we're talking about confronting this country's trade deficit with Germany.'

import for Australia. When Ford in Australia makes a car and sells it to a New Zealand resident, the sale is an import for New Zealand and an export for Australia.

The **net exports** of any country are the value of its exports minus the value of its imports. The Ford sale raises Australian net exports, and the Boeing purchase reduces Australian net exports. Because net exports tell us whether a country is, in total, a seller or a buyer in world markets for goods and services, net exports are also called the **trade balance**. If net exports are positive, exports are greater than imports, indicating that the country sells more goods and services abroad than it buys from other countries. In this case, the country is said to run a **trade surplus**. If net exports are negative, exports are less than imports, indicating that the country sells fewer goods and services abroad than it buys from other countries. In this case, the country is said to run a **trade deficit**. If net exports are zero, its exports and imports are exactly equal, and the country is said to have **balanced trade**.

In the next chapter, we develop a theory that explains an economy's trade balance, but even at this early stage it is easy to think of many factors that might influence a country's exports, imports and net exports. Those factors include:

- the tastes of consumers for domestic and foreign goods
- the prices of goods at home and abroad
- the rates at which people can exchange domestic currency for foreign currencies
- the cost of transporting goods from country to country
- the policies of the government towards international trade.

As these variables change over time, so does the amount of international trade.

net exports
the value of a nation's exports minus the value of its imports, also called the trade balance

trade balance
the value of a nation's exports minus the value of its imports, also called net exports

trade surplus
an excess of exports over imports

trade deficit
an excess of imports over exports

balanced trade
a situation in which exports equal imports

CASE STUDY THE IMPORTANCE OF TRADE IN THE AUSTRALIAN ECONOMY

International trade has always been a significant part of the Australian economy. Figure 14.1 shows the total value of goods and services exported to other countries and imported from other countries expressed as a percentage of gross domestic product. In the early 1950s, exports of goods and services averaged around 20% of GDP. In the mid-1950s, they levelled off to around 13% and have stayed around that level since then. Imports of goods and services have followed a similar pattern. After World War II, the fledgling Australian economy began to develop a manufacturing base so more goods were produced in the domestic economy for domestic production. But trade has remained an important part of the national economy.

Because Australia is a small economy, it has always relied on goods produced overseas for both investment and consumption. Many of the goods that Australians need to produce other goods or that Australians like to consume are not produced in the domestic economy. So we import these goods. Since Australia is physically a large country, well endowed with natural resources, our most important exports have been minerals and primary products, particularly wool, hence the expression 'riding on the sheep's back'.

Even though trade has always been important for Australia, trade has increased in importance globally. This increase in international trade is partly

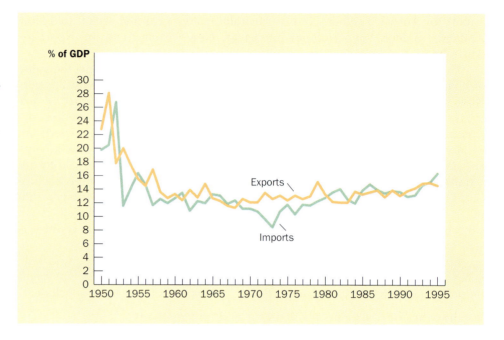

Figure 14.1

THE OPENNESS OF THE AUSTRALIAN ECONOMY. This figure shows exports and imports of the Australian economy as a percentage of Australian gross domestic product since 1950. The fairly steady percentages over time show the ongoing importance of international trade and finance.

SOURCE: Reserve Bank of Australia.

due to improvements in transportation. In 1950 the average merchant ship carried less than 10 000 tonnes of cargo; today, many ships carry more than 100 000 tonnes. The long-distance jet was introduced in 1958, and the wide-bodied jet in 1967, making air transport far cheaper. Because of these developments, goods that once had to be produced and consumed locally can now be traded around the world. Cut flowers, for instance, are now grown in Israel and flown to the United States to be sold. Fresh fruits and vegetables that can grow only in summer can now be consumed by consumers in the Northern Hemisphere in winter as well, because they can be shipped from countries in the Southern Hemisphere, such as Australia.

The increase in international trade has also been influenced by advances in telecommunications, which have allowed businesses to reach overseas customers more easily. Australia's first intercontinental telephone connection was created in 1902 when a submarine cable was laid across the Pacific, linking Australia with Canada. The first transatlantic telephone cable was not laid until 1956, though. As recently as 1966, the technology allowed only 138 simultaneous conversations between North America and Europe. Today, communications satellites permit more than 1 million conversations to occur at the same time.

Technological progress has also fostered international trade by changing the kinds of goods that economies produce. When bulky raw materials (such as steel) and perishable goods (such as wheat) were a large part of the world's output, transporting goods was often costly and sometimes impossible. In contrast, goods produced with modern technology are often light and easy to transport. Consumer electronics, for instance, have low weight for every dollar of value, which makes them easy to produce in one country and sell in another. An even more extreme example is the film industry. Once Fox Studios in Sydney makes a film, it can send copies of the film around the world at almost zero cost. And, indeed, films are an export of many countries including Australia, the United States and India.

The government's trade policies have also been a factor in increasing international trade. As we discussed in chapter 3, economists have long believed that free trade between countries is mutually beneficial. Over time, policymakers around the world have come to accept these conclusions. International agreements, such as the North American Free Trade Agreement (NAFTA) and the General Agreement on Tariffs and Trade (GATT), now governed by the World Trade Organisation (WTO), have gradually lowered trade barriers, such as tariffs and import quotas. Australia has been a leader both in lowering trade barriers and in encouraging other countries to do likewise. The pattern of increasing trade is a phenomenon that most economists and policymakers endorse and encourage. Because trade has always been a significant part of Australia's economy, these changes are to Australia's benefit.

THE FLOW OF CAPITAL: NET FOREIGN INVESTMENT

So far we have been discussing how residents of an open economy participate in world markets for goods and services. In addition, residents of an open economy participate in world financial markets. An Australian resident with $20 000 could use that money to buy a car from Toyota, but she could instead use that money to buy shares in the Toyota corporation. The first transaction would represent a flow of goods, whereas the second would represent a flow of capital.

The term **net foreign investment** refers to the purchase of foreign assets by domestic residents minus the purchase of domestic assets by foreigners. When an Australian resident buys shares in British Telecom, the British phone company, the purchase raises Australian net foreign investment. When a Japanese resident buys a bond issued by the Australian government, the purchase reduces Australian net foreign investment.

net foreign investment
the purchase of foreign assets by domestic residents minus the purchase of domestic assets by foreigners

Recall that foreign investment takes two forms. When the Australian Pie Company opens up a bakery in Moscow, that is an example of *foreign direct investment*. Alternatively, if an Australian buys shares in a Russian corporation, that is an example of *foreign portfolio investment*. In the first case, the Australian owner is actively managing the investment, whereas in the second case the Australian owner has a more passive role. So the distinction is the degree of control. In both cases, Australian residents are buying assets located in another country, so both purchases increase Australian net foreign investment.

We develop a theory to explain net foreign investment in the next chapter. Here, let's consider briefly some of the more important variables that influence net foreign investment:

- the real interest rates being paid on foreign assets
- the real interest rates being paid on domestic assets
- the perceived economic and political risks of holding assets abroad
- the government policies that affect foreign ownership of domestic assets.

For example, consider Australian investors deciding whether to buy Japanese government bonds or Australian government bonds. (Recall that a bond is, in effect, an IOU of the issuer.) To make this decision, Australian investors compare the real interest rates offered on the two bonds. The higher a bond's real interest rate, the more attractive it is. While making this comparison, however, Australian investors must also take into account the risk that one of these

IN THE NEWS

Do capital flows spread financial panic?

IT HAS BEEN TAKEN AS GIVEN THAT THE financial crisis in Asia will automatically mean a downturn in the Australian economy because of the importance of the region for Australia's trade. Warwick McKibbin laments that Australia may be heading towards an economic slump it didn't have to have.

Why We Should Not Panic About Asia

BY WARWICK MCKIBBIN

Over the past year, much media and market commentary has suggested the Asia crisis will cause a recession in Australia. Now, with Japan sinking under poor economic management and a banking crisis, Russia teetering on collapse, weakness on Wall Street and the $A plunging, the pessimism has turned into fears of a global recession perhaps as large as the 1930s Great Depression. But the evidence suggests the world economy remains reasonably robust. World growth in 1998 could easily be about 2 per cent, a slowdown of only about one-third relative to 1997. More important than the overall growth rate, however, are the disparities across countries. These raise policy challenges which, if badly handled, could increase the chances of serious problems.

As dramatically illustrated by Asia, confidence—the essence of capitalist systems—may be undermined by revised expectations about future prospects or by bad policy choices in major economies. As well, the reallocation of global capital flows out of Asia into the rest of the world is being reflected in a large increase in the current account deficits of the non-Asian, OECD economies. This could provoke protectionist sentiments in the US and Europe as their current accounts worsen. Despite these possible problems, global economic models that I have developed over the past decade suggest that, rather than a disaster, the Asian crisis will have a relatively modest impact on Australia because of some offsetting factors.

Although devastating for Asia, the region's crisis is shown in these models to provide a short-term stimulus to production in the rest of the world. The large slump in demand in Asia is reflected in a cut in exports to Asia—clearly negative for exporters outside Asia—and in lower commodity prices. But against this is the big outflow of capital from Asia which leads to a hefty drop in real long-term interest rates outside Asia. These lower interest rates are stimulating domestic demand through stronger investment and consumption.

---

governments might *default* on its debt (that is, not pay interest or principal when it is due), as well as any restrictions that the Japanese government has imposed, or might impose in the future, on foreign investors in Japan.

THE EQUALITY OF NET EXPORTS AND NET FOREIGN INVESTMENT

We have seen that an open economy interacts with the rest of the world in two ways—in world markets for goods and services and in world financial markets. Net exports and net foreign investment each measure a type of imbalance in these markets. Net exports measure an imbalance between a country's exports and its imports. Net foreign investment measures an imbalance between the amount of foreign assets bought by domestic residents and the amount of domestic assets bought by foreigners.

An important but subtle fact of accounting states that, for an economy as a whole, these two imbalances must offset each other. That is, net foreign investment (*NFI*) always equals net exports (*NX*):

$$NFI = NX$$

Whether the boost from lower interest rates is big enough to offset the loss of exports depends crucially on how important exports to Asia are relative to domestic demand for each non-Asian economy. The models suggest that only the most exposed countries such as Australia are hurt on balance.

Other economies such as the US and Europe benefit in the short term as capital and then production shifts from the crisis countries to the no-crisis countries. This further reduces the negatives for Australia because we also sell products into these other economies. The $A depreciation means stronger demand growth for our exports to regions outside Asia—we lose exports in Asia but we gain some exports in other economies. When these models produced such results in 1997, they were seen as improbable. Everyone focused on trade flows only and the negatives of Asia were clear. Yet the adjustment that has occurred through asset markets because of international capital flows has proven robust in the US and Europe and even for Australia.

The problem in Australia is that every piece of good economic news from when the crisis first began has been accompanied by commentary about the looming tidal wave from Asia. In fact, until recently, all broad indicators of actual economic performance in Australia had remained robust. The key negatives have been in certain highly exposed export industries. Yet the biggest damage has not occurred in overall economic activity but in indicators of business confidence, which have begun to fall sharply in the wake of the continued negative commentary in this country. Yet this commentary flies in the face of the facts (which both the Reserve Bank and Treasury have got about right).

True, Australian exports to Asia have been hurt, but some of our exports to the US and Europe have registered double digit growth in recent months. Low real interest rates have stimulated investment and domestic demand has remained strong. The latest $A depreciation is not a sign of panic because it continues to follow weakening commodity prices pretty well. More importantly, there has been no surge in long-term bond rates, which would reflect a rise in the risk premium on Australian assets. Thus the exchange rate adjustment is due to fundamentals and should be allowed to happen. The Reserve Bank is correct not to raise interest rates in order to hold the currency.

Unfortunately, confidence indicators point to an impending economic slowdown for Australia. This is not directly the result of Asia but stems from a loss of domestic confidence which will likely slow domestic demand. If it happens, it will be the economic slowdown that Australia really didn't have to have.

SOURCE: *Australian Financial Review*, 28 August 1998, p. 37.

This equation holds because every transaction that affects one side of this equation must also affect the other side by exactly the same amount. This equation is an *identity*—an equation that must hold by the way the variables in the equation are defined and measured.

To see why this accounting identity is true, consider an example. Suppose that Fisher & Paykel, the New Zealand white goods manufacturer, sells some refrigerators to a Japanese hotel. In this sale, a New Zealand company gives fridges to a Japanese company, and a Japanese company gives yen to a New Zealand company. Notice that two things have occurred simultaneously. New Zealand has sold to a foreigner some of its output (the refrigerators), and this sale increases New Zealand net exports. In addition, New Zealand has acquired some foreign assets (the yen), and this acquisition increases New Zealand net foreign investment.

Although Fisher & Paykel most likely will not hold onto the yen it has acquired in this sale, any subsequent transaction will preserve the equality of net exports and net foreign investment. For example, Fisher & Paykel may exchange its yen for New Zealand dollars with a New Zealand stockbroker that wants the yen to buy shares in Sony Corporation, the Japanese maker of consumer electronics. In this case, Fisher & Paykel's net export of refrigerators equals the stockbroker's net foreign investment in Sony shares. Hence, NX and NFI rise by an equal amount.

Alternatively, Fisher & Paykel may exchange its yen for New Zealand dollars with another New Zealand company that wants to buy computers from Toshiba, the Japanese computer maker. In this case, New Zealand imports (of computers) exactly offset New Zealand exports (of refrigerators). The sales by Fisher & Paykel and Toshiba together affect neither New Zealand net exports nor New Zealand net foreign investment. That is, NX and NFI are the same as they were before these transactions took place.

The equality of net exports and net foreign investment follows from the fact that every international transaction is an exchange. When a seller country transfers a good or service to a buyer country, the buyer country gives up some asset to pay for this good or service. The value of that asset equals the value of the good or service sold. When we add everything up, the net value of goods and services sold by a country (NX) must equal the net value of assets acquired (NFI). The international flow of goods and services and the international flow of capital are two sides of the same coin.

SAVING, INVESTMENT AND THEIR RELATIONSHIP TO THE INTERNATIONAL FLOWS

A nation's saving and investment are, as we have seen in previous chapters, crucial to its long-run economic growth. Let's therefore consider how these variables are related to the international flows of goods and capital, as measured by net exports and net foreign investment. We can do this most easily with the help of some simple mathematics.

As you may recall, the term *net exports* first appeared earlier in the book when we discussed the components of gross domestic product. The economy's gross domestic product (Y) is divided among four components: consumption (C), investment (I), government purchases (G) and net exports (NX). We write this as:

$$Y = C + I + G + NX$$

Total expenditure on the economy's output is the sum of expenditure on consumption, investment, government purchases and net exports. Because each dollar of expenditure is placed in one of these four categories, this equation is an accounting identity—it must be true because of the way the variables are defined and measured.

Recall that 'national saving' is the income of the nation that is left after paying for current consumption and government purchases. National saving (S) equals $Y - C - G$. If we rearrange the above equation to reflect this fact, we obtain:

$$Y - C - G = I + NX$$
$$S = I + NX$$

Because net exports (NX) also equal net foreign investment (NFI), we can also write this equation as:

$$S = I + NFI$$
$$\text{Saving} = \text{Domestic investment} + \text{Net foreign investment}$$

IN THE NEWS

Flows between the developing south and the industrial north

WILL THE WORLD'S DEVELOPING COUNtries, such as those in Latin America, flood the world's industrial countries with cheap exports while refusing to import goods from the industrial countries? Will the developing countries use the world's saving to finance investment and growth, leaving the industrial countries with insufficient funds for their own capital accumulation? Some people fear that both of these outcomes might occur. But an accounting identity, and economist Paul Krugman, tell us not to worry.

Fantasy Economics

BY PAUL KRUGMAN

Reports by international organizations are usually greeted with well deserved yawns. Occasionally, however, such a report is a leading indicator of a sea change in opinion.

A few weeks ago, the World Economic Forum—which every year draws an unmatched assemblage of the world's political and business elite to its conference in Davos, Switzerland—released its annual report on international competitiveness. The report made headlines because it demoted Japan and declared America the world's most competitive economy.

The revealing part of the report, however, is not its more or less meaningless competitiveness rankings but its introduction, which offers what seems to be a very clear vision of the global economic future.

That vision, shared by many powerful people, is compelling and alarming. It is also nonsense. And the fact that this nonsense is being taken seriously by many people who believe themselves to be sophisticated about economics is itself an ominous portent for the world economy.

The report finds that the spread of modern technology to newly industrializing nations is deindustrializing high-wage nations: Capital is flowing to the Third World and low-cost producers in these countries are flooding world markets with cheap manufactured goods.

The report predicts that these trends will accelerate, that service jobs will soon begin to follow the lost jobs in manufacturing and that the future of the high-wage nations offers a bleak choice between declining wages and rising unemployment.

This vision resonates with many people. Yet as a description of what has actually happened in recent years, it is almost completely untrue.

Rapidly growing Third World economies have indeed increased their exports of manufactured goods. But today these exports absorb only about 1 percent of First World income. Moreover, Third World nations have also increased their imports.

Overall, the effect of Third World growth on the number of industrial jobs in Western nations has been minimal: Growing exports to the newly industrializing countries have created about as many jobs as growing imports have displaced.

What about capital flows? The numbers sound impressive. Last year, $24 billion flowed to Mexico, $11 billion to China. The total movement of capital from advanced to developing nations was about $60 billion. But though this sounds like a lot, it is pocket change in a world economy that invests more than $4 trillion a year.

In other words, if the vision of a Western economy battered by low-wage competition is meant to describe today's world, it is a fantasy with hardly any basis in reality.

Even if the vision does not describe the present, might it describe the future? Well, growing exports of manufactured goods from South to North will lead to a net loss of northern industrial jobs only if they are not matched by growth in exports from North to South.

The authors of the report evidently envision a future of large-scale Third World trade surpluses. But it is an unavoidable fact of accounting that a country that runs a trade surplus must also be a net investor in other countries. So large-scale deindustrialization can take place only if low-wage nations are major exporters of capital to high-wage nations. This seems unlikely. In any case, it contradicts the rest of the story, which predicts huge capital flows into low-wage nations.

Thus, the vision offered by the world competitiveness report conflicts not only with the facts but with itself. Yet it is a vision that a growing number of the world's most influential men and women seem to share. That is a dangerous trend.

Not everyone who worries about low-wage competition is a protectionist. Indeed, the authors of the world competitiveness report would surely claim to be champions of free trade. Nonetheless, the fact that such ideas have become respectable—that much would-be sophisticated opinion apparently now agrees with Ross Perot about the 'great sucking sound' from the South—suggests that the intellectual consensus that has kept world trade relatively free, and that has allowed hundreds of millions of people in the Third World to get their first taste of prosperity, may be unraveling.

SOURCE: *New York Times*, 26 September 1994, p. A17.

This equation shows that a nation's saving must equal its domestic investment plus its net foreign investment. In other words, when Australian citizens save a dollar of their income for the future, that dollar can be used to finance accumulation of domestic capital or it can be used to finance the purchase of capital abroad.

This equation should look somewhat familiar. Earlier in the book, when we analysed the role of the financial system, we considered this identity for the special case of a closed economy. In a closed economy, net foreign investment is zero ($NFI = 0$), so saving equals investment ($S = I$). In contrast, an open economy has two uses for its saving—domestic investment and net foreign investment.

As before, we can view the financial system as standing between the two sides of this identity. For example, suppose the Barnes family decides to save some of its income for retirement. This decision contributes to national saving, the left-hand side of our equation. If the Barneses deposit their saving in a managed fund, the managed fund may use some of the deposit to buy shares issued by BHP, which uses the proceeds to build a processing factory in Victoria. In addition, the managed fund may use some of the Barnes family's deposit to buy shares issued by Toyota, which uses the proceeds to build a factory in Osaka. These transactions show up on the right-hand side of the equation. From the standpoint of Australian accounting, the BHP expenditure on a new factory is domestic investment, and the purchase of Toyota shares by an Australian resident is net foreign investment. Thus, all saving in the Australian economy shows up as investment in the Australian economy or as Australian net foreign investment.

CASE STUDY   SAVING, INVESTMENT AND NET FOREIGN INVESTMENT OF AUSTRALIA

Let's see what these macroeconomic accounting identities tell us about the Australian economy. Panel (a) of figure 14.2 shows national saving and domestic investment for the Australian economy as a percentage of GDP since 1960. Panel (b) shows net foreign investment as a percentage of GDP. Notice that, as the identities require, domestic investment plus net foreign investment always equals national saving.

The figure shows a change beginning in the late 1970s. Before 1975, national saving and domestic investment were very close, and so net foreign investment was small. After 1976, however, national saving fell dramatically. (This decline was due in part to increased government budget deficits and in part to a fall in private saving.) Yet the Australian economy did not experience a similar fall in domestic investment. As a result, net foreign investment became a large negative number, indicating that foreigners were buying more assets in Australia than Australians were buying abroad. Because net exports must equal net foreign investment, net exports were also negative. In other words, Australia ran a trade deficit—imports of goods and services exceeded exports. In 1996, the trade deficit was just over $8 billion.

Are these trade deficits a problem for the Australian economy? Most economists argue that they are not a problem in themselves, but are, perhaps, a symptom of a problem—reduced national saving. Reduced national saving is potentially a problem because it means that the nation is putting away less to

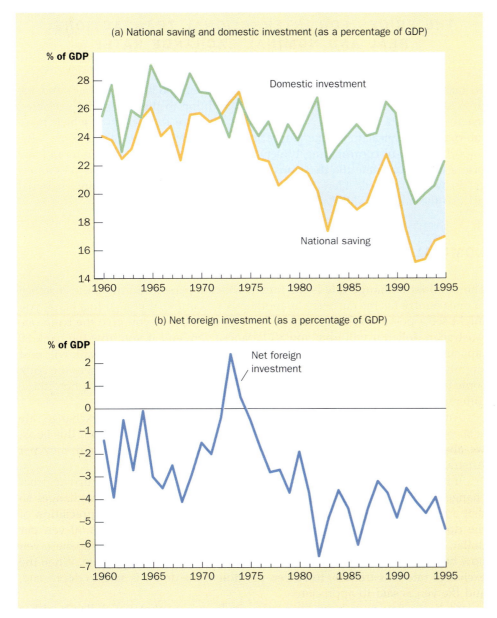

Figure 14.2

NATIONAL SAVING, DOMESTIC INVESTMENT AND NET FOREIGN INVESTMENT. Panel (a) shows national saving and domestic investment as a percentage of GDP. Panel (b) shows net foreign investment as a percentage of GDP. You can see from the figure that national saving has been lower since 1976 than it was before 1976. This fall in national saving has been reflected mainly in reduced net foreign investment rather than in reduced domestic investment.

SOURCE: Based on statistical data from the Australian Bureau of Statistics.

provide for its future. Once national saving has fallen, however, there is no reason to deplore the resulting trade deficits. If national saving fell without inducing a trade deficit, investment in Australia would have to fall. This fall in investment, in turn, would adversely affect the growth in the capital stock, labour productivity and real wages. In other words, given the fact that Australian citizens are not saving much, it is better to have foreigners invest in the Australian economy than no one at all.

QUICK QUIZ Define *net exports* and *net foreign investment*. Explain how they are related.

THE PRICES FOR INTERNATIONAL TRANSACTIONS: REAL AND NOMINAL EXCHANGE RATES

So far we have discussed measures of the flow of goods and services and the flow of capital across a nation's border. In addition to these quantity variables, macroeconomists also study variables that measure the prices at which these international transactions take place. Just as the price in any market serves the important role of coordinating buyers and sellers in that market, international prices help coordinate the decisions of consumers and producers as they interact in world markets. Here we discuss the two most important international prices—the nominal and real exchange rates.

NOMINAL EXCHANGE RATES

nominal exchange rate
the rate at which a person can trade the currency of one country for the currency of another

The **nominal exchange rate** is the rate at which a person can trade the currency of one country for the currency of another. For example, if you go to a bank, you might see a posted exchange rate of 80 yen per dollar. If you give the bank one Australian dollar, it will give you 80 Japanese yen; and if you give the bank 80 Japanese yen, it will give you one Australian dollar. (In reality, the bank will post slightly different prices for buying and selling yen. The difference gives the bank some profit for offering this service. For our purposes here, we can ignore these differences.)

An exchange rate can always be expressed in two ways. If the exchange rate is 80 yen per dollar, it is also 1/80 (0.0125) dollar per yen. Throughout this book, we always express the nominal exchange rate as units of foreign currency per Australian dollar, such as 80 yen per dollar.

appreciation
an increase in the value of a currency as measured by the amount of foreign currency it can buy

depreciation
a decrease in the value of a currency as measured by the amount of foreign currency it can buy

If the exchange rate changes so that a dollar buys more foreign currency, that change is called an **appreciation** of the dollar. If the exchange rate changes so that a dollar buys less foreign currency, that change is called a **depreciation** of the dollar. For example, when the exchange rate rises from 80 to 90 yen per dollar, the dollar is said to appreciate. At the same time, because a Japanese yen now buys less of the Australian currency, the yen is said to depreciate. When the exchange rate falls from 80 to 70 yen per dollar, the dollar is said to depreciate, and the yen is said to appreciate.

At times you may have heard the media report that the dollar is either 'strong' or 'weak'. These descriptions usually refer to recent changes in the nominal exchange rate. When a currency appreciates, it is said to *strengthen* because it can then buy more foreign currency. Similarly, when a currency depreciates, it is said to *weaken*.

For any country, there are many nominal exchange rates. The Australian dollar can be used to buy Japanese yen, British pounds, French francs, Thai baht and so on. When economists study changes in the exchange rate, they often use indexes that average these many exchange rates. Just as the consumer price index turns the many prices in the economy into a single measure of the price level, an exchange rate index turns these many exchange rates into a single measure of the international value of the currency. So when economists talk about the dollar appreciating or depreciating, they often are referring to an exchange rate index that takes into account many individual exchange rates.

REAL EXCHANGE RATES

The **real exchange rate** is the rate at which a person can trade the goods and services of one country for the goods and services of another. For example, suppose that you go shopping and find that a case of German beer is twice as expensive as a case of Australian beer. We would then say that the real exchange rate is ½ case of German beer per case of Australian beer. Notice that, like the nominal exchange rate, the real exchange rate is expressed as units of the foreign item per unit of the domestic item. But in this instance the item is a good rather than a currency.

real exchange rate
the rate at which a person can trade the goods and services of one country for the goods and services of another

Real and nominal exchange rates are closely related. To see how, consider an example. Suppose that a tonne of Australian rice sells for $100, and a tonne of Japanese rice sells for 16 000 yen. What is the real exchange rate between Australian and Japanese rice? To answer this question, we must first use the nominal exchange rate to convert the prices into a common currency. If the nominal exchange rate is 80 yen per dollar, then a price for Australian rice of $100 per tonne is equivalent to 8000 yen per tonne. Australian rice is half as expensive as Japanese rice. The real exchange rate is ½ tonne of Japanese rice per tonne of Australian rice.

We can summarise this calculation for the real exchange rate with the following formula:

$$\text{Real exchange rate} = \frac{\text{Nominal exchange rate} \times \text{Domestic price}}{\text{Foreign price}}$$

Using the numbers in our example, the formula applies as follows:

$$\text{Real exchange rate} = \frac{(80 \text{ yen per dollar}) \times (\$100 \text{ per tonne of Australian rice})}{16\,000 \text{ yen per tonne of Japanese rice}}$$

$$= \frac{8000 \text{ yen per tonne of Australian rice}}{16\,000 \text{ yen per tonne of Japanese rice}}$$

$$= \text{½ tonne of Japanese rice per tonne of Australian rice}$$

Thus, the real exchange rate depends on the nominal exchange rate and on the prices of goods in the two countries measured in the local currencies.

Why does the real exchange rate matter? As you might guess, the real exchange rate is a key determinant of how much a country exports and imports. When Woolworths is deciding whether to buy Australian rice or Japanese rice to put on its shelves, for example, it will ask which rice is cheaper. The real exchange rate gives the answer. As another example, imagine that you are deciding whether to take a seaside holiday in Cairns in Queensland or in Bali in Indonesia. You might ask your travel agent the price of a hotel room in Cairns (measured in dollars), the price of a hotel room in Bali (measured in rupiah), and the exchange rate between rupiah and dollars. If you decide where to holiday by comparing costs, you are basing your decision on the real exchange rate.

When studying an economy as a whole, macroeconomists focus on overall prices rather than the prices of individual items. That is, to measure the real exchange rate, they use price indexes, such as the consumer price index. By using a price index for Australia (P), a price index for prices abroad (P^*), and the nominal exchange rate between the Australian dollar and foreign currencies (e), we can calculate the overall real exchange rate between Australia and other countries as follows:

$$\text{Real exchange rate} = (e \times P)/P^*$$

This real exchange rate measures the price of a basket of goods and services available domestically relative to a basket of goods and services available abroad.

As we will see more fully in the next chapter, a country's real exchange rate is a key determinant of its net exports of goods and services. A depreciation (fall) in the Australian real exchange rate means that Australian goods have become cheaper relative to foreign goods. This change encourages consumers both at home and abroad to buy more Australian goods and fewer goods from other countries. As a result, Australian exports rise, and Australian imports fall, and both of these changes raise Australian net exports. Conversely, an appreciation (rise) in the Australian real exchange rate means that Australian goods have become more expensive compared with foreign goods, so Australian net exports fall.

QUICK QUIZ Define *nominal exchange rate* and *real exchange rate*, and explain how they are related. ◆ If the nominal exchange rate goes from 100 to 120 yen per dollar, has the dollar appreciated or depreciated?

A FIRST THEORY OF EXCHANGE-RATE DETERMINATION: PURCHASING-POWER PARITY

Exchange rates vary substantially over time. In 1974, an Australian dollar could be used to buy 1.49 US dollars, 402 Japanese yen, 0.579 of a British pound, or 703 Italian lire. In 1998, an Australian dollar bought 0.586 of a US dollar, 79 Japanese yen, 0.349 of a British pound, or 960 Italian lire. In other words, over this period the value of the dollar fell by more than half compared with the US dollar. The value of the dollar fell by over three-quarters relative to the Japanese yen. And yet it appreciated by nearly 40% compared with the Italian lira.

What explains these large changes? Economists have developed many models to explain how exchange rates are determined, each emphasising some of the many forces at work. Here we develop the simplest theory of exchange rates, called **purchasing-power parity**. This theory states that a unit of any given currency should be able to buy the same quantity of goods in all countries. Many economists believe that purchasing-power parity describes the forces that determine exchange rates in the long run. We now consider the logic on which this long-run theory of exchange rates is based, as well as the theory's implications and limitations.

purchasing-power parity
a theory of exchange rates whereby a unit of any given currency should be able to buy the same quantity of goods in all countries

THE BASIC LOGIC OF PURCHASING-POWER PARITY

The theory of purchasing-power parity is based on a principle called the *law of one price*. This law asserts that a good must sell for the same price in all locations. Otherwise, there would be opportunities for profit left unexploited.

IN THE NEWS

A baht depreciation and a tourist boom

When a currency depreciates, travel to that country becomes less expensive relative to travel to other countries. It also makes goods in the depreciating country cheaper. The following article explains how travellers switch from holidays in Europe and America to destinations in Asia when the Asian currencies depreciate.

Travellers Flock to New Asian Havens

BY IAN THOMAS

Australian travellers are making the most of cheap packages to South-East Asia and foreign exchange shifts in their favour. The increased demand is pushing airlines to their limit. The dollar-wise tourists are shunning expensive Europe and the US and making a beeline instead to the 'safe havens' of Thailand and Bali, where tour prices are at their lowest levels for years.

With the burgeoning demand, the bookings through major tour operators to Thailand have gone through the roof with increases of 200 to 300 per cent in the past 10 months. In sharp contrast to other parts of Asia, Australian visitor numbers to Bali have climbed by 43 per cent in the past year.

And the momentum is expected to continue into the peak Christmas–New Year travel season, underpinned by a recent strengthening in the Australian dollar. The immense pressure on seat availability on flights into and out of the leisure destinations was underlined by American Express's decision to cancel its planned annual networking conference in Bali later this year. Amex had tried to secure flights with its commercial partner Qantas for the 300 delegates at special rates, but the airline was unable to do so because it needed the seats for full fare-paying passengers.

Ansett has chalked up record loads on its Bali services with its planes close to 100 per cent full for the past two weekends. On last Saturday alone, 2600 passengers flew into and out of the Indonesian islands' airport at Denpasar. The carrier has deployed one of its Boeing 747–300s on the route out of Sydney at least until the end of November to inject extra capacity into the booming market, and will complement its operations with smaller aircraft.

A survey released this week by Tourism Council Australia listed Indonesia and Thailand at numbers one and two respectively in terms of price competitiveness as tourist destinations. Australia ranked ninth on the league table of 20 countries. The heavy devaluations in the baht and rupiah have made it cheaper, in some cases, to travel to South-East Asia than take domestic holidays, with Ansett offering five-night deals for Bali for $955 and Royal Orchid Holidays pushing nine nights in the Thai resort centre of Phuket for $1103. Royal Orchid recently announced a three-night package in Bangkok for $799, promoting it as an opportunity to take advantage of discounts of up to 80 per cent being offered on retail goods at shopping centres and stores in the Thai capital.

Mr Grant Symonds, the manager in NSW and the ACT for Thai Airways, said on Friday that passenger figures for Thailand had increased by 47 per cent in the past year with the airline's tour arm, Royal Orchid, experiencing a 300 per cent lift in bookings. 'With load factors up in the 80 per cents, we have been discussing with

Bangkok the possibility of expanding services out of Australia,' Mr Symonds said. 'However, that seems unlikely to happen until next March because of restraints on aircraft availability.'

He attributed the surge in business out of Australia to a combination of factors, from the fall in the baht and foreign exchange fluctuations to the relative political stability of Thailand against its Asian competitors such as Indonesia and Malaysia.

Thomas Cook has also seen a resurgence in travel to Thailand, citing a 226 per cent jump in bookings for the 12 months to August. Bali showed 14 per cent growth. However, in the same period bookings for the US fell 30 per cent and Hong Kong was down by 15 per cent. Europe, including the UK, posted growth of 4.6 per cent.

'Thailand has zoomed up with the focus on Asia becoming better value for Australians, and Bali has also been doing well,' said Mr Peter Hansen, communications manager for Thomas Cook.

Mr Graham Turner, the managing director of Flight Centre, said Australians travelling to popular Asian destinations should focus on buying packages with accommodation included, which are often cheaper than the air fares alone.

Tour operators also said prospective travellers should shop around, with many companies offering two-for-one deals on flights and accommodation, discounted room rates or sightseeing extras.

SOURCE: *Australian Financial Review*, 17 October 1998, p. 6.

For example, suppose that coffee beans sold for less in Brisbane than in Perth. A person could buy coffee in Brisbane for, say, $20 a kilo and then sell it in Perth for $30 a kilo, making a profit of $10 per kilo from the difference in price. The process of taking advantage of differences in prices in different markets is called *arbitrage*. In our example, as people took advantage of this arbitrage opportunity, they would increase the demand for coffee in Brisbane and increase the supply in Perth. The price of coffee would rise in Brisbane (in response to greater demand) and fall in Perth (in response to greater supply). This process would continue until, eventually, the prices were the same in the two markets, ignoring transactions costs.

Now consider how the law of one price applies to the international marketplace. If a dollar (or any other currency) could buy more coffee in Australia than in Japan, international traders could profit by buying coffee in Australia and selling it in Japan. This export of coffee from Australia to Japan would drive up the Australian price of coffee and drive down the Japanese price. Conversely, if a dollar could buy more coffee in Japan than in Australia, traders could buy coffee in Japan and sell it in Australia. This import of coffee into Australia from Japan would drive down the Australian price of coffee and drive up the Japanese price. In the end, the law of one price tells us that a dollar must buy the same amount of coffee in all countries.

This logic leads us to the theory of purchasing-power parity. According to this theory, a currency must have the same purchasing power in all countries. That is, an Australian dollar must buy the same quantity of goods in Australia and Japan, and a Japanese yen must buy the same quantity of goods in Japan and Australia. Indeed, the name of this theory describes it well. *Parity* means equality, and *purchasing power* refers to the value of money. *Purchasing-power parity* states that one unit of every currency must have the same real value in every country.

IMPLICATIONS OF PURCHASING-POWER PARITY

What does the theory of purchasing-power parity say about exchange rates? It tells us that the nominal exchange rate between the currencies of two countries depends on the price levels in those countries. If a dollar buys the same quantity of goods in Australia (where prices are measured in dollars) as in Japan (where prices are measured in yen), then the number of yen per dollar must reflect the prices of goods in Australia and Japan. For example, if a kilo of coffee costs 1500 yen in Japan and $20 in Australia, then the nominal exchange rate must be 75 yen per dollar (1500 yen/$20 = 75 yen per dollar). Otherwise, the purchasing power of the dollar would not be the same in the two countries.

To see more fully how this works, it is helpful to use just a bit of mathematics. Suppose that P is the price level in Australia (measured in dollars), P^* is the price level in Japan (measured in yen), and e is the nominal exchange rate (the number of yen a dollar can buy). Now consider the quantity of goods a dollar can buy at home and abroad. At home, the price level is P, so the purchasing power of $1 at home is $1/P$. Abroad, a dollar can be exchanged into e units of foreign currency, which in turn have purchasing power e/P^*. For the purchasing power of a dollar to be the same in the two countries, it must be the case that:

$$1/P = e/P^*$$

With rearrangement, this equation becomes:

$$1 = eP/P^*$$

Notice that the left-hand side of this equation is a constant, and the right-hand side is the real exchange rate. Thus, *if the purchasing power of the dollar is always the same at home and abroad, then the real exchange rate—the relative price of domestic and foreign goods—cannot change.* To see the implication of this analysis for the nominal exchange rate, we can rearrange the last equation to solve for the nominal exchange rate:

$$e = P^*/P$$

That is, the nominal exchange rate equals the ratio of the foreign price level (measured in units of the foreign currency) to the domestic price level (measured in units of the domestic currency). *According to the theory of purchasing-power parity, the nominal exchange rate between the currencies of two countries must reflect the different price levels in those countries.*

A key implication of this theory is that nominal exchange rates change when price levels change. As we saw in the preceding chapter, the price level in any country adjusts to bring the quantity of money supplied and the quantity of money demanded into balance. Because the nominal exchange rate depends on the price levels, it also depends on the money supply and money demand in each country. When a central bank in any country increases the money supply and causes the price level to rise, it also causes that country's currency to depreciate relative to other currencies in the world. In other words, when the central bank prints large quantities of money, that money loses value both in terms of the goods and services it can buy and in terms of the amount of other currencies it can buy.

We can now answer the question that began this section: Why has the Australian dollar lost value compared with the US dollar and gained value compared with the Italian lira? The answer is that the US has pursued a less inflationary monetary policy than Australia, and Italy has pursued a more inflationary monetary policy. From 1970 to 1998, inflation in Australia was 7.2% per year. In contrast, inflation was 5.3% in the United States, and 9.7% in Italy. As Australian prices rose relative to US prices, the value of the Australian dollar fell relative to the US dollar. Similarly, as Australian prices fell relative to Italian prices, the value of the Australian dollar rose relative to the lira.

CASE STUDY THE NOMINAL EXCHANGE RATE DURING HYPERINFLATION

Macroeconomists cannot conduct controlled experiments. Instead, they must glean what they can from the natural experiments that history gives them. One natural experiment is hyperinflation—the high inflation that arises when a government turns to the printing press to pay for large amounts of government spending. Because hyperinflations are so extreme, they illustrate some basic economic principles with clarity.

Consider the German hyperinflation of the early 1920s. Figure 14.3 shows the German money supply, the German price level and the nominal exchange

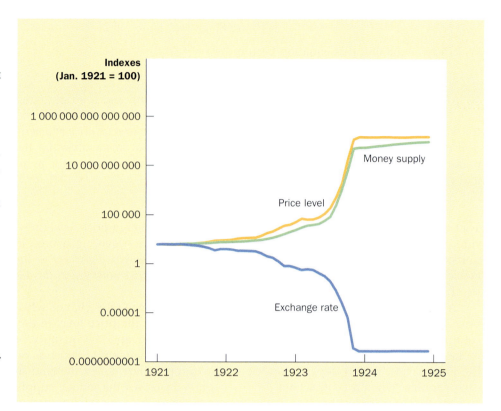

Figure 14.3

MONEY, PRICES AND THE NOMINAL EXCHANGE RATE DURING THE GERMAN HYPERINFLATION. This figure shows the money supply, the price level, and the exchange rate (measured as US cents per mark) for the German hyperinflation from January 1921 to December 1924. Notice how similarly these three variables move. When the quantity of money started growing quickly, the price level followed, and the mark depreciated relative to the dollar. When the German central bank stabilised the money supply, the price level and exchange rate stabilised as well.

SOURCE: Adapted from Thomas J. Sargent, 'The end of four big inflations', in Robert Hall, ed., *Inflation* (Chicago: University of Chicago Press, 1983), pp. 41–93.

rate (measured as US cents per German mark) for that period. Notice that these series move closely together. When the supply of money starts growing quickly, the price level also takes off, and the German mark depreciates. When the money supply stabilises, so does the price level and the exchange rate.

The pattern shown in this figure appears during every hyperinflation. It leaves no doubt that there is a fundamental link between money, prices and the nominal exchange rate. The quantity theory of money discussed in the previous chapter explains how the money supply affects the price level. The theory of purchasing-power parity discussed here explains how the price level affects the nominal exchange rate.

LIMITATIONS OF PURCHASING-POWER PARITY

Purchasing-power parity provides a simple model of how exchange rates are determined. For understanding many economic phenomena, the theory works well. In particular, it can explain many long-term trends, such as the depreciation of the Australian dollar against the US dollar and the appreciation of the Australian dollar against the Italian lira. It can also explain the major changes in exchange rates that occur during hyperinflations.

Yet the theory of purchasing-power parity is not completely accurate. That is, exchange rates do not always move to ensure that a dollar has the same real value in all countries all the time. There are two reasons that the theory of purchasing-power parity does not always hold in practice.

The first reason is that many goods are not easily traded. Imagine, for instance, that haircuts are more expensive in Paris than in Sydney. International travellers might avoid getting their haircuts in Paris, and some hairdressers might move from Sydney to Paris. Yet such arbitrage would probably be too limited to eliminate the differences in prices. Thus, the deviation from purchasing-power parity might persist, and a dollar (or franc) would continue to buy less of a haircut in Paris than in Sydney.

The second reason that purchasing-power parity does not always hold is that even tradable goods are not always perfect substitutes when they are produced in different countries. For example, some consumers prefer German beer, and others prefer Australian beer. Moreover, consumer tastes for beer change over time. If German beer suddenly becomes more popular, the increase in demand will drive up the price of German beer. As a result, a dollar (or a mark) might then buy more beer in Australia than in Germany. But despite this difference in prices in the two markets, there might be no opportunity for profitable arbitrage because consumers do not view the two beers as equivalent.

Thus, both because some goods are not tradable and because some tradable goods are not perfect substitutes with their foreign counterparts, purchasing-power parity is not a perfect theory of exchange-rate determination. For these reasons, real exchange rates do in fact fluctuate over time. Nonetheless, the theory of purchasing-power parity does provide a useful first step in understanding exchange rates. The basic logic is persuasive—as the real exchange rate drifts from the level predicted by purchasing-power parity, people have greater incentive to move goods across national borders. Even if the forces of purchasing-power parity do not completely fix the real exchange rate, they do provide a reason to expect that changes in the real exchange rate are most often small or temporary. As a result, large and persistent movements in nominal exchange rates typically reflect changes in price levels at home and abroad.

QUICK QUIZ Over the past 20 years, Spain has had high inflation, and Japan has had low inflation. What do you predict has happened to the number of Spanish pesetas a person can buy with a Japanese yen?

CONCLUSION

The purpose of this chapter has been to develop some basic concepts that macroeconomists use to study open economies. You should now understand why a nation's net exports must equal its net foreign investment, and why national saving must equal domestic investment plus net foreign investment. You should also understand the meaning of the nominal and real exchange rates, as well as the implications and limitations of purchasing-power parity as a theory of how exchange rates are determined.

The macroeconomic variables defined here offer a starting point for analysing an open economy's interactions with the rest of the world. In the next chapter, we develop a model that can explain what determines these variables. We can then discuss how various events and policies affect a country's trade balance and the rate at which nations make exchanges in world markets.

Summary

- Net exports are the value of domestic goods and services sold abroad minus the value of foreign goods and services sold domestically. Net foreign investment is the acquisition of foreign assets by domestic residents minus the acquisition of domestic assets by foreigners. Because every international transaction involves an exchange of an asset for a good or service, an economy's net foreign investment always equals its net exports.

- An economy's saving can be used either to finance investment at home or to buy assets abroad. Thus, national saving equals domestic investment plus net foreign investment.

- The nominal exchange rate is the relative price of the currency of two countries, and the real exchange rate is the relative price of the goods and services of two countries. When the nominal exchange rate changes so that each dollar buys more foreign currency, the dollar is said to *appreciate* or *strengthen*. When the nominal exchange rate changes so that each dollar buys less foreign currency, the dollar is said to *depreciate* or *weaken*.

- According to the theory of purchasing-power parity, a dollar (or a unit of any other currency) should be able to buy the same quantity of goods in all countries. This theory implies that the nominal exchange rate between the currencies of two countries should reflect the price levels in those countries. As a result, countries with relatively high inflation should have depreciating currencies, and countries with relatively low inflation should have appreciating currencies.

Key concepts

closed economy, p. 298
open economy, p. 298
exports, p. 298
imports, p. 298
net exports, p. 299
trade balance, p. 299
trade surplus, p. 299
trade deficit, p. 299

balanced trade, p. 299
net foreign investment, p. 301
nominal exchange rate, p. 308
appreciation, p. 308
depreciation, p. 308
real exchange rate, p. 309
purchasing-power parity, p. 310

Questions for review

1. Define net exports and net foreign investment. Explain how and why they are related.

2. Explain the relationship between saving, investment and net foreign investment.

3. If a Japanese car costs 500 000 yen, if a similar Australian car costs $10 000, and if a dollar can buy 100 yen, what is the nominal and real exchange rate?

4. Describe the economic logic behind the theory of purchasing-power parity.

5. If the Reserve Bank of Australia started printing large quantities of Australian dollars, what would happen to the number of Japanese yen a dollar could buy?

Problems and applications

1. How would the following transactions affect Australian exports, imports and net exports?
    a. An Australian art professor spends the summer touring museums in Europe.
    b. Students in London flock to see the latest Gillian Armstrong movie.
    c. Your uncle buys a new Volvo.
    d. The Australian designer Collette Dinnigan sells her latest collection in Paris.
    e. A New Zealand citizen shops at a store in Melbourne to avoid the New Zealand goods and services tax.

2. Suggest some specific reasons that each of the following products is traded internationally more today than in the past:
   a. wheat
   b. banking services
   c. computer software
   d. cars.

3. How would the following transactions affect Australian net foreign investment? Also, state whether each involves direct investment or portfolio investment.
   a. An Australian cellular phone company establishes an office in the Czech Republic.
   b. Harrod's of London sells shares to the AMP superannuation fund.
   c. Toyota expands its factory in Altona, South Australia.
   d. A Westpac mutual fund sells its Volkswagen shares to a French investor.

4. Holding national saving constant, does an increase in net foreign investment increase, decrease or have no effect on a country's accumulation of domestic capital?

5. The *Australian Financial Review* contains a table showing Australian exchange rates. Find such a table and use it to answer the following questions.
   a. Does this table show nominal or real exchange rates? Explain.
   b. What are the exchange rates between Australia and the United States and between Australia and Japan? Calculate the exchange rate between the United States and Japan.
   c. If Australian inflation exceeds US inflation over the next year, would you expect the dollar to appreciate or depreciate relative to the US dollar?

6. Would each of the following groups be happy or unhappy if the Australian dollar appreciated? Explain.
   a. Dutch pension funds holding Australian government bonds
   b. Australian manufacturing industries
   c. Australian tourists planning a trip to the United States
   d. An Australian firm trying to purchase property overseas

7. What is happening to the Australian real exchange rate in each of the following situations? Explain.
   a. The Australian nominal exchange rate is unchanged, but prices rise faster in Australia than abroad.
   b. The Australian nominal exchange rate is unchanged, but prices rise faster abroad than in Australia.
   c. The Australian nominal exchange rate declines, and prices are unchanged in Australia and abroad.
   d. The Australian nominal exchange rate declines, and prices rise faster abroad than in Australia.

8. List three goods for which the law of one price is likely to hold, and three goods for which it is not. Justify your choices.

9. A can of Pepsi costs $1.50 in Australia and 3 francs in France. What would the franc–dollar exchange rate be if purchasing-power parity holds?

10. Assume that Australian rice sells for $100 per tonne, Japanese rice sells for 16 000 yen per tonne, and the nominal exchange rate is 80 yen per dollar.
    a. Explain how you could make a profit from this situation. What would be your profit per tonne of rice? If other people exploit the same opportunity, what would happen to the price of rice in Japan and the price of rice in the Australia?
    b. Suppose that rice is the only commodity in the world. What would happen to the real exchange rate between the Australia and Japan?

11. The *Economist*, an international newsmagazine, regularly collects data on the price of a McDonald's Big Mac hamburger in different countries, in order to examine the theory of purchasing-power parity.
    a. Why might the Big Mac be a good product to use for this purpose?
    b. Based on the Big Mac data, purchasing-power parity appears to hold roughly across some countries, though not across others. Why might the assumptions underlying the theory of purchasing-power parity not hold exactly for Big Macs?

15

A MACROECONOMIC THEORY OF THE OPEN ECONOMY

IN THIS CHAPTER YOU WILL

Build a model to explain an open economy's trade balance and exchange rate

Use the model to analyse the effects of government budget deficits

Use the model to analyse the macroeconomic effects of trade policies

Use the model to analyse political instability and capital flight

Since the 1970s, Australia's trade balance has swung between surplus and deficit. Sometimes we export more goods and services than we import. Sometimes we import more than we export. Despite periods of trade surplus, economists debate whether the trade deficits are a problem for the Australian economy. The nation's business community, however, has a strong opinion. Many business leaders claim that the trade deficits reflect unfair competition—foreign firms are allowed to sell their products in Australian markets, they contend, while foreign governments impede Australian firms selling Australian products abroad.

Imagine that you are the prime minister and you want to end these trade deficits. What should you do? Should you try to limit imports, perhaps by increasing tariffs on the import of cars from Japan? Or should you try to influence the nation's trade deficit in some other way?

To understand what factors determine a country's trade balance and how government policies can affect it, we need a macroeconomic theory of the open economy. The preceding chapter introduced some of the key macroeconomic variables that describe an economy's relationship with other economies—including net exports, net foreign investment, and the real and nominal exchange rates. This chapter develops a model that shows what forces determine these variables and how these variables are related to one another.

To develop this macroeconomic model of an open economy, we build on our previous analysis in two important ways. First, the model takes the economy's GDP as given. The economy's output of goods and services, as measured by real GDP, is assumed to be determined by the supplies of the factors of production and by the available production technology that turns these inputs into output.

Second, the model takes the economy's price level as given. The price level is assumed to adjust to bring the supply and demand for money into balance. In other words, this chapter takes as a starting point the lessons learned in previous chapters about the determination of the economy's output and price level.

The goal of the model in this chapter is to highlight those forces that determine the economy's trade balance and exchange rate. In one sense, the model is simple—it merely applies the tools of supply and demand to an open economy. Yet the model is also more complicated than others we have seen because it involves looking simultaneously at two related markets—the market for loanable funds and the market for foreign-currency exchange. After we develop this model of the open economy, we use it to examine how various events and policies affect the economy's trade balance and exchange rate. We will then be able to determine the government policies that are most likely to reverse the trade deficits that the Australian economy has experienced from time to time over the past few decades.

SUPPLY OF AND DEMAND FOR LOANABLE FUNDS AND FOR FOREIGN-CURRENCY EXCHANGE

To understand the forces at work in an open economy, we focus on supply and demand in two markets. The first is the market for loanable funds, which coordinates the economy's saving and investment (including its net foreign investment). The second is the market for foreign-currency exchange, which coordinates people who want to exchange the domestic currency for the currency of other countries. In this section we discuss supply and demand in each of these markets. In the next section we put these markets together to explain the overall equilibrium for an open economy.

THE MARKET FOR LOANABLE FUNDS

When we first analysed the role of the financial system earlier in this book, we made the simplifying assumption that the financial system consists of only one market, called the *market for loanable funds*. All savers go to this market to deposit their saving, and all borrowers go to this market to get their loans. In this market, there is one interest rate, which is both the return on saving and the cost of borrowing.

To understand the market for loanable funds in an open economy, the place to start is the identity discussed in the preceding chapter:

$$S = I + NFI$$
$$\text{Saving} = \text{Domestic investment} + \text{Net foreign investment}$$

Whenever a nation saves a dollar of its income, it can use that dollar to finance the purchase of domestic capital or to finance the purchase of an asset abroad. The two sides of this identity represent the two sides of the market for loanable funds. The supply of loanable funds comes from national saving (S). The demand for loanable funds comes from domestic investment (I) and net foreign investment (NFI). Note that the purchase of a capital asset adds to the demand for loanable funds, regardless of whether that asset is located at home or abroad. Because net foreign investment can be either positive or negative, it can either add to or subtract from the demand for loanable funds that arises from domestic investment.

As we learned in our earlier discussion of the market for loanable funds, the quantity of loanable funds supplied and the quantity of loanable funds demanded depend on the real interest rate. A higher real interest rate encourages people to save and, therefore, raises the quantity of loanable funds supplied. A higher interest rate also makes borrowing to finance capital projects more costly; thus, it discourages investment and reduces the quantity of loanable funds demanded.

In addition to influencing national saving and domestic investment, the real interest rate in a country affects that country's net foreign investment. To see why, consider two managed funds—one in Australia and one in Canada—deciding whether to buy an Australian government bond or a Canadian government bond. The managed funds would make this decision in part by comparing the real interest rates in Australia and Canada. When the Australian real interest rate rises, the Australian bond becomes more attractive to both managed funds. Thus, an increase in the Australian real interest rate discourages Australians from buying foreign assets and encourages foreigners to buy Australian assets. For both reasons, a high Australian real interest rate reduces Australian net foreign investment.

We represent the market for loanable funds on the familiar supply-and-demand diagram in figure 15.1. As in our earlier analysis of the financial system, the supply curve slopes upwards because a higher interest rate increases the quantity of loanable funds supplied, and the demand curve slopes downwards because a higher interest rate decreases the quantity of loanable funds demanded. Unlike the situation in our previous discussion, however, the

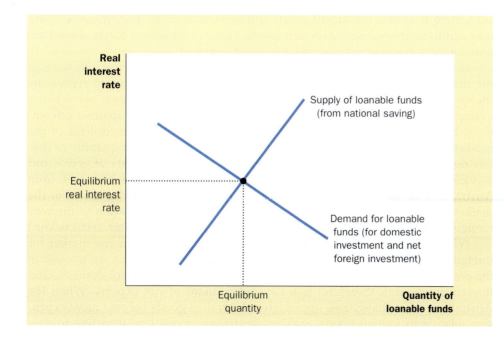

Figure 15.1

THE MARKET FOR LOANABLE FUNDS. The interest rate in a large, open economy, as in a closed economy, is determined by the supply of and demand for loanable funds. National saving is the source of the supply of loanable funds. Domestic investment and net foreign investment are the sources of the demand for loanable funds. At the equilibrium interest rate, the amount that people want to save exactly balances the amount that people want to borrow for the purpose of buying domestic capital and foreign assets.

demand side of the market now represents the behaviour of both domestic investment and net foreign investment. That is, in an open economy, the demand for loanable funds comes not only from those who want to borrow funds to buy domestic capital goods but also from those who want to borrow funds to buy foreign assets.

The interest rate adjusts to bring the supply of and demand for loanable funds into balance. If the interest rate were below the equilibrium level, the quantity of loanable funds supplied would be less than the quantity demanded. The resulting shortage of loanable funds would push the interest rate upwards. Conversely, if the interest rate were above the equilibrium level, the quantity of loanable funds supplied would exceed the quantity demanded. The surplus of loanable funds would drive the interest rate downwards. At the equilibrium interest rate, the supply of loanable funds exactly balances the demand. That is, *at the equilibrium interest rate, the amount that people want to save exactly balances the desired quantities of domestic investment and net foreign investment.*

THE MARKET FOR FOREIGN-CURRENCY EXCHANGE

The second market in our model of the open economy is the market for foreign-currency exchange. Participants in this market trade Australian dollars in exchange for foreign currencies. To understand the market for foreign-currency exchange, we begin with another identity from the last chapter:

$$NFI = NX$$
$$\text{Net foreign investment} = \text{Net exports}$$

This identity states that the imbalance between the purchase and sale of capital assets abroad (*NFI*) equals the imbalance between exports and imports of goods and services (*NX*). When net exports are positive, for instance, foreigners are buying more Australian goods and services than Australians are buying foreign goods and services. What are Australians doing with the foreign currency they are getting from this net sale of goods and services abroad? They must be using it to add to their holdings of foreign assets. These purchases of assets abroad are reflected in a positive value of net foreign investment.

We can view the two sides of this identity as representing the two sides of the market for foreign-currency exchange. Net foreign investment represents the quantity of dollars supplied for the purpose of buying assets abroad. For example, when an Australian managed fund wants to buy a Japanese government bond, it needs to change dollars into yen, so it supplies dollars in the market for foreign-currency exchange. Net exports represent the quantity of dollars demanded for the purpose of buying Australian net exports of goods and services. For example, when a Japanese steel mill wants to buy coal from Australia, it needs to change its yen into dollars, so it demands dollars in the market for foreign-currency exchange. (This view is a simplification of the way foreign exchange markets actually work. We discuss this in greater detail below.)

What is the price that balances the supply and demand in the market for foreign-currency exchange? The answer is the real exchange rate. As we saw in the preceding chapter, the real exchange rate is the relative price of domestic and foreign goods and, therefore, is a key determinant of net exports. When the Australian real exchange rate appreciates, Australian goods become more expensive relative to foreign goods, making Australian goods less attractive to con-

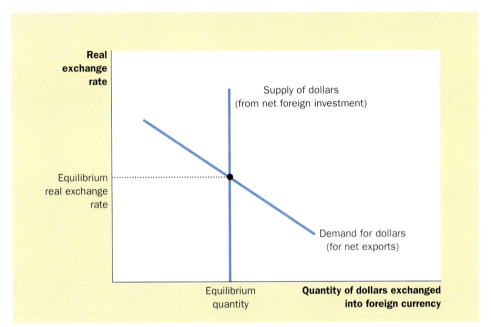

Figure 15.2

THE MARKET FOR FOREIGN-CURRENCY EXCHANGE. The real exchange rate is determined by the supply of and demand for foreign-currency exchange. The supply of dollars to be exchanged into foreign currency comes from net foreign investment. Because net foreign investment does not depend on the real exchange rate, the supply curve is vertical. The demand for dollars comes from net exports. Because a lower real exchange rate stimulates net exports (and thus increases the quantity of dollars demanded to pay for these net exports), the demand curve is downward-sloping. At the equilibrium real exchange rate, the number of dollars people supply to buy foreign assets exactly balances the number of dollars people demand to buy net exports.

sumers both at home and abroad. As a result, exports from Australia fall, and imports into Australia rise. For both reasons, net exports fall. Hence, an appreciation of the real exchange rate reduces the quantity of dollars demanded in the market for foreign-currency exchange.

Figure 15.2 shows supply and demand in the market for foreign-currency exchange. The demand curve slopes downwards for the reason we just discussed—a higher real exchange rate makes Australian goods more expensive and reduces the quantity of dollars demanded to buy those goods. The supply curve is vertical because the quantity of dollars supplied for net foreign investment does not depend on the real exchange rate. (As discussed earlier, net foreign investment depends on the real interest rate. When discussing the market for foreign-currency exchange, we take the real interest rate and net foreign investment as given.)

The real exchange rate adjusts to balance the supply of and demand for dollars just as the price of any good adjusts to balance supply of and demand for that good. If the real exchange rate were below the equilibrium level, the quantity of dollars supplied would be less than the quantity demanded. The resulting shortage of dollars would push the value of the dollar upwards. Conversely, if the real exchange rate were above the equilibrium level, the quantity of dollars supplied would exceed the quantity demanded. The surplus of dollars would drive the value of the dollar downwards. *At the equilibrium real exchange rate, the demand for dollars to buy net exports exactly balances the supply of dollars to be exchanged into foreign currency to buy assets abroad.*

At this point, it is worth noting that the division of transactions between 'supply' and 'demand' in this model is somewhat artificial. In our model, net exports are the source of the demand for dollars, and net foreign investment is the source of the supply. Thus, when an Australian resident imports a car made in Japan, our model treats that transaction as a decrease in the quantity of dollars demanded (because net exports fall) rather than an increase in the quantity

FYI

Purchasing-power parity as a special case

IN THE PRECEDING CHAPTER we developed a simple theory of the exchange rate called *purchasing-power parity*. This theory asserts that a dollar (or any other currency) must buy the same quantity of goods and services in every country. As a result, the real exchange rate is fixed, and all changes in the nominal exchange rate between two currencies reflect changes in the price levels in the two countries.

How is the model of the exchange rate developed here related to the theory of purchasing-power parity? According to the theory of purchasing-power parity, international trade responds quickly to international price differences. If goods were cheaper in one country than in another, they would be exported from the first country and imported into the second until the price differential disappeared. In other words, the theory of purchasing-power parity assumes that net exports are highly responsive to small changes in the real exchange rate. If net exports were in fact so responsive, the demand curve in figure 15.2 would be horizontal.

Thus, the theory of purchasing-power parity is a special case of the model considered here. In that special case, the demand curve for foreign-currency exchange, rather than being downward-sloping, is horizontal at the level of the real exchange rate that ensures parity of purchasing power at home and abroad.

---

of dollars supplied. Similarly, when a Japanese citizen buys an Australian government bond, our model treats that transaction as a decrease in the quantity of dollars supplied (because net foreign investment falls) rather than an increase in the quantity of dollars demanded. This use of language may seem somewhat unnatural at first, but it will prove useful when analysing the effects of various policies.

QUICK QUIZ Describe the sources of supply and demand in the market for loanable funds and the market for foreign-currency exchange.

EQUILIBRIUM IN THE OPEN ECONOMY

So far we have discussed supply and demand in two markets—the market for loanable funds and the market for foreign-currency exchange. Let's now consider how these markets are related to each other.

NET FOREIGN INVESTMENT: THE LINK BETWEEN THE TWO MARKETS

We begin by recapping what we've learned so far in this chapter. We have been discussing how the economy coordinates four important macroeconomic variables: national saving (*S*), domestic investment (*I*), net foreign investment (*NFI*) and net exports (*NX*).

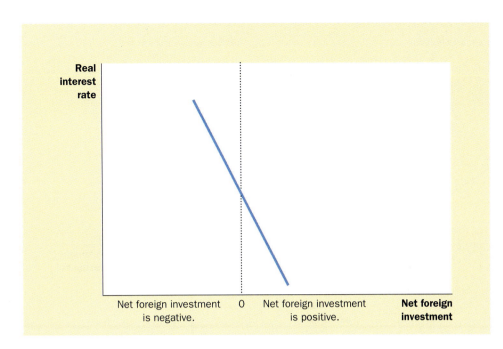

Figure 15.3

HOW NET FOREIGN INVESTMENT DEPENDS ON THE INTEREST RATE. Because a higher domestic real interest rate makes domestic assets more attractive, it reduces net foreign investment. Note the position of zero on the horizontal axis—net foreign investment can be either positive or negative.

Keep in mind the following identities:

$$S = I + NFI$$

and

$$NFI = NX$$

In the market for loanable funds, supply comes from national saving, demand comes from domestic investment and net foreign investment, and the real interest rate balances supply and demand. In the market for foreign-currency exchange, supply comes from net foreign investment, demand comes from net exports, and the real exchange rate balances supply and demand.

Net foreign investment is the variable that links these two markets. In the market for loanable funds, net foreign investment is a piece of demand. A person who wants to buy an asset abroad must finance this purchase by borrowing in the market for loanable funds. In the market for foreign-currency exchange, net foreign investment is the source of supply. A person who wants to buy an asset in another country must supply dollars in order to exchange them for the currency of that country.

The key determinant of net foreign investment, as we have discussed, is the real interest rate. When the Australian interest rate is high, owning Australian assets is more attractive, and Australian net foreign investment is low. Figure 15.3 shows this negative relationship between the interest rate and net foreign investment. This net-foreign-investment curve is the link between the market for loanable funds and the market for foreign-currency exchange.

SIMULTANEOUS EQUILIBRIUM IN TWO MARKETS

We can now put all the pieces of our model together in figure 15.4. This figure shows how the market for loanable funds and the market for foreign-currency

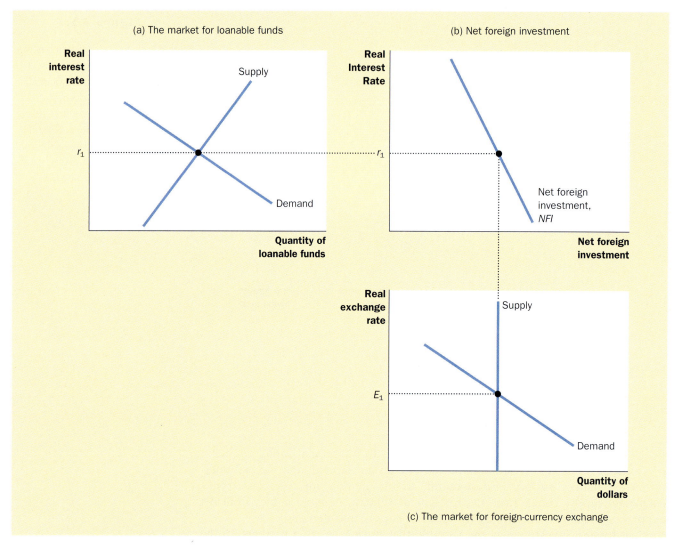

Figure 15.4

THE REAL EQUILIBRIUM IN AN OPEN ECONOMY. In panel (a), the supply of and demand for loanable funds determine the real interest rate. In panel (b), the interest rate determines net foreign investment, which provides the supply of dollars in the market for foreign-currency exchange. In panel (c), the supply of and demand for dollars in the market for foreign-currency exchange determine the real exchange rate.

exchange jointly determine the important macroeconomic variables of an open economy.

Panel (a) of the figure shows the market for loanable funds (taken from figure 15.1). As before, national saving is the source of the supply of loanable funds. Domestic investment and net foreign investment are the source of the demand for loanable funds. The equilibrium real interest rate (r_1) brings the quantity of loanable funds supplied and the quantity of loanable funds demanded into balance.

FYI

The classical dichotomy once again

THE MACROECONOMIC THEORY of the open economy that we have just developed is 'classical'. This term has two related meanings. First, the theory harks back to themes emphasised by economists of centuries past. Second, and more important, the theory uses the classical dichotomy and the assumption of monetary neutrality. Recall that the classical dichotomy is the theoretical separation of real and nominal variables. Our model of the open economy is written completely in terms of real variables, including quantities (saving, investment, net foreign investment and net exports) and relative prices (the real interest rate and the real exchange rate). The model explains these real variables without including a role for money.

How do changes in the money supply affect the economy? The answer is the same as in our analysis in previous chapters. Classical theory posits that the price level adjusts to balance money supply and money demand. If the central bank doubles the money supply, the price level doubles. If the central bank follows a policy of persistent growth in the money supply, the result is persistent inflation.

To ensure that real variables are not affected by monetary changes, all nominal variables must adjust to these changes. In particular, if the real exchange rate is not affected by monetary changes, then the nominal exchange rate (measured in units of foreign currency per dollar) must fall as the domestic price level rises. We first saw this effect of inflation on nominal exchange rates in the preceding chapter when we discussed the theory of purchasing-power parity. Nothing we have said about the open economy in this chapter alters these conclusions.

Recall that the assumption of monetary neutrality is best viewed as applying over the long run. To fully understand year-to-year changes in the economy, we need to incorporate reasons for short-run monetary non-neutrality. We cover that topic beginning in the next chapter. Throughout this chapter, we maintain the assumption of monetary neutrality in order to understand the implications of this classical model.

Panel (b) of the figure shows net foreign investment (taken from figure 15.3). It shows how the interest rate from panel (a) determines net foreign investment. A higher interest rate at home makes domestic assets more attractive, and this in turn reduces net foreign investment. Therefore, the net-foreign-investment curve in panel (b) slopes downwards.

Panel (c) of the figure shows the market for foreign-currency exchange (taken from figure 15.2). Because net foreign investment must be paid for with foreign currency, the quantity of net foreign investment from panel (b) determines the supply of dollars to be exchanged into foreign currencies. The real exchange rate does not affect net foreign investment, so the supply curve is vertical. The demand for dollars comes from net exports. Because a depreciation of the real exchange rate increases net exports, the demand curve for foreign-currency exchange slopes downwards. The equilibrium real exchange rate (E_1) brings into balance the quantity of dollars supplied and the quantity of dollars demanded in the market for foreign-currency exchange.

The two markets shown in figure 15.4 determine two relative prices—the real interest rate and the real exchange rate. The real interest rate determined in panel (a) is the price of goods and services in the present relative to goods and services in the future. The real exchange rate determined in panel (c) is the price of domestic goods and services relative to foreign goods and services. These two relative prices adjust simultaneously to balance supply and demand in these two markets. As they do so, they determine national saving, domestic investment, net foreign investment and net exports. In a moment, we will use this model to see how all these variables change when some policy or event causes one of these curves to shift.

> **QUICK QUIZ** In the model of the open economy just developed, two markets determine two relative prices. What are the markets? What are the two relative prices?

HOW POLICIES AND EVENTS AFFECT AN OPEN ECONOMY

Having developed a model to explain how key macroeconomic variables are determined in an open economy, we can now use the model to analyse how changes in policy and other events alter the economy's equilibrium. As we proceed, keep in mind that our model is just supply and demand in two markets—the market for loanable funds and the market for foreign-currency exchange. When using the model to analyse any event, we can apply the three steps outlined in chapter 4. First, we determine which of the supply and demand curves the event affects. Second, we determine which way the curves shift. Third, we use the supply-and-demand diagrams to examine how these shifts alter the economy's equilibrium.

GOVERNMENT BUDGET DEFICITS

When we first discussed the supply of and demand for loanable funds earlier in the book, we examined the effects of government budget deficits, which occur when government spending exceeds government revenue. Because a government budget deficit represents *negative* public saving, it reduces national saving (the sum of public and private saving). Thus, a government budget deficit reduces the supply of loanable funds, drives up the interest rate and crowds out investment.

Now let's consider the effects of a budget deficit in an open economy. First, which curve in our model shifts? As in a closed economy, the initial impact of the budget deficit is on national saving and, therefore, on the supply curve for loanable funds. Second, which way does this supply curve shift? Again as in a closed economy, a budget deficit represents *negative* public saving, so it reduces national saving and shifts the supply curve for loanable funds to the left. This is shown as the shift from S_1 to S_2 in panel (a) of figure 15.5.

Our third and final step is to compare the old and new equilibria. Panel (a) shows the impact of a Australian budget deficit on the Australian market for loanable funds. With fewer funds available for borrowers in Australian financial markets, the interest rate rises from r_1 to r_2 to balance supply and demand. Faced with a higher interest rate, borrowers in the market for loanable funds choose to borrow less. This change is represented in the figure as the movement from point A to point B along the demand curve for loanable funds. In particular, households and firms reduce their purchases of capital goods. As in a closed economy, budget deficits crowd out domestic investment.

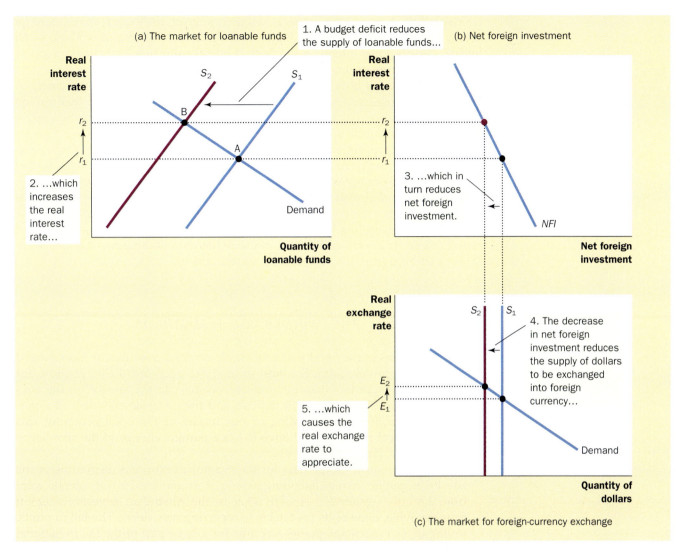

THE EFFECTS OF A GOVERNMENT BUDGET DEFICIT. When the government runs a budget deficit, it reduces the supply of loanable funds from S_1 to S_2 in panel (a). The interest rate rises from r_1 to r_2 to balance the supply of and demand for loanable funds. In panel (b), the higher interest rate reduces net foreign investment. Reduced net foreign investment, in turn, reduces the supply of dollars in the market for foreign-currency exchange from S_1 to S_2 in panel (c). This fall in the supply of dollars causes the real exchange rate to appreciate from E_1 to E_2. The appreciation of the exchange rate pushes the trade balance towards deficit.

Figure 15.5

In an open economy, however, the reduced supply for loanable funds has additional effects. Panel (b) shows that the increase in the interest rate from r_1 to r_2 reduces net foreign investment. (This fall in net foreign investment is also part of the decrease in the quantity of loanable funds demanded in the movement from point A to point B in panel (a).) Because saving kept at home now earns higher rates of return, investing abroad is less attractive, and domestic residents buy fewer foreign assets. Higher interest rates also attract foreign investors, who want to earn the higher returns on Australian assets. Thus, when budget deficits raise interest rates, both domestic and foreign behaviour cause Australian net foreign investment to fall.

Panel (c) shows how budget deficits affect the market for foreign-currency exchange. Because net foreign investment is reduced, people need less foreign currency to buy foreign assets, and this induces a leftward shift in the supply curve for dollars from S_1 to S_2. The reduced supply of dollars causes the real exchange rate to appreciate from E_1 to E_2. That is, the dollar becomes more valuable compared with foreign currencies. This appreciation, in turn, makes Australian goods more expensive compared with foreign goods. Because people both at home and abroad switch their purchases away from the more expensive Australian goods, exports from Australia fall, and imports into Australia rise. For both reasons, Australian net exports fall. Hence, *in an open economy, government budget deficits raise real interest rates, crowd out domestic investment, cause the dollar to appreciate, and push the trade balance towards deficit.*

CASE STUDY   THE TWIN DEFICITS IN AUSTRALIA

As we have seen, the fiscal policy of the Australian government has changed over the past few decades. For most of the 1960s and early 1970s, government expenditures were less than government revenue. In the late 1970s, the government began running budget deficits, and the government's debt as a percentage of GDP rose. According to our model of the open economy, this change in fiscal policy should have led to a parallel change in the economy's trade balance. And, in fact, it did.

Table 15.1 shows some data for the Australian economy. Beginning in the late 1970s, public saving (including federal, state and local governments) went from 2.6% to *negative* 1% of GDP. That is, the Australian government went from repaying some of its past debts to incurring new debts. The fall in public saving of 3.6 percentage points accounts for a large part of the fall in national saving of 5.2 percentage points during this period.

Table 15.1

THE TWIN DEFICITS IN AUSTRALIA. This table shows public saving, private saving, national saving, domestic investment and net foreign investment as a percentage of GDP. Note that negative values for public saving represent a budget deficit and negative values for net foreign investment represent a trade deficit.

	1960–1976	1977–1995	CHANGE
Public saving	2.6%	–1.0%	–3.6
Private saving	22.1	20.4	–1.7
National saving	24.6	19.5	–5.2
Domestic investment	26.3	23.6	–2.7
Net foreign investment	–1.6	–4.1	–2.5

SOURCE: Australian Bureau of Statistics. All data are gross nominal magnitudes as a percentage of nominal GDP. The numbers in the table may not satisfy the accounting identities exactly because of rounding.

In our model, reduced national saving means that a smaller supply of loanable funds is available for domestic investment and net foreign investment. In Australia, the fall in national saving has been associated with a fall in domestic investment of 2.7 percentage points. In other words, the crowding out of domestic investment has been fairly significant. But the fall in national saving was such a large decline that it also had a large effect on net foreign investment. In fact, Australian net foreign investment went from a small negative number to a large negative one, a fall of 2.5 percentage points.

Negative net foreign investment means that Australia is selling some of its assets to foreigners on world financial markets. Australia has always had a significant capital inflow, but the proportion of Australian assets owned by foreigners has increased significantly since the late 1970s. In 1974, Australian net foreign liabilities were about 10% of GDP. That is, foreigners owned more Australian assets than Australians owned overseas. Over time, with increasing negative values of net foreign investment, foreign ownership grew. In 1981, the Australian stock of net foreign liabilities had doubled to 21% of GDP, and by 1990 this figure was over 50% of GDP.

Because $NFI = NX$, negative net foreign investment must be accompanied by negative net exports. And, indeed, Australia did run a trade deficit throughout the recent period. This simultaneous switch in the late 1970s from budget surplus and trade surplus to budget deficit and trade deficit is, from the standpoint of our model, hardly a surprise. Because they are so closely related, the budget and trade deficits are sometimes called the *twin deficits*.

TRADE POLICY

A **trade policy** is a government policy that directly influences the quantity of goods and services that a country imports or exports. Trade policy takes various forms. One common trade policy is a *tariff*, a tax on imported goods. Another is an *import quota*, a limit on the quantity of a good that can be produced abroad and sold domestically. Trade policies are common throughout the world, although sometimes they are disguised. For example, the US government has often pressured Japanese car manufacturers to reduce the number of cars they sell in the United States. These so-called voluntary export restrictions are not really voluntary and, in essence, are a form of import quota. In Australia, tariffs and quotas have been used to restrict the import of cars into Australia.

Let's consider the macroeconomic impact of trade policy. Suppose that the Australian car industry, concerned about competition from Japanese car manufacturers, convinces the Australian government to increase tariffs on imported cars. The tariff would affect the number of cars that will be imported from Japan. (This is, in effect, what Australian car manufacturers did in the first term of the Howard government, when they convinced the government to limit planned reductions in tariffs on imported cars.) In making their case, lobbyists for the car industry assert that the trade restriction would shrink the size of the Australian trade deficit. Are they right? Our model, as illustrated in figure 15.6, offers an answer.

The first step in analysing the trade policy is to determine which curve shifts. The initial impact of the tariff is, not surprisingly, on imports. Because net exports equal exports minus imports, the policy also affects net exports. And because net

trade policy
a government policy that directly influences the quantity of goods and services that a country imports or exports

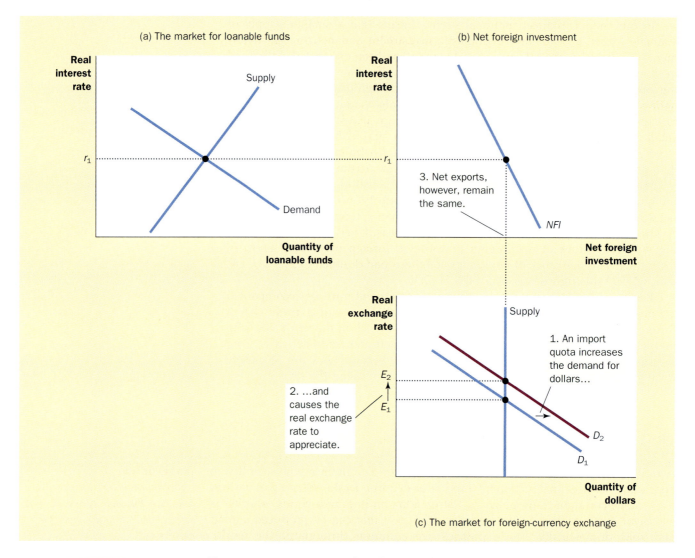

Figure 15.6

THE EFFECTS OF A TARIFF. When the Australian government imposes a tariff on the import of cars, nothing happens in the market for loanable funds in panel (a) or to net foreign investment in panel (b). The only effect is a rise in net exports (exports minus imports) for any given real exchange rate. As a result, the demand for dollars in the market for foreign-currency exchange rises, as shown by the shift from D_1 to D_2 in panel (c). This increase in the demand for dollars causes the value of the dollar to appreciate from E_1 to E_2. This appreciation of the dollar tends to reduce net exports, offsetting the direct effect of the import quota on the trade balance.

exports are the source of demand for dollars in the market for foreign-currency exchange, the policy affects the demand curve in this market.

The second step is to determine which way this demand curve shifts. Because the tariff reduces the number of Japanese cars sold in Australia, it reduces imports at any given real exchange rate. Net exports, which equal exports minus imports, will therefore rise for any given real exchange rate. Because foreigners need dollars to buy Australian net exports, there is an increased demand for dollars in the market for foreign-currency exchange. This increase in the demand for dollars is shown in panel (c) as the shift from D_1 to D_2.

The third step is to compare the old and new equilibria. As we can see in panel (c), the increase in the demand for dollars causes the real exchange rate to appreciate from E_1 to E_2. Because nothing has happened in the market for loanable funds in panel (a), there is no change in the interest rate. There is also no change in net foreign investment, shown in panel (b). And because there is no change in net foreign investment, there can be no change in net exports, even though the tariff has reduced imports.

The reason that net exports can stay the same while imports fall is explained by the change in the real exchange rate—when the dollar appreciates in value in the market for foreign-currency exchange, domestic goods become more expensive relative to foreign goods. This appreciation encourages imports and discourages exports—and both of these changes work to offset the direct increase in net exports due to the import quota. In the end, an import quota reduces both imports and exports, but net exports (exports minus imports) are unchanged.

We have thus come to a surprising implication—*trade policies do not affect the trade balance*. That is, policies that directly influence exports or imports do not alter net exports. This conclusion seems less surprising if one recalls the accounting identity:

$$NX = NFI = S - I$$

Net exports equal net foreign investment, which equals national saving minus domestic investment. Trade policies do not alter the trade balance because they do not alter national saving or domestic investment. For given levels of national saving and domestic investment, the real exchange rate adjusts to keep the trade balance the same, regardless of the trade policies the government puts in place.

Although trade policies do not affect a country's overall trade balance, these policies do affect specific firms, industries and countries. When the Australian government imposes a tariff on Japanese cars, General Motors–Holden has less competition from abroad and will sell more cars. At the same time, because the dollar has appreciated in value, Australian beef producers will find it harder to compete with Argentinian beef producers. Australian exports of beef will fall, and Australian imports of beef will rise. In this case, the tariff on Japanese cars will increase net exports of cars and decrease net exports of beef. In addition, it will increase net exports from Australia to Japan and decrease net exports from Australia to Argentina. The overall trade balance of the Australian economy, however, stays the same.

The effects of trade policies are, therefore, more microeconomic than macroeconomic. Although advocates of trade policies sometimes claim (incorrectly) that these policies can alter a country's balance of trade, they are usually more motivated by concerns about particular firms or industries. One should not be surprised, for instance, to hear an executive from General Motors–Holden advocating tariffs on imported cars. Economists almost always oppose such trade policies. As we saw in chapter 3, free trade allows economies to specialise in doing what they do best, making residents of all countries better off. Trade restrictions interfere with these gains from trade and, thus, reduce overall economic wellbeing.

POLITICAL INSTABILITY AND CAPITAL FLIGHT

The political instability in Indonesia and Malaysia have made world financial markets nervous. People began to view these countries as much less stable than they had previously thought. They decided to pull some of their assets out of Indonesia and Malaysia in order to move these funds to Australia, the United States and other 'safe havens'. Such a large and sudden movement of funds out of a country is called **capital flight**. To see the implications of capital flight for the Indonesian economy, we again follow our three steps for analysing a change in equilibrium, but this time we apply our model of the open economy from the perspective of Indonesia rather than Australia.

capital flight
a large and sudden reduction in the demand for assets located in a country

Consider first which curves in our model capital flight affects. When investors around the world observe political problems in Indonesia, they decide to sell some of their Indonesian assets and use the proceeds to buy Australian assets. This act increases Indonesian net foreign investment and, therefore, affects both markets in our model. Most obviously, it affects the net-foreign-investment curve, and this in turn influences the supply of rupiah in the market for foreign-currency exchange. In addition, because the demand for loanable funds comes from both domestic investment and net foreign investment, capital flight affects the demand curve in the market for loanable funds.

Now consider which way these curves shift. When net foreign investment increases, there is greater demand for loanable funds to finance these purchases. Thus, as panel (a) of figure 15.7 shows, the demand curve for loanable funds shifts to the right from D_1 to D_2. In addition, because net foreign investment is higher for any interest rate, the net-foreign-investment curve also shifts to the right from NFI_1 to NFI_2, as in panel (b).

To see the effects of capital flight on the economy, we compare the old and new equilibria. Panel (a) of figure 15.7 shows that the increased demand for loanable funds causes the interest rate in Indonesia to rise from r_1 to r_2. Panel (b) shows that Indonesian net foreign investment increases. (Although the rise in the interest rate does make Indonesian assets more attractive, this only partly offsets the impact of capital flight on net foreign investment.) Panel (c) shows that the increase in net foreign investment raises the supply of rupiahs in the market for foreign-currency exchange from S_1 to S_2. That is, as people try to get out of Indonesian assets, there is a large supply of rupiah to be converted into dollars. This increase in supply causes the rupiah to depreciate from E_1 to E_2. Thus, *capital flight from Indonesia increases Indonesian interest rates and decreases the value of the Indonesian rupiah in the market for foreign-currency exchange*. This is exactly what was observed in 1998. From January to May, the interest rate on short-term Indonesian government bonds rose from 19% to 44%, and the rupiah depreciated in value from 5300 to 9000 rupiah per Australian dollar from January to July.

Although capital flight has its largest impact on the country from which capital is fleeing, it also affects other countries. When capital flows out of Indonesia into Australia, for instance, it has the opposite effect on the Australian economy as it has on the Indonesian economy. In particular, the rise in Indonesian net foreign investment coincides with a fall in Australian net foreign investment. As the rupiah depreciates in value and Indonesian interest rates rise, the dollar appreciates in value and Australian interest rates fall. The size of this impact on the Australian economy is small, however, because flows of capital into Australia are relatively limited.

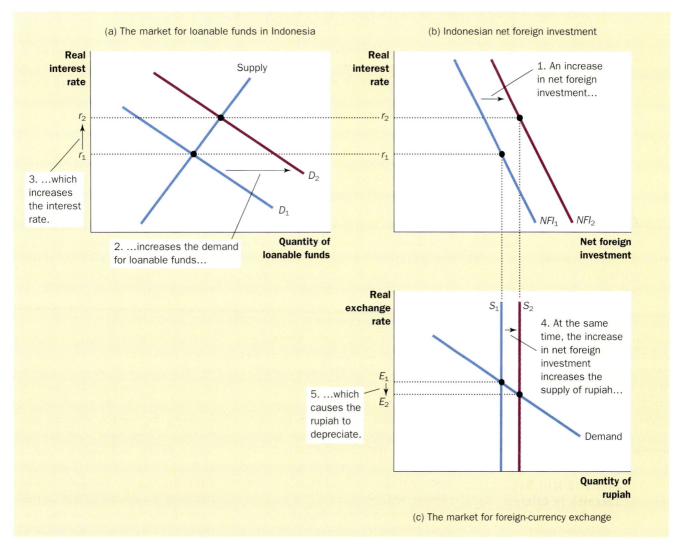

Figure 15.7

THE EFFECTS OF CAPITAL FLIGHT. If people in Indonesia decide that Indonesia is a risky place to keep their savings, they will move their capital to safer havens such as Australia, resulting in an increase in Indonesian net foreign investment. Consequently, the demand for loanable funds in Indonesia rises from D_1 to D_2, as shown in panel (a), and this drives up the Indonesian real interest rate from r_1 to r_2. Because net foreign investment is higher for any interest rate, that curve also shifts to the right from NFI_1 to NFI_2 in panel (b). At the same time, in the market for foreign-currency exchange, the supply of rupiah rises from S_1 to S_2, as shown in panel (c). This increase in the supply of rupiah causes the rupiah to depreciate from E_1 to E_2, so the rupiah becomes less valuable compared with other currencies.

Could the events that occurred in Indonesia ever happen in Australia? Although the Australian economy has long been viewed as a safe economy in which to invest, political developments in Australia have at times induced small amounts of capital flight. For example, when Paul Keating made his now infamous 'banana republic' statement in 1986, the effect of the announcement was,

IN THE NEWS

Australia and the Asian crisis: She'll be right, mate

IT'S BEEN DESCRIBED AS A TIDAL WAVE just offshore, but some have argued that the impact of the economic crisis in Asia will have little impact on the Australian economy. In this article from the *Australian Financial Review*, Frank Gelber, Chief Economist at BIS Shrapnel, discusses the impact of a fall in demand from some of Australia's major trading partners. Although the article discusses the impact of the financial crisis that began in 1997, the set of economic interactions described applies to any open economy.

Australia Will Not Succumb to Crisis

BY FRANK GELBER

She'll be right mate. The Australian economy is growing at rates strong enough to withstand the global financial shock, insists BIS Shrapnel's Frank Gelber.

The conventional wisdom has turned pessimistic. The Asian financial crisis, the argument goes, will translate into a global—and Australian—slump. But these pessimists have overstated the negatives and forgotten the positives.

True, the Asian crisis is hitting the world economy, with reduced demand, financial failures and concerns about over-investment in many markets leading to sustained weakness of prices and investment in those markets. This is leading to falls in commodity prices, rolling currency crises and a major re-alignment of world currencies.

The doomsayers point to the weakness of Japan offsetting the strength of Europe and America with shocks to stockmarkets and concern about deflation and world recession. In Australia, the shocks are in the form of reduced demand for exports, the fall in commodity prices, increased competition from Asian exports, the fall in the Australian dollar and the effects of uncertainty on consumption and investment expenditure. Certainly, the Australian economy cannot withstand a world recession. But that's far too early to call. For starters, the strength of demand in Europe and America will offset the negative impacts of the Asian crisis and the weakness of Japan. And while some industries, notably those set up in Asia for export markets, suffer from over-capacity, many others do not. The flow of funds has been a crucial driver of investment and was a major determinant of the over-investment in Asia.

With the demise of Asia as an investment destination and heightened awareness of risk, these funds are now looking for a safe haven, notably in America and Europe. While the Dow is now entering a bear phase, this is a long-overdue correction and will lead to a switch of new funds into fixed interest and property markets in America and Europe.

The conditions for a worldwide recession are not yet in place. The world economy can withstand this shock.

For Australia, too, the negative impacts have been overstated. There will be a major impact, but consider the strength of the Australian economy if there had not been an Asian economic crisis. On BIS Shrapnel's estimates, Australia would have experienced real GDP growth of between 5 and 6 per cent. And we don't have the same sorts of problems currently affecting Asia.

Although there has been a shock to exports and increased competition from Asian imports, the fall in the Australian dollar against Europe and America is leading to significant increases in market share in both exports and import competing markets. Interestingly, with Australia depreciating significantly against Europe and America, but appreciating against the worst-affected Asian countries, there is little guidance on the net impact of the consequent change in competitiveness against the different currency blocs.

If Australian production competed solely against Asia, the impacts would be negative, with a loss of competitiveness, loss of share and higher prices for imported products not manufactured in Australia. But that is not the case. Already we have seen significant gains against Europe and America in export markets and have started to see substitution for imports. But for Australian industries the effects of the currency realignments are idiosyncratic and depend on the countries with which individual producers compete. Will the shock to confidence become self-fulfilling? The upshot is that Australia will experience lower growth. Most expect growth to fall below Treasury's 2.75 per cent revised forecast.

But growth, as outlined by BIS Shrapnel, is forecasted for a respectable 3.75 per cent rate, with a major offsetting impact from import substitution. This is consistent with last week's national accounts which showed reasonable growth through the time most affected by the slide in confidence.

SOURCE: *Australian Financial Review*, 9 September 1998, p. 17.

in a small way, similar to that experienced by Indonesia in 1998. Over the course of a single day, the exchange rate fell more than US 5 cents, the largest devaluation in a 24-hour period. Thus, even the stable Australian economy is potentially susceptible to the effects of capital flight.

> **QUICK QUIZ** Suppose that Australians decided to spend a smaller fraction of their incomes. What would be the effect on saving, investment, interest rates, the real exchange rate and the trade balance?

CONCLUSION

International economics is a topic of growing importance. Australian citizens have always bought goods produced abroad and produced goods to be sold overseas. Through managed funds and other financial institutions, they borrow and lend in world financial markets. As a result, a full analysis of the Australian economy requires an understanding of how the Australian economy interacts with other economies in the world. This chapter has provided a basic model for thinking about the macroeconomics of open economies.

Although the study of international economics is valuable, we should be careful not to exaggerate its importance. Policymakers and commentators are often quick to blame foreigners for problems facing the Australian economy. In contrast, economists more often view these problems as homegrown. For example, politicians often discuss foreign competition as a threat to Australian living standards. Economists are more likely to lament the low level of national saving. Low saving impedes growth in capital, productivity and living standards, regardless of whether the economy is open or closed. Foreigners are a convenient target for politicians because blaming foreigners provides a way to avoid responsibility without insulting any domestic constituency. Whenever you hear popular discussions of international trade and finance, therefore, it is especially important to try to separate myth from reality. The tools you have learned in the past two chapters should help in that endeavour.

Summary

- To analyse the macroeconomics of open economies, two markets are central—the market for loanable funds and the market for foreign-currency exchange. In the market for loanable funds, the interest rate adjusts to balance the supply of loanable funds (from national saving) and the demand for loanable funds (from domestic investment and net foreign investment). In the market for foreign-currency exchange, the real exchange rate adjusts to balance the supply of dollars (for net foreign investment) and the demand for dollars (for net exports). Because net foreign investment is part of the demand for loanable funds and provides the supply of dollars for foreign-currency exchange, it is the variable that connects these two markets.

- A policy that reduces national saving, such as a government budget deficit, reduces the supply of loanable funds and drives up the interest rate. The higher interest rate reduces net foreign investment, which reduces the supply of dollars in the market for foreign-currency exchange. The dollar appreciates, and net exports fall.

- Although restrictive trade policies, such as a tariff or quota on imports, are sometimes advocated as a way to alter the trade balance, they do not necessarily have that effect. A trade restriction increases net exports for a given exchange rate and, therefore, increases the demand for dollars in the market for foreign-currency exchange. As a result, the dollar appreciates in value, making domestic goods more expensive relative to foreign goods. This appreciation offsets the initial impact of the trade restriction on net exports.

♦ When investors change their attitudes about holding assets of a country, the ramifications for the country's economy can be profound. In particular, political instability can lead to capital flight, which tends to increase interest rates and cause a country's currency to depreciate.

Key concepts

trade policy, p. 331

capital flight, p. 334

Questions for review

1. Describe supply and demand in the market for loanable funds and the market for foreign-currency exchange. How are these markets linked?

2. Why are budget deficits and trade deficits sometimes called the twin deficits?

3. Suppose that a union of textile workers encourages people to buy only Australian-made clothes. What would this policy do to the trade balance and the real exchange rate? What is the impact on the textile industry? What is the impact on the car industry?

4. Suppose that Parliament passes an investment tax credit, which subsidises domestic investment. How does this policy affect saving, domestic investment, net foreign investment, the interest rate, the exchange rate and the trade balance?

Problems and applications

1. Japan generally runs a significant trade surplus. Do you think this is most related to high foreign demand for Japanese goods, low Japanese demand for foreign goods, a high Japanese saving rate relative to Japanese investment, or structural barriers against imports into Japan? Explain your answer.

2. How would an increase in foreigners' income affect the Australian net exports curve? How would this affect the value of the dollar in the market for foreign-currency exchange?

3. The value of the Australian dollar has declined dramatically since John Howard became prime minister. Could the continued decline in the value of the dollar represent a signal that the government was solidly on course for deficit reduction by making the dollar more attractive to investors? Would deficit reduction in fact raise the value of the dollar? Explain.

4. Several successive governments in Australia have said they were implementing polices to encourage saving. What would be the effect of increased saving on the value of the dollar?

5. The chapter explains that the rise in the Australian trade deficit during the 1980s was due largely to the rise in the Australian budget deficit. On the other hand, the popular press sometimes claims that the increased trade deficit resulted from a decline in the quality of Australian products relative to foreign products.
   a. Assume that Australian products did decline in relative quality during the 1980s. How did this affect net exports *at any given exchange rate*?
   b. Use a three-panel diagram to show the effect of this shift in net exports on the Australian real exchange rate and trade balance.

c. Is the claim in the popular press consistent with the model in this chapter? Does a decline in the quality of Australian products have any effect on our standard of living? (*Hint:* When we sell our goods to foreigners, what do we receive in return?)

6. Economists have argued that removing trade restrictions benefits Australian industries that produce goods for *export*. They say that export industries would find it easier to sell their goods abroad—even if other countries didn't follow our example and reduce their trade barriers. Explain in words why Australian *export* industries would benefit from a reduction in restrictions on *imports* to Australia.

7. Suppose the French suddenly develop a strong taste for Australian wines. Answer the following questions in words and using a diagram.
    a. What happens to the demand for dollars in the market for foreign-currency exchange?
    b. What happens to the value of dollars in the market for foreign-currency exchange?
    c. What happens to the quantity of net exports?

8. Australia has been a strong supporter of world reductions in protectionism. The previous Labor governments reduced trade restrictions across the board, but particularly in car manufacturing and the textiles, clothing and footwear industries. However, there have been calls for the subsidising of exports instead of restricting imports. The argument is that if we subsidise Australian exports instead, we can reduce the deficit by increasing our competitiveness. Using a three-panel diagram, show the effect of an export subsidy on net exports and the real exchange rate. Do you agree with this strategy?

9. Suppose that real interest rates increase in the rest of the world. Explain how this will affect Australian net foreign investment. Then explain how this change will affect Australian net exports by using a formula from the chapter and by using a diagram. What will happen to the Australian real exchange rate?

10. Suppose that Australians decide to increase their saving.
    a. If the elasticity of Australian net foreign investment with respect to the real interest rate is very high, will this increase in private saving have a large or small effect on Australian domestic investment?
    b. If the elasticity of Australian exports with respect to the real exchange rate is very low, will this increase in private saving have a large or small effect on the Australian real exchange rate?

11. Suppose that Europeans suddenly become very interested in investing in New Zealand.
    a. What happens to New Zealand net foreign investment?
    b. What effect does this have on New Zealand private saving and New Zealand domestic investment?
    c. What is the long-run effect on New Zealand capital stock?

12. Over the past decade, some of Japanese saving has been used to finance Australian investment. That is, Australian net foreign investment in Japan has been negative.
    a. If the Japanese decided they no longer wanted to buy Australian assets, what would happen in the Australian market for loanable funds? In particular, what would happen to Australian interest rates, Australian saving and Australian investment?
    b. What would happen in the market for foreign-currency exchange? In particular, what would happen to the value of the dollar and the Australian balance of trade?

13. (This problem is challenging.) Most models of open economies show that a decline in national saving leads to a decline in net foreign investment and thus in net exports. Thus, the case study in this chapter referred to the Australian budget deficit and Australian trade deficit as 'twins'. At the same time, economists have found that national saving has equalled domestic investment over long time periods in virtually every country.
    a. In what way does this fact seem to contradict the models?
    b. Suppose that investors are unwilling to accumulate too many assets from a single foreign country. How does this behaviour help to reconcile the fact and the models?
    c. If investors are unwilling to accumulate too many assets from Australia, what would happen to the Australian trade deficit over time even if the Australian budget deficit remains large?

VII

SHORT-RUN ECONOMIC FLUCTUATIONS

16

AGGREGATE DEMAND AND AGGREGATE SUPPLY

IN THIS CHAPTER YOU WILL

Learn three key facts about short-run economic fluctuations

Consider how the economy in the short run differs from the economy in the long run

Develop a short-run theory called the model of aggregate demand and aggregate supply

See how shifts in either aggregate demand or aggregate supply can cause recessions

Economic activity fluctuates from year to year. In most years, the production of goods and services rises. Because of increases in the labour force, increases in the capital stock and advances in technological knowledge, the economy can produce more and more over time. This growth allows everyone to enjoy a higher standard of living. On average over the past 50 years, the production of the Australian economy as measured by real GDP has grown by about 2% per year.

In some years, however, this normal growth does not occur. Firms find themselves unable to sell all of the goods and services they have to offer, so they cut back on production. Workers are laid off, unemployment rises and factories are left idle. With the economy producing fewer goods and services, real GDP and other measures of income fall. Such a period of falling incomes and rising

recession
a period of declining real incomes and rising unemployment

depression
a severe recession

unemployment is called a **recession** if it is relatively mild and a **depression** if it is more severe.

What causes short-run fluctuations in economic activity? What, if anything, can public policy do to prevent periods of falling incomes and rising unemployment? When recessions and depressions do occur, how can policymakers reduce their length and severity? These are the questions that we take up in this and the next two chapters.

The variables that we study in the coming chapters are largely those we have already seen. They include GDP, unemployment, interest rates, exchange rates and the price level. Also familiar are the policy instruments of government spending, taxes and the money supply. What differs in the next few chapters is the time horizon of our analysis. Our focus in the previous seven chapters has been on the behaviour of the economy in the long run. Our focus now is on the economy's short-run fluctuations around its long-run trend.

Although there remains some debate among economists about how to analyse short-run fluctuations, most economists use the model of *aggregate demand and aggregate supply*. Learning how to use this model for analysing the short-run effects of various events and policies is the main task ahead. This chapter introduces the model's two key pieces—the aggregate-demand curve and the aggregate-supply curve. After getting a sense of the overall structure of the model in this chapter, we examine the pieces of the model in more detail in the next two chapters.

THREE KEY FACTS ABOUT ECONOMIC FLUCTUATIONS

Short-run fluctuations in economic activity occur in all countries. As a starting point for understanding these year-to-year fluctuations, let's discuss some of their most important properties.

FACT 1: ECONOMIC FLUCTUATIONS ARE IRREGULAR AND UNPREDICTABLE

Fluctuations in the economy are often called the *business cycle*. As this term suggests, economic fluctuations correspond to changes in business conditions. When real GDP grows rapidly, business is good. Firms find that customers are plentiful and that profits are growing. On the other hand, when real GDP falls, businesses have trouble. In recessions, most firms experience declining sales and profits.

The term *business cycle* is somewhat misleading, however, because it seems to suggest that economic fluctuations follow a regular, predictable pattern. In fact, economic fluctuations are not at all regular, and they are almost impossible to predict with any accuracy. Panel (a) of figure 16.1 shows the real GDP of the Australian economy since 1970. The shaded areas represent times of recession. As the figure shows, recessions do not come at regular intervals. Sometimes recessions are close together, such as the recessions of 1974 and 1977. Sometimes the economy goes many years without a recession.

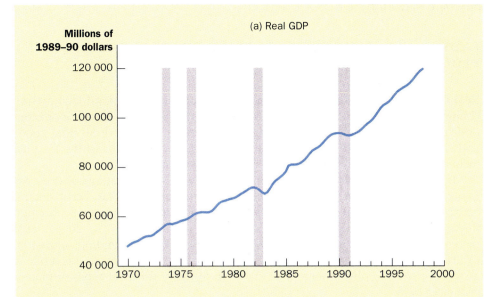
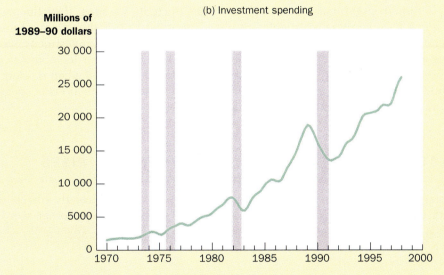

Figure 16.1

A LOOK AT SHORT-RUN ECONOMIC FLUCTUATIONS. This figure shows real GDP in panel (a), investment spending in panel (b), and unemployment in panel (c) for the Australian economy using quarterly data since 1970. Recessions are shown as the shaded areas. Notice that real GDP declines during recessions, while unemployment rises. Investment spending usually declines, as can be seen in the recessions of 1982–83 and 1991.

SOURCE: Reserve Bank of Australia.

FACT 2: MOST MACROECONOMIC QUANTITIES FLUCTUATE TOGETHER

Real GDP is the variable that is most commonly used to monitor short-run changes in the economy because it is the most comprehensive measure of economic activity. Real GDP measures the value in constant prices of all final goods and services produced within a given period of time. It also measures the total income (adjusted for inflation) of everyone in the economy.

It turns out, however, that for monitoring short-run fluctuations, it does not really matter which measure of economic activity one looks at. Most macroeconomic variables that measure some type of income, spending or production fluctuate closely together. When real GDP falls in a recession, so do personal income, corporate profits, consumer spending, investment spending, industrial production, retail sales, home sales, car sales and so on. Because recessions are economy-wide phenomena, they show up in many different types of macroeconomic data.

Although many macroeconomic variables fluctuate together, they fluctuate by different amounts. In particular, as panel (b) of figure 16.1 shows, investment spending varies greatly over the business cycle. Even though investment averages about one quarter of GDP, declines in investment account for about two-thirds of the declines in GDP during recessions. In other words, when economic conditions deteriorate, much of the decline is attributable to reductions in spending on new factories, housing and inventories.

FACT 3: AS OUTPUT FALLS, UNEMPLOYMENT RISES

Changes in the economy's output of goods and services are strongly correlated with changes in the economy's utilisation of its labour force. In other words,

'You're fired. Pass it on.'

> ## FYI
>
> ### Okun's law
>
>
>
> When the real GDP of the economy fluctuates, how much does unemployment typically change? Economists answer this question with Okun's law. This law can be described with the following equation:
>
> Change in unemployment rate = $-\frac{1}{2} \times$ (Percentage change in real GDP minus 3%).
>
> According to this equation, when real GDP grows at its average rate of 3%, the unemployment rate remains unchanged. When the economy expands more rapidly than 3%, the unemployment rate falls by about half as much. For example, if real GDP grows by 5% from one year to the next (2% higher than normal), Okun's law predicts a fall in the unemployment rate of 1 percentage point. When real GDP falls, or rises by less than 3%, the unemployment rate rises. For example, if real GDP falls by 1% from one year to the next, as it might during a recession, Okun's law predicts a rise in unemployment of 2 percentage points.
>
> Okun's law is named for economist Arthur Okun, who first studied the link between fluctuations in real GDP and fluctuations in unemployment for the US economy. Okun did not claim his law to be a fundamental truth of economic theory. The law is, instead, a simple description of US data on real GDP and unemployment. When economists look at data from other countries, they find that the numbers in the formula for Okun's law differ somewhat. Nonetheless, in all countries, there is a strong correlation between changes in GDP and changes in unemployment.
>
> As we study economic fluctuations in the next few chapters, we should keep Okun's law in mind. This law reminds us that the business cycle concerns related movements in the quantity of goods and services that the economy is producing (as measured by real GDP) and the number of people who cannot find jobs (as measured by the unemployment rate).

when real GDP declines, the rate of unemployment rises. This fact is hardly surprising—when firms choose to produce a smaller quantity of goods and services, they lay off workers, expanding the pool of unemployed.

Panel (c) of figure 16.1 shows the unemployment rate in the Australian economy since 1970. Once again, recessions are shown as the shaded areas in the figure. The figure shows clearly the impact of recessions on unemployment. In each of the recessions, the unemployment rate rises substantially. When the recession ends and real GDP starts to expand, the unemployment rate gradually declines. The unemployment rate never approaches zero; instead, it fluctuates around its natural rate. The natural rate in Australia has risen over time and is now about 7%.

> **QUICK QUIZ** List and discuss three key facts about economic fluctuations.

EXPLAINING SHORT-RUN ECONOMIC FLUCTUATIONS

Describing the regular patterns that economies experience as they fluctuate over time is easy. Explaining what causes these fluctuations is more difficult. Indeed, compared with the topics we have studied in previous chapters, the theory of economic fluctuations remains controversial. In this and the next two chapters, we develop the model that most economists use to explain short-run fluctuations in economic activity.

HOW THE SHORT RUN DIFFERS FROM THE LONG RUN

In previous chapters, we developed theories to explain what determines most important macroeconomic variables. Chapter 9 explained the level and growth of productivity and real GDP. Chapter 10 explained how the real interest rate adjusts to balance saving and investment. Chapter 11 explained the various causes of unemployment. Chapters 12 and 13 explained the monetary system and how changes in the money supply affect the price level, the inflation rate and the nominal interest rate. Chapters 14 and 15 extended this analysis to open economies in order to explain the trade balance and the exchange rate.

All of this previous analysis was based on two related ideas—the classical dichotomy and monetary neutrality. Recall that the classical dichotomy is the separation of variables into real variables (those that measure quantities or relative prices) and nominal variables (those measured in terms of money). According to classical macroeconomic theory, changes in the money supply affect nominal variables but not real variables. As a result of this monetary neutrality, chapters 9, 10 and 11 were able to examine the determinants of real variables (real GDP, the real interest rate and unemployment) without introducing nominal variables (the money supply and the price level).

Do these assumptions of classical macroeconomic theory apply to the world in which we live? The answer to this question is of central importance to understanding how the economy works—*most economists believe that classical theory describes the world in the long run but not in the short run*. Beyond a period of several years, changes in the money supply affect prices and other nominal variables but do not affect real GDP, unemployment or other real variables. When studying year-to-year changes in the economy, however, the assumption of monetary neutrality is no longer appropriate. Most economists believe that, in the short run, real and nominal variables are highly interrelated.

To understand the economy in the short run, therefore, we need a new model. To build this new model, we rely on many of the tools we have developed in previous chapters, but we have to abandon the classical dichotomy and the neutrality of money.

THE BASIC MODEL OF ECONOMIC FLUCTUATIONS

Our model of short-run economic fluctuations focuses on two variables. The first variable is the economy's output of goods and services, as measured by real GDP. The second variable is the overall price level, as measured by the CPI or the GDP deflator. Notice that output is a real variable, whereas the price level is a nominal variable. Hence, by focusing on the relationship between these two variables, we are highlighting the breakdown of the classical dichotomy.

Just as we analyse an individual market with a market demand curve and a market supply curve, we analyse fluctuations in the economy as a whole with the **model of aggregate demand and aggregate supply**. This model is illustrated

model of aggregate demand and aggregate supply
the model that most economists use to explain short-run fluctuations in economic activity around its long-run trend

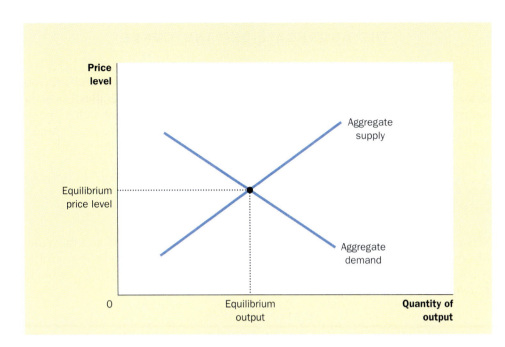

Figure 16.2

AGGREGATE DEMAND AND AGGREGATE SUPPLY. Economists use the model of aggregate demand and aggregate supply to analyse economic fluctuations. On the vertical axis is the overall level of prices. On the horizontal axis is the economy's total output of goods and services. Output and the price level adjust to the point at which the aggregate-supply and aggregate-demand curves intersect.

in figure 16.2. On the vertical axis is the overall price level in the economy. On the horizontal axis is the overall quantity of goods and services. The **aggregate-demand curve** shows the quantity of goods and services that households, firms and the government want to buy at any price level. The **aggregate-supply curve** shows the quantity of goods and services that firms produce and sell at any price level. According to this model, the price level and the quantity of output adjust to bring aggregate demand and aggregate supply into balance.

It may be tempting to view the model of aggregate demand and aggregate supply as nothing more than a large version of the model of market demand and market supply, which we introduced in chapter 4. Yet, in fact, this model is quite different. When we consider demand and supply in a particular market—ice-cream, for instance—the behaviour of buyers and sellers depends on the ability of resources to move from one market to another. When the price of ice-cream rises, the quantity demanded falls because buyers will use their incomes to buy products other than ice-cream. Similarly, a higher price of ice-cream raises the quantity supplied because firms that produce ice-cream can increase production by hiring workers away from other parts of the economy. This *microeconomic* substitution from one market to another is impossible when we are analysing the economy as a whole. After all, the quantity that our model is trying to explain—real GDP—includes the quantities produced in all of the economy's markets. To understand why the aggregate-demand curve is downward-sloping and why the aggregate-supply curve is upward-sloping, we need a *macroeconomic* theory. Developing such a theory is our next task.

aggregate-demand curve
a curve that shows the quantity of goods and services that households, firms and the government want to buy at any price level

aggregate-supply curve
a curve that shows the quantity of goods and services that firms choose to produce and sell at any price level

> **QUICK QUIZ** How does the economy's behaviour in the short run differ from its behaviour in the long run? ◆ Draw the model of aggregate demand and aggregate supply. What variables are on the two axes?

THE AGGREGATE-DEMAND CURVE

The aggregate-demand curve tells us the quantity of all goods and services demanded in the economy at any given price level. As figure 16.3 illustrates, the aggregate-demand curve is downward-sloping. This means that, other things being equal, a fall in the economy's overall level of prices (from, say, P_1 to P_2) tends to raise the quantity of goods and services demanded (from Y_1 to Y_2).

WHY THE AGGREGATE-DEMAND CURVE IS DOWNWARD-SLOPING

What lies behind this negative relationship between the price level and the quantity of goods and services demanded? To answer this question, it is useful to recall that GDP (Y) is the sum of consumption (C), investment (I), government purchases (G) and net exports (NX):

$$Y = C + I + G + NX$$

Each of these four components contributes to the aggregate demand for goods and services. Government spending is assumed to be a fixed policy variable, but the other three components of spending—consumption, investment and net exports—depend on economic conditions and, in particular, on the price level. To understand the downward slope of the aggregate-demand curve, therefore, we must examine how the price level affects the quantity of goods and services demanded for consumption, investment and net exports.

Figure 16.3

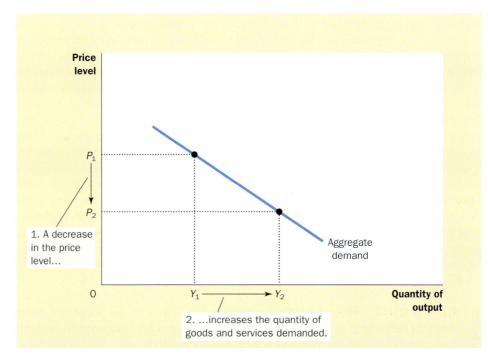

THE AGGREGATE-DEMAND CURVE. A fall in the price level from P_1 to P_2 increases the quantity of goods and services demanded from Y_1 to Y_2. There are three reasons for this negative relationship. As the price level falls, real wealth rises, interest rates fall and the exchange rate depreciates. These effects stimulate spending on consumption, investment and net exports. Increased spending on these components of output means a larger quantity of goods and services demanded.

Pigou's wealth effect Consider the money that you hold in your wallet and your bank account. The nominal value of this money is fixed, but its real value is not. When prices fall, these dollars are more valuable because then they can be used to buy more goods and services. Thus, *a decrease in the price level makes consumers feel more wealthy, which in turn encourages them to spend more. The increase in consumer spending means a larger quantity of goods and services demanded.* This wealth effect was emphasised by economist Arthur Pigou (1877–1959), and it is sometimes called the *Pigou effect*.

Keynes's interest-rate effect As we discussed in chapter 13, the price level is one determinant of the quantity of money demanded. The lower the price level, the less money households need to hold to buy the goods and services they want. When the price level falls, therefore, households try to reduce their holdings of money by lending some of it out. For instance, a household might use its excess money to buy interest-bearing bonds. Or it might deposit its excess money in an interest-bearing savings account, and the bank would use these funds to make more loans. In either case, as households try to convert some of their money into interest-bearing assets, they drive down interest rates. Lower interest rates, in turn, encourage borrowing by firms that want to invest in new plant and equipment and by households who want to invest in new housing. Thus, *a lower price level reduces the interest rate, encourages greater spending on investment goods, and thereby increases the quantity of goods and services demanded.* This interest-rate effect was emphasised by the famous economist John Maynard Keynes (1883–1946), and it is sometimes called the *Keynes effect*.

Mundell–Fleming's exchange-rate effect As we have just discussed, a lower price level in Australia lowers the Australian interest rate. In response, some Australian investors will seek higher returns by investing abroad. For instance, as the interest rate on Australian government bonds falls, a managed fund might sell Australian government bonds in order to buy German government bonds. As the managed fund tries to move assets overseas, it increases the supply of dollars in the market for foreign-currency exchange. The increased supply of dollars causes the dollar to depreciate relative to other currencies. (That is, each dollar buys fewer units of foreign currencies.) As a result of this depreciation, foreign goods become more expensive relative to domestic goods, and this change in relative prices increases Australian exports of goods and services and decreases Australian imports of goods and services. Net exports, which equal exports minus imports, also increase. Thus, *when a fall in the Australian price level causes Australian interest rates to fall, the real exchange rate depreciates, and this depreciation stimulates Australian net exports and thereby increases the quantity of goods and services demanded.* This exchange-rate effect was emphasised by economists Robert Mundell and Marcus Fleming.

Summary There are, therefore, three distinct but related reasons that a fall in the price level increases the quantity of goods and services demanded: (1) consumers feel wealthier, which stimulates the demand for consumption goods; (2) interest rates fall, which stimulates the demand for investment goods; and (3) the exchange rate depreciates, which stimulates the demand for net exports. For all three reasons, the aggregate-demand curve slopes downwards.

It is important to keep in mind that the aggregate-demand curve (like all demand curves) is drawn holding 'other things equal'. In particular, our three explanations of the downward-sloping aggregate-demand curve assume that the money supply is fixed. That is, we have been considering how a change in the price level affects the demand for goods and services, holding the amount of money in the economy constant. As we will see, a change in the quantity of money shifts the aggregate-demand curve. At this point, just keep in mind that the aggregate-demand curve is drawn for a given quantity of money.

WHY THE AGGREGATE-DEMAND CURVE MIGHT SHIFT

The downward slope of the aggregate-demand curve shows that a fall in the price level raises the overall quantity of goods and services demanded. Many other factors beyond the price level, however, affect the quantity of goods and services demanded. When one of these other factors changes, the aggregate-demand curve shifts.

There are many possible examples of events that shift aggregate demand. Here are a few:

- Australians suddenly become more concerned about saving for retirement and, as a result, reduce their current consumption. Because the quantity of goods and services demanded at any price level is lower, the aggregate-demand curve shifts to the left.

- The computer industry introduces a faster line of computers, and many firms decide to invest in new computer systems. Because the quantity of goods and services demanded at any price level is higher, the aggregate-demand curve shifts to the right.

- The government decides that, with the increase in political instability in the region, it will increase purchases of new weapon systems. Because the quantity of goods and services demanded at any price level is higher, the aggregate-demand curve shifts to the right.

- The Reserve Bank of Australia expands the money supply by printing more bank notes and dropping them by helicopter around the country. After people pick up this money, they spend some of it. Because the quantity of goods and services demanded at any price level is higher, the aggregate-demand curve shifts to the right.

The shifts in the aggregate-demand curve in the first two examples arise from changes in spending plans by consumers or firms. The shifts in the last two examples arise from changes in fiscal or monetary policy. In fact, shifts in aggregate demand sometimes come from private behaviour and sometimes come from public policy.

In the next chapter, we examine the aggregate-demand curve in more detail. There we examine, in particular, how the tools of monetary and fiscal policy can shift aggregate demand. At this point, however, you should have some idea about why the aggregate-demand curve slopes downwards and what kinds of events and policies can shift this curve.

QUICK QUIZ Explain the three reasons that the aggregate-demand curve slopes downwards. ◆ Give an example of an event that would shift the aggregate-demand curve. Which way would this event shift the curve?

THE AGGREGATE-SUPPLY CURVE

The aggregate-supply curve tells us the quantity of goods and services that firms produce and sell at any given price level. The relationship between the price level and the quantity supplied depends on the time horizon. In the long run, the aggregate-supply curve is vertical whereas, in the short run, the aggregate-supply curve is upward-sloping. To understand short-run economic fluctuations and how the short-run behaviour of the economy deviates from its long-run behaviour, we need to examine both the long-run aggregate-supply curve and the short-run aggregate-supply curve.

WHY THE AGGREGATE-SUPPLY CURVE IS VERTICAL IN THE LONG RUN

What determines the quantity of goods and services supplied in the long run? We implicitly answered this question earlier in the book when we analysed the process of economic growth. *In the long run, an economy's supply of goods and services depends on its supplies of capital and labour and on the available production technology used to turn capital and labour into goods and services.* Because the price level does not affect these long-run determinants of real GDP, the long-run aggregate-supply curve is vertical, as in figure 16.4. In other words, the economy's capital, labour and technology determine the quantity of goods and services supplied, and the quantity supplied is the same regardless of what the price level happens to be.

The vertical long-run aggregate-supply curve is, in essence, just an application of the classical dichotomy and monetary neutrality. As we have already discussed, classical macroeconomic theory is based on the assumption that real

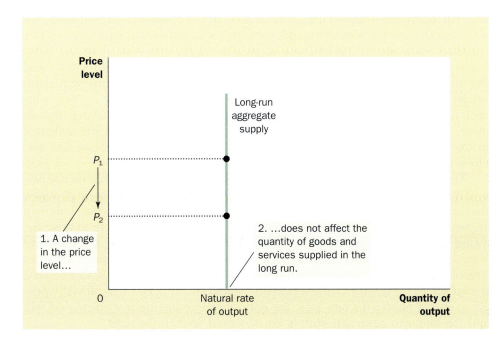

Figure 16.4

THE LONG-RUN AGGREGATE-SUPPLY CURVE. In the long run, the quantity of output supplied depends on the economy's quantities of capital and labour and on the technology for turning these inputs into output. The quantity supplied does not depend on the overall price level. As a result, the long-run aggregate-supply curve is vertical at the natural rate of output.

variables do not depend on nominal variables. The long-run aggregate-supply curve is consistent with this idea because it implies that the quantity of output (a real variable) does not depend on the level of prices (a nominal variable). As noted earlier, most economists believe that this principle works well when studying the economy over a period of many years, but not when studying year-to-year changes. Thus, the aggregate-supply curve is vertical only in the long run.

One might wonder why supply curves for specific goods and services can be upward-sloping if the long-run aggregate-supply curve is vertical. The reason is that the supply of specific goods and services depends on *relative prices*—the prices of those goods and services compared with other prices in the economy. For example, when the price of ice-cream rises, suppliers of ice-cream increase their production, taking labour, milk, chocolate and other inputs away from the production of other goods, such as frozen yogurt. In contrast, the economy's overall production of goods and services is limited by its capital, labour and technology. Thus, when all prices in the economy rise together, there is no change in the overall quantity of goods and services supplied.

WHY THE LONG-RUN AGGREGATE-SUPPLY CURVE MIGHT SHIFT

The position of the long-run aggregate-supply curve shows the quantity of goods and services predicted by classical macroeconomic theory. This level of production is sometimes called *potential output* or *full-employment output*. These terms are somewhat misleading, however, because in the short run output can either fall below or rise above this level. To be more accurate, we will call this level of output the *natural rate of output* because it shows what the economy produces when unemployment is at its natural, or normal, rate. The natural rate of output is the level of production towards which the economy gravitates in the long run.

Any change in the economy that alters the natural rate of output shifts the long-run aggregate-supply curve. An increase in the economy's capital stock, for instance, increases productivity and, thereby, the quantity of goods and services supplied. As a result, the long-run aggregate-supply curve shifts to the right. Conversely, a decrease in the economy's capital stock decreases productivity and the quantity of goods and services supplied, shifting the long-run aggregate-supply curve to the left. As we have previously discussed, many factors influence long-run economic growth, including policies concerning saving, investment, education, technology, international trade and so on. Whenever a change in one of these factors alters the economy's ability to produce goods and services, it shifts the long-run aggregate-supply curve.

The position of the long-run aggregate-supply curve also depends on the natural rate of unemployment. That is, if the natural rate of unemployment changes, the economy's natural rate of output changes as well, and the long-run aggregate-supply curve shifts. For example, if the government were to raise the award wage, the natural rate of unemployment would rise, and the economy would produce a smaller quantity of goods and services for any price level. As a result, the long-run aggregate-supply curve would shift to the left. Conversely, if a reform of the unemployment benefits system encouraged unemployed workers to search harder for new jobs, the natural rate of unemployment would fall, and the long-run aggregate-supply curve would shift to the right.

In sum, the long-run aggregate-supply curve merely provides a new way of describing the classical model of the economy we developed in previous chapters. Any policy or event that raised real GDP in previous chapters can now be viewed as increasing the quantity of goods and services supplied and shifting the long-run aggregate-supply curve to the right. Similarly, any policy or event that lowered real GDP in previous chapters can now be viewed as decreasing the quantity of goods and services supplied and shifting the long-run aggregate-supply curve to the left.

WHY THE AGGREGATE-SUPPLY CURVE IS UPWARD-SLOPING IN THE SHORT RUN

Although the model of aggregate demand and aggregate supply can be used to describe the economy in the long run, the model is designed to analyse short-run deviations from this long-run equilibrium. The key difference between the short run and the long run is the behaviour of aggregate supply. In the short run, the aggregate-supply curve is upward-sloping, as in figure 16.5. That is, over a period of a year or two, an increase in the overall level of prices in the economy tends to raise the quantity of goods and services supplied, and a decrease in the level of prices tends to reduce the quantity of goods and services supplied.

What causes this positive relationship between the price level and output? Macroeconomists have proposed three theories for the upward slope of the short-run aggregate-supply curve. In each theory, a specific market imperfection causes the supply side of the economy to behave differently in the short run than in the long run. Although each of the following theories differs in detail, they share a common theme—the quantity of output supplied deviates from its long-run, or 'natural', level when the price level deviates from the price level that people expected. When the price level rises above the expected level, output rises above

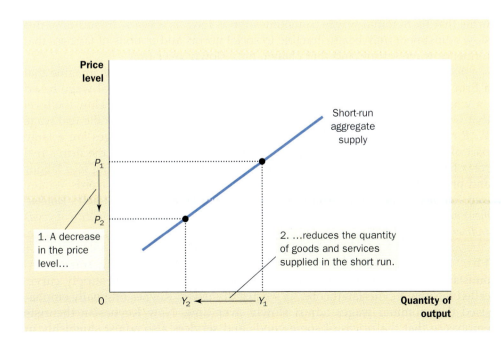

Figure 16.5

THE SHORT-RUN AGGREGATE-SUPPLY CURVE. In the short run, a fall in the price level from P_1 to P_2 reduces the quantity of output supplied from Y_1 to Y_2. This positive relationship could be due to misperceptions, sticky wages or sticky prices. Over time, perceptions, wages and prices adjust, so this positive relationship is only temporary.

its natural rate, and when the price level falls below the expected level, output falls below its natural rate.

The new classical misperceptions theory

One theory of the short-run aggregate-supply curve, which is based on the work of economists Milton Friedman and Robert Lucas, is the new classical misperceptions theory. According to this theory, changes in the overall price level can temporarily mislead suppliers about what is happening in the markets in which they sell their output. As a result of these short-run misperceptions, suppliers respond to changes in the level of prices, and this response leads to an upward-sloping aggregate-supply curve.

To see how this might work, suppose the overall price level falls below the level that people expected. When suppliers see the prices of their products fall, they may mistakenly believe that their *relative* prices have fallen. For example, wheat farmers may notice a fall in the price of wheat before they notice a fall in the prices of the many items they buy as consumers. They may infer from this observation that the reward for producing wheat is temporarily low, and they may respond by reducing the quantity of wheat they supply. Similarly, workers may notice a fall in their nominal wages before they notice a fall in the prices of the goods they buy. They may infer that the reward for working is temporarily low and respond by reducing the quantity of labour they supply. In both cases, *a lower price level causes misperceptions about relative prices, and these misperceptions induce suppliers to respond to the lower price level by decreasing the quantity of goods and services supplied.*

The Keynesian sticky-wage theory

Another explanation of the upward slope of the short-run aggregate-supply curve is based on the work of John Maynard Keynes. According to Keynes and many of his followers, the short-run aggregate-supply curve slopes upwards because nominal wages are slow to adjust, or 'sticky', in the short run. To some extent, the slow adjustment of nominal wages is attributable to long-term contracts between workers and firms that fix nominal wages, sometimes for as long as 3 years. In addition, this slow adjustment may be attributable to social norms and notions of fairness that influence wage setting and that change only slowly over time.

To see what sticky nominal wages mean for aggregate supply, imagine that a firm has agreed in advance to pay its workers a certain nominal wage based on what it expected the price level to be. If the price level P falls below the level that was expected and the nominal wage remains stuck at W, then the real wage W/P rises above the level the firm planned to pay. Because wages are a large part of a firm's production costs, a higher real wage means that the firm's real costs have risen. The firm responds to these higher costs by hiring less labour and producing a smaller quantity of goods and services. In other words, *because wages do not adjust immediately to the price level, a lower price level makes employment and production less profitable, which induces firms to reduce the quantity of goods and services supplied.*

The new Keynesian sticky-price theory

Recently, some economists have advocated a third theory of the short-run aggregate-supply curve, called the new Keynesian theory. As we just discussed, Keynes originally emphasised that nominal wages adjust slowly over time. New Keynesian theorists emphasise that the prices of some goods and services also adjust sluggishly in response to changing economic conditions. This slow adjustment of prices occurs in part because there are costs to adjusting prices, called *menu costs*. These menu costs include the cost of printing and distributing catalogues and the time required to change price tags. As a result of these costs, prices as well as wages may be sticky in the short run.

To see the implications of sticky prices for aggregate supply, suppose that each firm in the economy announces its prices in advance based on the economic conditions it expects to prevail. Then, after prices are announced, the economy experiences an unexpected contraction in the money supply, which (as we have learned) will reduce the overall price level in the long run. Although some firms reduce their prices immediately in response to changing economic conditions, other firms may not want to incur additional menu costs and, therefore, may temporarily lag behind. Because these lagging firms have prices that are too high, their sales decline. Declining sales, in turn, cause these firms to cut back on production and employment. In other words, *because not all prices adjust instantly to changing conditions, an unexpected fall in the price level leaves some firms with higher-than-desired prices, and these higher-than-desired prices depress sales and induce firms to reduce the quantity of goods and services they produce.*

Summary Thus, there are three alternative explanations for the upward slope of the short-run aggregate-supply curve: (1) misperceptions, (2) sticky wages and (3) sticky prices. Economists debate which of these theories is correct. For our purposes in this book, however, the similarities of the theories are more important than the differences. All three theories suggest that output deviates from its natural rate when the price level deviates from the price level that people expected.

Notice that each of these three theories of short-run aggregate supply emphasises a problem that is likely to be only temporary. Whether the upward slope of the aggregate-supply curve is attributable to misperceptions, sticky wages or sticky prices, these conditions will not persist forever. Eventually, as people adjust their expectations, misperceptions are corrected, nominal wages adjust, and prices become unstuck. In the long run, therefore, the aggregate-supply curve is vertical rather than upward-sloping.

WHY THE SHORT-RUN AGGREGATE-SUPPLY CURVE MIGHT SHIFT

The short-run aggregate-supply curve tells us the quantity of goods and services supplied in the short run for any given level of prices. Many events that shift the long-run aggregate-supply curve shift the short-run aggregate-supply curve as well. For example, when an increase in the economy's capital stock increases productivity, both the long-run and short run aggregate supply curves shift to the right. When an increase in the minimum wage raises the natural rate of unemployment, both the long-run and short-run aggregate-supply curves shift to the left.

There is, however, an important new variable that affects the position of the short-run aggregate-supply curve—people's expectation of the price level. As we have discussed, the quantity of goods and services supplied depends, in the short run, on misperceptions, sticky wages and sticky prices. Yet perceptions, wages and prices are set on the basis of expectations of the price level. For example, when people expect the price level to be high, they will tend to set wages high. High wages tend to raise firms' costs and, for any given actual price level, reduce the quantity of goods and services that firms supply. *Thus, a higher expected price level decreases the quantity of goods and services supplied and shifts the short-run aggregate-supply curve to the left. Conversely, a lower expected price level increases the quantity of goods and services supplied and shifts the short-run aggregate-supply curve to the right.*

As we will see, this influence of expectations on the position of the short-run aggregate-supply curve reconciles the economy's behaviour in the short run with its behaviour in the long run. In the short run, expectations are fixed, and the economy finds itself at the intersection of the aggregate-demand curve and the short-run aggregate-supply curve. In the long run, expectations adjust, and the short-run aggregate-supply curve shifts. This shift ensures that the economy eventually finds itself at the intersection of the aggregate-demand curve and the long-run aggregate-supply curve.

QUICK QUIZ Explain why the long-run aggregate-supply curve is vertical. ◆ Explain three theories for why the short-run aggregate-supply curve is upward-sloping.

TWO CAUSES OF RECESSION

Now that we have introduced the model of aggregate demand and aggregate supply, we have the basic tools we need to analyse short-run fluctuations in economic activity. In the next two chapters, we will refine our understanding of how to use these tools. But even now we can use what we have learned about aggregate demand and aggregate supply to examine the two basic causes of recession.

Figure 16.6 shows an economy in long-run equilibrium. Equilibrium output and the price level are determined by the intersection of the aggregate-demand curve and the long-run aggregate-supply curve, shown as point A in the figure. At this point, output is at its natural rate. The short-run aggregate-supply curve passes through this point as well, indicating that perceptions, wages and prices have fully adjusted to this long-run equilibrium. That is, when an economy is at its long-run equilibrium, perceptions, wages and prices must have adjusted so that the intersection of aggregate demand with short-run aggregate supply is the same as the intersection of aggregate demand with long-run aggregate supply.

THE EFFECTS OF A SHIFT IN AGGREGATE DEMAND

Suppose that for some reason a wave of pessimism suddenly overtakes the economy. The cause might be a decline in the world economy, a crash in the stock market, or the outbreak of a war overseas. Because of this event, many people lose confidence in the future and alter their plans. Households cut back on their spending and delay major purchases, and firms put off buying new equipment.

What is the impact of such a wave of pessimism on the economy? Such an event reduces the aggregate demand for goods and services. That is, for any

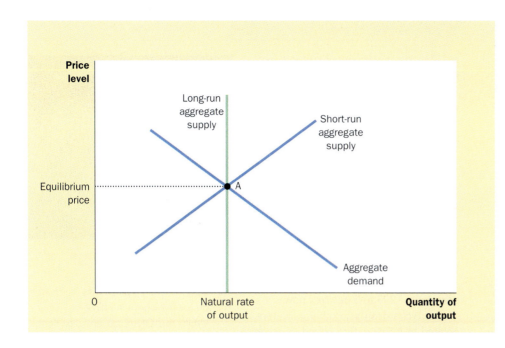

Figure 16.6

THE LONG-RUN EQUILIBRIUM. The long-run equilibrium of the economy is found where the aggregate-demand curve crosses the long-run aggregate-supply curve (point A). When the economy reaches this long-run equilibrium, perceptions, wages and prices will have adjusted so that the short-run aggregate-supply curve crosses this point as well.

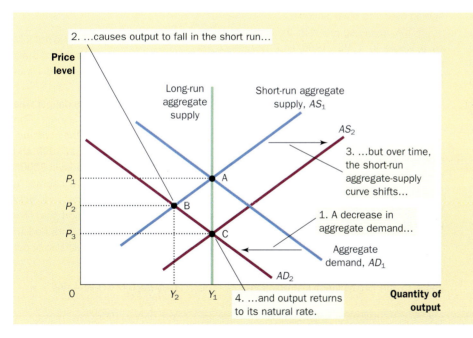

Figure 16.7

A CONTRACTION IN AGGREGATE DEMAND. A fall in aggregate demand, which might be due to a wave of pessimism in the economy, is represented with a shift to the left in the aggregate-demand curve from AD_1 to AD_2. The economy moves from point A to point B. Output falls from Y_1 to Y_2, and the price level falls from P_1 to P_2. Over time, as perceptions, wages and prices adjust, the short-run aggregate-supply curve shifts to the right from AS_1 to AS_2, and the economy reaches point C, where the new aggregate-demand curve crosses the long-run aggregate-supply curve. The price level falls to P_3, and output returns to its natural rate, Y_1.

given price level, households and firms now want to buy a smaller quantity of goods and services. As figure 16.7 shows, the aggregate-demand curve shifts to the left from AD_1 to AD_2.

In this figure, we can examine the effects of the fall in aggregate demand. In the short run, the economy moves along the initial short-run aggregate-supply curve AS_1, going from point A to point B. As the economy moves from point A to point B, output falls from Y_1 to Y_2, and the price level falls from P_1 to P_2. The

IN THE NEWS

Going for gold: How the Olympics building boom increases aggregate demand

AS WE HAVE SEEN, INVESTMENT IS A significant component of aggregate demand. For an event like the Sydney Olympics to occur, vast amounts of construction must take place. This has increased aggregate demand in New South Wales, the site of the 2000 Olympic Games. Whether this will lead to increased GDP for Australia is a matter of debate among economists, but most agree that economic activity will slow after the building boom ends.

Sydney's a City on Steroids

BY MARK ROBINSON

A boom stemming from the Olympics has kicked in 'with a vengeance' in NSW with huge increases in construction and industrial production according to a new report.

The Access Economics report also predicts the State's business will be more than double the long-term average this year.

'The Olympics was always going to do to NSW's economy what steroids did to (Canadian sprinter) Ben Johnson's 100m times', it says.

It says the massive boom 'has only now kicked in with a vengeance'. Access director Chris Richardson said construction was booming due to Olympic projects and office buildings under construction. That surge was prompted in part by a fall in the CBD vacancy rate from 22 per cent in 1993 to 5 per cent now.

Mr Richardson said other indicators pointed to NSW pulling ahead of other States with the 'construction bubble' spilling over into other sectors.

'NSW level-pegged with the nation as a whole in 1995, 1996 and 1997. However, in 1998 to date the Waratah State has finally pulled away from the pack.'

Access forecast economic growth would be 4.8 per cent in the 1998 calendar year, almost double the 2.8 10-year average. Also, industrial production covering the mining and manufacturing sectors was predicted to rise 6.6 per cent, against the long-term average rise of 0.6 per cent.

Treasurer Michael Egan welcomed the report yesterday, although he admitted he was a 'long-term sceptic' when it came to the organisation's predictions.

PARTIALLY BUILT OLYMPIC STADIUM IN SYDNEY

He said the Olympics was only one reason for the boom in NSW.

'While the Olympics are significant, we are getting 40 per cent of the national total of business building in NSW,' Mr Egan said.

'That is in a variety of forms, not just Olympic construction, not just hotels and motels, but new offices, new factories and new shops.'

According to Access the danger was the boom would precede a bust. The best scenario would be for the construction boom to 'peak gently' in 1999 and be followed by a tourism boom in 2000.

'However, our earlier concerns re the post-Olympics hangover are now less than (before),' the report said. Mr Richardson added that tax cuts tied to the federal tax package would also boost NSW.

SOURCE: *Daily Telegraph*, 9 October 1998, p. 9.

---

falling level of output indicates that the economy is in a recession. Although not shown in the figure, firms respond to lower sales and production by reducing employment. Thus, the pessimism that caused the shift in aggregate demand is, to some extent, self-fulfilling—pessimism about the future leads to falling incomes and rising unemployment.

What should policymakers do when faced with such a recession? One possibility is to take action to increase aggregate demand. As we noted earlier, an increase in government spending or an increase in the money supply would increase the quantity of goods and services demanded at any price and, therefore, would shift the aggregate-demand curve to the right. If policymakers can act with sufficient speed and precision, they can offset the initial shift in aggregate demand, return the aggregate-demand curve back to AD_1, and bring the economy back to point A. (The next chapter discusses in more detail the ways in which monetary and fiscal policy influence aggregate demand, as well as some of the practical difficulties in using these policy instruments.)

Even without action by policymakers, the recession eventually remedies itself. Over time, people correct the misperceptions, sticky wages and sticky prices that cause aggregate supply to slope upwards in the short run. In particular, as expectations of the price level fall, perceptions, wages and prices are adjusted, and the short-run aggregate-supply curve shifts to the right from AS_1 to AS_2 in figure 16.7. In the long run, the economy approaches point C, where the new aggregate-demand curve (AD_2) crosses the long-run aggregate-supply curve.

In the new long-run equilibrium, point C, output is back to its natural rate. Even though the wave of pessimism has reduced aggregate demand, the price level has fallen sufficiently (to P_3) to offset the shift in the aggregate-demand curve. Thus, in the long run, the shift in aggregate demand is reflected fully in the price level and not at all in the level of output. In other words, the long-run effect of a shift in aggregate demand is a nominal change (the price level is lower) but not a real change (output is the same).

To sum up, this story about shifts in aggregate demand has two important implications:

- In the short run, shifts in aggregate demand cause fluctuations in the economy's output of goods and services.
- In the long run, shifts in aggregate demand affect the overall price level but do not affect output.

THE EFFECTS OF A SHIFT IN AGGREGATE SUPPLY

Imagine once again an economy at its long-run equilibrium. Now suppose that suddenly some firms experience an increase in their costs of production. For example, droughts might reduce yields of some crops, driving up the cost of producing food products. Or an explosion at a gasworks might drastically reduce the supply of natural gas, driving up the cost of production as firms try to switch to alternative energy sources.

What is the macroeconomic impact of such an increase in production costs? For any given price level, firms now want to supply a smaller quantity of goods and services. Thus, as figure 16.8 shows, the short-run aggregate-supply curve shifts to the left from AS_1 to AS_2. (Depending on the event, the long-run aggregate-supply curve might also shift. To keep things simple, however, we will assume that it does not.)

In this figure, we can trace the effects of the leftward shift in aggregate supply. In the short run, the economy moves along the existing aggregate-demand curve, going from point A to point B. The output of the economy falls from Y_1 to Y_2, and the price level rises from P_1 to P_2. Because the economy is

Figure 16.8

AN ADVERSE SHIFT IN AGGREGATE SUPPLY. When some event increases firms' costs, the short-run aggregate-supply curve shifts to the left from AS_1 to AS_2. The economy moves from point A to point B. The result is stagflation—output falls from Y_1 to Y_2, and the price level rises from P_1 to P_2.

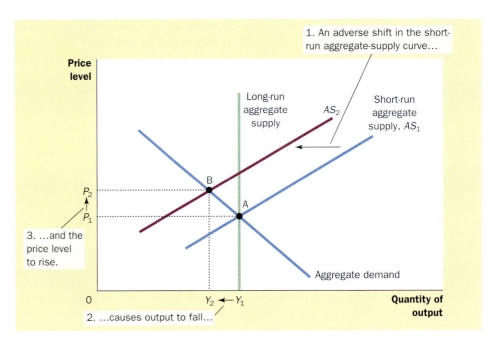

stagflation
a period of falling output and rising prices

experiencing both *stagnation* (falling output) and *inflation* (rising prices), such an event is sometimes called **stagflation**.

What should policymakers do when faced with stagflation? As we will discuss more fully later in this book, there are no easy choices. One possibility is to do nothing. In this case, the output of goods and services remains depressed at Y_2 for a while. Eventually, however, the recession will remedy itself as perceptions, wages and prices adjust to the higher production costs. A period of low output and high unemployment, for instance, puts downward pressure on workers' wages. Lower wages, in turn, increase the quantity of output supplied. Over time, as the short-run aggregate-supply curve shifts back towards AS_1, the price level falls, and the quantity of output approaches its natural rate. In the long run, the economy returns to point A, where the aggregate-demand curve crosses the long-run aggregate-supply curve.

Alternatively, policymakers who control monetary and fiscal policy might attempt to offset some of the effects of the shift in the short-run aggregate-supply curve by shifting the aggregate-demand curve. This possibility is shown in figure 16.9. In this case, changes in policy shift the aggregate-demand curve to the right from AD_1 to AD_2—exactly enough to prevent the shift in aggregate supply from affecting output. The economy moves directly from point A to point C. Output remains at its natural rate, and the price level rises from P_1 to P_3. In this case, policymakers are said to *accommodate* the shift in aggregate supply because they allow the increase in costs to affect the level of prices permanently.

To sum up, this story about shifts in aggregate supply has two important implications:

- Shifts in aggregate supply can cause stagflation—a combination of recession (falling output) and inflation (rising prices).
- Policymakers who can influence aggregate demand cannot offset both of these adverse effects simultaneously.

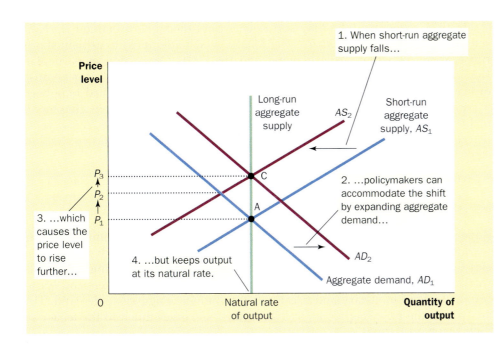

Figure 16.9

ACCOMMODATING AN ADVERSE SHIFT IN AGGREGATE SUPPLY. Faced with an adverse shift in aggregate supply from AS_1 to AS_2, policymakers who can influence aggregate demand might try to shift the aggregate-demand curve to the right from AD_1 to AD_2. The economy would move from point A to point C. This policy would prevent the supply shift from reducing output in the short run, but the price level would permanently rise from P_1 to P_3.

QUICK QUIZ Suppose that the passage of a referendum to make Australia a republic suddenly increases people's confidence in the future. Use the model of aggregate demand and aggregate supply to analyse the effect on the economy.

CONCLUSION: THE ORIGINS OF AGGREGATE DEMAND AND AGGREGATE SUPPLY

This chapter has achieved two goals. First, we have discussed some of the important facts about short-run fluctuations in economic activity. Second, we have introduced a basic model to explain those fluctuations, called the model of aggregate demand and aggregate supply. In the next two chapters we look at each piece of this model in more detail in order to understand more fully what causes fluctuations in the economy and how policymakers might respond to these fluctuations.

Now that we have a preliminary understanding of this model, it is worthwhile to step back from it and consider its history. How did this model of short-run fluctuations develop? The answer is that this model is, to a large extent, a by-product of the Great Depression of the 1930s. During this period, the Australian economy and most other major economies around the world experienced a deep downturn in economic activity. In Australia, real GDP fell by more than 10% from 1929 to 1932, and unemployment rose from 6% to 20%. Economists and policymakers at the time were puzzled about what had caused this event and were uncertain about how to deal with it.

In 1936, economist John Maynard Keynes published a book entitled *The General Theory of Employment, Interest, and Money*, which attempted to explain short-run economic fluctuations in general and the Great Depression in particular. Keynes's main message was that recessions and depressions can occur because of inadequate aggregate demand for goods and services. Keynes had long been a critic of classical economic theory—the theory we examined in chapters 9 to 15—because it could explain only the long-run effects of policies. A few years before offering *The General Theory*, Keynes had written the following about classical economics:

> The long run is a misleading guide to current affairs. In the long run we are all dead. Economists set themselves too easy, too useless a task if in tempestuous seasons they can only tell us when the storm is long past, the ocean will be flat.

Keynes's message was aimed at policymakers as well as economists. As the world's economies suffered from high unemployment, Keynes advocated policies to increase aggregate demand, including government spending on public works. In the next chapter, we examine in detail how policymakers can try to use the tools of monetary and fiscal policy to influence aggregate demand. The analysis in the next chapter, as well as in this one, owes much to the legacy of John Maynard Keynes.

Summary

- All societies experience short-run economic fluctuations around long-run trends. These fluctuations are irregular and largely unpredictable. When recessions do occur, real GDP and other measures of income, spending and production fall, and unemployment rises.

- Economists analyse short-run economic fluctuations using the model of aggregate demand and aggregate supply. According to this model, the output of goods and services and the overall level of prices adjust to balance aggregate demand and aggregate supply.

- The aggregate-demand curve slopes downwards for three reasons. First, a lower price level raises the real value of households' money holdings, which stimulates consumer spending. Second, a lower price level reduces the quantity of money households demand; as households try to convert money into interest-bearing assets, interest rates fall, which stimulates investment spending. Third, as a lower price level reduces interest rates, the dollar depreciates in the market for foreign-currency exchange, which stimulates net exports.

- The long-run aggregate-supply curve is vertical. In the long run, the quantity of goods and services supplied depends on the economy's labour, capital and technology, but not on the overall level of prices.

- The short-run aggregate-supply curve is upward-sloping. There are three theories to explain short-run aggregate supply. According to the new classical misperceptions theory, an unexpected fall in the price level leads suppliers to mistakenly believe that their relative prices have fallen, which induces them to reduce production. According to the Keynesian sticky-wage theory, an unexpected fall in the price level temporarily raises real wages, which induces firms to reduce employment and production. According to the new Keynesian sticky-price theory, an unexpected fall in the price level leaves some firms with prices that are temporarily too high, which reduces their sales and causes them to cut back production.

- One possible cause of recession is a fall in aggregate demand. When the aggregate-demand curve shifts to the left, output and prices fall in the short run. Over time, as perceptions, wages and prices adjust, the short-run aggregate-supply curve shifts to the right, and the economy returns to its natural rate of output at a new, lower price level.

- A second possible cause of recession is an adverse change in aggregate supply. When the aggregate-supply curve shifts to the left, the short-run effect is falling output and rising prices—a combination called stagflation. Over time, as perceptions, wages and prices adjust, the price level falls back to its original level, and output recovers.

Key concepts

recession, p. 344
depression, p. 344
model of aggregate demand and aggregate supply, p. 348
aggregate-demand curve, p. 349
aggregate-supply curve, p. 349
stagflation, p. 362

Questions for review

1. Draw a diagram with aggregate demand, short-run aggregate supply and long-run aggregate supply. Be careful to label the axes correctly.

2. List and explain the three reasons that the aggregate-demand curve is downward-sloping.

3. Explain why the long-run aggregate-supply curve is vertical.

4. List and explain the three theories for why the short-run aggregate-supply curve is upward-sloping.

5. What might shift the aggregate-demand curve to the left? Use the model of aggregate demand and aggregate supply to trace through the effects of such a shift.

6. What might shift the aggregate-supply curve to the left? Use the model of aggregate demand and aggregate supply to trace through the effects of such a shift.

Problems and applications

1. Why do you think that investment is more variable over the business cycle than consumer spending? Which category of consumer spending do you think would be most volatile: durable goods (such as furniture and car purchases), non-durable goods (such as food and clothing), or services (such as haircuts and medical care)? Why?

2. Suppose that the economy is undergoing a recession because of a fall in aggregate demand.
   a. Using an aggregate-demand/aggregate-supply diagram, depict the current state of the economy.
   b. If real GDP is now 1% below last year's value, how does the unemployment rate compare with last year's rate? (*Hint:* Review Okun's law.)
   c. 'Capacity utilisation' is a measure of how intensively the capital stock is being used. In a recession, is capacity utilisation above or below its long-run average? Explain.

3. Explain whether each of the following events will increase, decrease or have no effect on long-run aggregate supply.
   a. Australia experiences a wave of immigration.
   b. The ACTU wins an unexpectedly high increase in the award wage.
   c. Intel invents a new and more powerful computer chip.
   d. An earthquake destroys factories in Newcastle and Sydney.

4. In figure 16.7, how does the unemployment rate at points B and C compare with the unemployment rate at point A? Under the sticky-wage explanation of the short-run aggregate-supply curve, how does the real wage at points B and C compare with the real wage at point A?

5. Explain why the following statements are false.
   a. 'The aggregate-demand curve slopes downwards because it is the horizontal sum of the demand curves for individual goods.'
   b. 'The long-run aggregate-supply curve is vertical because economic forces do not affect long-run aggregate supply.'
   c. 'If firms adjusted their prices every day, then the short-run aggregate-supply curve would be horizontal.'
   d. 'Whenever the economy enters a recession, its long-run aggregate-supply curve shifts to the left.'

6. For each of the three theories for the upward slope of the short-run aggregate-supply curve, carefully explain the following:
   a. how the economy recovers from a recession and returns to its long-run equilibrium without any policy intervention
   b. what determines the speed of that recovery.

7. Suppose that the economy is currently in a recession. If policymakers take no action, how will the economy evolve over time? Explain in words and using an aggregate-demand/aggregate-supply diagram.

8. Suppose workers and firms suddenly believe that inflation will be quite high over the coming year. Suppose also that the economy begins in long-run equilibrium, and the aggregate-demand curve does not shift.
   a. What happens to nominal wages? What happens to real wages?
   b. Using an aggregate-demand/aggregate-supply diagram, show the effect of the change in expectations on both the short-run and long-run levels of prices and output.
   c. Were the expectations of high inflation accurate? Explain.

9. The chapter explains that the economy will eventually recover from a recession even without action by policymakers. Why might policymakers nevertheless want to take some action?

10. Explain whether each of the following events shifts the short-run aggregate-supply curve, the aggregate-demand curve, both, or neither. For each event that does shift a curve, use a diagram to illustrate the effect on the economy.
    a. Households decide to save a larger share of their income.
    b. Queensland orange groves suffer from an infestation of Mediterranean fruit flies.
    c. The birthrate shoots up 9 months after a particularly cold Melbourne winter.

11. Suppose that firms become very optimistic about future business conditions and invest heavily in new capital equipment.
    a. Use an aggregate-demand/aggregate-supply diagram to show the short-run effect of this optimism on the economy. Label the new levels of prices and real output. Explain in words why the aggregate quantity of output *supplied* changes.
    b. Use the diagram from part (a) to show the new long-run equilibrium of the economy. (For now, assume there is no change in the long-run aggregate-supply curve.) Explain in words why the aggregate quantity of output *demanded* changes between the short run and the long run.
    c. How might the investment boom affect the long-run aggregate-supply curve? Explain.

12. Assume that the economy begins in long-run equilibrium, and households decide to hold higher money balances than they did before.
    a. What happens to the interest rate? Explain.
    b. What happens to the quantity of investment demanded? Explain.
    c. What happens to the value of the dollar? Explain.
    d. What happens to the quantity of net exports demanded? Explain.
    e. What happens to aggregate demand? Explain.

17

THE INFLUENCE OF MONETARY AND FISCAL POLICY ON AGGREGATE DEMAND

IN THIS CHAPTER YOU WILL

Learn the theory of liquidity preference as a short-run theory of the interest rate

Analyse how fiscal policy affects interest rates and aggregate demand

Analyse how monetary policy affects interest rates and aggregate demand

Discuss the debate over whether policymakers should try to stabilise the economy

Reconsider how the economy behaves differently in the short run and in the long run

Imagine that you are a member of the Reserve Bank Board, which sets monetary policy. You observe that the Australian government has decided to cut government spending in order to eliminate the budget deficit. You and the other Board members decide what direction you think monetary policy should take. What policy recommendation should you make in response to this change in fiscal policy? Should the Reserve Bank of Australia (RBA) expand the money supply, contract the money supply, or leave the money supply the same?

To answer this question, you need to consider the impact of monetary and fiscal policy on the economy. In the preceding chapter, we saw how to explain short-run economic fluctuations using the model of aggregate demand and aggregate supply. When the aggregate-demand curve or the aggregate-supply curve shifts, the result is fluctuations in the economy's overall output of goods and services and in its overall level of prices. As we noted in the previous chapter, monetary and fiscal policy can each influence aggregate demand. Thus, a change in one of these policies can lead to short-run fluctuations in output and prices. Policymakers will want to anticipate this effect and, perhaps, adjust the other policy in response.

In this chapter we examine in more detail how the government's tools of monetary and fiscal policy influence the position of the aggregate-demand curve. We have previously discussed the long-run effects of these policies. In chapters 9 and 10 we saw how fiscal policy affects saving, investment and long-run economic growth. In chapters 12 and 13 we saw how the RBA influences the money supply in order to meet interest rate targets and how the money supply affects the price level in the long run. We now see how these policy tools can shift the aggregate-demand curve and, in doing so, affect short-run economic fluctuations.

As we have already learned, many factors influence aggregate demand besides monetary and fiscal policy. In particular, desired spending by households and firms determines the overall demand for goods and services. When desired spending changes, aggregate demand shifts. If policymakers do not respond, such shifts in aggregate demand cause short-run fluctuations in output and employment. As a result, monetary and fiscal policymakers sometimes use the policy levers at their disposal to try to offset these shifts in aggregate demand and thereby stabilise the economy. Here we discuss the theory behind these policy actions and some of the difficulties that arise in using this theory in practice.

HOW MONETARY POLICY INFLUENCES AGGREGATE DEMAND

The aggregate-demand curve shows the quantity of goods and services demanded for any price level. As you may recall from the preceding chapter, the aggregate-demand curve slopes downwards for three reasons:

- *Pigou's wealth effect:* A lower price level raises the real value of households' money holdings, and higher real wealth stimulates consumer spending.

- *Keynes's interest-rate effect:* A lower price level lowers the interest rate as people try to lend out their excess money holdings, and the lower interest rate stimulates investment spending.

- *Mundell–Fleming's exchange-rate effect:* When a lower price level lowers the interest rate, investors move some of their funds overseas and cause the domestic currency to depreciate relative to foreign currencies. This depreciation makes domestic goods cheaper compared with foreign goods and, therefore, stimulates net exports.

These three effects should not be viewed as alternative theories. Instead, they occur simultaneously to increase the quantity of goods and services demanded when the price level falls.

Although all three effects work together in explaining the downward slope of the aggregate-demand curve, they are not of equal importance. Because money holdings are a small part of household wealth, Pigou's wealth effect is the least important of the three. Because exports and imports represent a relatively large fraction of Australian GDP, Mundell–Fleming's exchange-rate effect can be significant for the Australian economy. (This effect is much less important for larger countries because larger countries typically export and import a smaller fraction of their GDP.) However, the most important reason for the downward slope of the aggregate-demand curve is Keynes's interest-rate effect.

To understand how policy influences aggregate demand, therefore, we examine Keynes's interest-rate effect in more detail. Here we develop Keynes's theory of how the interest rate is determined, called the **theory of liquidity preference**. After we develop this theory, we use it to understand the downward slope of the aggregate-demand curve and how monetary policy shifts this curve. By shedding new light on the aggregate-demand curve, the theory of liquidity preference expands our understanding of short-run economic fluctuations.

theory of liquidity preference
Keynes's theory that the interest rate adjusts to bring money supply and money demand into balance

THE THEORY OF LIQUIDITY PREFERENCE

In his classic book *The General Theory of Employment, Interest, and Money*, Keynes proposed the theory of liquidity preference to explain what factors determine the economy's interest rate. The theory is, in essence, just an application of supply and demand. According to Keynes, the interest rate adjusts to balance the supply of and demand for money. Let's therefore consider the supply of and demand for money and how each depends on the interest rate.

Money supply The first piece of the theory of liquidity preference is the supply of money. As we first discussed in chapter 12, the RBA conducts monetary policy by setting interest rates rather than controlling the money supply. It does not matter which one the RBA chooses, but it can control one or the other, but not both. Just as in the simple models of supply and demand that we studied in chapter 4, the RBA can set the quantity of money and allow the market to determine the 'price' of money, the interest rate, or it can set the the interest rate and allow the market to determine the quantity of money. In the chapters following chapter 12, we assumed that the RBA chooses to control the money supply by changing the quantity of reserves in the banking system through the purchase and sale of government bonds in open-market operations. When the RBA buys government bonds, the dollars it pays for the bonds are typically deposited in banks, and these dollars are added to bank reserves. When the RBA sells government bonds, the dollars it receives for the bonds are withdrawn from the banking system, and bank reserves fall. These changes in bank reserves, in turn, lead to changes in the ability of banks to make loans and create money. Because we assumed that the quantity of money supplied is fixed by RBA policy, we could therefore represent a fixed money supply with a vertical supply curve, as in figure 17.1 (p. 370).

These details of monetary control are important for the implementation of RBA policy, but they are not crucial in this chapter. Our goal here is to examine how changes in the money supply affect the aggregate demand for goods and services. For this purpose, we can ignore the details of how RBA policy is implemented and simply assume that the RBA controls the money supply directly. In other words, the quantity of money supplied in the economy is fixed at whatever level the RBA decides to set it.

Money demand The second piece of the theory of liquidity preference is the demand for money. As a starting point for understanding money demand, recall that any asset's *liquidity* refers to the ease with which that asset is converted into the economy's medium of exchange. Money is the economy's medium of exchange, so it is by definition the most liquid asset available. The liquidity of money explains the demand for it—people choose to hold money

Figure 17.1

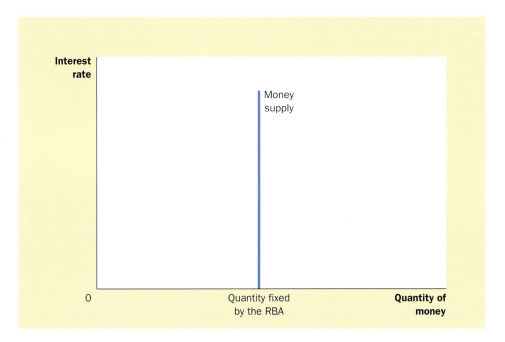

THE SUPPLY OF MONEY. The supply of money in an economy is fixed by the central bank, which in Australia is the Reserve Bank of Australia. Because the RBA is assumed to determine the supply of money, the supply curve is vertical.

instead of other assets that offer higher rates of return because money can be used to buy goods and services.

Although there are many determinants of the quantity of money demanded, the theory of liquidity preference emphasises that one of the most important is the interest rate. The reason is that the interest rate is the opportunity cost of holding money. That is, when you hold wealth as cash in your wallet, instead of as an interest-bearing bond, you lose the interest you could have earned. An increase in the interest rate raises the cost of holding money and, as a result, reduces the quantity of money demanded. Thus, as shown in figure 17.2, the money-demand curve is downward-sloping.

Equilibrium in the money market According to the theory of liquidity preference, the interest rate adjusts to balance the supply of and demand for money. This is shown in figure 17.3. There is one interest rate, called the *equilibrium interest rate*, at which the quantity of money demanded exactly balances the quantity of money supplied. If the interest rate is at any other level, people will try to adjust their portfolios of assets and, as a result, drive the interest rate towards the equilibrium.

For example, suppose that the interest rate is above the equilibrium level, such as r_1 in figure 17.3. In this case, the quantity of money that people want to hold, M_1^d, is less than the quantity of money that the RBA has supplied. Those people who are holding the excess supply of money will try to get rid of it by buying interest-bearing bonds or by depositing it in an interest-bearing bank account. Because bond issuers and banks prefer to pay lower interest rates, they respond to this excess supply of money by lowering the interest rates they offer. As the interest rate falls, people become more willing to hold money until, at the equilibrium interest rate, people are happy to hold exactly the amount of money the RBA has supplied.

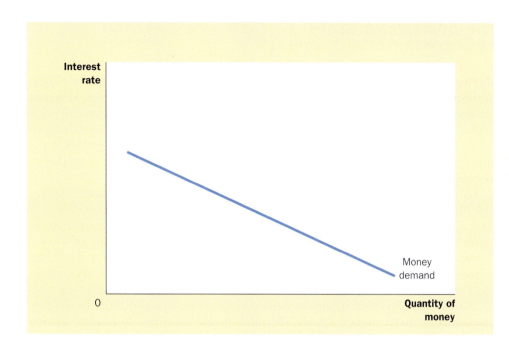

Figure 17.2

THE DEMAND FOR MONEY. Because the interest rate measures the opportunity cost of holding non-interest-bearing money instead of interest-bearing bonds, an increase in the interest rate reduces the quantity of money demanded. A downward-sloping demand curve represents this negative relationship.

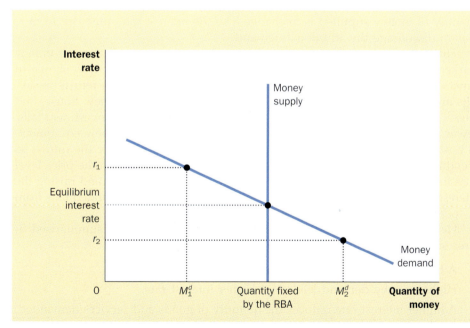

Figure 17.3

EQUILIBRIUM IN THE MONEY MARKET. According to the theory of liquidity preference, the interest rate adjusts to bring the quantity of money supplied and the quantity of money demanded into balance. If the interest rate is above the equilibrium level (such as at r_1), the quantity of money people want to hold (M_1^d) is less than the quantity the RBA has created, and this excess supply of money puts downward pressure on the interest rate. Conversely, if the interest rate is below the equilibrium level (such as at r_2), the quantity of money people want to hold (M_2^d) is greater than the quantity the RBA has created, and this excess demand for money puts upward pressure on the interest rate. Thus, the forces of supply and demand in the market for money push the interest rate towards the equilibrium interest rate, at which people are content holding the quantity of money the RBA has created.

Conversely, at interest rates below the equilibrium level, such as r_2 in figure 17.3, the quantity of money that people want to hold, M_2^d, is greater than the quantity of money that the RBA has supplied. As a result, people try to increase their holdings of money by reducing their holdings of bonds and other interest-bearing assets. As people cut back on their holdings of bonds, bond issuers find that they have to offer higher interest rates in order to attract buyers. Thus, the interest rate rises and approaches the equilibrium level.

THE DOWNWARD SLOPE OF THE AGGREGATE-DEMAND CURVE

Having seen how the theory of liquidity preference explains the economy's equilibrium interest rate, we now consider its implications for the aggregate demand for goods and services. We first use the model to explain the downward slope of the aggregate-demand curve. In particular, suppose that the overall level of prices in the economy rises. What happens to the interest rate that balances the supply of and demand for money, and how does that change affect the quantity of goods and services demanded?

As we discussed in chapter 13, the price level is one determinant of the quantity of money demanded. At higher prices, more money is exchanged every time a good or service is sold. As a result, people will choose to hold a larger quantity of money. That is, a higher price level increases the quantity of money demanded for any given interest rate. Thus, as panel (a) of figure 17.4 shows, an increase in the price level from P_1 to P_2 shifts the money-demand curve to the right from MD_1 to MD_2.

Notice how this shift in money demand affects the equilibrium in the money market. For a fixed money supply, the interest rate must rise to balance money supply and money demand. The higher price level has increased the amount of money people want to hold and shifted the demand curve to the right. Yet the quantity of money supplied is unchanged, so the interest rate must rise from r_1 to r_2 to discourage the additional demand.

This increase in the interest rate has ramifications not only for the money market but also for the quantity of goods and services demanded, as shown in panel (b). At a higher interest rate, the cost of borrowing and the return on savings are greater. Fewer households choose to borrow to buy a new house, and those who do buy smaller houses, so the demand for residential investment falls. Fewer firms choose to borrow to build new factories and buy new equipment, so business investment falls. Households choose to save more for the future, so spending on consumption goods falls. For all these reasons, when the price level rises from P_1 to P_2, increasing money demand from MD_1 to MD_2 and raising the interest rate from r_1 to r_2, the quantity of goods and services demanded falls from Y_1 to Y_2.

Hence, this analysis of Keynes's interest-rate effect can be summarised in three steps:

1. A higher price level raises money demand.
2. Higher money demand leads to a higher interest rate.
3. A higher interest rate reduces the quantity of goods and services demanded.

The end result of this analysis is a negative relationship between the price level and the quantity of goods and services demanded. This relationship is illustrated with a downward-sloping aggregate-demand curve.

CHANGES IN THE MONEY SUPPLY

So far we have used the theory of liquidity preference merely to explain more fully the downward slope of the aggregate-demand curve. The theory is useful, however, because it also sheds light on how the RBA shifts the aggregate-

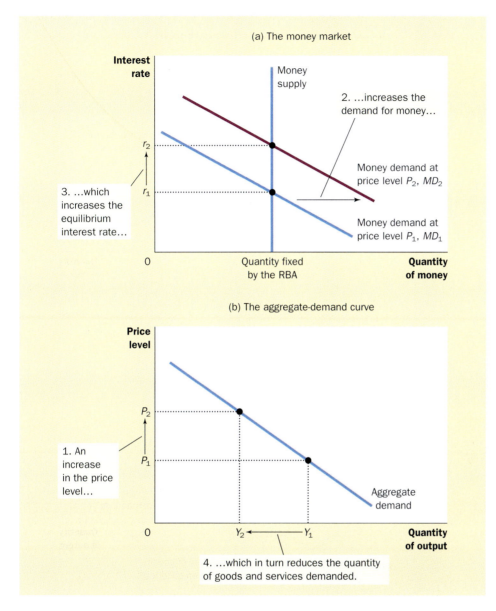

Figure 17.4

THE MONEY MARKET AND THE SLOPE OF THE AGGREGATE-DEMAND CURVE. An increase in the price level from P_1 to P_2 shifts the money-demand curve to the right, as in panel (a). This increase in money demand causes the interest rate to rise from r_1 to r_2. Because the interest rate is the cost of borrowing, the increase in the interest rate reduces the quantity of goods and services demanded from Y_1 to Y_2. This negative relationship between the price level and quantity demanded is represented with a downward-sloping aggregate-demand curve, as in panel (b).

demand curve when it changes monetary policy. Suppose that the RBA increases the money supply by buying government bonds in open-market operations. And suppose that the price level does not, in the short run, respond at all to this monetary injection. How does this monetary injection affect the equilibrium interest rate and the aggregate-demand curve?

As panel (a) of figure 17.5 shows, an increase in the money supply shifts the money-supply curve to the right from MS_1 to MS_2. Because the money-demand curve has not changed, the interest rate falls from r_1 to r_2 to balance money supply and money demand. That is, the interest rate must fall to induce people to hold the additional money the RBA has created.

Figure 17.5

A MONETARY INJECTION. In panel (a), an increase in the money supply from MS_1 to MS_2 reduces the equilibrium interest rate from r_1 to r_2. Because the interest rate is the cost of borrowing, the fall in the interest rate raises the quantity of goods and services demanded at a given price level from Y_1 to Y_2. Thus, in panel (b), the aggregate-demand curve shifts to the right from AD_1 to AD_2.

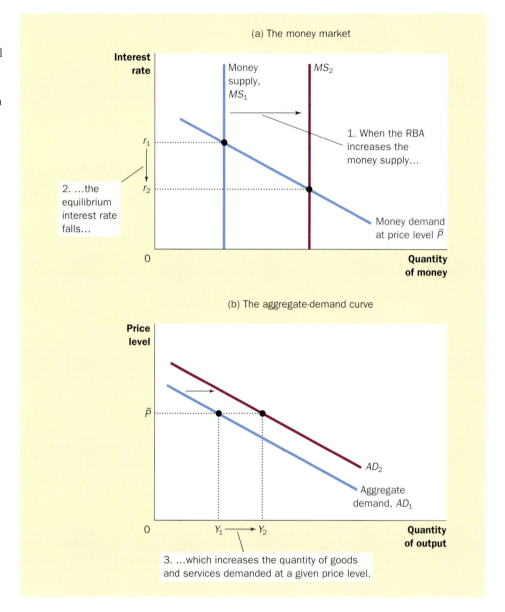

Once again, the interest rate influences the quantity of goods and services demanded, as shown in panel (b) of figure 17.5. The lower interest rate reduces the cost of borrowing and the return on savings. Households buy more and larger houses, stimulating the demand for residential investment. Firms spend more on new factories and new equipment, stimulating business investment. Households save less and spend more on consumption goods. For all of these reasons, the quantity of goods and services demanded at the given price level, $\bar{P}$, rises from Y_1 to Y_2.

To sum up—*a monetary injection by the RBA increases the money supply. For any given price level, a higher money supply leads to a lower interest rate, which in turn increases the quantity of goods and services demanded.* Thus, a monetary injection shifts the aggregate-demand curve to the right.

INTEREST-RATE TARGETS AND RBA POLICY

How does the RBA affect the economy? Our discussion here and earlier in the book has treated the money supply as the RBA's policy instrument. When the RBA buys government bonds in open-market operations, it increases the money supply and expands aggregate demand. When the RBA sells government bonds in open-market operations, it decreases the money supply and contracts aggregate demand. However, as we explained in chapter 12, the RBA treats the interest rate, rather than the money supply, as its policy instrument. As we described, the RBA conducts policy by setting a target for the *cash rate*—the interest rate that banks charge one another for overnight loans. This target is re-evaluated at the monthly meetings of the Reserve Bank Board, although the target is changed relatively infrequently. The RBA has chosen to set a target for the cash rate (rather than for the money supply, as it has done at times in the past) in part because the money supply is hard to measure with sufficient precision.

The RBA's decision to target an interest rate does not fundamentally alter our analysis of monetary policy. The theory of liquidity preference illustrates an important principle—*monetary policy can be described either in terms of the money supply or in terms of the interest rate*. When the Reserve Bank Board sets a target for the cash rate of, say, 5%, the RBA's bond traders are told: 'Conduct open-market operations to ensure that the equilibrium interest rate equals 5%.' That is, when the RBA sets a target for the interest rate, it commits itself to adjusting the money supply in order to make the equilibrium in the money market hit that target.

Similarly, changes in monetary policy can be viewed either in terms of a changing target for the interest rate or in terms of a change in the money supply. When the Reserve Bank Board lowers the target for the cash rate, the RBA's bond traders buy government bonds, and this purchase increases the money supply and lowers the equilibrium interest rate. When the Board raises the target, the bond traders sell government bonds, and this sale decreases the money supply and raises the equilibrium interest rate. Thus, a change in monetary policy that aims to expand aggregate demand can be described either as increasing the money supply or as lowering the interest rate. A change in policy that aims to contract aggregate demand can be described either as decreasing the money supply or as raising the interest rate.

> **QUICK QUIZ** Use the theory of liquidity preference to explain how a decrease in the money supply affects the equilibrium interest rate. How does this change in monetary policy affect the aggregate-demand curve?

HOW FISCAL POLICY INFLUENCES AGGREGATE DEMAND

The government can influence the behaviour of the economy not only with monetary policy but also with fiscal policy. Fiscal policy refers to the government's choices regarding the overall level of government purchases or taxes. Earlier in the book we examined how fiscal policy influences saving, investment and growth in the long run. In the short run, however, the main effect of fiscal policy is on the aggregate demand for goods and services.

CHANGES IN GOVERNMENT PURCHASES

When the government changes its own purchases of goods and services, it shifts the aggregate-demand curve directly. Suppose, for instance, that the Australian Department of Defence places a $5 billion order for new submarines with the Australian Submarine Corporation, a South Australian company. This order raises the demand for the output produced by Australian Submarine Corporation, which induces the company to hire more workers and increase production. Because Australian Submarine Corporation is part of the economy, the increase in the demand for their submarines is reflected in an increase in the aggregate demand for goods and services. The aggregate-demand curve shifts to the right.

By how much does this $5 billion order from the government shift the aggregate-demand curve? At first, one might guess that the aggregate-demand curve shifts to the right by exactly $5 billion. It turns out, however, that this is not correct. There are two macroeconomic effects that make the size of the shift in aggregate demand differ from the change in government purchases. The first—the multiplier effect—suggests that the shift in aggregate demand could be *larger* than $5 billion. The second—the crowding-out effect—suggests that the shift in aggregate demand could be *smaller* than $5 billion. We now discuss each of these effects in turn.

THE MULTIPLIER EFFECT

When the government buys $5 billion of goods from Australian Submarine Corporation, that purchase has repercussions. The immediate impact of the higher demand from the government is to raise employment and profits at Australian Submarine Corporation. But as the workers see higher earnings and the firm owners see higher profits, they respond to this increase in income by raising their own spending on consumer goods. As a result, the government purchase from Australian Submarine Corporation raises the demand for the products of many other firms in the economy as well. Because each dollar spent by the government can raise the aggregate demand for goods and services by more than a dollar, government purchases are said to have a **multiplier effect** on aggregate demand.

This multiplier effect continues even after this first round. When consumer spending rises, the firms that produce these consumer goods hire more people and experience higher profits. Higher earnings and profits stimulate consumer spending once again, and so on. Thus, there is positive feedback as higher demand leads to higher income, which in turn leads to even higher demand. Once all these effects are added together, the total impact on the quantity of goods and services demanded can be much larger than the initial impulse from higher government spending.

Figure 17.6 illustrates the multiplier effect. The increase in government purchases of $5 billion initially shifts the aggregate-demand curve to the right from AD_1 to AD_2, by exactly $5 billion. But when consumers respond by increasing their spending, the aggregate-demand curve shifts still further to AD_3.

This multiplier effect arising from the response of consumer spending can be strengthened by the response of investment to higher levels of demand. For instance, Australian Submarine Corporation might respond to the higher

multiplier effect
the additional shifts in aggregate demand that result when expansionary fiscal policy increases income and thereby increases consumer spending

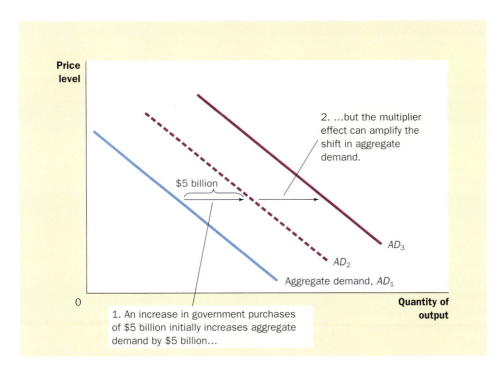

Figure 17.6

THE MULTIPLIER EFFECT. An increase in government purchases of $5 billion can shift the aggregate-demand curve to the right by more than $5 billion. This multiplier effect arises because increases in aggregate income stimulate additional spending by consumers.

demand for submarines by deciding to buy more equipment or build another plant. In this case, higher government demand spurs higher demand for investment goods. This positive feedback from demand to investment is sometimes called the *investment accelerator*.

THE CROWDING-OUT EFFECT

Although the multiplier effect suggests that the change in demand from fiscal policy can be larger than the change in government purchases, there is another effect that works in the opposite direction. Although an increase in government purchases stimulates the demand for goods and services, it also causes the interest rate to rise, and a higher interest rate tends to choke off the demand for goods and services. The reduction in demand that results when a fiscal expansion raises the interest rate is called the **crowding-out effect**.

To see why crowding out occurs, let's consider once again what happens when the government buys $5 billion of submarines from Australian Submarine Corporation. As we have discussed, this increase in demand raises the incomes of the workers and owners of this firm (and, because of the multiplier effect, of other firms as well). As incomes rise, households plan to buy more goods and services and, as a result, choose to hold more of their wealth in liquid form. That is, the increase in income caused by the fiscal expansion raises the demand for money.

The effect of the increase in money demand is shown in panel (a) of figure 17.7 (p. 379). Because the RBA has not changed the money supply, the vertical supply curve remains the same. When the higher level of income shifts the

crowding-out effect
the offset in aggregate demand that results when expansionary fiscal policy raises the interest rate and thereby reduces investment spending

FYI

A formula for the government-purchases multiplier

A LITTLE SECONDARY SCHOOL algebra permits us to derive a formula for the size of the multiplier effect that arises from consumer spending. An important number in this formula is the *marginal propensity to consume (MPC)*—the fraction of extra income that a household consumes rather than saves. For example, suppose that the marginal propensity to consume is ¾. This means that for every extra dollar that a household earns, the household saves $0.25 and spends $0.75. With an *MPC* of ¾, when the workers and owners of Australian Submarine Corporation earn $5 billion from the government contract, they increase their consumer spending by ¾ × $5 billion, or $3¾ billion.

To gauge the impact on aggregate demand of a change in government purchases, we follow the effects step by step. The process begins when the government spends $5 billion, which implies that income (earnings and profits) also rises by this amount. This increase in income in turn raises consumer spending by $MPC \times \$5$ billion, which in turn raises the income for the workers and owners of the firms that produce the consumption goods. This second increase in income again raises consumer spending, this time by $MPC \times (MPC \times \$5$ billion$)$. These feedback effects go on and on.

To find the total impact on the demand for goods and services, we add up all these effects:

Change in government purchases	=	$5 billion
First change in consumption	=	$MPC \times \$5$ billion
Second change in consumption	=	$MPC^2 \times \$5$ billion
Third change in consumption	=	$MPC^3 \times \$5$ billion
•		•
•		•
•		•

Total change in demand =
$(1 + MPC + MPC^2 + MPC^3 + \ldots) \times \$5$ billion

Here, '…' represents an infinite number of similar terms. We say that the government-purchases multiplier is:

$$\text{Multiplier} = 1 + MPC + MPC^2 + MPC^3 + \ldots$$

This multiplier tells us the demand for goods and services that each dollar of government purchases generates.

To simplify this equation for the multiplier, recall from maths lessons that this expression is an infinite geometric series. For x between -1 and $+1$:

$$1 + x + x^2 + x^3 + \ldots = 1/(1-x)$$

In our case, $x = MPC$. Thus:

$$\text{Multiplier} = 1/(1 - MPC)$$

For example, if *MPC* is ¾, the government-purchases multiplier is $1/(1 - ¾)$, which is 4. In this case, the $5 billion of government spending generates $20 billion of demand for goods and services.

---

money-demand curve to the right from MD_1 to MD_2, the interest rate must rise from r_1 to r_2 in order to keep supply and demand in balance.

The increase in the interest rate, in turn, reduces the quantity of goods and services demanded. In particular, because borrowing is more expensive, the demand for residential and business investment goods declines. That is, as the increase in government purchases increases the demand for goods and services, it may also crowd out investment. This crowding-out effect partially offsets the impact of government purchases on aggregate demand, as illustrated in panel (b) of figure 17.7. The initial impact of the increase in government purchases is to shift the aggregate-demand curve from AD_1 to AD_2, but once crowding out takes place, the aggregate-demand curve drops back to AD_3.

To sum up—*when the government increases its purchases by $5 billion, the aggregate demand for goods and services could rise by more or less than $5 billion, depending on whether the multiplier effect or the crowding-out effect is larger.*

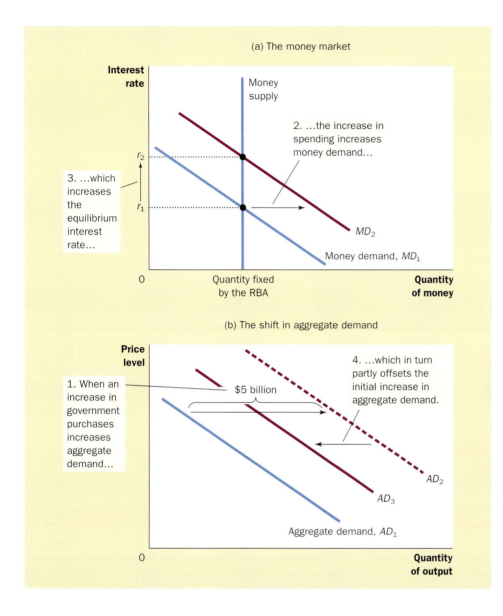

Figure 17.7

THE CROWDING-OUT EFFECT. Panel (a) shows the money market. When the government increases its purchases of goods and services, the resulting increase in income raises the demand for money from MD_1 to MD_2, and this causes the equilibrium interest rate to rise from r_1 to r_2. Panel (b) shows the effects on aggregate demand. The initial impact of the increase in government purchases shifts the aggregate-demand curve from AD_1 to AD_2. Yet because the interest rate is the cost of borrowing, the increase in the interest rate tends to reduce the quantity of goods and services demanded, particularly for investment goods. This crowding out of investment partially offsets the impact of the fiscal expansion on aggregate demand. In the end, the aggregate-demand curve shifts only to AD_3.

CHANGES IN TAXES

The other important instrument of fiscal policy is the level of taxation. When the government cuts taxes, it increases households' take-home pay. Households will save some of this additional income, but they will also spend some of it on consumer goods. Because it increases consumer spending, the tax cut shifts the aggregate-demand curve to the right. Similarly, a tax increase depresses consumer spending and shifts the aggregate-demand curve to the left.

The size of the shift in aggregate demand resulting from a tax change is also affected by the multiplier and crowding-out effects. When the government cuts taxes and stimulates consumer spending, earnings and profits rise, which further stimulates consumer spending. This is the multiplier effect. (The multiplier effect for a tax change will be less than the multiplier effect of an equivalent change in government spending.) At the same time, higher income leads to higher money demand, which tends to raise interest rates. Higher interest rates make borrowing more costly, which reduces investment spending. This is the crowding-out effect. Depending on the size of the multiplier and crowding-out effects, the shift in aggregate demand could be larger or smaller than the tax change that causes it.

In addition to the multiplier and crowding-out effects, there is another important determinant of the size of the shift in aggregate demand that results from a tax change—households' perceptions about whether the tax change is permanent or temporary. For example, suppose that the government announces a tax cut of $1000 per household. In deciding how much of this $1000 to spend, households must ask themselves how long this extra income will last. If households expect the tax cut to be permanent, they will view it as adding substantially to their financial resources and, therefore, increase their spending by a large amount. In this case, the tax cut will have a large impact on aggregate demand. In contrast, if households expect the tax change to be temporary, they will view it as adding only slightly to their financial resources and, therefore, will increase their spending by only a small amount. In this case, the tax cut will have a small impact on aggregate demand.

> **QUICK QUIZ** Suppose that the government reduces spending on highway construction by $10 billion. Which way does the aggregate-demand curve shift? Explain why the shift might be larger than $10 billion. Explain why the shift might be smaller than $10 billion.

FYI

How fiscal policy might affect aggregate supply

So far our discussion of fiscal policy has stressed how changes in government purchases and changes in taxes influence the quantity of goods and services demanded. Most economists believe that the short-run macroeconomic effects of fiscal policy work mainly through aggregate demand. Yet fiscal policy can potentially also influence the quantity of goods and services supplied.

For instance, consider the effects of tax changes on aggregate supply. One of the *Ten Principles of Economics* in chapter 1 is that people respond to incentives. When government policymakers cut tax rates, workers get to keep more of each dollar they earn, so they have a greater incentive to work and to produce goods and services. As a result, the quantity of goods and services supplied is greater at any given price level. This is represented by a shift to the right in the aggregate-supply curve. Some economists, called *supply-siders*, have argued that the influence of tax cuts on aggregate supply is very large. Indeed, some supply-siders claim the influence is so large that a cut in tax rates will actually increase tax revenue by increasing worker effort. Most economists, however, believe that the supply-side effects of tax cuts are much smaller.

Like changes in taxes, changes in government purchases can also potentially affect aggregate supply. Suppose, for instance, that the government increases expenditure on a form of government-provided capital, such as roads. Roads are used by private businesses to make deliveries to their customers; an increase in the quantity of roads increases these businesses' productivity. Hence, when the government spends more on roads, it increases the quantity of goods and services supplied at any given price level and, thus, shifts the aggregate-supply curve to the right. This effect on aggregate supply is probably more important in the long run than in the short run, however, because it would take some time for the government to build the new roads and put them into use.

USING POLICY TO STABILISE THE ECONOMY

We have seen how monetary and fiscal policy can affect the economy's aggregate demand for goods and services. These theoretical insights raise an important policy question: Should policymakers use these instruments in order to control aggregate demand and stabilise the economy? If so, when? If not, why not?

THE CASE FOR ACTIVE STABILISATION POLICY

Let's return to the question that began this chapter. When government spending is cut to eliminate the budget deficit, what should the RBA's advice be? As we have seen, government spending is one determinant of the position of the aggregate-demand curve. When the government cuts spending, aggregate demand will fall, which will depress production and employment in the short run. If the RBA is concerned about this adverse effect of the fiscal policy, it can recommend an expansion of aggregate demand by increasing the money supply. A monetary expansion would reduce interest rates and stimulate consumption and investment spending. If monetary policy responds appropriately, the combined change in monetary and fiscal policy leaves the aggregate demand for goods and services unaffected.

This analysis is exactly that followed by members of the Reserve Bank Board. They know that monetary policy is an important determinant of aggregate demand. They also know that there are other important determinants as well, including fiscal policy as set by the government. As a result, the Board watches the debates over fiscal policy with a keen eye.

This response of monetary policy to the change in fiscal policy is an example of a more general phenomenon—the use of policy instruments to stabilise aggregate demand and, as a result, production and employment. Economic stabilisation has been an explicit goal of Australian macroeconomic policy since the Reserve Bank Act of 1959. This Act states that the RBA should 'contribute to stability of the currency..., the maintenance of full employment; and the economic prosperity and welfare of the people of Australia'. In essence, the RBA is required to be accountable for short-run macroeconomic performance.

The Reserve Bank charter has two implications. The first, more modest, implication is that the RBA should avoid being a cause of economic fluctuations. Thus, most economists advise against large and sudden changes in monetary (or fiscal) policy, for such changes are likely to cause fluctuations in aggregate demand. Moreover, when large changes do occur, it is important that monetary and fiscal policymakers be aware and respond to the other's actions.

The second, more ambitious, implication of the charter is that the RBA should respond to changes in the private economy in order to stabilise aggregate demand. Although recent changes in emphasis of the RBA's responsibilities mean that it is less likely to get involved in management of short-run fluctuations of the economy, there is a strong history of central bank involvement in stabilisation policy.

The Reserve Bank Act was passed not long after the publication of John Maynard Keynes's *The General Theory of Employment, Interest, and Money*. As we discussed in the preceding chapter, *The General Theory* has been one of the most influential books ever written about economics. In it, Keynes emphasised the key role of aggregate demand in explaining short-run economic fluctuations. Keynes claimed that the government should actively stimulate aggregate demand when aggregate demand appeared insufficient to maintain production at its full-employment level. Government stimulus could take the form of expansionary fiscal policy or expansionary monetary policy.

Keynes (and his many followers) argued that aggregate demand fluctuates because of largely irrational waves of pessimism and optimism. He used the term *animal spirits* to refer to these arbitrary changes in attitude. When pessimism reigns, households reduce consumption spending, and firms reduce investment spending. The result is reduced aggregate demand, lower production and higher unemployment. Conversely, when optimism reigns, households and firms increase spending. The result is higher aggregate demand, higher production and inflationary pressure. Notice that these changes in attitude are, to some extent, self-fulfilling.

In principle, the government can adjust its monetary and fiscal policy in response to these waves of optimism and pessimism and, thereby, stabilise aggregate demand. For example, when people are excessively pessimistic, the RBA can expand the money supply; when they are excessively optimistic, it can contract the money supply. A former chairman of the US Federal Reserve described this view of monetary policy very simply: 'The Federal Reserve's job is to take away the punch bowl just as the party gets going.'

CASE STUDY   KEYNESIAN THINKING TODAY

Keynesian economics was declared dead and buried by Nobel prize winner Robert Lucas in 1980 when he said: 'One cannot find good, under-forty economists who identify themselves or their work as Keynesian...At research seminars, people don't take Keynesian theorizing seriously anymore: the audience starts to whisper and giggle to one another.' And yet Keynesian economists have been hiding away in governments around the world for decades, modelling the economy and influencing policy.

Keynes first published his book *The General Theory of Employment, Interest, and Money* in 1936. The height of its influence was in the United States in the 1960s and 1970s. When a reporter in 1961 asked President John F. Kennedy why he advocated a tax cut, Kennedy replied, 'To stimulate the economy. Don't you remember your Economics 101?' Kennedy's policy was, in fact, based on the analysis of taxes we have developed in this chapter. His goal was to increase aggregate demand in order to stimulate production and employment.

In choosing this policy, Kennedy was relying on his team of economic advisers. This team included such prominent economists as James Tobin and Robert Solow, who later would win Nobel prizes for their contributions to economics. As students in the 1940s, these economists had closely studied John Maynard Keynes's *General Theory*, which then was only a few years old. When the Kennedy advisers proposed cutting taxes, they were putting Keynes's ideas into action.

Although tax changes can have a potent influence on aggregate demand, they have other effects as well. In particular, by changing the incentives that people face, taxes can alter the aggregate supply of goods and services. Part

John Maynard Keynes

of the Kennedy proposal was an investment tax credit, which gives a tax break to firms that invest in new capital. Higher investment would not only stimulate aggregate demand immediately but would also increase the economy's productive capacity over time. Thus, the short-run goal of increasing production through higher aggregate demand was coupled with a long-run goal of increasing production through higher aggregate supply. The tax cut would help in this because it was an investment tax credit, not simply an across-the-board tax cut. And, indeed, when the tax cut Kennedy proposed was finally enacted in 1964, it helped usher in a period of robust economic growth.

Policymakers in various countries have, from time to time, proposed using fiscal policy as a tool for controlling aggregate demand. For example, some of the recently elected governments in Europe have a decidedly Keynesian outlook. Germany and France both have finance ministers who have advocated Keynesian-type expansionary fiscal policies to combat European unemployment of over 10%.

The Japanese government boosted government expenditure in 1998 to try to kick-start the Japanese economy. Both private consumption and investment demand were low and exports were down due to the downturn in the economies of Japan's trading partners in Asia. The Japanese government was urged by its trading partners to make up for the lack of aggregate demand by 'priming the pump'.

Similarly, when President Clinton moved into the White House in 1993, one of his first proposals was a 'stimulus package' of increased government spending. Many economists considered the Clinton proposal too late to be of much help. Moreover, deficit reduction to encourage long-run economic growth was considered a higher priority than a short-run expansion in aggregate demand. The elimination of the budget deficit reduces crowding out and therefore encourages private sector investment.

THE CASE AGAINST ACTIVE STABILISATION POLICY

Some economists argue that the government should avoid using monetary and fiscal policy to try to stabilise the economy. They claim that these policy instruments should be set to achieve long-run goals, such as rapid economic growth and low inflation, and that the economy should be left to deal with short-run fluctuations on its own. Although these economists may admit that monetary and fiscal policy can stabilise the economy in theory, they doubt whether it can do so in practice.

The main argument against active monetary and fiscal policy is that these policies affect the economy with a substantial lag. As we have seen, monetary policy works by changing interest rates, which in turn influence investment spending. But many firms make investment plans far in advance. Thus, changes in monetary policy are thought to take at least 6 months to have much effect on output and employment, and these effects can last for several years. Critics of stabilisation policy argue that, because of this lag, the RBA should not try to fine-tune the economy. They claim that the RBA often reacts too late to changing economic conditions and, as a result, ends up being a cause rather than a cure of economic fluctuations. They advocate a passive monetary policy, such as low and steady growth in the money supply.

Fiscal policy also works with a lag but, unlike the lag in monetary policy, the lag in fiscal policy is largely attributable to the political process. In Australia, this is because changes in fiscal policy involve adjustments to the government's spending and taxing behaviour that may not be fully supported by the Senate. So although the government budget is, by convention, usually accepted by the Senate, by the time it has been negotiated, passed and implemented, the condition of the economy may well have changed.

These lags in monetary and fiscal policy are a problem in part because economic forecasting is so imprecise. If forecasters could accurately predict the condition of the economy a year in advance, then monetary and fiscal policymakers could look ahead when making policy decisions. In this case, policymakers could stabilise the economy, despite the lags they face. In practice, however, recessions and depressions arrive without much advance warning. The best policymakers can do at any time is to respond to economic changes as they occur.

AUTOMATIC STABILISERS

All economists—both advocates and critics of stabilisation policy—agree that the lags in the implementation of policy render policy less useful as a tool for short-run stabilisation. The economy would be more stable, therefore, if policymakers could find a way to avoid some of these lags. In fact, they have. **Automatic stabilisers** are changes in fiscal policy that stimulate aggregate demand when the economy goes into a recession without policymakers having to take any deliberate action.

The most important automatic stabiliser is the tax system. When the economy goes into a recession, the amount of taxes collected by the government falls automatically because almost all taxes are closely tied to economic activity. Personal income tax depends on households' incomes, payroll tax depends on workers' earnings, and company income tax depends on firms' profits. Because incomes, earnings and profits all fall in a recession, the government's tax revenue falls as well. This automatic tax cut stimulates aggregate demand and, thereby, reduces the magnitude of economic fluctuations.

Government outlays also act as automatic stabilisers. In particular, when the economy goes into a recession and workers are laid off, more people apply for unemployment benefits and other forms of income support. This automatic increase in government outlays stimulates aggregate demand at exactly the time when aggregate demand is insufficient to maintain full employment. Indeed, when the unemployment benefits system was first introduced in 1945, economists who advocated this policy did so in part because of its power as an automatic stabiliser.

The automatic stabilisers in the Australian economy are not sufficiently strong to prevent recessions completely. Nonetheless, without these automatic stabilisers, output and employment would probably be more volatile than they are. For this reason, many economists oppose any sort of legislated requirement for a balanced budget. When the economy goes into a recession, taxes fall, government spending rises and the government's budget moves towards deficit. If the government faced a strict balanced-budget rule, it would be forced to look for ways to raise taxes or cut spending in a recession. In other words, a strict balanced-budget rule would eliminate the automatic stabilisers inherent in our current system of taxes and government spending.

---

automatic stabilisers

changes in fiscal policy that stimulate aggregate demand when the economy goes into a recession without policymakers having to take any deliberate action or rein in aggregate demand when the economy booms

IN THE NEWS

The independence of the Reserve Bank of Australia

CLOSELY RELATED TO THE QUESTION OF whether monetary and fiscal policy should be used to stabilise the economy is the question of who should set monetary and fiscal policy. In Australia, monetary policy is made by a central bank that operates free of most political pressures; the Governor of the RBA is increasing in importance. According to the following article, the RBA's power is greater than ever before, but it is being forced to rethink its management of the Australian economy.

Inside the Bank that Runs Australia

BY BRIAN TOOHEY

There are two signatures on Australia's bank notes. The squiggle in the top left corner is that of the Treasury Secretary, Ted Evans. The one below is that of the Reserve Bank Governor, Ian Macfarlane. Despite equal billing on the notes, there is no doubt that Macfarlane creates the bigger buzz in both the marketplace and the higher levels of government. And for good reason: rarely in Australia has so much been riding on the behaviour of a single public official.

It wasn't always like this. Two decades ago, no-one was in any doubt that the Treasury Secretary, Sir Frederick Wheeler, carried far more clout than the Governor, Sir John Phillips. Likewise, Wheeler's successor at Treasury, John Stone, clearly overshadowed his counterpart at the Reserve, Harry Knight.

All that has changed. A whole new industry exists to second-guess what Macfarlane will do next. How will he respond to the latest set of statistics? Has he phoned other members of the RBA board? Is he due to give a speech? Put out a statement? Drop a clue as to whether he will shift interest rates up or down a notch or two?

Thousands of finance industry economists, dealers and wire service journalists are now employed to provide the answers. Apart from altering the economic outlook for the entire nation, the answers can make or break those players who use the futures markets to punt on what is going on in Macfarlane's head.

In contrast, few people are even interested in whether Ted Evans turns up to work. This is not a comment on the respective abilities of the two men, merely a statement which recognises the enormous increase in power wielded by the Governor of the Reserve in the wake of financial deregulation in the mid-1980s.

Before then, the exchange rate was set in Canberra by an official committee on which Treasury was the dominant influence. Now, the price of the Australian dollar is set predominantly in the market, with any residual official influence residing solely within the Reserve's Martin Place headquarters in Sydney.

Before deregulation, official interest rates were set by a Cabinet subcommittee in which Treasury played a key role, especially in Stone's day. Back then, changes in official interest rates were announced by the Treasurer. Today, rate changes are indisputably within the Reserve's province, and Treasurers invite a swift rap over the knuckles if they try to muscle in on the action, let alone reveal the detail of any change.

Macfarlane does not act alone. He needs the support of a board which includes some of the nation's most confident business executives. He also takes advice from close colleagues such as a deputy governor, Stephen Grenville, and an assistant governor, Glenn Stevens. In the end, however, there is little doubt that Macfarlane is the dominant influence on interest rate policy.

SOURCE: *Australian Financial Review*, 27 September 1997, p. 23.

THE RESERVE BANK OF AUSTRALIA

> **QUICK QUIZ** Suppose firms become pessimistic about the future. What happens to aggregate demand? If the RBA wants to stabilise aggregate demand, how should it alter the money supply? If it does this, what happens to the interest rate?

THE ECONOMY IN THE LONG RUN AND THE SHORT RUN

At this point, we should pause and reflect on a seemingly awkward embarrassment of riches. It might appear as if we now have two theories for how interest rates are determined. Chapter 10 said that the interest rate adjusts to balance the supply of and demand for loanable funds (that is, national saving and desired investment). In contrast, this chapter said that the interest rate adjusts to balance the supply of and demand for money. Which of these theories is right? The answer is 'both'.

To understand how this can be true, we must consider the differences between the long-run and short-run behaviour of the economy. Three macroeconomic variables are of central importance—the economy's output of goods and services, the interest rate and the price level. According to the classical macroeconomic theory we developed in chapters 9, 10 and 13, these variables are determined as follows:

1. *Output* is determined by the supplies of capital and labour and the available production technology for turning capital and labour into output.

2. For any given level of output, the *interest rate* adjusts to balance the supply of and demand for loanable funds.

3. The *price level* adjusts to balance the supply of and demand for money. Changes in the supply of money lead to proportionate changes in the price level.

These are three of the essential propositions of classical economic theory. Most economists believe that these propositions do a good job of describing how the economy works *in the long run*.

Yet these propositions do not hold in the short run. As we discussed in the preceding chapter, many prices are slow to adjust to changes in the money supply. As a result, the overall price level cannot, by itself, balance the supply of and demand for money in the short run. This price inflexibility forces the interest rate to move in order to bring the money market into equilibrium. These changes in the interest rate, in turn, affect the aggregate demand for goods and services. As aggregate demand fluctuates, the economy's output of goods and services moves away from the level determined by factor supplies and technology.

For thinking about the economy in the short run, then, it is best to reverse the order of analysis:

1. The *price level* is stuck at some level and, in the short run, is relatively unresponsive to changing economic conditions.

2. For any given price level, the *interest rate* adjusts to balance the supply of and demand for money.

3. The level of *output* responds to changes in the aggregate demand for goods and services, which is in part determined by the interest rate that balances the money market.

Figure 17.8 (p. 388) summarises these propositions and highlights the differences between the economy in the long run and the economy in the short run.

Thus, the different theories of the interest rate are useful for different purposes. When thinking about the long-run determinants of interest rates, it is best to keep in mind the loanable-funds theory. This theory highlights the importance of an economy's saving propensities and investment opportunities. In contrast, when thinking about the short-run determinants of interest rates, it is best to keep in mind the liquidity-preference theory. This theory highlights the importance of monetary policy.

QUICK QUIZ Explain the difference between long-run and short-run macroeconomic analysis. ◆ What theory of the interest rate is best for analysing the economy in the long run? What theory is best for analysing the economy in the short run?

FYI

The long run and the short run: An algebraic explanation

A FEW MATHEMATICALLY inclined readers might find the following algebraic explanation helpful for clarifying the difference between the economy's behaviour in the long run and its behaviour in the short run. If you are not so inclined, just skip this box.

We can view the economy as described by two key markets: the money market and the goods market. Supply and demand in the money market are described by the equation:

$$M = L(r)P$$

where M is the money supply, P the price level and r the interest rate. $L(r)$ is a function showing how money demand responds to the interest rate. This is called the *LM* (liquidity-money) equation. Supply and demand in the goods market are described by the equation:

$$Y = C + I(r) + G$$

where Y is output, C consumption, I investment and G government purchases. (For simplicity, we assume here a closed economy, so net exports do not enter this equation.) Note that national saving, $Y - C - G$, represents the supply of loanable funds, and investment, $I(r)$, represents the demand for loanable funds, which depends on the interest rate. This is called the *IS* (investment–saving) equation. The *IS* and *LM* equations together describe two relationships among three variables: output Y, the interest rate r and the price level P.

Now let's compare the long run and short run. Over both time horizons, the *IS* and the *LM* equations must be satisfied to ensure equilibrium in both the goods market and the money market. But different variables move to maintain equilibrium in the long run and the short run. Here is the difference:

◆ In the long run, output Y is determined by factor supplies and technology. Given the fixed level of output, the interest rate r adjusts to satisfy the *IS* equation. Given this interest rate, the price level P adjusts to satisfy the *LM* equation.

◆ In the short run, the price level P is stuck at a level set in the past. Given the fixed price level, the interest rate r adjusts to satisfy the *LM* equation. Given this interest rate, the level of output Y adjusts to satisfy the *IS* equation.

The long-run case corresponds to our analysis in chapters 9, 10 and 13. The short-run case corresponds to our analysis of monetary and fiscal policy in this chapter.

Figure 17.8

HOW LONG-RUN AND SHORT-RUN MACROECONOMIC THEORIES DIFFER. This figure illustrates the differences between the long-run and short-run behaviour of the economy. In the long run, the interest rate and price level adjust to accommodate a fixed level of output. In the short run, the interest rate and output adjust to accommodate a predetermined level of prices.

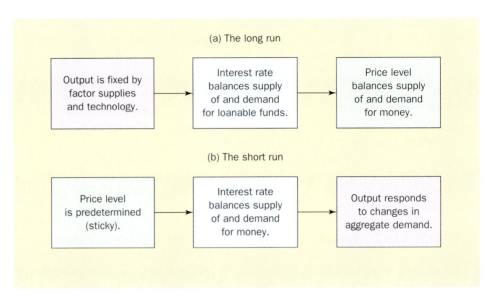

CONCLUSION

Before policymakers make any change in policy, they need to consider all the effects of their decisions. Earlier in the book we examined classical models of the economy, which describe the long-run effects of monetary and fiscal policy. There we saw how fiscal policy influences saving, investment, the trade balance and long-run growth, and how monetary policy influences the price level and the inflation rate.

In this chapter we examined the short-run effects of monetary and fiscal policy. We saw how these policy instruments can change the aggregate demand for goods and services and, thereby, alter the economy's production and employment in the short run. When governments reduce their spending in order to balance the budget, they need to consider both the long-run effects on saving and growth and the short-run effects on aggregate demand and employment. When the RBA reduces the growth rate of the money supply, it must take into account the long-run effect on inflation as well as the short-run effect on production. In the next chapter we discuss the transition between the short run and the long run more fully, and we see that policymakers often face a trade-off between long-run and short-run goals.

Summary

- In developing a theory of short-run economic fluctuations, Keynes proposed the theory of liquidity preference to explain the determinants of the interest rate. According to this theory, the interest rate adjusts to balance the supply of and demand for money.

- An increase in the price level raises money demand and increases the interest rate that brings the money market into equilibrium. Because the interest rate represents the cost of borrowing, a higher interest rate reduces investment and, thereby, the quantity of goods and services demanded. The downward-sloping aggregate-demand curve expresses this negative relationship between the price level and the quantity demanded.

- Policymakers can influence aggregate demand with monetary policy. An increase in the money supply reduces the equilibrium interest rate for any given price level. Because a lower interest rate stimulates investment spending, the aggregate-demand curve shifts to the right. Conversely, a decrease in the money supply raises the equilibrium interest rate for any given price level and shifts the aggregate-demand curve to the left.

- Policymakers can also influence aggregate demand with fiscal policy. An increase in government purchases or a cut in taxes shifts the aggregate-demand curve to the right. A decrease in government purchases or an increase in taxes shifts the aggregate-demand curve to the left.

- When the government alters spending or taxes, the resulting shift in aggregate demand can be larger or smaller than the fiscal change. The multiplier effect tends to amplify the effects of fiscal policy on aggregate demand. The crowding-out effect tends to dampen the effects of fiscal policy on aggregate demand.

- Because monetary and fiscal policy can influence aggregate demand, the government sometimes uses these policy instruments in an attempt to stabilise the economy. Economists disagree about how active the government should be in this effort. According to advocates of active stabilisation policy, changes in attitudes by households and firms shift aggregate demand; if the government does not respond, the result is undesirable and unnecessary fluctuations in output and employment. According to critics of active stabilisation policy, monetary and fiscal policy work with such long lags that attempts at stabilising the economy often end up being destabilising.

- The effects of monetary and fiscal policy depend on the time horizon. The aggregate-demand effects on output emphasised in this chapter hold only in the short run, over which prices are sticky. In the long run, output is determined by factor supplies and technology.

Key concepts

theory of liquidity preference, p. 369
multiplier effect, p. 376

crowding-out effect, p. 377
automatic stabilisers, p. 384

Questions for review

1. What is the theory of liquidity preference? How does it help explain the downward slope of the aggregate-demand curve?

2. Use the theory of liquidity preference to explain how a decrease in the money supply affects the aggregate-demand curve.

3. The government spends $3 billion to build new roads for the Olympics. Explain why aggregate demand might increase by more than $3 billion. Explain why aggregate demand might increase by less than $3 billion.

4. Suppose that survey measures of consumer confidence indicate a wave of pessimism is sweeping the country. If policymakers do nothing, what will happen to aggregate demand? What should the RBA do if it wants to stabilise aggregate demand? If the RBA does nothing, what might the government do to stabilise aggregate demand?

5. Give an example of a government policy that acts as an automatic stabiliser. Explain why this policy has this effect.

6. Why do changes in monetary policy have different effects over different time horizons?

Problems and applications

1. Explain how each of the following developments would affect the supply of money, the demand for money and the interest rate. Illustrate your answers with diagrams.
   a. A wave of optimism boosts business investment.
   b. The RBA is worried about the possibility of bad loans made by Australian banks and suggests they increase their holdings of reserves.
   c. An increase in oil prices shifts the short-run aggregate-supply curve upwards.
   d. Households decide to hold more money to use for holiday shopping.

2. Suppose banks install automatic teller machines on every block and, by making cash readily available, reduce the amount of money people want to hold.
   a. Assume the RBA does not change the money supply. According to the theory of liquidity preference, what happens to the interest rate? What happens to aggregate demand?
   b. If the RBA wants to stabilise aggregate demand, how should it respond?

3. Consider two policies—a tax cut that will last for only 1 year, and a tax cut that is expected to be permanent. Which policy will stimulate greater spending by consumers? Which policy will have the greater impact on aggregate demand? Explain.

4. The interest rate in Australia fell sharply during 1991. Many observers believed this decline showed that monetary policy was quite expansionary during the year. Could this conclusion be incorrect? (*Hint:* Australia was in the middle of a recession in 1991.)

5. In 1984, new legislation allowed banks to pay interest on cheque account deposits, which they could not do previously.
   a. If we define money to include cheque account deposits, what effect did this legislation have on money demand? Explain.
   b. If the RBA had maintained a constant money supply in the face of this change, what would have happened to the interest rate? What would have happened to aggregate demand and aggregate output?
   c. If the RBA had maintained a constant market interest rate (the interest rate on non-monetary assets) in the face of this change, what change in the money supply would have been necessary? What would have happened to aggregate demand and aggregate output?

6. This chapter explains that expansionary monetary policy reduces the interest rate and thus stimulates demand for consumption and investment goods. Explain how such a policy also stimulates the demand for net exports.

7. Suppose economists observe that an increase in government spending of $10 billion raises the total demand for goods and services by $30 billion.
   a. If these economists ignore the possibility of crowding out, what would they estimate the marginal propensity to consume (*MPC*) to be?
   b. Now suppose the economists allow for crowding out. Would their new estimate of the *MPC* be larger or smaller than their initial one?

8. Suppose the government reduces taxes by $20 million, that there is no crowding out, and that the marginal propensity to consume is ¾.
   a. What is the initial effect of the tax reduction on aggregate demand?
   b. What additional effects follow this initial effect? What is the total effect of the tax cut on aggregate demand?
   c. How does the total effect of this $20 million tax cut compare with the total effect of a $20 million increase in government purchases? Why?

9. Suppose consumers suddenly become more optimistic about their future incomes and decide to purchase $30 million of additional goods and services. Will this change have a 'multiplied' effect on total output? Explain.

10. Suppose government spending increases. Would the effect on aggregate demand be larger if the RBA took no action in response, or if the RBA were committed to maintaining a fixed interest rate? Explain.

11. In which of the following circumstances is expansionary fiscal policy more likely to lead to a short-run increase in investment? Explain.
    a. when the investment accelerator is large, or when it is small?
    b. when the interest sensitivity of investment is large, or when it is small?

12. Assume the economy is in a recession. Explain how each of the following policies would affect

consumption and investment. In each case, indicate any direct effects, any effects resulting from changes in total output, any effects resulting from changes in the interest rate, and the overall effect. If there are conflicting effects making the answer ambiguous, say so.
   a. an increase in government spending
   b. a reduction in taxes
   c. an expansion of the money supply

13. For various reasons, fiscal policy changes automatically when output and employment fluctuate.
    a. Explain why tax revenue changes when the economy goes into a recession.
    b. Explain why government spending changes when the economy goes into a recession.
    c. If the government were to operate under a strict balanced-budget rule, what would it have to do in a recession? Would that make the recession more or less severe?

14. In response to an increase in the money supply, would the following things be smaller, larger, or no different in the long run than in the short run?
    a. consumer expenditures
    b. the price level
    c. the interest rate
    d. aggregate output

15. Suppose that the RBA decides to expand the money supply.
    a. What is the effect of this policy on the interest rate in the short run? Illustrate your answer with an appropriate diagram.
    b. What is the effect of this policy on the interest rate in the long run? How do you know?
    c. What characteristic of the economy makes the short-run effect of monetary policy on the interest rate different from the long-run effect?

18

THE SHORT-RUN TRADE-OFF BETWEEN INFLATION AND UNEMPLOYMENT

IN THIS CHAPTER YOU WILL

Learn why policymakers face a short-run trade-off between inflation and unemployment

Consider why the inflation–unemployment trade-off disappears in the long run

See how supply shocks can shift the inflation–unemployment trade-off

Consider the short-run cost of reducing the rate of inflation

See how policymakers' credibility might affect the cost of reducing inflation

Two closely watched indicators of economic performance are inflation and unemployment. When the Australian Bureau of Statistics releases data on these variables each month, policymakers are eager to hear the news. Some commentators have added together the inflation rate and the unemployment rate to produce a *misery index*, which purports to measure the health of the economy.

How are these two measures of economic performance related to each other? Earlier in the book we discussed the long-run determinants of unemployment and the long-run determinants of inflation. We saw that the natural rate of unemployment depends on various features of the labour market, such as minimum-wage laws, the market power of unions, the role of efficiency wages, and the effectiveness of job search. In contrast, the inflation rate depends primarily on growth in the quantity of money, which the central bank influences. In the long run, therefore, inflation and unemployment are largely unrelated problems.

In the short run, just the opposite is true. One of the *Ten Principles of Economics* discussed in chapter 1 is that society faces a short-run trade-off between inflation and unemployment. If monetary and fiscal policymakers expand aggregate demand, they can lower unemployment in the short run, but only at the cost of higher inflation. If they contract aggregate demand, they can lower inflation, but only at the cost of temporarily higher unemployment.

In this chapter we examine this trade-off more closely. The relationship between inflation and unemployment is a topic that has attracted the attention of some of the most important economists of the last 50 years. The best way to understand this relationship is to see how thinking about it has evolved over time. As we will see, the history of thought regarding inflation and unemployment since the 1950s is inextricably connected to the history of the Australian economy. These two histories will show why the trade-off between inflation and unemployment holds in the short run, why it does not hold in the long run, and what issues it raises for economic policymakers.

THE PHILLIPS CURVE

The short-run relationship between inflation and unemployment is often called the *Phillips curve*. We begin our story with the discovery of the Phillips curve and its migration to Australia.

ORIGINS OF THE PHILLIPS CURVE

In 1958, economist A. W. Phillips from New Zealand published an article in the British journal *Economica* that would make him famous. The article was entitled 'The Relationship between Unemployment and the Rate of Change of Money Wages in the United Kingdom, 1861–1957'. In it, Phillips showed a negative correlation between the rate of unemployment and the rate of inflation. That is, Phillips showed that years with low unemployment tend to have high inflation, and years with high unemployment tend to have low inflation. (Phillips examined inflation in nominal wages rather than inflation in prices, but for our purposes that distinction is not important. These two measures of inflation usually move together.) Phillips concluded that two important macroeconomic variables —inflation and unemployment—were linked in a way that economists had not previously appreciated.

Although Phillips's discovery was based on data for the United Kingdom, researchers quickly extended his finding to other countries. Two years after Phillips published his article, economists Paul Samuelson and Robert Solow published an article in the *American Economic Review* called 'Analytics of Anti-Inflation Policy' in which they showed a similar negative correlation between inflation and unemployment in data for the United States. They reasoned that this correlation arose because low unemployment was associated with high aggregate demand and because high demand puts upward pressure on wages and prices throughout the economy. Samuelson and Solow dubbed the negative association between inflation and unemployment the **Phillips curve**. Figure 18.1 shows an example of a Phillips curve like the one found by Samuelson and Solow.

Phillips curve
a curve that shows the short-run trade-off between inflation and unemployment

As the title of their paper suggests, Samuelson and Solow were interested in the Phillips curve because they believed that it held important lessons for policymakers. In particular, they suggested that the Phillips curve offers policymakers a menu of possible economic outcomes. By altering monetary and fiscal policy to influence aggregate demand, policymakers could choose any point on this curve. Point A offers high unemployment and low inflation. Point B offers low unemployment and high inflation. Policymakers might prefer both low

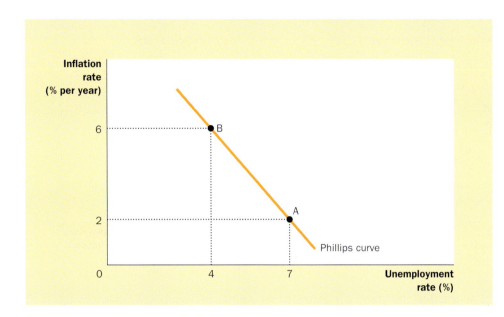

Figure 18.1

THE PHILLIPS CURVE. The Phillips curve illustrates a negative association between the inflation rate and the unemployment rate. At point A, inflation is low and unemployment is high. At point B, inflation is high and unemployment is low.

inflation and low unemployment, but the historical data as summarised by the Phillips curve indicate that this combination is impossible. According to Samuelson and Solow, policymakers face a trade-off between inflation and unemployment, and the Phillips curve illustrates that trade-off.

AGGREGATE DEMAND, AGGREGATE SUPPLY AND THE PHILLIPS CURVE

The model of aggregate demand and aggregate supply provides an easy explanation for the menu of possible outcomes described by the Phillips curve. *The Phillips curve simply shows the combinations of inflation and unemployment that arise in the short run as shifts in the aggregate-demand curve move the economy along the short-run aggregate-supply curve.* As we discussed in chapter 16, the greater the aggregate demand for goods and services, the greater the economy's output and the higher the overall price level. Okun's law tells us that greater output means a lower rate of unemployment. In addition, because the previous year's price level is already given, the higher the price level in the current year, the higher the rate of inflation. Thus, an increase in aggregate demand moves the economy along the Phillips curve to a point with lower unemployment and higher inflation.

To see how this works, let's consider an example. To keep the numbers simple, imagine that the price level (as measured, for instance, by the consumer price index) equals 100 in the year 2000. Figure 18.2 shows two possible outcomes that might occur in year 2001. Panel (a) shows the two outcomes using the model of aggregate demand and aggregate supply. Panel (b) illustrates the same two outcomes using the Phillips curve.

In panel (a) of the figure, we can see the implications for output and the price level in the year 2001. If the aggregate demand for goods and services is

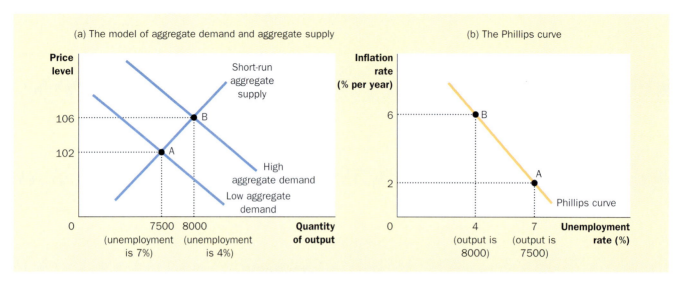

Figure 18.2

HOW THE PHILLIPS CURVE IS RELATED TO THE MODEL OF AGGREGATE DEMAND AND AGGREGATE SUPPLY. This figure assumes a price level of 100 for the year 2000 and charts possible outcomes for the year 2001. Panel (a) shows the model of aggregate demand and aggregate supply. If aggregate demand is low, the economy is at point A; output is low (7500) and the price level is low (102). If aggregate demand is high, the economy is at point B; output is high (8000) and the price level is high (106). Panel (b) shows the implications for the Phillips curve. Point A, which arises when aggregate demand is low, has high unemployment (7%) and low inflation (2%). Point B, which arises when aggregate demand is high, has low unemployment (4%) and high inflation (6%).

relatively low, the economy experiences outcome A. The economy produces output of 7500, and the price level is 102. In contrast, if aggregate demand is relatively high, the economy experiences outcome B. Output is 8000, and the price level is 106. Thus, higher aggregate demand moves the economy to an equilibrium with higher output and a higher price level.

In panel (b) of the figure, we can see what these two possible outcomes mean for unemployment and inflation. Because firms need more workers when they produce a greater output of goods and services, unemployment is lower in outcome B than in outcome A. In this example, when output rises from 7500 to 8000, unemployment falls from 7% to 4%. Moreover, because the price level is higher at outcome B than at outcome A, the inflation rate (the percentage change in the price level from the previous year) is also higher. In particular, since the price level was 100 in the year 2000, outcome A has an inflation rate of 2%, and outcome B has an inflation rate of 6%. Thus, we can compare the two possible outcomes for the economy either in terms of output and the price level (using the model of aggregate demand and aggregate supply) or in terms of unemployment and inflation (using the Phillips curve).

As we saw in the preceding chapter, monetary and fiscal policy can shift the aggregate-demand curve. Therefore, monetary and fiscal policy can move the economy along the Phillips curve. Increases in the money supply, increases in

IN THE NEWS

The effects of low unemployment

ACCORDING TO THE PHILLIPS CURVE, when unemployment falls to low levels, wages and prices start to rise more quickly. The following article illustrates this link between labour-market conditions and inflation.

Tighter Labor Market Widens Inflation Fears

BY ROBERT D. HERSHEY, JR

REMINGTON, VA—Trinity Packaging's plant here recently hired a young man for a hot, entry-level job feeding plastic scrap onto a conveyor belt. The pay was OK for unskilled labor—a good $3 or so above the federal minimum of $4.25 an hour—but the new worker lasted only one shift.

'He worked Friday night and then just told the supervisor that this work's too hard—and we haven't seen him since,' said Pat Roe, a personnel director for the Trinity Packaging Corporation, a producer of plastic bags for supermarkets and other users. 'Three years ago he'd have probably stuck it out.'

This is just one of the many examples of how a growing number of companies these days are facing something they have not seen for many years: a tight labor market in which many workers can be much more choosy about their job. Breaking a sweat can be reason enough to quit in search of better opportunities.

'This summer's been extremely difficult, with unemployment so low,' said Eleanor J. Brown, proprietor of a small temporary-help agency in nearby Culpeper, which supplies workers to Trinity Packaging. 'It's hard to find, especially, industrial workers and laborers.'

From iron mines near Lake Superior to retailers close to Puget Sound to construction contractors around Atlanta, a wide range of employers in many parts of the country are grappling with an inability to fill their ranks with qualified workers. These areas of virtually full employment hold important implications for household incomes, financial markets, and political campaigns as well as business profitability itself.

So far, the tightening labor market has generated only scattered—and in most cases modest—pay increases. Most companies, unable to pass on higher costs by raising prices because of intense competition from foreign and domestic rivals, are working even harder to keep a lid on labor costs, in part by adopting novel ways of coupling pay to profits.

'The overriding need is for expense control,' said Kenneth T. Mayland, chief financial economist at Keycorp, a Cleveland bank, 'at a time when revenue growth is constrained.'

But with unemployment already at a low 5.5 percent and the economy looking stronger than expected this summer, more analysts are worried that it may be only a matter of time before wage pressures begin to build again as they did in the late 1980s…

The labor shortages are widespread and include both skilled and unskilled jobs. Among the hardest occupations to fill are computer analyst and programmer, aerospace engineer, construction trades worker, and various types of salespeople. But even fast-food establishments in the St Louis area and elsewhere have resorted to signing bonuses as well as premium pay and more generous benefits to attract applicants…

So far, upward pressure on pay is relatively modest, a phenomenon that economists say is surprising in light of an uninterrupted business expansion that is now five and a half years old.

'We have less wage pressure than, historically, anyone would have guessed,' said Stuart G. Hoffman, chief economist at PNC Bank in Pittsburgh.

But wages have already crept up a bit and could accelerate even if the economy slackens from its recent rapid growth pace. And if the economy maintains significant momentum, some analysts say, all bets are off. If growth continues another six months at above 2.5 percent or so, Mark Zandi, chief economist for Regional Financial Associates, said, 'we'll be looking at wage inflation right square in the eye…'

One worker who has taken advantage of the current environment is Clyde Long, a thirty-year-old who switched jobs to join Trinity Packaging in May. He had been working about two miles away at Ross Industries, which makes food-processing equipment, and quit without having anything else lined up.

In a week, Mr Long had hired on at Trinity where, as a press operator, he now earns $8.55 an hour—$1.25 more than at his old job—with better benefits and training as well. 'It's a whole lot better here,' he said.

SOURCE: *New York Times*, 5 September 1996, p. D1.

government spending, or cuts in taxes shift the aggregate-demand curve to the right and move the economy to a point on the Phillips curve with lower unemployment and higher inflation. Decreases in the money supply, cuts in government spending, or increases in taxes shift the aggregate-demand curve to the left and move the economy to a point on the Phillips curve with lower inflation and higher unemployment. In this sense, the Phillips curve offers policymakers a menu of combinations of inflation and unemployment.

> **QUICK QUIZ** Draw the Phillips curve. Use the model of aggregate demand and aggregate supply to show how policy can move the economy from a point on this curve with high inflation to a point with low inflation.

SHIFTS IN THE PHILLIPS CURVE: THE ROLE OF EXPECTATIONS

The Phillips curve seems to offer policymakers a menu of possible inflation–unemployment outcomes. But does this menu remain stable over time? Is the Phillips curve a relationship on which policymakers can rely? These are the questions that economists took up in the late 1960s, shortly after Samuelson and Solow had introduced the Phillips curve into the macroeconomic policy debate.

THE LONG-RUN PHILLIPS CURVE

In 1968, economist Milton Friedman published a paper in the *American Economic Review*, based on an address he had recently given as president of the American Economic Association. The paper was entitled 'The Role of Monetary Policy'. It contained sections on 'What Monetary Policy Can Do' and 'What Monetary Policy Cannot Do'. Friedman argued that one thing monetary policy cannot do, other than for only a short time, is pick a combination of inflation and unemployment on the Phillips curve. At about the same time, another economist, Edmund Phelps, also published a paper denying the existence of a long-run trade-off between inflation and unemployment.

Friedman and Phelps reasoned from classical principles of macroeconomics, which we discussed in chapters 9 to 15. Recall that classical theory points to growth in the quantity of money as the main determinant of inflation. But classical theory also states that monetary growth does not have real effects—it merely alters all prices and nominal incomes proportionately. In particular, monetary growth does not influence those factors that determine the economy's unemployment rate, such as the market power of unions, the role of efficiency wages, or the process of job search. Friedman and Phelps concluded that there is no reason to think the rate of inflation would, *in the long run*, be related to the rate of unemployment.

Here, in his own words, is Friedman's view about what a central bank can hope to accomplish in the long run:

> The monetary authority controls nominal quantities—directly, the quantity of its own liabilities [currency plus bank reserves]. In principle, it can use this control

to peg a nominal quantity—an exchange rate, the price level, the nominal level of national income, the quantity of money by one definition or another—or to peg the change in a nominal quantity—the rate of inflation or deflation, the rate of growth or decline in nominal national income, the rate of growth of the quantity of money. It cannot use its control over nominal quantities to peg a real quantity—the real rate of interest, the rate of unemployment, the level of real national income, the real quantity of money, the rate of growth of real national income, or the rate of growth of the real quantity of money.

These views have important implications for the Phillips curve. In particular, they imply that monetary policymakers face a long-run Phillips curve that is vertical, as in figure 18.3. In Australia, if the RBA increases the money supply slowly, the inflation rate is low, and the economy finds itself at point A. If the RBA increases the money supply quickly, the inflation rate is high, and the economy finds itself at point B. In either case, the unemployment rate tends towards its normal level, called the *natural rate of unemployment*. The vertical long-run Phillips curve illustrates the conclusion that unemployment does not depend on money growth and inflation in the long run.

The vertical long-run Phillips curve is, in essence, one expression of the classical idea of monetary neutrality. As you may recall, we expressed this idea in chapter 16 with a vertical long-run aggregate-supply curve. Indeed, as figure 18.4 illustrates, the vertical long-run Phillips curve and the vertical long-run aggregate-supply curve are two sides of the same coin. In panel (a) of this figure, an increase in the money supply shifts the aggregate-demand curve to the right from AD_1 to AD_2. As a result of this shift, the long-run equilibrium moves from point A to point B. The price level rises from P_1 to P_2, but because the aggregate-supply curve is vertical, output remains the same. In panel (b), more rapid growth in the money supply raises the inflation rate by moving the economy from point A to point B. But because the Phillips curve is vertical, the rate of unemployment is the same at these two points. Thus, the vertical long-run aggregate-supply curve and the vertical long-run Phillips curve both imply that

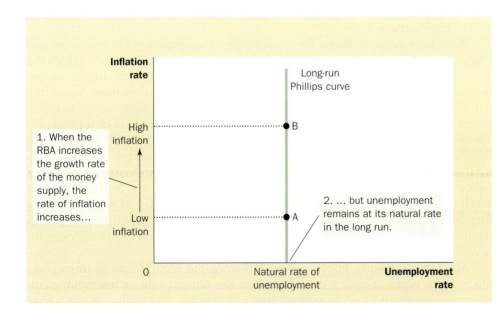

Figure 18.3

THE LONG-RUN PHILLIPS CURVE. According to Friedman and Phelps, there is no trade-off between inflation and unemployment in the long run. Growth in the money supply determines the inflation rate. Regardless of the inflation rate, the unemployment rate gravitates towards its natural rate. As a result, the long-run Phillips curve is vertical.

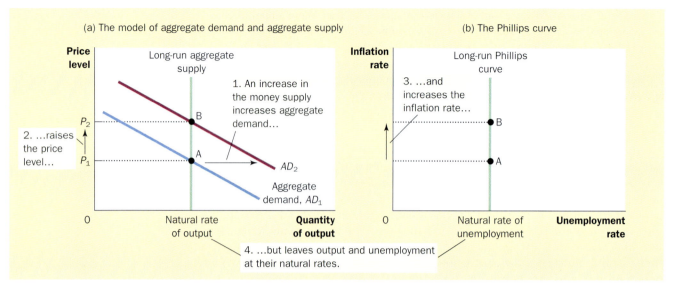

Figure 18.4

HOW THE LONG-RUN PHILLIPS CURVE IS RELATED TO THE MODEL OF AGGREGATE DEMAND AND AGGREGATE SUPPLY. Panel (a) shows the model of aggregate demand and aggregate supply with a vertical aggregate-supply curve. When expansionary monetary policy shifts the aggregate-demand curve to the right from AD_1 to AD_2, the equilibrium moves from point A to point B. The price level rises from P_1 to P_2, while output remains the same. Panel (b) shows the long-run Phillips curve, which is vertical at the natural rate of unemployment. Expansionary monetary policy moves the economy from lower inflation (point A) to higher inflation (point B) without changing the rate of unemployment.

monetary policy influences nominal variables (the price level and the inflation rate) but not real variables (output and unemployment). Regardless of the monetary policy pursued by the RBA, output and unemployment are, in the long run, at their natural rates.

What is so 'natural' about the natural rate of unemployment? Friedman and Phelps used this adjective to describe the unemployment rate towards which the economy tends to gravitate in the long run. Yet the natural rate of unemployment is not necessarily the socially desirable rate of unemployment. Nor is the natural rate of unemployment constant over time. For example, suppose that a newly formed union uses its market power to raise the real wages of some workers above the equilibrium level. The result is an excess supply of workers and, therefore, a higher natural rate of unemployment. This unemployment is 'natural' not because it is good but because it is beyond the influence of monetary policy. This level of unemployment is often referred to as the **'NAIRU' or non-accelerating inflation rate of unemployment**. It is the level of unemployment that does not result in increases in the inflation rate. More rapid money growth would not reduce the market power of the union or the level of unemployment; it would lead only to more inflation.

Although monetary policy cannot influence the natural rate of unemployment, other types of policy can. To reduce the natural rate of unemployment, policymakers should look to policies that improve the functioning of the labour

NAIRU or non-accelerating inflation rate of unemployment
the level of unemployment that does not result in increases in the inflation rate

market. Earlier in the book we discussed how various labour-market policies, such as minimum-wage laws, collective-bargaining laws, unemployment benefits and job-training programs, affect the natural rate of unemployment. A policy change that reduced the natural rate of unemployment would shift the long-run Phillips curve to the left. In addition, because lower unemployment means more workers are producing goods and services, the quantity of goods and services supplied would be larger at any given price level, and the long-run aggregate-supply curve would shift to the right. The economy could then enjoy lower unemployment and higher output for any given rate of money growth and inflation.

EXPECTATIONS AND THE SHORT-RUN PHILLIPS CURVE

At first, the denial by Friedman and Phelps of a long-run trade-off between inflation and unemployment might not seem persuasive. Their argument was based on an appeal to theory. In contrast, the negative correlation between inflation and unemployment documented by Phillips, Samuelson and Solow was based on *data*. Why should anyone believe that policymakers faced a vertical Phillips curve when the world seemed to offer a downward-sloping one? Shouldn't the findings of Phillips, Samuelson and Solow lead us to reject the classical conclusion of monetary neutrality?

Friedman and Phelps were well aware of these questions; they offered a way to reconcile classical macroeconomic theory with the findings of a downward-sloping Phillips curve in data from the United Kingdom and the United States. They claimed that a negative relationship between inflation and unemployment holds in the short run but that it cannot be used by policymakers in the long run. In other words, policymakers can pursue expansionary monetary policy to achieve lower unemployment for a while, but eventually unemployment returns to its natural rate, and more expansionary monetary policy leads only to higher inflation.

Friedman and Phelps reasoned as we did in chapter 16 when we explained the difference between the short-run and long-run aggregate-supply curves. (In fact, the discussion in that chapter drew heavily on the legacy of Friedman and Phelps.) As you may recall, the short-run aggregate-supply curve is upward-sloping, indicating that an increase in the price level raises the quantity of goods and services that firms supply. In contrast, the long-run aggregate-supply curve is vertical, indicating that the price level does not influence quantity supplied in the long run. Chapter 16 presented three theories to explain the upward slope of the short-run aggregate-supply curve: misperceptions about relative prices, sticky wages and sticky prices. Because perceptions, wages and prices adjust to changing economic conditions over time, the positive relationship between the price level and quantity supplied applies in the short run but not in the long run. Friedman and Phelps applied this same logic to the Phillips curve. Just as the aggregate-supply curve slopes upwards only in the short run, the trade-off between inflation and unemployment holds only in the short run. And just as the long-run aggregate-supply curve is vertical, the long-run Phillips curve is also vertical.

To help explain the short-run and long-run relationship between inflation and unemployment, Friedman and Phelps introduced a new variable into the analysis—*expected inflation*. Expected inflation measures how much people expect the overall price level to change. As we discussed in chapter 16, the expected price level affects the perceptions of relative prices that people form and the wages and prices that they set. As a result, expected inflation is one factor that determines the position of the short-run aggregate-supply curve. In the short run, the RBA can take expected inflation (and thus the short-run aggregate-supply curve) as already determined. When the money supply changes, the aggregate-demand curve shifts, and the economy moves along a given short-run aggregate-supply curve. In the short run, therefore, monetary changes lead to unexpected fluctuations in output, prices, unemployment and inflation. In this way, Friedman and Phelps explained the Phillips curve that Phillips, Samuelson and Solow had documented.

Yet the RBA's ability to create unexpected inflation by increasing the money supply exists only in the short run. In the long run, people come to expect whatever inflation rate the RBA chooses to produce. Because perceptions, wages and prices will eventually adjust to the inflation rate, the long-run aggregate-supply curve is vertical. In this case, changes in aggregate demand, such as those due to changes in the money supply, do not affect the economy's output of goods and services. Thus, Friedman and Phelps concluded that unemployment returns to its natural rate in the long run.

The analysis of Friedman and Phelps can be summarised in the following equation:

$$\text{Unemployment rate} = \text{Natural rate of unemployment} - a\left(\text{Actual inflation} - \text{Expected inflation}\right)$$

This equation relates the unemployment rate to the natural rate of unemployment, actual inflation and expected inflation. In the short run, expected inflation is already given. As a result, higher actual inflation is associated with lower unemployment. (How much unemployment responds to unexpected inflation is determined by the size of a, a number that in turn depends on the slope of the short-run aggregate-supply curve.) In the long run, however, people come to expect whatever inflation the RBA produces. Thus, actual inflation equals expected inflation, and unemployment is at its natural rate.

According to Friedman and Phelps, it is dangerous to view the Phillips curve as a menu of options available to policymakers. To see why, imagine an economy at its natural rate of unemployment with low inflation and low expected inflation, shown in figure 18.5 as point A. Now suppose that policymakers try to take advantage of the trade-off between inflation and unemployment by using monetary or fiscal policy to expand aggregate demand. In the short run when expected inflation is given, the economy goes from point A to point B. Unemployment falls below its natural rate, and inflation rises above expected inflation. Over time, people get used to this higher inflation rate, and they raise their expectations of inflation. When expected inflation rises, the short-run trade-off between inflation and unemployment shifts upwards. The economy ends up at point C, with higher inflation than at point A but with the same level of unemployment.

Thus, Friedman and Phelps concluded that policymakers do face a trade-off between inflation and unemployment, but only a temporary one. If policymakers use this trade-off, they lose it.

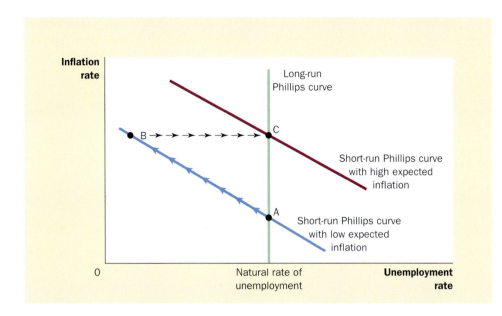

Figure 18.5

HOW EXPECTED INFLATION SHIFTS THE SHORT-RUN PHILLIPS CURVE. The higher the expected rate of inflation, the higher the short-run trade-off between inflation and unemployment. At point A, expected inflation and actual inflation are both low, and unemployment is at its natural rate. If the RBA pursues an expansionary monetary policy, the economy moves from point A to point B in the short run. At point B, expected inflation is still low, but actual inflation is high. Unemployment is below its natural rate. In the long run, expected inflation rises, and the economy moves to point C. At point C, expected inflation and actual inflation are both high, and unemployment is back to its natural rate.

CASE STUDY **THE US ECONOMY AS THE NATURAL EXPERIMENT FOR THE NATURAL-RATE HYPOTHESIS**

Friedman and Phelps had made a bold prediction in 1968—if policymakers try to take advantage of the Phillips curve by choosing higher inflation in order to reduce unemployment, they will succeed at reducing unemployment only temporarily. This view—that unemployment eventually returns to its natural rate, regardless of the rate of inflation—is called the **natural-rate hypothesis**. A few years after Friedman and Phelps proposed this hypothesis, monetary and fiscal policymakers inadvertently created a natural experiment to test it. Their laboratory was the US economy.

Before we see the outcome of this test, however, let's look at the data that Friedman and Phelps had when they made their prediction in 1968. Figure 18.6 shows the unemployment rate and the inflation rate for the period from 1961 to 1968 in the United States. These data trace out a Phillips curve. As inflation rose over these 8 years, unemployment fell. The economic data from this era seemed to confirm the trade-off between inflation and unemployment.

The apparent success of the Phillips curve in the 1960s made the prediction of Friedman and Phelps all the more bold. In 1958 Phillips had suggested a negative association between inflation and unemployment. In 1960 Samuelson and Solow had showed it in US data. Another decade of data had confirmed the relationship. To some economists at the time, it seemed ridiculous to claim that the Phillips curve would break down once policymakers tried to use it.

But, in fact, that is exactly what happened. Beginning in the late 1960s, the US government followed policies that expanded the aggregate demand for goods and services. In part, this expansion was due to fiscal policy—government spending rose as the Vietnam War heated up. In part, it was due to monetary policy—because the Federal Reserve was trying to hold down

natural-rate hypothesis
the claim that unemployment eventually returns to its normal, or natural, rate, regardless of the rate of inflation

Figure 18.6

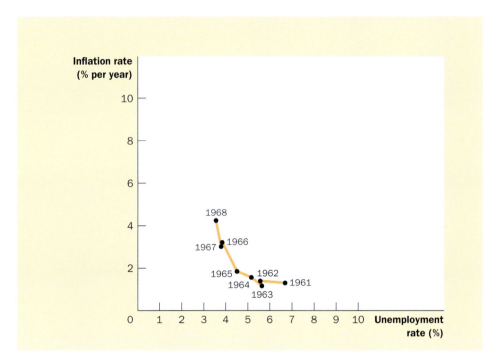

THE PHILLIPS CURVE IN THE 1960S IN THE UNITED STATES. This figure uses annual data from 1961 to 1968 on the unemployment rate and on the inflation rate (as measured by the GDP deflator) to show the negative relationship between inflation and unemployment.

SOURCE: US Department of Labor; US Department of Commerce.

Figure 18.7

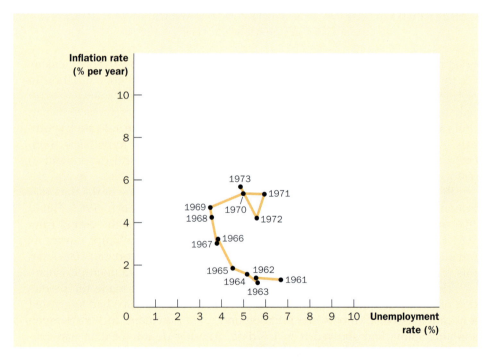

THE BREAKDOWN OF THE PHILLIPS CURVE IN THE UNITED STATES. This figure shows annual data from 1961 to 1973 on the unemployment rate and on the inflation rate (as measured by the GDP deflator). Notice that the Phillips curve of the 1960s breaks down in the early 1970s.

SOURCE: US Department of Labor; US Department of Commerce.

interest rates in the face of expansionary fiscal policy, the quantity of money rose about 13% per year during the period from 1970 to 1972, compared with 7% per year in the early 1960s. As a result, inflation stayed high (about 5–6% per year in the late 1960s and early 1970s, compared with about 1–2% per year in the early 1960s). But, as Friedman and Phelps had predicted, unemployment did not stay low.

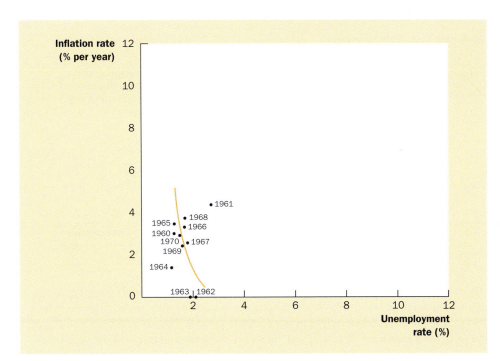

Figure 18.8

THE PHILLIPS CURVE IN AUSTRALIA FROM 1960 TO 1970. This figure uses annual data from 1960 to 1970 on the unemployment rate and on the inflation rate (as measured by the implicit price deflator for GDP) to show the negative relationship between inflation and unemployment.

SOURCE: Reserve Bank of Australia, Occasional Paper No. 8.

Figure 18.7 shows the history of inflation and unemployment from 1961 to 1973 in the United States. Notice that the simple negative relationship between these two variables started to break down around 1970. In particular, as inflation remained high in the early 1970s, people's expectations of inflation caught up with reality, and the unemployment rate reverted to the 5–6% range that had prevailed in the early 1960s. By 1973, policymakers had learned that Friedman and Phelps were right—there is no trade-off between inflation and unemployment in the long run.

Australia experienced a similar breakdown in the Phillips curve. Figure 18.8 shows the Phillips curve for the 1960s. As you can see, the trade-off between inflation and unemployment is not straightforward. Australia, like the United States, had a fairly stable Phillips curve during the 1960s, but the oil shocks of the 1970s, along with increases in wages due to indexation of wages to inflation, helped shift the Australian Phillips curve to the right (see figure 18.11 on page 412). These events are described below.

> **QUICK QUIZ** Draw the short-run Phillips curve and the long-run Phillips curve. Explain why they are different.

SHIFTS IN THE PHILLIPS CURVE: THE ROLE OF SUPPLY SHOCKS

Friedman and Phelps had suggested in 1968 that changes in expected inflation shift the short-run Phillips curve, and the experience of the early 1970s convinced

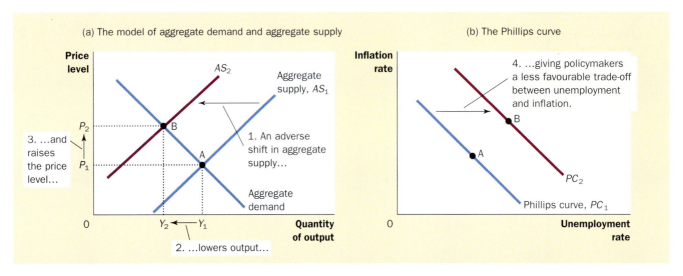

Figure 18.9

AN ADVERSE SHOCK TO AGGREGATE SUPPLY. Panel (a) shows the model of aggregate demand and aggregate supply. When the aggregate-supply curve shifts to the left from AS_1 to AS_2, the equilibrium moves from point A to point B. Output falls from Y_1 to Y_2, and the price level rises from P_1 to P_2. Panel (b) shows the short-run trade-off between inflation and unemployment. The adverse shift in aggregate supply moves the economy from a point with lower unemployment and lower inflation (point A) to a point with higher unemployment and higher inflation (point B). The short-run Phillips curve shifts to the right from PC_1 to PC_2. Policymakers now face a worse trade-off between inflation and unemployment.

most economists that Friedman and Phelps were right. Within a few years, however, the economics profession would turn its attention to a different source of shifts in the short-run Phillips curve—shocks to aggregate supply.

This time, the shift in focus came not from two American economics professors but from a group of Arab sheiks. In 1974, the Organization of Petroleum Exporting Countries (OPEC) began to exert its market power as a cartel in the world oil market in order to increase its members' profits. The countries of OPEC, such as Saudi Arabia, Kuwait and Iraq, restricted the amount of crude oil they pumped and sold on world markets. Within a few years, this reduction in supply caused the price of oil to almost double.

This OPEC price increase had major macroeconomic effects in countries around the world. Because an increase in the price of oil raises the cost of producing many goods and services, it reduces the quantity of goods and services supplied at any given price level. (This is true even for a country like Australia that is generally a net exporter of oil. The increase in the price of oil may be good for oil producers, but it still raises the costs of production of just about everything else in the economy.) As panel (a) of figure 18.9 shows, this reduction in supply is represented by the shift to the left in the aggregate-supply curve from AS_1 to AS_2. The price level rises from P_1 to P_2, and output falls from Y_1 to Y_2. The result is called *stagflation*.

This shift in aggregate supply is associated with a similar shift in the short-run Phillips curve, shown in panel (b). Because firms need fewer workers to produce the smaller output, employment falls and unemployment rises. Because the price level is higher, the inflation rate—the percentage change in the price level from the previous year—is also higher. Thus, the shift in aggregate supply leads to higher unemployment and higher inflation. The short-run trade-off between inflation and unemployment shifts to the right from PC_1 to PC_2.

Confronted with an adverse shift in aggregate supply, policymakers face a difficult choice. If they contract aggregate demand to fight inflation, they will raise unemployment further. If they expand aggregate demand to fight unemployment, they will raise inflation further. In other words, policymakers face a less favourable trade-off between inflation and unemployment than they did before the shift in aggregate supply—they have to live with a higher rate of inflation for a given rate of unemployment, a higher rate of unemployment for a given rate of inflation, or some combination of higher unemployment and higher inflation.

An important question is whether this adverse shift in the Phillips curve is temporary or permanent. The answer depends on how people adjust their expectations of inflation. If people view the event as a temporary aberration, expected inflation does not change, and the Phillips curve will soon revert to its former position. But if people view the shock as leading to a new era of higher inflation, then expected inflation rises, and the Phillips curve remains at its new, less desirable position.

In Australia during the 1970s, actual inflation did rise substantially, particularly in 1973–74, and this led to increases in expected inflation. The rise in actual inflation was the result of two factors—a wage explosion and the increase in oil prices. From the late 1960s to 1973–74, wages increased rapidly, increasing by nearly 30% in 1974 alone. Gough Whitlam's government debated trying a 'short, sharp shock' to bring down inflation in 1974, but the policy was never

'Remember the good old days when all the economy needed was a little fine-tuning?'

implemented. The Labor government became more concerned about increasing unemployment rather than inflation, and reversed its restrictive fiscal measures.

When Malcolm Fraser became prime minister in 1975, his government attempted to slow inflation by trying to put on the monetary brakes. In 1978, inflation dropped from over 13% to below 10%, but the impact of the second oil shock in 1979 and continued increases in commodity prices led to another round of high inflation. In 1983, after an extended period of wage explosion and two OPEC supply shocks, the Australian economy had an inflation rate of more than 11% and an unemployment rate of nearly 10%. This combination of inflation and unemployment was not at all near the trade-off that seemed possible in the 1960s. (In the 1960s, the Phillips curve suggested that an unemployment rate of 6% would be associated with an inflation rate of less than 1%. Inflation of more than 10% was unthinkable in the 1960s.) With the misery index in 1983 near an historic high, the public was widely dissatisfied with macroeconomic performance. Something had to be done, and soon it would be.

QUICK QUIZ Give an example of a favourable shock to aggregate supply. Use the model of aggregate demand and aggregate supply to explain the effects of such a shock. How does it affect the Phillips curve?

THE COST OF REDUCING INFLATION

Despite the Fraser government's efforts to bring inflation down, it hovered around 10% until 1983, when Bob Hawke brought a Labor government to power. Inflation in Australia was mostly the result of the rise in wages, but with a Labor government negotiating with the Australian Council of Trade Unions (ACTU), a brake was applied to the wage increases. The government was committed to a Prices and Incomes Accord (known as the Accord) which would limit wage increases, and guarantee productivity increases while maintaining worker incomes. The era of the Accords had begun.

To understand the importance of the Accords in bringing down wages, we need to understand how wages were determined before the Accord and why they were allowed to rise so rapidly. From 1921 to 1953, a centrally arbitrated minimum wage was set. A significant component of this wage was indexed to inflation. But as inflation increased to levels of 25% in 1953, this indexation was removed. By the 1970s a system of arbitrated collective bargaining had developed that determined wages in the major industries, such as oil and metal trades, by bargaining between the big unions and employer groups. These wages then formed the benchmark for increases in wages in other industries.

Wage indexation was reintroduced in 1975 as a means of controlling the wages outbreak. The objective was to strictly limit increases in wages that were not based on indexation. But this was not successful—wages continued to rise, although more slowly. Partial indexation was used until 1980, when there was a move back to decentralised wage determination. Strong unions bargained to obtain wage increases in excess of the increase in prices so that workers' real wages would not fall. This led to greater increases in prices, which led to increases in wages and so on. It was this wage–price spiral that the newly elected government intended to change in 1983.

The ACTU had been advocating a centralised wage fixation system based on 'prices and productivity'. This meant that wages should rise in line with inflation to stop the real wage falling and also to reflect productivity gains so that workers would get a share of the increased profit that their productivity helped generate. However, this approach to wage increases was difficult to maintain in the face of rising inflation. The traditional approach to solving inflation problems was to slam on the brakes and slow the economy down. According to accepted thinking on the Phillips curve, this would mean a rise in unemployment, an unpalatable outcome for the unions. As the Australian economy went into recession in 1982–83, there were two possibilities for lowering inflation. One was to lower aggregate demand through a combination of tight monetary policy and restrictive fiscal policy, and the other was to come to some agreement with the unions over wage restraint. We consider these two possibilities in turn.

THE SACRIFICE RATIO

To reduce the inflation rate, the RBA could pursue contractionary monetary policy. Figure 18.10 shows some of the effects of such a decision. When the RBA slows the rate of money growth, it contracts aggregate demand. The fall in aggregate demand, in turn, reduces the quantity of goods and services that firms produce, and this fall in production leads to a fall in employment. The economy begins at point A in the figure and moves along the short-run Phillips curve to point B, which has lower inflation and higher unemployment. Over time, as people come to understand that prices are rising more slowly, expected inflation falls, and the short-run Phillips curve shifts downwards. The economy moves from point B to point C. Inflation is lower, and unemployment is back at its natural rate.

Thus, if an economy is to reduce inflation, it must endure a period of high unemployment and low output. In figure 18.10, this cost is represented by the movement of the economy through point B as it travels from point A to point

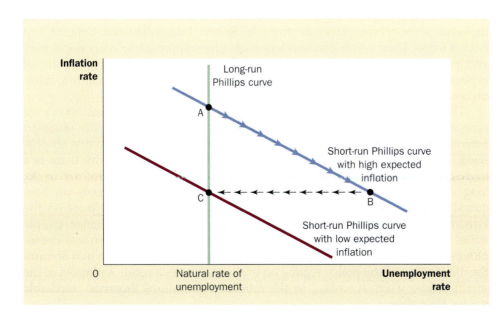

Figure 18.10

DISINFLATIONARY MONETARY POLICY IN THE SHORT RUN AND LONG RUN. When the RBA pursues contractionary monetary policy to reduce inflation, the economy moves along a short-run Phillips curve from point A to point B. Over time, expected inflation falls, and the short-run Phillips curve shifts downwards. When the economy reaches point C, unemployment is back at its natural rate.

sacrifice ratio
the number of percentage points of annual output lost in the process of reducing inflation by 1 percentage point

C. The size of this cost depends on the slope of the Phillips curve and how quickly expectations of inflation adjust to the new monetary policy.

Many studies have examined the data on inflation and unemployment in order to estimate the cost of reducing inflation. The findings of these studies are often summarised in a statistic called the **sacrifice ratio**. The sacrifice ratio is the number of percentage points of annual output lost in the process of reducing inflation by 1 percentage point. A typical estimate of the sacrifice ratio is 5. That is, for each percentage point that inflation is reduced, 5% of annual output must be sacrificed in the transition.

Such estimates surely must have made the Fraser government apprehensive as it confronted the task of reducing inflation. Inflation was running at almost 10% per year. To reach moderate inflation of, say, 4% per year would mean reducing inflation by 6 percentage points. If each percentage point cost 5% of the economy's annual output, then reducing inflation by 6 percentage points would require sacrificing 30% of annual output.

According to studies of the Phillips curve and the cost of disinflation, this sacrifice could be paid in various ways. An immediate reduction in inflation would depress output by 30% for a single year, but that outcome was surely too harsh even for the most ardent inflation 'hawks' in Treasury. It would surely be better to spread out the cost over several years. If the reduction in inflation took place over 5 years, for instance, then output would have to average only 6% below trend during that period to add up to a sacrifice of 30%. An even more gradual approach would be to reduce inflation slowly over a decade, so that output would have to be only 3% below trend. Whatever path was chosen, however, it seemed that reducing inflation would not be easy.

RATIONAL EXPECTATIONS AND THE POSSIBILITY OF COSTLESS DISINFLATION

Just as the Fraser government was pondering how costly reducing inflation might be, a group of economics professors was leading an intellectual revolution that would challenge the conventional wisdom on the sacrifice ratio. This group included such prominent economists as Robert Lucas, Thomas Sargent and Robert Barro. Their revolution was based on a new approach to economic theory and policy called **rational expectations**. According to the theory of rational expectations, people optimally use all the information they have, including information about government policies, when forecasting the future.

rational expectations
the theory according to which people optimally use all the information they have, including information about government policies, when forecasting the future

This new approach has had profound implications for many areas of macroeconomics, but none is more important than its application to the trade-off between inflation and unemployment. As Friedman and Phelps had first emphasised, expected inflation is an important variable that explains why there is a trade-off between inflation and unemployment in the short run but not in the long run. How quickly the short-run trade-off disappears depends on how quickly expectations adjust. Proponents of rational expectations built on the Friedman–Phelps analysis to argue that when economic policies change, people adjust their expectations of inflation accordingly. Studies of inflation and unemployment that tried to estimate the sacrifice ratio had failed to take into account the direct effect of the policy regime on expectations. As a result, estimates of the sacrifice ratio were, according to the rational-expectations theorists, unreliable guides for policy.

In a 1981 paper entitled 'The End of Four Big Inflations', Thomas Sargent described this new view as follows:

> An alternative 'rational expectations' view denies that there is any inherent momentum to the present process of inflation. This view maintains that firms and workers have now come to expect high rates of inflation in the future and that they strike inflationary bargains in light of these expectations. However, it is held that people expect high rates of inflation in the future precisely because the government's current and prospective monetary and fiscal policies warrant those expectations…An implication of this view is that inflation can be stopped much more quickly than advocates of the 'momentum' view have indicated and that their estimates of the length of time and the costs of stopping inflation in terms of foregone output are erroneous…This is not to say that it would be easy to eradicate inflation. On the contrary, it would require more than a few temporary restrictive fiscal and monetary actions. It would require a change in the policy regime…How costly such a move would be in terms of foregone output and how long it would be in taking effect would depend partly on how resolute and evident the government's commitment was.

According to Sargent, the sacrifice ratio could be much smaller than suggested by previous estimates. Indeed, in the most extreme case, it could be zero. If the government made a credible commitment to a policy of low inflation, people would be rational enough to lower their expectations of inflation immediately. The short-run Phillips curve would shift downwards, and the economy would reach low inflation quickly without the cost of temporarily high unemployment and low output.

THE ACCORD APPROACH

Although no one in the Hawke government or the ACTU would have claimed to be advocates of the theory of rational expectations, the idea of reducing inflationary expectations was fundamental to the approach of the Accord. If the government could get the ACTU to accept some form of wage reductions, then prices would not need to increase as much to pay for the wage increases. Wage earners would begin to expect a lower level of inflation and not demand large wage increases in the next round of wage negotiation. Then the cycle of increasing wages and prices could be broken. The first Accord still had full indexation, but by the second round (Accord Mark II), indexation had been removed. In return for productivity gains, workers at all levels would be granted superannuation coverage. So the emphasis had been changed from wage increases to other forms of benefits for workers that would be less inflationary, including tax cuts and reductions in the Medicare levy. Costs of production could be kept low by the productivity gains that were promised in return for these benefits.

Inflation did indeed come down in 1984 and 1985. But in 1986, Australia suffered a significant depreciation of its dollar that caused inflation to rise again. Figure 18.11 shows the inflation rate and unemployment rate during this period. Without the Accord, the inflation rate might have been much higher, but by the late 1980s, fears of escalating inflation were again strong. The government decided to use restrictive monetary policy to bring inflation down, as well as continuing to rely on the Accord to prevent a wages blow-out from the higher inflation rates. This led to the recession of 1990–91, dubbed by the then Treasurer,

Figure 18.11

THE PHILLIPS CURVE IN AUSTRALIA IN THE 1970S AND THE 1980S. This figure uses annual data from 1974 to 1983 on the unemployment rate and on the inflation rate (as measured by the implicit price deflator for GDP) to show the shift to the right of the Phillips curve.

SOURCE: Reserve Bank of Australia, Occasional Paper No. 8.

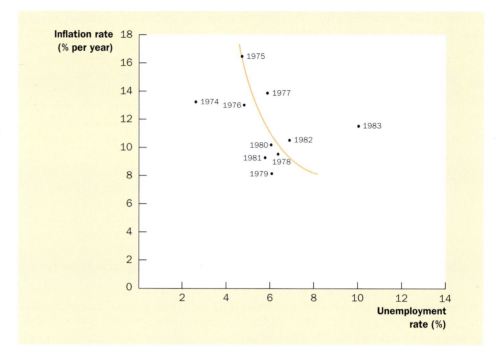

Figure 18.12

A PERIOD OF DISINFLATION. This figure uses annual data from 1984 to 1998 on the unemployment rate and on the inflation rate (as measured by the implicit price deflator for GDP). The reduction in inflation during this period came at the cost of very high unemployment in 1992 and 1993. Note that the points labelled A, B and C in this figure correspond roughly to the points in figure 18.10.

SOURCE: Reserve Bank of Australia, Occasional Paper No. 8.

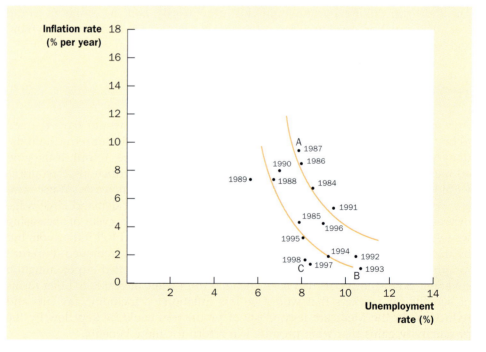

Paul Keating, as the 'recession we had to have'. This recession did get the inflation rate under control—it was down to 1% by 1993. However, the cost was a significant increase in unemployment. Unemployment reached 10.7% in 1993, its highest level since the Depression.

Does this experience refute the possibility of costless disinflation as suggested by the rational-expectations theorists? Some economists have argued that the answer to this question is a resounding yes. Indeed, the pattern of disinflation shown in figure 18.12 is very similar to the pattern predicted in figure 18.10. To make the transition from high inflation (point A in both figures) to low inflation (point C), the economy had to experience a painful period of high unemployment (point B).

Yet there are two reasons not to reject the conclusions of the rational-expectations theorists so quickly. First, even though disinflation did impose a cost of temporarily high unemployment, the cost was not as large as many economists had predicted. Most estimates of the sacrifice ratio based on the disinflation experienced from 1987 to 1993 are smaller than estimates that had been obtained from previous data. Perhaps Treasurer Keating was right. We did have to have a recession to see some direct effect on expectations, as the rational-expectations theorists claimed.

A LOW INFLATION ERA

Since the wages inflation of the 1970s and the disinflation of the early 1990s, the Australian economy has experienced relatively mild fluctuations in inflation, but unemployment has stayed fairly high. Figure 18.12 shows inflation and unemployment from 1984 to 1998. The high unemployment figures in 1996 helped remove the Keating Labor government from power and brought in a Coalition government for the first time in 13 years.

Since then, the RBA has been careful to avoid repeating the policy mistakes of the 1960s, when excessive aggregate demand pushed unemployment below the natural rate and raised inflation. Unemployment has remained around 8%, which is still higher than most economists estimate the natural rate for the Australian economy to be. When unemployment fell and inflation rose in 1989 and 1990, the RBA contracted aggregate demand, leading to the recession of 1991 and 1992. Unemployment then rose above the natural rate, and inflation fell. The economy gradually recovered from this recession in the mid-1990s, and inflation stabilised at about 2%.

What does the future hold? Macroeconomists are notoriously bad at forecasting, but several lessons of the past are clear. First, as long as the RBA remains vigilant in its control over interest rates and, thereby, aggregate demand, there is no reason for inflation to heat up, as it did in the late 1960s. Second, the possibility always exists for the economy to experience adverse shocks to aggregate supply, as it did in the 1970s. If that unfortunate development occurs, policy-makers will have little choice but to confront a less desirable trade-off between inflation and unemployment.

> **QUICK QUIZ** What is the sacrifice ratio? How might the credibility of the RBA's commitment to reduce inflation affect the sacrifice ratio?

CONCLUSION

This chapter has examined how economists' thinking about inflation and unemployment has evolved over time. We have discussed the ideas of many of the best economists of the twentieth century—from the Phillips curve of Phillips,

IN THE NEWS

Unemployment and its natural rate

As the US presidential election of 1996 neared, the unemployment rate fell to 5.1%, its lowest level in years. The Federal Reserve faced a difficult question: Was this rate of unemployment below the natural rate?

Trying to Figure Out How Low Unemployment Figures Can Go

By Richard W. Stevenson

WASHINGTON—Beyond the clear political gain it represents for President Clinton, the decline in unemployment to its lowest level in seven years has focused added attention on an issue that increasingly dominates policy debates and financial markets: whether the economy has changed so fundamentally in recent years that it can accommodate a lower rate of unemployment, and the resulting wage increases, without re-igniting inflation.

Over the last two years, as the unemployment rate edged below 6 percent and slid gradually down to its current level of 5.1 percent, economists have had to reassess one of their most widely accepted assumptions: that the natural rate of unemployment was a little more than 6 percent. Below that rate, the assumption held, labor markets would become so tight that wages would surge, sending prices upward.

As unemployment has fallen below that level, the Federal Reserve [the Fed] and the bond markets have strained mightily to detect the expected signs of inflation, and have so far found almost nothing. While wages have been creeping up, most companies have reported an inability to push through price increases to customers, keeping inflation quiescent.

The resulting economic mix—low unemployment, low inflation, steady growth, and signs that wages might be edging up after a long period of stagnation—could not be more ideal for Mr Clinton as he confronts a Republican nominee, Bob Dole, who has built his campaign on the argument that the nation is being shortchanged economically.

Indeed, the economic gods have smiled on Mr Clinton since 1992, when it was George Bush's bad fortune to preside over an economy that came out of recession in a slow and faltering way. While unemployment generally drifted upward throughout Mr Bush's presidency, it has moved down during Mr Clinton's term.

Whether Mr Clinton deserves any credit for the economic record of the last three years and eight months is a matter of intense partisan debate, and Mr Clinton could remain vulnerable to widespread if dissipating economic anxiety and resentment about stagnant wages and job insecurity. But Mr Clinton is maintaining his big lead in the polls, and the unemployment report will make it that much harder for Mr Dole to get a hearing for his argument that the nation needs to improve its long-run economic performance...

Although the Fed has indicated that it is leaning toward raising rates if the economy does not show signs of cooling off, Fed officials over the last week have said they remain undecided whether they need to act, and if so, by how much they will need to raise rates.

Clinton administration officials stuck today to their position that they do not comment on the Fed's monetary policy. But they said they saw no signs of inflation, and left little doubt that they would view any rate increase before the election as unjustified, even though it takes months before higher rates begin working to slow the economy.

They also argued that the Fed should continue to engage in what has amounted to an experiment in determining just how low unemployment can go before signs of inflation emerge. Despite its reputation for taking a hard line on inflation, the Fed, in the view of some analysts, has been remarkably restrained in allowing unemployment to go so low and economic growth to remain so strong without raising rates.

'In the presence of such strong stability in the economy, it should be possible at low cost to reverse any slight overheating,' said Joseph E. Stiglitz, the chairman of the president's Council of Economic Advisers.

SOURCE: *New York Times*, 7 September 1996, p. 35.

Samuelson and Solow, to the natural-rate hypothesis of Friedman and Phelps, to the rational-expectations theory of Lucas, Sargent and Barro. Four of this group have already won Nobel prizes for their work in economics, and more are likely to be so honoured in the years to come.

Although the trade-off between inflation and unemployment has generated much intellectual turmoil over the past 40 years, certain principles have developed that today command consensus. Here is how Milton Friedman expressed the relationship between inflation and unemployment in 1968:

> There is always a temporary tradeoff between inflation and unemployment; there is no permanent tradeoff. The temporary tradeoff comes not from inflation per se, but from unanticipated inflation, which generally means, from a rising rate of inflation. The widespread belief that there is a permanent tradeoff is a sophisticated version of the confusion between 'high' and 'rising' that we all recognize in simpler forms. A rising rate of inflation may reduce unemployment, a high rate will not.
>
> But how long, you will say, is 'temporary'?...I can at most venture a personal judgment, based on some examination of the historical evidence, that the initial effects of a higher and unanticipated rate of inflation last for something like two to five years.

Today, about 30 years later, this statement still summarises the view of most macroeconomists.

Summary

- The Phillips curve describes a negative relationship between inflation and unemployment. By expanding aggregate demand, policymakers can choose a point on the Phillips curve with higher inflation and lower unemployment. By contracting aggregate demand, policymakers can choose a point on the Phillips curve with lower inflation and higher unemployment.

- The trade-off between inflation and unemployment described by the Phillips curve holds only in the short run. In the long run, expected inflation adjusts to changes in actual inflation, and the short-run Phillips curve shifts. As a result, the long-run Phillips curve is vertical at the natural rate of unemployment.

- The short-run Phillips curve also shifts because of shocks to aggregate supply. An adverse supply shock, such as the increase in world oil prices during the 1970s, gives policymakers a less favourable trade-off between inflation and unemployment. That is, after an adverse supply shock, policymakers have to accept a higher rate of inflation for any given rate of unemployment, or a higher rate of unemployment for any given rate of inflation.

- When the RBA contracts monetary growth to reduce inflation, it moves the economy along the short-run Phillips curve, which results in temporarily high unemployment. The cost of disinflation depends on how quickly expectations of inflation fall. Some economists argue that a credible commitment to low inflation can reduce the cost of disinflation by inducing a quick adjustment of expectations.

Key concepts

Phillips curve, p. 394
NAIRU or non-accelerating inflation rate of unemployment, p. 400

natural-rate hypothesis, p. 403
sacrifice ratio, p. 410
rational expectations, p. 410

Questions for review

1. Draw the short-run trade-off between inflation and unemployment. How might the RBA move the economy from one point on this curve to another?

2. Draw the long-run trade-off between inflation and unemployment. Explain how the short-run and long-run trade-offs are related.

3. Why might the natural rate of unemployment differ across countries?

4. Suppose a drought destroys farm crops and drives up the price of food. What is the effect on the short-run trade-off between inflation and unemployment?

5. The RBA decides to reduce inflation. Use the Phillips curve to show the short-run and long-run effects of this policy. How might the short-run costs be reduced?

Problems and applications

1. Suppose the natural rate of unemployment is 6%. On one graph, draw two Phillips curves that can be used to describe the four situations listed here. Label the point that shows the position of the economy in each case:
   a. actual inflation is 5% and expected inflation is 3%
   b. actual inflation is 3% and expected inflation is 5%
   c. actual inflation is 5% and expected inflation is 5%
   d. actual inflation is 3% and expected inflation is 3%.

2. Illustrate the effects of the following developments on both the short-run and long-run Phillips curves. Give the economic reasoning underlying your answers.
   a. a rise in the natural rate of unemployment
   b. a decline in the price of imported oil
   c. a rise in government spending
   d. a decline in expected inflation

3. Suppose that reduced consumer spending causes a recession.
   a. Illustrate the changes in the economy using both an aggregate-supply/aggregate-demand diagram and a Phillips-curve diagram.
   b. What will happen in the long run if expected inflation is unchanged? What will happen in the long run if expected inflation changes in the same direction that actual inflation changes in the short run? Illustrate your answers using your diagrams from part (a).

4. Suppose the economy is in a long-run equilibrium.
   a. Draw the economy's short-run and long-run Phillips curves.
   b. Suppose a wave of business pessimism reduces aggregate demand. Show the effect of this shock on your diagram from part (a). If the RBA undertakes expansionary monetary policy, can it return the economy to its original inflation rate and original unemployment rate?
   c. Now suppose the economy is back in long-run equilibrium, and then the price of imported oil rises. Show the effect of this shock with a new diagram like that in part (a). If the RBA undertakes expansionary monetary policy, can it return the economy to its original inflation rate and original unemployment rate? If the RBA undertakes contractionary monetary policy, can it return the economy to its original inflation rate and original unemployment rate? Explain why this situation differs from that in part (b).

5. Suppose the RBA believed that the natural rate of unemployment was 7% when the actual natural rate was 6.5%. If the RBA based its policy decisions on its belief, what would happen to the economy?

6. Suppose the RBA announced that it would pursue contractionary monetary policy in order to reduce the inflation rate. Would the following conditions make the ensuing recession more or less severe? Explain.
   a. Wage contracts have short durations.
   b. There is little confidence in the RBA's determination to reduce inflation.
   c. Expectations of inflation adjust quickly to actual inflation.

7. Some economists believe that the short-run Phillips curve is relatively steep and shifts quickly in response to changes in the economy. Would these economists be more or less likely to favour contractionary policy in order to reduce inflation than economists who had the opposite views?

8. According to one version of Okun's law (discussed in chapter 16), when real GDP is 1% below its trend level, the unemployment rate is half a percentage point above its natural rate. If the sacrifice ratio in Australia is 5, the natural rate of unemployment is 6%, and the RBA wants to reduce inflation by 2%, what rate of unemployment would be necessary for the RBA to reach its goal in 5 years?

9. Imagine an economy in which all wages are set in 3-year contracts. In this world, the RBA announces a

disinflationary change in monetary policy to begin immediately. Everyone in the economy believes the RBA's announcement. Would this disinflation be costless? Why or why not? What might the RBA do to reduce the cost of disinflation?

10. Given the unpopularity of inflation, why don't elected leaders always support efforts to reduce inflation? Economists believe that countries can reduce the cost of disinflation by letting their central banks make decisions about monetary policy without interference from politicians. Why might this be so?

VIII

FINAL THOUGHTS

19

FIVE DEBATES OVER MACROECONOMIC POLICY

IN THIS CHAPTER YOU WILL

Consider whether policymakers should try to stabilise the economy

Consider whether monetary policy should be made by rule rather than by discretion

Consider whether the central bank should aim for zero inflation

Consider whether the government should balance its budget

Consider whether the tax laws should be reformed to encourage saving

It is hard to open a newspaper without finding some politician or editorial writer advocating a change in economic policy. The government should cut government spending to reduce the budget deficit, or we all should stop worrying about the budget deficit. The Reserve Bank of Australia (RBA) should cut interest rates to stimulate a flagging economy, or it should avoid such moves in order not to risk higher inflation. Government should reform the tax system to promote faster economic growth, or it should reform the tax system to achieve a more equitable distribution of income. Economic issues are central to the continuing political debate in Australia and other countries around the world. Heads of governments around the world should heed the advice of US presidential candidate Bill Clinton's chief strategist in 1992—he posted a sign to remind the staff of the central campaign issue: 'The economy, stupid.'

The previous dozen chapters have developed the tools that economists use when analysing the behaviour of the economy as a whole and the impact of policies on the economy. This final chapter presents both sides in five leading debates over macroeconomic policy. The knowledge you have accumulated in this course provides the background with which we can discuss these important, unsettled issues. It should help you choose a side in these debates or, at least, help you see why choosing a side is so difficult.

THAT MONETARY AND FISCAL POLICYMAKERS SHOULD TRY TO STABILISE THE ECONOMY

In chapters 16, 17 and 18 we saw how changes in aggregate demand and aggregate supply can lead to short-run fluctuations in production and employment. We also saw how monetary and fiscal policy can shift aggregate demand and, thereby, influence these fluctuations. But even if policymakers *can* influence short-run economic fluctuations, does that mean they *should*? Our first debate concerns whether monetary and fiscal policymakers should use the tools at their disposal in an attempt to smooth the ups and downs of the business cycle.

PRO: POLICYMAKERS SHOULD TRY TO STABILISE THE ECONOMY

Left on their own, economies tend to fluctuate. When households and firms become pessimistic, for instance, they cut back on spending, and this reduces aggregate demand for goods and services. The fall in aggregate demand, in turn, reduces the production of goods and services. Firms lay off workers, and the unemployment rate rises. Real GDP and other measures of income fall. Rising unemployment and falling income help confirm the pessimism that initially generated the economic downturn.

Such a recession has no benefit for society—it represents a sheer waste of resources. Workers who become unemployed because of inadequate aggregate demand would rather be working. Business owners whose factories are left idle during a recession would rather be producing valuable goods and services and selling them at a profit.

There is no reason for society to suffer through the booms and busts of the business cycle. The development of macroeconomic theory has shown policymakers how to reduce the severity of economic fluctuations. By 'leaning against the wind' of economic change, monetary and fiscal policy can stabilise aggregate demand and, thereby, production and employment. When aggregate demand is inadequate to ensure full employment, policymakers should boost government spending, cut taxes and expand the money supply. When aggregate demand is excessive, risking higher inflation, policymakers should cut government spending, raise taxes and reduce the money supply. Such policy actions put macroeconomic theory to its best use by leading to a more stable economy, which benefits everyone.

CON: POLICYMAKERS SHOULD NOT TRY TO STABILISE THE ECONOMY

Although monetary and fiscal policy can be used to stabilise the economy in theory, there are substantial obstacles to the use of such policies in practice.

One problem is that monetary and fiscal policy do not affect the economy immediately but instead work with a substantial lag. Monetary policy affects aggregate demand by changing interest rates, which in turn affects spending, especially residential and business investment. But many households and firms

set their spending plans in advance. As a result, it takes time for changes in interest rates to alter the aggregate demand for goods and services. Many studies indicate that changes in monetary policy have little effect on aggregate demand until about 6 months after the change is made.

Fiscal policy works with a lag because of the long political process that governs changes in spending and taxes.

Because of these long lags, policymakers who want to stabilise the economy need to look ahead to economic conditions that are likely to prevail when their actions will take effect. Unfortunately, economic forecasting is highly imprecise, in part because macroeconomics is such a primitive science and in part because the shocks that cause economic fluctuations are intrinsically unpredictable. Thus, when policymakers change monetary or fiscal policy, they must rely on educated guesses about future economic conditions.

All too often, policymakers trying to stabilise the economy do just the opposite. Economic conditions can easily change between the time when a policy action begins and when it takes effect. Because of this, policymakers can inadvertently exacerbate rather than mitigate the magnitude of economic fluctuations. Some economists have claimed that many of the major economic fluctuations in history, including the Great Depression of the 1930s, can be traced to destabilising policy actions.

One of the first rules taught to doctors is 'do no harm'. The human body has natural restorative powers. Confronted with a sick patient and an uncertain diagnosis, often a doctor should do nothing but leave the patient's body to its own devices. Intervening in the absence of reliable knowledge merely risks making matters worse.

The same can be said about treating an ailing economy. It might be desirable if policymakers could eliminate all economic fluctuations, but that is not a realistic goal given the limits of macroeconomic knowledge and the inherent unpredictability of world events. Economic policymakers should refrain from intervening often with monetary and fiscal policy and be content if they do no harm.

> **QUICK QUIZ** Explain why monetary and fiscal policy work with a lag. Why do these lags matter in the choice between active and passive policy?

THAT MONETARY POLICY SHOULD BE MADE BY RULE RATHER THAN BY DISCRETION

As we first discussed in chapter 12, the Reserve Bank Board sets monetary policy in Australia in consultation with the government. The committee meets every month to evaluate the state of the economy. Based on this evaluation and forecasts of future economic conditions, it chooses whether to raise, lower or leave unchanged the level of short-term interest rates. The RBA then adjusts the money supply to reach that interest-rate target until the next meeting, when the target is re-evaluated.

The Reserve Bank Board operates with almost complete discretion over how to conduct monetary policy. As we saw, the charter of the RBA gives the institution only vague recommendations about what goals it should pursue; and the Act does not tell the RBA how to pursue whatever goals it might choose. Once members are appointed to the Board, they have little mandate but to 'do the right thing'.

Some economists are critical of this institutional design. Our second debate over macroeconomic policy, therefore, focuses on whether the RBA should have its discretionary powers reduced and, instead, be committed to following a rule in how it conducts monetary policy.

PRO: MONETARY POLICY SHOULD BE MADE BY RULE

Discretion in the conduct of monetary policy has two problems. The first is that it does not limit incompetence and abuse of power. When the government sends police into a community to maintain order, it gives them strict guidelines about how to carry out their job. Because police have great power, allowing them to exercise that power in whatever way they want would be dangerous. Yet when the government gives central bankers the authority to maintain economic order, it gives them no guidelines. Monetary policymakers are allowed undisciplined discretion.

As an example of abuse of power, central bankers are sometimes tempted to use monetary policy to affect the outcome of elections. Suppose that the vote for the government is based on economic conditions at election time. A central banker sympathetic to the incumbent government might be tempted to pursue expansionary policies just before the election to stimulate production and employment, knowing that the resulting inflation will not show up until after the election. Thus, to the extent that central bankers ally themselves with politicians, discretionary policy can lead to economic fluctuations that reflect the electoral calendar. Economists call such fluctuations the *political business cycle*.

The second, more subtle, problem with discretionary monetary policy is that it might lead to more inflation than is desirable. Central bankers, knowing that there is no long-run trade-off between inflation and unemployment, often announce that their goal is zero inflation. Yet they rarely achieve price stability. Why? Perhaps it is because, once the public forms expectations of inflation, policymakers face a short-run trade-off between inflation and unemployment. They are tempted to renege on their announcement of price stability in order to achieve lower unemployment. This discrepancy between announcements (what policymakers *say* they are going to do) and actions (what they subsequently in fact do) is called the *time inconsistency of policy*. Because policymakers are so often time-inconsistent, people are sceptical when central bankers announce their intentions to reduce the rate of inflation. As a result, people always expect more inflation than monetary policymakers claim they are trying to achieve. Higher expectations of inflation, in turn, shift the short-run Phillips curve upwards, making the short-run trade-off between inflation and unemployment less favourable than it otherwise might be.

One way to avoid these two problems with discretionary policy is to commit the central bank to a policy rule. For example, suppose that Parliament passed a law requiring the RBA to increase the money supply by exactly 3% per year. (Why 3%? Because real GDP grows on average about 3% per year and because money demand grows with real GDP, 3% growth in the money supply is roughly the rate necessary to produce long-run price stability.) Such a law would eliminate incompetence and abuse of power on the part of the RBA, and it would make the political business cycle impossible. In addition, policy could no longer be time-inconsistent. People would now believe the RBA's announcement of low inflation because the RBA would be legally required to pursue a low-inflation monetary policy. With low expected inflation, the economy would face a more favourable short-run trade-off between inflation and unemployment.

Other rules for monetary policy are also possible. A more active rule might allow some feedback from the state of the economy to changes in monetary policy. For example, a more active rule might require the RBA to increase monetary growth by 1 percentage point for every percentage point that unemployment rises above its natural rate. Regardless of the precise form of the rule, committing the RBA to some rule would yield advantages by limiting incompetence, abuse of power and time inconsistency in the conduct of monetary policy.

CON: MONETARY POLICY SHOULD NOT BE MADE BY RULE

Although there may be pitfalls with discretionary monetary policy, there is also an important advantage to it: flexibility. The RBA has to confront various circumstances, not all of which can be foreseen. In the 1930s, banks failed in record numbers. In the 1970s, the price of oil skyrocketed around the world. In October 1987, the stock market fell by 22% in a single day. The RBA must decide how to respond to these shocks to the economy. A designer of a policy rule could not possibly consider all the contingencies and specify in advance the correct policy response. It is better to appoint good people to conduct monetary policy and then give them the freedom to do the best they can.

Moreover, the alleged problems with discretion are largely hypothetical. The practical importance of the political business cycle, for instance, is far from clear. In some cases, just the opposite seems to occur. For example, Prime Minister Keating appointed Bernie Fraser to head the RBA in 1990. Nonetheless, Fraser continued the contraction of monetary policy initiated in April 1988 in order to combat the high rate of inflation. The predictable result of Fraser's decision was a recession, and the predictable result of the recession was a decline in Keating's popularity. Rather than using monetary policy to help the politician who had appointed him, Fraser helped with Keating's defeat in the 1996 election.

The practical importance of time inconsistency is also far from clear. Although most people are sceptical of central bank announcements, central bankers can achieve credibility over time by backing up their words with actions. In the 1990s, the RBA achieved and maintained a low rate of inflation, despite the ever-present temptation to take advantage of the short-run trade-off between inflation and unemployment. This experience shows that low inflation does not require that the RBA be committed to a policy rule.

Any attempt to replace discretion with a rule must confront the difficult task of specifying a precise rule. Despite much research examining the costs and benefits of alternative rules, economists have not reached a consensus about what a good rule would be. Until there is a consensus, society has little choice but to give central bankers discretion to conduct monetary policy as they see fit.

QUICK QUIZ Give an example of a monetary policy rule. Why might your rule be better than discretionary policy? Why might it be worse?

THAT THE CENTRAL BANK SHOULD AIM FOR ZERO INFLATION

One of the *Ten Principles of Economics* discussed in chapter 1, and developed more fully in chapter 13, is that prices rise when the government prints too much money. Another of the *Ten Principles of Economics* discussed in chapter 1, and developed more fully in chapter 18, is that society faces a short-run trade-off between inflation and unemployment. Put together, these two principles raise a question for policymakers: How much inflation should the central bank be willing to tolerate? Our third debate is whether zero is the correct target for the inflation rate.

PRO: THE CENTRAL BANK SHOULD AIM FOR ZERO INFLATION

Inflation confers no benefit to society, but it does impose several real costs. As we discussed in chapter 13, economists have identified six costs of inflation:

- shoeleather costs associated with reduced money holdings
- menu costs associated with more frequent adjustment of prices
- increased variability of relative prices

- unintended changes in tax liabilities due to non-indexation of the tax laws
- confusion and inconvenience resulting from a changing unit of account
- arbitrary redistributions of wealth associated with dollar-denominated debts.

Some economists argue that these costs are small, at least for moderate rates of inflation, such as the 2% inflation experienced in Australia during the first half of the 1990s. But other economists claim these costs can be substantial, even for moderate inflation. Moreover, there is no doubt that the public dislikes inflation. When inflation heats up, opinion polls identify inflation as one of the nation's leading problems.

Of course, the benefits of zero inflation have to be weighed against the costs of achieving it. Reducing inflation usually requires a period of high unemployment and low output, as illustrated by the short-run Phillips curve. But this disinflationary recession is only temporary. Once people come to understand that policymakers are aiming for zero inflation, expectations of inflation will fall, which improves the short-run trade-off. Because expectations adjust, there is no trade-off between inflation and unemployment in the long run.

Reducing inflation is, therefore, a policy with temporary costs and permanent benefits. That is, once the disinflationary recession is over, the benefits of zero inflation would persist into the future. If policymakers are farsighted, they should be willing to incur the temporary costs for the permanent benefits. This is precisely the calculation made by Bernie Fraser in the early 1990s, when he reduced inflation from about 8% in 1989 to about 2% in 1991. Fraser was following in the footsteps of Paul Volcker, the Chairman of the US Federal Reserve who performed a similar feat for the US economy in the 1980s. Volcker is considered a hero among central bankers.

Moreover, the costs of reducing inflation need not be as large as some economists claim. If the RBA announces a credible commitment to zero inflation, it can directly influence expectations of inflation. Such a change in expectations can improve the short-run trade-off between inflation and unemployment, allowing the economy to reach lower inflation at a reduced cost. The key to this strategy is credibility—people must believe that the RBA is actually going to carry through its announced policy. Parliament could help in this regard by passing legislation that made price stability the RBA's main goal, much as the New Zealand Parliament has done. Such a law would make it less costly to achieve zero inflation without reducing any of the resulting benefits.

One advantage of a zero-inflation target is that zero provides a more natural focal point for policymakers than any other number. Suppose, for instance, that the RBA were to announce that it would keep inflation at 2%—the rate experienced during the first half of the 1990s. Would the RBA really stick to that 2% target? If events inadvertently pushed inflation up to 4% or 5%, why wouldn't the RBA just raise the target? There is, after all, nothing special about the number 2. In contrast, zero is the only number for the inflation rate at which the RBA can claim that it achieved price stability and fully eliminated the costs of inflation.

CON: THE CENTRAL BANK SHOULD NOT AIM FOR ZERO INFLATION

Although price stability may be desirable, the benefits of zero inflation compared with moderate inflation are small, whereas the costs of reaching zero inflation are large. Estimates of the sacrifice ratio suggest that reducing inflation by 1 percentage point requires giving up about 5% of 1 year's output. Reducing inflation from, say, 4% to zero requires a loss of 20% of a year's output. At the current level of gross domestic product of about $500 billion, this cost translates into $9 billion of lost output, which is about $500 per person. Although people might dislike inflation, it is not at all clear that they would (or should) be willing to pay this much to get rid of it.

The social costs of disinflation are even larger than this $500 figure suggests, for the lost income is not spread equitably over the population. When the economy goes into recession, all incomes do not fall proportionately. Instead, the fall in aggregate income is concentrated on those workers who lose their jobs. The vulnerable workers are often those with the least skills and experience. Hence, much of the cost of reducing inflation is borne by those who can least afford to pay it.

Although economists can list several costs of inflation, there is no professional consensus that these costs are substantial. The shoeleather costs, menu costs and others that economists have identified do not seem great, at least for moderate rates of inflation. It is true that the public dislikes inflation, but the public may be misled into believing the inflation fallacy—the view that inflation erodes living standards. Economists understand that living standards depend on productivity, not monetary policy. Because inflation in nominal incomes goes hand in hand with inflation in prices, reducing inflation would not cause real incomes to rise more rapidly.

Moreover, policymakers can reduce many of the costs of inflation without actually reducing inflation. They can eliminate the problems associated with the non-indexed tax system by rewriting the tax laws to take account of the effects of inflation. They can also reduce the arbitrary redistributions of wealth between creditors and debtors caused by unexpected inflation by issuing indexed government bonds, as in fact the Australian government did in 1985. Such an act insulates holders of government debt from inflation. In addition, by setting an example, it might encourage private borrowers and lenders to write debt contracts indexed for inflation.

Reducing inflation might be desirable if it could be done at no cost, as some economists argue is possible. Yet this trick seems hard to carry out in practice. When economies reduce their rate of inflation, they almost always experience a period of high unemployment and low output. It is risky to believe that the central bank could achieve credibility so quickly as to make disinflation painless.

Indeed, a disinflationary recession can potentially leave permanent scars on the economy. Firms in all industries reduce their spending on new plant and equipment substantially during recessions, making investment the most volatile component of GDP. Even after the recession is over, the smaller stock of capital reduces productivity, incomes and living standards below the levels they otherwise would have achieved. In addition, when workers become unemployed in recessions, they lose valuable job skills. Even after the economy has recovered, their value as workers is diminished. Some economists have argued that the high unemployment in many European economies during the past decade is the aftermath of the disinflations of the 1980s.

Why should policymakers put the economy through a costly, inequitable disinflationary recession to achieve zero inflation, which may have only modest benefits? American economist Alan Blinder argued forcefully in his book *Hard Heads, Soft Hearts* that policymakers should not make this choice:

The costs that attend the low and moderate inflation rates experienced in the United States and in other industrial countries appear to be quite modest—more like a bad cold than a cancer on society…As rational individuals, we do not volunteer for a lobotomy to cure a head cold. Yet, as a collectivity, we routinely prescribe the economic equivalent of lobotomy (high unemployment) as a cure for the inflationary cold.

Blinder concludes that it is better to learn to live with moderate inflation.

QUICK QUIZ Explain the costs and benefits of reducing inflation to zero. Which are temporary and which are permanent?

THAT THE GOVERNMENT SHOULD BALANCE ITS BUDGET

Perhaps the most persistent macroeconomic debate in recent years has been over the Australian government's budget deficit. As you may recall, a budget deficit is an excess of government spending over government revenue. The government finances a budget deficit by issuing government debt. When we studied financial markets in chapter 10, we saw how budget deficits affect saving, investment and interest rates. But how big a problem are budget deficits? Our fourth debate concerns whether fiscal policymakers should make balancing the government's budget a high priority.

PRO: THE GOVERNMENT SHOULD BALANCE ITS BUDGET

Since the early 1980s, the Australian government has usually spent more than it has received in tax revenue. Because of these budget deficits, the debt of the Australian government rose from $30 billion in 1980 to $106 billion in 1995. If we divide today's debt by the size of the population, we learn that each person's share of the government debt is about $9000.

The most direct effect of the government debt is to place a burden on future generations of taxpayers. When these debts and accumulated interest come due, future taxpayers will face a difficult choice. They can pay higher taxes, enjoy less government spending, or both, in order to make resources available to pay off the debt and accumulated interest. Or they can delay the day of reckoning and put the government into even deeper debt by borrowing once again to pay off the old debt and interest. In essence, when the government runs a budget deficit, it allows current taxpayers to pass the bill for some of their government spending on to future taxpayers. Inheriting such a large debt cannot help but lower the living standard of future generations.

In addition to this direct effect, budget deficits also have various macroeconomic effects. Because budget deficits represent *negative* public saving, they lower national saving (the sum of private and public saving). Reduced national saving causes real interest rates to rise and investment to fall. Reduced investment leads over time to a smaller stock of capital. A lower capital stock reduces labour productivity, real wages and the economy's production of goods and services. Thus, when the government increases its debt, future generations are born into an economy with lower incomes as well as higher taxes.

There are, nevertheless, situations in which running a budget deficit is justifiable. Throughout history, the most common cause of increased government debt is war. When a military conflict raises government spending temporarily, it is reasonable to finance this extra spending by borrowing. Otherwise, taxes during wartime would have to rise precipitously. Such high tax rates would greatly distort the incentives faced by those who are taxed, leading to large efficiency losses. In addition, such high tax rates would be unfair to current generations of taxpayers, who already have to make the sacrifice of fighting the war.

Similarly, it is reasonable to allow a budget deficit during a temporary downturn in economic activity. When the economy goes into a recession, tax revenue falls automatically, because the income tax and the payroll tax are levied on measures of income. If the government tried to balance its budget during a recession, it would have to raise taxes or cut spending at a time of high unemployment. Such a policy would tend to depress aggregate demand at precisely the time it needed to be stimulated and, therefore, would tend to increase the magnitude of economic fluctuations.

CON: THE GOVERNMENT SHOULD NOT BALANCE ITS BUDGET

The problem of the budget deficit is often exaggerated. Although government debt does represent a tax burden on younger generations, it is not large compared with the average person's lifetime income. The debt of the Australian government is about $9000 per person. A person who works 40 years for $25 000 a year will earn $1 million over his lifetime. His share of the government debt represents less than 1% of his lifetime resources.

Moreover, it is misleading to view the effects of budget deficits in isolation. The budget deficit is just one piece of a large picture of how the government chooses to raise and spend money. In making these decisions about fiscal policy, policymakers affect different generations of taxpayers in many ways. The budget deficit should be considered together with these other policies.

For example, suppose the government reduces the budget deficit by cutting spending on education. Does this change in policy make young generations better off? The government debt will be smaller when they enter the labour force, which means a smaller tax burden. Yet if they are less well educated, their productivity and incomes will be lower. Many estimates of the return on education (the increase in a worker's wage that results from an additional year of learning) find that it is quite large. Reducing the budget deficit by cutting education spending could, all things considered, make future generations worse off.

Single-minded concern about the budget deficit is also dangerous because it draws attention away from various other policies that redistribute income across generations. For example, in the 1970s, the Australian government decided not to charge fees for university education. That meant an increase in Commonwealth government spending on education. It financed this higher spending by increasing borrowing, which was a burden on future generations. This policy resulted in a redistribution of income for the generation receiving the benefit of free university education. Instead of paying for their education out of current income, they would pay for it in the future by paying off government debt. This occurred even though the policy did not affect the budget deficit. Thus, the budget deficit is only a small piece of the larger issue of how government policy affects the welfare of different generations.

To some extent, the adverse effects of government budget deficits can be reversed by forward-looking parents. Suppose parents are worried about the impact of the government debt on their children. Parents can offset the impact simply by saving and leaving a larger bequest. The bequest would enhance the children's ability to bear the burden of future taxes. Some economists claim that people do, in fact, behave this way. If this were true, higher private saving by parents would offset the public dissaving of budget deficits, and deficits would not affect the economy. (As chapter 10 noted, this theory is called *Ricardian equivalence*.) Most economists doubt that parents are so farsighted, but some people probably do act this way, and anyone could. Deficits give people the opportunity to consume at the expense of their children, but deficits do not require them to do so. If the government debt were actually a great problem facing future generations, some parents would help to solve it.

Critics of budget deficits sometimes assert that the government debt cannot continue to rise forever, but in fact it can. Just as a bank evaluating a loan application would compare a person's debts with his income, we should judge the burden of the government debt relative to the size of the nation's income. Population growth and technological progress cause the total income of the Australian economy to grow over time. As a result, the nation's ability to pay the interest on the government debt grows over time as well. As long as the government debt grows more slowly than the nation's income, there is nothing to prevent the government debt from growing forever.

Some numbers can put the budget deficit into perspective. The real output of the Australian economy grows on average about 3% per year. If the inflation rate is 4% per year, then nominal income grows at a rate of 7% per year. The government debt, therefore, can rise by 7% per year without increasing the ratio of debt to income. In 1995 the Australian government debt was $106 billion; 7% of this figure is $7 billion. As long as the budget deficit is smaller than $7 billion, as it has been in recent years, the policy is sustainable. There will never be any day of reckoning that forces budget deficits to end or the economy to collapse.

> **QUICK QUIZ** Explain how a budget deficit makes future generations worse off. Explain how reducing the budget deficit might make future generations worse off.

THAT THE TAX LAWS SHOULD BE REFORMED TO ENCOURAGE SAVING

A nation's standard of living depends on its ability to produce goods and services. This was one of the *Ten Principles of Economics* in chapter 1. As we saw in chapter 9, a nation's productive capability, in turn, is determined largely by how much it saves and invests for the future. Our fifth debate is whether policy-makers should reform the tax laws in order to encourage greater saving and investment.

PRO: THE TAX LAWS SHOULD BE REFORMED TO ENCOURAGE SAVING

A nation's saving rate is a key determinant of its long-run economic prosperity. When the saving rate is higher, more resources are available for investment in new plant and equipment. A larger stock of plant and equipment, in turn, raises labour productivity, wages and incomes. It is, therefore, no surprise that international data show a strong correlation between national saving rates and measures of economic wellbeing.

Another of the *Ten Principles of Economics* presented in chapter 1 is that people respond to incentives. This lesson should apply to people's decisions about how much to save. If a nation's laws make saving attractive, people will save a higher fraction of their incomes, and this higher saving will lead to a more prosperous future.

Unfortunately, the Australian tax system discourages saving by taxing the return on saving quite heavily. For example, consider Julie, a 25-year-old worker, who saves $1000 of her income in order to have a more comfortable retirement at the age of 70. If she buys a bond that pays an interest rate of 10%, the $1000 will accumulate at the end of 45 years to $72 900 in the absence of taxes on interest. But suppose she faces a marginal tax rate on interest income of 40%, which is typical for many workers. In this case, her after-tax interest rate is only 6%, and the $1000 will accumulate at the end of 45 years to only $13 800. That is, accumulated over this long span of time, the tax rate on interest income reduces the benefit of saving $1000 from $72 900 to $13 800—or by about 80%.

In addition to the tax laws, many other policies and institutions in our society reduce the incentive for households to save. Some government benefits, such as social welfare, age pensions and sickness benefits, are means-tested; that is, the benefits are reduced for those who, in the past, have been prudent enough to save some of their income. Austudy payments for students are granted as a function of the wealth of the students and their parents. Such a policy is like a tax on wealth and, as such, discourages students and parents from saving.

There are various ways in which the tax laws could provide an incentive to save, or at least reduce the disincentive that households now face. Already the tax laws give preferential treatment to some types of retirement saving. When a taxpayer puts income into a superannuation fund, for instance, that income and the interest it earns are taxed at much lower rates than ordinary earned income, if the funds are not withdrawn until retirement. Because there are penalties for withdrawal before retirement age, these retirement plans provide little incentive for other types of saving, such as saving to pay for education. A small step to encourage greater saving would be to expand the ability of households to use such tax-advantaged savings accounts.

A more comprehensive approach is what the Howard government advocated in 1998–99, that is, to reconsider the entire basis upon which the government collects revenue. The centrepiece of the Australian tax system is income tax. A dollar earned is taxed the same whether it is spent or saved. An alternative advocated by many economists is a consumption tax. Under a consumption tax, a household pays taxes only on the basis of what it spends. Income that is saved is exempt from taxation until the saving is later withdrawn and spent on consumption goods. In essence, a consumption tax puts all saving automatically into a tax-advantaged savings account, much like funds in a superannuation account. A switch from income to consumption taxation would greatly increase the incentive to save.

CON: THE TAX LAWS SHOULD NOT BE REFORMED TO ENCOURAGE SAVING

Although increasing saving may be desirable, it is not the only goal of tax policy. Policymakers also must be sure to distribute the tax burden fairly. The problem with proposals to increase the incentive to save is that they increase the tax burden on those who can least afford it.

It is an undeniable fact that high-income households save a higher fraction of their income than low-income households. As a result, any tax change that favours people who save will also tend to favour people with high income. Policies such as tax-advantaged retirement accounts may seem appealing, but they lead to a less egalitarian society. By reducing the tax burden on the wealthy who can take advantage of these accounts, they force the government to raise the tax burden on the poor.

The same argument applies to the tax laws governing inheritances. There are no death duties in Australia, so individuals who want to leave their accumulated wealth to their children (or anyone else) rather than consuming it during their lifetime are advantaged. To a large extent, concern about national saving is motivated by a desire to ensure economic prosperity for future generations. The tax laws already encourage the most direct way in which one generation can help the next.

Moreover, it is not clear if tax policies designed to encourage saving are effective at achieving that goal. Many studies have found that saving is relatively inelastic—that is, the amount of saving is not very sensitive to the rate of return on saving. If this is indeed the case, then tax provisions that raise the effective return by reducing the taxation of capital income will further enrich the wealthy without inducing them to save more than they otherwise would. What's more, a reduction in tax will lower public saving and, on balance, national saving may actually *fall*.

From the standpoint of economic theory, it is not clear whether a higher rate of return would increase saving. The outcome depends on the relative size of two conflicting effects, called the *substitution effect* and the *income effect*. On the one hand, a higher rate of return raises the benefit of saving—each dollar saved today produces more consumption in the future. This substitution effect tends to raise saving. On the other hand, a higher rate of return lowers the need for saving—a household has to save less to achieve any target level of consumption in the future. This income effect tends to reduce saving. If the substitution and income effects approximately cancel each other, as some studies suggest, then saving will not change when lower taxation of capital income raises the rate of return.

There are other ways to raise national saving than by giving tax breaks to the rich. National saving is the sum of private and public saving. Instead of trying to alter the tax laws to encourage greater private saving, policymakers can simply raise public saving by reducing the budget deficit. Reducing the budget deficit, perhaps by raising taxes on the wealthy, offers a direct way of raising national saving and increasing prosperity for future generations.

Indeed, once public saving is taken into account, it seems that tax provisions to encourage saving might backfire. Tax changes that reduce the taxation of capital income reduce government revenue and, thereby, increase the budget deficit. To increase national saving, such a change in the tax laws must stimulate private saving by more than it increases the budget deficit. If this is not the case, so-called saving incentives can potentially make matters worse.

QUICK QUIZ Give three examples of how our society discourages saving. What are the drawbacks of eliminating these disincentives?

CONCLUSION

This chapter has considered five debates over macroeconomic policy. For each, it began with a controversial proposition and then offered the arguments pro and con. If you find it hard to choose a side in these debates, you may find some comfort in the fact that you are not alone. The study of economics does not always make it easy to choose among alternative policies. Indeed, by clarifying the inevitable trade-offs that policymakers face, it can make the choice more difficult.

Difficult choices, however, have no right to seem easy. When you hear politicians or commentators proposing something that sounds too good to be true, it probably is. If they sound like they are offering you a free lunch, you should look for the hidden price tag. Few if any policies come with benefits but no costs. By helping you see through the fog of rhetoric so common in political discourse, the study of economics should make you a better informed participant in our national debates.

Summary

- Advocates of active monetary and fiscal policy view the economy as inherently unstable and believe that policy can manage aggregate demand in order to offset the inherent instability. Critics of active monetary and fiscal policy emphasise that policy affects the economy with a lag and that our ability to forecast future economic conditions is quite bad. As a result, attempts to stabilise the economy can end up being destabilising.

- Advocates of rules for monetary policy argue that discretionary policy can suffer from incompetence, abuse of power and time inconsistency. Critics of rules for monetary policy argue that discretionary policy is more flexible in responding to changing economic circumstances.

- Advocates of a zero-inflation target emphasise that inflation has many costs and few if any benefits. Moreover, the cost of eliminating inflation—depressed output and employment—is only temporary. Even this cost can be reduced if the central bank announces a credible plan to reduce inflation, thereby directly lowering expectations of inflation. Critics of a zero-inflation target claim that moderate inflation imposes only small costs on society, whereas the recession necessary to reduce inflation is quite costly.

- Advocates of a balanced government budget argue that budget deficits impose an unjustifiable burden on future generations by raising their taxes and lowering their incomes. Critics of a balanced government budget argue that the deficit is only one small piece of fiscal policy. Single-minded concern about the budget deficit can obscure the many ways in which policy, including various spending programs, affects different generations.

◆ Advocates of tax incentives for saving point out that our society discourages saving in many ways, such as by heavily taxing the income from capital and by reducing benefits for those who have accumulated wealth. They endorse reforming the tax laws to encourage saving, perhaps by switching from an income tax to a consumption tax. Critics of tax incentives for saving argue that many proposed changes to stimulate saving would primarily benefit the wealthy, who do not need a tax break. They also argue that such changes might have only a small effect on private saving. Raising public saving by eliminating the government's budget deficit would provide a more direct and equitable way to increase national saving.

Questions for review

1. What causes the lags in the effect of monetary and fiscal policy on aggregate demand? What are the implications of these lags for the debate over active versus passive policy?

2. What might motivate a central banker to cause a political business cycle? What does the political business cycle imply for the debate over policy rules?

3. Explain how credibility might affect the cost of reducing inflation.

4. Why are some economists against a target of zero inflation?

5. Explain two ways in which a government budget deficit hurts a future worker.

6. What are two situations in which a budget deficit is justifiable?

7. Give an example of how the government might hurt young generations, even while reducing the government debt they inherit.

8. Some economists say that the government can continue running a budget deficit forever. How is that possible?

9. Some income from capital is taxed twice. Explain.

10. Give an example, other than tax policy, of how our society discourages saving.

11. What adverse effect might be caused by tax incentives to increase saving?

Problems and applications

1. The chapter suggests that the economy, like the human body, has 'natural restorative powers'.
   a. Illustrate the short-run effect of a fall in aggregate demand using an aggregate-demand/aggregate-supply diagram. What happens to total output, income and employment?
   b. If the government does not use stabilisation policy, what happens to the economy over time? Illustrate on your diagram. Does this adjustment generally occur in a matter of months or a matter of years?
   c. Does the economy restore itself? How quickly do the economy's restorative powers work?

2. Policymakers who want to stabilise the economy must decide how much to change the money supply, government spending or taxes. Why is it difficult for policymakers to choose the appropriate strength of their actions?

3. Suppose that people suddenly wanted to hold more money balances.
   a. What would be the effect of this change on the economy if the RBA followed a rule of increasing the money supply by 3% per year? Illustrate your answer with a money market diagram and an aggregate-demand/aggregate-supply diagram.
   b. What would be the effect of this change on the economy if the RBA followed a rule of increasing the money supply by 3% per year *plus* 1 percentage point for every percentage point that unemployment rises above its normal level? Illustrate your answer.
   c. Which of the foregoing rules better stabilises the economy? Would it help to allow the RBA to respond to predicted unemployment instead of current unemployment? Explain.

4. The problem of time inconsistency applies to fiscal policy as well as to monetary policy. Suppose the government announced a reduction in taxes on income from capital investments, such as new factories.
   a. If investors believed that capital taxes would remain low, how would the government's action affect the level of investment?
   b. After investors have responded to the announced tax reduction, does the government have an incentive to renege on its policy? Explain.
   c. Given your answer to part (b), would investors believe the government's announcement? What can the government do to increase the credibility of announced policy changes?
   d. Explain why this situation is similar to the time inconsistency problem faced by monetary policymakers.

5. Chapter 2 explains the difference between positive analysis and normative analysis. In the debate about whether the central bank should aim for zero inflation, which areas of disagreement involve positive statements and which involve normative judgements?

6. Why are the benefits of reducing inflation permanent and the costs temporary? Why are the costs of increasing inflation permanent and the benefits temporary? Use Phillips-curve diagrams in your answer.

7. Explain how each of the following policies redistributes income across generations. Is the redistribution from young to old, or from old to young?
   a. an increase in the budget deficit
   b. more generous subsidies for education loans
   c. greater investments in highways and bridges
   d. indexation of pension benefits to inflation

8. Surveys suggest that most people are opposed to budget deficits, but these same people elect representatives who pass budgets with significant deficits anyway. Why might the opposition to budget deficits be stronger in principle than in practice?

9. The chapter says that budget deficits reduce the income of future generations, but can boost output and income during a recession. Explain how both of these statements can be true.

10. The chapter says that tax changes that encourage saving will tend to favour people with high incomes. If the government cut taxes on capital income, what could it do at the same time to avoid redistributing income?

11. What is the fundamental trade-off that society faces if it chooses to save more?

12. Suppose the government reduced the tax rate on income from savings.
    a. Who would benefit from this tax reduction most directly?
    b. What would happen to the capital stock over time? What would happen to the capital available to each worker? What would happen to productivity? What would happen to wages?
    c. In light of your answer to part (b), who might benefit from this tax reduction in the long run?

13. For several of the policy debates discussed in this chapter, the costs of certain choices are borne primarily by a narrow segment of the population.
    a. Give several examples, and explain why the costs are unevenly distributed.
    b. How does the uneven distribution of costs affect your view of these debates?

GLOSSARY

absolute advantage—the comparison among producers of a good according to their productivity

aggregate-demand curve—a curve that shows the quantity of goods and services that households, firms and the government want to buy at any price level

aggregate-supply curve—a curve that shows the quantity of goods and services that firms choose to produce and sell at any price level

appreciation—an increase in the value of a currency as measured by the amount of foreign currency it can buy

automatic stabilisers—changes in fiscal policy that stimulate aggregate demand when the economy goes into a recession without policymakers having to take any deliberate action or rein in aggregate demand when the economy booms

awards—the minimum wage rates that can be paid to particular workers in particular industries

balanced trade—a situation in which exports equal imports

bond (security)—a certificate of indebtedness

budget deficit—when government spending exceeds tax revenue

budget surplus—an excess of tax revenue over government spending

capital flight—a large and sudden reduction in the demand for assets located in a country

cash—the amount of currency and bank reserves in the economy

cash rate—the interest rate that financial institutions can earn on overnight loans of their currency or reserves

catch-up effect—the property whereby countries that start off poor tend to grow more rapidly than countries that start off rich

central bank—an institution designed to oversee the banking system and regulate the quantity of money in the economy

ceteris paribus—a Latin phrase, translated as 'other things being equal', used as a reminder that all variables other than the ones being studied are assumed to be constant

circular-flow diagram—a visual model of the economy that shows how dollars flow through markets among households and firms

classical dichotomy—the theoretical separation of nominal and real variables

closed economy—an economy that does not interact with other economies in the world

collective bargaining—the process by which unions and firms agree on the terms of employment

commodity money—money that takes the form of a commodity with intrinsic value

comparative advantage—the comparison among producers of a good according to their opportunity cost

competitive market—a market in which there are many buyers and many sellers so that each has a negligible impact on the market price

complements—two goods for which a decrease in the price of one good leads to an increase in the demand for the other good

consumer price index (CPI)—a measure of the overall cost of the goods and services bought by a typical consumer

consumption—spending by households on goods and services, with the exception of purchases of new housing

crowding out—a decrease in investment that results from government borrowing

crowding-out effect—the offset in aggregate demand that results when expansionary fiscal policy raises the interest rate and thereby reduces investment spending

currency—the plastic notes and coins in the hands of the public

current deposits—balances in bank accounts that depositors can access on demand by using a debit card or writing a cheque

cyclical unemployment—the deviation of unemployment from its natural rate

demand curve—a graph of the relationship between the price of a good and the quantity demanded

demand schedule—a table that shows the relationship between the price of a good and the quantity demanded

depreciation—a decrease in the value of a currency as measured by the amount of foreign currency it can buy

depression—a severe recession

diminishing returns—the property whereby the benefit from an extra unit of an input declines as the quantity of the input increases

discouraged workers—individuals who would like to work but have given up looking for a job

economics—the study of how society manages its scarce resources

efficiency—the property of society getting the most it can from its scarce resources

efficiency wages—above-equilibrium wages paid by firms in order to increase worker productivity

elasticity—a measure of the responsiveness of quantity demanded or quantity supplied to one of its determinants

equilibrium—a situation in which supply and demand have been brought into balance

equilibrium price—the price that balances supply and demand

equilibrium quantity—the quantity supplied and the quantity demanded when the price has adjusted to balance supply and demand

equity—the property of distributing economic prosperity fairly among the members of society

excess demand—a situation in which quantity demanded is greater than quantity supplied

excess supply—a situation in which quantity supplied is greater than quantity demanded

exports—goods and services that are produced domestically and sold abroad

externality—the impact of one person's actions on the wellbeing of a bystander

fiat money—money without intrinsic value that is used as money because of government decree

financial intermediaries—financial institutions through which savers can indirectly provide funds to borrowers

financial markets—financial institutions through which savers can directly provide funds to borrowers

financial system—the group of institutions in the economy that help to match one person's saving with another person's investment

Fisher effect—the one-for-one adjustment of the nominal interest rate to the inflation rate

fractional-reserve banking—a banking system in which banks hold only a fraction of deposits as reserves

GDP deflator—a measure of the price level calculated as the ratio of nominal GDP to real GDP times 100

government purchases—spending on goods and services by local, state and federal governments

gross domestic product (GDP)—the market value of all final goods and services produced within a country in a given period of time

gross national product (GNP)—the market value of all final goods and services produced by permanent residents of a nation within a given period of time

human capital—the knowledge and skills that workers acquire through education, training and experience

imports—goods and services that are produced abroad and sold domestically

income elasticity of demand—a measure of how much the quantity demanded of a good responds to a change in consumers' income, calculated as the percentage change in quantity demanded divided by the percentage change in income

indexation—the automatic correction of a dollar amount for the effects of inflation by law or contract

inferior good—a good for which, other things being equal, an increase in income leads to a decrease in quantity demanded

inflation—an increase in the overall level of prices in the economy

inflation rate—the percentage change in the price index from the preceding period

inflation tax—the revenue the government raises by creating money

investment—spending on new capital equipment, inventories and structures, including household purchases of new housing

job search—the process by which workers find appropriate jobs given their tastes and skills

labour force—the total number of workers, including both the employed and the unemployed

labour-force participation rate—the percentage of the adult population that is in the labour force

law of demand—the claim that, other things being equal, the quantity demanded of a good falls when the price of the good rises

law of supply—the claim that, other things being equal, the quantity supplied of a good rises when the price of the good rises

law of supply and demand—the claim that the price of any good adjusts to bring the supply of and demand for that good into balance

liquidity—the ease with which an asset can be converted into the economy's medium of exchange

liquidity conditions—the price and availability of funding for the economy's expenditure

macroeconomics—the study of economy-wide phenomena, including inflation, unemployment and economic growth

managed fund—a type of financial investment that allows investors to own a portfolio of various types of shares and/or bonds

marginal changes—small incremental adjustments to a plan of action

market—a group of buyers and sellers of a particular good or service

market economy—an economy that allocates resources through the decentralised decisions of many firms and households as they interact in markets for goods and services

market failure—a situation in which a market left on its own fails to allocate resources efficiently

market for loanable funds—the market in which those who want to save supply funds and those who want to borrow to invest demand funds

market power—the ability of a single economic actor (or small group of actors) to have a substantial influence on market prices

medium of exchange—an item that buyers give to sellers when they want to purchase goods and services

menu costs—the costs of changing prices

microeconomics—the study of how households and firms make decisions and how they interact in markets

model of aggregate demand and aggregate supply—the model that most economists use to explain short-run fluctuations in economic activity around its long-run trend

monetary neutrality—the proposition that changes in the money supply do not affect real variables

monetary policy—the management by the central bank of liquidity conditions in the economy

money—the set of assets in an economy that people regularly use to buy goods and services from other people

money multiplier—the amount of money the banking system generates with each dollar of reserves

money supply—the quantity of money circulating in the economy

multiplier effect—the additional shifts in aggregate demand that result when expansionary fiscal policy increases income and thereby increases consumer spending

NAIRU or non-accelerating inflation rate of unemployment—the level of unemployment that does not result in increases in the inflation rate

national saving (saving)—the total income in the economy that remains after paying for consumption and government purchases

natural rate of unemployment—unemployment accounted for by structural factors around which the actual unemployment rate fluctuates

natural-rate hypothesis—the claim that unemployment eventually returns to its normal, or natural, rate, regardless of the rate of inflation

natural resources—the inputs into the production of goods and services that are provided by nature, such as land, rivers and mineral deposits

net exports—the value of a nation's exports minus the value of its imports, also called the trade balance

net foreign investment—the purchase of foreign assets by domestic residents minus the purchase of domestic assets by foreigners

nominal exchange rate—the rate at which a person can trade the currency of one country for the currency of another

nominal GDP—the production of goods and services valued at current prices

nominal interest rate—the interest rate as usually reported without a correction for the effects of inflation

nominal variables—variables measured in monetary units

normal good—a good for which, other things being equal, an increase in income leads to an increase in quantity demanded

normative statements—claims that attempt to prescribe how the world should be

open economy—an economy that interacts freely with other economies around the world

open-market operations—the purchase and sale of Australian government securities by the Reserve Bank of Australia (RBA)

opportunity cost—whatever must be given up to obtain some item

Phillips curve—the short-run trade-off between inflation and unemployment

physical capital—the stock of equipment and structures that are used to produce goods and services

positive statements—claims that attempt to describe the world as it is

price ceiling—a legal maximum on the price at which a good can be sold

price elasticity of demand—a measure of how much the quantity demanded of a good responds to a change in the price of that good, calculated as the percentage change in quantity demanded divided by the percentage change in price

price elasticity of supply—a measure of how much the quantity supplied of a good responds to a change in the price of that good, calculated as the percentage change in quantity supplied divided by the percentage change in price

price floor—a legal minimum on the price at which a good can be sold

private saving—the income that households have left after paying for taxes and consumption

producer price index—a measure of the cost of a basket of goods and services bought by firms

production possibilities frontier—a graph that shows the various combinations of output that the economy can possibly produce given the available factors of production and the available production technology

productivity—the amount of goods and services produced from each hour of a worker's time

public saving—the tax revenue that the government has left after paying for its spending

purchasing-power parity—a theory of exchange rates whereby a unit of any given currency should be able to buy the same quantity of goods in all countries

quantity demanded—the amount of a good that buyers are willing and able to purchase

quantity equation—the equation $M \times V = P \times Y$, which relates the quantity of money, the velocity of money and the dollar value of the economy's output of goods and services

quantity supplied—the amount of a good that sellers are willing and able to sell

quantity theory of money—a theory asserting that the quantity of money available determines the price level and that the growth rate in the quantity of money available determines the inflation rate

rational expectations—the theory according to which people optimally use all the information they have, including information about government policies, when forecasting the future

real exchange rate—the rate at which a person can trade the goods and services of one country for the goods and services of another

real GDP—the production of goods and services valued at constant prices

real interest rate—the interest rate corrected for the effects of inflation

real variables—variables measured in constant units

recession—a period of declining real incomes and rising unemployment

Reserve Bank of Australia (RBA)—the central bank of Australia

reserve ratio—the fraction of deposits that banks hold as reserves

reserve requirements—regulations on the minimum amount of reserves that banks must hold against deposits

reserves—deposits that banks have received but have not lent out

sacrifice ratio—the number of percentage points of annual output lost in the process of reducing inflation by 1 percentage point

scarcity—the limited nature of society's resources

share—a claim to partial ownership in a firm

shoeleather costs—the resources wasted when inflation encourages people to reduce their money holdings

stagflation—a period of falling output and rising prices

store of value—an item that people can use to transfer purchasing power from the present to the future

strike—the organised withdrawal of labour from a firm by a union

substitutes—two goods for which a decrease in the price of one good leads to a decrease in the demand for the other good

supply curve—a graph of the relationship between the price of a good and the quantity supplied

supply schedule—a table that shows the relationship between the price of a good and the quantity supplied

tax incidence—the study of who bears the burden of taxation

technological knowledge—society's understanding of the best ways to produce goods and services

theory of liquidity preference—Keynes's theory that the interest rate adjusts to bring money supply and money demand into balance

total revenue (in a market)—the amount paid by buyers and received by sellers of a good, calculated as the price of the good times the quantity sold

trade balance—the value of a nation's exports minus the value of its imports, also called net exports

trade deficit—an excess of imports over exports

trade policy—a government policy that directly influences the quantity of goods and services that a country imports or exports

trade surplus—an excess of exports over imports

unemployment benefits—a government program that partially protects workers' incomes when they become unemployed

unemployment rate—the percentage of the labour force that is unemployed

union—a worker association that bargains with employers over wages and working conditions

unit of account—the yardstick people use to post prices and record debts

value added—the value of a firm's output minus the value of its inputs

velocity of money—the rate at which money changes hands

CREDITS

Photos and cartoons
p. 5 © Universal Press Syndicate
p. 8 Reprinted by permission of The Wall Street Journal © 1990 Dow Jones and Company, Inc.; all rights reserved worldwide
p. 11 Steiner, Cartoonists and Writers Syndicate
p. 13 © 1978 Stayskal and the Chicago Tribune
p. 18 © United Media
p. 27 Drawing by Stevenson; © 1981 The New Yorker Magazine, Inc.
p. 54 Corbis-Bettman
p. 69 © Michael Newman/Photo Edit
p. 82 Drawing by Robert Day; © The New Yorker Magazine, Inc.
p. 94 © Swanson/Gamma Liaison
p. 159 Reprinted by permission of The Wall Street Journal © 1990 Dow Jones and Company, Inc.; all rights reserved worldwide
p. 161 The Kobal Collection
p. 176 © Michael Newman/Photo Edit
p. 179 © Jeff Greenberg/Photo Edit
p. 185 AAP Image Archive
p. 187 Andomeda Interactive
p. 198 © J. P. Laffont/Sygma
p. 212 Drawing by Robert Weber; © 1989 The New Yorker Magazine, Inc.
p. 215 Photograph courtesy of the Parliament of Australia
p. 226 © Jeff Greenberg/Photo Edit
p. 252 Cartoon by Rod Clement from his book *The Economic Rationalist's Guide to Sex*, with the permission of HarperCollins Publishers
p. 253 Reprinted by permission of The Wall Street Journal © 1984 Dow Jones and Company, Inc.; all rights reserved worldwide
p. 254 Cartoon by Rod Clement from his book *The Economic Rationalist's Guide to Sex*, with the permission of HarperCollins Publishers
p. 255 Photograph courtesy of the Commonwealth Bank of Australia
p. 260 Drawing by M. Stevens; © 1989 The New Yorker Magazine, Inc.
p. 290 The Kobal Collection
p. 298 Drawing by Mort Gerberg; © 1992 The New Yorker Magazine, Inc.
p. 311 Digital Stock
p. 346 Drawing by Mankoff; © 1990 The New Yorker Magazine, Inc.
p. 360 Photograph courtesy of the Olympic Co-ordination Authority
p. 382 Corbis-Bettmann
p. 385 Photograph courtesy of the Reserve Bank of Australia
p. 401 Cartoon by David Messer/*Sydney Morning Herald*, 8 May 1999; reproduced with permission
p. 407 Drawing by Dana Fradon; © 1983 The New Yorker Magazine, Inc.
p. 423 Drawing by Modell; © 1983 The New Yorker Magazine, Inc.
p. 433 Cartoon by Rod Clement from his book *The Economic Rationalist's Guide to Sex*, with the permission of HarperCollins Publishers

Literary
p. 83 The Boston Globe/Jerry Ackerman; reprinted by permission
p. 96 Kylie Hansen/*Herald Sun*; reprinted by permission
p. 115 © *Economist*; reprinted by permission
pp. 154, 155 Ross Gittins/*Sydney Morning Herald*; reprinted by permission
pp. 156, 157 Alan Mitchell/*Australian Financial Review*; reprinted by permission
pp. 178, 179 Copyright © 1996 by The New York Times Co.; reprinted by permission
p. 182 Copyright © 1996 by The New York Times Co.; reprinted by permission
pp. 186, 187 © *Economist*; reprinted by permission
p. 199 Share tables reprinted by permission of *Sydney Morning Herald*
pp. 214, 215 John Pitchford/*Australian*; reprinted by permission
pp. 216, 217 Reprinted by permission of The Wall Street Journal © Dow Jones and Company, Inc.; all rights reserved worldwide
pp. 230, 231 Ross Gittins/*Sydney Morning Herald*; reprinted by permission
p. 253 Reprinted by permission of The Wall Street Journal © 1984 Dow Jones and Company, Inc.; all rights reserved worldwide
p. 280 Reprinted by permission of The Wall Street Journal © 1993 Dow Jones and Company, Inc.; all rights reserved worldwide
pp. 288, 289 Copyright © 1996 by The New York Times Co.; reprinted by permission
p. 289 Edna Carew/*Personal Investment*; reprinted by permission
pp. 302, 303 Warwick McKibbin/*Australian Financial Review*; reprinted by permission
p. 305 Copyright © 1994 by The New York Times Co.; reprinted by permission
p. 311 Ian Thomas/*Australian Financial Review*; reprinted by permission
p. 336 Frank Gelber/*Australian Financial Review*; reprinted by permission
p. 360 Mark Robinson/*Daily Telegraph*; reprinted by permission
p. 385 Brian Toohey/*Australian Financial Review*; reprinted by permission
p. 397 Copyright © 1996 by The New York Times Co.; reprinted by permission
p. 414 Copyright © 1996 by The New York Times Co.; reprinted by permission

INDEX

Note: Page numbers in **bold** refer to pages where key terms are defined.

Absolute advantage **51**
Absolute value 89
ACCC (Australian Competition and Consumer Commission) 27
Accord, Prices and Income 231, 234, 236, 408–9, 411–13
Account, money as unit of 251
Accounting 201
Ackerman, Jerry 83
ACTU (Australian Council of Trade Unions) 408–9, 411
Adverse selection **240**
Africa. *See also specific countries*
    economic growth 186–7
Aggregate demand. *See also* Aggregate-demand curve; Model of aggregate demand and aggregate supply
    crowding-out effect 377–8
    fiscal policy 375–80
    government purchases 376
    liquidity preference 369–71
    monetary policy 368–76
    money supply changes 372–4
    multiplier effect 376–7
    taxes 378–80
Aggregate-demand curve **349**, 350–2. *See also* Model of aggregate demand and aggregate supply
    downward slope 350–2, 372
    money supply changes 372–4
    shifts 352, 358–61
Aggregate-supply curve **349**, 353–8. *See also* Model of aggregate demand and aggregate supply
    long-run 353–4
    shifts 361–2
    short-run 355–8
AIRC (Australian Industrial Relations Commission) 116–17, 234, 235
American Forest and Paper Association 83
American Stock Exchange (ASE) 198
'Analytics of Anti-inflation Policy' (Samuelson and Solow) 394
Anderson, Malcolm 31
Animal spirits 382
Ansett 311
APEC (Asia–Pacific Economic Cooperation) 30–1
Appreciation, of currency **308**
APRA (Australian Prudential Regulation Authority) 257
Arbitrage 312
Argentina, economic growth in 170–1, 172
Art gallery admission, pricing 94
Asia–Pacific Economic Cooperation (APEC) 30–1
Asian financial crisis 302–3, 336
Assembly lines 238–9
Assumptions 19–20
ASX (Australian Stock Exchange) 198
Asymmetric information **240**
AT&T 198
Australia
    car industry 331–3
    budget deficits 12, 210, 211–13, 330–1

economic growth 11, 171, 181
    effect of Asian crisis 302–3, 336
    financial institutions 196–201
    GDP and quality of life 145
    inflation 12–13
    international trade 299–301
    labour-force participation rate 225–7
    money 252–4
    net foreign investment 306–7
    productivity slowdown 189–90
    standard of living 11
Australian Bureau of Statistics 27
Australian Competition and Consumer Commission (ACCC) 27
Australian Council of Trade Unions (ACTU) 408–9, 411
Australian Industrial Relations Commission (AIRC) 116–17, 234, 235
Australian Prudential Regulation Authority (APRA) 257
Australian Research Council 189
Australian Stock Exchange (ASX) 198
Austria, inflation in 279
Austudy 432
Automatic stabilisers **384**
Award wages 231, 235
Awards **116**

Baht, depreciation of 311
Balanced trade **299**
Bangladesh
    economic growth 171–2
    GDP and quality of life 145
Banks 198–9, 200
    central **256**, 426–9. *See also* Reserve Bank of Australia (RBA)
    money supply. *See* Money supply
    reserves 258–60, 263
    runs on 264–5
Bar graphs 34
Barro, Robert J. 409, 410, 415
Barter 249–50
Baum, L. Frank 289–90
Blandy, Richard 31
Blinder, Alan 289, 428–9
Bolivia, inflation in 283–4
Bonds (securities) **197**
    inflation-indexed 288–9
    inflation-linked 289
    junk 197
    market 196–7
    municipal 197
Brain drain 184
Brazil, economic growth in 172
Brinkmanship 234
Britain
    economic growth 172
    productivity slowdown 190
Broad money 254
Brown, Eleanor J. 397
Bryan, William Jennings 288–9
Budget deficits 12, **203**
    of Australia 12, 210, 330–1
    Australia and United States compared 211–13

    economic crisis 214–15
    market for loanable funds 209–10
    in open economy 328–31
Budget, government
    balancing 429–31
    deficits. *See* Budget deficits
    surpluses **203**
Budget surpluses **203**
Bush, George 30
Business cycles. *See* Economic fluctuations; Great Depression; Recessions
Buyers, taxes on, market outcomes 120–1

Campbell, John Y. 288–9
Canada
    economic growth 172
    productivity slowdown 190
Capital
    flow 301–3, 305
    human **174**
    physical **174**
Capital flight **334**
    in open economies 334–7
Car industry, Japanese–Australian competition in 331–3
Car-safety laws 7
Carew, Edna 289
Cartels, unions as 232
Cash **261**
Cash rate **261**, 263–4
Catch-up effect **181**
Causality 41–3
Central banks **256**, 426–9. *See also* Reserve Bank of Australia (RBA)
Ceteris paribus **66**
Chad, economic growth in 169
China
    capital flow to 305
    economic growth 170
    GDP and quality of life 145
Chodad, John 253
Cigarettes, as commodity money 251–2
Circular-flow diagram **21**, 21–2
Classical dichotomy 274–6, **275**
Cleveland, Grover 290
Clinton, Bill 421
Closed economies 202, **298**
Coca-Cola Company 176, 198
Collective bargaining **232**
Commodity money **251**, 252
Commonwealth Bank of Australia 256
Communism, collapse of 9
Comparative advantage 50–5, **52**
    applications 53–5
    opportunity cost 51–2
    trade 52
Competition 8–9
    monopolistic 63
    oligopoly 63
Competitive markets **62**
Complements **64**
Compounding 172
Computers, productivity and 178–9
Constant returns to scale 177

Consumer price index (CPI) 149, **150**, 150–9
    accuracy 155–6
    biases 156–7
    calculation 150–2
    composition of basket 153
    GDP deflator versus 157–9
    microeconomic reform 154–5
    problems in measuring cost of living 153–7
Consumption **137**
    marginal propensity to consume 378
Coordinate system 34
Correlation 36
Cost of living, measuring. *See* Consumer price index (CPI)
Costs
    of inflation. *See* Inflation
    menu **284**
    opportunity. *See* Opportunity cost
CPI. *See* Consumer price index (CPI)
Credit cards 255
Credit risk 197
Crowding out **210**
Crowding-out effect **377**, 377–8
CSIRO 189
Currency **252**, 254–5. *See also* Exchange rates
    appreciation (strengthening) 308
    change to decimal 218
    depreciation (weakening) 308, 310–11
Current deposits 253
Curves 37–9. *See also specific curves*
    movements along versus shifts 39, 79–80
Cyclical unemployment 222, **225**

Date of maturity, of bonds 197
Debelle, Gary 231
Debit cards 252, 255
Debt finance 198
Debt, government 209
Decimal currency, change to 218
Decisions 3–8
    incentives 7–8
    marginal changes 6–7
    opportunity cost 6
    trade-offs 4–5
Default 197
Deficits
    budget. *See* Budget deficits
    trade **299**
Deflation 269
Demand 63–9
    aggregate. *See* Aggregate demand; Aggregate-demand curve; Model of aggregate demand and aggregate supply
    change 78, 80–1
    elastic 88, 90, 95
    excess **78**
    individual. *See* Individual demand
    inelastic 88, 90, 95
    law 644
    for loanable funds 204–6
    market. *See* Market demand
    for money. *See* Money demand

Demand curve 37–9, **65**
    aggregate. *See* Aggregate-demand curve
    applications 98–105
    ceteris paribus 66
    elasticity 90–2, 95
    shifts 68–9
Demand schedule **65**
Deposits, current 253
Depreciation, of currency **308**
    baht 311
Depressions 264, **344**, 364
Deregulation 385
Developed countries, flows of goods and capital to and from 305
Developing countries, flows of goods and capital to and from 305
Diminishing returns **181**
    economic growth 180–1
Discouraged workers **227**
Discretion, rule versus 424–6
Discretionary expenditure
    income elasticity of demand 96
    price elasticity of demand 88
Disinflation 410–11
Dividend yield 199
Dividends 199
Double coincidence of wants 250
Dow Jones Industrial Average 198
Drug bans and supply, demand and elasticity 103–5

Eastern Europe. *See also specific countries*
    collapse of communism 9
Economic fluctuations 344–9. *See also* Recessions
    aggregate-demand and aggregate-supply model for analysis 348–9
    irregular and unpredictable nature 344
    output and unemployment 346–7
    short-run versus long-run 348
    simultaneous fluctuation of macroeconomic quantities 346
Economic growth 11, 169–73, 178–89
    in Africa 186–7
    compounding and the rule of 70 172
    diminishing returns and catch-up effect 180–1
    education 183–4
    famine 185
    foreign investment 181–3
    free trade 185–8
    population control 188–9
    productivity. *See* Productivity
    property rights and political stability 184–5
    research and development 189
    saving and investment 178–80
    World Bank 182
Economic models 20. *See also specific models*
Economic welfare, and the GDP 143–5
Economics 4
    as science 18–25, 28–9
Economists
    disagreement among 28–31
    in government 26–8
Education, and economic growth 183–4

Efficiency **5**
Efficiency wages **236**, 236–9
    worker effort theory 237
    worker health theory 236–7
    worker quality theory 237–8
    worker turnover theory 237
EFTPOS 252
Egan, Michael 360
Einstein, Albert 18
Elastic demand 88, 90, 95
Elastic supply 97, 97–8
Elasticity 40–1, **88**
    of supply. *See* Price elasticity of supply
    tax incidence 124–5
    unit 90
Elasticity of demand 88–96
    applications 98–105
    income 94–8, 96
    price. *See* Price elasticity of demand
Empire Paper Company 83
Environmental quality, exclusion from GDP 144
Equilibrium **76**
    change 78–81
    market supply and market demand at 76–8
    monetary 271–2
    in money market 370–1
    in open economy 324–8
Equilibrium interest rate 370
Equilibrium price **76**
Equilibrium quantity **76**
Equity **5**
Equity finance 198
Ethiopia, economic growth in 169
European Union 30–1
Evans, Ted 385
Excess demand **78**
Excess supply **76**, 76–7
Exchange, mediums of 200, 251
Exchange rates 308–10
    market for foreign–currency exchange 322–4
    Mundell–Fleming's exchange-rate effect 351, 368
    nominal. *See* Nominal exchange rates
    purchasing-power parity 310–15
    real **308**, 309–10
Expectations
    individual demand 64
    individual supply 71
    Phillips curve 401–2
    reverse causality 43
Expenditure. *See also* Consumption
    equality with income 132–4
Exports **53**, **298**, 298–9. *See also* International flows; International trade
    net. *See* Net exports
    voluntary restriction 331
Externalities **10**

Factors of production 21–2. *See also specific factors and factor markets*
    prices, and individual supply 71
    productivity 174
Fad economics 29–30
Famine, causes of 185

Federal Reserve (US) 27, 257
Fiat money **252**
Film industry, and price indexes 161
Final goods 135
Finance, debt versus equity 198
Finance, Department of 27
Financial intermediaries **198**, 198–201. *See also* Banks
Financial markets **196**, 196–8
Financial system **196**
First World, flows of goods and capital to and from 305
Fiscal policy
    aggregate demand 375–80
    crowding-out effect 377–8
    government purchases 376
    multiplier effect 376–7
    stabilisation using. *See* Stabilisation policy
    taxes 378–80
Fisher effect 280–2, **282**
Fisher, Irving 289
Fleming, Marcus 351
Flows, international. *See* International flows
Ford, Henry 176, 238–9
Ford Motor Company 238–9
Foreign-currency exchange market 322–4
Foreign investment
    direct 182, 301
    economic growth 181–3
    net **301**, 301–3, 306–7
    portfolio 182, 301
Fractional-reserve banking **259**, 259–60
France
    controlling aggregate demand 383
    productivity slowdown 190
Fraser, Bernie 427
Fraser, Malcolm 270, 408, 410, 426
Free-silver debate 287–90
Free trade, and economic growth 185–8
Friedman, Milton 273, 289, 356, 398–9, 401–5, 410, 415
FTSE (London) 198
Full-employment output 354

Gains from trade 48–50
GDP. *See* Gross domestic product (GDP)
GDP deflator **142**
    consumer price index versus 157–9
GDP(I) and GDP(P) approaches 138
Gelber, Frank 336
Gender, and labour-force participation rate 225–7
General Electric 198
General Motors Corporation 198
General Theory of Employment, Interest, and Money, The (Keynes) 364, 369, 381, 382
Generational accounting 215
Germany
    controlling aggregate demand 383
    GDP and quality of life 145
    inflation 12, 270, 279, 280, 287, 313–14
    productivity slowdown 190
Ghettos 243
Gittins, Ross 154–5, 230–1
GNP (gross national product) **136**

Gold
    as commodity money 251
    free-silver debate 287–90
Gold standard 251
Goods
    final 135
    flow 298–9, 305
    inferior **64**, 96
    intermediate 135
    new, and consumer price index 155
    normal **64**, 94, 96
    public 189
Government budget
    balancing 429–31
    deficits. *See* Budget deficits
    surpluses **203**
Government debt 209
Government economists 26–8
Government purchases **137**
    changes in, and aggregate demand 376
    crowding-out effect 377–8
    multiplier effect 376–7
Graphs 34–43
    cause and effect 41–3
    curves 37–9
    elasticity 41
    of single variable 34
    slope 39–41
    of two variables 34, 36
Great Britain. *See* Britain
Great Depression 264, 364
Greenspan, Alan 289
Gregory, Bob 242–3
Grenville, Stephen 385
Griliches, Zvi 179
Gross domestic product (GDP) 132, **134**, 134–45, 202
    components 137–8
    economic wellbeing 143–5
    GDP deflator 142, 157–9
    international differences 145
    nominal **140**, 140–2
    real. *See* Real GDP
Gross domestic product income approach (GDP(I)) 138
Gross domestic product production approach (GDP(P)) 138
Gross national product (GNP) **136**

Hang Seng (Hong Kong) 198
Hanna, Marcus Alonzo 290
Hard Heads, Soft Hearts (Blinder) 428–9
Hawke, Bob 236, 408
Hershey, Robert D., Jr 397
Hoffman, Stuart G. 397
Hong Kong, economic growth in 169
Horton, Virgil 83
Households, decisions faced by 3
Human capital **174**
Hume, David 275
100%-reserve banking 258
Hungary, inflation in 279
Hunter, Boyd 243
Hyperinflation 287
    in Austria 279
    in Bolivia 283–4
    in Germany 12, 270, 279, 313–14

    in Hungary 279
    money and prices during 278–9
    nominal exchange rates during 313–14
    in Poland 279
    in Serbia 280

IBM 198
Identities 137, 202–3
IMF (International Monetary Fund) 183, 186
Import quotas 331
Imports **53**, **298**, 298–9. *See also* International flows; International trade
Incentives 7–8
    for saving 433
Income effect, on saving 433
Income elasticity of demand **94**, 94–8, 96
Income, equality with expenditure 132–4
Income taxes. *See entries beginning with* Tax
Index funds 201
Indexation **160**, 235–6, 408–9
India
    economic growth 170–1
    GDP and quality of life 145
Individual demand
    demand schedule and demand curve 64–6
    determinants 63–4
    market demand versus 66–8
Individual supply
    determinants 71
    market supply versus 72–3
    supply schedule and supply curve 71–2
Indonesia
    GDP and quality of life 145
    political instability and capital flight 333–7
    tourism 311
Industrial disputes 232, 234
Industry Commission 27
Inelastic demand 88, 90, 95
Inelastic supply 97
'Infant industry' argument 185–6
Inferior goods **64**
    income elasticity of demand 96
Inflation **12**, 12–14, 150, 269–91. *See also* Hyperinflation
    causes 270–82
    comparing dollar figures from different times 159–60
    confusion and inconvenience due to 286
    costs 282–90
    expected, and unemployment 401–2
    free-silver debate 287–90
    indexation 160
    menu costs 284
    non-accelerating inflation rate of unemployment (NAIRU) 400
    protecting savings from 287–8
    purchasing power 282–3
    real and nominal interest rates 160–2
    reducing 408–13
    relative-price variability and resource misallocation due to 284–5
    shoeleather costs 282–3, **283**
    tax distortions induced 285–6
    unemployment. *See* Phillips curve

unexpected, wealth redistribution due to 287–8
zero, as aim of central bank 426–9
Inflation-indexed bonds 288–9
Inflation-linked securities 289
Inflation rate 150, **152**
Inflation tax 279, **279**
Information, asymmetric 240
Inheritances 433
Injections, monetary 272–3
Inputs. *See* Factors of production
Inquiry into the Nature and Causes of the Wealth of Nations, An (Smith) 9, 54
Insiders, unions and 233
Interest rates
    cash rate **261**
    equilibrium 370
    Keynes effect 351, 368
    in long and short runs 386–7
    as monetary policy instrument 375
    real and nominal 160–2, **162**
Interest, tax treatment of 285–6
Intermediate goods 135
International comparisons
    economic growth 171
    GDP 144–5
    quality of life 144–5
International flows
    of capital 301–3
    equality of net exports and net foreign investment 302–4
    of goods 298–9
    saving and investment 304–6
    between South and North 305
International Monetary Fund (IMF) 183, 186
International trade 53–4
    Australia 299–301
    balance 299, 333
    comparative advantage. *See* Comparative advantage
    flows. *See* International flows
    free, and economic growth 185–8
    gains from 48–50
    restriction 331
    trade policy 331–3
Intrinsic value 251
Investment **137**
    economic growth 178–80
    foreign. *See* Foreign investment
    international flows of goods and capital 304–6
    meaning 203
    taxes 208–9
Investment accelerator 377
Inward-oriented policies 185–6, 187–8
Italy
    inflation 313–14
    productivity slowdown 190

Japan
    car industry 331–3
    controlling aggregate demand 383
    economic growth 11, 171, 180
    GDP and quality of life 145
    productivity slowdown 190
Jevons, William Stanley 289

Job search **239**, 239–43
    inevitability of search unemployment 239–41
    location of unemployment 242–3
    public policy 241
    unemployment benefits 241–2
Jordan, Michael 53
Junk bonds 197

Keating, Paul 335, 413, 426
Kennedy, Robert 143
Keynes effect 351, 368
Keynes, John Maynard 28, 32, 351, 356, 364, 369, 381–2
Keynesian economists 382–3
Knight, Harry 385
Korea 11, 169
Krueger, Alan 178–9
Krugman, Paul 305

Labour force **223**
Labour-force participation rate **223**, 223–7
Labour Force Survey 222
Labour market, tightening of 397
Latin America, inflation 287. *See also specific countries*
Law of demand **64**
Law of supply **71**
Law of supply and demand **78**
Legislation
    car safety 7
    Reserve Bank Act (1959) 381
Leisure, exclusion from GDP 144
Lender of last resort 257
Lewis, Paul 182
Lindbaek, Jannik 182
Liquidity **251**
Liquidity conditions **257**
Liquidity preference 369–71, 375
Living standards, determinants of 11–12
Loanable funds, market for. *See* Market for loanable funds
London Stock Exchange 198
Long, Clyde 397
Long run
    algebraic explanation 387
    short run versus 348, 386–7
Long-run aggregate-supply curve 353–4
    shifts 354–5
    vertical slope 353–4
Lowe, Joseph 289
Lucas, Robert 170, 409, 415

M3 254
Macfarlane, Ian 385
McKibbin, Warwick 302–3
McKinley, William 289, 290
Macroeconomics 24–5, **25**, **132**
Malaysia, political instability and capital flight in 334
Managed funds **200**, 200–8
Marginal changes **6**, 6–7
Marginal propensity to consume (*MPC*) 378
Market demand
    at equilibrium 76–8
    individual demand versus 66–8

Market economies **9**, 9–10
Market failure **10**
Market for loanable funds **204**, 204–13
    budget deficits 209–10
    in open economy 320–2
    supply and demand 204–6
    taxes and investment 208–9
    taxes and saving 206–8
Market power **10**
Market supply
    in competitive markets 62
    at equilibrium 76–8
    individual supply versus 72–3
Markets **62**. *See also specific markets*
    competitive **62**. *See also* Competition
    definition, and price elasticity of demand 88–9
    efficiency 5
    for factors of production 21–2
    financial **196**, 196–8
    for goods and services 21–2
    price ceiling effects on 110–11
    price floor effects on outcomes 114–18
Maturity date, of bonds 197
Mayland, Kenneth T. 397
Medium of exchange **200**, **251**
Menu costs **284**, 357
Mexico
    capital flow to 305
    economic growth 171
Microeconomic reform, effect on CPI 154–5
Microeconomics 24–5, **25**, **132**
Midpoint method, for calculating elasticities 90
Minimum wage
    rates 116–18
    unemployment 229–32
Misery index 393
Mitchell, Alan 156–7
Model of aggregate demand and aggregate supply 343–64, **348**
    aggregate-demand curve 349, 350–2
    aggregate-supply curve 349, 353–8
    economic fluctuations. *See* Economic fluctuations
    Phillips curve 395–8
Model T Ford 238
Models 20. *See also specific models*
Monetary equilibrium 271–2
Monetary injections 272–3
    adjustment to 273–4
Monetary neutrality **275**
Monetary policy **257**
    aggregate demand 368–76
    Australia 261–3
    interest-rate targets 375
    liquidity preference 369–71
    money supply changes 372–4
    problems in controlling money supply 263–4
    by rule versus discretion 424–6
    stabilisation using. *See* Stabilisation policy
Money 249–65, **250**. *See also* Money supply; Reserve Bank of Australia (RBA)
    in Australian economy 252–4
    commodity **251**, 252

credit cards and debit cards 255
fiat **252**
functions 250–1
kinds 251–2
quantity theory. *See* Quantity theory of money
value, and price level 271
velocity **276**, 276–7
on Yap Island 253
Money demand
determinants 271–2
liquidity preference 369–70
Money market, equilibrium in 370–1
Money multiplier 260–1, **261**
Money supply **252**, 258–65
bank runs 264–5
control. *See* Monetary policy
determinants 271–2
liquidity preference 369
money multiplier 260–1
Monopolistic competition 63
Monopoly 10, 63
Moral hazard 240
Movie industry, and price indexes 161
MPC (marginal propensity to consume) 378
Multiplier effect **376**, 376–7
Multiplier, money 260–1, **261**
Mumbai (India), rent controls in 115
Mundell, Robert 351
Mundell–Fleming's exchange-rate effect 351, 368
Municipal bonds 197

Nader, Ralph 7
NAFTA (North American Free Trade Agreement) 30–1
NAIRU (non-accelerating inflation rate of unemployment) **400**
Nakayama, Tosiho 253
National Association of Securities Dealers Automated Quotations (NASDAQ) system 198
National Health and Medical Research Council 189
National income accounts, saving in 202–3
National saving **202**. *See also* Saving
Nationals 136
Natural-rate hypothesis **403**, 403–5
Natural rate of output 354
Natural rate of unemployment 221–2, **225**, 399–401, 414
natural-rate hypothesis **403**, 403–5
Natural resources **175**
productivity 175–7
Necessities
income elasticity of demand 96
price elasticity of demand 88
Negative correlations 36
Net exports **137**, 299
equality with net foreign investment 302–4
Net foreign investment **301**, 301–3
of Australia 306–7
equality with net exports 302–4
equilibrium in open economy 324–5

Neutrality, monetary **275**
New classical misperceptions theory 356
New goods, consumer price index and 155
New Keynesians, sticky-price theory of 356–7
New York Stock Exchange (NYSE) 198
New Zealand
inflation 12–13, 270
inflation-linked securities 289
Newspapers, share tables in 199
Newton, Isaac 18
Nigeria
economic growth 169
GDP and quality of life 145
standard of living 11
Nikkei share index (Tokyo) 198
Nominal exchange rates **308**
during hyperinflation 313–14
real exchange rates related to 309
Nominal GDP **140**
real GDP versus 140–2
Nominal interest rate 160–2, **162**
Nominal variables **275**
Non-accelerating inflation rate of unemployment (NAIRU) **400**
Normal goods **64**
income elasticity of demand 94, 96
Normative statements **26**
North American Free Trade Agreement (NAFTA) 30–1

Oil prices
OPEC increases 111–12, 405–8
OPEC's failure to keep high 102–3
price ceilings 111–12
Okun, Arthur 347
Okun's law 347, 395
Oligopoly 63
Olympic Games, building boom 360
Omitted variables, causality and 41–2
OPEC. *See* Organization of Petroleum Exporting Countries (OPEC)
Open economies 202, **298**. *See also* International flows
budget deficits 328–31
equilibrium 324–8
market for loanable funds 320–2
political instability and capital flight 333–7
trade policy 331–3
Open-market operations 257, **262**
Opportunity cost **6**, 51
comparative advantage 51–2
production possibilities frontier 23–4
Ordered pairs 36
Organization of Petroleum Exporting Countries (OPEC)
failure to keep oil prices high 102–3
oil price increases 111–12, 405–8
Phillips curve 406–8
Output. *See also* Gross domestic product (GDP); Real GDP
in long and short runs 386–7
natural rate (full employment; potential) 354
Outsiders, unions and 233
Outward-oriented policies 186–7

P/E (price–earnings) ratio 199
Packer, Kerry 250
Pakistan
economic growth 171
GDP and quality of life 145
Paper market, prices in 83
Papua-New Guina, famine in 185
Payroll taxes 123
Peltzman, Sam 8
Perception versus reality 30–1
Perfect competition 62–3
Perfectly competitive markets 62
Perot, Ross 305
Perpetuities 197
Phar Lap 149, 159–60
Phelps, Edmund 398, 401–5, 410, 415
Philips, Sir John 385
Phillips, A. W. 394, 401
Phillips curve **13**, 393–415, **394**
aggregate demand and aggregate supply 395–8
disinflation 410–11
expectations 401–2
long-run 398–401
natural-rate hypothesis 403–5
origins 394–5
supply shocks 405–8
Physical capital **174**
Pie charts 34
Pigou, Arthur C. 351
Pigou effect 351, 368
Pine, Art 253
Pitchford, John 214–15
Poland, inflation in 279
Political stability
economic growth 184–5
lacking, in open economies 333–7
Population growth, control of, economic growth and 188–9
Populists 288–9
Portfolios 200
Positive correlations 36
Positive statements **26**
Potential output 354
Poverty, effect on job search 242
Price ceilings **110**, 110–14
evaluation 118–19
Price–earnings ratio (P/E) 199
Price elasticity of demand **88**, 88–9
calculating 90–1
demand curves 90–2
total revenue 92–4
Price elasticity of supply 96–8, **97**
calculating 97–8
supply curves 98
Price floors **110**, 114–18
evaluation 118–19
Price indexes. *See* Consumer price index (CPI)
Price level. *See also* Hyperinflation; Inflation
in long and short runs 386–7
value of money 271
Price takers 62
Prices
of art gallery admissions 94
equilibrium **76**

individual demand 63–4
individual supply 71
in paper market 83
of related goods, individual demand 64
relative 284–5
resource allocation 82–4
of shares 199
Prices and Incomes Accord 231, 234, 236, 408–9, 411–13
Principles of Political Economy and Taxation (Ricardo) 54
Private saving **203**
Producer price index **152**
Production
assembly lines 238–9
factors. *See* Factors of production; *also specific factors and factor markets*
possibilities 46–8
Production function 177
Production possibilities frontier **22**, 22–4
Productivity **11**, **173**, 173–8
computers 178–9
determination 174–7
importance 173–4
production function 177
slowdown 189–91
Property rights, and economic growth 184–5
Prudential supervision 256
Public goods 189
Public policy. *See also* Fiscal policy; Legislation; Monetary policy; *also specific types of policy*
job search 241
Public saving **203**
Purchases, government. *See* Government purchases
Purchasing power, inflation and 282–3
Purchasing-power parity **310**, 310–15
implications 312–13
limitations 314–15
logic 310–12

Quality, change in, and consumer price index 155–6
Quantity demanded **63**, 69
Quantity equation 276–7, **277**
Quantity, equilibrium **76**
Quantity supplied **70**, 70–4
Quantity theory of money 270–82, **273**
adjustment process 273–4
classical dichotomy and monetary neutrality 274–6
Fisher effect 280–2
hyperinflation 278–9
inflation tax 279
monetary injections 272–3
money supply, money demand, and monetary equilibrium 271–2
price level and value of money 271
velocity and quantity equation 276–7
Quiggan, Professor John 230–1
Quotas, import 331

Rational expectations **410**
disinflation and 410–11
Reagan, Ronald 28, 29–30
Real exchange rates **309**, 309–10

Real GDP **140**
historical record 142
nominal GDP versus 140–3
unemployment 347
Real interest rate 160–2, **162**
Real variables **275**
Recessions 142, **344**, 358–63
shift in aggregate demand 358–61
shift in aggregate supply 361–2
'Relationship between Unemployment and the Rate of Change of Money Wages in the United Kingdom, The' (Phillips) 394
Relative prices 284–5
Rent controls, in short run and long run 113–14, 115
Research and development, economic growth and 189
Reservation wage 238
Reserve Bank Act (1959) 381
Reserve Bank Board 256, 375, 381
Reserve Bank of Australia (RBA) 215, **255**, 255–8
active stabilisation policy 381–2
changing role 256–8
independence 385
interest-rate targets 375
monetary policy 261–3
organisation 256
reducing inflation 409, 413
zero inflation as aim 426–9
Reserve ratio **259**
money multiplier 261
Reserve requirements **262**, 262–3
Reserves **258**
fractional-reserve banking 259–60
100%-reserve banking 258
Resources
allocation by prices 82–4
misallocation, and inflation 284–5
natural **175**, 175–7
Retained earnings 199
Retirement saving 432
Returns to scale, constant 177
Revenue, total 92–4
Reverse causality 41, 42–3
Ricardian equivalence 210, 431
Ricardo, David 54, 210
Richardson, Chris 360
Risk, credit 197
Robinson, Mark 360
Rockoff, Hugh 289–90
Roe, Pat 397
'Role of Monetary Policy, The' (Friedman) 398
Rosenbloom, Edward 83
Ross Industries 397
Rubin, Robert 289
Rule, discretion versus 424–6
Rule of 70 172
Rum as commodity money 252
Russell, Bill 231
Russia, GDP and quality of life in 145

Sachs, Jeffrey 186–7
Sacrifice ratio 409–10, **410**
Samuelson, Paul 394, 401, 403, 415
Sargent, Thomas J. 410, 410–11, 415

Saving **202**
economic growth 178–80
inflation's discouragement 285–6
international flows of goods and capital 303–6
meaning 203
in national income accounts 202–3
net foreign investment 306–7
private **203**
protecting from inflation 287–8
public **203**
for retirement 432
taxes 206–8, 431–4
Scale, constant returns to 177
Scarcity **4**
Scatterplots 36
Scientific method 18–19
Scullin, Prime Minister 149, 160
Seasonal adjustments 136
Secrets of the Temple: How the Federal Reserve Runs the Country 265
Sectoral shifts 241
Securities. *See* Bonds
Sellers, taxes on, market outcomes 121–2
Serbia, hyperinflation in 280
70, rule of 172
Shakespeare, William 214
Share indexes 198
Share market 197–8
Shares **197**
newspaper share tables 199
Shaw, George Bernard 28
Shiller, Robert J. 288–9
Shoeleather costs 282–3, **283**
Short run
algebraic explanation 387
long run versus 348, 386–7
Short-run aggregate-supply curve 355–8
shifts 357–8
upward slope 355–8
Silver, free-silver debate and 287–90
Singapore, economic growth in 169, 180, 181
Slope 39–41
Smith, Adam 9, 54, 187
Smoking, reducing quantity demanded 69
Society, decisions faced by 3
Solow, Robert 191, 394, 401, 403, 415
South Korea 11, 169
Soviet Union, collapse of communism 9
Specialisation 48–50
Spending. *See* Consumption; Expenditure
Squatters 115
Stabilisation policy 381–6
automatic stabilisers 384
case against 383–4, 422–4
case for 381–2, 422
Stagflation **362**, 406
Standard & Poor's 500 Index 198
Standard of living, determinants of 11–12
Stevens, Glenn 385
Stevenson, Richard W. 414
Sticky-price theory 356–7
Sticky-wage theory 356
Stiglitz, Joseph E. 414
Stock Exchange of Hong Kong 198
Stock market 197–8

Stone, John 385
Store of value **251**
Strikes **232**, 234
Substitutes **64**
  price elasticity of demand 88
Substitution bias 154
Substitution effect, on saving 433
Superannuation 432
Supply
  aggregate. *See* Aggregate-supply curve; Model of aggregate demand and aggregate supply
  change 80–1
  elastic 97, 97–8
  excess **76**, 76–7
  individual 71–3
  inelastic 97
  law **71**
  of loanable funds 204–6
  market. *See* Competitive markets; Market supply
  of money. *See* Monetary policy; Money supply
Supply curve **72**
  aggregate. *See* Aggregate-supply curve
  applications 98–105
  in competitive markets 62
  shifts 73–4
Supply schedule **71**
Supply shocks, Phillips curve and 405–8
Supply-side economics 380
Surpluses
  budget **203**
  trade **299**
Sydney, Olympic building boom in 360
Symonds, Grant 311

Taiwan, economic growth in 169
Targets, interest-rate 375
Tariffs 331
Tastes, individual demand and 64
Tax incidence 119–25, **120**
  elasticity 124–5
  government distribution 123
  market outcomes 120–1
Taxes
  aggregate demand 379–80
  bonds 197
  inflation 279
  inflation-induced distortions 285–6
  investment 208–9
  saving 206–8, 432–4
Tease, Warren 231
Technological knowledge **176**, 176–7
Technology, individual supply and 71
Term, of bonds 197
Thailand, tourism in 311
Theory of liquidity preference **369**, 369–71

Third World, flows of goods and capital to and from 305
Thomas, Ian 311
Thurow, Roger 280
Time horizon, price elasticity of demand and 89
Time inconsistency of policy 425
Time-series graphs 34
Tobin, James 289
Tokyo Stock Exchange 198
Toohey, Brian 385
Total revenue **92**
  and price elasticity of demand 92–4
Tourism Council Australia 311
Trade 48–50. *See also* International trade
  benefits 8–9
  comparative advantage 52
Trade balance **299**
  trade policies 333
Trade deficits **299**
Trade policy **331**
  in open economies 331–3
Trade restriction, tariffs 331
Trade surpluses **299**
Trade-offs 4–5
  between inflation and unemployment. *See* Phillips curve
Transfer payments 137
Treasury 27
Truman, Harry 27
Turner, Graham 311
Twin deficits 331

Uchitelle, Louis 178–9
Unemployment 221–43
  cyclical 222, **225**
  duration 227–8
  efficiency wages 236–9
  job search 239–43
  location 242–3
  low, effects of 397
  measurement 222–7
  minimum-wage laws 229–32
  non-accelerating inflation rate of unemployment (NAIRU) 400
  real GDP 347
  reasons 228, 230–1
  trade-off between inflation. *See* Phillips curve
  unions 232–5
Unemployment benefits **241**
Unemployment rate **223**
  natural 221–2, **225**, 399–401, 403–5, 414
Unions **232**, 232–6
  economics 232–3
  evaluation 233–5
  membership rate 232
  strikes 234

Unit elasticity 90
Unit of account **251**
United Kingdom. *See* Britain
United States
  budget deficits 211–13
  GDP and quality of life 145
  government economists 27
  inflation 313
  natural experiment for the natural-rate hypothesis 403–5
  productivity slowdown in 190
Unsafe at Any Speed (Nader) 7

Value
  absolute 89
  intrinsic 251
  of money, and price level 271
  stores 200, 251
Value added **138**
Values, differences among 29
Variables
  nominal **275**
  real **275**
Velocity of money **276**, 276–7
Vickery, James 231
Volcker, Paul 427
Voluntary export restrictions 331
'Voodoo economics' 30

Wages
  efficiency. *See* Efficiency wages
  indexation 160, 273–4, 408–9
  minimum rates 116–18
  reservation 238
Wants, double coincidence of 250
Wealth 250, 251
  Pigou effect 351, 368
  redistribution, and inflation 287–8
Wealth of Nations, The (Smith) 9, 54
Weekly volume of shares traded 199
Welfare, economic, and the GDP 143–5
Wheat market, supply, demand and elasticity and 100–1
Wheeler, Sir Frederick 385
Wizard of Oz, The (Baum) 289–90
Wolfensohn, James D. 182
Women, labour-force participation rate of 225–7
World Bank 182, 183
  economic growth 186
World Economic Forum 305

x-coordinate 36

y-coordinate 36
Yap Island money 253

Zandi, Mark 397

TO THE OWNER OF THIS BOOK

We are interested in your reaction to *Principles of Macroeconomics* by Stonecash, Gans, King and Mankiw.

1. What was your reason for using this book?
   - ____ university course
   - ____ college course
   - ____ TAFE course
   - ____ continuing education course
   - ____ personal interest
   - ____ other (please specify)

2. In which school are you enrolled? _____

3. Approximately how much of the book did you use?
   ____ ¼   ____ ½   ____ ¾   ____ all

4. What is the best aspect of the book?

5. Have you any suggestions for improvement?

6. Would more diagrams/ illustrations help?

7. Is there any topic that should be added?

Fold here

(Tape shut)

No postage stamp required
if posted in Australia

Reply Paid 5
The Marketing Manager, College Division
Harcourt Australia Pty Limited
Locked Bag 16
ST PETERS 2044

Suggestions for Reading

*If you enjoyed the economics course you have just finished,
you might like reading more about economic issues in the following books.*

■ **Getting It Right: Markets and Choices in a Free Society**, Robert J. Barro (Cambridge, Mass.: MIT Press, 1996). In this collection of essays based on his *Wall Street Journal* columns, conservative economist Robert Barro offers his view about the workings of the economy and the proper scope of economic policy.

■ **Hard Heads, Soft Hearts: Tough-minded Economics for a Just Society**, Alan S. Blinder (Reading, Mass.: Addison-Wesley, 1987). How should government policymakers balance economic efficiency and social compassion? Alan Blinder, who has served as an economic adviser to President Clinton, offers his answers in this wide-ranging book.

■ **New Ideas from Dead Economists**, Todd G. Buchholz (New York: Penguin Books, 1989). This amusing book provides an overview of the history of economic thought.

■ **Thinking Strategically: A Competitive Edge in Business, Politics, and Everyday Life**, Avinash Dixit and Barry Nalebuff (New York: Norton, 1991). This introduction to game theory discusses how all people—from corporate executives to arrested criminals—should and do make strategic decisions that affect themselves and others.

■ **Co-opetition**, Adam M. Brandenburger and Barry J. Nalebuff (New York: Doubleday, 1996). This book explains the usefulness of game theory for business decision making in a competitive environment.

■ **The Winner-take-all Society: How More and More Americans Compete for Fewer and Bigger Prizes, Encouraging Economic Waste, Income Inequality, and an Impoverished Cultural Life**, Robert H. Frank and Philip J. Cook (New York: The Free Press, 1995). This book examines some of the reasons for, and the effects of, increasing inequality of incomes in the United States.

■ **Capitalism and Freedom**, Milton Friedman (Chicago: University of Chicago Press, 1962). In this classic book, one of the most important economists of the twentieth century argues that society should rely less on the government and more on the free market.

■ **The Worldly Philosophers**, Robert L. Heilbroner (New York: Touchstone, 1953). This classic book discusses the lives, times and ideas of the great economic thinkers, including Adam Smith, David Ricardo and John Maynard Keynes.